# Getting Started with Linux:
# Novell's Guide to CompTIA's Linux+ (Course 3060)

## Novell & Jason W. Eckert

D0074259

THOMSON

COURSE TECHNOLOGY

Australia • Canada • Mexico • Singapore • Spain • United Kingdom • United States

**THOMSON**

**COURSE TECHNOLOGY**

**Getting Started with Linux: Novell's Guide to CompTIA's Linux+ (Course 3060)**

is published by Course Technology.

**Vice President, Technology and Trades**
Dave Garza

**Managing Editor**
William Pitkin III

**Product Manager**
Amy Lyon

**Technical Editor**
Ed Sawicki

**Manufacturing Coordinator**
Susan Carroll

**Text Design**
GEX Publishing Services

**Editorial Director**
Sandy Clark

**Acquisitions Editor**
Nick Lombardi

**Product Manager**
John Bosco

**Marketing Director**
Deborah Yarnell

**Senior Editorial Assistant**
Dawn Daugherty

**Compositor**
GEX Publishing Services

**Executive Editor**
Stephen Helba

**Product Manager**
Manya Chylinski

**Production Editor**
Brooke Booth

**Senior Channel Marketing Manager**
Dennis Williams

**Cover Design**
Laura Rickenbach

Disclaimer
Course Technology reserves the right to revise this publication and make changes from time to time in its content without notice.

The Novell and SUSE names and trademarks are the exclusive property of, and are licensed from, Novell, Inc. Linux is a registered trademark of Linus Torvalds.

ISBN-13: 978-1-4188-3730-3
ISBN-10: 1-4188-3730-X

# BRIEF
# Contents

# TABLE OF
# Contents

# SECTION EIGHT
## Processes, Jobs, and Runlevels                                            **337**

# Preface

Open source software such as Linux has radically changed how the computer industry approaches software development. One of the largest changes since 2000 was Novell's switch to SUSE Linux as their main enterprise platform. Today, there are millions of Linux users, administrators, and developers, and this trend continues as companies adopt Linux and open source technologies. To provide benchmarks for hiring, many vendors such as CompTIA, Novell, and Red Hat have released Linux certification exams geared toward different skill sets required for common Linux job functions. One of the most common entry-level Linux certifications is CompTIA's Linux+, which tests Linux skills in many different areas of usage and systems administration. Using carefully constructed examples, questions, and practical exercises, the *Getting Started with Linux: Novell's Guide to CompTIA's Linux+ (Course 3060)* text introduces you to the concepts required to success-fully use and administer a Linux system as well as prepare for the CompTIA Linux+ certification examination.

## The Intended Audience

This book is appropriate for anyone who wishes to learn how to administer, use, or develop programs for SUSE Linux. The concepts introduced in this book do not assume prior Linux experience and are geared toward the objectives on the CompTIA Linux+ certification exam. Furthermore, many of the concepts and procedures introduced in this book are transferable to most other Linux distributions.

## Section Descriptions

**Section 1**, "Linux Basics and SLES 9 Installation," introduces the history and features of the Linux operating system with a focus on the SUSE Linux distribution. As well, this section examines the installation of SUSE Linux Enterprise Server (SLES).

**Section 2**, "Use the Linux Desktop," examines the navigation of the KDE and GNOME desktop environments. This section also introduces the Linux command-line interface.

**Section 3**, "Locate and Use Help Resources in the Linux System," discusses the various tools used to obtain help in SLES, including the manual pages, info pages, howto files, and the SUSE HelpCenter.

**Section 4**, "Use the YaST Management Utility," walks through the procedures used to administer software, users, groups, printers, and hardware using the YaST utility. In addition, this section examines the structure of the X Window System and its configuration.

**Section 5**, "Manage Directories and Files in Linux," covers the structure of the Linux file system as well as the commands used to navigate the file system directory structure. As well, this section introduces the commands that may be used to locate, view, search, archive, compress, and manage files on the file system.

**Section 6**, "Work with the Linux Shell and Edit Text Files," discusses the various features of your shell, including filename completion, command history, variables, special characters, piping, and redirection. Following this, you will examine the usage of the vi editor as well as the sed and awk text utilities.

**Section 7**, "Use the Command-Line Interface to Administer the System," examines the commands used to administer users, groups, passwords, file permissions, file ownership, disk quotas, file systems, software, and boot managers.

**Section 8**, "Processes, Jobs, and Runlevels," discusses the administration of daemon and user processes on the system. More specifically, this section discusses how to view, manage, kill, and schedule processes as well as configure them to start and stop upon entering various runlevels.

**Section 9**, "Manage the Network Configuration," covers the basics of the TCP/IP protocol and its configuration in SLES using YaST and command-line utilities. In addition, this section examines the hostname, alias, and route configuration along with the utilities used to troubleshoot SLES network configuration.

**Section 10**, "Manage Network Services: DNS, File, and Print Services," covers the structure and configuration of the DNS service in SLES. This section also discusses the configuration of the NFS, Samba, and CUPS services to provide file and printer sharing on a TCP/IP network.

**Section 11**, "Manage Network Services: NIS, Mail, and xinetd," details the configuration of the Network Information Service in SLES as well as the configuration of e-mail services and clients (Postfix, Sendmail, Procmail). Following this, the configuration of the Internet Super Daemon, Secure Shell (SSH), Dynamic Host Configuration Protocol (DHCP), and Apache Web server (HTTPD) is examined.

**Section 12**, "Manage Security," describes the utilities, services, and procedures used to secure a Linux environment. More specifically, this section describes how to use the sudo command, secure file permissions, configure the syslog daemon, audit log files, configure firewalls, and implement Intrusion Detection Systems.

**Section 13**, "Hardware Basics," discusses the configuration of hardware devices in SLES as well as the procedures and tools used to troubleshoot hardware and multimedia devices.

Focus is placed on hotplug devices, hard disks (SCSI, IDE, RAID), recordable media, and ACPI.

**Appendix A** details the various functions and commands that can be used in the vi editor.

## Features

To ensure a successful learning experience, this book includes the following pedagogical features:

- **Section Objectives:** Each section in this book begins with a detailed list of the concepts to be mastered within that section. This list provides you with a quick reference to the contents of the section, as well as a useful study aid.

- **Screenshots, Illustrations, and Tables:** Wherever applicable, screenshots and illustrations are used to aid you in the visualization of common installation, administration, and management steps; theories; and concepts. In addition, many tables provide command options that may be used in combination with the specific command being discussed.

- **Exercises:** Exercises are distributed throughout the body of each section. They contain specific step-by-step instructions that enable you to apply the knowledge gained in the section.

- **End-of-Chapter Material:** The end of each section includes the following features to reinforce the material covered in the section:
  - Chapter Summary: Gives a brief but complete summary of the section
  - Key Terms List: Lists all new terms and their definitions
  - Review Questions: Test your knowledge of the most important concepts covered in the section
  - Discovery Exercises: Include theoretical, research, or scenario-based projects that allow you to expand on your current knowledge of the concepts that you learned in the section

## Text and Graphic Conventions

Wherever appropriate, additional information and exercises have been added to this book to help you better understand what is being discussed. Icons throughout the text alert you to additional materials. The icons used in this textbook are as follows:

 Notes present additional helpful material related to the subject being discussed.

**NOTE**

The Caution icon identifies important information about potential mistakes or hazards.

Each Discovery Exercise in this book is preceded by the Discovery Exercise icon.

**On the DVDs:** On the DVDs included with this text you will find a copy of SLES 9, VMWare emulation software for lab setup, the Student Manual PDF, files used for chapter exercises, and a Self-Study Workbook.

## INSTRUCTOR'S MATERIALS

The following supplemental materials are available when this book is used in a classroom setting. All of the supplements available with this book are provided to the instructor on a single CD.

**Electronic Instructor's Manual:** The Instructor's Manual that accompanies this textbook includes additional instructional material to assist in class preparation, including suggestions for classroom activities, discussion topics, and additional projects.

**Solutions:** Answers to all end-of-chapter materials are provided, including the Review Questions, and, where applicable, Discovery Exercises.

**ExamView®:** This textbook is accompanied by ExamView, a powerful testing software package that allows instructors to create and administer printed, computer (LAN-based), and Internet exams. ExamView includes hundreds of questions that correspond to the topics covered in this text, enabling students to generate detailed study guides that include page references for further review. The computer-based and Internet testing components allow students to take exams at their computers, and also save the instructor time by grading each exam automatically.

**PowerPoint presentations:** This textbook comes with Microsoft PowerPoint slides for each chapter. These are included as a teaching aid for classroom presentation, to make available to students on the network for chapter review, or to be printed for classroom distribution. Instructors, please feel at liberty to add your own slides for additional topics you introduce to the class.

**Figure Files:** All of the figures in this textbook are reproduced on the Instructor's Resource CD in bitmapped format. Similar to the PowerPoint presentations, these are included as a teaching aid for classroom presentation, to make available to students for review, or to be printed for classroom distribution.

## LAB REQUIREMENTS

The following hardware is required for the Discovery Exercises at the end of each section and should be listed on the Hardware Compatibility List available at *www.novell.com/linux/suse/*:

- Pentium CPU (Pentium II 400 or higher recommended)
- 256 MB RAM (512 MB RAM recommended)
- 4 GB hard disk
- A DVD drive (or a combination CD/DVD drive)
- Network Interface Card
- Internet connection

Similarly, the following lists the software required for the Discovery Exercises at the end of each section:

- SUSE Linux Enterprise Server 9

## ACKNOWLEDGMENTS

First, I wish to thank the staff at Course Technology and Novell for an overall enjoyable writing experience. More specifically, I wish to thank my Project Managers, Manya Chylinski and Amy Lyon, for their coordination and insight, as well as my Production Editor, Brooke Booth, for the long hours spent pulling everything together to transform the text into its current state. As well, I wish to thank Frank Gerencser, of triOS College for freeing me up to write this textbook, and Apple Computer Inc. for the amazing computer I wrote it on.

Readers are encouraged to e-mail comments, questions, and suggestions regarding *Getting Started with Linux: Novell's Guide to CompTIA's Linux+ (Course 3060)* to Jason W. Eckert: jason.eckert@trios.com

# INTRODUCTION

This textbook is based on Novell Authored Courseware *Getting Started with Linux: Novell's Guide to CompTIA's Linux+ (Course 3060),* which Novell sells and distributes to commercial and academic institutions, as well as self-study customers.

Utilizing the strength of Novell's original content, software, and hands-on exercises, Course Technology has reformatted and enhanced the texts for an academic audience. Additional end of chapter exercises, student labs, and instructor tools — including test banks, slide decks, and online deliverables — have been added to produce quality courseware based on Novell's SUSE Linux.

The Novell course developers have reviewed the manuals from Course Technology to ensure that, although in a new format, the content is consistent with Novell's own manuals, meeting the objectives to prepare students to take the Certification Exams.

To learn more about Novell Academic Programs, visit *www.novell.com/natp.*

In the *Getting Started with Linux: Novell's Guide to CompTIA's Linux+* (3060) course, you learn the basic Linux skills you need to perform administrative tasks in SUSE Linux Enterprise Server 9 (SLES 9). The subject matter covered in this course covers the objectives outlined by CompTIA for its Linux+ exam.

This manual covers many topics covered in these objectives, but there will probably not be enough time to discuss them all in class. To prepare for the exam you should read and practice outside class whatever could not be covered in class.

YaST is an integral part of the SUSE Linux Enterprise Server, so it is covered in this course in various sections. However, there are no questions on YaST included in the CompTIA Linux+ exam.

The skills you learn in this course, along with those taught in the *SUSE Linux Enterprise Server Administration* (3037) and *Advanced SUSE Linux Enterprise Server Administration* (3038) courses, prepare you to take the Novell Certified Linux Professional (Novell CLP) certification practicum test.

The contents of your student kit include two DVDs. The first DVD is your Course DVD and contains the following:

- *Getting Started with Linux: Novell's Guide to CompTIA's Linux+ (Course 3060)* Student Manual

- *Getting Started with Linux: Novell's Guide to CompTIA's Linux+ (Course 3060)* Self-Study Workbook

- *Getting Started with Linux: Novell's Guide to CompTIA's Linux+ (Course 3060)* Self-Study Files

- SLES 9 VMWare Server

The second DVD contains a full evaluation version of SUSE Linux Enterprise Server 9. To accommodate this academic deliverable, the original software has been modified from CD to DVD and is distributed on an "AS IS" basis. Please note that this software is for classroom use only and is not to be used in a production environment.

To download a fully functional, supported, and upgradeable version of the SUSE Linux Enterprise Server and other Novell Open Source products, visit *www.novell.com/downloads*.

The *SLES 9 VMware Server* DVD contains two VMware Workstation SLES 9 servers that you can use with the *Getting Started with Linux: Novell's Guide to CompTIA's Linux+ Self-Study Workbook* (in PDF format on your DVD) outside the classroom to practice the skills you need to prepare for Course 3060 and the Linux+ exam. On one machine you do all the exercises; the other (da1) offers services, for instance a DNS server, needed in certain exercises in the second half of the course.

**NOTE**

Instructions for setting up a self-study environment are included in the *Getting Started with Linux: Novell's Guide to CompTIA's Linux+ Self-Study Workbook*.

If you do not own a copy of VMware Workstation, you can obtain a 30-day evaluation version at *www.vmware.com*. If you want to dedicate a machine to install SLES 9, instructions are also provided in the Self-Study Workbook.

## COURSE OBJECTIVES

This course teaches you the following concepts and skills fundamental to understanding SLES 9:

- Linux basics and SLES 9 installation

- Using the Linux desktop

- Locating and using Help resources in the Linux system

- Using the YaST management utility to administer the system

- Managing directories and files in the Linux system

- Working with the Linux shell and editing text files
- Using the command-line interface to administer the system
- Understanding processes, jobs, and runlevels in the Linux system
- Managing the network configuration
- Managing network services
- Managing security
- Hardware basics

Understanding these concepts is necessary to learn the skills of an entry- to medium-level SUSE Linux administrator or help desk technician in an enterprise environment.

## AUDIENCE

The primary audience for this course are students preparing for CompTIA's Linux+ exam. Current Novell CNESM certification candidates with experience in other operating systems can also use this course to begin preparing for the Novell CLP Practicum.

## LINUX CERTIFICATION

With Novell® and Linux, you are going places! Industry-recognized certification exams are available to leverage your Linux experience and training. Novell's commitment to the open source community is evident by our support of CompTIA's Linux+ vendor-neutral exam.

### CompTIA Linux+

The CompTIA Linux+ certification is an international industry credential that validates the knowledge of individuals with at least six months of practical Linux experience. Professionals who want to certify their technical knowledge in basic installation, operation, and troubleshooting for Linux operating systems should consider this certification. The skills and knowledge measured by this examination were developed with global input to assure accuracy, validity, and reliability. Earning the CompTIA Linux+ designation means that the candidate can explain fundamental open source resources/licenses, demonstrate knowledge of user administration, understand file permissions/software configurations, and manage local storage devices and network protocols.

## Novell Certified Linux Professional (Novell CLP)

The Novell Certified Linux Professional is for people interested in being Linux administrators. Skills demonstrated by someone holding a Novell CLP certification include: installing Linux servers into a network environment, managing users and groups, managing the SUSE® Linux file system, managing printing, managing software, and managing network processes and services — just to name a few. As with all Novell certifications, course work is never required, but you must pass a Novell Practicum exam (050-689) in order to achieve the certification. *www.novell.com/training/certinfo/*

## Novell Certified Linux Engineer 9 (Novell CLE 9)

This is for those wanting engineer-level skills to operate SUSE Linux Enterprise Servers in a network. The Novell Certified Linux Engineer 9 certification will help you master all aspects of SUSE Linux Enterprise Servers for an enterprise environment that is not already covered in the CLP curriculum. With this certification, you will be in high demand as more and more employers seek talented Linux engineers. This certification will require you to have completed your Novell CLP certification before you take the Novell Practicum for your Novell CLE 9 certification. (So if you're already a Novell CLP, you're more than halfway done with the Novell CLE 9 certification.) *www.novell.com/training/certinfo/*

## Novell Practicum Exams

Both Novell CLP and CLE 9 certifications are Practicum based exams. These performance-based exams are designed to test not only a student's knowledge but also their skills. The 2.5-hour exam requires students to perform real-world tasks on one or more SUSE Linux servers. At the end of the exam, each server environment is evaluated and the student is scored with a pass or fail grade. These exams are available through testing partners world-wide. *http://practicum.novell.com*

Novell and SUSE are registered trademarks of Novell, Inc. in the United States and other countries.

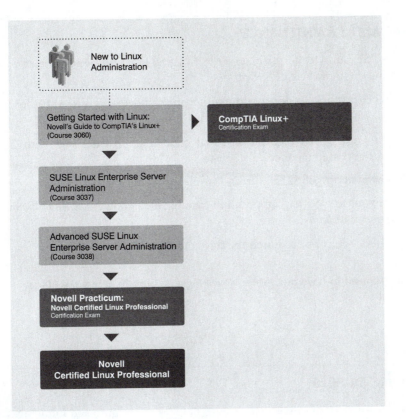

**Figure I-1**

# ONLINE RESOURCES FOR GETTING STARTED WITH LINUX — NOVELL'S GUIDE TO COMPTIA'S LINUX+

For additional exercises, errata, and further information around this course, please visit:

*www.novell.com/training/train_product/linuxplus.html*

## SLES 9 Support and Maintenance

The copy of SUSE Linux Enterprise Server 9 (SLES 9) you receive in your student kit is a fully functioning copy of the SLES 9 product.

However, to receive official support and maintenance updates, you need to do one of the following:

- Register for a free registration/serial code that provides you with 30 days of support and maintenance.
- Purchase a copy of SLES 9 from Novell (or an authorized dealer).

You can obtain your free 30-day support and maintenance code at *www.novell.com/products/linuxenterpriseserver/eval.html*.

Obtaining such a code is not required for this course.

You will need to have or create a Novell login account to access the 30-day evaluation.

**NOTE**

## SLES 9 Online Resources

Novell provides a variety of online resources to help you configure and implement SLES 9.

These include the following:

- www.novell.com/products/linuxenterpriseserver/

  This is the Novell home page for SLES 9.
- www.novell.com/documentation/sles9/index.html

  This is the Novell Documentation Web site for SLES 9.
- http://support.novell.com/linux/

  This is the home page for all Novell Linux support, and includes links to support options such as the Knowledgebase, downloads, and FAQs.
- www.novell.com/coolsolutions

  This Novell Web site provides the latest implementation guidelines and suggestions from Novell on a variety of products, including SUSE Linux.

## AGENDA

The following is the agenda for this 5-day course:

Table I-1

| | Section | Duration |
|---|---|---|
| Day 1 | Introduction | 00:30 |
| | **Section 1:** Linux Basics and SLES 9 Installation | 02:00 |
| | **Section 2:** Use the Linux Desktop | 00:45 |
| | **Section 3:** Locate and Use Help Resources in the Linux System | 00:45 |
| | **Section 4:** Use the YaST Management Utility | 02:00 |
| Day 2 | **Section 5:** Manage Directories and Files in Linux | 03:00 |
| | **Section 6:** Work with the Linux Shell and Edit Text Files | 03:00 |
| Day 3 | **Section 7:** Use the Command-Line Interface to Administer the System | 04:00 |
| | **Section 8:** Processes, Jobs, and Runlevels | 02:00 |
| Day 4 | **Section 9:** Manage the Network Configuration | 02:00 |
| | **Section 10:** Manage Network Services: DNS, File, and Print Services | 02:00 |
| | **Section 11:** Manage Network Services: NIS, Mail, and xinetd | 02:00 |
| Day 5 | **Section 12:** Manage Security | 03:00 |
| | **Section 13:** Hardware Basics | 02:00 |

## SCENARIO

You are the system administrator for your Digital Airlines office. The management is considering migrating some network services to SLES 9 servers.

As system administrator, you decide to do the following:

- Install SLES 9 on a test workstation.
- Become familiar with the graphical user interface and the command-line interface.
- Learn how to get help for all problems you might have.
- Learn how to manage users and software packages with the configuration tool YaST2 and at the command line.
- Understand the structure of the Linux file system.
- Understand basic shell commands for working in the file system (such as copying, moving, and archiving files), and learn how to edit configuration files with a graphical editor or the command-line editor vi.
- Become familiar with command-line tools used for system administration in Linux.
- Understand processes, jobs, runlevels, and the initprocess.

- Learn how to configure networking and network services on SLES 9 and Linux.

- Become familiar with basic security management tasks.

- Understand hardware issues as they relate to Linux.

Once you complete this training, you will be able to install SLES 9 and set up a system for further tests.

## EXERCISE CONVENTIONS

When working through an exercise, you will see conventions that indicate information you need to enter that is specific to your server.

The following describes the most common conventions:

- *italicized/bolded text*. This is a reference to your unique situation, such as the host name of your server.

  For example, if the host name of your server is DA50, and you see the following:

  **hostname.digitalairlines.com**

  you would enter:

  **DA50.digitalairlines.com**

- **10.0.0.xx**. This is the IP address that is assigned to your SLES 9 server.

  For example, if your IP address is 10.0.0.50, and you see the following:

  **10.0.0.xx**

  you would enter:

  **10.0.0.50**

- **Select.** The word *select* is used in exercise steps to indicate a variety of actions including clicking a button on the interface and selecting a menu item.

- **Enter and Type.** The words *enter* and *type* have distinct meanings.

  The word *enter* means to type text in a field or at a command line and press the Enter key when necessary. The word *type* means to type text without pressing the Enter key.

  If you are directed to type a value, make sure you do not press the Enter key or you might activate a process that you are not ready to start.

# LINUX BASICS AND SLES 9
# INSTALLATION

**This section provides background information about Linux and guides you through an installation of SLES 9.**

- The History of Linux
- Understand the Multiuser Environment
- Identify the Components of SLES 9
- Perform a Simple Installation of SLES 9
- Document Installation, Configuration, and Baseline System Performance

## OBJECTIVE 1    THE HISTORY OF LINUX

Linux is closely related to the UNIX operating system. To understand the history of Linux, you need to know the following:

- The Historical Development of UNIX
- The Development of Linux
- Differences Between SUSE Linux and SUSE Linux Enterprise Server

## The Historical Development of UNIX

At the end of the 1960s, most operating systems were only designed for batch operations. If you wanted to run a program, you inserted a pile of punch cards or a roll of perforated strips into a reading device and waited until the result was sent to a printer.

If there was an error in the program or if you did not get the required result, you had to rewrite the perforated roll or replace one or several punch cards, reread the stack, and again wait for the result.

This procedure was not only long-winded, but also inefficient, which led computer developers to look for a way to allow a number of users to simultaneously use a dialog-oriented way of working with the system.

MULTICS was one of the first programs created to meet this demand. It allowed you to work in a dialog with the computer, but it was still very strongly influenced by the batch operation, and it was difficult to operate.

In 1969, one of the MULTICS developers, Ken Thompson, began creating an operating system that, apart from a dialog-oriented operation, aimed to provide a high functionality and structural simplicity.

The first version of UNIX was written in Assembler, a programming language close to the machine-level. To be machine-independent in its further development, UNIX was rewritten in 1971 in the programming language C, developed by Dennis Ritchie.

Because Bell Laboratories (a subsidiary company of AT&T) provided documentation and the source code of UNIX to universities almost at cost, the system spread relatively quickly.

The simple operation of the system, the almost unlimited availability of the source code, and its relative portability motivated many users and companies to become actively engaged in its development, so functionalities were very quickly added to UNIX and it reached a very high level of maturity.

At the same time, a series of commercial UNIX derivatives were developed including versions from IBM, DEC, and HP (HP-UX, 1982), as well as BSD UNIX (Berkeley Software Distribution, 1978), developed by the University of California in Berkeley.

In 1983, AT&T began marketing UNIX System V commercially via its sister company USL, proclaiming System V as "the" UNIX standard.

As a consequence of this, the licensing of UNIX changed considerably, leading, among other things, to a long-lasting legal battle with BSD. At the same time, with never-ending quarrels between UNIX vendors, a genuine standardization of the UNIX operating system family was prevented.

Modern UNIX operating systems can still be separated as either more System V or more BSD types, although there are no "pure" systems of one kind or the other.

Linux tries to combine the best of both worlds.

## The Development of Linux

In the spring of 1991, Linus Benedict Torvalds, a Finnish student, began to take a closer look at the memory management of his 386 PC.

A few months later he had developed a rudimentary kernel that he passed on as a source text to others who were interested via the Internet with the following message:

```
From: torvalds@klaava.Helsinki.FI (Linus Benedict Torvalds)

Newsgroups: comp.os.minix

Subject: What would you like to see most in minix?

Summary: small poll for my new operating system

Message-ID: <1991Aug25.205708.9541@klaava.Helsinki.FI>

Date: 25 Aug 91 20:57:08 GMT

Organization: University of Helsinki

Hello everybody out there using minix -

I'm doing a (free) operating system (just a hobby, won't be big
and professional like gnu) for 386(486) AT clones. This has been
brewing since april, and is starting to get ready. I'd like any
feedback on things people like/dislike in minix, as my OS
resembles it somewhat (same physical layout of the file-system
(due to practical reasons) among other things).

I've currently ported bash(1.08) and gcc(1.40), and things seem
to work. This implies that I'll get something practical within
a few months, and I'd like to know what features most people
would want. Any suggestions are welcome, but I won't promise
I'll implement them :-)
```

```
Linus (torvalds@kruuna.helsinki.fi) PS. Yes - it's free of any
minix code, and it has a multi-threaded fs. It is NOT portable
(uses 386 task switching etc), and it probably never will
support anything other than AT-harddisks, as that's all I
have :-(.
```

Linus Torvalds made the source code of his Linux kernel available with the GPL (GNU General Public License). The GPL allows everyone to read and edit the source code. The GPL license also requires any edited source code to be made available to the public.

Linux rapidly developed into a project involving many people, although the development of the system's core (Linux kernel) is still coordinated by Linus Torvalds. All kernel modifications are integrated by him.

The functions of the kernel include input and output control, device control, process management, and file management. Other system components (shell utilities, network programs, and implementations of the kernel for non-Intel processors) are maintained by other people or groups.

As a rule, there are two current versions of Linux development: a stable one, identified by an even number after the first dot; and developer versions, identified by an odd number.

Linux distributions—consisting of the Linux kernel, applications (such as office packages, databases, and network services), and manuals—are based on the even-numbered versions, but they often provide current development kernels, which, under certain circumstances, are needed for the integration of new hardware components.

Because Linux is written in C, it is available for a lot of different hardware platforms, including the following:

- i386: 32 bit
- Intel/AMD: 64 bit
- PowerPC (Macintosh, RS/6000)
- SPARC (Sun)
- IBM pSeries
- IBM zSeries (S/390)
- Embedded

## Differences Between SUSE Linux and SUSE Linux Enterprise Server

SUSE Linux Enterprise Server (SLES) is based on the SUSE Linux Professional distribution. The time between release of the Professional distribution and release of SLES is used for intensive testing and applying patches that improve security and stability of the system.

Additionally, SLES contains some features that will be made available in future versions of the Professional distribution.

Figure 1-1 illustrates the relationships between open source code, SUSE Linux Professional, and SUSE Linux Enterprise Server.

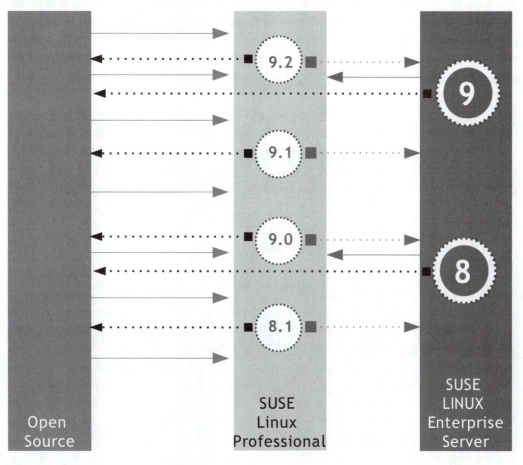

**Figure 1-1**

SUSE Linux Enterprise Server 9 has fewer packages (about 1,000) than the SUSE Linux Professional distribution (about 3,500). Most packages that have been removed are desktop applications.

SLES has a guaranteed life cycle of 5 years. During this time, you are provided patches and fixes that help you maintain SLES. In addition, you can choose from a range of support offers.

Only the SLES product is certified by independent hardware and software vendors.

## OBJECTIVE 2    UNDERSTAND THE MULTIUSER ENVIRONMENT

One of the goals of UNIX was to enable a number of users to use the system simultaneously (multiuser capability).

Because several users might also want to use several different programs simultaneously, mechanisms must be available to allow these programs to run simultaneously (multitasking capability).

The implementation of a multiuser and multitasking system in a single processor system only appears to be simultaneous. Truly simultaneous processing is only possible in a multiprocessor system.

Even in a single-processor system, advantages can be gained through multitasking because waiting times for input or output from other processes can be used.

UNIX implements *preemptive multitasking*—each process is allowed a maximum time with which it can work. When this time has expired, the operating system stops processing that process and allocates processing time to another process waiting to run.

Other operating systems (such as versions of MAC OS older than version X) do not intervene in this process cycle. Instead, control over the processor must be released by the running process before another process can run.

This can lead to one process hijacking the processor, leaving other processes without processing time and blocking the system.

The operating system coordinates access to the resources available in the system (hard drives, tapes, interfaces). If there is competition among processes for access to a tape device, only one process can be granted access. The others must be rejected.

This coordination task is very complex and no operating system is able to implement an ideal solution. The classic problem involves a situation in which two or more processes exclusively need the same resources, as illustrated in the resource conflict shown in Figure 1-2.

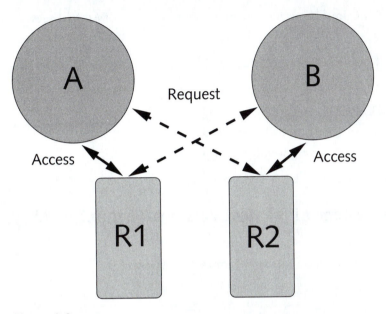

**Figure 1-2**

The following describes the resource conflict:

- Process A needs resources R1 and R2.
- Process B needs resources R2 and R1.
- Process A has received access to R1 and would now also like access to R2. In the meantime, however, B has already gained access to R2 and, in turn, would like access to R1 as well.

  If these two processes now wait until what they need is available, nothing more will happen—they are deadlocked.

Multithreading is an extension of multitasking and helps solve this problem.

In multithreading, a number of parts independent from one another (*threads*) can be produced within a process. Multithreading increases the level of parallel processes with each thread needing to be administered, which makes the use of a multiprocessor system more valuable.

A clear distinction should be made here between programs and processes: as a rule, a program exists only once in the system, but there can be several processes that perform the same program.

If a number of users are active, both programs and processes can be used independently of one another (such as a program used to display directories).

## OBJECTIVE 3    IDENTIFY THE COMPONENTS OF **SLES 9**

SLES 9 has several new and improved features, including the following:

- Updated Core System with Latest Versions/Features of All Packages
- New and Improved YaST Modules
- Next Generation Linux Kernel 2.6.5
- Improved High Availability Support
- Full Enablement and Support of UTF-8
- Inclusion of Red Carpet Enterprise Daemon
- New Type of Installation Source: SLP
- POSIX-Compliant, High-Performance Threads Support (NPTL)

## Updated Core System with Latest Versions/Features of All Packages

The following are updated core system features and versions:

- SUSE Linux kernel (version 2.6.5)
- Main C library (glibc 2.3.3)
- GNU compiler collection (GCC 3.3.3)
- XFree X11 graphical user interface (XFree 4.3.99)
- KDE Desktop Environment (3.2.1)
- GNOME Desktop Environment (2.4.2)
- File, print, and other services for Windows (Samba 3.0.4)
- Apache Web server version 2.*x* (Apache 2.0.49)
- Domain name server (BIND 9.2.3)

## New and Improved YaST Modules

YaST is the installation and administration tool for SLES 9. It includes the following improvements:

- New YaST license (GPL)
- New and improved installation methods (NFS, HTTP, FTP, VNC, SSH, and SLP)
- New and improved configuration modules (such as DNS)

# Next Generation Linux Kernel 2.6.5

Linux kernel 2.6.5 includes several improvements over the 2.4.*x* kernel versions, such as the following:

- Performance
- Improved hyper threading (one processor can handle more processes at the same time) and NUMA (Non-Uniform Memory Access) support (memory architecture for multiprocessor systems)
- Full enablement and support of UTF-8
- Better support of big SMP (symmetric multiprocessing) systems
- Fine granular locking to boost parallel execution
- Multiple kernel tuning parameters (like I/O scheduler)
- Scalability
- Support for more than 64 CPUs
- Support for thousands of devices and disks (64-bit major/minor)
- Improved block I/O layer
- Improved network stack with IPv6, IPSEC, and Mobile IPv6
- Hotplug support (SCSI, USB, Firewire, PCI, and CPU)
- Persistent device names and unified device handling
- Class-based kernel resource management (CKRM)
- ACPI improvements (such as suspend to disk/RAM)
- Infiniband support (high-speed serial computer bus)

# Improved High Availability Support

The following are high availability supported features:

- Cluster volume manager (EVMS)
- Cluster IP alias
- "Lustre" cluster file system

## Full Enablement and Support of UTF-8

SLES 9 supports Asian characters and fonts with UTF–8 support, which includes translations and commercial fonts.

## Inclusion of Red Carpet Enterprise Daemon

SLES 9 includes the Red Carpet daemon.

## New Type of Installation Source: SLP

SLES 9 now supports a Service Location Protocol (SLP) installation source and can send an SLP request for service install.suse to the network and prompt you to select an entry from the list of returned URLs.

## POSIX-Compliant, High-Performance Threads Support (NPTL)

SLES 9 features a new thread implementation called NPTL, which is faster and better than the old implementation (called linuxthreads).

---

## OBJECTIVE 4    PERFORM A SIMPLE INSTALLATION OF SLES 9

The process of installing the SUSE Linux Enterprise Server 9 can be divided into the following steps:

- Pre-Installation Requirements and Guidelines
- Installation Options
- Basic Installation
- Manual Software Selection
- Configuration

## Pre-Installation Requirements and Guidelines

The following are basic system requirements for SLES 9:

- Minimum system requirements for operation:
    - 256 MB RAM
    - 500 MB hard disk space for software
    - 500 MB hard disk space for user data

- Recommended system requirements:

    - 512 MB to 3 GB RAM, at least 256 MB per CPU

    - 4 GB hard disk space

    - Network interface (Ethernet or modem)

After installing SLES 9, some system configurations can be hard to change.

In order to make sure you are prepared to install SLES 9 with the configuration settings you need, you should consider the following:

- **Hardware compatibility.** SUSE Linux Enterprise Server 9 supports most enterprise hardware for servers. It also supports hardware for desktops. Some laptop computer hardware might not be compatible with SUSE Linux Enterprise Server 9.

    To verify that your hardware is compatible with SUSE Linux Enterprise Server 9, you can use the following Web site:

    *www.novell.com/partnerguide/section/481.html*

- **File system types.** SUSE Linux Enterprise Server 9 supports various file system types.

    Make sure you select the file system type that is right for your particular needs and requirements.

- **Partitioning scheme.** Make sure you plan for the appropriate partitions and partition sizes before starting your installation (if you are using traditional instead of virtual partitions).

    Modifying partition sizes after installation can be impossible or difficult to achieve.

    It's also easier to configure Software RAID or LVM during installation. This is especially true of configuring the root file system.

- **Software package selection.** Although you can install software packages after installation, it can be easier to decide ahead of time which packages you want installed and do the configuration during SUSE Linux installation.

To increase the security of your system, make sure you install only required services on your computer.

- **Dual-boot system.** If you plan on installing a dual-boot system on your computer (with SUSE Linux Enterprise Server 9 as one of the systems), it is often better to install SUSE Linux Enterprise Server 9 first.

For example, if you install SUSE Linux Enterprise Server 9, and then install a Windows operating system, SUSE Linux recognizes the Windows operating system and automatically provides a dual boot screen after installing Windows.

## Installation Options

Do the following:

1. Boot your computer from the SLES 9 DVD. Figure 1-3 appears.

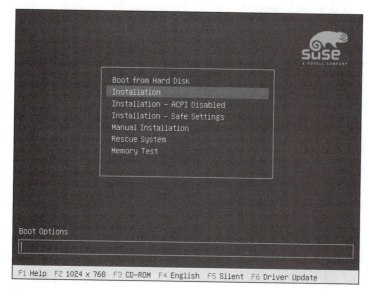

**Figure 1-3**

2. Select the installation option you want to use or wait for the installation program to choose one automatically.

   If you do not choose an option within 20 seconds, the first entry in the list (Boot from Hard Disk) is chosen automatically. To stop this countdown, simply press the **Tab** key once.

   The following describes options on this screen:

   - **Boot from Hard Disk.** Boots the standard operating system installed on your hard disk.

   - **Installation.** Starts the normal installation process.

   - **Installation – ACPI Disabled.** Some old computers don't have ACPI power management. This can lead to problems during the installation. If you select this option, you can disable the ACPI features of SLES 9.

**1**

- **Installation – Safe Settings.** Some older computers don't have any kind of power management or hard disk acceleration. If you have problems with your installation, select this option.

- **Manual Installation.** All automatic features of YaST (such as hardware detection) are disabled. You must configure everything manually.

- **Rescue System.** A minimal Linux system (without a graphical user interface) starts from the SLES CD or DVD so you can repair the Linux installation on the hard disk.

- **Memory Test.** Select this option to test the RAM for physical errors.

Function keys, indicated in the bar at the bottom of the screen, let you change the following installation settings:

- **F1.** Opens context-sensitive help for the currently selected option of the boot screen.

- **F2.** Lets you select a graphical display mode (such as 640x480 or 1024x768) for the installation. You can select one of these or select the text mode, which is useful if the graphical mode causes display problems.

- **F3.** Lets you select an installation media type. Normally, you install from the SLES 9 DVD, but in some cases you might want to select another source, such as FTP, HTTP, or NFS.

The installation method and media you select are generally determined by what is the most efficient use of your time.

For example, if you do not want to bother burning the installation images to CD-ROMs or DVDs, you can store them in a central location on the network and access them using one of the network protocols. If your network performance is not too slow, this option can save you a lot of time.

**NOTE**

Most Linux distributions allow various methods of installation. For example, you can install from a CD, from another local media source, boot the system from a floppy, or install from a server on the network using HTTP, FTP, NFS, or SMB.

Using FTP, HTTP, NFS, or SMB for installation requires an installation repository on another machine. Setting up such a repository is relatively easy with SLES 9. (There is a YaST module to do this, but it is beyond the scope of this course.)

- **F4.** Lets you select an installation language.

- **F5.** Lets you select the debugging output level. By default, diagnostic messages of the Linux kernel are not displayed during system startup. To display these messages, select **Native**. For maximum information, select **Verbose**.

- **F6.** Lets you add a driver update CD to the installation process. You are asked to insert the update CD at the appropriate point in the installation process.

3. Press **Enter**. The installation program YaST starts.

## Basic Installation

Do the following:

1. Read and accept the Novell Software License Agreement by selecting **I Agree**.

2. Select the language to be used during the installation process; then select **Accept** (see Figure 1-4).

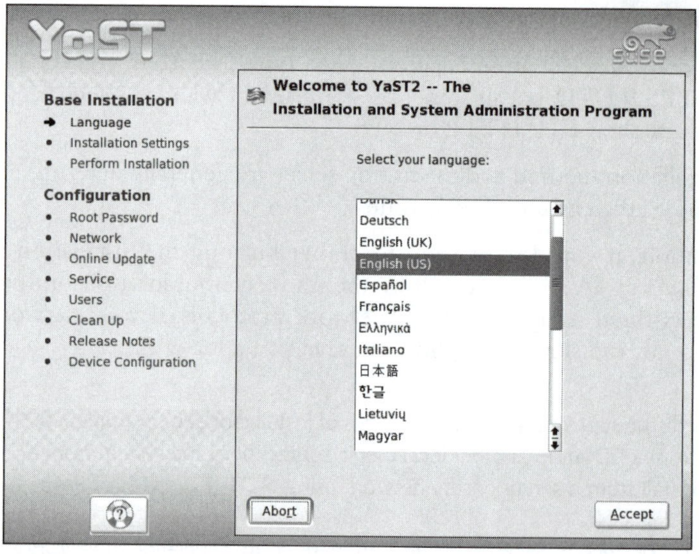

**Figure 1-4**

If Linux is already installed on your computer, the dialog box shown in Figure 1-5 appears.

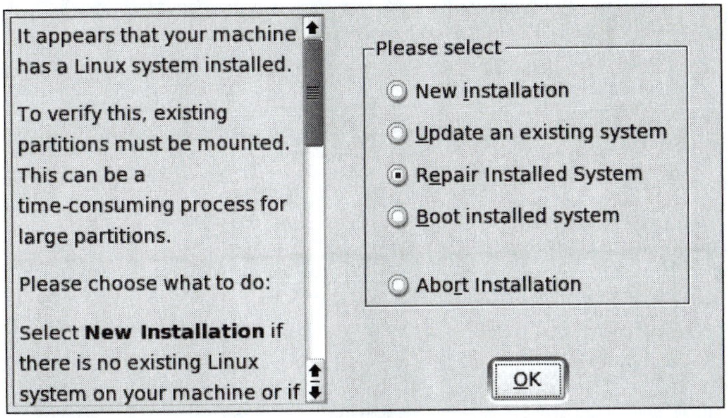

It appears that your machine has a Linux system installed.

To verify this, existing partitions must be mounted. This can be a time-consuming process for large partitions.

Please choose what to do:

Select **New Installation** if there is no existing Linux system on your machine or if

Please select
- New installation
- Update an existing system
- Repair Installed System
- Boot installed system

- Abort Installation

OK

**Figure 1-5**

3. In this dialog box, select one of the following:

   - **New Installation** (to install SLES 9)
   - **Update an Existing System**
   - **Repair Installed System**
   - **Boot installed system**
   - **Abort installation**

4. Select **OK**.

YaST displays the information shown in Figure 1-6 about your hardware and makes suggestions for the installation.

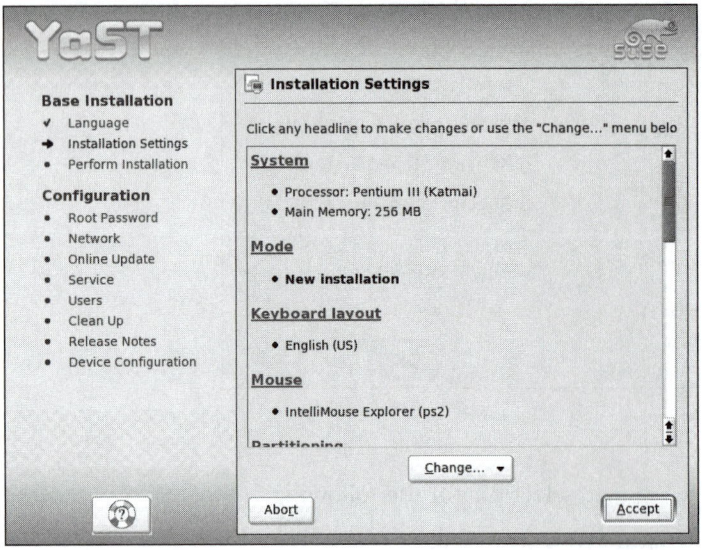

**Figure 1-6**

5. If you need to change a setting, select its headline or select the **Change** button; then select **Accept**.

The following sections are available:

- **System.** Lists details about your hardware.

- **Mode.** Lists the available installation modes.

- **Keyboard layout.** Identifies the layout of your keyboard.

- **Mouse.** Identifies your mouse type.

- **Partitioning.** Lets you create and change the partitioning table of your hard disk. If you have free space on your hard disk, the configuration program tries to use it for the installation.

If a Windows partition exists, YaST tries to resize it. An existing Linux partition is overwritten. In any case, you should make a backup of any needed partitions.

- **Software.** Lets you select the software to be installed (see the following section).

- **Booting.** Lets you install and configure the GRUB boot loader.

- **Time zone.** Lets you select your time zone.

■ **Language.** Lets you select the default language for your installation.

■ **Default Runlevel.** Lets you select your default runlevel for SLES 9.

Runlevels are different modes your system can work in. Runlevel 5 offers full networking capabilities and starts the graphical user interface.

You will usually have to change the software and partitioning recommendations made by YaST depending on the intended purpose of your computer. See *Pre-Installation Requirements and Guidelines* for details.

If another operating system is already installed on the computer but the hard drive has free, unpartitioned space left, YaST automatically recommends installing SLES 9 in that free space and creating a dual boot configuration for both operating systems.

6. After selecting **Accept**, you need to confirm your settings again. Select **Yes, Install** to start the installation process.

The installation can take some time, depending on your hardware.

## Manual Software Selection

1. If you want to install software that is not included in the default installation, select the **Change** drop-down list and select **Software**.

Figure 1-7 appears.

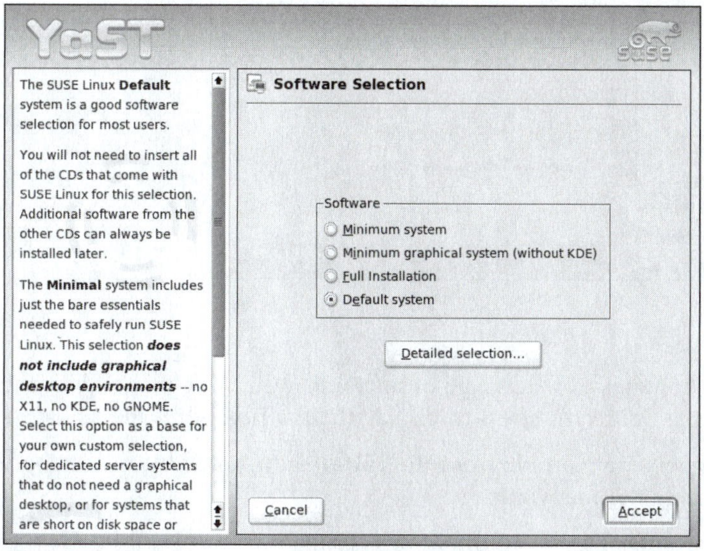

Figure 1-7

2. Select one of the following:

- **Minimum System.** Installs a minimum SUSE Linux configuration with-out a graphical system.

- **Minimum Graphical System (without KDE).** Installs a standard soft-ware selection but with limited graphical capabilities. Instead of the power-ful KDE or GNOME environments, only the basic window manager fvwm2 is installed.

- **Full Installation.** Installs most packages available on the SUSE Linux Enterprise Server CDs or DVD.

- **Default System.** Installs a standard software selection, including KDE as the desktop environment.

3. If you want to select individual packages, select **Detailed Selection**.

Figure 1-8 appears.

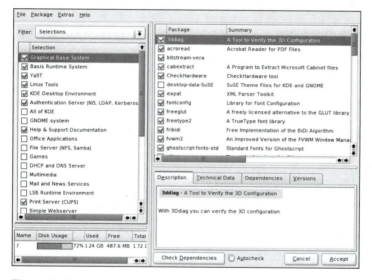

**Figure 1-8**

SLES 9 contains a broad range of software. When selecting individual packages, you can use different filters to display the available software packages.

These filters are available from the **Filter** drop-down list in the top left corner and include the following:

- **Selections.** Displays grouped selections of packages.

- **Package Groups.** Displays all software packages that are available on the installation media.

■ **Search.** Lets you enter a search term and select where you want YaST to search.

Enter the full package name, part of the name, or keywords in the Search text field and select **Search**. The results are listed in the right window. The installation state is shown by a small symbol in front of the package name.

The most important symbols are shown in Figure 1-9 (view a complete list by selecting **Help > Symbols**).

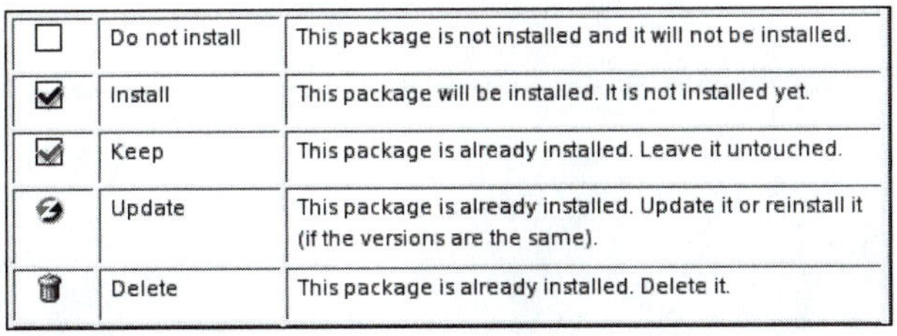

| | Do not install | This package is not installed and it will not be installed. |
|---|---|---|
| ☑ | Install | This package will be installed. It is not installed yet. |
| ☑ | Keep | This package is already installed. Leave it untouched. |
| ⟳ | Update | This package is already installed. Update it or reinstall it (if the versions are the same). |
| 🗑 | Delete | This package is already installed. Delete it. |

**Figure 1-9**

Select the symbol of the package you want to install until the "install" symbol appears.

■ **Installation Summary.** Displays all the packages with the status marked.

4. Once your software selection is complete, select **Accept**.

You might see a dialog box indicating that the dependencies between the packages cannot be resolved and that some other packages need to be installed, too. In most cases, you can simply confirm this dialog box.

If you are installing SLES from CDs, a warning appears if the wrong CD is in the drive.

## Configuration

During the configuration phase of the installation, you configure the following:

■ Root Password

■ Network Devices

■ Services

■ Users

■ Hardware

### Root Password

If the installation was successful, the computer reboots. YaST starts again because you need to configure some basic settings.

Do the following:

1. Specify the password for the administrator root in as shown in Figure 1-10.

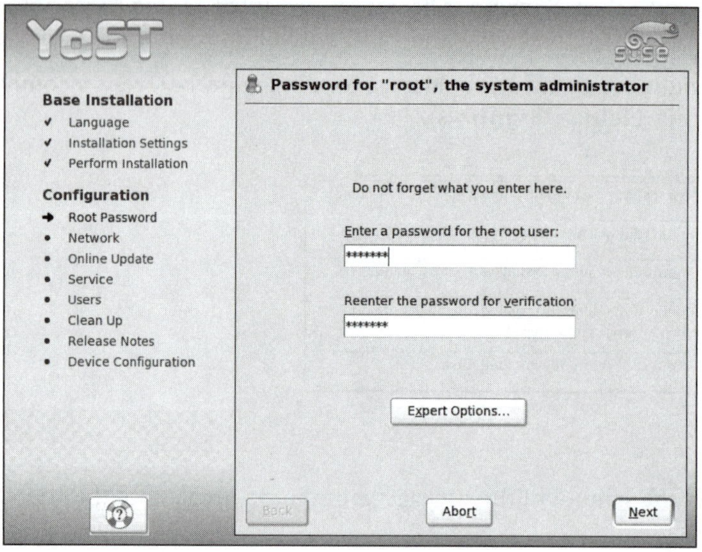

**Figure 1-10**

Warnings appear if the selected password is too simple.

1

handwritten: rescue com . Com

v your network configuration.

vices it has discovered (see Figure 1-11).

re displayed:

- Network interfaces
- DSL connections
- ISDN adapters
- Modems

2. By default, YaST selects the DHCP configuration for the network interfaces. If you need to change the network configuration, select the headline of the section or select the Change.

3. Select **Next**.

4. Test your Internet connection in the Test Internet Connection shown in Figure 1-12.

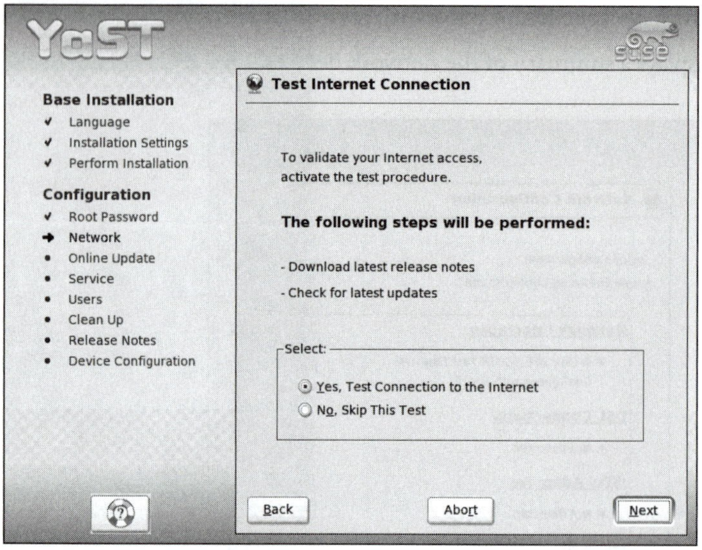

**Figure 1-12**

5. Select **Yes, Test Connection to the Internet** if you want the latest release notes to be downloaded and if you want YaST to check for new updates.

   If new updates are found, YaST asks you to verify the download and installation. You should apply any updates to ensure your new system has the latest patches applied.

## Services

Do the following:

1. In the Service Configuration dialog box, you can configure two very important services (see Figure 1-13).

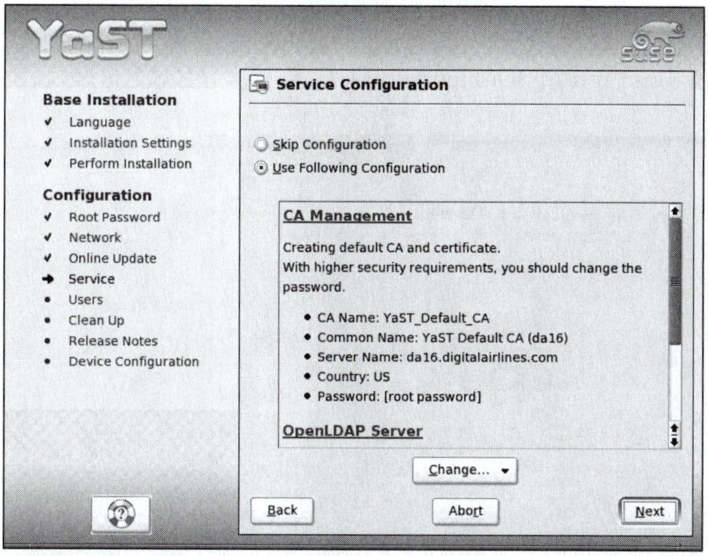

**Figure 1-13**

These services are:

- **CA Management.** A CA (Certificate Authority) guarantees a trust relationship among all network services communicating with each other.

- **OpenLDAP Server.** You run an LDAP server on your host to provide a central facility managing a range of configuration files.

   Typically, an LDAP server handles user account data, but with SUSE Linux Enterprise Server, it is also used for mail-, DHCP-, and DNS-related data.

   If you decide not to use an LDAP server, the YaST mail server module will not work because it depends on LDAP functionality. Nevertheless, you can still set up a mail server on your system with the help of the "Mail Transfer Agent" module.

   By default, a CA is created and an LDAP server is set up during the installation.

2. Select **Next**.

Make sure the **Server Name** is set correctly before selecting **Next**, because it is in the CA and the LDAP server configuration. If the server name is incorrect, select **Back** to return to the **Network Configuration** dialog box and set the name in the **Network Interface** dialog boxes.

## Users

After you configure the services, you configure user authentication. First, select the authentication method you want to use (see Figure 1-14).

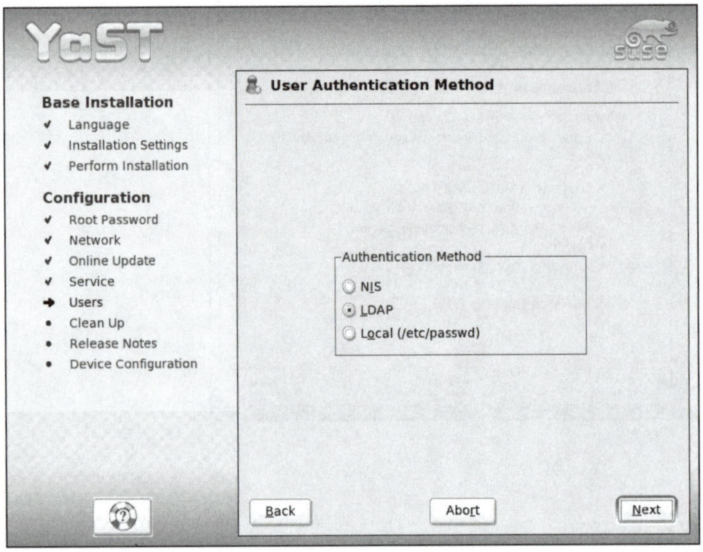

**Figure 1-14**

Three different methods are available:

- **NIS.** User account data is managed centrally by a NIS server. NIS can only be used in pure UNIX environments.

- **LDAP.** User account data is managed centrally by an LDAP server. Users should be authenticated via LDAP if you are working in a network environment that has both UNIX and Windows computers.

- **Local (/etc/passwd).** This setup is used for systems where no network connection is available or where users are not supposed to log in from a remote location at all. User accounts are managed using the local file /etc/passwd.

The next dialog box displayed depends on the authentication method you select. Figure 1-15 shows the dialog box for the LDAP authentication method.

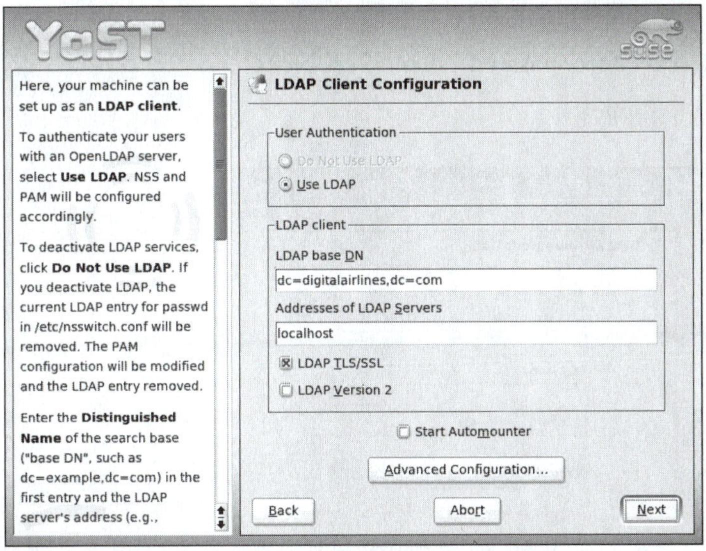

**Figure 1-15**

NOTE

LDAP authentication isn't used in this course. The topic is covered in the *Advanced SUSE Linux Enterprise Server Administration* course (3038). In this course, only the local authentication is explained.

For this course, do the following:

1. Select **Local (/etc/passwd)**, then select **Next**.

   Figure 1-16 appears.

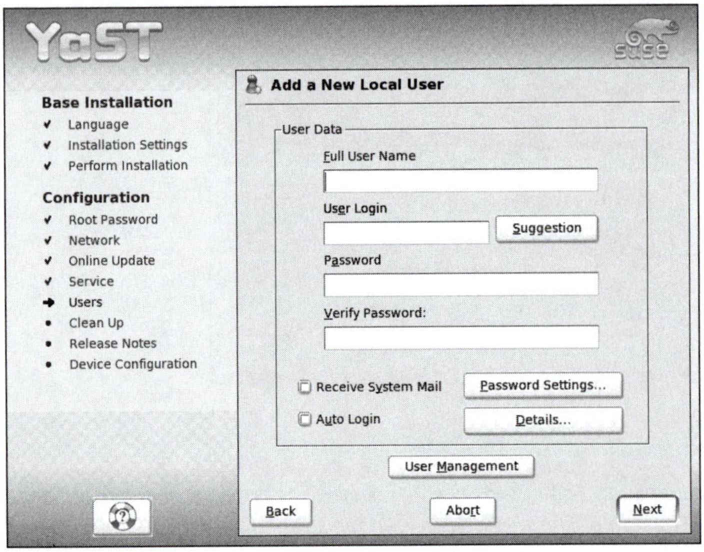

**Figure 1-16**

2. Add a user by providing the following information:

   ▪ **Full User Name.** The complete name of the user.

   ▪ **User Login.** The login name of the user. This name must be unique on the system.

   ▪ **Password** and **Verify Password.** The case-sensitive login password for the user. You have to enter the password twice for verification. For security reasons, the letters of the password are shown as stars. YaST displays warnings if the password is insecure.

3. If you want the user to receive automatically generated email for root, select **Receive System Mail**.

4. If you use your Linux computer only at your own desk and you want to avoid the login after startup, select **Auto Login**.

For security reasons, we recommended that you deselect this option.

5. After setting up one or more users, the system information is written to disk. YaST opens a window with the release notes. Select **Next** to go to the next step of the installation.

## Hardware

At this point, the final configuration dialog box appears (the hardware configuration dialog box, as shown in Figure 1-17).

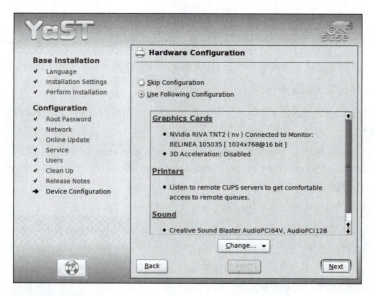

**Figure 1-17**

Do the following:

1. Configure additional hardware items such as the following:

   - Graphics cards

   - Printers

   - Sound cards

   YaST configures the graphics card and the sound card automatically.

2. YaST also detects most printers automatically. Confirm the settings and write them to the system by selecting **Next**.

3. A dialog box appears, explaining that the installation was successful. Select **Finish**.

SUSE Linux Enterprise Server 9 is now ready for use.

## Exercise 1-1    Install SUSE Linux Enterprise Server 9

The purpose of this exercise is to guide you through an installation of SLES 9. A working installation of SLES 9 is basic to all further exercises.

To install SLES 9, do the following:

1.  Insert the SLES 9 DVD into your DVD drive.

2.  Reboot your computer.

3.  From the Installation menu, select **Installation**.

4.  From the Novell Software License Agreement dialog box, select **I Agree**.

5.  From the Language dialog box, select *your language*; then select **Accept**.

6.  Select **New Installation**; then select **OK**.

7.  Verify that the correct keyboard layout is selected in the section **Keyboard Layout**.

8.  (Conditional) If the correct keyboard layout is not selected, from the Change drop-down list select **Keyboard Layout**; then select the correct layout and select **Accept**.

9.  From the Change drop-down list, select **Software**.

10.  Select **Detailed Selection**; then from the Filter drop-down list select **Selections**.

11.  In the left window, select **GNOME system** and **C/C++ Compiler and Tools**; then select **Accept**.

12.  Confirm the YaST installation suggestions by selecting **Accept**.

13.  Confirm the installation settings by selecting **Yes, Install**.

14.  (Conditional) If you are installing SLES 9 from CDs and YaST indicates that another installation CD is needed, insert the correct CD.

     After copying files and finishing a basic installation, YaST reboots your computer to a Password for root dialog box.

15.  Specify the root password by entering **novell** (twice); then select **Next**.

16.  Confirm the two warning messages by selecting **Yes**.

**CAUTION**

You should use an insecure password (such as novell) only for the purpose of training. Choose a more secure password on a live system.

17.  Confirm the network configuration by selecting **Next**.

18. Select **Yes, Test Connection to the Internet**; then test your Internet connection by selecting **Next**.

19. Do one of the following:

    ■ If the connection test fails (you see a failed message for the release notes), select **OK**.

    *or*

    ■ If the connection test is successful, select **Next**.

20. Do not install the updates found by selecting **No, Skip Update**; then select **OK**.

 You should install the updates on production systems. You do not install the updates during training because the updates require a maintenance key and they might change menus and user interfaces from the ones shown in this manual.

21. In the Service Configuration dialog box, make sure that **Use Following Configuration** is selected; then select **Next**.

22. In the User Authentication Method dialog box, select **Local (/etc/passwd)**; then select **Next**.

23. Add a local user by entering the following:

    ■ Full Name: **Geeko Novell**

    ■ User Login: **geeko**

    ■ Password: **N0v3ll** (use a zero, not an uppercase O)

    ■ Verify Password: **N0v3ll**

24. When you finish, select **Next**.

    YaST begins configuring your SLES 9 system.

25. Confirm that you want to view the release notes by selecting **Next**.

26. Accept the default hardware configuration by selecting **Next**.

27. When the installation is complete, select **Finish**.

    The GUI login screen appears. Leave this screen open for the next exercise.

## Objective 5    Document Installation, Configuration, and Baseline System Performance

As your Linux system grows, you will find your documentation of installation decisions, configuration options, and baseline performance to be invaluable.

There is no set rule where to keep such a documentation. If there is no company policy to follow you might want to keep it in a binder near the machine itself. A copy of it should be kept at another place, so that the documentation is not destroyed in a disaster.

Documentation makes it easier to add new systems, to troubleshoot most problems, and to optimize system and network performance.

In this objective you learn to:

- Document Installations and Maintenance
- Document Configuration Changes
- Document System Baseline Performance

## Document Installations and Maintenance

You should document every aspect of each of your Linux installations.

For each computer, you should document the following:

- Hardware specifications for the computer Linux is installed on
- Installation sources (such as an installation server, a DVD, or CDs)
- Installation options you used
- Installed packages
- Services configured during installation
- TCP/IP assignment
- Network settings
- Who performed the installation and when it was done

You can facilitate the installation documentation process by creating a form where you just fill in the blanks as you go through the installation steps. You can also set up a database where this information is stored.

As important as it is to record information pertaining to the installation of each new system, it is also important to keep the information up to date as you maintain each system on your network.

This means that your documentation should reflect maintenance procedures that are performed on each system, such as:

- Upgrades to or maintenance of hardware
- Packages that are added, removed, or updated
- Changes made to the configuration of services
- Changes made to TCP/IP assignments
- Changes made to network settings
- The order of steps used in the maintenance procedure
- Who performed the maintenance procedure and when it was done
- Tools that were used to facilitate or perform the procedure

Much of the time, maintenance procedures are performed in response to a user or customer complaint.

In these cases you should also document information about:

- Information about the user or customer, such as name, phone number, and department
- The date the problem was reported
- A brief description of the problem (for example, user cannot log in)
- A detailed description of the problem (for example, the user is a member of the Accounting department, has recently upgraded to the latest version of the desktop, and cannot log in to the accounting server)
- Steps taken to resolve the issue, including steps that didn't work as well as those that did
- The name of the technician who resolved the issue and when it was resolved
- Confirmation from the customer that the problem is resolved

## Document Configuration Changes

Documenting changes made to the configuration of hardware and software is so important a topic that it deserves more discussion.

Documentation of configuration changes should be kept as though it is a history of each system. All records of changes made to a system should be kept together and in chronological order of when the changes were made.

This documentation will help you when troubleshooting a problem as well as when you want to refer to configurations that are tested and known to work the way you want them to.

Details regarding configuration changes must include a history of the following:

- Operating system distributions and version numbers
- Software configuration changes
- Software version numbers
- Hardware configuration changes
- Hardware brand names and version numbers
- System behavior before the change and system behavior after the change

Keeping a history of this information helps you review and compare original settings and new settings, similar to before and after snapshots of your systems.

## Document System Baseline Performance

To accurately identify system performance problems you must start with a knowledge of the system's baseline performance. Baseline performance is established by regularly analyzing the performance of a healthy system during normal operating hours.

Once you have recorded a system's baseline performance information, you have something to refer to if you suspect that a system has started to perform poorly.

With this baseline information in hand, you can analyze the system's performance statistics and compare them with the baseline statistics.

First, this tells you if the system is performing poorly and how far from the baseline it is. Second, it tells you which specific components of the system are having a problem, so you know where to start looking for solutions.

Examples of command-line utilities that you can use to analyze system performance are

- top
- free
- vmstat

These utilities are discussed in more detail later in the course.

**NOTE**

# CHAPTER SUMMARY

❏ Linux is an advanced multiuser and multitasking operating system developed by Linus Torvalds. It can run on nearly any hardware platform and is based on the UNIX operating system, developed largely by Ken Thompson and Dennis Ritchie.

❏ The Linux source code is protected under the GNU Public License (GPL), which allows it to be publicly developed and distributed.

❏ There are many different distributions of the Linux operating system; one of the most prominent distributions is SUSE Linux. SUSE Linux Professional contains about 3500 packages that are updated frequently. SUSE Linux Enterprise Server (SLES) contains a fully-supported subset of the packages included in SUSE Linux Professional and has a useful life cycle of five years; the latest version of SLES is 9.

❏ Before installing SLES 9, you should verify that your computer hardware meets minimum installation requirements; in general, SLES has more support for server-class computers and less support for portable laptop computers.

❏ The SLES 9 installation process involves selecting a language, verifying hardware information, choosing software packages, and selecting a hard disk partitioning scheme. On the first boot following installation, you are prompted for a root user password, as well as network, service, user, and device settings.

❏ You should document all hardware, software, configuration settings, and baseline performance of your Linux system immediately following installation for use in future troubleshooting and maintenance.

# KEY TERMS

**baseline performance** — The average performance of a computer under normal working conditions.

**Dennis Ritchie** — The creator of the C programming language that was adopted by the UNIX operating system.

**free command** — A utility that can be run within a command-line Linux interface; it displays information about memory usage on your system.

**GNU Public License (GPL)** — A legal license under which the Linux kernel and most Linux software is published; it allows for open development and distribution of software.

**Ken Thompson** — The original creator of the UNIX operating system.

**kernel** — The core component of the Linux operating system; SLES uses the 2.6.5 version of the Linux kernel.

**Linus Torvalds** — The creator of the Linux operating system kernel.

**MULTICS** — An operating system that originated in 1965 and developed into the UNIX operating system.

**multiuser** — A feature of the Linux operating system that allows multiple users to interact with it simultaneously.

**platform** — A set of common hardware components on which an operating system can be run. The most common one today is the Intel i386 32-bit platform.

**preemptive multitasking** — A feature of the Linux operating system that allows several processes to run simultaneously; the Linux kernel determines how much time each process has to execute.

**top command** — A utility that can be run from a command-line Linux interface; it displays the processes that are currently using the most CPU time on your system.

**UNIX** — The operating system developed in 1969 that provided the basis for modern operating systems such as Linux.

**vmstat command** — A utility that can be run from a command-line Linux interface; it displays process, memory, paging, and CPU activity statistics for your system.

**YaST** — The main system configuration utility in SUSE Linux. It is also used to perform the SUSE Linux installation process. YaST stands for Yet another Setup Tool.

## REVIEW QUESTIONS

1. Which of the following operating systems is closely related to Linux?

   a. MULTICS

   b. OS X

   c. Windows

   d. UNIX

2. Which of the following are benefits of using the Linux operating system? (Choose all that apply.)

   a. Linux supports multiple hardware platforms.

   b. Linux is only developed by Linus Torvalds.

   c. Linux is a multiuser and multitasking operating system.

   d. Linux is developed under the GPL.

3. How does SUSE Linux Enterprise Server differ from SUSE Linux Professional?

   a. It contains more packages and has a shorter life cycle.

   b. It contains fewer packages and has a shorter life cycle.

   c. It contains more packages and has a longer life cycle.

   d. It contains fewer packages and has a longer life cycle.

4. Which of the following are the minimum system requirements for SLES?

   a. 256 MB RAM, 1 GB hard disk space

   b. 512 MB RAM, 1 GB hard disk space

   c. 256 MB RAM, 4 GB hard disk space

   d. 512 MB RAM, 4 GB hard disk space

5. The SLES Linux kernel contains many new features compared to older Linux kernels, including support for multiple CPUs. How many CPUs can the SLES Linux kernel support?

   a. 2

   b. 4

   c. 8

   d. More than 64

6. You are planning the hard disk configuration of a Linux installation. Which of the following is the best practice when planning partitions that will be used by Linux?

   a. Use a large number of partitions for redundancy.

   b. Use only a single partition for simplicity.

   c. Use RAID partitions whenever possible.

   d. Select the number and size of partitions depending on the purpose of your Linux system.

7. You are planning a new SUSE Linux installation and wish to verify that your computer hardware is compatible with SLES 9. Where can you find this information?

   _____

8. Which of the following keys can you press at the initial SUSE Linux installation screen to select the location of the SUSE source files?

   a. F1

   b. F3

   c. F4

   d. F6

9. You are having difficulty performing a standard installation of SUSE Linux on an older computer in your organization. Which option could you try next at the initial installation screen?

   a. Installation — ACPI Disabled

   b. Installation — Safe Settings

   c. Manual Installation

   d. Rescue System

10. Which of the following are configured after the first boot following a SUSE Linux installation? (Choose all that apply.)

   a. The root user's password

   b. Hard disk partitioning

   c. Software package selection

   d. Network configuration parameters

11. Which services are set up by default following an SLES installation? (Choose all that apply.)

    a. Certificate Authority (CA)

    b. Dynamic Host Configuration Protocol (DHCP)

    c. Sendmail mail relay agent

    d. Lightweight Directory Access Protocol (LDAP)

12. Following an SLES installation, you are prompted to choose how users will authenticate to your system. Which method should you select if you wish to allow authentication requests from Windows computers?

    a. Kerberos

    b. NIS

    c. LDAP

    d. Local (/etc/passwd)

13. After you have successfully installed SLES, you should create documentation that may help you in future troubleshooting and maintenance. Which items should you document? (Choose all that apply.)

    a. Installation choices

    b. Configuration settings

    c. Configuration changes

    d. System baseline performance information

14. Several months following installation, your SLES system is exhibiting poor performance. How can you use system baseline performance information to find the solution to the performance problem? _____

## Discovery Exercises

### Linux History

Although Linux was evolved from the UNIX operating system, it is very different from UNIX in that its source code is freely available to software developers. As a result, Linux is called open source software (OSS) and is protected under the GNU Public License (GPL) that evolved from Richard Stallman's Free Software Foundation (FSF) and GNU (GNU's Not Unix) project. Using the Internet, research how the FSF, GNU project, and GPL set the stage for the introduction of Linux.

### Exploring Linux Distributions

All Linux operating system distributions share the same core Linux kernel and operating system libraries, yet implement different software components and applications. SUSE Linux is a Linux distribution that is specialized for an enterprise organization. Using the Internet, research five other Linux distributions. Summarize their key features and usage in a short memo.

## Open Source Software

One of Linux's largest advantages on the operating system market is that it is open source software. Furthermore, most software that is available for use on Linux systems is also open source software. Read the book *The Cathedral and the Bazaar* by Eric S. Raymond and summarize why open source software is a valuable resource to organizations today. You can read an online copy of this book on the Internet at *www.catb.org/~esr/writings/cathedral-bazaar/*.

## Checking for Memory Errors

During the interactive and noninteractive sections of an SLES installation, your computer may suddenly reboot, hang, or display a Fatal Signal 11 (Segmentation Fault) error. Although these problems may be the result of incompatible or malfunctioning hardware devices, they are most often the result of defective RAM. The SLES installation program can use all of the available locations in your RAM during the installation process. Hence, even if your system worked well before you started the SLES installation, the installation program may still detect bad locations in your RAM. As a result, it is good form to use the memtest86 utility that is included on your SLES DVD to check your RAM before starting the installation. Boot your computer from the SLES DVD and select **Memory Test** from the menu to run the memtest86 utility on your computer. Were any errors found? When one full series of tests has been performed, press **Esc** to stop the utility.

## Text-Based Installation

Some video adapter cards are incompatible with the SLES installation program. In this case, you can install SLES using a text-based menu interface (called ncurses) rather than a graphical interface; on the first boot following installation, SLES will then detect and install your video card. Some administrators choose to perform a text-based installation because it is faster than a graphical installation, since the graphical subsystem does not need to be loaded. Perform Exercise 1-1 again, but instead of selecting Installation in Step 3, press the **F2** key and choose to perform a **Text Mode** installation of SLES. You will need to use the **Tab** key to navigate through screen options during the installation.

## Documentation

After completing the SLES installation in this chapter, prepare a sample documentation set that outlines your system hardware, installation choices, and software packages.

## System Baseline Performance Utilities

There are several available Linux utilities in addition to **top**, **free**, and **vmstat** that can measure different aspects of your computer's performance to determine your system baseline performance. Use Internet resources such as the *www.novell.com* Web site to find three other SLES utilities that may be used to obtain performance data, and summarize their usage and features.

# USE THE LINUX DESKTOP

**This section gives an overview of two different graphical user interfaces of SLES and explains how to access the command line.**

♦ Overview of the Linux Desktop

♦ Use the KDE Desktop Environment

♦ Use the GNOME Desktop Environment

♦ Access the Command-Line Interface from the Desktop

## INTRODUCTION

You cannot install Microsoft Windows without its graphical user interface (GUI). However, in Linux, the GUI is a normal application that you can choose whether or not to install.

You can configure most services in Linux by editing an ASCII text file, so you do not need a GUI if you want your computer to act only as a server.

While a GUI is convenient, not installing a GUI has the following advantages:

- **Stability.** Every program contains errors that can make your system unstable. The fewer programs are installed, the more stable your system will be. A graphical user front end is a large program that might contain a large number of undiscovered programming errors, even if the error ratio is low.

- **Performance.** Every running program needs system resources. Fewer programs running on your computer means increased performance.

- **Security.** The points mentioned under Stability above are also relevant from a security perspective. The fewer programs installed, the fewer the potential security vulnerabilities there are. You need not worry about the vulnerabilities of programs you have not installed on you system.

## OBJECTIVE 1    OVERVIEW OF THE LINUX DESKTOP

The base of any GUI on Linux is the X Window System (simply called X or X11). It allows you to control the input and output of several applications in different windows of a graphical interface.

You need to distinguish here between graphical applications, which run in their own windows, and text-based applications, which are carried out in a terminal window.

The X Window System was created in 1984 at **Massachusetts Institute of Technology**. The aim of the development was to be able to use graphical applications across a network, independent of hardware.

The X Window System allows graphical applications to be displayed and operated on any monitor, without running the applications on the machines to which these monitors are connected.

The basis for this is the separation into a server component (X server) and the application itself (client application). The X server and client application communicate with each other by way of various communication channels.

- **X server.** The X server controls the graphical screen. This corresponds roughly to what would be called a graphics driver on other systems. In addition, it manages the input devices, such as keyboard and mouse, and transmits their actions to the X client.

The X server, however, has nothing to do with the appearance of the window and the desktop; this is the task of the window manager. XFree86 3.3.x and its successor XFree86 4.x are free implementations of the X server. SUSE Linux Enterprise Server defaults to using XFree86 4.*x*.

- **Client application.** The client application is a graphical application that uses the services of the X server to receive keyboard and mouse actions and to have its own output displayed on the screen.

As shown in Figure 2-1, the X server is running on computer **da5**, while the X client applications are running on computers **da1** and **da2**.

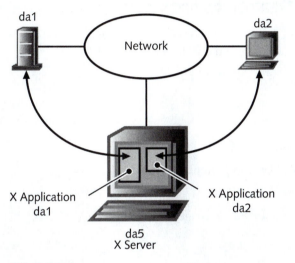

**Figure 2-1**

The display of the client applications, however, is performed by the X server on the machine **da5**. All of these computers can be running different operating systems.

The communication between X server and X client uses the network protocol TCP/IP—even if the server and client run on the same computer.

**NOTE**

Window managers are specialized client applications. A window manager works together with the X server and provides additional functionality. The window manager:

- Provides control elements
- Manages virtual desktops
- Provides functionality of window frames (for example, changing their size)

The X Window System is not linked to any specific window manager and thus it is not linked to any particular look and feel.

The current version of SLES 9 has several window managers, including kwin (the KDE window manager), the GNOME window manager, and twm (Tab Window Manager).

Desktop environments go far beyond the look and feel window managers provide for desktops and manipulating windows. The aim is to provide clients with a unified look and feel. KDE is the standard graphical desktop for SLES 9, but you can install the GNOME desktop instead.

## OBJECTIVE 2    USE THE KDE DESKTOP ENVIRONMENT

One of the most frequently used graphical desktop environments is KDE. This desktop environment is installed by default during the installation of SLES 9.

The following explains how to use KDE on SLES 9:

- How to Log In
- How to Log Out
- How to Shut Down and Reboot the Linux System
- How to Identify KDE Desktop Components
- How to Manage Icons in the KDE Environment
- How to Use the Konqueror File Manager

## How to Log In

If computer users want to work with a multiuser operating system, they must first identify themselves to the operating system. For this purpose, they need:

- A *login string* or *username*
- A *password* (usually assigned by the system administrator when a new user is added)

**2**

When the computer is booted and ready for work, the login dialog box shown in Figure 2-2 appears.

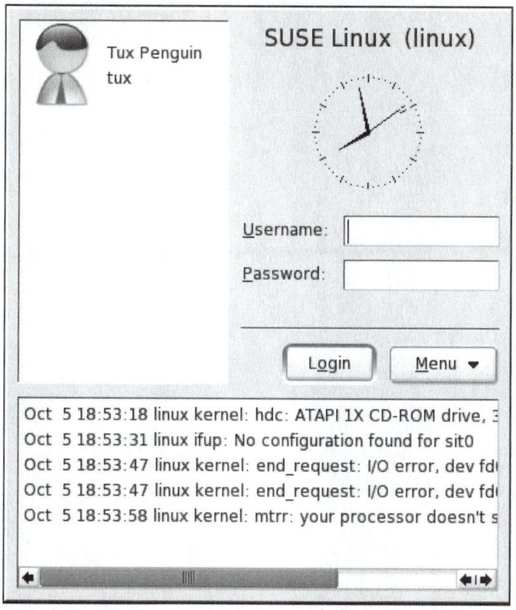

**Figure 2-2**

After entering a username and password, select **Login**. If the login is successful, the KDE desktop environment shown in Figure 2-3 appears, as well as a welcome screen and some useful tips.

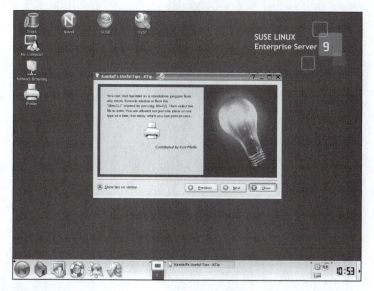

**Figure 2-3**

You can read the information or just close the window by selecting the **X** button in the top right corner of the window, as shown in Figure 2-4.

**Figure 2-4**

## How to Log Out

When you are ready to log out of the system, open the KDE menu by selecting the first (left) icon in the bottom panel, as shown in Figure 2-5.

2

**Figure 2-5**

At the bottom of the KDE menu, select **Logout**. You can also right-click on the window background and select the same option from the popup menu.

After selecting Logout, a confirmation dialog box appears. If you select **Logout** again, you are logged out and the login screen reappears, allowing you or another person to log in.

## How to Shut Down and Reboot the Linux System

If you are at the login screen, you can open the **Menu** menu you select from several choices, including the following:

- **Session Type.** You can choose a window manager other than KDE. In this manual, we cover only KDE (the default window manager).

- **Restart X Server.** You can restart the program that is responsible for the GUI. Remember, SLES 9 does not need a GUI to work.

  The GUI is clearly separated from the operating system. However, in this course we work from the GUI interface.

- **Shutdown Type.** If you select this option, you are asked if you want to shut down or restart your computer (see Figure 2-6).

Figure 2-6

For security reasons, you have to enter the root password because only root is allowed to restart or shut down the computer.

If you select **Turn Off Computer** and select **OK**, Linux closes all the (system) programs currently running.

Older computers that do not have power management and cannot switch themselves off can be switched off manually when the following message appears:

Master Resource Control: runlevel 0 has been    reached

If you switch the machine off too soon, this could possibly lead to loss of data.

**NOTE** You should *always* shut down your computer before you turn it off.

## How to Identify KDE Desktop Components

After you log in, your system will by default start the KDE desktop environment. It is composed of:

- The Desktop
- The KDE Control Panel (Kicker)
- The KDE Menu
- Virtual Desktops

### The Desktop

The desktop shows only a few icons. You can start the applications associated with these icons by selecting them once with the left mouse button.

You can move the icons by dragging them with the mouse.

### The KDE Control Panel (Kicker)

You control the KDE desktop by using the KDE control panel (also called the Kicker), located at the bottom of the desktop (see Figure 2-7).

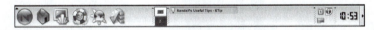

**Figure 2-7**

The following are the most commonly used icons and their functions (from left to right):

- **Green button with red "N".** Menu of all *configured* programs and functions (not of all programs and functions installed on the machine). This menu is called the *KDE menu*.
- **Blue house.** Konqueror, the preferred KDE file manager.
- **Shell in front of monitor.** A terminal window in which to type commands directly.
- **Lifesaver with a chameleon head.** The SUSE Help Center.
- **Globe with gear wheel teeth.** Konqueror, as the preferred Web browser.
- **"E" with letter.** The KMail e-mail program.
- **The white and gray box.** Virtual desktops.
- **The empty area right of the virtual desktops.** Task Manager area.

- **Clipboard with "k".** Clipboard.
- **Loudspeaker.** A sound mixer.
- **Sheet with "i".** SuSEwatcher for automatic updates.
- **Computer card.** SuSEplugger for plug and play.
- **Clock.** Current time.

## The KDE Menu

Programs are normally started from the KDE menu. You can select the KDE menu button to open the KDE menu, as shown in Figure 2-8.

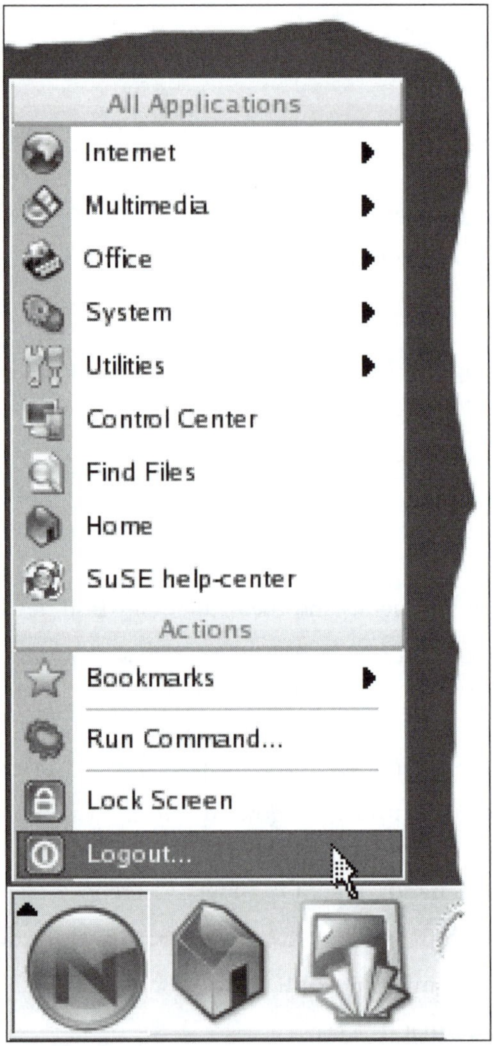

Figure 2-8

This menu consists of the following three sections:

- **Most Frequently Used Applications.** As indicated by the name, this section lists the five most frequently used applications. Accordingly, the listed entries can change from time to time.

- **All Applications.** This section features an overview of various applications sorted by subjects (such as **Multimedia**).

- **Actions.** This section provides a command line interface, an overview of the bookmarks, an option for locking the screen, and the option for logging out.

A submenu in the KDE menu is marked by a small black arrow in the right-hand corner. To open a submenu, move the mouse cursor over the menu entry. To start a program, select the corresponding entry once with the left mouse button.

### Virtual Desktops

If you are working with several programs concurrently, the screen can quickly become cluttered with open windows. In Linux, you can bring order to this chaos by changing to another (virtual) desktop. You can switch between the various desktops via the control panel.

By default, two virtual desktops are configured. In the KDE control center, you can increase the number of usable virtual desktops up to sixteen. Every virtual desktop can host a virtually unlimited number of applications. Using these virtual desktops, you can easily organize your work.

## How to Manage Icons in the KDE Environment

Three areas in your KDE environment contain icons:

- Desktop
- Kicker
- KDE Menu

### Desktop

There are several ways to create a new icon on your desktop; however, for simplicity, only one method is used in this course.

To create an icon for an application on your desktop, do the following:

1. Select the item in your KDE menu.

2. Hold down the left mouse button, move the mouse pointer to free space on your desktop, and release the mouse button.

3. In the menu that appears, select **Copy Here**.

## Kicker

You can add new programs to the control panel by right-clicking a free area of the panel and then selecting **Add**.

You can remove a program from the control panel by right-clicking its icon in the control panel and then selecting **Remove** *program name*.

You can move icons in the panel by holding down the middle mouse button or by choosing **Move** from the Context menu.

## KDE Menu

To make changes in your KDE menu, do the following:

1. Start the KDE Menu Editor by selecting the KDE menu icon with the right mouse button and selecting **Menu Editor**.

   The dialog box in Figure 2-9 appears, where you can edit the KDE menu.

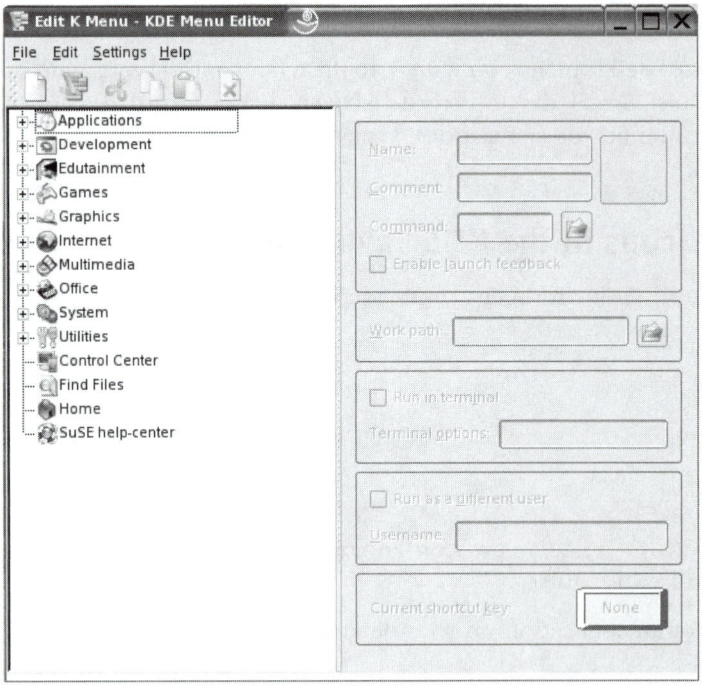

**Figure 2-9**

## How to Use the Konqueror File Manager

You can do nearly all work on the file system by using the KDE Konqueror program. To start Konqueror, select the *blue house* icon in Kicker. Figure 2-10 appears.

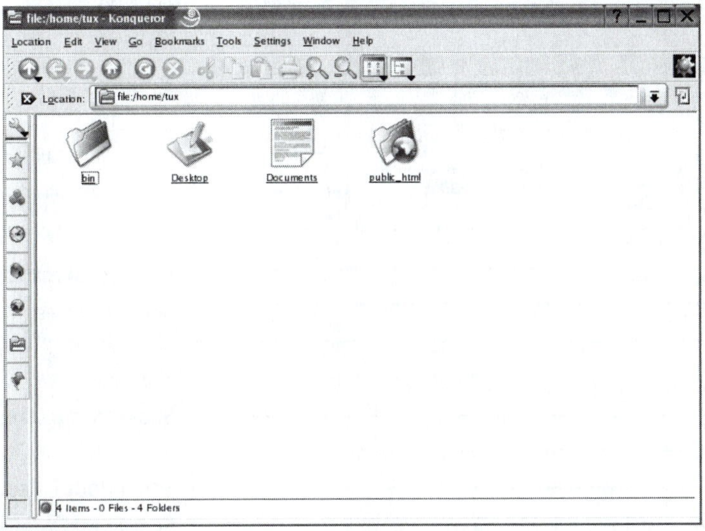

**Figure 2-10**

To navigate quickly through the file system, activate the *navigation panel* (select **Window > Show Navigator Panel**), which splits the main window and displays the directory tree.

The icon with the blue house on the navigation panel displays the directory tree starting from the user's home directory. The icon with the folder displays the directory tree starting from the root directory.

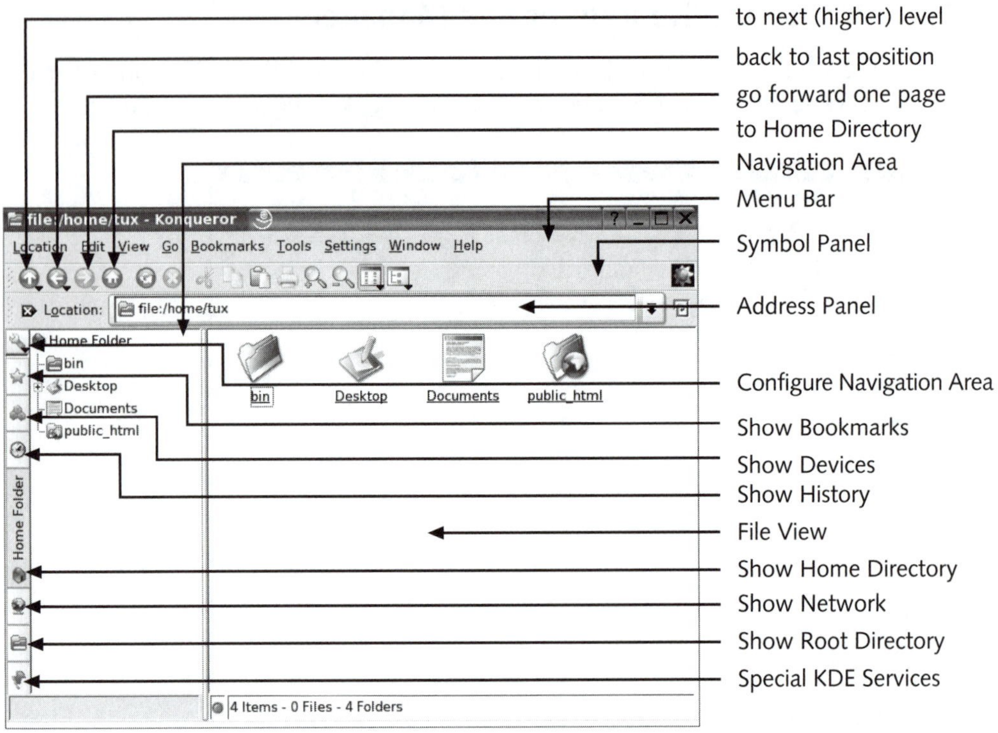

**Figure 2-11**

The Konqueror window is divided into three sections:

- The **top section** contains a menu bar, a toolbar, and an address panel. The bar to the left is the preset navigation panel, which serves primarily for navigation and orientation.

- After you select the blue house or folder icon, the navigation area is split into a **left window** and a right window. You can use the left window for quicker navigation through the file system tree.

- The **right window** displays the contents of the directory you selected in the left window. This is the file view.

There are several ways to navigate in the file system: using three arrows on the left side of the toolbar is the simplest way. The current position can be seen in the text window of the URL panel (in the above example, **/home/tux/**).

If you select the arrow pointing up, you will move from the current directory to the next highest directory (from **/home/tux/** to **/home/**). The arrow pointing to the left returns you to the previously visited location. You can move forward again with the right arrow.

- You can open a directory and view its contents by selecting the directory in the file view. If you select a normal file, KDE tries to open it or starts a program to open it.

- Selecting the house symbol in the toolbar takes you directly to your own home directory (for example, **/home/tux/**).

- If you select a directory in the navigation area, its contents are displayed in the file view.

You can double-click the directory in the navigation area to open it and view all subdirectories in it. Double-click the directory again to close it.

**NOTE**

If you prefer a detailed list that displays information about each file in the tree, activate the tree view by selecting the second icon from the right in the toolbar.

## Exercise 2-1    Explore Your KDE Desktop

It is possible to administer SLES 9 without a graphical user interface. However, sometimes a GUI is much more convenient than a pure text console. The purpose of this exercise is to familiarize you with KDE.

To explore your KDE desktop, do the following from the GUI login screen (where you were left after installing SLES 9):

1. In the Username field, enter **geeko**.

2. In the Password field, enter **N0v3ll** (use a zero, *not* an uppercase O).

    For security reasons, asterisks are displayed instead of the actual letters when you enter the password.

3. Select **Login**.

    The KDE desktop environment starts, and initial dialog boxes appear.

4. Close the SUSE Linux welcome screen and the Kandolf's Useful Tips dialog box by selecting the **X** in the upper right corner of the windows.

5. (Conditional) If a new hardware dialog box appears, deselect **Keep Me Informed about New Hardware**; then select **No**.

6. Start the file manager Konqueror by selecting the *blue house* icon in Kicker.

7. View the navigation area by selecting the *red folder* icon on the left side of the Konqueror window.

8. View the contents of the /etc/ directory by selecting **etc** in the side panel (a single mouse click).

9. Copy the file /etc/DIR_COLORS to the directory /tmp/ by scrolling down and selecting the **DIR_COLORS** file icon, dragging it over the **tmp** folder icon in the navigation area, and releasing the mouse button.

10. From the popup menu, select **Copy Here**.

11. View the contents of the directory /tmp/ by selecting **tmp** in the side panel (a single mouse click).

12. Rename the copied file by right-clicking the **DIR_COLORS** file icon, and then selecting **Rename** from the popup menu.

13. For the new filename, type **example.txt**; then press **Enter**.

14. Quit Konqueror by selecting the **X** button in the top right corner of the window.

15. Open the KDE menu by selecting the leftmost icon in the bottom panel.

16. Select **Logout**; then select **Logout** again.

    You are returned to the GUI login screen.

17. Open the **Menu** drop-down list; then select **Shutdown**.

18. Select **Restart computer**; then enter the root password **novell** in the Password field and select **OK**.

    After the computer has restarted, the login screen appears.

19. Log in as **geeko** with a password of **N0v3ll**; then select **Login**.

20. Close all windows that open automatically by selecting the **X** button in the top right corner of the window.

## OBJECTIVE 3    USE THE GNOME DESKTOP ENVIRONMENT

Both GNOME and KDE are comfortable desktop environments. Like KDE, GNOME supports drag and drop. Numerous programs are specifically designed for GNOME.

To use the GNOME desktop environment, you need to know the following:

- How to Start GNOME
- How to Navigate in GNOME
- How to Manage Icons in GNOME
- How to Use the GNOME File Manager (Nautilus)

## How to Start GNOME

Before you select Login at the login screen, you can start GNOME instead of KDE by selecting **Session Type > GNOME** from the Menu drop-down list. Figure 2-12 appears.

**Figure 2-12**

## How to Navigate in GNOME

Besides the main window, the GNOME desktop includes the following two panels:

- **Top panel.** The panel at the top of the desktop is responsible for launching applications. The following features are available (left to the right):
  - Applications menu for launching applications
  - Actions menu for basic actions (such as logging out)
  - The Nautilus file manager (house icon)
  - The terminal emulation window (monitor icon)
  - A clock
  - A speaker icon for volume
  - A menu listing all open windows
- **Bottom panel.** The panel at the bottom of the desktop provides the following:
  - An icon to close all open windows
  - A task manager
  - A pager for the four virtual desktops

You can start a program with an icon on the desktop by double-clicking the icon. You can set preferences for the desktop environment by selecting the **Start Here** icon.

To quit GNOME, select **Actions > Log Out** in the GNOME panel. Figure 2-13 appears.

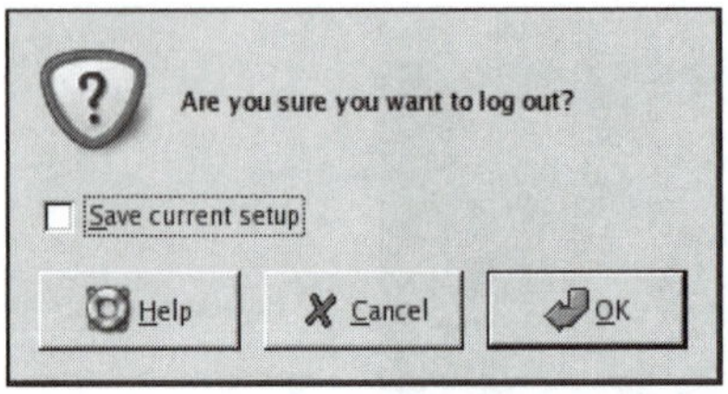

**Figure 2-13**

If you select **Save Current Setup**, your current desktop environment settings are saved.

## How to Manage Icons in GNOME

You can find icons in the following three areas on your desktop:

- Desktop
- Panel
- Application Menu

### Desktop

There are several ways to create a new icon on your desktop; however, in this course only one method is described.

To create an icon for an application on your desktop, select the item in your Applications menu, drag it to a free space on your desktop, release the mouse button; then select **Copy Here**.

### Panel

You can add new programs to the control panel by right-clicking a free area of the panel and then selecting **Add to Panel**. From the submenus displayed, select the application you want to add.

You can remove a program from the control panel by right-clicking its icon in the control panel and then selecting **Remove from Panel**.

You can move icons in the panel by holding down the right mouse button and selecting **Move** from the context menu.

2

### Application Menu

To add an entry to a menu, do the following:

1. Double-click the **Start Here** icon on the desktop.

   The Start Here location appears.

2. In the file manager window, double-click the icon that represents the menu (**Applications** or **Menu SuSE**) to which you want to add the launcher.

3. Select **File > Create Launcher**.

   A Create Launcher dialog box is displayed.

4. Enter the properties of the launcher in the Create Launcher dialog box; then select **OK**.

## How to Use the GNOME File Manager (Nautilus)

GNOME provides its own file manager, called Nautilus, shown in Figure 2-14.

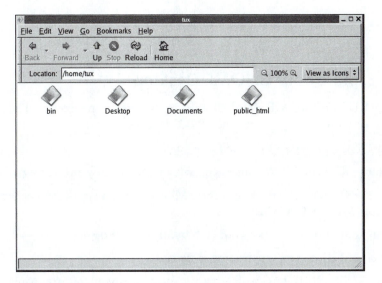

**Figure 2-14**

You can start Nautilus by selecting the house icon in the top panel or by selecting the **username Home** icon on the desktop. Although Nautilus does not provide as many features as some other file managers, it has the features you need for most file navigation tasks.

To display the file system tree view, select **View > Side Panel**; then select **Tree** from the side panel drop-down list. A window similar to Figure 2-15 appears.

**Figure 2-15**

## Exercise 2-2    Explore Your GNOME Desktop

Whether you use KDE or GNOME is entirely a matter of personal preference. The purpose of this exercise is to familiarize you with the GNOME desktop.

To explore your GNOME desktop, do the following:

1. From the KDE menu, log out as geeko by selecting **Logout > Logout**.
2. From the GUI login screen, select the **Menu** drop-down list; then select **Session Type > GNOME**.
3. Log in as **geeko** with a password of **N0v3ll** (select **Login**).

   The GNOME desktop environment starts.
4. From the GNOME desktop, select the **Applications** menu (top panel) and view the applications available.
5. Start the Nautilus file manager by selecting the *house icon* in the top panel.
6. Display the side pane by selecting **View > Side Pane**.
7. View the file system tree in the side pane by selecting **Tree** from the drop-down list at the top of the side pane.
8. Display the contents of the directory /tmp/ by expanding **Filesystem**; then select **tmp**.

2

9.  Delete the file **example.txt** by right-clicking the file icon and selecting **Move to Trash**.

10. Close the Nautilus file manager window.

11. From the top of the GNOME desktop, select the **Actions** menu; then select **Log Out**.

12. Select **OK**.

    You are returned to the GUI login screen.

13. From the **Menu** drop-down list, select **Session Type > KDE**.

14. Log in as **geeko** with a password of **N0v3ll** (select **Login**).

---

# OBJECTIVE 4    ACCESS THE COMMAND-LINE INTERFACE FROM THE DESKTOP

You can implement the classic multiuser environment by connecting several terminals (dialog stations)—monitor and keyboard units—to the serial interface of a single computer.

You can also connect several terminals to the serial interface in a Linux system. However, because in general not more than one person sits in front of one computer at any given time, usually only one physical keyboard is needed. *Virtual terminals* were created in Linux to allow a user to run tasks in parallel.

With virtual terminals, you can work in Linux as if you had several classic terminals available at the same time.

By default, you have six virtual terminals (F1–F6) running on your computer. By pressing **Ctrl + Alt + Fx**, you can switch between individual terminals. By pressing **Ctrl + Alt + F7**, you can switch back to your graphical user interface.

You can determine the terminal currently being used from the tty number (tty1–tty6). tty is an abbreviation for *teletype*, which is another word for terminal.

When you switch to a virtual terminal, a login prompt appears:

```
Welcome to SUSE LINUX Enterprise Server 9 (i586) - Kernel 2.6.4-
27-
default (tty1).

da10 login:
```

From here you can enter your login name and password. To log out enter **exit**.

**NOTE**

The file /etc/issue contains the text that is displayed before you log in to the system (see above). When you log in to a host via the network, the contents of the file /etc/issue.net are used.

To display a welcome message after the successful login to the system, you can enter the text in the file /etc/motd with the help of a text editor such as vi.

Besides using the virtual terminals, you can start a terminal emulation (called Konsole) from your KDE desktop Kicker by selecting the icon shown in Figure 2-16.

**Figure 2-16**

The terminal opens inside a window with options you can select to modify the display of the terminal (such as font and background color).

## Exercise 2-3   Access the Command Line Interface

As has been stated before, SLES 9 does not need a GUI for its administration. And even with a graphical desktop environment running you can switch to the text consoles any time if you like to. This exercise shows you how.

To access the command line interface, do the following:

1. Switch to the first virtual terminal by pressing **Ctrl + Alt + F1**.

2. (Conditional) If you see a SUSE - A Novell Company splash screen, display the command line by pressing **F2**.

3. Enter **geeko** as a login name.

4. Enter **N0v3ll** as the password.

5. Switch to the second virtual terminal by pressing **Ctrl + Alt + F2**.

   Notice that you are not logged in at this terminal.

6. Press **Ctrl + Alt + F1** to switch back to the first terminal.

   You are still logged in as geeko.

7. Log out by entering **exit**.

8. Switch back to the graphical user interface by pressing **Ctrl + Alt + F7**.

# CHAPTER SUMMARY

❑ You can interact with a Linux system using a graphical user interface (GUI) or command-line interface. Unlike Windows systems, the GUI is optional.

❑ The Linux GUI is provided by the X Window System, which consists of an X server, window manager, and client applications. The X server used by SLES is XFree86 version 4, and communicates with client applications using the TCP/IP protocol. As a result, the X server and client applications may reside on different computers across a network.

❑ A desktop environment such as KDE or GNOME can be used to standardize the X Window System. The default desktop environment in SLES is KDE.

❑ The KDE Control Panel at the bottom of the KDE desktop may be used to start applications, switch virtual desktops, or open the KDE menu. The default file and Web browser in the KDE desktop is Konqueror.

❑ The top panel in the GNOME desktop may be used to start applications, whereas the bottom panel may be used to switch virtual desktops or control applications. The default file browser in GNOME is Nautilus.

❑ You can obtain a command-line interface in SLES by interacting with one of six virtual terminals. To start a virtual terminal, you may use the Ctrl + Alt + F$x$ key combination, where $x$ is number 1 through 6. Alternatively, you can invoke the Konsole application in the KDE desktop to obtain a command-line interface within your desktop environment.

❑ To switch from a command-line interface to a GUI interface, you can use the Ctrl + Alt + F7 key combination.

# KEY TERMS

**/etc/issue** — A text file containing banner text that is displayed before you log into a command-line virtual terminal.

**/etc/issue.net** — A text file containing banner text that is displayed before you log in to a command-line terminal from across the network.

**/etc/motd** — A text file containing banner text that is displayed after you log in to a command-line terminal.

**client application** — The application program that receives keyboard and mouse input from the X server and sends screen output to the X server. It may run on the same or a different computer than the X sever. It is also called the X client.

**desktop environment** — A set of software components that standardize the look and feel of the desktop. There are two standard GUI desktop environments available in most Linux distributions: KDE and GNOME.

**GNOME** — A common Linux desktop environment that uses the GNOME window manager. GNOME stands for GNU Object Model Environment.

**GNOME window manager** — The window manager used by the GNOME desktop.

**graphical applications** — Programs that send their output to a graphical user interface.

**graphical user interface (GUI)** — An interface that allows users to manipulate icons to control the operating system and run application programs.

**KDE** — A common Linux desktop environment that uses the KDE window manager. KDE stands for K Desktop Environment.

**KDE Control Panel** — The panel at the bottom of the KDE desktop that is used to start applications. It is also called the KDE Kicker.

**KDE Kicker** — See KDE Control Panel.

**KDE menu** — The main menu used to start applications in the KDE desktop. It is invoked by pressing the leftmost button on the KDE Control Panel.

**KDE window manager (kwin)** — The window manager used by the KDE desktop.

**Konqueror** — The default directory navigation utility and Web browser that is included with KDE.

**Konsole** — An application that emulates a command-line terminal within the KDE desktop.

**Nautilus** — The default directory navigation utility that is included with GNOME.

**Tab Window Manager (twm)** — A small, stand-alone window manager that uses few system resources and which may be used instead of the KDE or GNOME desktop. When you invoke the Tab Window Manager, you are said to be in failsafe mode.

**TCP/IP** — The default network protocol used on Linux systems. It stands for Transmission Control Protocol / Internet Protocol.

**text-based applications** — Programs that send their output to a command-line user interface.

**virtual desktops** — Separate workspaces that you can use within a desktop environment such as KDE or GNOME.

**virtual terminals** — The system components that allow you to log in to and interact with a command-line user interface. You can use and switch between six virtual terminals by default on most Linux systems (tty1–tty6).

**window manager** — The component of the X Window System that controls the look and feel of windows on the desktop.

**X server** — The component of the X Window System that accepts information from client applications and draws graphical images to the screen.

**X Window System** — The set of software components that provides a graphical user interface in Linux.

**XFree86** — A free version of the X Window System that is used by SLES.

# REVIEW QUESTIONS

2

1. Which of the following is not a reason to install Linux without a GUI?
   a. To increase the security of your system
   b. To improve the usability of your system
   c. To improve the performance of your system
   d. To increase the stability of your system

2. Which X Window System component is used to draw the actual graphical images on your screen?
   a. X server
   b. Window manager
   c. Client application
   d. Desktop environment

3. Which X Window System component is used to change the size of window frames?
   a. Desktop environment
   b. Client application
   c. Window manager
   d. X server

4. What version of the X Window System is used in SLES 9? _____

5. What two desktop environments are available in SLES 9? _____

6. What is the purpose of a desktop environment?
   a. It provides elements that control the windows on the desktop.
   b. It standardizes the look and feel of the desktop.
   c. It allows you to use virtual desktops.
   d. It manages the size of window frames.

7. What is the default desktop environment in SLES 9? _____

8. Which of the following statements are true? (Choose two answers.)
   a. The X server and client applications must reside on the same computer.
   b. The X server and client applications typically reside on the same computer.
   c. The X server and client applications communicate using the TCP/IP protocol.
   d. The X server and client applications must communicate using the window manager.

9. Which of the following can you use to start applications in the KDE desktop environment? (Choose all that apply.)

    a. Virtual desktops

    b. The KDE Kicker

    c. Konqueror

    d. The KDE menu

10. How many virtual desktops are configured by default in SLES 9?

    a. 1

    b. 2

    c. 3

    d. 4

11. You wish to add an icon for a recently installed application to your KDE menu. What should you do?

    a. Drag an existing icon to the KDE menu icon on the KDE Kicker.

    b. Right-click the KDE menu icon and choose Menu Editor.

    c. Drag an existing icon to the KDE Kicker.

    d. Right-click the KDE Kicker and choose Menu Editor.

12. Which icon on your KDE Kicker can you use to start the Konqueror file manager?

    _____

13. How can you start the GNOME desktop environment from the login screen?

    _____

14. Which key combination can you use to switch to your first virtual terminal in order to obtain a command-line interface login prompt?

    a. Ctrl + Alt + F1

    b. Ctrl + C

    c. Ctrl + T + 1

    d. Ctrl + Alt + 1

15. Which virtual terminal refers to your GUI?

    a. tty1

    b. tty6

    c. tty7

    d. tty8

## DISCOVERY EXERCISES

### Desktop Security

All network programs use a port number to identify information that is sent to them. The X Window System is a network application that listens to information addressed to TCP/UDP port 0. Hackers can use this information to breach the security of the X Window System, and this threat is heightened when the X Window System is run as the root user, which has all rights to the Linux system.

As a result, it is good form to log in to a GUI environment as a regular user and only switch to the root user as necessary to perform system administration. Log in to the KDE desktop as the root user. Does the interface warn that you are logged in as the root user? When finished, log out of the KDE desktop.

### Exploring Window Managers

Although the KDE and GNOME desktop environments are the most common GUI interfaces used today, many Linux distributions ship with stand-alone window managers such as FVWM (Feeble Virtual Window Manager) and the TWM (Tab Window Manager). These window managers can be used to obtain a small GUI that uses less system resources than KDE and GNOME.

At the login screen, choose a FVWM session type from the Menu drop-down box and log in to the system as geeko. What elements exist in this desktop? How is this desktop different from KDE and GNOME? Right-click the desktop background and view the KDE menu. Left-click the desktop background and select WindowManager and **Exit** to return to the login screen.

At the login screen, choose a TWM session type from the Menu drop-down box and log in to the system as geeko. What elements exist in this desktop? How is this desktop different from KDE and GNOME? Left-click the desktop background, choose **Xterm** while holding down the mouse button, and click an area of the desktop in order to place it there. Left-click the desktop background and select **Exit** while holding down the mouse button to return to the login screen.

### Virtual Desktops

Virtual Desktops allow you to organize several open applications and hence improve your productivity. Log in to the KDE desktop as geeko. What virtual desktop are you using? Open a Konsole application. Next, click on the second virtual desktop icon in the KDE Kicker. Is your application available? Does the icon for your first virtual desktop indicate a running application?

Next, right-click your desktop background, click **Create New**, **File**, **Text File**, type the name **sample**, and press **OK**. Switch back to your first virtual desktop by clicking on the appropriate icon on the KDE Kicker. Is your application available? Is your desktop file available? Explain.

## Virtual Terminals

There are six command-line virtual terminals available in SLES by default. Ensure that you are not logged in to a desktop environment and use the appropriate key combination discussed in this chapter to switch to tty1. Log in as the root user. What prompt do you get? Type **who** and press Enter. What terminal does the who command indicate that you are on?

Next, switch to tty2 and log in as the geeko user. What prompt do you get? Type **who** and press Enter. Who is logged in, and on which terminals?

Switch to tty7 and log in to the KDE desktop as the geeko user. Following this, open the Konsole application, type **who**, and press Enter. How does the who command indicate that you have a GUI session? Why? (*Hint*: See the first Discovery Exercise.)

Log out of tty7. Use the **exit** command to log out of tty1 and tty2.

## Understanding X Windows

Becoming familiar the X Window System (commonly called X Windows) is key to understanding how the GUI is implemented in Linux. Use the Internet to answer the following questions:

1. There are two X Windows packages available for use on Linux systems today: XFree86 and X.org. What is the difference between them? How did they develop? What are the latest versions of each?

2. What other operating systems use X Windows? What window managers and desktop environments do they use?

3. How does X Windows differ from the GUI that is included with the Microsoft Windows operating system?

## KDE versus GNOME

When Linux was in the early stages of development in the 1990s, two competing desktop environments were created: KDE and GNOME. Use the Internet to answer the following questions:

1. Which desktop environment was created first?

2. What developmental libraries did each desktop environment use? Were they open source?

3. What parallel features exist in both desktop environments? What are some differences between them?

# 3

# LOCATE AND USE HELP RESOURCES IN THE LINUX SYSTEM

**Linux is one of the best documented operating systems. This section shows you how to find and use several sources of help information.**

♦ Access and Use Manual Pages

♦ Use info Pages

♦ Access Release Notes and White Papers

♦ Use GUI-Based Help in the Linux System

♦ Find Help on the Web

## OBJECTIVE 1    ACCESS AND USE MANUAL PAGES

The most important command for online help is *man* (an abbreviation of manual or man page).

All manual pages are available in English and many have been translated into other languages. Because these translations are often incomplete or not maintained, we recommend using the English versions.

If the English manual pages are not shown automatically with the command **man**, you can display the English version of the manual page by setting LANG=en_EN.

For example, to display the English version of the manual page for the command man, you would enter the following:

```
tux@da10:~ > LANG=en_EN man man
```

Using the parameter LANG=en_EN switches to the English language for the requested man pages only.

The following is the first page of the manual pages for the command man:

```
man(1)          Manual pager utils               man(1)



NAME
   man  an interface to the on-line reference manuals



SYNOPSIS
   man [-c|-w|-tZT device] [-adhu7V] [-m system[,...]]
   [-L locale] [-p string] [-M path] [-P pager] [-r prompt]   [-S list] [-e
extension] [[section] page ...] ...
   man -l [-7] [-tZT device] [-p string] [-P pager]
   [-r prompt] file ...
   man -k [apropos options] regexp ...
   man -f [whatis options] page ...

DESCRIPTION
   man is the system's manual pager. Each page
   argument given to man is normally the name of
   a program, utility or function. The manual
   page associated with each of these arguments
   is then found and displayed. A section, if
   provided, will direct man to look only in that
   section of the manual. The default action
   is to search in all of the available sections,
   following a pre-defined order and to show
   only the first page found, even if page exists
   in several sections.
```

The header of each manual page contains the command name at the left and right sides and the section number to which the manual page belongs. The center of the header shows the name of the section. The last line usually contains the date of the last changes.

A manual page is always divided into the parts shown in Table 3–1.

**Table 3-1**

| Part | Contents |
|---|---|
| NAME | Name and short description of the command |
| SYNOPSIS | Description of the syntax |
| DESCRIPTION | Detailed description of the command |
| OPTIONS | Description of all options available |
| COMMANDS | Instructions that can be given to the program while it is running |
| FILES | Files connected in some way to the command |
| SEE ALSO | References to related commands |
| DIAGNOSTICS | Possible error messages of the program |
| EXAMPLE | Examples of how to use a command |
| BUGS | Known errors and problems with the command |

Not every manual page has all parts.

The manual pages are organized in the sections shown in Table 3–2.

**Table 3-2**

| Section | Contents |
|---|---|
| 1 | Executable programs and shell commands (user commands) |
| 2 | System calls |
| 3 | Functions and library routines |
| 4 | Device files |
| 5 | Configuration files and file formats |
| 6 | Games |
| 7 | Macro packages and file formats |
| 8 | System administration commands |

For example, entering the following displays general information about the command crontab:

**man 1 crontab**

Entering the following displays information about the configuration file for the command crontab (which also has the name crontab):

**man 5 crontab**

It is especially important to know to which section a command belongs when there is more than one manual page for a command.

For example, the command uname is both a user command and a system call. Entering the following displays information about the user command:

**man 1 uname**

Entering the following displays information about the system call used to get name and information about the current kernel:

**man 2 uname**

You can display a brief description of all the available manual pages for a command or utility by using the command whatis (as shown in the following):

```
tux@da10:~ > whatis uname
uname (1)  - print system information
uname (2)  - get name and information about current kernel
uname (1p) - return system name
uname (3p) - get the name of the current system
tux@da10:~>
```

**NOTE**

Manual pages whose output is marked with "p" are POSIX manual pages of the command uname (**uname (1p)**) and the function (**uname (3p)**).

To display manual pages on the screen, **man** uses the program **less** which displays one screen of information at a time. The keys listed in Table 3–3 are available to use with command less.

**Table 3-3**

| Key Name | Description |
|---|---|
| Space | Page one screen forward. |
| b | Page one screen backward. |
| PageDown | Page half a screen forward. |
| PageUp | Page half a screen backward. |
| Down-Arrow, Enter | Jump one line forward. |
| Up-Arrow | Jump one line backward. |
| End | Go to the end of the manual page. |
| Home | Go to the beginning of the manual page. |
| /expression | Search forward from the current cursor position for *expression*; matching line is displayed as first line on the screen. |
| ?expression | Search backward from the current cursor position for *expression*; matching line is displayed as first line on the screen. |
| n | Move to the next instance of expression in the search. |
| N | Move to the previous instance of expression in the search. |
| q | Close the manual page. |

In SUSE Linux Enterprise Server (SLES), the manual pages are located in the directory /usr/share/man/.

If you enter **man –k** *keyword* or **apropos** *keyword*, a list of manual pages in which the keyword appears in the NAME section is displayed. For example:

```
tux@da10:~ > man -k printf
vasprintf (3) - print to allocated string
vwprintf (3p) - wide-character formatted output of a stdarg
argument list
vfprintf (3)   - formatted output conversion
snprintf (3)   - formatted output conversion
format (n)     - format a string in the style of sprintf
swprintf (3)   - formatted wide character output conversion
asprintf (3)   - print to allocated string
vsprintf (3p)  - format output of a stdarg argument list
printf (3p)    - print formatted output
sprintf (3p)   - print formatted output
wprintf (3p)   - print formatted wide-character output
vdprintf (3)   - print to a file descriptor
fwprintf (3)   - formatted wide character output conversion
sprintf (3)    - formatted output conversion
dprintf (3)    - print to a file descriptor
wprintf (3)    - formatted wide character output conversion
printf (3)     - formatted output conversion
```

## Exercise 3-1   Access and Use Manual Pages

Manual pages are ideal for getting a quick information on command-line commands. This is a resource you will probably use very often.

To use manual pages, do the following:

1. Select the *monitor* icon in the Kicker to start **Konsole**.

2. Find the sections of the manual pages for the command info by entering:

   **whatis info**

3. Read the first section (executable programs and shell commands) of the manual pages of the command info by entering:

   **man 1 info**

4. Scroll through the text by using **Up-arrow** and **Down-arrow**.

5. When you finish viewing the information, exit (quit) the manual page by typing **q**.

6. *(Optional)* Look at the manual page of a command of your choice.

   Leave the Konsole window open for the next exercise.

## OBJECTIVE 2    USE INFO PAGES

Unfortunately, a whole series of GNU programs no longer have manual pages (or the pages have become outdated). Instead, info files are used, which can be read with the command **info**.

In SLES 9, the info files are located in the directory /usr/share/info/.

The following is the beginning of the info file for the command info:

```
File: info.info, Node: Top, Next: Getting Started, Up: (dir)

Info: An Introduction
*********************

 Info is a program, which you are using now, for reading
documentation of computer programs.
 The GNU Project distributes most of its on-
line manuals in the Info format, so you need a program called
"Info reader" to read the manuals. One of such
programs you are using now.

 If you are new to Info and want to learn how to use it, type
the command 'h' now. It brings you to a programmed instruction
sequence.

 To learn advanced Info commands, type 'n' twice.
 This brings you to'Info for Experts', skipping over the 'Getting
Started' chapter.

 * Menu:

 * Getting Started::  Getting started using an Info reader.
 * Advanced Info::    Advanced commands within Info.
 * Creating an Info File:: How to make your own Info file.
 * Index::     An index of topics, commands, and variables.
```

The following are advantages of the info file format:

- It uses a structured document setup.

- Specific sections can be reached directly from the table of contents.

- Specific sections can be linked.

Table 3-4 lists the most commonly used keys for the command info.

**Table 3-4**

| Key Name | Description |
| --- | --- |
| Space, PageDown | Page down one screen. |
| Backspace, PageUp | Page up one screen. |
| b | Move the cursor to the beginning of the current info page. |
| e | Move the cursor to the end of the current info page. |
| Tab | Move the cursor to the next reference (*). |
| Enter | Follow the reference. |
| n | Move to the next info page of the same level (Next:). |
| p | Move to the previous info page of the same level. |
| u | Move one level higher. |
| l | Move back to the last text displayed; end help. |
| s | Search in the info page. |
| h | Display help. |
| ? | List a summary of commands. |
| q | Close the info document. |

## Exercise 3-2   Access and Use info Pages

Sometimes manual pages have only very little information and refer to info pages for more complete information. The purpose of this exercise is for you to get used to the format, which might need a little time.

To use info pages, do the following:

1. From the Konsole terminal window, display the info pages for the command info by entering

   **info info**

2. Move the cursor to the first reference (Getting Started) by pressing **Tab**.

3. Follow the reference by pressing **Enter**.

4. Move the cursor to the reference **Quitting Info** by pressing **Tab** eight times.

5. Follow the reference by pressing **Enter**.

6. Return to the page Getting Started by typing **l** (lowercase L).

7. Exit the info file by typing **q**.

8. *(Optional)* Look at the info page of a command of your choice.

9. Close the Konsole terminal window.

## Objective 3    Access Release Notes and White Papers

Release notes, white papers, and other helpful information are stored in the directory /usr/share/doc/. This directory contains the following:

- Release Notes
- Howto Files
- Help for Installed Packages

## Release Notes

When you complete the SLES 9 installation (just before the Login screen is displayed), the release notes appear in a window.

If you want to access these release notes later, you can find them in the directory /usr/share/doc/release-notes/.

Two release note files are available:

- RELEASE-NOTES.en.html
- RELEASE-NOTES.en.rtf

The content of these files is identical. Only the file format is different.

## Howto Files

You can find additional information (including background material) in the ***howto*** files. There is a howto for almost every topic in Linux.

The howto files are available in different formats, such as ASCII, PostScript, and HTML. In addition, many of the howto files have been translated into various languages.

SLES 9 contains a large number of howto files. The howto files of the Linux Documentation Project in HTML format are installed during the SLES 9 installation. You can access these files in the directory.

**/usr/share/doc/howto/en/html/**

You can also install the howto files in ASCII format (package howto, ASCII format). After installation, you can find them in the directory.

**/usr/share/doc/howto/en/txt/**

You can find a list of all current howto files (together with available translations) at:

www.tldp.org/

## Help for Installed Packages

Help files are available in the following directory for most installed packages:

**/usr/share/doc/packages/*package-name***

These help files are written by the programmers of the package. Therefore, the format of these files is not standardized. Some packages provide help files in HTML, while others are in pure ASCII.

## Exercise 3-3    Access Release Notes and White Papers

Sometimes you may want to look at the release notes again after installation. The purpose of this exercise is to show you how to access them, as well as to give you a first idea on how to navigate in the Linux file system and use the file manager Konqueror.

To access the release notes, do the following:

1. Start the file manager Konqueror by selecting the *blue house* icon in Kicker.

2. Open the navigation panel by selecting the **root folder** icon (red folder) on the left side of the Konqueror window.

3. Display the content of the directory /usr/ by selecting the **usr** folder icon in the Navigation Panel.

4. Display the content of the directory /usr/share/ by selecting the the **share** folder icon in File View (right window).

   Select the icon once; you do not need to double-click.

5. Display the content of the directory /usr/share/doc/ by selecting the **doc** folder icon in the File View.

6. Display the content of the directory /usr/share/doc/release-notes/ by selecting the **release-notes** folder icon in the file view.

7. Read the release notes by selecting **RELEASE-NOTES.en.html** in the File View.

8. Close the Konqueror window.

## OBJECTIVE 4    USE GUI-BASED HELP IN THE LINUX SYSTEM

Two important applications for getting help in SUSE Linux Enterprise Server are the SUSE HelpCenter and Konqueror. To get help, you can do the following:

- Display the SUSE HelpCenter
- Use Help Commands with Konqueror

## Display the SUSE HelpCenter

SUSE provides its own help system—the *SUSE HelpCenter*. To access the HelpCenter, select the lifesaver icon, shown in Figure 3-1, in the Kicker.

**Figure 3-1**

The HelpCenter starts and displays help information, as shown in Figure 3-2.

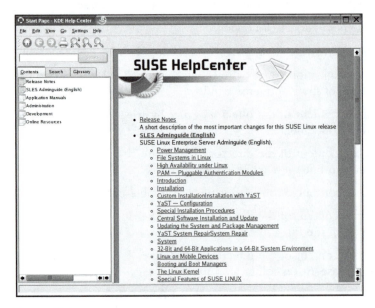

**Figure 3-2**

Help programs are available in most KDE applications and can be started by pressing **F1**. Because the help programs use HTML format, you can follow any embedded hyperlinks by selecting an entry in the table of contents.

The first time you use the Search feature, you see a message telling you that you have to create an index. If you want to use the Search feature, select **Yes > OK**.

**NOTE**

## Use Help Commands with Konqueror

Konqueror is a Web and file browser. You can use it to display manual pages and info pages.

To view a manual page, enter **man:***command* (such as **man:info**) in the address bar. Konqueror lists any available man pages for that command, as shown in Figure 3-3.

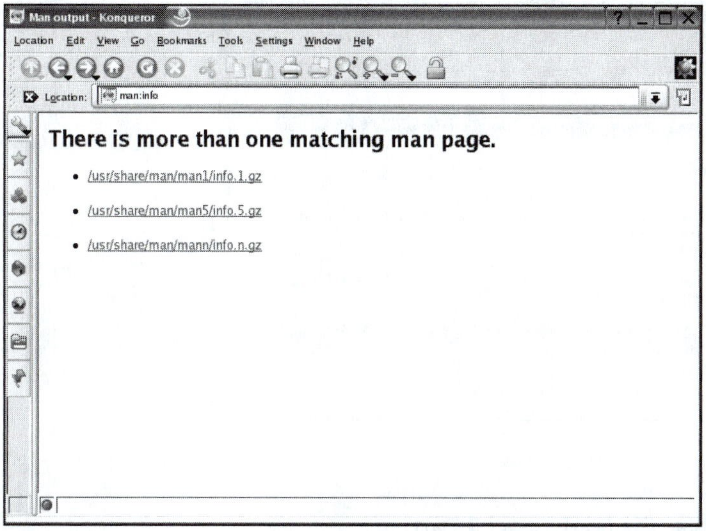

**3**

**Figure 3-3**

To use the info command with Konqueror, enter **info:*command*** in the address bar; Konqueror displays the info page, as shown in Figure 3-4.

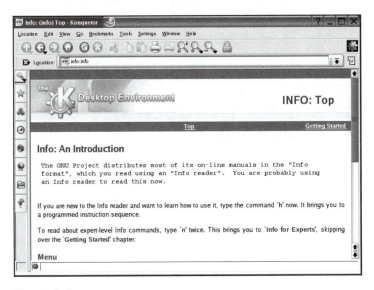

**Figure 3-4**

# Exercise 3-4   Use GUI-Based Help

Most of the time you will probably get along fine with manual and info pages. The purpose of this exercise is to show you additional help resources, in case, for example, the manual pages don't fit your needs.

To use GUI-based help, do the following:

1. Start the SUSE HelpCenter by selecting the *lifesaver* icon in Kicker.

2. Create a search index by selecting the **Search** tab.

3. Start the creation by selecting **Yes**.

4. Confirm the creation by selecting **OK**.

   A dialog box appears requesting the root password to create the search index.

5. Enter a password of **novell** and select **OK**.

6. After the creation process finishes, close the dialog box by selecting **Close**.

7. Find information about printing with Linux by entering **printer** in the text field above the Search tab; then select **Search**.

8. In the Help information window (to the right) select the link under the Release Notes heading.

9. To find the paragraph about printer configuration, select:

   **Edit > Find**

10. In the Text to find field, enter **printer**; then select **Find**.

11. After viewing the information, close the Find dialog box by selecting **Cancel**.

12. Close the SUSE HelpCenter window.

## OBJECTIVE 5    FIND HELP ON THE WEB

You can find an extensive collection of information about Linux on the Internet. The following are some of the more frequently used Linux sites:

- www.novell.com/linux/suse

- www.linux.org

- www.linux.com

- www.tldp.org

- www.linuxplanet.com

- www.cert.org (security issues)

- www.securityfocus.com (security issues)

- www.kernel.org (Linux kernel issues)

To find other sources of information, you can use a Web search site such as Google. Google offers a special Web search site for questions about Linux at *www.google.com/linux*.

Be careful with information you find on personal home pages. This information can be old or wrong.

## Exercise 3-5    Find Help on the Web

The help information on the installation CD-ROMs or DVD mirrors what was known at the time of the release. However since that time things have likely happened—errors were found, as well as solutions or work-arounds for these errors, etc.

Most of this information can be found in the Internet. The purpose of this exercise is to give you a first start into using this resource.

To find help on the Web, do the following:

1. Start Konqueror by selecting the *globe* icon in Kicker.

2. In the Location bar, enter **support.novell.com**.

   The Novell Support home page appears.

3. Under Technical Resource Search, select **SUSE** from the Choose a Product drop-down list.

4. In the empty Search field, enter:

   **SLES 9 Installation**

   Notice that you can search the Knowledgebase and Documentation.

5. Search both by selecting **Documentation**; then select **Search**.

6. (Conditional) If you receive a warning message about unencrypted transmission of data, select **Do Not Ask Again**; then select **Yes**.

7. (Conditional) If you see a cookie alert warning message, select **All Cookies**; then select **Accept**.

   A Search Results page appears, showing several pages of links.

8. Select one or more links, then select the **Back** icon arrow until you return to the Support home page.

9. Take some time to explore other links such as **Download Patches** or **Downloads**.

10. When you finish, in the Location field enter:

    **www.google.com/linux**

11. In the text field at the top of the page, enter **kde and sles9**; then select **Google Search**.

12. Select one or more of the displayed links.

13. When you finish, close the Konqueror window.

## CHAPTER SUMMARY

❑ There are several help resources available locally on your SLES system as well as on the Internet.

❑ The manual pages contain the syntax and usage of most commands and files on your system. The manual page database contains eight sections that organize commands and files based on type and function. You can search the manual pages from a command-line interface by using the **man** command or from a GUI by using the **man:** syntax within Konqueror.

**3**

❏ The info pages are an alternative to the manual pages; they format information differently and can contain links to other sections. You can search the info pages from a command-line interface by using the **info** command or from a GUI by using the **info:** syntax within Konqueror.

❏ The /usr/share/doc directory on your SLES system contains release notes for the SLES installation, howto files that guide you through various Linux tasks, and help files for installed software packages.

❏ You can use the F1 key in most GUI applications to obtain application-specific help, or invoke the SUSE HelpCenter from within the KDE or GNOME desktop environment to obtain SUSE-specific help.

## KEY TERMS

**/usr/share/doc** — A directory that stores most command, file, system, and program information on a Linux system.

**apropos command** — Used to search the manual pages by keyword.

**howto files** — A document that contains the steps for common Linux procedures.

**info command** — Used to search the info pages.

**info pages** — A database that contains information about the syntax and usage of commands and files, organized in a document-like format with links to other information.

**less command** — Used to display text files in a page-by-page fashion. It also is used to display the contents of manual pages.

**man command** — Used to search the manual pages.

**manual pages** — A database that contains information about the syntax and usage of commands and files.

**POSIX** — An industry standard that defines operating system interface components. It stands for Portable Operating System Interface.

**SUSE HelpCenter** — A GUI help program that contains information about the SUSE Linux operating system.

**whatis command** — Used to display the basic usage of a command from the manual pages database.

## REVIEW QUESTIONS

1. Which of the following commands can you use to obtain a brief description of the **find** command?

   a. man find

   b. info find

   c. help find

   d. whatis find

2. Which manual page section contains system administration commands that require root user access?

    a. 1

    b. 5

    c. 7

    d. 8

3. Which section of a manual page contains the syntax of the command?

    a. Synopsis

    b. Options

    c. Files

    d. Example

4. What command could you type at a command prompt to search Section 5 of the manual pages for help on the **inittab** file? _____

5. Which commands can be used to search the manual pages database for entries that have the word **logged** in the name or description? (Choose two answers.)

    a. man –k logged

    b. man logged

    c. apropos logged

    d. whatis –k logged

6. What character can you press in the **info** utility to display a help screen?

_____

7. You are attempting to locate documentation for a program that you have recently installed on your system. Where should you look?

    a. /usr/share/doc

    b. /usr/share/doc/howto

    c. /usr/share/doc/release-notes

    d. /usr/share/doc/packages

8. You wish to search the Internet for a step-by-step list of instructions that will allow you to create a new filesystem. Where should you look?

    a. *www.linux.org*

    b. *www.tldp.org*

    c. *www.kernel.org*

    d. *www.help.org*

9. Which key can you press to obtain help in most graphical programs?

   a. F1

   b. F2

   c. F3

   d. F4

10. What would you type in the Location bar of Konqueror to search the info pages for information about the **who** command? _____

---

## DISCOVERY EXERCISES

### Using the Manual Pages

Use the manual pages to find help on the **top**, **free**, and **vmstat** command-line utilities that you learned about in Chapter 1. What manual page section are these commands listed in? What are some common options for each command? Next, use these commands to obtain system baseline performance information about your system.

### Using apropos to Search the Manual Pages

Use the **apropos** command to find any utilities that have the word **who** in their name or description. How many utilities are there? What section of the manual pages are they from? Which utility may be used to see who is logged onto the system and what programs they are running? View the regular manual page for this command and note any options that can be used. Run the command to verify its purpose.

### Using the Info Pages

The info pages provide an alternative to the manual pages for finding command and file information, but not all commands on your system have info pages available. Use the info command to find help on the **top**, **free**, and **vmstat** command line utilities in the previous Discovery Exercise. Do info pages exist for all three utilities?

### Using the Help Utility

Another utility that can be used to obtain information about commands on the system is the help utility. However, the help utility only lists help for commands that are built into your command-line interpreter (or shell). Type **help** at a command prompt and observe the various commands for which you can obtain help. Next, type **help echo** to learn the syntax and usage of the echo command in your shell. Use the help command to learn about three more commands of your choice.

## Obtaining Online Help Using LDP

There are many Linux help resources on the Internet. One of the most comprehensive is the Linux Documentation Project (LDP). LDP hosts a complete collection of howto documents that describe how to perform most user and administrative tasks in Linux. In addition, LDP hosts online manual pages as well as longer and more in-depth guides to different Linux technologies. Search the latest howto documents at the LDP (*www.tldp.org*) or for information on how to play DVDs in Linux. What is the name of the howto document? How is the howto document organized? Does it contain information specific to different Linux distributions such as SUSE? Check for the same howto document in /usr/share/doc/howto/en/html. Is the same version available on your local computer?

## Using the SUSE HelpCenter

Open the SUSE HelpCenter by clicking on the appropriate icon in your KDE Kicker. Using the left pane, navigate the various HelpCenter areas. What categories of information exist? Can you access the manual pages and info pages?

# 4

# USE THE YaST MANAGEMENT UTILITY

**This section introduces the YaST graphical administration tool and some of the more frequently used modules. It also covers the configuration of the X Window system.**

- ◆ Get to Know YaST
- ◆ Understand the YaST Software Management Feature
- ◆ Manage User Accounts with YaST
- ◆ Configure a Printer in the Linux System
- ◆ Use YaST to Configure a Modem
- ◆ Use YaST to Obtain Hardware Configuration Information
- ◆ Configure the X Window System

## OBJECTIVE 1    GET TO KNOW YaST

YaST stands for Yet another Setup Tool. You can use YaST to complete many configuration tasks as a SUSE Linux Enterprise Server (SLES) administrator.

The appearance of the user interface (ncurses or Qt) depends on which command you use to start YaST and on whether you use the graphical system or the command line, as indicated in Table 4-1.

**Table 4-1**

| Command | Terminal in X Windows | Command Line |
|---------|-----------------------|--------------|
| yast2   | Qt                    | ncurses      |
| yast    | ncurses               | ncurses      |

Except for the controls and the appearance, the graphical mode and the text mode of YaST are identical.

In the graphical interface, shown in Figure 4-1, you can control YaST with the mouse.

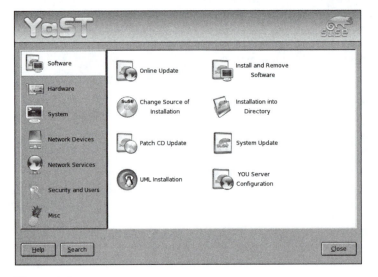

**Figure 4-1**

In the ncurses interface, shown in Figure 4-2, you control YaST2 with the keyboard.

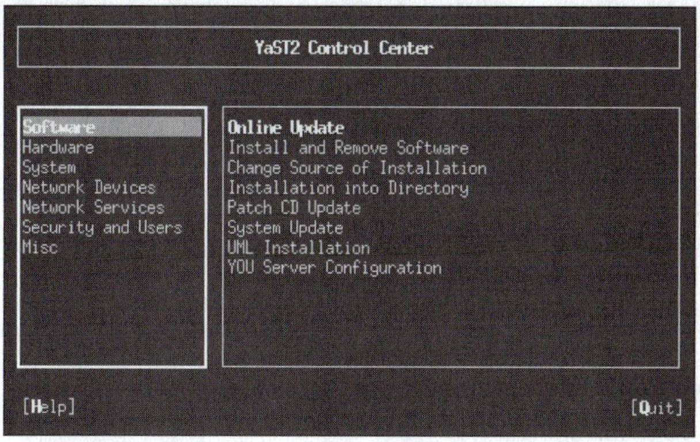

**Figure 4-2**

Use the following keys to navigate in this window:

- Press **Tab** to move from one box to another or to the text buttons.
- To go back to the previous box, press **Alt+Tab**.
- Use the arrow keys to navigate within the box.
- Select highlighted menu items by pressing the **Spacebar**.
- To select a menu item, press **Enter**.
- Press **Alt** and the highlighted letter to access an item directly.

To display a list of YaST modules, enter:

**yast –l**

To start an individual module, specify its name. For example, to start the software installation module, enter:

**yast sw_single**

You can enter the software module name with the command yast or yast2, as in the following:

- **yast sw_single** (text mode)
- **yast2 sw_single** (graphical mode)

To display a list of YaST options, enter one of the following:

- **yast --help**
- **yast –h**

## Exercise 4-1    Get to Know YaST

While YaST is not relevant for CompTIA's Linux+ exam it is nevertheless a tool used very frequently when administering SLES 9.

The purpose of this exercise is to give you a first idea of what can be done with YaST. During the remainder of this course, you will see that it is a very powerful tool.

To use the graphical version of YaST, do the following:

1. From the KDE desktop, start YaST by selecting the **YaST** icon.

2. Enter the root password **novell** in the Run As Root dialog box; then select **OK**.

    The YaST Control Center appears.

3. Select **Misc > View System Log**.

4. From the top drop-down list, select **/proc/version**.

5. Close the log window by selecting **OK**.

6. Select **System > Date and Time**.

7. Select **Change Time or Date**.

8. Enter the current time (such as **08:00:00**) and the current date (such as **27.09.2005**).

9. Select **Apply**.

10. Select **Accept**.

11. Switch to console 1 by pressing **Crtl + Alt + F1**.

12. Log in as **root** with a password of **novell**.

13. View a list of the available YaST modules by entering:

    **yast –l**

14. Log out by entering **exit**.

15. Switch back to the graphical interface by pressing **Crtl + Alt + F7**.

16. Close the YaST Control Center.

---

## OBJECTIVE 2    UNDERSTAND THE YaST SOFTWARE MANAGEMENT FEATURE

To understand the YaST software management feature, you need to know the following:

- How to Select Software Packages to Install
- How to Manage Installation Sources

## How to Select Software Packages to Install

After performing a standard SLES 9 installation, you will often need to install additional software. To do this, start the YaST module **Software > Install and Remove Software**.

YaST analyzes the installed packages and the packages that are available on the installation media and checks the dependencies between packages.

After this check, the dialog box for selecting packages to install, shown in Figure 4-3, appears.

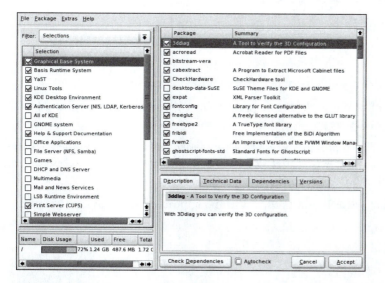

**Figure 4-3**

To help you find the software you want to install, you can select the different filters from the drop-down list in the top left corner of the window. The following filters are available:

- **Selections.** Displays grouped selections of packages.
- **Package Groups.** Displays all software that is available on the known installation media.
- **Search.** Lets you enter a search term and specify where you want YaST to search for the software package.
- **Installation Summary.** Displays all the packages and their status.

To find a package, enter the package name or part of the package name or keywords in the Search field; then select **Search**.

Matching packages are listed in the right pane. The installation state is shown by a small symbol in front of the package name. The most commonly displayed symbols include those shown in Figure 4-4.

| | | |
|---|---|---|
| ☐ | Do not install | This package is not installed and it will not be installed. |
| ☑ | Install | This package will be installed. It is not installed yet. |
| ☑ | Keep | This package is already installed. Leave it untouched. |
| ⟳ | Update | This package is already installed. Update it or reinstall it (if the versions are the same). |
| 🗑 | Delete | This package is already installed. Delete it. |

**Figure 4-4**

To view a list of all possible symbols, select **Help > Symbols**.

Select the symbol of the package you want to install several times until the Install symbol appears; then select **Accept**.

You might see a dialog box indicating that the dependencies between the packages cannot be resolved and that other packages also need to be installed. In most cases you can simply confirm this dialog box.

If you are installing SLES from CDs, a warning appears if the wrong CD is in the drive.

## How to Manage Installation Sources

The software installation dialog box lists only the packages that are on the current installation media.

If you want to add more installation sources, you need to select **Software > Change Source of Installation** from the YaST Control Center. Figure 4-5 appears.

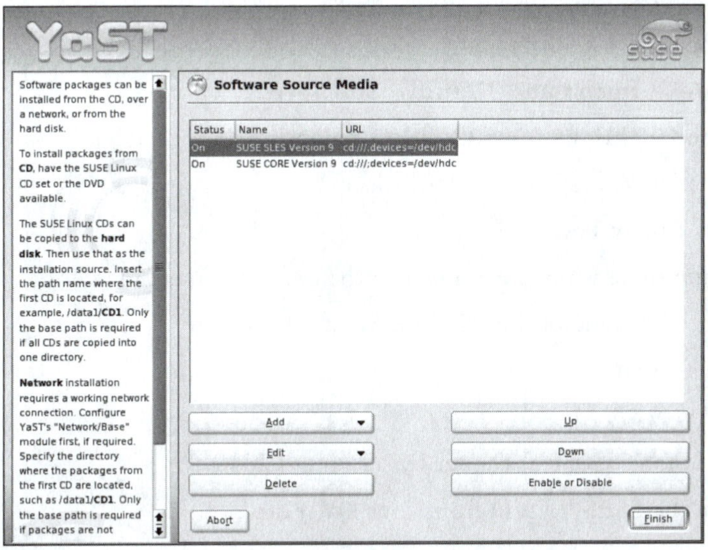

**4**

**Figure 4-5**

To add a new source, select the **Add** drop-down list and select the type of installation source. Depending on the type of source, you might have to provide additional information (such as the IP address of an installation server).

To edit the configuration of an existing installation source, select the source in the list; then select **Edit**.

If you want to disable an installation source temporarily, select the source in the list; then select **Enable or Disable**.

To remove an installation source permanently, select the source from the list; then select **Delete**.

YaST uses the first installation source in the list that has the software package you want to install. To change the order of a source in the list, select the source; then select **Up** or **Down**.

## Exercise 4-2     Install New Software

Installing and removing software is a very common task of a system administrator. YaST offers a convenient way to do this. Other procedures are covered later in this course as well.

To install new software, do the following:

1. From the KDE desktop, select the **YaST** icon; then enter a password of **novell** and select **OK**.

2. From the YaST Control Center, select

   **Software > Install and Remove Software**

3. From the Filter drop-down list, select **Selections**.

4. From the left side of the window, select

   **Various Linux Tools**

   Make sure there is no check mark to the left of Various Linux Tools.

5. From the right side of the window, select the package

   **findutils-locate**

6. Select **Accept**.

7. Close the YaST Control Center by selecting **Close**.

8. Remove the SLES 9 DVD from your DVD drive.

---

## OBJECTIVE 3     MANAGE USER ACCOUNTS WITH YaST

Using YaST, you can manage users and groups. To do this, you need to understand the following:

- Basics about Users and Groups
- User and Group Administration with YaST

## Basics about Users and Groups

Linux is a multiuser system. In other words, several users can work on the system at the same time. For this reason the system must be able to uniquely identify all users. To achieve this, every user must log in with the following:

- A user name
- A password

Because the operating system can handle numbers much better than words, users are handled internally as numbers. The number that a user receives is a ***UID*** (UserID).

Every Linux system has a privileged user, the user root. This user always has the UID 0.

Users can be grouped together based on shared characteristics or activities. For example:

- Normal users are usually in the group ***users***.
- You can place all users who will create Web pages in a group ***webedit***.

    Of course, file permissions for the directory in which the Web pages are located must be set so that the group webedit can create and save files.

As with users, each group is also allocated a number called the ***GID*** (GroupID). The GID can be one of the following types:

- Normal groups
- All groups used by the system
- The root group (GID = 0)

## User and Group Administration with YaST

You can access YaST user and group account administration in the following ways:

- **User administration.** From the YaST Control Center, select:

    **Security and Users > Edit and create users**

    or from a terminal window, enter:

    **yast2 users**

- **Group administration.** From the YaST Control Center, select:

    **Security and Users > Edit and create groups**

    or from a terminal window, enter:

    **yast2 groups**

If you have selected LDAP for authentication during the SLES 9 installation you are asked for the LDAP server administrator password.

You can switch back and forth between administering users and administering groups by selecting the **Users** and **Groups** radio buttons at the top of the module window.

The User and Group Administration window, shown in Figure 4-6, lists the existing user accounts.

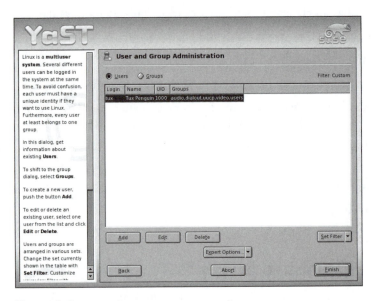

**Figure 4-6**

To create a new user account, select **Add** in the User and Group Administration window. Figure 4-7 appears.

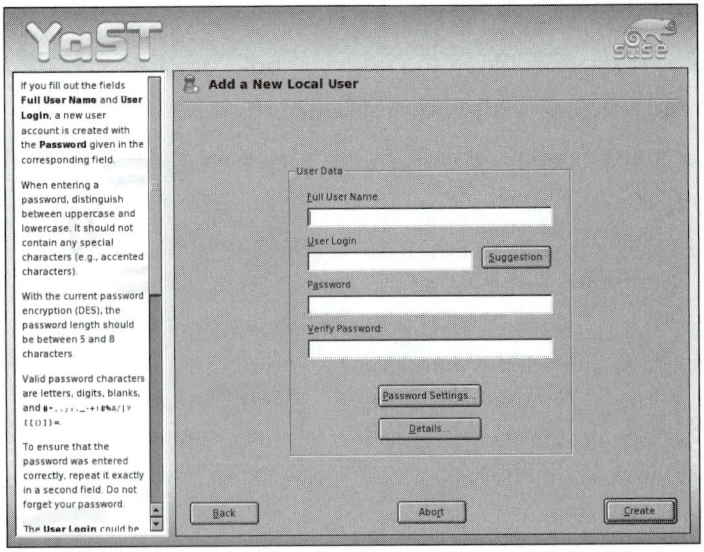

**Figure 4-7**

To set password parameters (such as duration of a password), select **Password Settings**. Figure 4-8 appears.

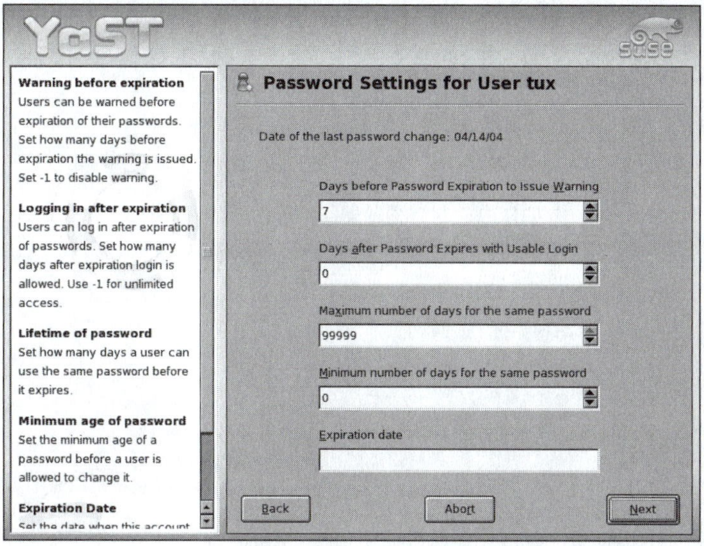

**Figure 4-8**

To set the properties of the user (such as the UID, the home directory, the login shell, group affiliation, and additional user account comments), select **Details**. Figure 4-9 appears.

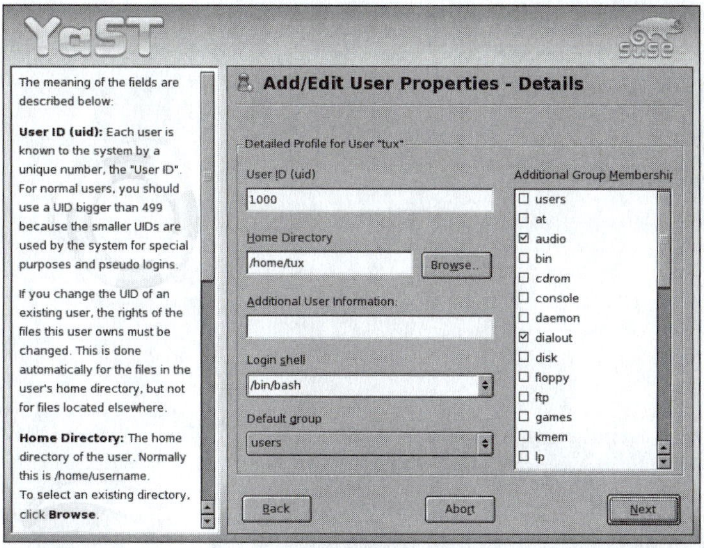

**Figure 4-9**

You can modify the settings of an existing user account by selecting **Edit** in the user account management window. Figure 4-10 appears.

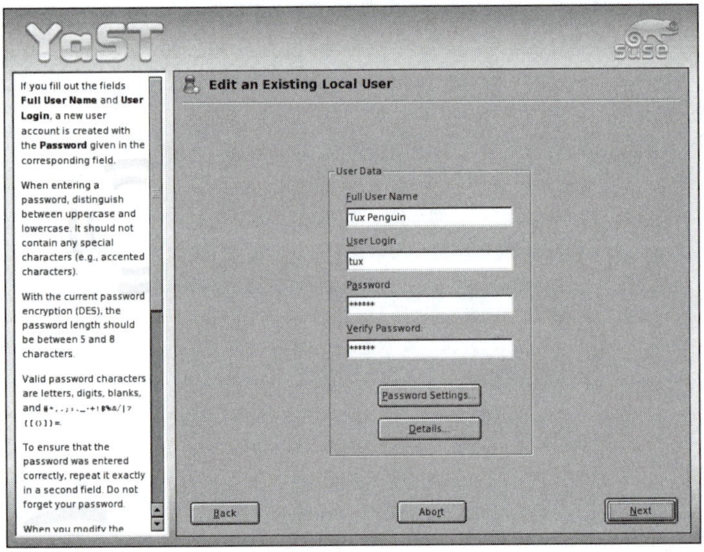

**Figure 4-10**

You can administer groups from the User and Group Administration window, shown in Figure 4-11.

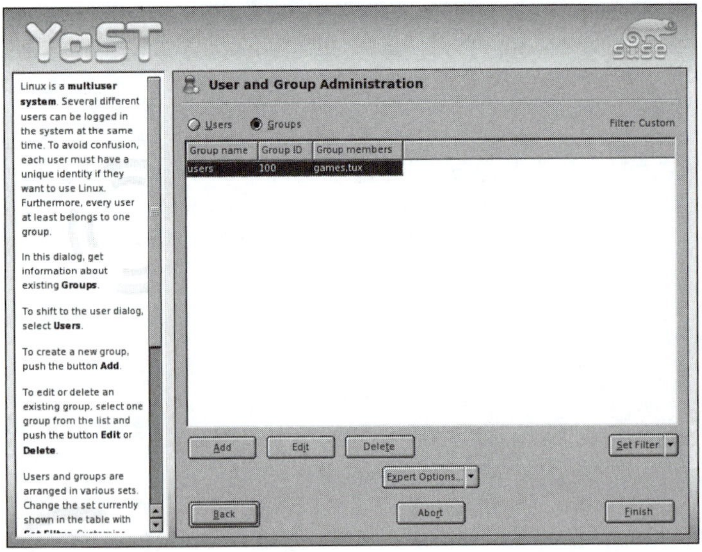

**Figure 4-11**

To create a new group, select **Add**. Figure 4-12 appears.

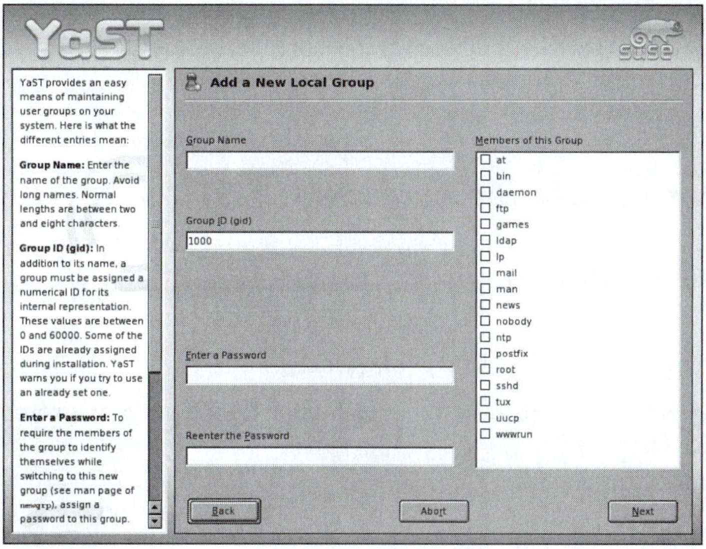

**Figure 4-12**

You can edit an existing group to perform tasks such as adding or deleting members of the group by selecting **Edit** in the Users and Group Administration window. Figure 4-13 appears.

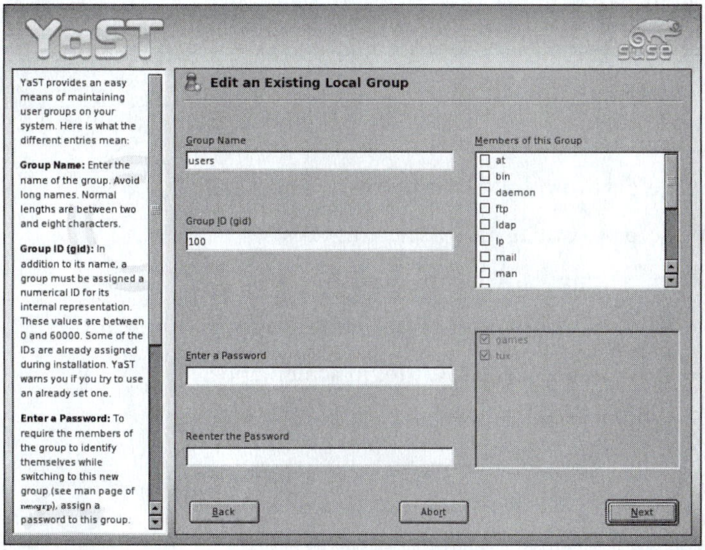

**Figure 4-13**

The information you enter when creating or editing users and groups with YaST is normally saved to the following user administration files:

- /etc/passwd
- /etc/shadow
- /etc/group

## Exercise 4-3    Manage User Accounts with YaST

Managing user accounts is a common task for a system administrator. The purpose of this exercise is to show you how it is done using YaST. (In a later exercise the same task is done using command-line tools.)

To manage user accounts with YaST, do the following:

1. From the KDE desktop, select the **YaST** icon; then enter a password of **novell** and select **OK**.

    The YaST Control Center appears.

2. From the YaST Control Center, select:

    **Security and Users > Edit and Create Users**

3. Add a new user by selecting **Add**.

4. Enter the following information:

   - Full User Name: **Tux Linux**
   - User Login: **tux**
   - Password: **novell**
   - Verify Password: **novell**

5. When you finish, select **Create**.

6. Confirm the password by selecting **Yes**.

7. Confirm the password again by selecting **Yes**.

8. Save the new settings by selecting **Finish**.

9. From the KDE menu, log out by selecting **Logout > Logout**.

    X Windows restarts and the GUI login screen appears.

10. In the User Name field, enter **tux**.

11. In the Password field, enter **novell**.

12. Select **Login**.

13. Close or cancel any open dialog boxes.

14. Start the Konqueror file manager by selecting the *blue house* icon in Kicker.

    The content of Tux's home directory is displayed.

15. Browse to the directory **/etc/**.

16. Select the file **passwd**.

    Notice the entries for users tux and geeko at the end of the file.

17. Close the Konqueror window.

18. From the KDE menu, log out by selecting **Logout > Logout**.

19. Log in as **geeko** with a password of **N0v3ll**.

20. Start YaST from the desktop by selecting the **YaST** icon.

21. Enter a root password of **novell**; then select **OK**.

22. From the YaST Control Center, select

    **Security and Users > Edit and Create Users**

23. From the list of users, select **tux**; then select **Delete**.

24. Select **Delete Home Directory /home/tux**; then select **Yes**.

25. Select **Finish**.

26. Confirm that the user tux has been removed by doing the following:

    a. Start the Konqueror file manager by selecting the *blue house* icon in Kicker.

       The content of Geeko's home directory is displayed.

    b. Browse to the directory **/etc/**.

    c. Select the file **passwd**.

       Notice the entry for tux has been removed from the end of the file.

    d. Close the Konqueror window.

27. Close the YaST Control Center.

## OBJECTIVE 4  CONFIGURE A PRINTER IN THE LINUX SYSTEM

YaST provides printer installation and configuration functionality. To configure a printer, you need to know the following:

- When to Configure a Printer
- How to Change a Printer Configuration

# When to Configure a Printer

You can configure your printer at the following times:

- **During installation.** If you are at the Hardware Configuration dialog box during installation (see Figure 4-14) and your automatic detection is not correct, select the Printers headline or use the **Change** drop-down list.

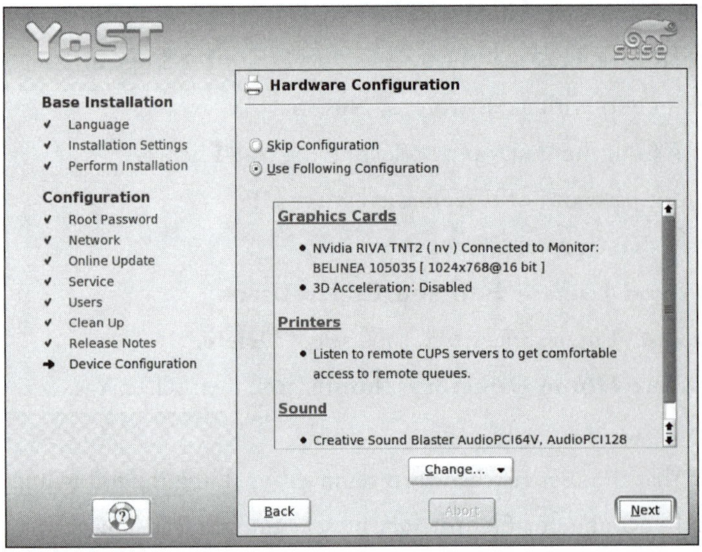

**Figure 4-14**

Note that during installation, only locally connected printers are detected automatically and listed under Printers.

- **After installation.** You can change your printer configuration settings from the YaST Control Center by selecting **Hardware > Printer**.

## How to Change a Printer Configuration

After accessing printer configuration during or after installation, you use the Printer Configuration dialog box to configure your printer, as shown in Figure 4-15.

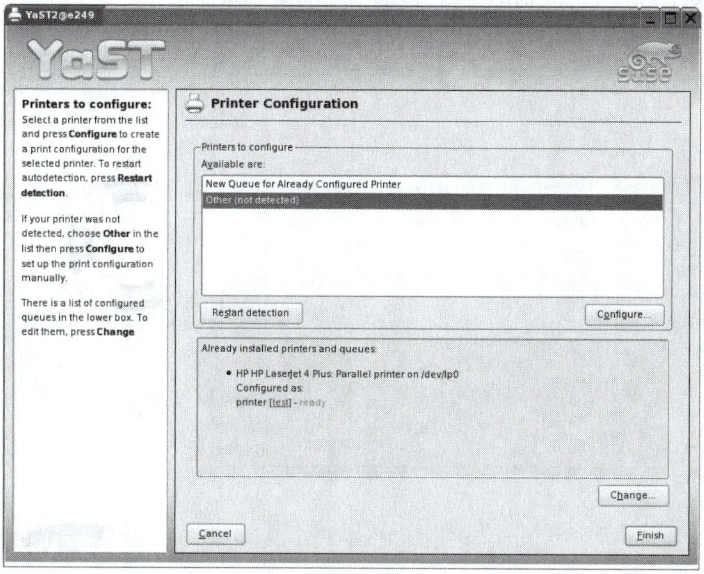

**Figure 4-15**

The upper part of the Printer Configuration dialog box lists all automatically detected printers that have not been configured.

If the printers cannot be detected automatically or if all printers are already configured, this text area displays only the Other (Not Detected) option.

The lower part of the dialog box lists all configured printers.

To configure your printer, select **Configure**. Figure 4-16 appears.

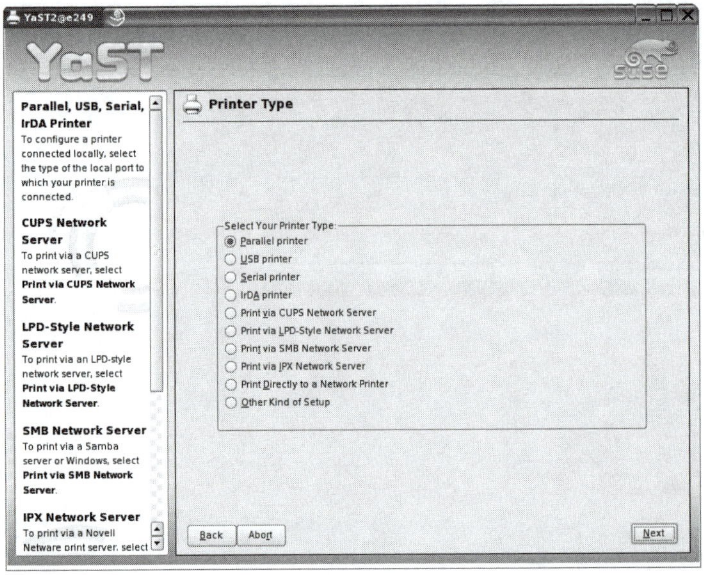

**Figure 4-16**

From here you select your printer type. If the printer is directly connected to your computer, you select one of the following:

- Parallel printer
- USB printer
- Serial printer
- IrDA printer

The other printer types are used to configure a printer in your network. Network Printing Services is covered in Section 10.

In the next step, you select the interface your printer is connected to. The dialog box varies, depending on what you previously selected.

For example, the dialog box in Figure 4-17 is used to configure a parallel printer connection.

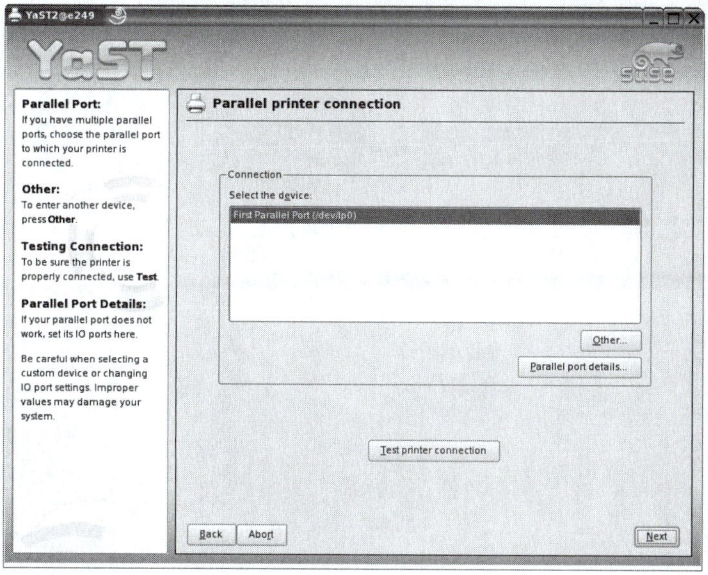

**Figure 4-17**

Select a device; then select **Next**. Figure 4-18 appears.

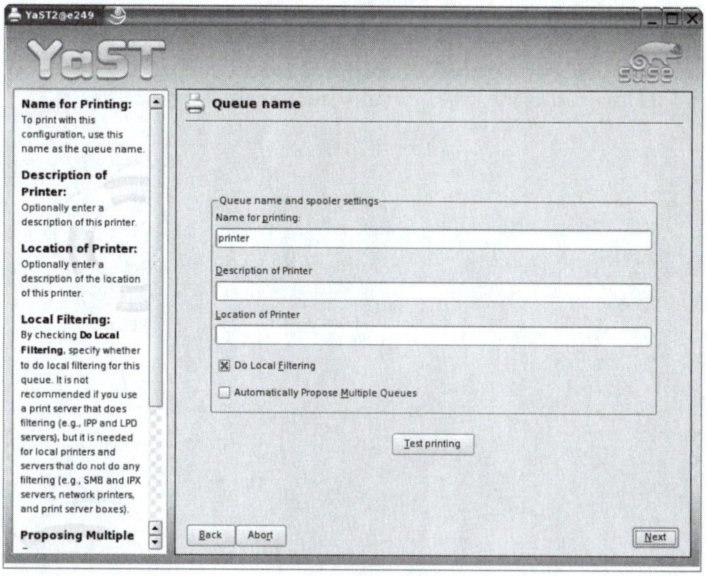

**Figure 4-18**

Enter a name for your print queue in the Name for printing field. You can also enter a description of your printer in the Description of Printer field and the printer location in the Location of Printer field.

Select **Next** to display the Printer Model dialog box, shown in Figure 4-19.

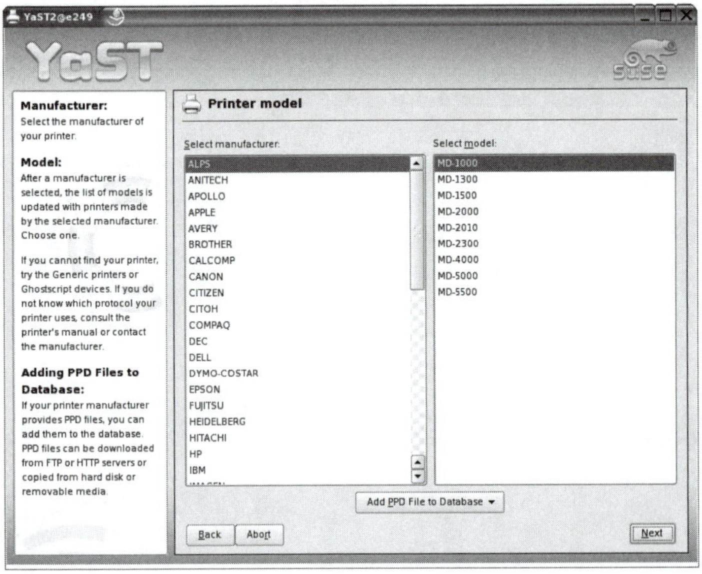

**Figure 4-19**

Select the name of the printer manufacturer from the list on the left side of the window. Select the printer model from the list on the right side of the window.

After selecting **Next**, the Edit configuration dialog box appears, as shown in Figure 4-20.

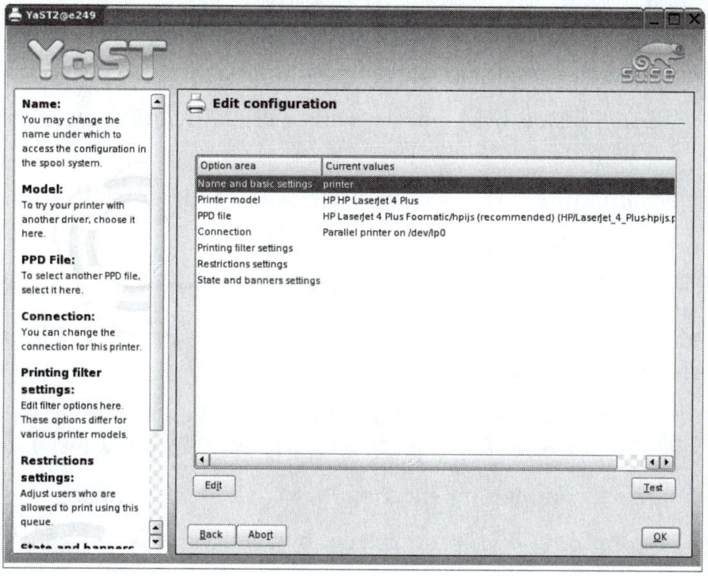

**Figure 4-20**

From this dialog box, you can test your printer configuration by selecting **Test**.

If you want to change any settings, select the appropriate line and select **Edit**. For example, you might want to change the default page size or the default paper tray.

If everything is correct, select **OK**.

## Exercise 4-4   Change Your Printer Configuration

Configuring a printer is made remarkably simple with YaST in SLES 9. There is no real alternative to it, as the printer configuration involves various files and directories and configuring them "by hand" would be rather complex.

The purpose of this exercise is to familiarize you with the YaST printer module.

In this exercise, you change your printer configuration by adding a new printer.

Do the following:

1. Start YaST from the desktop by selecting the **YaST** icon.

2. Enter a root password of **novell**; then select **OK**.

3. From the YaST Control Center, select **Hardware > Printer**.

   The Printer Configuration dialog box appears.

4. Add a new queue for a printer by selecting **Configure**.

5. For the printer type, make sure **Parallel Printer** is selected (even if no printer is connected to your machine); then select **Next**.

6. Accept **First Parallel Port (/dev/lp0)** as the printer device by selecting **Next**.

7. In the Name for Printing field, enter **hplj4**; then continue by selecting **Next**.

   A Printer Model dialog box appears, with a list of manufacturers and a list of models.

8. From the Manufacturer list, select **HP**; from the Model list, select **Laserjet 4**.

9. When you finish, select **Next**.

   An Edit Configuration dialog box appears.

10. Change the settings of the printing filter by selecting **Printing Filter Settings**; then select **Edit**.

11. Change the number of pages that should be printed on one sheet of paper by selecting **Pages per Sheet** in the Options list and **2** in the Values list.

12. When you finish, continue by selecting **Next**.

13. Return to the list of known print queues by selecting **OK**.

14. Finish the configuration by selecting **Finish**.

15. Confirm that the printer has been added by doing the following:

    a. From the KDE menu, select **Utilities > Printing > Printers**.

       A Printing Manager dialog box appears.

       Notice that hplj4 is listed as a printer.

    b. Select one or more tab pages (such as **Properties**) for the printer.

    c. When you finish, close the Printing Manager dialog box.

16. Close the YaST Control Center.

## OBJECTIVE 5    USE YaST TO CONFIGURE A MODEM

To configure a modem, you need to know the following information:

- The port over which the modem is connected to the machine (/dev/ttyS0, /dev/modem)

- The phone number of the dial-in host

- Authentication data: login name and password

- The IP assignment method: dynamic or static (most providers assign IP addresses dynamically)

- The IP address of the DNS server (only if the IP address is not transmitted when the connection is established)

You can use YaST to configure the modem and the provider access data.

Do the following:

1. To start the YaST module, select:

   **yast2 > Network Devices > Modem > Configure**

   The following dialog box appears:

2. To access the initialization settings of the modem, select **Details**.

The following dialog box appears:

Normally nothing needs to be changed here.

3. Select **Next** in the Modem Parameter dialog box.

4. If your provider is not listed, select **New**.

   The following dialog box appears.

5. Enter the information necessary to access your ISP; then select **Next**.
6. The following dialog box appears:

If **Dial on Demand** is selected, the connection will be established automatically whenever necessary, for example, when a page requiring an Internet connection is opened in the browser.

Connections can be controlled manually:

- By selecting the **Kinternet** icon in KDE

  or

- By entering **cinternet --start** in a console window

The connection can be terminated:

- By selecting the **Kinternet** connection in the control panel

  or

- By entering **cinternet --stop** in a console window

 You can find information about additional cinternet options in the cinternet man pages.

The data entered in the individual screens are written to several files:

- **/etc/sysconfig/network/ifcfg-ppp0.** Information about the modem, such as initialization strings or the interface speed.

- **/etc/sysconfig/network/providers/***providername*. The access data including the user name and password, DNS server, and phone number.

- **/etc/sysconfig/network/config.** General options, such as the activation of the firewall or whether the file /etc/resolv.conf is to be modified.

## OBJECTIVE 6    USE YaST TO OBTAIN HARDWARE CONFIGURATION INFORMATION

To obtain information about the configuration of your hardware, from the YaST Control Center, select **Hardware > Hardware Information**.

After scanning the hardware for a few moments, YaST displays a dialog box similar to Figure 4-21 that summarizes the information about the detected hardware.

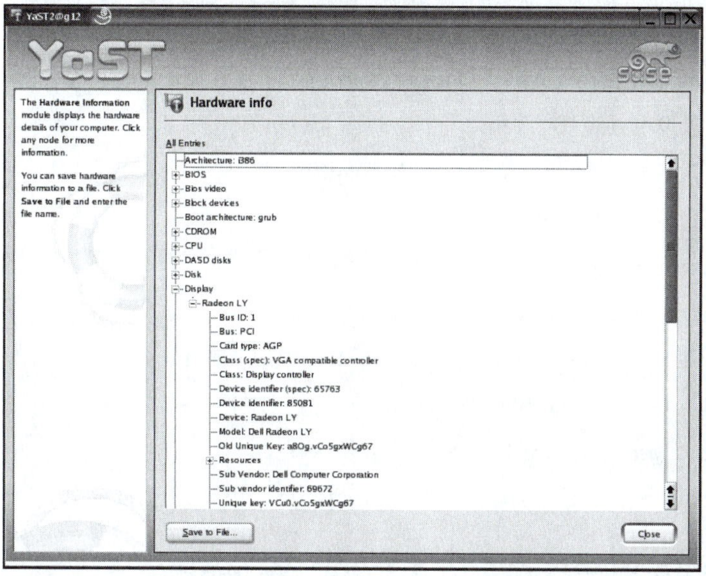

**Figure 4-21**

# Exercise 4-5    Obtain Hardware Configuration Information

It is not always feasible to take a screwdriver and to open a machine to see what is in it. The purpose of this exercise is to show you a way to obtain information on hardware more easily.

To obtain hardware configuration information about your computer, do the following:

1. Open the YaST Control Center; then select:

    **Hardware > Hardware Information**

    Wait until YaST has scanned your hardware.

2. Check the results of the detection.

3. When you finish, close the Hardware info window by selecting **Close**.

4. Close the YaST Control Center.

## OBJECTIVE 7    CONFIGURE THE X WINDOW SYSTEM

To configure the X Window System, you need to:

- Describe the Components of the X Window System
- Understand the Structure of Display Names
- Start the X Window System
- Start the X Server with a Window Manager
- Start a Second X Server
- Understand the Structure of X Server's Log File
- Understand the Function of a Login Manager
- Provide a Login Screen of the X Server to a Remote Host
- Use SSH for Secure Display Forwarding
- Know the Configuration File of the X Server
- Know Tools for Configuring the X Server

## Describe the Components of the X Window System

The X Window System (or simply X or X11) allows you to control the input and output of several applications in different windows of a graphical interface. X Server and X clients do not have to run on the same computer.

As shown in Figure 4–22, the X server is running on da5, while the X applications are running on da1 and da2. The display of the client applications, however, is performed by the X server on da5. These computers might have different architectures.

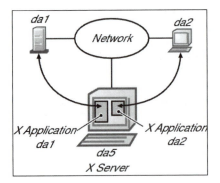

**Figure 4-22**

The relationship between X server and X client was already covered in *Overview of the Linux Desktop*.

## Understand the Structure of Display Names

On one computer, a number of X servers might be running to which a number of monitors can be connected.

For a client application to know which X server performs input and output, it is informed of the display name.

The syntax for this is:

*host:display_no.screen_no*

The parameters are defined in the following:

- *host*. Name (or IP address) of the computer to which the monitor is connected.

  *If no computer is given, the local monitor is used.*

- *display_no*. Defines the number of the display.

  A display is a unit consisting of a monitor (or several monitors), a keyboard, and a mouse.

  Normally, the display is 0, because computers only have one display.

  Large multiuser systems can have a number of displays, each of which has a unique number. Normally they are counted upward, starting with 0 for the first display, 1 for the second display, etc.

  To start a second X server on a computer with only one display, you also need to set the display number for this to another value (such as 1) (see "Start a Second X Server").

- *screen_no*. A display can have more than one monitor as its display unit. This number specifies on which monitor client applications should display their output.

Normally the display name is given in the environment variable DISPLAY, but it can be passed on to a client application with the option:

**–display** *display_name*

## Start the X Window System

The distinction of the X server, client application, and window manager is not perceivable during normal operation; once you have logged in by using the graphical login, the entire environment is at your command.

However, in order to identify the structure more clearly, the individual components can also be started individually.

For this purpose, terminate the running X server by entering:

```
da5:~ # init 3
```

Then start the X server by entering in a text console:

```
da5:~ # X &
```

/usr/X11R6/bin/X is a link to /var/X11R6/bin/X. This, in turn, is a link to the actual X server /usr/X11R6/bin/XFree86.

The result of this command is a gray area with a mouse pointer cross. Users cannot use the pure X server in a meaningful way, but X applications can use the X server for the graphical output.

You can terminate the X server by pressing **Ctrl + Alt + Backspace**.

If you start a graphical application from the same console from which the X server was started in the background, the following error message is displayed:

```
tux@da5:~> xterm
xterm Xt error: Can't open display:
```

The application lacks the information on which X server to use.

The X server needs to be addressed specifically, as it might be active on the same machine or on a different machine, or several X servers might be active on one machine.

Graphical applications interpret the variable DISPLAY, which contains the needed information.

However, in the above example this variable is not set. If this variable is set, the program command will work and an xterm window will appear on the gray surface.

To do this, enter:

```
tux@da5:~> DISPLAY=localhost:0 xterm &
```

or:

```
tux@da5:~> DISPLAY=:0 xterm &
```

Figure 4-23 appears.

```
tux@da5:~>
```

**Figure 4-23**

If you move the mouse pointer over the window, you can enter commands in the window.

Once the X window is open, you can do the following:

- Start an Application
- Start a Window Manager

## Start an Application

To start an application on this X server (such as xterm), enter:

```
tux@da5:~> xterm -g 80x25-0+30 &
```

Figure 4-24 appears.

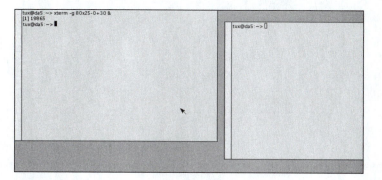

**Figure 4-24**

The numbers after –g define the geometry of the application that started.

- **80x25.** Defines the size of the application window.

  This means the window is 80 characters wide and 25 characters high.

- **–0+30.** Defines the position of the application.

  This means the window is 0 points away from the right edge and 30 points from the upper edge of the display.

  - **+**: distance from the left or upper margin

  - **-**: distance from the right or lower margin

**CAUTION**

Processes in the terminal should only be started in the background so the shell is available for other processes.

The size and the position of the window cannot be changed after. A window manager is required to do this.

### Start a Window Manager

To start a window manager (such as twm), enter in the terminal:

```
tux@da5:~> twm &
```

Figure 4-25 appears.

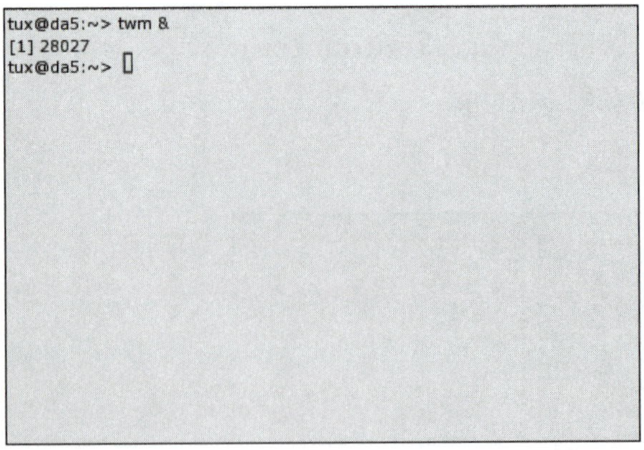

```
tux@da5:~> twm &
[1] 28027
tux@da5:~> ▯
```

**Figure 4-25**

The window manager changes the appearance of the desktop, the frames of existing windows, and title bar.

The functionality and behavior of the X desktop are also redefined when the window manager is started.

## Start the X Server with a Window Manager

Without a window manager, the X desktop is restricted in its use. For this reason, the X server is normally started together with a window manager.

In runlevel 3 (no graphical login), use the script **startx** to start the X server.

To ensure a secure start-up of the X server, the script /usr/X11R6/bin/startx performs a system check.

Then it starts the application **xinit**, which in turn starts the X server.

The environment variable WINDOWMANAGER is interpreted.

Upon start-up, startx activates the shared plain-text cookies that play a role in connection with the security mechanism xauth (see **man Xsecurity**).

If necessary, you can replace startx with a custom script.

## Start a Second X Server

Normally, only one X server is started.

To start a second X server, for example, as root, enter:

```
da5:~ # startx -- :1
```

This starts a second X server with its output on tty8.

The output can be reached by pressing **Ctrl + Alt + F8**.

The first X server can be reached, as before, by pressing **Ctrl + Alt + F7**.

You can also start a third or fourth X server.

To start another X server with output on tty9, enter:

```
da5:~ # startx -- :2
```

Toggle to this X server by pressing **Ctrl + Alt + F9**.

## Understand the Structure of X Server's Log File

When the X server starts, it generates a detailed log file, which can be helpful in finding problems with the X server.

The XFree86 4.x X server creates this file according to the following pattern:

**/var/log/XFree86.*display_no*.log**

Because the first X server that was started automatically has the display number 0, the name of its log file is:

**/var/log/XFree86.0.log**

The beginning of this log file looks like this:

```
XFree86 Version 4.3.99.902 (4.4.0 RC 2)
Release Date: 18 December 2003
X Protocol Version 11, Revision 0, Release 6.6
Build Operating System: SuSE Linux [ELF] SuSE
Current Operating System: Linux erde 2.6.5-7.21-default #1 Mon
May 3 20:49:14 UTC 2004
i686
Build Date: 25 April 2004
Changelog Date: 29 February 2004
        Before reporting problems, check http://www.XFree86.Org/
        to make sure that you have the latest version.
Module Loader present
Markers: (--) probed, (**) from config file, (==) default  setting,
         (++) from command line, (!!) notice, (II) informational,
         (WW) warning, (EE) error, (NI) not implemented, (??) unknown.
(==) Log file: "/var/log/XFree86.0.log", Time: Wed May  5 09:08:36 2004
(==) Using config file: "/etc/X11/XF86Config"
(==) ServerLayout "Layout[all]"
(**) |-->Screen "Screen[0]" (0)
(**) |    |-->Monitor "Monitor[0]"
(**) |    |-->Device "Device[0]"
(**) |-->Input Device "Keyboard[0]"
...
```

The first line shows the version of the X server.

You can see on what system the X server was compiled in the line beginning with Build Operating System.

Log entries include the following:

- **Markers**. Lists what the markers before individual entries mean.

  The most important are:

  - **(--)**. Values derived from system hardware detection.

  - **(\*\*)**. Settings taken from the configuration file.

  - **(==)**. Default settings for the X server.

  - **(++)**. Values passed from the command line.

  - **(WW)**. Hints about settings the X server does not carry out.

- **(EE).** Messages that caused the start process or the X server to crash.

  In these lines, you will normally find the reason why the X server did not start correctly.

  **(II).** Information messages about the X server, such as version numbers of X server modules.

- **Log file.** Displays the name of this log file.
- **Time.** States when this log file was created (when this X server was started).
- **Using config file.** Displays the name of the configuration file for the X server.

## Understand the Function of a Login Manager

If the Linux system is configured correctly and an X server is running on the local machine, after the system has booted, the welcome window of the X interface appears instead of the login prompt at a virtual console.

This login window is generated by the following login managers:

- xdm
- gdm
- kdm

These programs do not have to run on the local host. They can also use it as an X terminal.

To understand the function of a login manager, you need to know the following:

- Startup Files Used by the Login Manager

### xdm

The configuration files of xdm are located in the directory.

/etc/X11/xdm/

The central configuration file is:

/etc/X11/xdm/xdm-config

### gdm

gdm is the login manager of GNOME.

The configuration files of gdm are located in the directory.

/etc/opt/gnome/gdm/

The central configuration file is:

/etc/opt/gnome/gdm/gdm.conf

In other Linux distributions, these files are in the directory /etc/X11/gdm/.

## kdm

kdm is the login manager of KDE.

The configuration files of kdm are located in the directories:

- /etc/opt/kde3/share/config/kdm/
- /opt/kde3/share/config/kdm/

The central configuration files are:

- /etc/opt/kde3/share/config/kdm/kdmrc
- /opt/kde3/share/config/kdm/kdmrc

In other Linux distributions these files are in the directory /etc/X11/kdm/.

## Startup Files Used by the Login Manager

The kdm login manager gives every user who has logged in to the system a choice of window managers.

After a user name and password have been entered, the display manager executes the instructions of the file ~/.xsession plus (in SUSE Linux) the instructions of the file ~/.xinitrc, and starts the window manager or user interface selected by the user.

By default, both files are not present in SLES 9. However, there is a template for the file ~/.xinitrc named .xinitrc.template located in the home directory of the user account.

When the last X client entered in ~/.xsession (usually the window manager) is terminated, the X server, too, is terminated and restarted, after which the login screen of the X server is displayed.

If the file ~/.xsession does not exist, only the file ~/.xinitrc is evaluated.

If this file is not available, the file /etc/X11/xdm/sys.xsession is read.

If this file is also missing, the file xinitrc (without the dot) in /usr/X11R6/lib/X11/xinit/ or in /etc/X11/xinit/ is read.

## Provide a Login Screen of the X Server to a Remote Host

The login screen of the X server can also be relayed to a remote host.

To perform this, do the following:

1. Open the file /etc/sysconfig/displaymanager on the host whose login screen should be used; then set the following:

   ```
   DISPLAYMANAGER_REMOTE_ACCESS="yes"
   ```

2. Run **SuSEconfig**.

   This program will disable the following line in the configuration file of xdm /etc/X11/xdm/xdm-config (the character introducing a comment is !):

   ```
   !DisplayManager.requestPort: 0
   ```

3. Open the login screen by entering the following command on the remote host:

   **X -query** *host* **:1**

   Enter :1 if you already have a running X server on your local host (that can be accessed by pressing **Ctrl + Alt + F7**).

   You can then access the login screen from the remote host by pressing **Ctrl + Alt + F8**.

## Use SSH for Secure Display Forwarding

Due to the following characteristics of the X Window System, a series of security problems arises:

- It is divided into server and client components.
- It communicates across a network.
- It is easy for a client application to make a connection to an X server.

To avoid such security problems, several mechanisms provide protection from unauthorized access (see **man Xsecurity**).

One of them is SSH, network access via a secure shell.

With the secure shell, an encrypted communication between hosts is possible over a potentially insecure network.

Each host has a private host key and a public host key. Authentication between hosts is carried out by one host encrypting its request with the public key of the other host and sending it to that host.

Only the other host can decrypt the request with its private key.

The entire session between the hosts is additionally secured via a session key, which, for security reasons, is only located in the main memory of the computer and is regularly regenerated.

If, for example, the user tux wants to log in via SSH on the machine da10, he has to enter:

```
tux@da5:~> ssh da10
```

The following is displayed:

```
The authenticity of host 'da10 (10.0.0.10)' can't be established.
RSA key fingerprint is ea:79:90:9a:d4:bf:b6:a2:40:ee:72:56:f8:d9:
e5:76.
Are you sure you want to continue connecting (yes/no)? yes
Warning: Permanently added 'da10,10.0.0.10' (RSA) to the list
of known hosts.
password:
tux@da10:~>
```

User tux can use the option -l to specify the user name:

```
tux@da5:~> ssh -l geeko da10
```

To redirect X input and output on the host da10 to the host da5 (automatic display redirection), user tux can enter:

```
tux@da5:~> ssh -X da10
```

The X protocol is forwarded through a secure tunnel (X11 forwarding).

 With SSH, such an X tunnel is set up by default. With OpenSSH, you must specify -X to achieve this.

**CAUTION**

The forerunners of SSH were the r-tools.

Due to various security issues, such as cleartext passwords over the network or authentication based on IP address only, they should not be used anymore.

SSH and SCP offer the same functionality with added security by cryptographic means.

The r-tools are the following:

- **rlogin** (remote login). Allows you to log in on computers, similar to telnet.

  Depending on the entries in the files /etc/hosts.equiv or ~/.rhosts on the remote machine, a password might not be required at all.

- **rsh** (remote shell). Starts programs on the remote computer.

  If no command is passed to rsh, an interactive session using rlogin is started.

■ **rcp** (remote copy). Is used to copy files from one machine to another.

The syntax is similar to scp.

No password is required if suitable entries exist in /etc/hosts.equiv and/or ~/.rhosts.

## Know the Configuration File of the X Server

The configuration file of the X server is **/etc/X11/XF86Config**.

This file contains specifications such as the mouse settings, the keyboard, the resolution, and the frequency.

The file is divided in several sections:

- **Section "Files".** File pathnames.
- **Section "Module".** Dynamic module loading.
- **Section "ServerFlags".** Server flags.
- **Section "Input Device".** Input device description.
- **Section "Device".** Graphics device description.
- **Section "VideoAdaptor".** X video adapter description.
- **Section "Monitor".** Monitor description.
- **Section "Modes".** Video modes descriptions.
- **Section "Screen".** Screen configuration.
- **Section "ServerLayout".** Overall layout.
- **Section "DRI".** DRI-specific configuration (Direct Rendering Infrastructure).
- **Section "Vendor".** Vendor-specific configuration.

An example for this configuration file is/usr/X11R6/lib/X11/XF86Config.eg.

For more information about the configuration file XF86Config, see the manual page. Enter **man XF86Config**.

## Know Tools for Configuring the X Server

Various tools are available for configuring the X server (XFree86 4.x):

- **SaX2.** SaX2 (SuSE advanced X configuration) supports the X server and can be used with the mouse (package sax2).

■ **/usr/X11R6/bin/xf86config.** In contrast to SaX2, this is a text-based program for configuring the X server.

■ **/usr/X11R6/bin/xvidtune.** This program can be used to configure the screen dimension (width, height).

The modelines that define the screen size are contained in the file /etc/X11/ XF86Config under **section "Modes"**.

You can configure X Server version 3.3.*x* with XF86Setup.

Default values for some X applications (such as xterm and xclock) are defined in the file ~/.Xdefaults and can also be modified here, if necessary. There is also a file called ~/.Xresources. However, this is merely a link to ~/.Xdefaults. Neither file exists on SLES 9 by default. If these files are modified, restart the X server or enter **xrdb** to reread the file ~/.Xdefaults. You can view options by entering **xrdb --help**. KDE and GNOME applications use different configuration files.

## Exercise 4-6   Optional: Explore the Components of the X Window System

X Server is a program of its own, as is are the various window managers. The purpose of this exercise is to demonstrate the separate components to you.

1. Log out from the graphical environment and switch to a text console using **Ctrl + Alt + F1**. Log in as root with a password of *novell*.

2. Switch to runlevel 3 by entering **init 3** (runlevels are explained in more detail later in the course).

3. Start the X server by entering **X &**. A graphical surface with some grey pattern and a mouse cursor appears.

4. Switch back to the text console using **Ctrl + Alt + F1**. Try to start an xterm by entering **xterm &**. You will get an error message: "Can't open display".

5. Start the xterm again, this time setting the display variable:**DISPLAY=:0 xterm &**.

6. Switch to the graphical screen using **Alt + F7**.

7. Move the mouse cursor above the xterm window and enter **fvwm &**.

8. Explore the features of fvwm if you like. Start with clicking on the background with the left mouse button. Choose from the menu. Do the same with the right button.

9. Kill the X server by pressing **Ctrl + Alt + Backspace**.

10. Switch back to runlevel 5 by entering **init 5** in the text console. When the graphical login screen appears, log in as geeko with a password of *N0v3ll*.

## CHAPTER SUMMARY

□ The main system configuration utility in SLES is YaST. You can use a menu-based YaST interface from within a command-line terminal or a GUI YaST interface from within a desktop environment.

□ You can use the Software section of YaST to install and manage software packages on your SLES system. YaST can install from various sources and can check package dependencies.

□ Each user account on your system has a unique User ID (UID). Similarly, each group account is identified by a unique Group ID (GID). The root user and root group always have the UID and GID of 0, respectively. You can create, edit, or delete users and groups using YaST.

□ Although printers are typically configured during SLES installation, you can add or change printers on your system using the Printer module in YaST.

□ The Modem module of YaST may be used to configure a modem connection to the Internet on your SLES system. You can configure your modem to dial your Internet connection on demand, or you can manually initiate a modem Internet connection using the Kinternet utility or cinternet command.

□ By navigating to the Hardware Information module in YaST, you can view information about your computer hardware that is useful in troubleshooting hardware devices.

□ The X Window System uses display names to determine which computer, monitor, keyboard, and mouse are used by the X server.

□ Every X client application must know the display on which it can start. By default, most X client applications start on the first display (tty7). You can specify an alternate display name by modifying the DISPLAY variable or passing the –display argument to a graphical client application. Furthermore, by passing the appropriate arguments to the X client application, you can specify the window dimensions and location of an X client application relative to the upper right corner of the screen.

□ You can use the startx command to start the X server and the default window manager or desktop environment. Alternatively, you can stop the X server by using the Ctrl + Alt + Backspace key combination.

□ An X server can be started on more than one local terminal by specifying an alternate display name when starting the X server program.

□ The X server configuration is stored in the /etc/X11/XF86Config file. You can change the contents of this file by using the YaST, SaX2, xf86config, and xvidtune utilities.

❏ Login managers provide a graphical login screen that you can use to log in to your system or a remote system and start a GUI. The default login manager in SLES is kdm.

❏ SSH can be used to obtain a secure command-line or GUI interface on a remote computer. It replaces the nonsecure r-tools that were used in the past on Linux computers.

## KEY TERMS

**.rhosts** — A file that lists user accounts on certain remote UNIX or Linux computers. These users can connect to your computer using the r-tools without specifying a username or password; instead, they will be automatically logged in as your user account.

**.xinitrc** — A file that contains information used to control the X Window System.

**.xsession** — A file that contains the default window manager or desktop environment to load when starting the X Window System.

**/dev/modem** — A file that is used to identify the port that a modem uses. It is typically a shortcut to /dev/ttyS0 or /dev/ttyS1.

**/dev/ttyS0** — A file that is used to identify the first serial port on a Linux computer. It is called COM1 in Windows.

**/dev/ttyS1** — A file that is used to identify the second serial port on a Linux computer. It is called COM2 in Windows.

**/etc/group** — A file that stores the list of system groups, their GIDs, and members.

**/etc/hosts.equiv** — A file that contains a list of remote Linux or UNIX computers. Users on these computers can run the r-tools and specify your computer without providing a username or password; instead, they will be automatically logged in as the same user on your computer.

**/etc/passwd** — A file that stores information about user accounts on the Linux system including the UID, primary GID, home directory, and login shell.

**/etc/shadow** — A file that stores the encrypted password and account expiry information for user accounts on the Linux system.

**/etc/sysconfig/network/config** — A file that stores information about how network interfaces are handled by the system.

**/etc/sysconfig/network/ifcfg-ppp0** — A file that stores the configuration of your modem for use when connecting to the Internet.

**/etc/sysconfig/network/providers/***providername* — A file that stores the information used to connect to an Internet Service Provider including the username, password, and phone number.

**/etc/X11/XF86Config** — The configuration file used by the X server.

**/etc/X11R6/bin/xvidtune** — A utility that can be used to fine tune X server settings such as screen dimensions and screen refresh rates.

**/use/X11R6/bin/XFree86** — The X server program in SLES. The /usr/X11R6/bin/X and /var/X11R6/bin/X files are shortcuts to this file that are used for program compatibility.

**/usr/X11R6/bin/xf86config** — A text-based X server configuration utility that comes with XFree86 version 4.

**~** — A special character that refers to the current user's home directory.

**cinternet command** — Typically used to dial your modem to establish an Internet connection. It can also be used to close an Internet connection.

**dependencies** — The prerequisite software required by a software package.

**DISPLAY** — A variable that stores the default display name for your system.

**display name** — A name used by the X Window System to determine the location of the X server to use.

**gdm** — A program that is used to display a GNOME-style graphical login screen.

**Group ID (GID)** — A number that is used by the Linux operating system to uniquely identify a system group. The root group always has a GID of 0.

**home directory** — The directory on your hard disk that you have full permissions to and are placed in by default. It is typically /home/*username*.

**init command** — Used to change system states.

**kdm** — A program that is used to display a KDE-style graphical login screen. It is the default login manager in SLES.

**Kinternet** — A graphical utility that can be used to dial your modem to establish an Internet connection. It can also be used to close an Internet connection.

**login manager** — A program that provides a graphical login screen for users to log in. Following a successful log in, the login manager starts an X server, window manager, and desktop environment.

**login shell** — The program that provides a command prompt and executes user commands. The default shell in SLES is the Bourne Again Shell (/bin/bash).

**ncurses** — A standard used by menu-based programs that are run within a command-line terminal.

**package** — A group of software programs that provide a certain functionality on an SLES system.

**private host key** — A string of characters that is used to decrypt information that is encrypted using a public host key.

**public host key** — A string of characters that is used to encrypt information.

**Qt** — A standard toolkit used to create GUI programs within a desktop environment.

**rcp command** — Used to copy files from one remote Linux or UNIX computer to another across a network.

**rlogin command** — Used to obtain a command-line interface from a remote Linux or UNIX computer on the network.

**rsh command** — Used to run programs on remote Linux or UNIX computers.

**r-tools** — A series of utilities that was commonly used to access, copy files to, and run programs on remote UNIX and Linux computers. The most common r-tools are rlogin, rsh, and rcp.

**runlevel 3** — A system state that allows you to log in to tty1 through tty6, but does not contain a graphical login screen on tty7.

**runlevel 5** — A system state that allows you to log in to tty1 through tty7. It is the default system state in SLES.

**SaX2** — The main X server configuration utility in SLES.

**SSH** — A utility that can be used to access a remote computer in a secure manner by encrypting any data it sends across the network. SSH stands for Secure Shell.

**startx command** — Used to start the X server and default desktop environment from a command-line terminal.

**User ID (UID)** — A number that is used by the Linux operating system to uniquely identify a user account. The root user always has a UID of 0.

**users** — The default group that all new users are placed in on an SLES system.

**xdm** — A program that is used to display a graphical login screen.

**XF86Setup** — An X server configuration utility used in older versions of XFree86.

**YaST** — The main system configuration utility in SUSE Linux.

## REVIEW QUESTIONS

1. What keys can you use in the menu-based (ncurses) YaST interface to navigate between selections? (Choose two answers.)

   a. Tab

   b. Spacebar

   c. Alt

   d. Alt+Tab

2. Which command could you execute at a command prompt to start the user management module?

   a. yast users

   b. yast /users

   c. yast sw_users

   d. yast -u

3. What option to the **yast** command could you use to display a list of YaST modules?

   _____

4. You wish to install another software package using YaST from your SLES installation media. How can you verify that your system has the appropriate prerequisite packages?

   a. Start the YaST program using the **--dependencies** option.

   b. Click the **Check Dependencies** button within YaST.

   c. View the Description tab within YaST.

   d. Right-click the package in YaST and select **Verify**.

5. How can you change the default source location for packages within YaST?
   _____

6. What UID is used by the root user account? _____

7. What is the default Login Shell that is used when you create a new user account using YaST?
   a. /bin/shell
   b. /bin/bash
   c. /home/tux
   d. /home/users

8. What is the default group that new users are assigned to when you create them using YaST?
   a. users
   b. root
   c. system
   d. home

9. What two files are modified when you add a new user using YaST?
   _____

10. What file is modified when you add a new group using YaST?
    _____

11. Which of the following types of printers can you configure on your system using YaST? (Choose all that apply.)
    a. USB
    b. IrDA
    c. Parallel
    d. Network

12. What modem device do you normally specify when configuring a modem using YaST? _____

13. Which utilities may be used to connect your computer to an Internet Service Provider using a modem? (Choose all that apply.)
    a. ttyS0
    b. Kinternet
    c. cinternet
    d. dial-connect

14. Which of the following is a valid display name?

    a. DisplayNumber.ScreenNumber

    b. DisplayNumber.ScreenNumber:Hostname

    c. Hostname:DisplayNumber.ScreenNumber

    d. Hostname-ScreenNumber-DisplayNumber

15. You wish to start a graphical application using the command: **application −g 100x90−10+60**. What does the **−10+60** in this command refer to?

    a. The width of the application window

    b. The location of the application window from the upper right corner of the screen

    c. The height of the application window

    d. The location of the application window from the upper left corner of the screen

16. Which of the following commands can be used to start the X server, window manager, and desktop environment from a command-line interface?

    a. X

    b. X --start

    c. Xinitialize

    d. startx

17. What marker in the /var/log/XFree86.0.log file indicates values that were obtained from hardware detection? _____

18. Which of the following are valid Login Managers in SLES? (Choose all that apply.)

    a. kdm

    b. xdm

    c. rdm

    d. gdm

19. Which command would you use to connect to a computer across a network in order to run graphical programs remotely?

    a. rlogin hostname

    b. rsh −X hostname

    c. rcp hostname

    d. ssh −X hostname

20. Which of the following configuration utilities may be used to configure your X server settings using a text-based interface?

    a. SaX2

    b. xvidtune

    c. xf86config

    d. XF86Setup

4

# DISCOVERY EXERCISES

## Exploring YaST Interfaces

Log in to the KDE desktop as geeko and open the Konsole application. Next, type **/sbin/yast2** and observe the YaST utility. What tools are you allowed to configure and why? Close the YaST utility. At the Konsole command prompt, switch to the root user by typing **su root** and supply the root user's password. Next, type **/sbin/yast2** and observe the YaST utility. What tools are you allowed to configure and why? Close the YaST utility.

Switch to tty1 and log in as the root user. At the command prompt, type **/sbin/yast** and observe the menu-based version of YaST. Use the Tab key to navigate to Quit and press Enter to close the application. Log out of tty1 and switch back to tty7.

At the Konsole command prompt, type **/sbin/yast** and observe the menu-based version of YaST. Why did you get the menu-based version of YaST? Close all open applications and log out of the KDE desktop.

## Starting a Second X Server

Log in to the KDE desktop on tty7 as the geeko user. Next, switch to tty1 and log in as the root user. At the command prompt, type **startx -- :1** and press Enter. What happens? What terminal are you on? Switch back to tty7 and open the Konsole application. Type **who** and note which terminals are being used. Switch back to tty1. Is your command prompt available? Explain.

Switch to tty8 and terminate the X server by using the **Ctrl + Alt + Backspace** key combination. What terminal are you on and why? Log out of tty1. Switch to tty8 and log out of the KDE desktop.

## Starting X Client Applications

Log in to the KDE desktop as the geeko user and open the Konsole application. At the command prompt, type **DISPLAY=:0 xcalc &** and press Enter. What does this command do? Where is the X Windows calculator placed on your screen and why? Next, type **DISPLAY=:0 xcalc −g 400x450−300+300 &** and press Enter. What does this command do? Where is the X Windows calculator placed on your screen and what are its dimensions? When finished, log out of the KDE desktop.

## Viewing the X Server Log

Log in to the KDE desktop as the geeko user. Use Konqueror to navigate to the /var/log/XFree86.0.log file. How can you tell which lines contain information from the X server and which lines indicate settings that were loaded from the X server configuration file? When finished, log out of the KDE desktop.

## Starting Login Managers

Log in to tty1 as the root user. At the command prompt, type **init 3** and press Enter to switch to system runlevel 3. Switch to tty7. Is a login manager running in runlevel 3? Switch back to tty1, type **kdm** at the command prompt and press Enter. What happens? What terminal are you on?

Switch back to tty1 and type **killall kdm** at the command prompt to stop the kdm login manager. Next, type **gdm** and press Enter. How is the gdm login manager similar to the kdm login manager? How is it different?

Switch back to tty1 and type **killall gdm** at the command prompt to stop the gdm login manager. Next, type **xdm** and press Enter. How is the xdm login manager similar to the kdm and gdm login managers? How is it different?

Switch back to tty1 and type **killall xdm** at the command prompt to stop the xdm login manager. Next, type **init 5** and press Enter to return your system to system runlevel 5 (the default runlevel). What login manager is started by default?

## Configuring the X Server

Log in to the KDE desktop as the geeko user. Use Konqueror to navigate to the /etc/X11/XF86Config file. What is this file used for? By looking at the comments at the beginning of this file, can you tell what utility was used to create it and when? Close Konqueror.

Open the Konsole application. At the command prompt, type **sax2** and press Enter. Supply the root user's password when prompted. What X components can be configured in the SaX2 utility? Click on **Color and Resolution** and add an additional resolution and color depth to your display that is supported by your video adapter card and monitor. Apply your settings and exit the SaX2 utility.

Next, use Konqueror to navigate to the /etc/X11/XF86Config file again. Can you tell that SaX2 modified this file? (Hint: Look at the modification date near the top of the file.)

## Modifying Screen Options

Log in to the KDE desktop as the geeko user and open the Konsole application. At the command prompt, type **xvidtune** and press Enter. Press OK when you see the warning message. Use the appropriate buttons to fine tune the position of the X server on your screen. What other X server options can you change using xvidtune? Apply your changes and quit the xvidtune utility.

**DISCOVERY**

## Using SSH to Run Remote Programs

Log in to the KDE desktop as the geeko user and open the Konsole application. At the command prompt, type **ssh localhost** and press Enter to connect to your own computer across the network using the encrypted SSH utility. When prompted to accept the RSA key fingerprint, type **yes** and press Enter. Supply the password for your geeko user account when prompted. At the command prompt, type **who** and press Enter. Can you tell that you are connected remotely to your own computer? Type **xcalc &** and press Enter. What error message did you receive and why? Type **exit** and press Enter to end your SSH session.

At the command prompt, type **ssh −X localhost** and press Enter. Supply the password for your geeko user account when prompted. Type **xcalc &** and press Enter. Why were you allowed to run this utility? Close the xcalc window. Type **exit** and press Enter to end your SSH session.

# 5

# MANAGE DIRECTORIES AND FILES IN LINUX

> **In this section you learn about the structure of the Linux file system and the most important file operation commands for working at the command line.**
>
> ♦ Understand the Filesystem Hierarchy Standard (FHS)
> ♦ Identify File Types in the Linux System
> ♦ Change Directories and List Directory Contents
> ♦ Create and View Files
> ♦ Manage Files and Directories
> ♦ Find Files
> ♦ Search File Content
> ♦ Archive, Back up, Compress, and Decompress Files

## Objective 1    Understand the Filesystem Hierarchy Standard (FHS)

The file system concept of Linux (and, in general, of all UNIX systems) is considerably different than that of other operating systems.

To understand the concept of the Linux file system, you need to know the following:

- The Hierarchical Structure of the File System
- FHS (Filesystem Hierarchy Standard)
- Root Directory /
- Essential Binaries for Use by All Users (/bin/)
- Boot Directory (/boot/)
- Device Files (/dev/)
- Configuration Files (/etc/)
- User Directories (/home/)
- Libraries (/lib/)
- Mount Points for Removable Media (/media/*)
- Application Directory (/opt/)
- Home Directory of the Administrator (/root/)
- System Binaries (/sbin/)
- Data Directories for Services (/srv/)
- Temporary Area (/tmp/)
- The Hierarchy below /usr/
- Variable Files (/var/)
- Process Files (/proc/)
- System Information Directory (/sys/)
- Mount Point for Temporarily Mounted File Systems (/mnt/)
- Directories for Mounting Other File Systems

## The Hierarchical Structure of the File System

The file system concept of Linux involves a hierarchical file system that can be depicted in the form of a tree.

This tree is not limited to a local partition. It can stretch over several partitions, which can be located on different computers in a network. It begins at the root, from where the name for the system administrator comes, and branches out like the branches of a tree.

Figure 5-1 shows part of a typical file system tree.

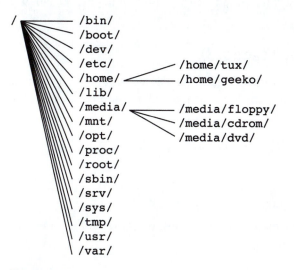

**Figure 5-1**

A file in this directory tree is uniquely defined by its path. A path refers to the directory names that lead to this file

The separation character between individual directory names is the slash ("/"). The path can be specified in two ways:

- As a *relative path* starting from the current directory

- As an *absolute path* starting from the root of the entire file system tree

The absolute path always begins with a slash (/), the symbol for the root directory, as in Figure 5-2.

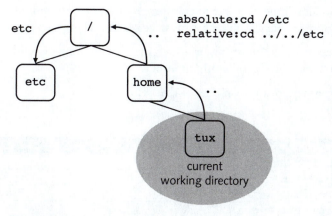

**Figure 5-2**

Sometimes it is necessary to specify the absolute path because certain files can only be uniquely addressed in this way. The length of the path cannot exceed 4096 characters, including the slashes.

## FHS (Filesystem Hierarchy Standard)

The structure of the file system is described in the Filesystem Hierarchy Standard (FHS). FHS specifies which directories must be located on the first level after the root directory and what they contain.

FHS does not specify all details. In some areas, it allows leeway for your own definitions. FHS defines a two-layered hierarchy:

- The directories in the top layer (immediately below the root directory "/")
- As a second layer, the directories under /usr/ and /var/

You can find information about FHS at *www.pathname.com/fhs/* on the Internet.

## Root Directory /

The root directory refers to the highest layer of the file system tree. Only directories are located here, not files. When the system is booted, the partition on which this directory is located is the first one mounted.

Because the kernel cannot complete all the tasks of the operating system, all programs that are run on the system start must be available on this partition; they cannot be located on another partition.

The following directories always have to be on the same partition as the root directory: /bin/, /dev/, /etc/, /lib/, and /sbin/.

## Essential Binaries for Use by All Users (/bin/)

The directory /bin/ contains important executable programs that are required when no other file systems are mounted, such as all programs necessary for the system start.

These include the various shells, the most important commands for working with files, and several commands for system analysis and configuration.

Table 5-1 provides an overview of the contents of the /bin/ directory.

**Table 5-1**

| File | Description |
|------|-------------|
| /bin/bash | The bash shell |
| /bin/cat | Display files |
| /bin/cp | Copy files |
| /bin/dd | Copy files byte-wise |

**Table 5-1**   (continued)

| File | Description |
|------|-------------|
| /bin/gzip | Compress files |
| /bin/mount | Mount file systems |
| /bin/rm | Delete files |
| /bin/vi | vi editor |

## Boot Directory (/boot/)

The directory /boot/ contains static files of the boot loader (GRUB or LILO). These are files required for the boot process (with the exception of configuration files).

The backed-up information for the Master Boot Record (MBR) and the system map files are also stored here. These contain information about where exactly the kernel is located on the partition. This directory also contains the kernel.

According to FHS, however, the kernel can also be located directly in the root directory.

## Device Files (/dev/)

Each hardware component existing in the system (such as hard drive partitions, CD drives, printer, and mouse) is represented as a file in the directory /dev/. (An exception is network cards, which are not represented by a device file.)

The hardware components are addressed via these files by writing to or reading from one of these files. Two kinds of device files are included:

- Character-oriented device files (for devices working sequentially, such as printer, mouse, or tape drive)
- Block-oriented device files (such as floppy disks and hard drives)

The connection to device drivers in the kernel is implemented via numbered channels, which correspond to the number of the device driver in question. These are referred to as *major device numbers*.

A driver might be responsible for several devices of the same type. To distinguish between these devices, the *minor device number* is used.

Instead of the size of the files, these two numbers are displayed (the files do not occupy any space on the hard drive):

```
da10:~ # ls -l /dev/hda*
brw-rw---- 1 root disk 3,  0 Mar 22 06:12 /dev/hda
brw-rw---- 1 root disk 3,  1 Mar 22 06:12 /dev/hda1
brw-rw---- 1 root disk 3, 10 Mar 22 06:12 /dev/hda10
brw-rw---- 1 root disk 3, 11 Mar 22 06:12 /dev/hda11
brw-rw---- 1 root disk 3, 12 Mar 22 06:12 /dev/hda12
brw-rw---- 1 root disk 3, 13 Mar 22 06:12 /dev/hda13
```

```
brw-rw---- 1 root disk 3, 14 Mar 22 06:12 /dev/hda14
brw-rw---- 1 root disk 3, 15 Mar 22 06:12 /dev/hda15
brw-rw---- 1 root disk 3, 16 Mar 22 06:12 /dev/hda16
brw-rw---- 1 root disk 3, 17 Mar 22 06:12 /dev/hda17
brw-rw---- 1 root disk 3, 18 Mar 22 06:12 /dev/hda18
brw-rw---- 1 root disk 3, 19 Mar 22 06:12 /dev/hda19
brw-rw---- 1 root disk 3, 2 Mar 22 06:12 /dev/hda2
brw-rw---- 1 root disk 3, 20 Mar 22 06:12 /dev/hda20
```

In this example, the major device number 3 is listed for all files. This refers to the driver for IDE hard drives on the first IDE channel. The minor device numbers for the first disk run from 1 to 15 (for SCSI hard drives) and up to 63 (for IDE hard drives) and refer to the various possible partitions.

Many device files are already available by default. Some of these, however, are never needed. If special device files are required for specific devices, these can be generated with the command **mknod**. The necessary parameters must be provided by the hardware manufacturer.

The null device /dev/null is also located in this directory. Program output that would normally be sent to the screen can be redirected to this device (for example, using redirects). The redirected data will be discarded.

Table 5-2 lists some important device files.

**Table 5-2**

| Device | Device File | Description |
|---|---|---|
| Terminals | dev/console | The system console. |
|  | /dev/tty1 | The first virtual console, reachable by pressing **Ctrl + Alt + F1**. |
| Serial ports | /dev/ttyS0 /dev/ttyS* | The first serial port. |
| Parallel ports | /dev/lp0 /dev/lp* | The first parallel port. |
| Floppy disk drives | /dev/fd0 /dev/fd* | The first floppy disk drive. If the drives are addressed via the device files fd0 and fd1, the kernel tries to recognize the floppy disk format itself. |
| IDE hard drives | /dev/hda | The first IDE hard drive on the first IDE controller. |
|  | /dev/hdc | The first IDE hard drive on the second IDE controller. |
|  | /dev/hd* | To label the partitions, the device names are given numbers. Numbers 1 to 4 refer to the primary partitions, higher numbers to logical partitions. Example: **/dev/hda1** is the first primary partition on the first IDE hard drive. |

**Table 5-2**   (continued)

| Device | Device File | Description |
|---|---|---|
| IDE CD-ROM/DVD drives | /dev/hd* | The drives are named in the same way as the IDE hard drives. This means that the CD-ROM/DVD drive **/dev/hdd** is the second drive on the second IDE controller. |
| SCSI hard drives | /dev/sda | The first SCSI hard drive. |
| | /dev/sda* | With SCSI hard drives, the device names are given numbers to label the various partitions. For example, **/dev/sda1** is the first primary partition on the first SCSI hard drive. |
| SCSI CD-ROM/DVD drives | /dev/scd0 /dev/scd* | The first SCSI CD-ROM/DVD drive. |

5

## Configuration Files (/etc/)

This directory and its subdirectories contain system configuration files. Almost all these files are ASCII files, which can be processed with any editor.

Normal users can read most of these files, but they cannot edit any of them. According to the FHS, no executable programs can be located here.

However, the subdirectories contain many shell scripts. Some important configuration files are listed in Table 5-3.

**Table 5-3**

| File | Description |
|---|---|
| /etc/SuSE-release | Version number of the installed SUSE Linux Enterprise Server |
| /etc/inittab | Configuration file for the init process |
| /etc/init.d/* | Scripts for starting services |
| /etc/grub.conf | Configuration file of GRUB |
| /etc/modprobe.conf | Configuration file of the kernel modules |
| /etc/DIR_COLORS | Specifies the colors for ls |
| /etc/X11/ XF86Config | Configuration file of the X Window System |
| /etc/fstab | Table of the file systems automatically mounted at system start |
| /etc/profile | Startup file to configure the shell |
| /etc/passwd | User database; all information except passwords |
| /etc/shadow | Encrypted passwords of users |
| /etc/group | Database of user groups |
| /etc/cups/* | Files for the CUPS printing system |
| /etc/hosts | Allocation of computer names to IP addresses |
| /etc/motd | Welcome message after a user logs in (message of the day) |

**Table 5-3**   (continued)

| File | Description |
|------|-------------|
| /etc/issue | Linux welcome message before the login prompt |
| /etc/sysconfig/* | System configuration files |

Most installed services have at least one configuration file in the directory /etc/ or a subdirectory.

## User Directories (/home/)

Every user on a Linux system has his own area in which to create and remove files. This area is called the home directory of the user. When a user logs in, she is in his own home directory.

Individual configuration files can be found in the user's home directory. These files have names that begin with a dot. These configuration files are hidden files, because files with names starting with a dot are normally not displayed by the command **ls**.

Table 5-4 shows the most important files in a user's home directory.

**Table 5-4**

| File | Description |
|------|-------------|
| .profile | User's private login script |
| .bashrc | Configuration file for bash |
| .bash_history | List of commands previously run in bash |

If there are no special settings, the home directories of all users are located beneath the directory /home/. The home directory of a user can also be addressed via the short cut "~", so **~/.bashrc** refers to the file .bashrc in the user's home directory.

In many cases, the directory /home/ is located on a different partition or can even be located on a different computer (with central administration of home directories).

## Libraries (/lib/)

Many programs use specific functions that are also used by other programs. Such standard functions are removed from the actual program, stored in the system, and only called up when the program runs. They are called **shared libraries**.

The directory /lib/ contains the libraries that are used by programs in the directories /bin/ and /sbin/. The kernel modules (hardware drivers not compiled into the kernel) are located in the directory /lib/modules/.

You can find additional libraries below the directory /usr/.

## Mount Points for Removable Media (/media/*)

SUSE Linux creates directories such as the following in the directory /media/ (depending on your hardware) for mounting removable media:

- **/media/cdrom/.** Created for mounting CD-ROMs.
- **/media/cdrecorder/.** Created for mounting CDs in a CD burner.
- **/media/dvd/.** Created for mounting DVDs.
- **/media/floppy/.** Created for mounting floppy disks.

## Application Directory (/opt/)

Installed programs can store their static files in the directory /opt/. First, a directory with the name of the application is created. The files are then stored in that directory.

Examples include GNOME (/opt/gnome/) and KDE3 (/opt/kde3/).

## Home Directory of the Administrator (/root/)

The home directory of the system administrator is not located beneath /home/ like that of a normal user. Preferably, it should be on the same partition as the root directory, "/". Only then is it guaranteed that the user root can always log in without a problem and have her own configured environment available.

## System Binaries (/sbin/)

The directory /sbin/ contains important programs for system administration. Programs that are run by normal users as well are located in /bin/.

Programs in the directory /sbin/ can also, as a rule, be run by normal users, but only to display the configured values. Changes to the configuration can only be made by the user root.

Table 5-5 gives an overview of important files in the directory /sbin/.

**Table 5-5**

| File | Description |
| --- | --- |
| /sbin/SuSEconfig | Used to configure the overall system; evaluates entries in the configuration files in the directory /etc/sysconfig/ and writes further configuration files |
| /sbin/conf.d/* | Contains more scripts from the SuSEconfig family; they are called up by /sbin/SuSEconfig |
| /sbin/yast | Administration tool for SUSE Linux Enterprise Server |
| /sbin/fdisk | Modifies partitions |
| /sbin/fsck | Checks file systems (file system check) |
| /sbin/init | Initializes the system |

**Table 5-5**   (continued)

| File | Description |
|------|-------------|
| /sbin/mkfs | Creates a file system (formatting) |
| /sbin/shutdown | Shuts down the system |

## Data Directories for Services (/srv/)

The directory /srv/ contains subdirectories filled with data of various services. For example, the files of the Apache web server are located in the directory /srv/www/ and the FTP server files are located in the directory /srv/ftp/.

## Temporary Area (/tmp/)

Various programs create temporary files that are stored in /tmp/ until they are deleted.

## The Hierarchy below /usr/

The directory /usr/, in accordance with the FHS, represents a second hierarchical layer.

This is the location for all application programs, graphical interface files, additional libraries, locally installed programs, and commonly shared directories containing documentation.

Table 5-6 lists some of the directories.

**Table 5-6**

| Directory | Description |
|-----------|-------------|
| /usr/X11R6/ | Files of the X Window System |
| /usr/bin/ | Almost all executable programs |
| /usr/lib/ | Libraries |
| /usr/local/ | Locally installed programs, now frequently found in the directory /opt/ |
| /usr/sbin/ | Programs for system administration |
| /usr/share/doc/ | Documentation |
| /usr/share/man/ | The manual pages (command descriptions) |
| /usr/src/ | Source files of all programs and the kernel (if installed) |

## Variable Files (/var/)

The directory /var/ contains a hierarchy that is described in the FHS. This directory and its subdirectories contain files that can be modified while the system is running.

Table 5-7 provides an overview of the most important directories beneath /var/.

**Table 5-7**

| Directory | Description |
|---|---|
| **/var/lib/** | Variable libraries (such as databases for the commands locate and rpm) |
| **/var/log/** | Log files for most services |
| **/var/run/** | Files with information on running processes |
| **/var/spool/** | Directory for queues (printers, e-mail) |
| **/var/lock/** | Lock files to protect devices from multiple use |

5

## Process Files (/proc/)

Linux handles process information that is made available to users via the directory /proc/. This directory does not contain any real files and therefore does not occupy any space on the hard disk.

It is generated dynamically when it is accessed (for example, with

**ls /proc/**). Each process has its own directory. The values in these directories can be read out as if they were in a file. Some values can also be set by writing to the corresponding "files." Changes to this virtual file system only have an effect as long as the system is running, however.

For example, the process **init** always has the process number "1." Information about it is therefore found in the directory /proc/1/. This directory contains the following files:

```
da10:~ # ls -l /proc/1
total 0
dr-xr-xr-x  3 root root 0 Apr  5 17:28 .
dr-xr-xr-x 62 root root 0 Mar 30 15:09 ..
dr-xr-xr-x  2 root root 0 Apr  5 17:36 attr
-r--------  1 root root 0 Apr  5 17:36 auxv
-r--r--r--  1 root root 0 Apr  5 17:28 cmdline
lrwxrwxrwx  1 root root 0 Apr  5 17:36 cwd -> /
-r--r--r--  1 root root 0 Apr  5 17:36 delay
-r--------  1 root root 0 Apr  5 17:36 environ
lrwxrwxrwx  1 root root 0 Apr  5 17:28 exe -> /sbin/init
dr-x------  2 root root 0 Apr  5 17:36 fd
-rw-------  1 root root 0 Apr  5 17:36 map_base
-r--r--r--  1 root root 0 Apr  5 17:36 maps
-rw-------  1 root root 0 Apr  5 17:36 mem
-r--r--r--  1 root root 0 Apr  5 17:36 mounts
lrwxrwxrwx  1 root root 0 Apr  5 17:36 root -> /
-r--r--r--  1 root root 0 Apr  5 17:28 stat
-r--r--r--  1 root root 0 Apr  5 17:36 statm
-r--r--r--  1 root root 0 Apr  5 17:36 status
dr-xr-xr-x  3 root root 0 Apr  5 17:36 task
-r--r--r--  1 root root 0 Apr  5 17:36 wchan
```

The contents of the files can be viewed with the command **cat**, which shows the status of the process, shown in the following:

```
da10:~ # cat /proc/1/status
Name:  init
State: S (sleeping)
SleepAVG:     26%
Tgid:  1
Pid:   1
PPid:  0
TracerPid:   0
Uid:  0     0     0     0
Gid:  0     0     0     0
FDSize: 32
Groups:
VmSize:    588 kB
VmLck:      0 kB
VmRSS:     108 kB
VmData:    136 kB
VmStk:      8 kB
VmExe:     432 kB
VmLib:      0 kB
Threads:    1
SigPnd: 0000000000000000
ShdPnd: 0000000000000000
SigBlk: 0000000000000000
SigIgn: fffffffd770d8fc
SigCgt: 00000000288b2603
CapInh: 0000000000000000
CapPrm: 00000000ffffffff
CapEff: 00000000fffffeff
da10:~ #
```

In this example, a list is displayed of what the process is called (**init**), what state it is in (**sleeping**), and to which user it belongs (**Uid: 0** for root).

In addition to directories for each individual process, /proc/ also includes directories and files containing information about the state of the system.

Table 5-8 lists the most important files and directories.

**Table 5-8**

| File | Description |
|---|---|
| /proc/cpuinfo | Information about the processor |
| /proc/dma | Use of the DMA ports (Direct Memory Access) |
| /proc/interrupts | Use of the interrupts |
| /proc/ioports | Use of the intrasystem I/O ports |
| /proc/filesystems | File system formats that the kernel understands |
| /proc/modules | Active modules |

**Table 5-8** (continued)

| File | Description |
|------|-------------|
| **/proc/mounts** | Mounted file systems |
| **/proc/net/*** | Network-specific information and statistics in human-readable form, for example, **ip_fwchains**, **ip_fwnames**, and **ip_masquerade** (IP firewall chains for kernels older than 2.4, meanwhile replaced by iptables for kernels 2.4 and 2.6) |
| **/proc/partitions** | Existing partitions |
| **/proc/pci** | Existing PCI devices |
| **/proc/scsi/** | Connected SCSI devices |
| **/proc/sys/*** | System and kernel information |
| **/proc/version** | Kernel version |

**5**

## System Information Directory (/sys/)

The directory /sys/ provides information in the form of a tree structure on various hardware buses, hardware devices, active devices, and their drivers.

## Mount Point for Temporarily Mounted File Systems (/mnt/)

The standard directory for integrating file systems is /mnt/. It should only be used for temporary purposes. For permanent mounts, you should create an appropriately named directory.

In the following example, the hard drive partition /dev/hda7 is mounted at the position /mnt/ in the directory tree using the command mount:

```
da10:~ # mount /dev/hda7 /mnt
```

All files on this partition can now be reached via the directory /mnt/. To remove this partition again, you use the command umount:

```
da10:~ # umount /mnt
```

If you do not include any options with the command mount, the program tries out several file system formats. If you want to specify a specific file system, use the option -t.

If the file system format is not supported by the kernel, the command is aborted, and you receive an error message. In this case, you must compile a new kernel that supports the file system format.

## Directories for Mounting Other File Systems

Other file systems such as other hard drive partitions, directories from other computers on the network, or removable media (floppy disk, CD-ROM, or removable hard drive) can be mounted to the file system at any point.

A directory must exist at the point where you intend to mount the file system. This directory is referred to as the ***mount point***. Once mounted, the complete directory structure of the mounted file system can be found beneath this directory.

In most cases, only the user root can mount and unmount directories. Removable media, such as floppy disks and CDs, can be changed by a normal user.

To mount a file system, enter the command **mount**, specifying the device file and the directory to which the file system should be mounted.

A file system can be removed again with the command **umount**. The file /etc/mtab, which is updated by the command mount, shows which file systems are currently mounted.

You can mount file systems to directories that are not empty. The existing contents of these directories, however, will no longer be accessible. After the file system is removed, this data will become available again.

Because the mounted file system does not have to be on a local hard disk, directories can be shared with many computers. This approach is often used for the home directories of users, which are located centrally on one machine and exported to other computers in the network.

The directories listed in Table 5-9 cannot be imported from other machines; they must always be located locally on each computer.

**Table 5-9**

| Directory | Description |
|-----------|-------------|
| /bin/ | Important programs |
| /boot/ | Kernel and boot files |
| /dev/ | Device files |
| /etc/ | Configuration files |
| /lib/ | Libraries |
| /sbin/ | Important programs for system administration |

Some of the directories that can be shared are listed in Table 5-10.

**Table 5-10**

| Directory | Description |
|-----------|-------------|
| /home/ | Home directories |
| /opt/ | Applications |
| /usr/ | The hierarchy below /usr/ |

## Exercise 5-1   Mount Removable Media

In past versions of Linux it was necessary to mount removable media with some command to access them and to unmount them afterwards. This has been automated in current kernel versions.

To access removable media, do the following:

1. From the KDE desktop, open a terminal window.
2. Log in as root by entering **su –** with a password of **novell**.
3. Insert the *SLES 9 DVD* into your DVD drive.
4. (Conditional) If a dialog box appears indicating that a data CD was found, close the dialog box by selecting **No**.
5. Display the contents of the directory /media/dvd/ by entering:

   **ls /media/dvd**

**NOTE**

If your CD-ROM drive is also a CD recorder, enter **ls /media/cdrecorder**.

If the DVD mounts automatically, the contents of the DVD are listed; if not, the directory is empty.

6. Mount the DVD manually by entering:

   **mount /dev/dvd/mnt**

**NOTE**

If your CD-ROM drive is also a CD recorder, enter **mount /dev/cdrecorder /mnt**.

A message appears indicating that the device is write-protected and is mounted as read-only.

7. Display the contents of the directory /mnt by entering:

   **ls /mnt**

   The contents of the DVD are listed.

8. Try to remove the DVD from the drive by pushing the eject button on the drive.

   The DVD unmounts automatically and the DVD tray opens.

9. (*Conditional*) If the DVD tray does not open, unmount the DVD manually by entering:

**umount /mnt**

Then push the eject button.

10. Remove the DVD from your DVD drive.

11. Display the contents of the directory /mnt by entering:

**ls /mnt**

The directory is now empty.

12. Log out as user root by entering **exit**.

13. Close the terminal window by entering **exit**.

---

# OBJECTIVE 2    IDENTIFY FILE TYPES IN THE LINUX SYSTEM

The Linux file system is distinct from the file systems of other operating systems because of the various file types.

The file types in Linux referred to as normal files and directories are also familiar to other operating systems:

- Normal Files
- Directories

Additional types of files are UNIX-specific:

- Device Files
- Links
- Sockets
- FIFOs

## Normal Files

*Normal files* refer to files as they are also known to other operating systems: a set of contiguous data addressed with one name. This includes all the files normally expected under this term (such as ASCII texts, executable programs, or graphics files).

You can use any names you want for these files—there is no division into filename and file type (such as report.txt).

A number of filenames still retain this structure, but these are requirements of the corresponding applications, such as a word processing program or a compiler.

## Directories

Directories contain two entries with which the structure of the hierarchical file system is implemented.

One of these entries (".") points to the directory itself. The other entry ("..") points to the entry one level higher in the hierarchy.

## Device Files

**5**

Each piece of hardware (with the exception of network cards) in a Linux system is represented by a *device file*. These files represent links between the hardware components or the device drivers in the kernel and the applications.

Every program that wants to access hardware must access it through the corresponding device file. The programs write to or read from a device file. The kernel then ensures that the data finds its way to the hardware or can be read from the file.

## Links

*Links* are references to files located at other points in the file system. Data maintenance is simplified through the use of such links. Changes only need to be made to the original file. The changes are then automatically valid for all links.

## Sockets

A *socket* refers to a special file with which data exchange between two locally running processes can be implemented through the file system.

## FIFOs

*FIFO* (first in first out) or *named pipe* is a term used for files used to exchange data between processes. However, the file can exchange data in one direction only.

---

## OBJECTIVE 3   CHANGE DIRECTORIES AND LIST DIRECTORY CONTENTS

The prompt of a shell terminal contains the current directory (such as **tux@da10:~**). The tilde (~) indicates that you are in the user's home directory.

You can use the following commands to list the contents of a directory, change directory and display the current directory:

- ls
- cd
- pwd

## ls

The command **ls** (list) lists the specified files. If a directory is included with ls, the directory's contents are displayed. Without an option, the contents of the current directory are listed.

Table 5-11 shows the most important options you can use with **ls**.

**Table 5-11**

| Option | Meaning |
|---|---|
| **(none)** | Displays the contents of the current directory in several columns (file and directory names only). |
| **-a** | Also displays hidden files (such as **.bashrc**) |
| **-F** | After each name, a character indicates the file type. (/ for directories, * for executable files, l for FIFO files, @ for symbolic links). This is helpful when the terminal does not display colors. |
| **-l** | (long list) Gives a detailed list of all files. For each filename, information about permissions, modification time, and size is included. |
| **-t** | Files are sorted by date of modification. Combined with the option -r, the output is in reverse order (the newest file is displayed last). |
| **-R** | Output is recursive, including all subdirectories. |
| **-u** | Sorted by date of last access. |

The following is an example of using ls:

```
tux@da10:/ > ls var/
adm cache games lib lock log mail opt run spool tmp X11R6 yp
tux@da10:/ > ls -l var/
total 2
drwxr-xr-x 10 root  root  272 2007-03-29 12:31 adm
drwxr-xr-x  6 root  root  144 2007-03-29 11:58 cache
drwxrwxr-x  2 games games  48 2007-03-23 18:41 games
drwxr-xr-x 22 root  root  624 2007-04-13 04:17 lib
drwxrwxr-x  4 root  uucp   96 2007-04-06 14:45 lock
drwxr-xr-x  6 root  root  800 2007-04-05 17:29 log
lrwxrwxrwx  1 root  root   10 2007-03-29 11:23 mail -> spool/mail
drwxr-xr-x  3 root  root   72 2007-03-29 11:26 opt
drwxr-xr-x 12 root  root  776 2007-04-08 11:21 run
drwxr-xr-x 11 root  root  296 2007-03-29 12:00 spool
drwxrwxrwt  5 root  root  144 2007-04-06 14:44 tmp
drwxr-xr-x  4 root  root  120 2007-03-29 11:47 X11R6
drwxr-xr-x  3 root  root  104 2007-03-29 11:46 yp
tux@da10:/ >
```

Each line shows the file permissions (covered in *Manage File Permissions and Ownership* in Section 7), the number of hard links to the file (covered in *Link Files*), owner and owning group, file size, time of last modification of content, and the filename.

## cd

You can use the command **cd** (change directory) to change between directories. Some examples are listed in Table 5-12.

**Table 5-12**

| Command | Meaning |
|---|---|
| cd plan | Change to the subdirectory plan. |
| cd /etc | Change directly to the directory /etc/ (absolute path). |
| cd | Change from any directory to the home directory. |
| cd .. | Move one directory level higher. |
| cd ../.. | Move two directory levels higher. |
| cd - | Move to the last valid directory. |

**5**

## pwd

You can use the command **pwd** (print working directory) to display the path of the current directory. If you enter pwd with the -P option, pwd prints the physical directory without any symbolic links, as shown in the following:

```
tux@da10:~ > ls -l doc/
lrwxrwxrwx  1 tux users  15 2007-02-12 08:43 doc -> /usr/share/
doc/
tux@da10:~ > cd doc/
tux@da10:~ > pwd
/home/tux/doc
tux@da10:~ > pwd -P
/usr/share/doc
tux@da10:~ >
```

## Exercise 5-2   Change Directories and List Directory Contents

Smooth administration of a Linux system requires familiarity with the directory tree and how to move within it. The purpose of this exercise is to show you how to orient yourself and move about within that tree.

To change the current directory and list the directory contents, do the following:

1. Describe what directories the following characters refer to:

   - /

   - ~

   - .

   - ..

2. From the KDE desktop, open a terminal window (Konsole).

3. Change to the directory /tmp/ by entering cd **/tmp**.

4. Change to the home directory by entering **cd ~**.

5. Display the name of the current directory by entering **pwd**.

6. Change to the directory /usr/share/doc by entering:

   **cd /usr/share/doc**

7. Display the name of the current directory by entering **pwd**.

8. Change back to the last directory (home) by entering **cd –**.

9. Display the name of the current directory by entering **pwd**.

10. Display the content of the current directory by entering **ls**.

11. Display the content of the current directory including the hidden files by entering **ls –a**.

12. Display the permissions and the file size of the directories starting with "D" in the current directory by entering:

    **ls –ld D***

13. View the permissions and the file size of all the files in the current directory by entering **ls –la**.

14. Close the terminal window by entering **exit**.

---

## OBJECTIVE 4    CREATE AND VIEW FILES

To create and view files, you need to know how to do the following:

- Create a New File with touch
- View a File with cat
- View a File with less
- View a File with head and tail

## Create a New File with touch

You can use the command **touch** to change the time stamp of a file or create a new file with a size of 0 bytes. The most important touch options are shown in Table 5-13.

**Table 5-13**

| Command | Description |
|---------|-------------|
| -a | Changes only the time of the last read access (**access time**) |
| -m | Changes only the time of the last modification of file content (**modification time**) |
| -r *file* | Sets the time stamp of *file* instead of the current time |
| -t *time* | Instead of the current time, sets *time* <br><br> (structure: [[CC]YY]MMDDhhmm.[ss] ([Century]Year] Month Day Hour Minute [Seconds], (use two digits for each variable)) |

The following is an example of using touch:

```
tux@da10:~> ls
bin Desktop Documents public_html
tux@da10:~> touch example
tux@da10:~> ls
bin Desktop Documents example public_html
tux@da10:~>
```

## View a File with cat

You can use the command **cat** to view the contents of a file (comparable to the command "type" in DOS). The command must include the filename of the file you want to see, as shown in the following:

```
tux@da10:~> cat /etc/HOSTNAME
da10.digitalairlines.com
tux@da10:~>
```

## View a File with less

You can use the command **less** to displays the contents of a file page by page. Even compressed files (such as .gz and .bz2) can be displayed. You can use the keystrokes in Table 5-14 with less.

**Table 5-14**

| Keystroke | Description |
|-----------|-------------|
| Spacebar | Move one screen down. |
| b | Move one screen up. |
| Down-arrow | Move one line down. |
| Up-arrow | Move one line up. |

**Table 5-14**  (continued)

| Keystroke | Description |
|---|---|
| */pattern* | Search forward for a pattern from current cursor position. |
| *?pattern* | Search backward for a pattern from the current cursor position. |
| n | Move to the next instance in the search for the pattern. |
| N | Move to the previous instance in the search for the pattern. |

## View a File with head and tail

With the command **head**, you can view only the first few lines of a file. The command **tail** shows you only the last few lines of a file.

By default, these commands only show ten lines. To change this number, just append the option *–number*, like *–20*.

When used with the command tail, the option **-f** displays a continuously updated view of the last lines of a file. If a line is added at the end of the file while **tail -f** is running, the line is displayed. This is a very useful feature for observing log files.

The following is an example of using the command head:

```
tux@da10:~> head /usr/share/doc/release-notes/RELEASE-NOTES.en.html
<H1>Release Notes for SUSE Linux Enterprise Server 9 for x86</H1>

<P>
These release notes cover the following areas:
<ul>
<li>General: Information that everybody should read.</li>
<li>Update: Explains changes that are not mentioned in the Admin Guide,
chapter 2.</li>
<li>Installation: Additional pertinent information for the
Installation.</li>
<li>Updates and Features: This section contains a number of
technical changes and enhancements for the experienced user.</li>
<li>Providing Feedback</li>
tux@da10:~> tail -5 /usr/share/doc/release-notes/RELEASE-NOTES.en.html
http://www.suse.com/feedback.
</P>
<P>
Your SUSE Linux Enterprise Team
</P>
tux@da10:~>
```

## Exercise 5-3   Create and View Files

To be able to view configuration and log files is a necessary part of system administration. Various tools exist for this purpose, and you choose the appropriate one depending on whether you want to view the complete file or only part of it.

To create and view files or parts of them, do the following:

1. Open a terminal window, log in as root (**su –**) with a password of **novell**.

2. Create a new, empty file by entering:

   **touch new_file**

3. Display the contents of the file /var/log/messages by entering:

   **cat /var/log/messages**

4. Display the contents of /var/log/messages page by page by entering:

   **less /var/log/messages**

5. Find the first occurrence of the word "root" by entering **/root**.

6. Find the next occurrence of the word "root" by typing **n**.

7. Navigate through the output by using the cursor keys and the **Page Up** and the **Page Down** keys.

8. Quit the display and return to the command line by typing **q**.

9. Display the first five lines of the file /var/log/messages by entering:

   **head –n 5 /var/log/messages**

10. View a continuously-updated display of the last lines of the file /var/log/messages by entering:

    **tail –f /var/log/messages**

11. Open a second terminal window.

12. Arrange the terminal windows on the desktop so that you can see the content of both.

13. In the second terminal window, log in as root (**su –**); then enter an invalid password (such as **suse**).

    Notice that the failed login attempt is logged in the first terminal window.

14. In the second terminal window, log in as root (**su –**) with a password of **novell**.

    The login is logged in the first terminal window.

15. Log out as root in the second terminal window by entering **exit**.

16. Close the second terminal window by entering **exit**.

17. Stop the tail process in the first terminal window by pressing **Ctrl + c**.

18. Log out as root by entering **exit**.

19. Close the terminal window.

## Objective 5    Manage Files and Directories

In this objective, you learn how to:

- Copy and Move Files and Directories
- Create Directories
- Delete Files and Directories
- Link Files

# Copy and Move Files and Directories

To copy and move files and directories, you need to know how to:

- Move Files with mv
- Copy Files with cp

## Move Files with mv

You can use the command **mv** (move) to move one or more files to another directory, as in the following:

**mv *.txt /tmp**

You can also use the command mv to rename a file, as in the following:

**mv recipe new_recipe**

Table 5-15 shows two options you can use with mv.

**Table 5-15**

| Option | Description |
|--------|-------------|
| -i | Asks for confirmation before moving or renaming a file. This prevents existing files with the same name from being overwritten. |
| -u | Only moves files that are newer than the target files of the same name. |

## Copy Files with cp

You can copy files and directories with the command **cp** (copy). The syntax for using cp is:

**cp** *source destination*

When using the command cp, you need to remember the following:

- The command cp overwrites existing files without confirmation.

- You can avoid automatic overwriting by using the option -i. This option requires confirmation before overwriting occurs.

- If you want to copy just the contents of a directory (without the directory itself), the target directory must already exist. An example is making a backup copy of a directory using a directory with a different name.

  For example, to copy the directory /tmp/quarterly-1/ with all its subdirectories to the directory /tmp/expenses/ (which already exists), you would enter the following:

  **cp –R /tmp/quarterly-1 /tmp/expenses**

  The result is a directory /tmp/expenses/quarterly-1/.

To copy the contents of the directory proposals/ and all its files, including hidden files and subdirectories, to the existing directory proposals_old/, do the following:

```
tux@da10:~ > ls -a proposals
.  ..  .hidden quarterly-1 quarterly-2 quarterly-3 quarterly-4
tux@da10:~ > cp -r proposals/. proposals_old
tux@da10:~ > ls -a proposals_old
.  ..  .hidden quarterly-1 quarterly-2 quarterly-3 quarterly-4
```

To avoid copying the hidden files, do the following:

```
tux@da10:~ > cp -r proposals/* proposals_old
tux@da10:~ > ls -a proposals_old
.  ..   quarterly-1 quarterly-2 quarterly-3 quarterly-4
```

You can use the options in Table 5-16 with cp.

**Table 5-16**

| Option | Description |
|---|---|
| -a, --archive | Copies a directory and subdirectories (compare with -R); symbolic links, file permissions, owners, and time stamps are not changed |
| --help | Displays the options of cp |
| -i, --interactive | Asks before overwriting |
| -l, --link | Links files instead of copying them |
| -R, -r, --recursive | Copies directories recursively (the directory and any subdirectories) |
| -s, --symbolic-link | Makes symbolic links instead of copying files |
| -u, --update | Copies a file only when the source file is newer than the destination file or when the destination file is missing |

## Exercise 5-4    Copy and Move a File and a Directory

Copying, moving and renaming files are basic and frequent operations done with files. Most probably you are already very familiar with these operations on a graphical desktop environment.

The purpose of this exercise is to get used to performing these operations on the command line.

To copy and move files and directories, do the following:

1. Open a terminal window and log in as root (**su -**) with a password of **novell**.

2. Rename new_file to my_file by entering:

   **mv new_file my_file**

3. Verify that the file was renamed by entering **ls -l**.

4. Copy my_file by entering **cp my_file my_file1**.

5. Verify that my_file1 was created by entering **ls -l my***.

6. Copy the files /usr/bin/rename and /usr/bin/mcopy to the directory /tmp/ by entering:

   **cp /usr/bin/rename /usr/bin/mcopy /tmp**

7. Verify that the files were copied by entering:

   **ls -l /tmp**

8. Move the file /tmp/mcopy to the home directory by entering:

   **mv /tmp/mcopy ~**

9. Verify the move by entering **ls -l**.

10. Move and rename the file /tmp/rename to ~/my_file2 by entering:

    **mv /tmp/rename ~/my_file2**

11. Verify that the file my_file2 exists by entering **ls -l**.

12. Copy the complete directory /bin/ to the home directory with the new directory named my_dir by entering:

    **cp -r /bin /home/my_dir**

13. Verify that the files were copied by entering:

    **ls -l /home/my_dir**

14. Close the terminal window.

## Create Directories

You can use the command **mkdir** (make directory) to create new directories (such as **mkdir proposal**). Use the option -p to create a complete path, as shown in the following:

**mkdir -p proposal/january**

## Exercise 5-5   Create Directories

The purpose of this exercise is to show you how to create directories.

To create directories, do the following:

1. Open a terminal window and su to root (**su -**) with a password of **novell**.
2. Create a directory named new_dir inside the directory my_dir by entering:

   **mkdir /home/my_dir/new_dir**
3. Verify that the directory was created by entering:

   **ls /home/my_dir**
4. Create a directory new_dir that includes a new directory empty_dir by entering:

   **mkdir -p ~/new_dir/empty_dir**
5. Verify that new_dir was created by entering **ls**.
6. Verify that empty_dir was created by entering:

   **ls new_dir**
7. Close the terminal window.

## Delete Files and Directories

In this section you learn how to:

- Use rmdir to Delete Empty Directories
- Use rm to Delete Files and Directories

### Use rmdir to Delete Empty Directories

You can use the **rmdir** (remove directory) command to remove the indicated directory or directories (for example, **rmdir proposal**). The directory or directories must be empty before you can delete them.

### Use rm to Delete Files and Directories

You can use the command **rm** (remove) to delete files, as shown in the following:

**rm part***

The command in this example deletes all files in the current directory that begin with **part** without asking for confirmation. If the user does not have sufficient permissions to delete a file, this file is ignored.

To delete directories, use the option **-r**, as shown in the following example:

```
tux@da10:~ > mkdir -p testdir/subdir
tux@da10:~ > rm testdir
rm: cannot remove 'testdir': Is a directory
tux@da10:~ > rmdir testdir
rmdir: 'testdir': Directory not empty
tux@da10:~ > rm -r testdir
tux@da10:~ >
```

 Files deleted with the command rm cannot be restored.

**CAUTION**

You can use the two options in Table 5-17 with rm.

**Table 5-17**

| Option | Description |
|--------|-------------|
| -i | Asks for confirmation before deleting |
| -r | Allows directories and their contents to be deleted |

# Exercise 5-6    Delete Files and Directories

The purpose of this exercise is to show you how to delete files and directories on the command line.

When deleting files and directories it is especially important to work only with the permissions necessary for the task and not as root, if possible. As root, you can easily destroy your installation with the rm command, and there is no undelete in Linux.

Think twice before hitting enter on an rm command issued as root!

To delete files and directories, do the following:

1. Open a terminal window and su to root (**su -**) with a password of **novell**.

2. Try to remove the directory ~/new_dir by entering:

    **rmdir new_dir**

    A message is displayed indicating that the directory cannot be removed. This is because the directory is not empty.

3. Remove the directory ~/new_dir/empty_dir by entering:

   **rmdir new_dir/empty_dir**

4. Verify that the directory /empty_dir has been removed by entering:

   **ls new_dir**

5. Remove the directory ~/new_dir by entering:

   **rmdir new_dir**

6. Verify that the directory was removed by entering **ls**.

7. Remove the file /home/my_dir/login by entering:

   **rm /home/my_dir/login**

8. Verify that the file has been removed by entering:

   **ls /home/my_dir/login**

9. Remove all files with names that begin with "a" in the directory /home/my_dir/ by entering:

   **rm –i /home/my_dir/a***

10. Confirm every warning by entering **y**.

11. Remove the directory /home/my_dir/ and its content by entering:

    **rm –r /home/my_dir**

12. Verify that the directory has been removed by entering:

    **ls /home/**

13. Close the terminal window.

## Link Files

File system formats in Linux keep data and administration information separate. How data organization takes place differs from one file system format to the next.

Each file is described by an inode (index node or information node). To see the inode number you can enter **ls –i**.

Each inode has a size of 128 bytes and contains all the information about this file besides the filename. This includes information such as owner, access permissions, size, time details (such as time of modification of content of file, time of access, and time of modification of the inode), and pointers to the data blocks of this file.

The command **ln** creates a link. A *link* is a reference to a file. You can use a link, to access a file from anywhere in the file system using different names for it. The file itself exists only once on the system, but it can be found under different names.

Linux recognizes two kinds of links: hard links and symbolic links (also called *soft links*).

You create a *hard link* by using the command ln, which points to the inode of an already existing file. Thereafter, the file can be accessed under both names—that of the file and that of the link—and you can no longer discern which name existed first or how the original file and the link differ.

The following is an example of using the command ln:

```
tux@da10:~/sell > ls -li
total 4
88658 -rw-r--r-- 1 tux users 82 2007-04-06 14:21 old
tux@da10:~/sell > ln old new
tux@da10:~/sell > ls -li
total 8
88658 -rw-r--r-- 2 tux users 82 2007-04-06 14:21 old
88658 -rw-r--r-- 2 tux users 82 2007-04-06 14:21 new
tux@da10:~/sell >
```

The link counter (shown after the file permissions) has changed from 1 to 2 because of the additional hard link to the file.

Hard links can only be used when both the file and the link are in the same file system, because inode numbers are only unique within the same file system.

You can create a *symbolic link* with the command ln and the option -s. A symbolic link is assigned its own inode—the link refers to a file, so a distinction can always be made between the link and the actual file.

The following is an example of creating a symbolic link:

```
tux@da10:~/sell > ls -li
total 4
88658 -rw-r--r-- 1 tux users 82 2007-04-06 14:21 old
tux@da10:~/sell > ln -s old new
tux@da10:~/sell > ls -li
total 4
88658 -rw-r--r-- 1 tux users 82 2007-04-06 14:21 old
88657 lrwxrwxrwx 1 tux users 3 2007-04-06 14:27 new -> old
tux@da10:~/sell >
```

The link counter (shown after the file permissions) has not changed, because only hard links are counted here.

If you use symbolic links, you are not limited by the boundaries of the file system, because the name of the object is shown, not the object itself. The disadvantage is that a symbolic link can point to a non-existing object if the object and its corresponding name no longer exist.

For e ample, if you erase the file **old** in the preceding *example,* in SLES 9 **new** will be shown in a different color in the output of ls, indicating that it points to a non-existent file:

```
tux@da10:~/sell > rm old
tux@da10:~/sell > ls -li
```

```
total 0
88657 lrwxrwxrwx 1 tux users 3 2007-04-06 14:27 new -> old
tux@da10:~/sell >
```

Another advantage of symbolic links is that you can create links to directories.

## Exercise 5-7    Link Files

Links are very convenient in administration, as they help to avoid having different versions of the same file within the file system.

The purpose of this exercise is to learn how to set hard and symbolic links and know the difference between those two.

To link a file, do the following:

1. Open a terminal window and su to root (**su -**) with a password of **novell**.

2. Enter the following to create a symbolic link to the howto index file in the directory /usr/share/doc/howto/en/html:

   **ln -s /usr/share/doc/howto/en/html/index.html howto-sym**

3. Enter the following to create a hard link to the howto index file in the directory /usr/share/doc/howto/en/html:

   **ln /usr/share/doc/howto/en/html/index.html howto-hard**

4. Display the links by entering **ls -l**.

   The symbolic link identifies the file it is linked to.

5. View the contents of the file /usr/share/doc/howto/en/html/index.html by entering:

   **cat howto-hard**

6. Create a file named **hello** by entering:

   **echo hello > hello**

7. Create a symbolic link to the file by entering:

   **ln -s hello hello-symlink**

8. View the content of the file hello via its symbolic link by entering:

   **cat hello-symlink**

9. Delete the original file by entering **rm hello**.

10. View the link by entering:

    **ls -l hello-symlink**

    Note that the link is now highlighted to indicate that it points to a non-existant file.

11. Delete the link by entering:

    **rm hello-symlink**

12. Close the terminal window.

---

## OBJECTIVE 6    FIND FILES

In this objective you learn how to find files and programs using the following commands:

- KFind
- find
- locate
- whereis
- which
- type command

## KFind

Sometimes you need to find a file so you can edit it, but you do not know exactly where it is located in the file system. You might know the name of this file or only a part of the name.

At another time, you might need a list of all files that have been modified in the last two days or that exceed a certain size.

You can use the KFind program to find files with specific features. You can start KFind from the KDE menu with the **Find Files** entry.

You can also start KFind directly in Konqueror by selecting **Tools > Find File**.

Figure 5-3 shows the Kfind dialog box.

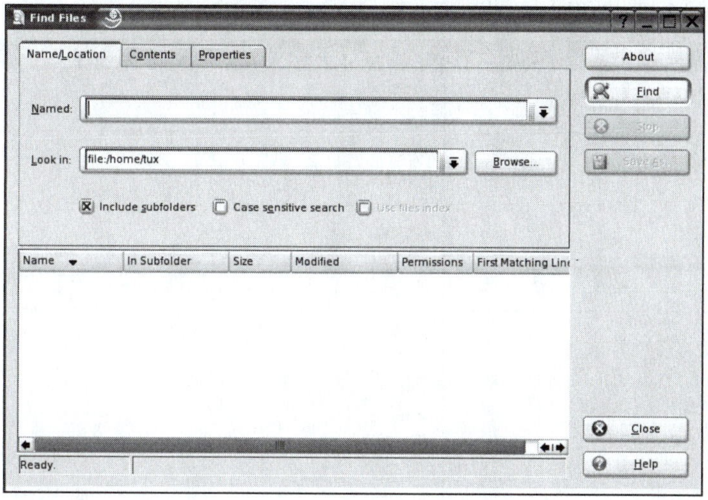

**Figure 5-3**

In the Named field, enter the name of the file you want to find. If you don't know the entire name of the file, you can use the wildcards "?" for one character and "*" for none, one, or several characters.

For example, suppose the following files exist:

- File
- file
- File1
- File1a
- File1b
- File2
- File2a
- MyFile

Table 5-18 shows the results of three different search strings.

**Table 5-18**

| Search String | Files Found |
|---|---|
| File? | File1 |
|  | File2 |
| File* | File |
|  | File1 |
|  | File1a |
|  | File1b |
|  | File2 |
|  | File2a |
| ?ile* | File |
|  | file |
|  | File1 |
|  | File1a |
|  | File1b |
|  | File2 |
|  | File2a |

Enter the directory you want to search in the Look In field. If you want to include all subdirectories in the search, select **Include Subfolders**.

Select the **Find** button to start the search process. All matching files and directories are shown in the lower window with details of their locations, as in Figure 5-4.

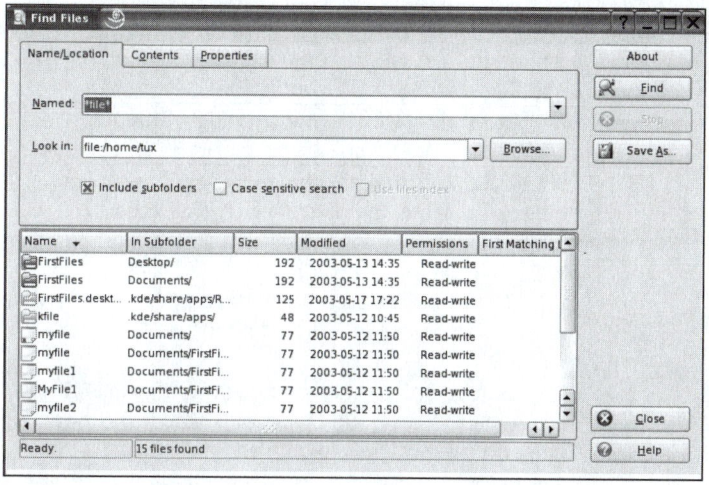

**Figure 5-4**

You can narrow the search by specifying certain criteria in Contents and Properties. In Contents, you can specify the file type, a string contained in the file, or the file size. In Properties, you can specify the date when the file to find was created or modified.

## find

To search for files on the command line, you can use the command **find**. The following is the syntax for the command find:

**find path** *criteria action*

This command has many options, a few of which are explained here. You can use the following arguments with the command:

- *path.* The section of the file system to search (the specified directory and all its subdirectories). If nothing is specified, the file system below the current directory is used.

■ *criteria.* The properties the file should have (refer to Table 5-19).

**Table 5-19**

| Option | Description |
|---|---|
| --mtime *number* | Searches for files whose content changed no earlier than a specified *number* x 24 hours ago. |
| --gid *number* | Searches for files with the numeric GID (Group ID) *number*. |
| --group *name* | Searches for files that are owned by the group *name*. Instead of a name, the numeric GID is allowed. |
| --name *pattern* | Searches for files whose names contain the given *pattern*. If the pattern contains meta characters or wildcards, it must be enclosed by quotation marks. Otherwise the wildcards will be interpreted by the shell and not by find. |
| --size [+/-]*size* | Matches files that are above or below a certain *size*. As an argument, the size (in blocks of 512 bytes) is given. The suffix "c" switches to byte and "k" to blocks of 1024 bytes. A preceding "+" stands for all larger files and a "-" for all smaller files. |
| --type *file_type* | Searches for a *file type*. A file type can be one of the following: "d" for a directory, "f" for a file, or "l" for a symbolic link. |
| --uid *number* | Searches for files with the numeric UID (User ID) *number*. |
| --user *name* | Searches for files, which are owned by user *name*. Instead of a name, the numeric UID is allowed. |

Examples:

To find files with a certain extension beneath the /usr/share/doc/ directory, enter the following:

```
tux@da10:~ > find /usr/share/doc/ -name "*.txt" -type f
/usr/share/doc/xine/faq/faq.txt
. . .
```

To find files that were changed within the last 24 hours,

```
tux@da10:~ > find ~ -mtime 0
.
./.xsession-errors
. . .
```

enter:

■ *action.* Options that influence the following conditions or control the search as a whole, such as the following:

  ■ --print

  ■ --exec *command*

You can use the option -exec to call up another command. This option is frequently used to link **find** and **grep**, as shown in the following:

```
tux@da10:~ > find ~ -name 'letter*' -type f -exec grep  appointment {} \; \
-print appointment for next meeting: 23.08.
/home/tux/letters/letter_Meier
tux@da10:~ >
```

In this example, the command find searches for files containing letters in their names, and then passes the names of the files found with -exec to the following command (in this case, **grep appointment {}**).

The two brackets {} are placeholders for the filenames that are found and passed to the command grep. The semicolon closes the -exec instruction. Because this is a special character, it is masked by placing a backslash in front of it.

When grep is used alone, it searches for a specific expression in a file whose exact position in the file system is known. When used in combination with find, the search is for a file that contains a certain expression but whose location is unknown.

## locate

The command **locate** is an alternative to **find –name** (the package findutils-locate must be installed). The command find must search through the selected part of the file system, a process that can be quite slow.

On the other hand, locate searches through a database previously created for this purpose (/var/lib/locatedb), making it much faster.

The database is automatically created and updated daily by SLES 9. But changes made after the update has been performed are not taken into account by locate, unless the database is updated manually using the command **updatedb**.

The following example shows the output of locate:

```
tux@da10:~ > locate letter_Miller
/home/tux/letters/letter_Miller
```

The following example shows that a search with locate returns all files whose names contain the search string:

```
tux@da10:~ > locate umount
/bin/umount
/lib/klibc/bin/umount
/opt/kde3/share/icons/crystalsvg/scalable/devices/3floppy_umount.svgz
/opt/kde3/share/icons/crystalsvg/scalable/devices/5floppy_umount.svgz
/opt/kde3/share/icons/crystalsvg/scalable/devices/camera_umount.svgz
/opt/kde3/share/icons/crystalsvg/scalable/devices/cdaudio_umount.svgz
```

```
/opt/kde3/share/icons/crystalsvg/scalable/devices/cdrom_umount.svgz
/opt/kde3/share/icons/crystalsvg/scalable/devices/cdwriter_umount.svgz
/opt/kde3/share/icons/crystalsvg/scalable/devices/dvd_umount.svgz
/opt/kde3/share/icons/crystalsvg/scalable/devices/hdd_umount.svgz
/opt/kde3/share/icons/crystalsvg/scalable/devices/mo_umount.svgz
/opt/kde3/share/icons/crystalsvg/scalable/devices/nfs_umount.svgz
/opt/kde3/share/icons/crystalsvg/scalable/devices/zip_umount.svgz
/usr/bin/humount
/usr/bin/smbumount
/usr/share/man/man1/humount.1.gz
/usr/share/man/man2/umount.2.gz
/usr/share/man/man2/umount2.2.gz
/usr/share/man/man8/smbumount.8.gz
/usr/share/man/man8/umount.8.gz
tux@da10:~ >
```

To learn more about locate, enter **man locate**.

## whereis

The command **whereis** returns the binaries (option **-b**), manual pages (option **-m**), and the source code (option **-s**) of the specified command.

If no option is used, all this information is returned, if the information is available. This command is faster than find, but it is less thorough.

The following is an example of using whereis:

```
tux@da10:~ > whereis grep
grep: /bin/grep /usr/bin/grep
/usr/share/man/man1/grep.1.gz
/usr/share/man/man1p/grep.1p.gz
tux@da10:~ > whereis -b grep
grep: /bin/grep /usr/bin/grep
tux@da10:~ > whereis -m grep
grep: /usr/share/man/man1/grep.1.gz
/usr/share/man/man1p/grep.1p.gz
tux@da10:~ > whereis -s grep
grep:
tux@da10:~ >
```

For more information about whereis, enter **man whereis**.

## which

The command **which** searches all paths listed in the variable PATH for the specified command and returns the full path of the command.

This command is especially useful if several versions of a command exist in different directories and you want to know which version is executed when entered without specifying a path.

The following is an example of using the command which:

```
tux@da10:~ > which find
/usr/bin/find
tux@da10:~ > which cp
/bin/cp
tux@da10:~ > which grep
/usr/bin/grep
tux@da10:~ >
```

For more information on which, enter **man which**.

## type command

The command **type** *command* can be used to find out what kind of command is executed when command is entered—a shell built-in command or an external command. The option **-a** delivers all instances of a command bearing this name in the file system.

The following is an example of using the command type:

```
tux@da10:~ > type type
type is a shell built in
tux@da10:~ > type grep
grep is /usr/bin/grep
tux@da10:~ > type -a grep
grep is /usr/bin/grep
grep is /bin/grep
tux@da10:~ >
```

## Exercise 5-8    Find Files

With around 100,000 files in a usual installation it is essential to be able to find files effectively within the file system. It is possible to search using part of the file name, but also to look for files that contain a certain string, as covered in the exercise after this one.

To find files and directories, do the following:

1. Open a terminal window (you do not need to su to root).
2. Find the type of the command ll by entering **type ll**.

3. Find the manual pages of the command find by entering:

   **whereis -m find**

4. Find the path of the program KFind by entering:

   **which kfind**

5. Start KFind by entering **kfind &**.

   A Find Files dialog box appears on the KDE desktop.

6. Find all files in the home directory whose names start with "my" by entering **my\*** in the Named field; then select **Find**.

7. Find all files in the directory /bin/ whose names consist of two characters by entering **??** in the Named field and **/bin** in the Look in field; then select **Find**.

8. Find all files in the directory /tmp/ that were changed or created in the last 24 hours by doing the following:

   a. Enter **\*** in the Named field and **/tmp** in the Look In field.

   b. Select the **Properties** tab.

   c. Select **Find All Files Created or Modified**.

   d. Select **During the Previous**; then enter **24** in the text field.

   e. Select **Find**.

9. Close the Find Files dialog box.

10. From the terminal window command line, find all files in the home directory whose names start with "my" by entering:

    **find ~ -name "my\*"**

11. Find all files in the directory /tmp/ that were changed or created in the last 24 hours by entering:

    **find /tmp -ctime -1**

12. Su to root (**su -**) with a password of **novell**.

13. Create the locate database by entering **updatedb**.

    Notice that the updatedb utility also searches for any files located on your CD-ROM or floppy drive to add to the database.

14. When the database is updated, find all files in your file system whose names contain the string "my" by entering:

    **locate my**

15. Log out as root by entering **exit**.

16. Close the terminal window by entering **exit**.

# Objective 7    Search File Content

Suppose you have dozens of text files and you need to find all files that include a particular word, phrase, or item. To scan these files without opening them in an editor, you need to know the following:

- How to Use the Command grep
- How to Use Regular Expressions

**5**

## How to Use the Command grep

The command **grep** and its variant **egrep** are used to search files for certain patterns using the syntax **grep** *search_pattern filename*. The command searches filenames for all text that matches *search_pattern* and prints the lines that contains the pattern.

If you specify several files, the output will not only print the matching line but also the corresponding filenames.

There are options to specify that only the line number should be printed, for instance, or that the matching line should be printed together with leading and trailing context lines.

You can specify search patterns in the form of regular expressions, although the basic grep command is limited in this regard. To search for more complex patterns, use the egrep command (or **grep -E**) instead, which accepts extended regular expressions.

As a simple way to deal with the difference between the two commands, make sure you use egrep in all of your shell scripts.

The regular expressions used with egrep need to comply with the standard regex syntax. For more information, see the manual page of grep.

To prevent the shell from interpreting special characters in search patterns, enclose the pattern in quotation marks.

The following is an example of using egrep and grep:

```
tux@da10:~> egrep (b|B)lurb file*
bash: syntax error near unexpected token '|'
tux@da10:~> grep "(b|B)lurb" file*
tux@da10:~> egrep "(b|B)lurb" file*
file1:blurb
filei2:Blurb
```

Table 5-20 shows options you can use with the command grep.

**Table 5-20**

| Option | Description |
|---|---|
| -i | Ignores case |
| -l | Shows only the names of files that contain the search string |
| -r | Searches entire directory trees recursively |
| -v | Gives all lines that do not contain the search string |
| -n | Shows the line numbers |

# How to Use Regular Expressions

Regular expressions are strings consisting of metacharacters and literals (regular characters and numerals). In the context of regular expressions, **metacharacters** are characters that do not represent themselves but have special meanings.

They can act as placeholders for other characters or can be used to indicate a position in a string.

Many commands (such as egrep) rely on regular expressions for pattern matching. It is important to remember, however, that some metacharacters used by the shell for filename expansion have a meaning different from the one discussed here.

To learn more about the structure of regular expressions, see the manual page **man 7 regex**.

Table 5-21 lists the most important metacharacters and their meanings.

**Table 5-21**

| Character | Meaning | Example |
|---|---|---|
| ^ | Beginning of the line | **^The: The** is matched if at the beginning of the line |
| $ | End of the line | **eighty$: eighty** is matched if at the end of line |
| \< | Beginning of the word | **\<thing\>**:matches the whole word **thing** |
| \> | End of the word | **\<thing\>**:matches the whole word **thing** |
| [abc] | One character from the set | **[abc]**: matches any one of "a", "b", and "c" |
| [a-z] | Any one character from the specified range | **[a-z]**: matches any one character from "a" to "z"<br>**[-:+]**: any one of "-", ":" and "+" |
| [^xyz] | None of the characters | **[^xyz]**: "x", "y", and "z" are not matched |
| . | Any single character | **file.**: matches file1 and file2, but not file10 |
| + | One or more of the preceding expression | **[0-9]+**: matches any number |

**Table 5-21**   (continued)

| Character | Meaning | Example |
|---|---|---|
| * | Any number (including none) of preceding single character | **file.***: matches file, file2, and file10 |
| {min,max} | The preceding expression min times at minimum and max times at maximum | **[0-9]{1,5}**: matches any one-digit to five-digit number |
| I | The expression before or after | **fileIFile**: matches file and File |
| ( ...) | Enclose alternatives for grouping with others | **(fIF)ile**: matches file and File |
| ? | Zero or one of the preceding | **file1?2**: matches both file2 and file12 |
| \ | Escape the following metacharacter to remove its special meaning | **www\.novell\.com**: matches www.novell.com, literally (with the dot not being treated as a metacharacter); this is also necessary for parentheses, e.g., matching a parenthetical pattern would require the expression \([a-zA-Z]+\) |

# Exercise 5-9   Search File Content

Sometimes all you know is some string that appears within a certain file, but you do not know in which file exactly. The purpose of this exercise is to show you how to find such a file.

To search file content, do the following:

1. Open a terminal window.

2. Find all HTML headings of hierarchy 2 in the file /usr/share/doc/release-notes/RELEASE-NOTES.en.html by entering (on one line):

   **grep "<H2>" /usr/share/doc/release-notes/RELEASE-NOTES.en.html**

3. Find all locations in the HTML files of the directory /usr/share/doc/packages/cups/ that include the word "management" by entering:

   **grep management /usr/share/doc/packages/cups/*.html**

4. Find all locations in the HTML files of the directory /usr/share/doc/packages/cups/ that include lines beginning with a number by entering:

   **egrep "^[0-9]" /usr/share/doc/packages/cups/*.html**

5. Find all locations in the HTML files of the directory /usr/share/doc/
packages/cups/ that include lines beginning with a four-digit number by
entering:

**egrep "^[0-9]{4}" /usr/share/doc/packages/cups/*.html**

6. Close the terminal window.

---

## OBJECTIVE 8    ARCHIVE, BACK UP, COMPRESS, AND DECOMPRESS FILES

To save a part of the file system structure, you need to create archives. When attaching files
to an e-mail or saving files on a removable storage, it is useful to compress them to
conserve space.

In this objective, you learn how to:

- Archive Files with ark
- Archive Files with tar
- Restore Files from tar Archives
- Copy Files to and from an Archive
- Use Data Backup Command-Line Tools
- Compress Files with gzip
- Decompress Files with gunzip
- Compress Files with bzip2
- Decompress Files with bunzip2
- View Compressed Files with zcat

## Archive Files with ark

The program **ark** lets you collect multiple files or even entire directories into an archive.
This can be very useful for:

- Backing up data
- Preparing data to be sent via floppy disk or e-mail

One big advantage of using ark to back up files is that the directory structure in an archive
is recreated when the archive is unpacked.

You can start ark from the KDE menu by selecting **Utilities > Archiving**. Figure 5-5 appears.

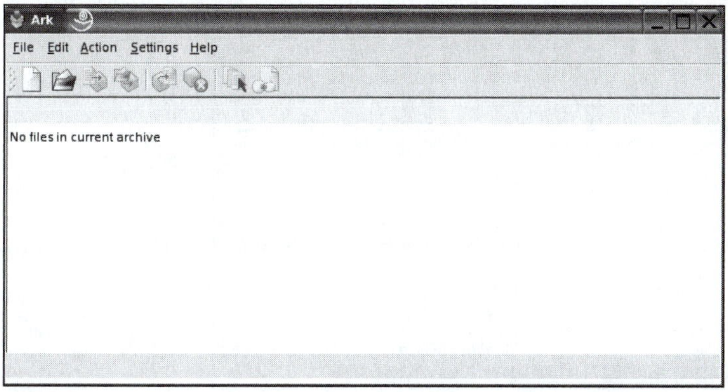

**Figure 5-5**

Before you can begin archiving files, you must create a new archive. Select **File > New** to open a window in which to specify the path and name of the archive. The standard file format for archives in Linux is .tar (from tape archiver; originally this was developed for data backup on magnetic tape).

Tar files can be quite large, but you can compress them. ark archives and compresses in one step if you use .tar.gz as the file format. ark can also handle the .zip format that is commonly used in Windows environments.

ark supports file formats such as the following:

- Tar archives (*.tar, *.tar.gz, *.tar.Z, *.tar.bz2, etc.)
- Compressed files (*.gz, *.bz, *.bz2, *.lzo, *.Z)
- Zip archives (*.zip)
- Lha archives (*.lzh)
- Zoo archives (*.zoo)
- Rar archives (*.rar)
- Ar archives (*.a)

When you select **Save**, an empty archive is created at the given location. To fill the archive, drag the files you want to archive with the mouse from Konqueror into the empty window.

You can open an existing archive (whether it is compressed or not) by selecting the file in Konqueror or by starting ark and then selecting **File > Open**. The contents of the archive are displayed in Figure 5-6.

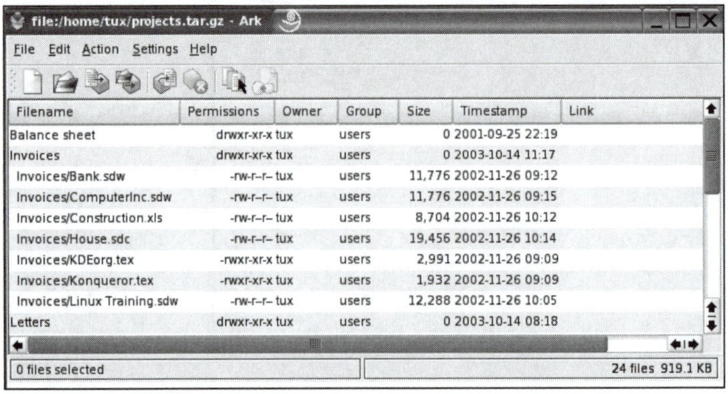

**Figure 5-6**

You can drag individual files from the archive window and place them in a Konqueror window. You can also unpack the entire archive by selecting **Action > Extract**.

## Archive Files with tar

The program **tar** (tape archiver) is the most commonly used tool for data backup. It archives files in a special format, either directly to a corresponding medium (such as magnetic tape or formatted floppy disk) or to an archive file.

Normally, the data is not compressed. Names of archive files end in .tar. If archive files are compressed (usually with the command gzip, then the extension of the filename is either *.tar.gz* or *.tgz*.

The command **tar** requires an option (which is why you don't need to use a minus sign), the name of the archive (or the device file) to be written to, and the name of the directory to back up.

All directories and files beneath the specified directory are also saved. Directories are typically backed up with a command similar to the following:

```
da10:~ # tar -cvf /dev/st0 /home
```

This command backs up the complete contents of the directory /home to the tape device /dev/st0 (this is the first SCSI tape drive).

The option **-c** (create) creates the archive. The option **-v** (verbose) provides a detailed list; that is, the name of each file just backed up is displayed. The name of the archive to be created is specified after the option **-f** (file). This can either be a device file (such as a tape drive) or a standard file, as in the following:

```
da10:~ # tar -cvf /backup/etc.tar /etc
```

In this example, the archive /backup/etc.tar is created. It contains all files from the directory /etc. When an archive is created, absolute paths are by default made relative; that is, the leading "/" is removed and the following message appears:

```
tar: Removing leading '/' from member names
```

To reduce the file size of the resulting archive, you can create a gzip compressed archive by adding the option **-z**, as in the following example:

```
da10:~ # tar -czvf /backup/etc.tgz /etc
```

You can use the options in Table 5-22 with tar.

**Table 5-22**

| Option | Description |
|--------|-------------|
| -c | Creates an archive |
| -C | Changes to the specified directory |
| -d | Compares files in the archive with those in the file system |
| -f | Uses the specified archive file or device |
| -j | Directly compresses or decompresses the tar archive using bzip2 |
| -r | Appends files to an archive |
| -u | Update only includes files in an archive that are newer than the version in the archive |
| -v | Verbose mode, displays the files that are being processed |
| -x | Extracts files from an archive |
| -X | Excludes files listed in a file |
| -z | Directly compresses or decompresses the tar archive using gzip |

If you want to exclude specific files from the backup, you must create a file that lists the names of the files to exclude, with each filename on a separate line. You then specify this list with the option -X, as in the following:

```
da10:~ # cat exclude.files
/home/user1/.bashrc
/home/user2/Text*
da10:~ # tar -cvf /dev/st0 /home -X exclude.files
```

In this example, the file /home/user1/.bashrc and all files in the directories of the user user2 that start with the string Text are not saved to tape.

You can display the contents of an archive by entering a command similar to the following:

```
da10:~ # tar -tvf /dev/st0
```

If you want to back up only files with a certain extension within your home directory and its subdirectories, you could use a combination of the commands find and tar, as in the following:

```
tux@da10:~> find . -name "*.txt" -type f -print0 | \
           tar --null -cvf txt.tar -T -
```

In this example, the command archives all files (-type f) with the extension .txt (-name "*.txt) in the current directory. The options -print0 and --null ensure that files featuring spaces in their names are also archived. The option **-T -** specifies that files piped to stdin are will be included in the archive.

Information on stdin, stdout and stderr and how to combine commands using the pipe character (|) is in Section 6 under *Use Piping and Redirection.*

In the following example only files that are more recent than a specific file are backed up:

```
da10:~ # find /home -type f -newer last_backup -print0 | \
      tar --null -cvf new.tar -T -
```

In this example, the command archives all files (-type f) in the directory /home/ that are younger than the file last_backup. Again, the options -print0 and --null ensure that files featuring spaces in their names are also archived. The option -T - specifies that files piped to stdin are included in the archive.

## Restore Files from tar Archives

To restore or extract files from an archive, enter:

**tar –xvf /dev/st0**

This writes all files in the archive to the current directory. Due to the relative path specifications in the tar archive, the directory structure of the archive is created here.

If you want to extract the files to another directory, you can use the option -C, followed by the directory name.

If you want to extract just one file, you can specify the name of the file with the –C option, as in the following:

**tar –xvf /test1/backup.tar –C /home/user1/.bashrc**

## Exercise 5-10    Archive Files

Files are frequently put into archives as they then can be sent more easily as attachements to e-mails. Backups also often make use of archives.

Various tools exist for this purpose in Linux and the purpose of this exercise is to show you the more common ones.

To archive files, do the following:

1. Start the ark program from the KDE menu by selecting:

   **Utilities > Archiving**

   An Ark dialog box appears on the KDE desktop.

2. From the dialog box, create a new archive by doing the following:

   a. Select **File > New**.

      A Create New Archive - Ark dialog box appears.

   b. Change to the geeko home directory by selecting the *Up-Arrow* button once.

   c. In the Location field, enter **unzipped_file**.

   d. From the Archive Format drop-down list, select **Tar Archive**.

   e. Select **Save**.

3. Copy all the files in the directory /bin to the tar archive by doing the following:

   a. Start Konqueror by selecting the icon in the Kicker.

   b. Display the files in directory **/bin**.

   c. Select all files in the directory by selecting:

      **Edit > Selection > Select All**

      (or press **Ctrl + a**).

   d. Copy the files in the directory /bin to the Ark window by dragging and dropping the files.

   e. Close the Konqueror window.

4. From the Ark dialog box, select **File > Quit**; then select **Save** (twice).

5. Open a terminal window (do not su to root).

6. Create a zipped archive of the same files at the command line by entering:

   **tar czvf zipped_file.tar.gz /bin**

7. Start Konqueror by selecting the *blue house* icon in the Kicker.

8. Select the icon of the file **zipped_file.tar.gz**.

9. Select the **bin** directory icon.

10. View the navigation area by selecting the *red folder* icon at the left side of the Konqueror window.

11. Drag and drop the file **df** to the directory **/tmp**.

12. Close the Konqueror window.

13. From the terminal window, copy the file unzipped_file.tar to the directory /tmp by entering:

    **cp unzipped_file.tar /tmp**

14. Switch to the directory /tmp by entering **cd /tmp**.

15. Verify that the file was copied by entering **ls –l un\***.

16. Extract the files of the archive /tmp/unzipped_file.tar by entering:

    **tar xvf unzipped_file.tar**

17. Switch to the home directory by entering **cd –**.

18. Close the terminal window.

# Copy Files to and from an Archive

The **cpio** command copies files into or out of a cpio or tar archive. The archive can be another file on the disk, a magnetic tape, or a pipe. cpio has three operating modes:

- Copy-Out Mode
- Copy-In Mode
- Copy-Pass Mode

## Copy-Out Mode

In copy-out mode, cpio copies files into an archive.

It reads a list of filenames, one per line, on the standard input, and writes the archive onto the standard output.

A typical way to generate the list of filenames is with the find command (find can be used with the -depth option to minimize problems with permissions on directories that are unwritable or not searchable).

The following is an example of using find with cpio in copy-out mode:

**find mystuff/ | cpio –o > mystuff.cpio**

## Copy-In Mode

In copy-in mode, cpio copies files out of an archive or lists the archive contents.

It reads the archive from the standard input.

Any non-option command-line arguments are shell globbing patterns; only files in the archive whose names match one or more of those patterns are copied from the archive.

Unlike in the shell, an initial "." in a filename does match a wildcard at the start of a pattern, and a "/" in a filename can match wildcards. If no patterns are given, all files are extracted.

The following is an example of using cpio in copy-in mode:

**cat mystuff.cpio | cpio –idvm**

## Copy-Pass Mode

In copy-pass mode, cpio copies files from one directory tree to another, combining the copy-out and copy-in steps without actually using an archive.

It reads the list of files to copy from the standard input; the directory it will copy them into is given as a non–option argument.

Table 5-23 lists cpio options.

**Table 5-23**

| Option | Description |
|---|---|
| **--block-size=BLOCK-SIZE** | Set the I/O block size to BLOCK-SIZE * 512 bytes. |
| **-d, --make-directories** | Create leading directories where needed. |
| **-i, --extract** | Run in copy-in mode. |
| **-l, --link** | Compress and decompress files in all subdirectories. |
| **-m, --preserve-modification-time** | Retain previous file modification times when creating files. |
| **-o, --create** | Run in copy-out mode. |
| **-p, --pass-through** | Run in copy-pass mode. |
| **-r, --rename** | Interactively rename files. |
| **-t, --list** | Print a table of contents of the input. |
| **-u, --unconditional** | Replace all files, without asking whether to replace existing newer files with older files. |
| **-v, --verbose** | List the files processed, or with -t, give an "ls -l" style table of the contents listing. In a verbose table of contents of a ustar archive, user and group names in the archive that do not exist on the local system are replaced by the names that correspond locally to the numeric UID and GID stored in the archive. |
| **--version** | Print the cpio program version number and exit. |

## Use Data Backup Command-Line Tools

In addition to tar, Linux has several command-line tools for data backup, including the following:

- **rsync (remote synchronization).** The command rsync creates copies of complete directories across a network to a different computer.

  rsync can also be used to carry out local mirroring of directories. The only files that are copied are those that are not already in the target directory or only exist in older versions. In fact, only parts of a file that have changed are copied, not the entire file.

  For example, you can mirror all home directories by entering a command similar to the following:

  **rsync –a /home /shadow**

  In this example, the mirroring is made to the directory shadow. The directory home is created first, and then the actual home directories of the users are created below it.

  If you want the home directories created directly beneath the target directory specified (such as **/shadow/geeko/**), enter:

  **rsync –a /home/. /shadow**

  Specifying /. at the end of the directory to be mirrored indicates that this directory is not included in the copy.

  The -a option switches rsync to archive mode. This is a combination of other options (–rlptg), which ensures that the characteristics of the files to be copied are identical to the originals.

**NOTE**

For additional details on rsync, enter **man rsync**, refer to /usr/share/doc/packages/rsync/tech_report.ps, or connect to the rsync project Web site at *http://rsync.samba.org/*.

- **dd.** You can use the dd command to convert and copy files byte-wise.

  Normally dd reads from the standard input and writes the result to the standard output.

  You can copy all kinds of files with this command, including device files, which means entire partitions. You can easily create exact copies of an installed system, or just parts of it.

  In the simplest case, you can copy a file by entering a command similar to the following:

  **dd if=/etc/protocols of=protocols.org**

Use the option if= (input file) to specify the file to be copied. Use the option of= (output file) to specify the name of the copied file.

For additional details on using dd to copy, convert, or format files, see **man dd**.

5

- **mt.** The mt command lets you work with magnetic tapes.

  You can use this command to position tapes, switch compression on or off (with some SCSI-2 tape drives), and query the status of the tape.

  Magnetic tape drives in Linux are always SCSI devices and can be addressed by names such as the following:

  - **/dev/st0**. Refers to the first tape drive.

  - **/dev/nst0.** Addresses the same tape drive in the no rewind mode. In other words, after writing or reading, the tape remains at that position and is not rewound back to the beginning.

For compatibility with other Unix conversions, two symbolic links exist: /dev/rmt0 and /dev/nrmt0.

You can view the status of a tape by entering a command similar to the following:

**mt –f /dev/st0 status**

For more information on the mt command, enter **man mt**.

Backing up data is a task that you should do regularly. You can automate backup from the command line with the **cron** service.

System jobs are controlled by the file /etc/crontab and the files in the directory /etc/cron.d/. Other jobs are defined by the scripts in the following directories:

- /etc/cron.hourly/
- /etc/cron.daily/
- /etc/cron.weekly/
- /etc/cron.monthly/

You specify which users can create cron jobs by using the following files, which are accessed in the order they are listed in:

- /var/spool/cron/allow
- /var/spool/cron/deny

If both files do not exist, then only root can define jobs.

The jobs of individual users are stored in files in the directory /var/spool/cron/tabs/ with names matching the user names.

Users can edit their own crontab files by entering **crontab –e** (see **man crontab**).

The following is an example of a defined cron job:

```
0 22 * * 5 /root/bin/backup
```

The script /root/bin/backup is started every Friday at 10:00 P.M. The format for the line is described in **man 5 crontab**.

**NOTE**

More information on scheduling jobs is in Section 8, *Processes, Jobs, and Runlevels.*

## Compress Files with gzip

Linux offers various tools for compressing and decompressing data. One tool is called **gzip**, which uses the following syntax:

**gzip** *options file*

You can use the command gzip to compress and decompress data. The compressed data is marked with the suffix *.gz*.

gzip only suitable for compressing individual files. To save several files or entire directories in a compressed file, use the command tar.

Table 5-24 shows some useful options of gzip.

**Table 5-24**

| Option | Description |
|---|---|
| -c, --stdout, --to-stdout | Compresses the file without modifying the original file. The result is written to the standard output (usually the screen). From there, it can be redirected to a file with the >symbol. |
| -d, --decompress, --uncompress | Decompresses the specified file (compare with gunzip; see below). |

**Table 5-24**    (continued)

| Option | Description |
|---|---|
| -1 to -9, --fast, --best | Controls the compression speed. **-1** means **--fast** and causes a quick compression but produces larger files; **-9** corresponds to **--best** and requires more computing time but produces smaller files. The default setting is -6. |
| -r, --recursive | Compresses and decompresses files in all subdirectories. |

5

In the following example, the command gzip compresses all .tex files in the current directory, resulting in files with the suffix .tex.gz:

**gzip *.tex**

In the following example, the command gzip compresses the file price_list:

**gzip –c price_list > price_list_backup.gz**

The file itself is not modified. The result of the compression is written to the file price_list_backup.gz.

## Decompress Files with gunzip

The command **gunzip** decompresses a file compressed with gzip and removes the suffix **.gz**.

This function corresponds to the command **gzip –d** *file*.

The syntax for the command gunzip is:

**gunzip** *file***.gz**

Combining tar and gzip has been covered under Archive Files with tar.

## Compress Files with bzip2

The command **bzip2** is another command for compressing files. Files compressed with bzip2 are usually twenty to thirty percent smaller than the files compressed with gzip.

The syntax for the command bzip2 is:

**bzip2** *options file*

The disadvantage of using this command is that more computing time is required for the compression.

Some important options you can use with bzip2 are shown in Table 5-25.

**Table 5-25**

| Option | Description |
| --- | --- |
| **-c, --to-stdout** | Compresses the file without modifying the original file. The result is written to the standard output (usually the screen). From there, it can be redirected to a file with a > symbol. |
| **-d, --decompress, --uncompress** | Decompresses the specified file (compare with bunzip2). |
| **-1 to -9** | Determines how much memory is allocated for the compression. -1 requires 1.1 MB; -9 requires 6.7 MB. -9 is the default setting and produces the best result. |

You can also use bzip2 with tar to reduce the size of the tar archive. Use the tar option **-j**, as in the following example:

```
da10:~ # tar -cjvf /backup/etc.tar.bz2 /etc
```

The same result can be achieved using a pipe character (|):

```
da10:~ # tar -cf - /etc | bzip2 > /backup/etc.tar.bz2
```

More information on combining commands using the pipe character (|) is in Section 6 under *Use Piping and Redirection*.

## Decompress Files with bunzip2

The command **bunzip2** decompresses files compressed with bzip2 and removes the suffix *bz2*.

Its function corresponds to the command **bzip2 -d** *file*.

The syntax for the command bunzip2 is:

**bunzip2** *file*.**bz2**

To unpack a bzip2-compressed tar archive, use the tar option **-j**, as in the following example:

```
da10:~ # tar -xjvf /backup/etc.tar.bz2
```

This unpacks the contents of the archive in the current directory.

The same result can be achieved using a pipe character (|):

```
da10:~ # bzip2 -d /backup/etc.tar.bz2 -c | tar -xf -
```

More information on combining commands using the pipe character (|) can be found in Section 6 under *Use Piping and Redirection*.

## View Compressed Files with zcat

You can use the command **zcat** to decompress files compressed with gzip and write them to the standard output (usually the screen). The compressed file is not modified.

The function of zcat corresponds to the command **gunzip -c -d**.

The syntax for the command zcat is:

**zcat** *file*.**gz**

**5**

## Exercise 5-11    Compress and Decompress Files with gzip and bzip2

Usually files are not just put into archives, but they are compressed as well to save on bandwidth and/or storage capacity.

To compress and uncompress files, do the following:

1. Open a terminal window.

2. Copy the file

   /usr/share/doc/release-notes/RELEASE-NOTES.en. html

   to the home directory by entering the following (on one line):

   **cp**

   **/usr/share/doc/release-notes/RELEASE-NOTES.en. html ~**

   The tilde (~) indicates to copy the file to the home directory.

3. Verify that the file was copied by entering:

   **ls RELEASE-NOTES.en.html**

4. Use gzip to compress the file RELEASE-NOTES.en.html by entering:

   **gzip RELEASE-NOTES.en.html**

5. Verify that the file was compressed by entering **ls**.

   Notice that the file RELEASE-NOTES.en.html.gz has replaced RELEASE-NOTES.en.html.

6. Display the contents of the file RELEASE-NOTES.en.html.gz by entering:

   **zcat RELEASE-NOTES.en.html.gz**

7. Decompress the file RELEASE-NOTES.en.html.gz with gunzip by entering:

   **gunzip RELEASE-NOTES.en.html.gz**

8. Verify that the file was decompressed by entering **ls**.

   Notice that the file RELEASE-NOTES.en.html has replaced RELEASE-NOTES.en.html.gz.

9. Compress the file unzipped_file.tar in the geeko home directory using bzip2 by entering:

   **bzip2 unzipped_file.tar**

10. Compare the size of the files unzipped_file.tar.bz2 and zipped_file.tar.gz by entering:

    **ls –l *zipped_file.tar.***

11. Close the terminal window.

---

## CHAPTER SUMMARY

❑ The Linux filesystem is arranged hierarchically, using a series of directories to store files.

❑ Regardless of the number of filesystems, there is only one root directory in Linux, denoted by a "/" character.

❑ Linux directories and files follow the Filesystem Hierarchy Standard (FHS); their locations can be described using absolute or relative pathnames.

❑ The /dev directory contains character and block-oriented device files that are used to identify most hardware devices on the Linux system. Each device file contains a major number that identifies the device driver in the Linux kernel and a minor number that identifies the instance of the particular device. You can use the **mknod** command to create device files.

❑ The /media and /mnt directories typically contain mount point subdirectories that are used to mount and access removable media such as CD-ROMs, CD-RWs, DVDs, and floppies. The system typically automounts these devices, but you can manually mount and unmount devices to these directories using the **mount** and **umount** commands.

❑ Most system configuration information is stored in text files under the /etc directory; shared libraries are stored under the /lib directory.

❑ The /usr directory stores most system applications, whereas the /opt directory stores most user applications. In addition, most applications store application data in the /srv directory and temporary files in the /tmp directory.

❑ Log files, spool directories, and application-specific files are typically stored under the /var directory.

❑ The /boot directory contains information used to load the Linux kernel.

❑ Home directories are typically located under the /home directory and named for their user account (e.g., /home/geeko). The root user's home directory is always /root.

- The /bin and /sbin directories contain executable binary programs. There are many directories throughout the filesystem that have the name bin and sbin.

- The /proc and /sys directories are virtual directories in system memory that contain information that is exposed by the Linux kernel, including process, hardware, network, and version information. As a result, files in these directories are often used in system troubleshooting.

- Many types of files may exist on the Linux filesystem, such as normal files (text files, data files, executable programs), directories, linked files, device files, sockets, and named pipes. You can use various options to the **ls** command to view filename information.

- Text files are the most common file type whose contents may be viewed by several utilities such as **head**, **tail**, **cat**, and **less**.

- There are many file management commands that can be used to create, change the location of, or remove files and directories. The most common of these include **cp**, **mv**, **rm**, **rmdir**, and **mkdir**.

- Every file and directory has an inode that contains all file information other than the data and filename.

- Files may be a link to another file by name or by inode. These are called symbolic and hard links, respectively. You can create linked files using the **ln** command.

- You may find files on the filesystem using a variety of utilities, including **KFind**, **find**, **locate**, **whereis**, and **which**. The **type** command can be used to determine the type of an executable file.

- Regular expression metacharacters can be used to specify certain patterns of text when used with certain programming languages and text tool utilities such as **grep**.

- You can use the **ark**, **tar**, and **cpio** utilities to archive data to a file or backup device. Alternatively, you can use the **rsync** or **dd** commands to copy data to a remote location or backup device. The **mt** command may be used to manage tape backup devices.

- Programs such as backup utilities can be scheduled to occur on a repetitive basis using the cron service.

- Files may be compressed to save disk space using a compression utility. Two common compression utilities are **gzip** and **bzip2**. You may use the **gunzip** and **bunzip2** utilities to decompress files.

## Key Terms

**. (period)** — A special character used to indicate the user's current directory in the directory tree.

**.. (double period)** — Special characters used to represent the user's parent directory in the directory tree.

**/** — The single root directory in Linux.

**/bin directory** — Contains binary commands for use by all users.

**/boot directory** — Contains the Linux kernel and files used by the boot loader.

**/dev directory** — Contains device files.

**/etc directory** — Contains system-specific configuration files.

**/etc/mtab** — A file that contains a list of mounted filesystems.

**/home directory** — Default location for user home directories.

**/lib directory** — Contains shared program libraries (used by the commands in /bin and /sbin) as well as kernel modules.

**/media directory** — Used for accessing (mounting) disks such as floppy disks and CD-ROMs.

**/mnt directory** — Used for accessing (mounting) disks such as floppy disks and CD-ROMs.

**/opt directory** — Stores additional software programs.

**/proc directory** — Contains process and kernel information.

**/root directory** — The root user's home directory.

**/sbin directory** — Contains system binary commands used for administration.

**/sys directory** — Contains current system information.

**/tmp directory** — Holds temporary files created by programs.

**/usr directory** — Contains most system commands and utilities.

**/var directory** — Contains log files and spools.

**~ (tilde)** — A character used to represent a user's home directory.

**absolute path** — The full name to a certain file or directory, starting from the root directory.

**ark** — A graphical program that may be used to archive files and directories.

**ASCII files** — Files that contain text that adheres to the American Standard Code for Information Interchange.

**block-oriented device file** — A device file which specifies that information be transferred to the device in a block-by-block manner to a formatted filesystem.

**bunzip2 command** — Used to decompress files that have been compressed with **bzip2**.

**bzip2 command** — A common compression utility in Linux.

**cat command** — Used to display (or concatenate) the entire contents of a text file to the screen.

**cd command** — Used to change the current directory in the directory tree.

**character-oriented device file** — A device file which specifies that information be transferred to the device in a character-by-character manner.

**cp command** — Used to create copies of files and directories.

**cpio (copy in and out) command** — A command-line utility that may be used to archive files and directories.

**cron** — A system service that can be used to run command on a repetitive schedule.

**crontab command** — Used to schedule commands using the cron service.

**dd command** — Used to copy files to an alternate location using a particular format or method.

**device file** — A file used to identify hardware devices such as hard disks and serial ports.

**directories** — Special files that are used to organize other files on the filesystem.

**egrep command** — A variant of the **grep** command used to search files for patterns using extended regular expressions.

**FIFOs** — See named pipes.

**Filesystem Hierarchy Standard (FHS)** — A standard outlining the location of set files and directories on a Linux system.

**find command** — Used to find files on the filesystem using various criteria.

**grep (Global Regular Expression Print) command** — Searches files for patterns of characters using regular expression metacharacters.

**gunzip command** — Used to decompress files that have been compressed with **gzip**.

**gzip command** — A common compression utility in Linux.

**hard link** — A file that points to another file's inode.

**head command** — Displays the first set of lines of a text file; by default, the head command displays the first 10 lines.

**hidden files** — Files that are not normally displayed to the user via common filesystem commands; hidden files have filenames that start with a period.

**home directory** — A directory on the filesystem set aside for users to store personal files and information.

**inode** — The portion of a file that stores information on the file's attributes, access permissions, location, ownership, and file type.

**KFind** — A graphical utility that may be used to find files and directories on the filesystem.

**less command** — Used to display a text file page-by-page on the terminal screen; users may then use the cursor keys to navigate the file.

**links** — Files that point to other files on the filesystem.

**ll command** — An alias for the ls —l command; it gives a long file listing.

**ln (link) command** — Used to create hard and symbolic links.

**locate command** — Used to locate files from a file database.

**ls command** — Used to list the files in a given directory.

**major device number** — A number used in a device file that determines the location of the device driver in the Linux kernel for a particular device.

**metacharacters** — Characters that have special meaning on your system when typed at a command prompt.

**minor device number** — A number used in a device file that determines the instance of the particular device.

**mkdir command** — Used to create directories.

**mount command** — Used to mount a device to a mount point directory.

**mount point** — The directory to which a device is mounted.

**mounting** — The process of associating a device (e.g., CD-ROM) to a directory (e.g., /media/cdrom). Once a device has been mounted, it may be accessed by navigating to the appropriate directory.

**mt (magnetic tape) command** — Used to manage tape devices.

5

**mv (move) command** — Used to move/rename files and directories.

**named pipes** — Temporary connections that send information from one command or process in memory to another; they are also represented by files on the filesystem. Named pipes are also called FIFO (First In First Out) files.

**normal files** — Commonly used files such as text files, graphic files, data files, and executable programs.

**PATH** — A variable that stores a list of directories that will be searched in order when commands are executed without an absolute or relative pathname.

**pwd (print working directory) command** — Used to display the current directory in the directory tree.

**regular expressions** — Special metacharacters used to match patterns of text within text files; they are commonly used by many text tool commands such as **grep**.

**relative path** — The name of a target directory relative to your current directory in the tree.

**rm command** — Used to remove files and directories.

**rmdir command** — Used to remove empty directories.

**rsync command** — Used to copy files and directories to a different location on the local computer or to a remote computer across a network.

**shared libraries** — Files that store common functions used by most programs on the system.

**sockets** — Named pipes connecting processes on two different computers; they can also be represented by files on the filesystem.

**soft link** — See symbolic link.

**symbolic link** — A pointer to another file on the same or another filesystem; commonly referred to as a shortcut or soft link.

**tail command** — A Linux command used to display the last set number of lines of text in a file; by default, the tail command displays the last 10 lines of the file.

**tar (tape archiver) command** — A command-line utility that may be used to archive files and directories.

**touch command** — Used to create new files. It was originally used to update the timestamp on a file.

**type command** — Used to determine the type of program for a command.

**umount command** — Used to unmount a device from a mount point directory.

**updatedb** — Used to create and update the database used by the **locate** command.

**whereis command** — Displays the location, manual pages, and source code for a command.

**which command** — Used to locate files that exist within directories listed in the PATH variable.

**zcat command** — Used to view the contents of text files that have been compressed with **gzip**.

## REVIEW QUESTIONS

1. Where can you find the detail specifications of FHS? _____

2. How long can the total path name to a particular file be in Linux (from the root directory)?
   a. 512 characters
   b. 1024 characters
   c. 2048 characters
   d. 4096 characters

3. What directories must reside on the same filesystem partition as the root directory? _____

4. Which of the following are absolute pathnames? (Choose all that apply.)
   a. ../bin
   b. /home/bin
   c. /
   d. bin

5. Which of the following devices can be referenced using device files? (Choose all that apply.)
   a. printers
   b. mice
   c. network cards
   d. hard disk partitions

6. When you do a long listing of the file /dev/fd0, you notice the following output:

   `brw-rw---- 1 root disk 2, 0 Jun 30 2007 /dev/fd0`

   Which of the following statements are true regarding this file? (Choose all that apply.)
   a. The file is a block-oriented device file that has a major number of 0 and a minor number of 2.
   b. The file is a block-oriented device file that has a major number of 2 and a minor number of 0.
   c. The file is a character-oriented device file that has a major number of 0 and a minor number of 2.
   d. The file is a character-oriented device file that has a major number of 2 and a minor number of 0.root

7. What device file is used to refer to the first partition on your first IDE hard disk? _____

8. What three hidden files exist in user home directories? _____

9. Which directory stores administrative programs?

   a. /bin

   b. /sbin

   c. /usr

   d. /opt

10. You are troubleshooting a system problem and believe that there is a duplicate interrupt being used on the system. What file can you view to verify this? _____

11. What command could you type at a command prompt to mount a CD-ROM filesystem to the /mnt/cdrom directory? _____

12. Which option to the **ls** command can you use to view a long listing of files in your current directory, including hidden files?

   a. –al

   b. –lR

   c. –Fa

   d. –Ru

13. Which of the following commands can be used to change your present working directory (/etc/sysconfig) to /home/geeko, using a relative path?

   a. cd ../geeko

   b. cd ../../home/geeko

   c. cd /home/geeko

   d. cd home/geeko/../..

14. What command could you type at a command prompt to view the first 25 lines of the file /etc/hosts? _____

15. Which option to the **tail** command is useful when viewing logfiles and why? _____

16. Which key combination can you use to cancel your current command?

   a. Ctrl + F1

   b. Ctrl + x

   c. Ctrl + c

   d. Ctrl + Del

17. Which command could you use to copy the directory /data/secret to the /var directory?

    a. cp –s /var /data/secret

    b. cp /data/secret /var

    c. cp –s /var –d /data/secret

    d. cp –R /data/secret /var

18. Which command can be used to remove a directory and all of the files within?

    a. rmdir

    b. deltree

    c. rm

    d. touch

19. Which of the following commands would you use to undelete a file that was accidentally deleted using the **rm** command?

    a. restore

    b. undelete

    c. crt

    d. none of the above

20. What command could you type in a command prompt window to create a new symbolic link called **shortcut** in your current directory that points to the /etc/inittab file? _____

21. Which of the following statements regarding file linking are true? (Choose all that apply)

    a. Symbolic links point to the inode of an existing file.

    b. To determine whether a file is hard linked, you can view the link counter in a long file listing.

    c. Symbolic links are given a different color in your terminal window.

    d. Hard links share the same inode.

22. Which command can be used to search the PATH variable for executable programs?

    a. which

    b. locate

    c. find

    d. KFind

23. What command may be used to search the /etc directory for files that are owned by the user geeko? _____

5

24. You are attempting to locate a new file on the filesystem using the locate command, however no results are displayed. What command could you run to remedy the problem? _____

25. Which command may be used to search the /etc/hosts file for lines that start with 127.0.0.1?

    a. grep /etc/hosts "127.0.0.1"

    b. egrep "$127.0.0.1" /etc/hosts

    c. grep /etc/hosts —E "127.0.0.1"

    d. grep "^127.0.0.1" /etc/hosts

26. Which of the following archive utilities must be run in a GUI environment?

    a. cpio

    b. ark

    c. tar

    d. dd

27. What **tar** command would you use to create a gzip-compressed archive file called /root/myfile.tar.gz that contains the entire contents of the /opt directory?

    _____

28. You have created a script that contains **cpio** commands used to create a daily backup of your system. What directory could you place this script in to allow the cron daemon to execute it each day? _____

29. After downloading a file, you note that it has a .bz2 extension. Which command could you use to extract the contents of this file?

    a. gunzip

    b. bunzip2

    c. bunzip

    d. gzip

30. Many file management commands support the –R (Recursive) option. How does this option change the operation of the command? _____

## DISCOVERY EXERCISES

**5**

### Navigating the Filesystem

Log into tty1 as the root user and perform the following actions in order. For each action, write the command(s) that you used. When finished, log out of tty1.

1. Change to the /etc/sysconfig directory using an absolute path and verify that it has been changed.

2. Use a relative path to change to the / directory.

3. Use a relative path to change to the /var/lib directory.

4. Use a relative path to change to the /etc/sysconfig directory.

5. Change to your home directory.

6. Without changing directories, perform a long listing of the /dev/log file using a relative path. What type of file is it?

### Managing Files and Directories

Log into tty1 as the root user and perform the following actions in order. For each action, write the command(s) that you used. When finished, log out of tty1.

1. Copy the file **/etc/issue** to your current directory and verify that the copy was successful.

2. Copy the file **/etc/issue** to your current directory and rename it **newissue** with one command. Verify that the copy was successful.

3. Rename the file **newissue** in your current directory to **newissue2** and verify that the file was renamed successfully.

4. Make a copy of the **Desktop** directory (in your home directory) called **Desktop2** and verify that the contents of each directory are identical.

5. Rename the **Desktop2** directory **Desktop3** and verify that the rename operation was successful.

6. Remove the **newissue2** file in your home directory and verify that you were successful.

7. Remove the **Desktop3** directory in your home directory with a single command and verify that you were successful.

### Exploring the /dev Directory

Log into tty1 as the geeko user. Type the command **ls –l /dev/fd0 /dev/fd1** to perform a long listing of the device files for your first and second floppy devices. What type are the files (block or character)? Do they share the same device driver? How can you tell?

Do a long listing of the device files associated with the local command-line terminals on your system by typing **ls -l /dev/tty[1-6]** at the command prompt. What type are these files? Do they all share the same major number? Do they share the same minor number? Why?

Log out of tty1.

## Viewing and Testing Hidden Environment Files

Your home directory contains several hidden files that contribute to your user environment. Log into tty1 as the geeko user and run the **ls -a** command. How can you identify the hidden files?

Type the command **less .bash_history** and press Enter. What is stored in this file? Press **q** when finished.

The .profile file is used to create variables and load programs when you log in to your system and obtain a login shell. If you create additional shells following login, the .bashrc file is used to perform the same function. Use the **less** command to view each of these files in turn. Be sure to read the commented sections at the top of the files (comment lines start with a # character).

Type the command **echo "echo Welcome to your Login Shell" >> .profile** and press Enter to add a line to the bottom of your .profile. Type the command **tail .profile** to verify that it was added successfully. Next, log out of tty1 and log in again as the geeko user. What happened? Following this, log out of tty1 and log in again as the root user. Why didn't you see the greeting?

## Mounting Media

Log in to tty1 as the root user. Insert the SLES DVD into your DVD drive. In a few seconds, it should mount automatically. Type **mount** and press Enter to see which mount point directory it was mounted to (it will be /media/cdrom, /media/cdrecorder or /media/dvd, depending on your computer hardware).

Switch your current directory to the mount point directory (e.g., /media/cdrom) and use the **ls** command to view the files on your DVD. Type **umount *mount point directory*** (e.g., **umount /media/dvd**) and press Enter. What error did you receive? Switch your current directory back to your home directory and type **umount *mount point directory*** to unmount your DVD. Type the **mount** command to verify that your DVD was unmounted.

Type **mount -r -t iso9660 /dev/dvd /mnt** and press Enter. What does this command do? Type the **mount** command and press Enter to see which directory your DVD was mounted to. Next, type **umount /mnt** and press Enter. Log out of tty1.

## Exploring the more Command to View /proc

The **more** command is nearly identical to the **less** command in that it can view a file page-by-page or line-by-line, but it lacks the ability to scroll text using the cursor keys. The command gets its name from the fact that it can do "more" than the **cat** command. Similarly, the **less** command can do "more" than the **more** command (and "less is more"...more or less.).

Log into tty1 as the root user and view the contents of the following files using the **more** command (use the Enter key and Spacebar key to navigate the file and the **q** key to quit). For each file, write the type of information that is contained within it.

1. /proc/cpuinfo
2. /proc/partitions
3. /proc/swaps
4. /proc/ioports
5. /proc/dma
6. /proc/devices
7. /proc/interrupts
8. /proc/mounts

## Locating Files

Log into tty1 as the root user.

Create a new file called **file1** in your current directory. Use the **locate** command to locate this file. Why were you unsuccessful? Update the locate database using the **updatedb** command (this will take several minutes). When it is finished updating, use the **locate** command to locate the file. Were you successful?

Use the **which** command to locate the **who**, **grep**, and **cp** executable files. What directories are the files in? Type **echo $PATH** and press Enter to view the PATH variable. Are these directories listed? Use the **which** command to find the file called **file1** in your home directory. Why were you not successful?

Use the appropriate **find** commands to perform the following actions. For each action, write the command that you used.

1. Find all files on the system called "hosts".
2. Find all files under the /etc directory and subdirectories that are larger than 100K in size.
3. Find all files in the /etc directory and subdirectories that are less than 2K in size.
4. Find all symbolic links underneath the /usr directory.

5. Find all files in the /usr directory and subdirectories that were modified less than one day ago.

6. Find all files in the /tmp directory and subdirectories that are owned by the root user.

## File Linking

Log in to tty1 as the geeko user and copy the file **/etc/issue** to your current directory. Next, perform a long listing of the **issue** file in your current directory. Is it hard linked? Is it soft linked? How can you tell?

Create a hard link to **issue** called **hardissue**. Next, do a long listing of both files. What are their sizes? What are their modification dates? What are their link counters? Why? Next, use the **ls –li** command to view their inodes. Are they the same? Remove the file **hardissue**. Was **issue** removed as well? What is the link count of **issue** now? Explain.

Create a soft link to **issue** called **softissue**. Next, do a long listing of both files. What are their sizes? What are their modification dates? What are their link counts? What is the file type of **softissue**? What does the filename of softletter indicate? Next, use the **ls –li** command to view their inodes. Are they the same? Explain.

## Creating, Viewing, and Extracting Archives

Log in to tty1 as the geeko user and perform the following actions in order. For each action, write the command(s) that you used. When finished, log out of tty1.

1. Use the **tar** utility to create a gzip-compressed tar archive (also known as a tarball) called **sample.tar.gz** in your current directory that contains the entire contents of the **Desktop** directory.

2. View the contents of your tarball.

3. Extract the contents of your tarball to the **/tmp** directory and verify that the action was successful.

4. Insert a floppy disk into your computer and use the **cpio** utility to create an archive on it that contains the entire contents of the **Desktop** directory. (Instead of using a filename, specify the /dev/fd0 device file.)

5. View the contents of the cpio archive on your floppy.

6. Extract the contents of your cpio archive to the **/tmp** directory and verify that the action was successful.

**DISCOVERY**

## Comparing Compression Utilities

Log in to tty1 as the geeko user and copy the file **/etc/services** to your current directory. Next, perform a long listing of this file and note its size. Use the **gzip** command with the **-1** option to compress the **services** file and perform a long listing to note its size. Next, uncompress the **services.gz** file and use the **gzip** command with the -9 option to compress it. Perform a long listing and note its size. Which option provides the best compression? Uncompress the **services.gz** file.

Use the **bzip2** command with the -1 option to compress the **services** file and perform a long listing to note its size. Next, uncompress the **services.bz2** file and use the **bzip2** command with the -9 option to compress it. Perform a long listing and note its size. Which option provides the best compression? Does bzip2 have better compression than gzip? Uncompress the **services.bz2** file and log out of tty1.

**5**

## Comparing Compression Utilities

# 6

# WORK WITH THE LINUX SHELL AND EDIT TEXT FILES

> **In this section you learn about the basic features of the bash shell. You also learn about some of the text editors available on SUSE Linux Enterprise Server 9 (SLES 9).**
>
> ◆ Get to Know the Command Shells
> ◆ Get to Know Common Command-Line Tasks
> ◆ Understand Command Syntax and Special Characters
> ◆ Use Piping and Redirection
> ◆ Use Terminal Based Editors to Edit Files
> ◆ Manipulate Text Non-Interactively

## Objective 1   Get to Know the Command Shells

You cannot communicate directly with the operating system kernel—you need to use a program that serves as an interface between the user and the operating system.

In the operating systems of the UNIX family, this program is called the shell.

The shell accepts a user's entries, interprets them, converts them to system calls, and delivers system messages back to the user, making it a command interpreter.

To work efficiently with command shells, you need to know about:

- Types of Shells
- Bash Configuration Files
- Filename Restrictions
- Command and Filename Completion
- History Function
- Switch to User root

## Types of Shells

UNIX has many shells, most of which are provided by Linux in freely usable versions. The following are examples of some popular shells:

- The Bourne shell (**/bin/sh**)
- The Bourne again shell (**/bin/bash**)
- The Korn shell (**/bin/ksh**)
- The C shell (**/bin/csh**)
- The TC shell (**/bin/tcsh**)

The various shells provide different functionality.

Each shell can be started like a program, and you can switch at any time to a different shell. For example, you can switch to the C shell by entering **csh**; you can switch to the TC shell by entering **tcsh**; or you can switch to the bash shell by entering **bash**.

Unlike most other programs, the shell does not close on its own. You need to enter the command **exit** to return to the previous shell.

A shell is started at a text console right after a user logs in. This is called the login shell. The shell that is started for each user is determined in the user database.

The standard Linux shell is bash, so we will cover only the Bourne again shell in this objective.

## Bash Configuration Files

To customize bash for an interactive session, you need to know about the configuration files and about the order in which they are processed.

To understand how shells work, you need to know the difference between the following:

- Login Shells
- Non-Login Shells

### Login Shells

6

A login shell is started whenever a user logs in to the system. By contrast, any shell started from within a running shell is a non-login shell.

The only differences between these two shells are the configuration files that are read when starting the shell.

A login shell is also started whenever a user logs in through an X display manager. Therefore, all subsequent terminal emulation programs run non-login shells.

The following files are read when a login shell starts:

- **/etc/profile.** A system-wide configuration file read by all shells.

  It sets global configuration options.

- **~/.bash_profile.** The first user-level configuration file that bash tries to find.

  It contains user customizations (for example, to change the command prompt).

  By default, this file is not present on SLES 9.

  **~/.bash_login.** The second user-specific file that bash tries to find if there is no ~/.bash_profile.

  By default, this file is not present on SLES 9.

  The counterpart to the file ~/.bash_login is the file ~/.bash_logout. In this file, you can set the actions to be performed when the user logs out.

  By default, this file is not present on SLES 9.

- **~/.profile.** The third user-specific file that bash tries to find if there is no ~/.bash_login.

  ~/.profile is created for each new user by default on SLES 9.

  This file can store any user-specific customizations.

  It will be read not only by bash, but also by other shells.

- **~/.bashrc.** A configuration file in which users store their customizations for the bash.

  By default, it is not read by bash when it is started as a login shell.

  However in SLES 9 the file /etc/profile causes ~/.bashrc to be read anyway.

### Non-Login Shells

Only the ~/.bashrc file is read when a non-login shell is started.

Most Linux distributions have a default setup that ensures users do not see any difference between a login shell and a non-login shell. In most cases, this is achieved by also reading the ~/.bashrc file when a login shell is started.

If you change any settings and want them to be applied during the same shell session, the changed configuration file needs to be read in again.

The proper way to read in a changed configuration file and to apply the changes to the current session is by using the internal shell command **source**, as in the following example:

**source .bashrc**

You can also use the short form of this command, which is included in many configuration files, where it is used to read in other configuration files, as in the following (put a space between the periods):

**. .bashrc**

## Filename Restrictions

A filename in Linux can be up to 255 characters long. It can contain any number of special characters (such as "_" or "%").

Certain special characters (for example, the dollar sign $, the semicolon ;, or the space) have a specific meaning. If you want to use one of these characters without the associated special meaning, the character must be preceded by a \ (backslash) so its special meaning is masked (switched off).

You can use umlauts, letters with diacritical marks, or other country-specific characters. Using them, however, can lead to problems when exchanging data with people in other countries using other settings if these characters are not present on their keyboards.

Linux differentiates between uppercase and lowercase letters. For example, **Invoice**, **invoice**, and **INVOICE** identify three different files.

## Command and Filename Completion

The bash shell can complete commands and filenames. Just enter the first characters of a command (or a filename) and press the **Tab** key. The bash shell completes the name of the command.

If there is more than one possibility, the bash shell shows all possibilities when you press the Tab key a second time. This feature makes entering long filenames very easy.

## History Function

bash stores the commands you enter so you have easy access to them again later when needed. By default, the commands are written to the file **.bash_history** in the user's home directory. In SLES 9, the size of this file is set to 1,000 entries.

You can display the contents of the file by using the command **history**.

You can display the commands stored in the history cache (one at a time) by using the arrow keys. **Up-Arrow** shows the previous command; the **Down-Arrow** shows the next command. After finding the desired command, edit it as needed; then execute it by pressing **Enter**.

When browsing the entries of the history, you can also select specific commands. Typing one or several letters and then pressing **Page Up** or **Page Down** displays the preceding or next command in the history cache, beginning with these letters.

If you enter part of the command (not necessarily the beginning of the command), pressing **Ctrl+R** searches the history list for matching commands and displays them. Searching starts backward from the last command executed.

## Switch to User root

If you are working with a shell, you can become root by entering **su –** and the root password. If you want to start a graphical application from the shell, enter **sux –** instead.

You can check to make sure you are root by entering **id** or **whoami**. To leave the root administrator shell, enter **exit**, as shown in the following:

```
tux@da10:~> sux -
Password:
da10:~ # whoami
root
da10:~ # exit
logout
tux@da10:~> whoami
tux
```

6

If you are working with Konsole, you can start a separate root shell by selecting **Session > New Root Console**, as shown in Figure 6-1.

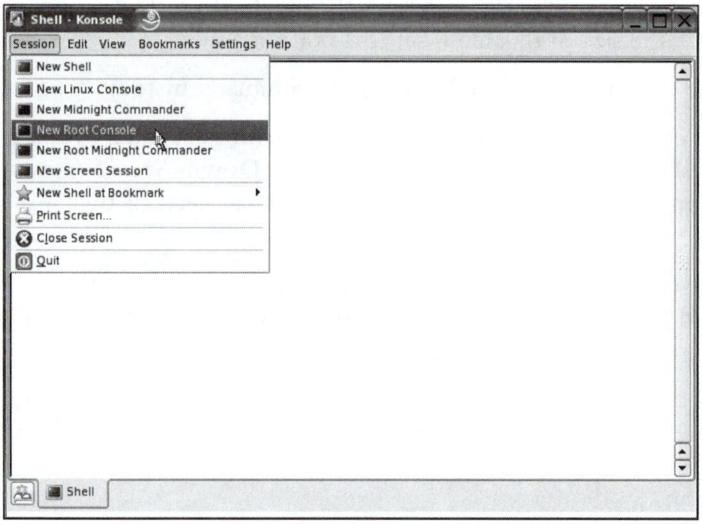

**Figure 6-1**

# Exercise 6-1    Execute Commands at the Command Line

By now you have of course already executed some commands at the command line. The purpose of this exercise is to highlight some of the features of the shell that make using the command line easier.

To execute commands at the command line, do the following:

1. Open a terminal window.

2. View the history cache by entering **history**.

3. Press **Up-arrow** until you see an ls command you would like to execute; then press **Enter**.

4. Type **h** and press **Page Up** once.

   You should see the command history at the command line again.

5. Press **Enter** to execute the **history** command.

6. Switch to root by entering **sux –**; then enter a password of **novell**.

7. Start YaST by entering **yast2**.

   YaST should start in QT mode.

8. Quit YaST by selecting **Close**.

9. Become the user geeko again by entering **exit**.

10. Su to root by entering **su –**; then enter a password of **novell**.

11. Check to make sure you are logged in as root by entering **id**.

12. Start YaST by entering **yast2**.

    YaST should start in ncurses mode.

13. Quit YaST by entering **Alt + q**.

14. Log out as root by entering **exit**.

15. Close the terminal window by entering **exit**.

6

## Objective 2  Get to Know Common Command-Line Tasks

To understand the features that make the bash shell more powerful, you need to know the following:

- Variable Basics
- Use Variables
- Define Aliases

## Variable Basics

With shell and environment variables, you can configure the behavior of the shell and adjust its environment to your own requirements.

The convention is to write variables such as PATH in uppercase letters. If you set your own variables, they should also be written in uppercase for the sake of clarity.

To display the value of a shell or environment variable, enter:

**echo $variable**, as in the following:

```
tux@da10:~> echo $HOME
/home/tux
```

To set the value of a variable or to crate a new variable, use the syntax *variable=value*, as in the following:

```
da10:~ # MYVAR=myvalue
da10:~ # echo $MYVAR
myvalue
da10:~ #
```

The value can be a number, a character or a string. If the string includes a space, you have to write the value in full quotes, as in the following:

```
da10:~ # MYVAR="my value"
da10:~ # echo $MYVAR
```

```
my value
da10:~ #
```

## Use Variables

The behavior of the shell is largely influenced by its internal (built-in) variables.

Users can also define their own variables and then use them as needed; for instance, in shell scripts.

There is an important differences between the shell variables and the environment variables:

- **Shell variables.** They control the behavior of the shell itself and are only relevant locally (for the currently active shell).

  Examples for shell variables are PS1 and UID.

- **Environment variables.** They have a larger scope and also influence any other programs started from within the current shell. In other words, they are inherited by any subshells or child processes.

  Some important environment variables are the following:

  - **PATH.** When a program is called up, the program is searched for in the directories specified here (each separated by :). The order in which directories are listed is important, since they are searched in turn.

  - **HOME.** The user's home directory.

  - **USER.** The login name of the actual user.

To understand better how shell variables and environment variables behave differently, it is useful to have a closer look at the way a shell executes a command:

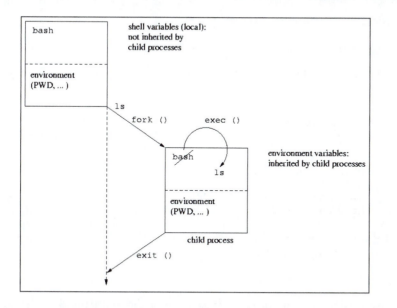

When an external command is called by the shell, the shell starts a subshell—it loads an image of itself into memory.

The frames in the figure each represent a process as present in memory when this first step has happened.

So the process has actually doubled itself, a mechanism called *forking.*

Now when the process is forked, the environment of the parent process (which in this example is the PWD variable—the name of the current working directory) is inherited by the child process.

However, since the actual command that has been called is the ls command, the shell replaces the second bash process with the ls process. The shell does so using its internal exec call.

This is done without changing the original environment variables (such as PWD).

When the command has finished its job, the process is terminated through the exit call, and control is handed over to the original shell again, which will always wait for the child process to come to an end.

Changes to the environment of the child process cannot have any influence on the environment of the parent shell.

The following are described:

- Work with Variables
- Describe Important Internal Bash Variables

## Work with Variables

The syntax to set a shell variable is:

*variable=value*

by which the contents of ***value*** are directly assigned to the new variable.

Since it is a shell variable, it will not be inherited by any subshells.

An example is shown in the following:

```
tux@da10:~> VARIABLE1="Good morning"
tux@da10:~> echo $VARIABLE1
Good morning
tux@da10:~> bash
tux@da10:~> echo $VARIABLE1

tux@da10:~>
```

To refer to an existing value, the variable must be prefixed with the $ sign. Thus, the command **echo $VARIABLE** will return the value of that variable.

To turn a shell variable into an environment variable, use the **export** command.

Also use the **export** command to immediately define an environment variable. The variable can then be inherited by any subshells.

The following is an example:

```
tux@da10:~> export VARIABLE2="Good afternoon"
tux@da10:~> bash
tux@da10:~> echo $VARIABLE2
Good afternoon
tux@da10:~>
```

To see which variables have been set for your shell, you can use these commands:

- **export.** Lists all environment variables.
- **set.** Lists all variables as well as functions that have been declared.

 Use **set *variable value*** to modify the shell attributes during runtime. See **man 1 bash** for more information.

**NOTE**

- **env.** Displays a list of all currently defined environment variables and their content.

Use *variable=value command* to execute commands in a modified environment, such as an environment in which special variables are set.

For example, you can use this command to read manual pages in a different language (if available):

```
tux@da10:~> LANG=de_DE man man
```

or

```
tux@da10:~> LANG=en_US man man
```

Use the command **unset** *variable* to delete a variable, as shown in the following:

```
tux@da10:~> a=10
tux@da10:~> echo $a
10
tux@da10:~> unset a
tux@da10:~> echo $a

tux@da10:~>
```

> **CAUTION**
>
> When defining variables within shell scripts, always make sure that they are different from any existing variables, such as UID or HOME. Otherwise, you might have to deal with conflicts and error messages.

In summary, if you want a variable to take effect on a local basis only, you should set it as a shell variable. If you want a variable to be inherited by subshells as well, use **export** to define it as an environment variable.

## Describe Important Internal Bash Variables

It is helpful to understand the important internal bash variables when customizing the shell for interactive sessions or for shell scripting.

Table 6-1 lists some of the important internal bash variables.

**Table 6-1**

| Variable | Description |
|---|---|
| HOME | The user's home directory |
| PATH | The search path for commands |
| PWD | The current working directory |
| IFS | The internal field separator (the character that separates individual arguments from each other) |
| PS1 | The primary shell prompt |
| PS2 | The secondary shell prompt |
| PS3 | The tertiary shell prompt |
| ? | The exit status (return value) of the most recent child process |

**Table 6-1**   (continued)

| Variable | Description |
|---|---|
| $ | The process ID of the current shell itself |
| # | The number of arguments passed to the shell |
| 0-9 | Argument 0 (usually the command itself), argument 1, and so on, as passed to the shell |
| * | All arguments (with the exception of argument 0) as a single word or argument |
| @ | All arguments (with the exception of argument 0) as separate words or arguments |

# Exercise 6-2    Create a Shell and an Environment Variable and Examine the Exit Status

Variables and the exit status are more frequently used within shell scripts than directly on the command line. Within scripts they are, however, vital.

The purpose of this exercise is to show you the difference between shell and environment variables and how to use them.

To create a shell and an environment variable and examine the exit status, do the following:

- Part I: Create a Shell and an Environment Variable
- Part II: Examine the Exit Status

## Part I: Create a Shell and an Environment Variable

Do the following:

1. As user geeko, open a terminal window and create a shell variable called USERNAME that holds your user name by entering:

   **USERNAME=*your_name***

2. Log in as root by entering **su –** and a password of **novell**.

3. What is the content of the variable USERNAME?

   (Find out by entering **echo $USERNAME**.)

4. Return to the original shell of the user by entering **exit**.

5. Change the variable USERNAME to an environment variable by entering:

   **export USERNAME**

6. Switch to user root again by entering **su –** and a password of **novell**.

7. What is the content of the variable USERNAME now?

8. *(Optional)* Change the primary bash prompt (variable PS1) so it displays the current time. (See **man bash** and search for PROMPTING. Several solutions are possible, such as **PS1="\u@\h – \A :\w> "**.)

### Part II: Examine the Exit Status

Do the following:

1. As a regular user, enter **ls** in your home directory.

2. Check the exit status by entering:

   **echo $?**

3. As a regular user, enter **ls** for the home directory of user root (/root/).

4. Check the exit status again.

## Define Aliases

Defining aliases allows you to create shortcuts for commands and their options or to create commands with entirely different names.

On a SUSE Linux system, whenever you enter the commands **dir**, **md**, or **ls**, for instance, you use aliases.

You can find out about the aliases defined on your system by using the command **alias**.

This will show you that **dir**, for instance, is an alias for **ls –l** and **md** is an alias for **mkdir –p**.

The following are examples of aliases that define new commands:

```
tux@da10:~> alias md
alias md='mkdir -p'
tux@da10:~> alias dir
alias dir='ls -l'
```

To see whether a given command is an alias for something else, use the **type** command.

For each command specified, type will tell you whether it is:

- A built-in shell command
- A regular command
- A function
- An alias

For regular commands, the output of type lists the path to the corresponding executable. For aliases, it lists the elements aliased:

```
tux@da10:~> type -a ls
ls is aliased to '/bin/ls $LS_OPTIONS'
ls is /bin/ls
```

The above example shows that ls is an alias although, in this case, it is only used to add some options to the command.

The -a option is used to show both the contents of the alias and the path to the original ls command. The output shows that ls is always run with the options stored in the variable LS_OPTIONS.

These options cause ls to list different file types in different colors (among other things).

Most of the aliases used on a system-wide basis are defined in the file /etc/bash.bashrc.

Aliases are defined by using the alias command and can be removed by using the unalias command.

For example, entering:

**unalias ls**

removes the alias for ls, causing ls to stop coloring its output.

The following is the syntax for defining aliases:

**alias** *alias_name*=**'***command options***'**

An alias defined in this way is only valid for the current shell and will not be inherited by subshells, as in the following:

```
tux@da1:~> alias ps="echo Hello"
tux@da1:~> ps
Hello
tux@da1:~> bash
tux@da1:~> ps
  PID TTY        TIME CMD
  858 pts/0   00:00:00 bash
  895 pts/1   00:00:00 bash
  . . .
```

To make an alias persistent, you need to store the definition in one of the shell's configuration files.

On SLES 9, the file **~/.alias** is intended for personal aliases defined by each user.

If it exists, this file is read in by **~/.bashrc**, where a command is included to that effect.

Aliases are not relevant to shell scripts at all, but can be a real time saver when using the shell interactively.

## Exercise 6-3   Use the alias Command

You will most likely get along well without aliases, but they can make life easier. An alias for a long command can sometimes come quite handy.

To get familiar with the alias command, do the following:

1. Open a terminal window.

2. View all defined aliases by entering:

   **alias**

3. Define a new alias by entering:

   **alias hello='echo "hello $USER"'**

4. Check the functionality of the alias hello by entering:

   **hello**

5. Check the command type of the command hello by entering:

   **type hello**

6. Remove the alias by entering:

   **unalias hello**

7. Close the terminal window.

6

---

## OBJECTIVE 3   UNDERSTAND COMMAND SYNTAX AND SPECIAL CHARACTERS

You can use specific characters to provide special functionality. Using them can save you a lot of time and effort. In this objective you will learn how to do the following:

- Use Search Patterns
- Prevent the Shell from Interpreting Special Characters

## Use Search Patterns

Occasionally, you might want to perform operations on a series of files without having to name all the files separately. In this case, you could make use of the following search patterns:

**Table 6-2**

| Search Pattern | Description |
|---|---|
| ? | Any single character (except /) |
| * | Any string length, including zero characters (except . at the beginning of a file name and /) |
| [a-z] | Any of the characters enclosed (here: lowercase letters from a to z) |
| [a-ek-s] | Any character from the ranges a–e and k–s |

**Table 6-2**    (continued)

| Search Pattern | Description |
|---|---|
| [abcdefg] | Any of these characters |
| [!abc] | None of these characters |

The following is an example of using some of these search patterns:

```
tux@da10:/usr/X11/bin > ls xc*
xcalc xclipboard xclock xcmsdb xconsole xcursorgen xcutsel
tux@da10:/usr/X11/bin > ls xc[alo]*
xcalc xclipboard xclock xconsole
tux@da10:/usr/X11/bin > ls xc[!o]*
xcalc xclipboard xclock xcmsdb xcursorgen xcutsel
tux@da10:/usr/X11/bin > ls xc*l*
xcalc xclipboard xclock xconsole xcutsel
```

If search patterns (wildcards) are used on the command line, the shell tries to compare these with the filenames in the file system. If they match, the expression is replaced with the matching filenames.

## Prevent the Shell from Interpreting Special Characters

To prevent the shell from interpreting special characters in the command line, these characters must be "masked" by using the following:

- \—The backslash protects exactly one character from being interpreted by the shell, as in the following:

  **mkdir new\ directory**

- "..."—Double quotes protect all special characters except $, \, and ´ (back tick) from being interpreted by the shell, as in the following:

  ```
  tux@da10:~> echo "$HOME"
  /home/tux
  tux@da10:~>
  ```

- '...'—In addition to regular expressions, variables are also protected with single quotes, as in the following:

  ```
  tux@da1:~> echo '$HOME'
  $HOME
  ```

## Exercise 6-4    Work with Command Syntax and Special Characters

More often than not you will want to manipulate more than one file at a time—move all .txt files below a certain directory somewhere else, etc. This is where special characters come into play and the purpose of this exercise is to get you used to them. Play around with these special characters to really get familiar with them.

To understand how to use command syntax and special characters, do the following:

1. Open a terminal window.

2. List all filenames in the directory /bin/ that start with the character "a" by entering:

   **ls /bin/a***

3. List all filenames in the directory /bin/ that consist of four characters by entering:

   **ls /bin/????**

6

4. List all filenames in the directory /bin/ that consist of four or more characters by entering:

   **ls /bin/????***

5. List all filenames in the directory /bin/ that do not start with one of the characters from a to r by entering:

   **ls /bin/[!a-r]***

6. Start the file manager Konqueror by selecting the *blue house* icon in Kicker.

7. Create a new file by right-clicking the file view window and selecting **Create New > File > Text File**.

8. Enter a filename of **My**; then select **OK**.

9. Create a new file by right-clicking the file view window and selecting **Create New > File > Text File**.

10. Enter a filename of **File**; then select **OK**.

11. Create a new file by right-clicking the file view window and selecting **Create New > File > Text File**.

12. Enter a filename of **My File**; then select **OK**.

13. Close the Konqueror window.

14. From the terminal window, list the files My and File by entering:

    **ls –l My File**

15. List the file My File by entering:

    **ls –l My\ File**

16. Remove the files My, File, and My File by entering:

    **rm My File My\ File**

17. Verify that the files have been removed by entering **ls –l**.

18. Close the terminal window.

# OBJECTIVE 4    USE PIPING AND REDIRECTION

Linux has three standard data channels, shown in Figure 6-2.

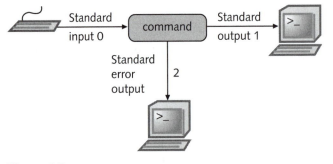

**Figure 6-2**

The following describes these channels:

- **Standard input (stdin).** The program currently running reads the input from this channel (usually the keyboard).

- **Standard output (stdout).** The program sends its output to this channel (usually the screen).

- **Standard error (stderr).** Errors are issued through this channel (usually to the monitor).

These input and output channels are assigned the numbers listed in Table 6-3.

**Table 6-3**

| Channel | Number Assigned |
|---|---|
| Standard input (stdin) | 0 |
| Standard output (stdout) | 1 |
| Standard error output (stderr) | 2 |

Each channel can be redirected by the shell. For example, stdin can come from a file, and stdout and stderr can be piped to a file. Table 6-4 shows the redirection characters.

**Table 6-4**

| Redirection Character | Description |
|---|---|
| < | Redirects standard input |
| > | Redirects standard output (> without a preceding number is just an abbreviation for 1>) |
| 2> | Redirects standard error output |

**CAUTION**

> overwrites an existing file. If the output should be appended to an existing file, you have to use >> or 2>>.

The following is an example of a standard input, standard output, and standard error output:

```
tux@da10:~> ls /opt /recipe
/bin/ls: /recipe: No such file or directory
/opt:
gnome kde3
```

If the standard error output is redirected to **/dev/null**, only the standard output is displayed on the screen, as shown in the following:

```
tux@da10:~> ls /opt /recipe 2> /dev/null
/opt:
gnome kde3
```

To redirect standard output and standard error output to a file, such as list, enter:

**ls /opt /recip > list 2>&1**

First, the standard output is redirected to the file list (> list); then the standard error output is directed to the standard output (2>&1). The & refers to the file descriptor that follows (1 for the standard output).

**CAUTION**

The sequence is important: first **>list**, then **2>&1**.

All known files in the system can be used as input or output. To display the contents of the file list, use the cat command, as shown in the following:

```
tux@da10:~> cat list
/bin/ls: /recipe: No such file or directory
/opt:
gnome
kde3
```

Occasionally, you might want to give programs that expect input from the keyboard data from a file instead. To do this, the standard input is redirected, as in the following:

```
da10:~ # echo "Hello Tux,
>
> how are you?
> Is everything okay?" >greetings
da10:~ # mail tux < greetings
```

First, the text is redirected to the file greetings through the redirector >. The mail program, mail, receives its input from the file greetings (not the keyboard), and then the e-mail program sends the e-mail to the user tux.

This option of redirecting data channels is available not only in the shell, but it can also be used by programs directly. One process uses the standard output of another process as its standard input. The pipe character "|" is used for this purpose:

*command1 | command2*

For example:

```
tux@da10:~> ls -l /etc | less
```

In a pipe, a maximum of 4 KB of unprocessed data can exist. If the process creating the output tries to write to a full pipe, it is stopped and only allowed to continue if the writing process can be completed. On the other side, the reading process is stopped if it tries to read an empty pipe.

Occasionally you might want output from a command displayed on the screen as well as written to a file. To do this, use the pipe character and the **tee** command:

**ls –l | tee output–file**

In this example, the output of the command is displayed on the screen as well as written to the file output-file.

To redirect the output of several consecutive commands on the command line, the commands must be separated with semicolons (;) and enclosed in parentheses, as shown in the following:

```
tux@da10:~> (id ; ls ~) > output-file
tux@da10:~> cat output-file
uid=1000(tux) gid=100(users)
groups=14(uucp),16(dialout),17(audio),33(video),100(users)
bin
Desktop
Documents
output
public_html
tux@da10:~>
```

The shell starts a separate subshell for processing the individual commands. To redirect the linked commands, the shell must be forced to execute the command chain in the same subshell by enclosing the expression in parentheses.

Upon completion, every program returns a value that states the success of the execution. If this return value is 0, the command completed successfully. If an error occurred, the return value is greater than 0. (Depending on the program, different return values indicate different errors.)

You can use the command **echo $?** to display a return value.

The return value can be used to trigger the execution of another command, as explained in Table 6-5.

**Table 6-5**

| Link | Result |
|------|--------|
| *command1* **&&** *command2* | *command2* is executed only if *command1* is completed without any errors. |
| *command1* **‖** *command2* | *command2* is executed only if *command1* is completed with an error. |

The following illustrates using both || and &&:

```
tux@da10:~> ls recipe || ls ~
/bin/ls: recipe: No such file or directory
bin  Desktop  Documents  output  public_html  test
tux@da10:~> ls recipe && ls ~
/bin/ls: recipe: No such file or directory
tux@da10:~>
```

The file recipe does not exist and the command **ls recipe** leads to an error. Because of this, the command **ls ~** in the first line is executed but the command in the fourth line is not.

## Exercise 6-5   Use Piping and Redirection

Piping the long output of some program into less to view it page by page is a frequently seen scenario. But there are many other uses of piping and redirecting, like sorting, counting lines, showing only certain columns of the output, etc.

To understand piping and redirection, do the following:

1. Open a terminal window.

2. Pipe the output of the ls command for the home directory (~) to a file by entering:

   **ls ~ > home_directory**

3. Display the content of the file by entering:

   **cat home_directory**

4. Append the output of the ls command for the root directory (/) to the file home_directory by entering:

   **ls / >> home_directory**

5. Display the content of the file by entering:

   **cat home_directory**

6. Overwrite the file home_directory with the output of the ls command by entering:

   **ls / > home_directory**

7. Display the content of the file by entering:

   **cat home_directory**

8. Write the output of the ls command on the screen and into the file home_directory by entering:

   **ls ~ | tee home_directory**

9. Count the number of files in your home directory by entering:

   **ls ~ | wc -l**

10. Remove the file home_directory by entering:

    **rm home_directory**

11. Verify that the file was removed by entering **ls -l**.

12. Close the terminal window.

---

# Objective 5   Use Terminal Based Editors to Edit Files

Because most of Linux services are configured by editing ASCII files, you need a text editor. A text editor is one of the most important tools a Linux system administrator uses.

Generally speaking, there are two kinds of editors are available:

- Text (or terminal) based editors
- Graphical editors

The main advantage of terminal based editors is that you do not need a graphical user interface to use them. A large number of terminal based editors are available for Linux.

The following are some examples of non-graphical text editors that are available:

VIM
- vi
- emacs
- xemacs
- joe
- e3
- pico

There are also several graphical text editors that you can use to edit files in Linux. The following are some examples:

- gedit
- jedit
- kate
- kedit
- kwrite
- nedit
- xedit
- xemacs

Although many factors are involved when selecting an editor for everyday use, the reason **vi** is used by most administrators is that it is available on every Linux and UNIX system. Because of this, you should be able to use vi.

In SLES 9, vim (vi improved) by Bram Moolenaar is the standard vi editor. When you enter **vi**, vim is started via a link to it.

In this objective, you learn how to:

- Start the Editor vi
- Use the Editor vi
- Get to Know the Working Modes

## Start the Editor vi

You can start vi by entering **vi** or **vim**, followed by various options, and the name of a file to edit, as in the following example:

**vi exercise**

If a file does not exist, it is created. The text of the file appears in an editor within the terminal window, as shown in Figure 6-3.

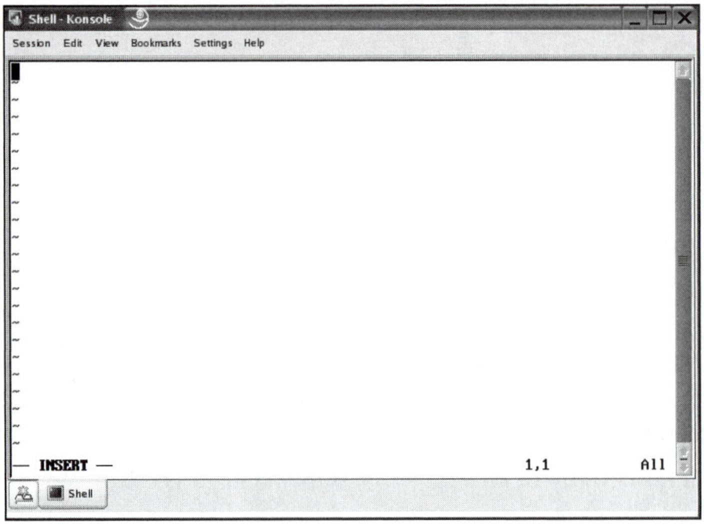

**Figure 6-3**

The sign ~ indicates lines that do not exist yet. The cursor is on the first line.

## Use the Editor vi

You can move the cursor by pressing **k**, **j**, **h**, and **l** (k one line up, j one line down, h to the left, l to the right) or by pressing the arrow keys (**Up-arrow**, **Down-arrow**, **Left-arrow**, **Right-arrow**).

## Get to Know the Working Modes

Unlike many other editors, vi is mode-oriented.

When vi is first started, it is in command mode. Anything you enter in this mode is considered a command. You must switch to input mode before you can type any text. This can be frustrating to users who are unfamiliar with vi.

In addition to switching modes, you must learn which keys perform which actions, because you cannot use the mouse.

The number of commands needed for everyday work is fairly small, however, and you can get used to them quickly.

When vi starts, it is in command mode. Everything now entered is interpreted by vi as a command.

To enter text, you must first switch the editor to input mode by pressing **i** (insert) or **Insert**. At the bottom of the screen, you see the message --INSERT--.

Press **Esc** once to go back to the command mode. From command mode you can switch to command-line mode by entering **:**. The cursor jumps to the last line after : and waits for a command entry.

A command will only be carried out in command-line mode after you press **Enter**. Then you are automatically back in command mode.

The following is a summary of the available modes:

■ **Command mode.** When vi starts, it is automatically in this mode.

In command mode, vi can be given commands.

The command **i** puts it into insert mode and the command **:** switches it to command-line mode.

■ **Insert mode.** In this mode (keyword --INSERT--), vi accepts all input as text.

Return to command mode with **Esc**.

■ **Command-line mode.** In this mode (keyword :), vi accepts commands from the command line.

Pressing **Enter** causes the command to be executed and automatically switches back to the command mode.

You can use the commands in Table 6-6 in command mode.

**Table 6-6**

| Command | Result |
| --- | --- |
| i or Insert | Switches vi to insert mode |
| x or Delete | Deletes the character where the cursor is |
| dd | Deletes the line the cursor is in and copies it to the buffer |
| D | Deletes the rest of the current line from the cursor position and copies it to the buffer |
| yy | Copies the line the cursor is in to the buffer |
| p, P | Inserts the contents of the buffer after/before current cursor position |
| ZZ | Saves the current file and ends vi |
| u | Undoes the last operation |
| /pattern | Searches forward from the cursor position for *pattern* |
| ?pattern | Searches backward from the cursor position for *pattern* |
| n | Repeats the search in the same direction |
| N | Repeats the search in the opposite direction |

If you want to use a command for several units, place the corresponding number in front of the command. For example, **3x** deletes three characters, **5dd** deletes five lines, and **7yy** copies seven lines to the buffer.

You can use the commands in Table 6-7 command-line mode.

**Table 6-7**

| Command | Result |
|---------|--------|
| :q | Ends vi (if no changes were made) |
| :q! | Ends vi without saving changes in the file |
| :wq or :x | Saves the current file and ends vi |
| :w | Saves the current file |
| :w *file* | Saves the current file under the name *file* (you continue editing the original file, not the new file) |

The commands shown here are just those needed for basic text editing. vi offers a lot more functions; for instance, syntax highlighting, search and replace, editing several files in separate windows, placing the output of programs directly into the text file, and others.

There is an overview of vi commands in Appendix A.

**NOTE**

# Exercise 6-6    Use vi to Edit Files in the Linux System

It will most likely take some time for you to get used to **vi**. It is very different from any graphical text editors you might already be familiar with.

Its biggest advantage is certainly that it is available on practically any Unix or Linux you will come across. Additionally, if you keep at it, you will find out that beyond simple editing of text files it is extremely versatile and powerful.

The purpose of this exercise is to help you with your first steps with vi.

To use the command-line editor vi, do the following:

1. Open a terminal window.

2. Start vim by entering **vi**.

3. Switch to insert mode by typing **i**.

4. Type the following two paragraphs of text (press **Enter** at the end of each line):

   **Administrator training for SLES 9 will be held**

   **in Training Room 4 of Building B on Tuesday**

**6**

of next week.

**Make sure you bring your SLES 9 Administration Manual. There will be wireless Internet access available in the training room.**

5. Exit insert mode by pressing **Esc**.
6. Move the cursor to the middle of the second line of the first paragraph.
7. Delete text to the right of the cursor by typing **D** (uppercase d).
8. Undo the deletion by typing **u**.
9. Delete the character directly under the cursor by pressing **Delete**.
10. Copy the current line to the internal buffer by typing **y** twice.
11. Move the cursor to the beginning the first line of the second paragraph.
12. Insert the content of the internal buffer after the current line by typing **p**.
13. Save the file with filename vi_test by entering:

    **:w vi_test**

14. Exit vi by entering **:q**.
15. Close the terminal window.

## Exercise 6-7  Optional: Work Through the vim Tutorial

The last exercise was only a brief introduction to vi. There is a tutorial that comes with vim and takes about 30 minutes to work through. It provides you increased familiarity with the possibilities vim offers.

To work through the tutorial, do the following

1. As the user geeko, open a terminal window.
2. Start vim and the tutorial by entering:

   **vimtutor**

   vim starts displaying the tutorial.

3. Work through the lessons of the tutorial as explained in the text.
4. When finished, close the terminal window.

## OBJECTIVE 6    MANIPULATE TEXT NON-INTERACTIVELY

When you need to make the same changes in a lot of files, non-interactive editors or text manipulation programs can speed up the task considerably. They are also useful within shell scripts.

To manipulate text non-interactively, you have to

- Understand the Stream Editor sed
- Understand the Text Manipulator awk

## Understand the Stream Editor sed

The sed program is a stream editor—an editor used from the command line rather than interactively.

sed performs text transformations on a line-by-line basis.

The sed commands can be specified either directly on the command line or in a special command script loaded by the program on execution.

The sed command requires the following syntax:

```
sed "editing-command" filename
```

The available editing commands are single-character arguments; for example:

- **d.** Delete
- **s.** Substitute (replace)
- **p.** Output line
- **a.** Append after

As with other commands, the output of sed normally goes to standard output, but it can also be redirected to a file.

Apart from the single-character commands for text transformations, you can also specify options to influence the overall behavior of the sed program.

The following are some important command-line options for sed:

- **–n, --quiet, --silent.** By default, sed will print all lines on standard output after they have been processed.

  This option suppresses the output, so sed only prints those lines for which the p editing command has been given to explicitly re-enable printing.

- **–e** *command1* **–e** *command2* **...** This option is necessary when specifying two or more editing commands.

  It must be inserted before each additional editing command.

■ **–f** *filename.* With this option, you can specify a script file from which sed should read its editing commands.

For many editing commands, it is important to specify the exact line or lines that will be processed by the command.

One of the more frequently used address labels is **$**, which stands for the last line.

The following are some examples:

■ To print only lines 1 through 9 on stdout, enter:

```
tux@da10:~> sed -n '1,9p' somefile
```

■ To delete everything from line 10 to the end and print the first 9 lines of the file somefile, enter:

```
tux@da10:~> sed '10,$d' somefile
```

You can use a regular expression to define the address or address range for an editing command.

Regular expressions must be enclosed in forward slashes.

If an address is defined with such an expression, sed processes every line that includes the given pattern.

In the following example, the command prints all lines that contain Murphy:

```
tux@da10:~> sed -n '/Murphy.*/p' somefile
```

To negate an address, put an exclamation point before it.

Also, if you want sed to perform several editing commands for the same address, you need to enclose the commands in braces:

**sed '1,10{*command1* ; *command2*}'**

As a general rule, editing commands need to be separated either by a line break or a semicolon.

Finally, you can also use a leading exclamation point to negate editing commands.

This can be used to tell sed that it should ***not*** perform the command on any lines matched by the address.

In the following example, sed will not delete any lines that are commented (those with a leading "#" in them), but it will print them:

```
tux@da10:~> sed '/^#/!d' somefile
```

Table 6-8 lists the most important editing commands of sed.

**Table 6-8**

| Command | Example | Editing action |
|---|---|---|
| d | sed '10,$d' *file* | Delete line. |
| a | sed 'a\<br><br>*text*\<br><br>*text*' *file* | Append text after the specified line, with line breaks and backslashes included as shown in the example. |
| i | sed 'i\<br><br>*text*\<br><br>text' *file* | Insert **text** before the specified line. |
| c | sed '2000,$c*text*'\*file* | Replace specified lines with the **text**. |
| s | sed s/*x*/*y*/*option* | Search and replace—the search pattern *x*' is replaced with pattern *y*'.<br><br>The search and the replacement patterns are regular expressions in most cases, and the search and replace behavior can be influenced through various options. |
| y | sed y/*abc*/*yxz*/ | (yank) Replace every character from the set of source characters with the character that has the same position in the set of destination characters. |

The following options can be used with s (search and replace):

- **I.** Do not distinguish between uppercase and lowercase letters.
- **g.** Replace globally wherever the search pattern is found in the line (instead of replacing only the first instance).
- **n.** Replace the *n*th matching pattern only.
- **p.** Print the line after replacing.
- **w *file*.** Write the resulting text to the specified file rather than printing it on stdout.

The following are some examples:

- To replace the first colon in each line with a space, enter:
  ```
  tux@da10:~> sed 's/:/ /' /etc/passwd
  ```
- To replace all colons in all lines with a space, enter:
  ```
  tux@da10:~> sed 's/:/ /g' /etc/passwd
  ```
- To replace only the second colon in each line with a space, enter:
  ```
  tux@da10:~> sed 's/:/ /2' /etc/passwd
  ```

- To replace all single vowels with double vowels, enter:

  ```
  tux@da10:~> sed -n 's/\([aeiou]\)/\1\1/Igp'
  ```

  The example shows how matched patterns can be referenced with \1 if the search pattern is given in parentheses (which in turn have to be escaped).

  The I option ensures that sed ignores the case.

  g ensures that characters are replaced globally.

  Finally, the p option tells sed to print all lines processed in this way.

- To change all uppercase characters to lowercase, enter (on one line):

  ```
  tux@da10:~> sed
  'y/ABCDEFGHIJKLMNOPQRSTUVWXYZ/abcdefghijklmnopqrstuvwxyz/'
  ```

## Understand the Text Manipulator awk

**awk** got its name from its developers Alfred V. **A**ho, Peter J. **W**einberger, and Brian W. **K**ernighan.

The main difference between awk and other script languages (such as bash) is the data oriented workflow.

An awk procedure is an indefinite loop. Exiting the loop is possible in two cases:

- There are no more data at input.
- You exit the loop deliberately.

awk is very similar to a stream editor, but you can also define such things as variables, functions, and loops.

To use awk, you need to know the following:

- General Structure of an awk Program
- Start an awk Program

### General Structure of an awk Program

An awk program consists of three main parts:

- An optional command that is executed once **before** computing the input data
- The **main program** consisting of one or more directives. It is executed for each line of the input data
- An optional command that is executed once **after** computing the input data

An awk directive consists of

- An optional pattern
- A list of commands included into braces

*/pattern/* { *command1*[; *command2*] }

For larger command lists, you should divide the directive into several lines:

*/pattern/* {

> *command1*;
>
> *command2*;
>
> ...
>
> }

A semicolon must be at the end of each command.

A pattern can be a regular expression or a comparison of variables.

The pattern is compared with the actual input line. If the comparison is true, the directive is executed. If there is no pattern, the directive is executed in all cases.

The commands executed before the main program are marked by **BEGIN**. This part is normally used to initialize variables.

The commands executed after the main program are marked by **END**. This part is normally used for output.

In the following, a simple awk script shows the structure:

```
BEGIN   {
        print "Counting lines";
        number=0;
        }

{ number++; }

END   { print "Result: " number; }
```

## Start an awk Program

You can start an awk program in the following ways:

- Start an awk Program at the Command Line
- Start an awk Program by Using awk Scripts

**Start an awk Program at the Command Line**    You can start short programs that are used only once at the command line:

**awk '***program***'** *file* **[***file***]**

To extract the first field from the password file, enter:

```
tux@da10> awk 'BEGIN {FS = ":"} {print NR,$1}' /etc/passwd
1 root
2 bin
```

```
3 daemon
4 lp
5 mail
...
```

The following variables are used:

- **FS.** An internal variable defining the field separator. In /etc/passwd fields are separated by **:**.

- **NR.** An internal variable including the number of the current line.

- **$1.** The content of the first field.

You can also pipe the output of another command to awk:

**command | awk 'program'**

For example:

```
tux@da10> date | awk '{print "Today is " $2". the "$3".",$6}'
Today is Jan. the 31., 2007
```

**Start an awk Program by Using awk Scripts**    For more complex problems, write the awk commands into a file and execute it by entering

**awk -f** *script file* [*file*]

You can also use pipe:

**command | awk -f** *script*

Another way is to write an awk script in the same way as a bash script.

In this case, the first line of the script is:

```
#!/usr/bin/awk -f
```

If you have permission to execute the script, you can call it directly by entering the filename at the command prompt.

# Exercise 6-8    Optional: Using sed

**sed** is a very powerful tool that can be used in various ways when working with text files. A common one is searching and replacing text strings.

When you first use sed, its syntax will probably seem rather cryptic. Don't get discouraged.

The purpose of this exercise is to give you some idea of what can be done with sed.

1. As the user geeko, open a terminal window.

2. Display the first 15 lines of the file /etc/init.d/skeleton by entering:
   **sed 1,15p /etc/init.d/skeleton**.

3. You will notice that lines 1 to 15 have indeed been displayed, but all other lines of the file as well (lines 1 to 15 therefore appear twice in the output).

   Improve your command line by suppressing those lines that do not match the pattern:

   **sed –n 1,15p /etc/init.d/skeleton**.

4. Now print all lines on the screen except lines 1 to 15:

   **sed 1,15d /etc/init.d/skeleton**.

5. A simple search and replace consists of inserting additional spaces at the beginning of each line. This can be achieved as follows:

   **sed –n –e 's/^/ /p' /etc/init.d/skeleton**.

6. The file /etc/init.d/skeleton contains the string "FOO" in places where the name of a program could be inserted. Let's assume the program you want to start using this start script is called "bar" and you want to replace FOO by bar:

   **sed –e 's/FOO/bar/g' /etc/init.d/skeleton > /etc/init.d/bar**.

   (Writing to /etc/init.d/bar works only as root, as a normal user may not create files in /etc/init.d/. You can redirect standard out to a file in your home directory instead.)

7. If you want to experiment more with sed, try to:

   ▪ Show only the comments (lines with a #).

   ▪ Show lines that are not comments and are not empty.

   ▪ Show the lines that belong to the "start" section of the case statement.

   ▪ Find out how to insert another textfile after a certain line.

## CHAPTER SUMMARY

❏ Once you log in to a Linux system, a login shell is started to provide your user environment, execute your commands, and display your output. If you use a GUI, the X Window system runs on top of a login shell. Any additional shells that you start following login are called nonlogin shells.

❏ Although there are many shells available for use in Linux, the default shell is the Bourne again shell (bash). The bash shell in SLES reads the /etc/profile, ~/.profile, and ~/.bashrc files at login to create variables and run programs. In addition, the ~/.bashrc file is read each time a nonlogin shell is started.

❏ The bash shell is case-sensitive, may be used to perform filename completion, and can execute previously entered commands.

6

- Processes that are started by typing a command at a command prompt are called child processes and are typically executed by a subshell via a process called forking. Although regular shell variables are only defined in one shell, environment variables are automatically exported to subshells and hence available to child processes.

- Aliases are special shell variables that contain commands. When you invoke an alias, the commands defined within it will be executed.

- Wildcards may be used to represent patterns when specifying file or directory names on the filesystem.

- There are three data channels available to commands: stdin, stdout, and stderr. Not all commands use every data channel. The stdin typically represents user input taken from the keyboard, whereas stdout and stderr are sent to the terminal screen by default.

- You may redirect the stdout and stderr of a command to a file using redirection symbols. Similarly, you may use redirection symbols to redirect a file to the stdin of a command.

- To direct the stdout from one command to the stdin of another, you must use the pipe symbol.

- All commands give a return value when they are finished executing on the system. A return value greater than 0 indicates that the command encountered an error.

- You can use the && operator to execute additional commands if a particular command gives a return value (or exit status) of 0. Similarly, you can use the || operator to execute additional commands if a particular command gives a return value that is greater than 0.

- Although there are many text-based and graphical text editors available for Linux systems, the **vi** editor is the most commonly used editor across different distributions of Linux and versions of UNIX. By default, SLES includes **vim** (vi improved), which uses different modes for inserting text, editing text, and saving document changes.

- The **sed** and **awk** utilities may be used with text files noninteractively; **sed** uses search-and-replace functions to edit text, whereas **awk** searches for text and formats it for a particular purpose.

# KEY TERMS

**&&** — A special operator that executes the command on the right side if the command on the left side exited with a zero exit status.

**. command** — Used to execute a file in the current shell environment.

**/etc/bash.bashrc** — A bash shell configuration file used to create aliases for all users on the system.

**/etc/profile** — A bash shell configuration file that is read for all users on the system.

**;** — A special character that acts as a command terminator and can be used to chain commands together on the command line.

**\** — A special character used to protect the following character from shell interpretation.

**|** — A special character used to send Standard Output from one command to the Standard Input of another command.

**| |** — A special operator that executes the command on the right side if the command on the left side exited with a nonzero exit status.

**~/.alias** — A bash shell configuration file that is used to store aliases.

**~/.bash_history** — A bash shell configuration file that is used to store previously executed commands.

**~/.bash_login** — A bash shell configuration file that is read if ~/.bash_profile does not exist.

**~/.bash_profile** — A bash shell configuration file that is read following /etc/profile.

**~/.bashrc** — A bash shell configuration file that is read at login and when nonlogin shells are started.

**~/.profile** — A bash shell configuration file that is read if ~/.bash_profile and ~/.bash_login do not exist.

**'...' (single quotes)** — Used to protect all enclosed text from shell interpretation.

**"..." (double quotes)** — Used to protect all enclosed text except $, \, and ' characters from shell interpretation.

**<** — A special character used to redirect Standard Input from a file.

**>** — A special character used to redirect Standard Output and Standard Error to a file.

**alias command** — Used to create special alias variables.

**aliases** — Special variables that may be used to execute commands in a shell.

**awk command** — Used to search for and display text using a variety of different formatting options.

**child process** — A program that is executed by another process, such as a shell.

**command mode** — A mode in the vi editor that allows you to perform any available text editing task that is not related to inserting text into the document.

**echo command** — Used to display or echo output to the terminal screen; it may be used to view the contents of variables.

**env command** — Used to display a list of exported environment variables.

**environment variables** — Variables that are available to subshells and which store information commonly accessed by the system or programs executing on the system.

**exit command** — Quits the current shell.

**exit status** — The hidden value that is returned by a program following execution. It is also called the **return value**.

**export command** — Used to create and view environment variables.

**forking** — The process whereby a shell creates a subshell to execute a child process.

**history command** — Used to view and recall previously executed commands.

**id command** — Displays the UID and GIDs for the current user account.

**insert mode** — A mode in the vi editor that allows you to insert text into the document.

**login shell** — A shell that is started immediately following login.

**nonlogin shell** — A shell that is started by an existing shell.

**pipe** — A string of commands connected by pipe (|) characters.

**redirection** — The process of changing the default locations of Standard Input, Standard Output, and Standard Error to or from a file.

**return value** — See **exit status**.

**search patterns** — Special characters that may be used to match multiple filenames. Also known as **wildcards**.

**sed command** — Used to search for and manipulate text.

**set command** — A command used to view all variables in the shell.

**shell** — The Linux command interpreter.

**shell variables** — Variables that are only available in the current shell and which store information commonly accessed by the system or your current shell.

**source command** — Used to execute a file in the current shell environment.

**Standard Error** — Represents any error messages generated by a command.

**Standard Input** — Represents information inputted to a command during execution.

**Standard Output** — Represents the desired output from a command.

**stderr** — See **Standard Error**.

**stdin** — See **Standard Input**.

**stdout** — See **Standard Output**.

**su (switch user) command** — Used to open a new shell as a different user account.

**subshell** — A shell started by the current shell.

**sux (switch user X) command** — Used to open a new shell that can execute graphical programs as a different user account.

**tee command** — Used to copy data from Standard Input to both Standard Output and a specified file.

**type command** — Used to determine the type of program for a command. The type command can be used to identify aliases and their target commands.

**unalias command** — Used to destroy an alias in memory.

**unset command** — Used to destroy a variable in memory.

**variable** — An area of memory used to store information; variables are created from entries in files when the shell is first created after login and are destroyed when the shell is exited upon logout.

**vi editor** — The most common text editor on Linux and UNIX systems.

**vim (vi improved) editor** — An enhanced version of the vi editor that is common on Linux systems today.

**whoami command** — Displays the name for the current user account.

**wildcards** — See **search patterns**.

## REVIEW QUESTIONS

1. Which of the following are valid shells that are available in Linux? (Choose all that apply.)
   a. /bin/bash
   b. /bin/zysh
   c. /bin/ksh
   d. /bin/tcsh

2. Which of the following files are executed when you start another shell following login?
   a. ~/.bash_profile
   b. ~/.profile
   c. ~/.bashrc
   d. /etc/profile

3. Which of the following files could you edit to create a variable that must exist in all shells that are started by users on your system?
   a. ~/.profile
   b. /etc/profile
   c. ~/.bash_login
   d. ~/.bashrc

4. You have just edited your ~/.bashrc file and added a line that loads a variable. How can you read this file into your current shell environment? (Choose all that apply.)
   a. Run the command **. ~/.bashrc**
   b. Run the command **bash ~/.bashrc**
   c. Run the command **load ~/.bashrc**
   d. Run the command **source ~/.bashrc**

5. Which of the following may be used to protect the $ character in the phrase $DIR from being interpreted specially by the bash shell? (Choose all that apply.)
   a. \$DIR
   b. '$DIR'
   c. -$DIR
   d. "$DIR"

6. You wish to recall a previous command that starts with the letters "cron". After you type the letters "cron" on the command line, what key combination could you use to search the command history for previous commands that start with "cron"?

   _____

7. Which key may be used to complete the name of a file or directory on the command line?

   a. F1

   b. Tab

   c. Delete

   d. Spacebar

8. Which of the following commands can be used to view the contents of the $NOVELL variable?

   a. echo NOVELL$

   b. echo $NOVELL

   c. echo $novell

   d. echo novell

9. What command could you use to create a variable called TEST that is available to child processes in subshells? _____

10. What function call is used by a shell to create a subshell for program execution? _____

11. Which of the following commands may be used to view all shell and environment variables on the system?

    a. env

    b. sys

    c. set

    d. export

12. What command could you use to create an alias called **c** that runs the **clear** command in your current shell? _____

13. Which of the following files are best suited to storing aliases? (Choose all that apply.)

    a. /etc/profile

    b. ~/.aliases

    c. ~/.bashrc

    d. /etc/bash.bashrc

14. Which command can be used to view all files in the /etc directory that are three characters long and start with either A or B?

    a. ls /etc/[AB]??

    b. ls /etc/A|B**

    c. ls /etc/{A}|{B}??

    d. ls /etc/[!A!B]??

6

15. Which of the following output redirection symbols will not overwrite an existing file?

    a. >

    b. <

    c. <<

    d. >>

16. What command could you enter at a command prompt to view a long listing of files in the /proc directory and save the stdout and stderr to the file **results** in your current directory? _____

17. Which of the following demonstrates correct syntax? (Choose all that apply.)

    a. command > command

    b. command > file

    c. file > command

    d. command | command

18. To which device file can you redirect stderr in order to ignore stderr completely? _____

19. Which of the following will run the command **echo "I found it!"** only if the command **grep localhost /etc/hosts** is successful?

    a. echo "I found it!" && grep localhost /etc/hosts

    b. echo "I found it!" || grep localhost /etc/hosts

    c. grep localhost /etc/hosts && echo "I found it!"

    d. grep localhost /etc/hosts || echo "I found it!"

20. What command accepts information from stdin and sends it to both a file and stdout? _____

21. Which key can you use to switch from command mode to insert mode in the vi editor?

    a. n

    b. i

    c. c

    d. Esc

22. Which key sequence in the vi editor will allow you to save your changes and quit? (Choose two answers.)

    a. :wq

    b. :z

    c. :x

    d. :q!

23. What **sed** command would you use to replace all occurrences of the word **mom** with **dad** in the file **letter**? _____

24. What **sed** command would you use to delete all lines that begin with a **#** character in the file **/etc/samba/smb.conf**? _____

25. What **awk** command would you use to print the third and fifth fields of the colon-delimited **/etc/passwd** file? _____

6

## Discovery Exercises

## Using the Filename Completion Feature

You can use the Tab key at a command prompt to allow your login shell to autocomplete the next part of a command. Log in to tty1 as the geeko user, then type **cd /e** and press the Tab key. What happens? Type **s** and press the Tab key. Press the Tab key again to see the possible choices. Type **y** and press the Tab key. Type **net** and press the Tab key. Press Enter to execute your command. What directory are you in? Log out of tty1.

## Protecting Characters from Shell Interpretation

Log in to tty1 as the geeko user and perform the following commands in order. For each command, note whether the $ character was protected from shell interpretation and explain why. When finished, log out of tty1.

1. echo My name is $USER

2. echo "My name is $USER"

3. echo 'My name is $USER'

4. echo My name is \$USER

## Working with Variables and Aliases

Log in to tty1 as the geeko user and perform the following actions in order. For each action, write the command(s) that you used. When finished, log out of tty1.

1. Create a shell variable called VAR1 that contains the value "test" without exporting it. Verify that you were successful by displaying the contents of the variable on the terminal screen.

2. Run the **set** command and use the appropriate keys to view all of the contents on the terminal screen. Does VAR1 appear in the output? Why?

3. Run the **env** command and use the appropriate keys to view all of the contents on the terminal screen. Does VAR1 appear in the output? Why?

4. Export the VAR1 variable. Next, run the **env** command and use the appropriate keys to view all of the contents on the terminal screen. Does VAR1 appear in the output? Why?

5. Remove the VAR1 variable from memory and verify that you were successful.

6. Create an alias called **dir** which runs the commands **pwd** and **ls -l** in that order. Test your alias and then remove it from the system.

## Editing Environment Files Using the vi Editor

Log in to tty1 as the geeko user. Use the **vi** editor to open the ~/.profile file. Add a line to the bottom of the file that creates the VAR1 environment variable and sets its value to "test2". When finished, save your changes and quit the **vi** editor. Log out of tty1. Log in to tty1 again as the geeko user. Display the value of the VAR1 variable on the terminal screen to ensure that the ~/.profile file was read when a login shell was created.

Next, use the **vi** editor to open the ~/.bashrc file. Add a line to the bottom of the file that creates the **dir** alias to run the commands **pwd** and **ls -l**, in that order. When finished, save your changes and quit the **vi** editor. Log out of tty1. Log in to tty1 again as the geeko user. Execute the **dir** variable to ensure that the ~/.bashrc file was read when a login shell was created.

Again, use the **vi** editor to open the ~/.bashrc file. Add a line to the bottom of the file that runs the command **echo Hi**. When finished, save your changes and quit the **vi** editor. Next, type the **bash** command to start another bash shell on top of your current bash shell. What was displayed and why? Use the **vi** editor to remove the **echo Hi** line from the bottom of the file and log out of tty1. Note: You will need to use the **exit** command twice, since you have two bash shells running.

## Testing the Forking Process

For nearly all commands that you execute, a subshell is forked to run the command itself. Log in to tty1 as the geeko user. Next, type the command **ls -l** and press Enter. Could you tell that the ls -l command ran in a subshell? Next, type the command **exec ls -l** and press Enter. What happened? Using the forking diagram from this chapter, explain how this result proves that the **ls -l** command normally runs in a subshell.

## Redirecting and Piping Command Output

Log in to tty1 as the root user and perform the following actions in order. For each action, write the command(s) that you used. When finished, log out of tty1.

1. Save the stdout of the **df** command to a file called **diskspace** in your current directory and verify that you were successful.

2. Append the output of the **date** command to the **diskspace** file in your current directory and verify that you were successful.

3. Use the **find** command to locate all files starting from the / directory that start with the word **host**. Save the stdout to a file called **hostfiles** in your current directory and the stderr to a file called **errors** in your current directory. When the command has completed, view the contents of each file.

4. Send the output of the **mount** command to the **wc –l** command to display only the number of mounted filesystems. Describe what the –l option to the wc command is used for.

5. Send the output of the **ls –l /dev** command to the **less** command.

6. Send the output of the **ls –l /dev** command to the **grep tty** command, which should send its output to the **less** command.

7. Send the output of the **ls –l /dev** command to the **grep tty** command, which should send its output to file **ttyfile** in your current directory. View the contents of **ttyfile** to verify its contents.

## Redirection Problems

Log in to tty1 as the geeko user. Make a copy of the **/etc/hosts** file in your home directory by typing the command **cp /etc/hosts ~** at a command prompt. Verify that you have the hosts file in your current directory. Next, use the **sort** command to sort the file by typing **sort hosts** and view the output on your terminal screen. Following this, type the command **sort hosts > hosts** at the command prompt to save the sorted output back into the file. View the contents of the **hosts** file. What are the contents? Explain what happened, using your knowledge of output redirection, and how it could have been remedied. When finished, log out of tty1.

## Piping stderr

Only stdout is sent across a pipe to another command by default. Log in to tty1 as the geeko user and verify this by trying the following commands and noting the absence of stderr in file1:

ls /etc/hosts /etc/h | tee file1

cat file1

Using the information presented in this chapter, how could you send stderr across the pipe in these commands?

## Working with awk and sed

Log in to tty1 as the root user and perform the following actions in order. For each action, write the command(s) that you used. When finished, log out of tty1.

1. Make a copy of the **/etc/passwd** file in your home directory called **passwd**.

2. Use the **sed** command to replace all occurrences of the string "/bin/bash" with "/bin/false" and save the results to a file called **passwd2** in your current directory.

3. Use the **sed** command to delete all lines in the **passwd2** file that have the string "/home" in them.

4. Use the **awk** command to print the first, sixth, and seventh fields of the **passwd** file to the terminal screen. Each field should be separated by a space character.

# 7

# USE THE COMMAND-LINE INTERFACE TO ADMINISTER THE SYSTEM

**In this section, you will focus on using command-line utilities to administer various parts of your SLES system.**

- ◆ Understand User and Group Configuration Files
- ◆ Manage User Accounts and Groups from the Command-Line
- ◆ Manage File Permissions and Ownership
- ◆ Set up and Configure Disk Quotas
- ◆ Decide Which File System Format to Use
- ◆ Manage Local Storage Devices and File Systems
- ◆ Execute RPM Package-Related Operations
- ◆ Perform a Standard Software Build from Source
- ◆ Understand and Configure a Boot Manager

## Objective 1    Understand User and Group Configuration Files

Information on users and groups on a Linux system is kept in the following files:

- /etc/passwd
- /etc/shadow
- /etc/group

Whenever possible, you should not modify these files with an editor. Instead, use the Security and Users modules in YaST or the command-line tools described in the next objective, Manage User Accounts and Groups from th.

Modifying these files with an editor can lead to errors (especially in /etc/shadow), such as a user—including the user root—no longer being able to log in.

To ensure consistency of these files, you need to understand how to:

- Check /etc/passwd and /etc/shadow
- Convert Passwords to and from Shadow

## /etc/passwd

The file **/etc/passwd** stores information for each user. In the past, UNIX and Linux users were handled in a single file: /etc/passwd. The user name, the UID, the home directory, the standard shell, and the encrypted password were all stored in this file.

The password was encrypted using the function crypt (**man 3 crypt**). In principle, the plain text password could not be deciphered from the encrypted password.

However, there are programs (such as john) that use dictionaries to encrypt various passwords with crypt, and then compare the results with the entries in the file /etc/passwd.

With the calculation power of modern computers, simple passwords can be "guessed" within minutes.

The main problem with the file /etc/passwd is that it has to be readable by any user. Because only the UID is saved in the inode of a file, /etc/passwd is used to map UIDs to user names.

The logical solution to this problem has been to store the password field in its own file (/etc/shadow), which can only be read by root.

Figure 7-1 shows a sample /etc/passwd file.

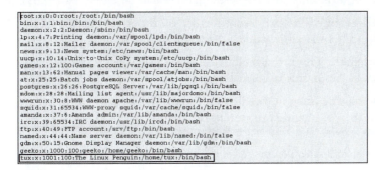

```
root:x:0:0:root:/root:/bin/bash
bin:x:1:1:bin:/bin:/bin/bash
daemon:x:2:2:Daemon:/sbin:/bin/bash
lp:x:4:7:Printing daemon:/var/spool/lpd:/bin/bash
mail:x:8:12:Mailer daemon:/var/spool/clientmqueue:/bin/false
news:x:9:13:News system:/etc/news:/bin/bash
uucp:x:10:14:Unix-to-Unix CoPy system:/etc/uucp:/bin/bash
games:x:12:100:Games account:/var/games:/bin/bash
man:x:13:62:Manual pages viewer:/var/cache/man:/bin/bash
at:x:25:25:Batch jobs daemon:/var/spool/atjobs:/bin/bash
postgres:x:26:26:PostgreSQL Server:/var/lib/pgsql:/bin/bash
mdom:x:28:28:Mailing list agent:/usr/lib/majordomo:/bin/bash
wwwrun:x:30:8:WWW daemon apache:/var/lib/wwwrun:/bin/false
squid:x:31:65534:WWW-proxy squid:/var/cache/squid:/bin/false
amanda:x:37:6:Amanda admin:/var/lib/amanda:/bin/bash
irc:x:39:65534:IRC daemon:/usr/lib/ircd:/bin/bash
ftp:x:40:49:FTP account:/srv/ftp:/bin/bash
named:x:44:44:Name server daemon:/var/lib/named:/bin/false
gdm:x:50:15:Gnome Display Manager daemon:/var/lib/gdm:/bin/bash
geeko:x:1000:100:geeko:/home/geeko:/bin/bash
tux:x:1001:100:The Linux Penguin:/home/tux:/bin/bash
```

**Figure 7-1**

Each line in the file /etc/password represents one user, and contains the following information:

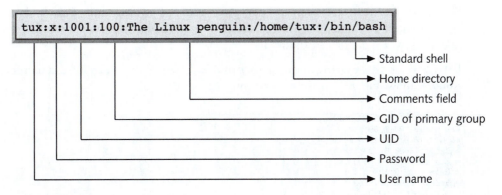

**Figure 7-2**

Note the following about the fields in each line:

- **User name.** This is the name a user enters to log in to the system (login name).

  Although Linux can handle longer user names, in this file they should be restricted to a maximum of eight characters for backward compatibility with older programs.

- **Password.** The x in this field means that the password is stored in the file /etc/shadow.

- **UID.** In compliance with the Linux standards, two number ranges are reserved:

  - **0–99** for the system itself

  - **100–499** for special system users (such as services and programs)

    On SLES 9, normal users start from UID 1000.

- **Comments field.** Normally, the full name of the user is stored here. Information such as a room number or telephone number can be entered as well.

- **Home directory.** The personal directory of a user is normally in the directory /home/ and has the same name as the user (login) name.

- **Standard shell.** This is the shell that is started for a user after he has successfully logged in. In Linux this is normally bash.

  The shell must be listed in the file **/etc/shells**. Each user can change her standard shell with the command chsh (see **man chsh**).

For additional information on this file, enter **man 5 passwd**.

## /etc/shadow

The **/etc/shadow** file stores encrypted user passwords and password expiration information. Most Linux systems use **shadow passwords**. Shadow passwords are stored in /etc/shadow instead of /etc/passwd.

This file can only be changed by the user root and read by the user root and members of the group shadow. Figure 7-3 shows a sample /etc/shadow file.

```
mailman:!:12608:0:99999:7:::
man:*:8902:0:10000::::
mdom:!:12 08:0:99999:7:::
mysql:!:12608:0:99999:7:::
named:!:12608:0:99999:7:::
news:*:8902:0:10000::::
nobody:*:8902:0:10000::::
ntp:!:12608:0:99999:7:::
pop:!:12608:0:99999:7:::
postfix:!:12608:0:99999:7:::
postgres:!:12608:0:99999:7:::
quagga:!:12608:0:99999:7:::
radiusd:!:12608:0:99999:7:::
root:X0QeyibhsgHj2:12608:0:10000::::
snort:!:12608:0:99999:7:::
squid:!:12608:0:99999:7:::
sshd:!:12608:0:99999:7:::
stunnel:!:12608:0:99999:7:::
uucp:*:8902:0:10000::::
vscan:!:12608:0:99999:7:::
wwwrun:*:8902:0:10000::::
tux:svSIYQsFoEwKg:12608:0:99999:7:-1::
geeko:mostStlzd1451:12623:1:99999:14:-1:12134:
```

Figure 7-3

Each line in the file /etc/shadow belongs to one user and contains the following fields:

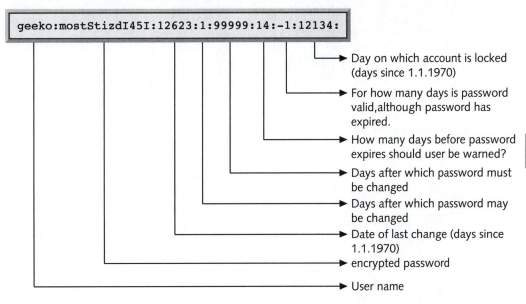

**Figure 7-4**

This figure shows the entry for the user **geeko** with his encrypted password. (Technically, it is more correct to speak of a hashed password.)

The encrypted password is coded with the crypt function and is always 13 characters long. The encrypted word consists of letters, numbers, and the special characters . and /.

If an invalid character occurs in the password field (such as * or !), then the user cannot log in.

Many users, such as wwwrun (Apache Web server) or bin have an asterisk (*) in the password field. This means that these users do not log in to the system, but instead play a role for specific programs.

If the password field is empty, then the user can log in to the system without entering a password. You should always set a password in a multiuser system.

## /etc/group

The file **/etc/group** stores group information.

Figure 7-5 shows a sample /etc/group file.

```
root:x:0:
bin:x:1:daemon
daemon:x:2:
sys:x:3:
tty:x:5:
disk:x:6:
lp:x:7:
www:x:8:
kmem:x:9:
uucp:x:14:geeko,tux
shadow:x:15:
dialout:x:16:geeko,tux
audio:x:17:geeko,tux
floppy:x:19:
cdrom:x:20:
console:x:21:
utmp:x:22:
at:!:25:
postgres:!:26:
mdom:!:28:
public:x:32:
video:x:33:geeko,tux
nobody:x:65533:
nogroup:x:65534:nobody
users:x:100:
novell:!:1000:
```

**Figure 7-5**

Each line in the file represents a single group record and contains the group name, a field for the password hash, the GID (group ID) and the members of the group. For example:

video:x:33:geeko,tux

This is the entry for the group video in /etc/group and has a GID of **33**. Users geeko and tux are members of this group. The **x** in the second field indicates that no password has been set.

The /etc/groups file shows secondary group memberships only; it does not identify the primary group for a user.

**NOTE**

In older versions of SUSE LINUX (such as SUSE LINUX Enterprise Server 8), group passwords are stored in the file /etc/gshadow.

## Check /etc/passwd and /etc/shadow

Because user configuration is handled by two files (/etc/passwd and /etc/shadow), these files have to match each other. Both files have to contain an entry for each user.

However, discrepancies can occur—especially if you are configuring these files in an editor. There are programs you can use to check for discrepancies in /etc/passwd and /etc/shadow.

For example, to view the contents of both files at once, you can enter the following:

```
da10:~ # tail -3 /etc/passwd /etc/shadow
==> /etc/passwd <==
cyrus:x:96:12:User for cyrus-imapd:/usr/lib/cyrus:/bin/bash
tux:x:1000:100:tux:/home/tux:/bin/bash
geeko:x:1001:100:geeko:/home/geeko:/bin/bash
==> /etc/shadow <==
postfix:!:12543:0:99999:7:::
cyrus:!:12543:0:99999:7:::
tux:0C9zaAMz3p72g:12551:0:99999:7:::
da10:~ #
```

In the above example, the user geeko is entered in /etc/passwd but not in /etc/shadow.

In order to correct this type of error, you can enter the command pwconv:

```
da10:~ # pwconv
da10:~ # tail -3 /etc/passwd /etc/shadow
==> /etc/passwd <==
cyrus:x:96:12:User for cyrus-imapd:/usr/lib/cyrus:/bin/bash
tux:x:1000:100:tux:/home/tux:/bin/bash
geeko:x:1001:100:geeko:/home/geeko:/bin/bash
==> /etc/shadow <==
cyrus:!:12543:0:99999:7:::
tux:0C9zaAMz3p72g:12551:0:99999:7:::
geeko:x:12566:0:99999:7:::0
da10:~ #
```

You can also use the command pwck:

```
da10:~ # pwck
Checking '/etc/passwd'
User 'geeko': directory '/home/geeko' does not exist.
Checking '/etc/shadow'.
da10:~ #
```

## Convert Passwords to and from Shadow

To convert passwords to and from /etc/shadow, you can use the **pwconv** command.

This command will also resolve discrepancies where an entry exists in /etc/passwd but not in /etc/shadow.

The following is described:

- Convert Password to Shadow
- Convert Shadow to Password

## Convert Password to Shadow

Since /etc/shadow did not exist in early Linux distributions, pwconv was written to help system administrators use the added security that /etc/shadow provides.

The pwconv command converts the passwd file to the shadow file. When you enter pwconv at the command-line, it creates /etc/shadow with information from /etc/passwd.

pwconv moves the user password from /etc/passwd to /etc/shadow and replaces the password in /etc/passwd with the special character *x*.

Password aging information (PASS_MIN_DAYS, PASS_MAX_DAYS, PASS_WARN_AGE) is pulled from login.defs and added to /etc/shadow.

If you already have both /etc/passwd and /etc/shadow but the shadow file does not have all the entries that are in the passwd file, pwconv adds the missing entries to the shadow file.

pwconv looks for the special character *x* in /etc/passwd so that it does not modify entries that are already in /etc/shadow.

## Convert Shadow to Password

To remove /etc/shadow and convert your user accounts to /etc/passwd only, use the **pwunconv** command. Passwords are moved from /etc/shadow to /etc/passwd and password aging information is lost.

There is no real reason to convert shadow to password. You should avoid doing it, because a separate /etc/shadow is more secure.

---

## OBJECTIVE 2 MANAGE USER ACCOUNTS AND GROUPS FROM THE COMMAND-LINE

In addition to the YaST modules **users** and **groups**, you can use the following commands to add, change, and delete users and groups:

- useradd
- passwd
- usermod
- userdel
- groupadd, groupmod, and groupdel

To prevent individual users from using system resources too excessively, use the following command:

- ulimit

## useradd

You can use the command useradd to add users. In the simplest case, you enter a user name as an argument, as in the following:

**useradd geeko**

By entering useradd geeko, the user geeko is created in /etc/passwd and /etc/shadow.

If you don't specify an option, in SLES the command useradd creates a user without a home directory and without a valid password.

The following are the most important options of the command useradd:

- **–m.** This option automatically generates the home directory for the user.

  Without further arguments, the directory is created under /home/.

  In addition, a series of files and directories are copied to this directory.

  The directory /etc/skel/ (from skeleton) is used as a template for the user home directory.

- **–c.** When creating a new user, you can enter text for the comment field by using the option **–c** *"comment"*.

- **–g.** This option defines the primary group of the user.

  You can specify either the GID or the name of the group.

- **–G.** This option defines any supplementary groups (separated by a comma) the user should be a member of.

  You can specify either the GID or the name of the group.

- **–p.** This option lets you create a password for a new user.

  The following is an example:

  **useradd –m –p "ghvkuzfFGW6cw" geeko**

**NOTE**

The encrypted password must be given here, not the plain text password. The program **mkpasswd** can be used to generate encrypted passwords. It is located in the package whois.

- **–e.** The option –e (expiredate) lets you set an expiration date for the user account, in the form of YYYY-MM-DD, as in the following:

  **useradd –m –e 2005-09-21 geeko**

You can see a description of additional options by entering **man 8 useradd**.

When creating a user account, the necessary standard configuration information (such as primary group, location of the home directory, and default shell) is derived from the files /etc/default/useradd (which is also used by YaST) and /etc/login.defs.

The following is an example of the file /etc/default/useradd:

```
GROUP=1001
HOME=/home
INACTIVE=-1
EXPIRE=
SHELL=/bin/bash
SKEL=/etc/skel
GROUPS=audio,dialout,uucp,video
```

## passwd

You can change a user's password with the command **passwd**.

If a user enters **passwd** without a username as an argument, the user can change her own password.

Besides being able to change a user password, the passwd command provides the following features:

- **Lock a user account.** With the option -l (lock), a user can be kept from logging in. With the option -u (unlock), he can log in again:

```
da10:~ # passwd -l tux
Password changed.
```

- **Show the status of a user account.** The option -S lists the status of a user account:

```
da10:~ # passwd -S tux
tux LK 04/19/2007 0 99999 7 0
```

The status follows directly after the user name. In the above example, LK (locked) means that the user cannot log in. Other options are NP (no password) or PS (valid password).

These are followed by the date of the last password change, the minimum amount of time a password is valid, the maximum amount of time a password is valid, and the warning periods and inactivity periods when a password expires.

- **Change password times.** You can change the password times by using the options in Table 7-1.

**Table 7-1**

| Option | Description |
|---|---|
| -i *number* | Disables an account after the password has been expired for number of days |
| -n *number* | Sets the minimum number of days before a password can be changed |
| -w *number* | Warns the user that in number of days her password will expire |
| -x *number* | Sets the maximum number of days a password remains valid; after number of days the password must be changed |

The following is an example:

**passwd -x 30 -w 5 tux**

In this example, the password of the user tux remains valid for 30 days. After this time, the password is required to be changed by tux. Tux receives a warning five days before the password expires.

When the command passwd is used to establish or change the password of a user account, the file /etc/default/passwd is checked for the encryption method to be used:

```
# This file contains some information for
# the passwd (1) command and other tools
# creating or modifying passwords.

 Define default crypt hash
# CRYPT={des,md5,blowfish}
CRYPT=des
...
```

The default setting for the variable CRYPT is DES. Other possible encryption methods include MD5 and Blowfish. YaST also uses the file /etc/default/passwd.

In SLES 9, a different algorithm (like blowfish) configured in /etc/security/pam_unix2.conf takes precedence over the one given in /etc/default/passwd.

The default option DES supports only passwords with a length up to eight characters long.

MD5 and Blowfish support longer passwords.

The quickest way to create a new user from a command-line is to use useradd and passwd, as in the following:

```
da1:~ # useradd -m -c "Geeko Chameleon" geeko
da1:~ # passwd geeko
New password:
Re-enter new password:
Password changed
```

With useradd the user is created, and with passwd the password is entered.

## usermod

With **usermod**, you can modify information such as the UID, the standard shell, the home directory, and the primary group in an existing user account.

The usermod options are nearly the same as the options of the command useradd.

The following are some examples of usermod:

- Change the home directory:

  **usermod –d /newhome/tux –m tux**

- Change the UID:

  **usermod –u 1504 tux**

## userdel

You can use the **userdel** command to delete user accounts.

To remove user accounts from the system, use a command similar to the following:

**userdel tux**

If you don't specify any options, userdel removes the user from the files:

- /etc/passwd
- /etc/shadow
- /etc/group

If the file /var/spool/cron/tabs/**username** exists, it is deleted.

However, the home directory and the data in the home directory is not deleted.

If you want to delete the user's home directory and the data it contains, use the option -r:

**userdel –r tux**

## groupadd, groupmod, and groupdel

You can use the following command-line commands to perform the same group management tasks available with YaST (and some tasks not available with YaST):

You need to be logged in as root (or switch to root by entering **su -**) to use these commands.

- **groupadd.** You can create a new group by entering **groupadd** *group_name*.

  In this case, the next free GID is used.

Using the option –g (such as **groupadd –g 200 sports**) lets you specify a GID.

Using the option –p (such as **groupadd –p SHIXKBmugEhdk sports**) lets you specify a password. You can use the command mkpasswd to create the encrypted password.

You can verify that the group has been added to the system by entering **tail /etc/group**.

- **groupmod.** You can modify the settings (such as GID, group name, and users) for an existing group.

  The following are examples:

  - Change the GID:

    **groupmod –g 201 sports**

  - Change the group name from sports to water:

    **groupmod –n water sports**

  - Add the user tux to the group:

    **groupmod –A tux sports**

- **groupdel.** You can delete a group by entering **groupdel** *group_name*. There are no options for this command.

  You can delete a group only if no user has this group assigned as a primary group.

**NOTE**

You can learn more about these commands by referring to the manual pages (such as **man groupadd**) or the online help page (such as **groupadd --help**).

## Exercise 7-1    Manage User Accounts

In this exercise command-line tools are employed to manager user accounts. Especially if there are many accounts to manage, the command-line tools usually get the job done faster than YaST.

However, usually you have to use more than one tool, whereas in YaST everything is within one or two dialog boxes.

To manage user accounts, do the following:

1. Open a terminal window; then su to root (**su –**) with a password of **novell**.

2. Create a new local user by entering:

   **useradd –c "Tux Linux" –m tux**

3. Verify that a home directory for tux was created by entering:

   **ls /home**

4. Verify that there is a entry for the tux user in /etc/shadow by entering:

   **cat /etc/shadow**

   Notice the ! in the second field, indicating that there is no password for tux. You did not use the option −p when creating tux, so no password is set.

5. Add a password for the user tux by entering:

   **passwd tux**

6. Enter the password **suse** twice.

7. Log out as root by entering:

   **exit**

8. Log in as tux by entering:

   **su – tux**

9. Enter the tux password (**suse**).

10. Change the password of the user tux by entering:

    **passwd**

11. Enter the old password of the user tux (**suse**).

12. Try to change the password to novell by entering:

    **novell**

    You see a warning that the password is too simple.

13. Enter **d1g1t@l** as new password (twice).

14. Log out as user tux by entering:

    **exit**

15. Switch to user root (**su –**) with a password of **novell**.

16. Delete the user tux by entering:

    **userdel –r tux**

17. Verify that the home directory for tux has been removed by entering:

    **ls /home**

18. Verify that there is no entry for tux in /etc/passwd by entering:

    **cat /etc/passwd**

19. Close the terminal window.

## ulimit

The ulimit command does not have a direct impact on the system performance.

Rather, ulimit prevents individual users from using system resources excessively at the expense of other users.

Accordingly, ulimit can be used to configure:

- The memory usage
- The number of possible processes
- Other factors

7

You can view the current limits by entering:

**ulimit -a**

The output looks like the following:

```
core file size          (blocks, -c) 0
data seg size           (kbytes, -d) unlimited
file size               (blocks, -f) unlimited
max locked memory       (kbytes, -l) unlimited
max memory size         (kbytes, -m) unlimited
open files                      (-n) 1024
pipe size         (512 bytes, -p) 8
stack size              (kbytes, -s) unlimited
cpu time               (seconds, -t) unlimited
max user processes              (-u) 1023
virtual memory          (kbytes, -v) unlimited
```

Individual values can also be reset for the current shell and its child processes by using ulimit with one of the options given above, as in the following example:

```
da10:~ # ulimit -u
1023
da10:~ # ulimit -u 100
da10:~ # ulimit -u
100
```

The details of the individual options are described in the manual pages of bash, section ulimit.

You can change the settings globally for the entire system.

The configuration can be performed:

- By means of the file /etc/profile

  or

- By way of the PAM configuration

  (PAM stands for Pluggable Authentication Modules and is the framework used to perform and configure authentication for various programs requiring authentication, such as login, xdm, or ftp.)

The advantages of using PAM to make configuration changes are:

- The file /etc/security/limits.conf enables user- or group-specific configuration.

- The files in the directory /etc/pam.d/ allow application-specific (login, sshd, etc.) configuration.

The file /etc/profile contains preconfigured entries that you can customize according to your needs, as shown in the following:

```
...
# Adjust some size limits (see bash(1) -> ulimit)
# Note: You may use /etc/initscript instead to set up ulimits
and your PATH.
#
if test "$is" != "ash" ; then
    #ulimit -c 20000       # only core-files less than 20 MB
are written
    #ulimit -d 15000       # max data size of a program is 15 MB
    #ulimit -s 15000       # max stack size of a program is 15 MB
    #ulimit -m 30000       # max resident set size is 30 MB

    ulimit -Sc 0           # don't create core files
    ulimit -Sd unlimited
    # ksh does not support this command.
    test "$is" != "ksh" && ulimit -Ss unlimited
    ulimit -Sm unlimited
fi
...
```

The corresponding configuration in the file /etc/security/limits.conf appears as follows:

```
# /etc/security/limits.conf
#
#Each line describes a limit for a user in the form:
#<domain>        <type>   <item>          <value>
...
#*              soft     core            0
#*              hard     rss             10000
#@student       hard     nproc           20
#@faculty       soft     nproc           20
```

```
#@faculty           hard    nproc           50
#ftp                hard    nproc           0
#@student           -       maxlogins       4

# Max number of processes for the members
# of the group users
@users              hard    nproc           100
```

This file also contains an explanation of what you can enter in the individual columns.

## Exercise 7-2    Use ulimit

The program ulimit is useful when there are several users on a machine and you want to prevent them from giving each other a hard time by using too many of the available resources.

To use ulimit, do the following:

1. Enter the following:

   ```
   tux@da10:~> echo "main() {for(;;)fork();}" > fork.c
   tux@da10:~> gcc fork.c
   ```

   The program (a.out) is for demonstration purposes only.

   This kind of program is referred to as *fork bomb*.

   The program continuously starts new instances of itself, making the computer virtually unusable due the multitude of processes—unless suitable precautions are taken before the program is started.

 Do not execute this program on productive systems!

**CAUTION**

2. Set ulimit to 10.

3. Start a.out.

4. Switch to another console and look at the process table by entering:

   **ps aux**

5. Terminate a.out by pressing **Ctrl + c**.

6. Change the ulimit value.

7. Execute a.out again.

8. Observe the change in the processes.

   If the default ulimit value of 1023 is used, the computer will be virtually unusable following the execution of a.out.

   Often, the only thing you can do in such a case is to reboot the system.

## OBJECTIVE 3    MANAGE FILE PERMISSIONS AND OWNERSHIP

The current file permissions and ownership are displayed using ls -l, as shown in the following example:

```
geeko@da10:~ > ls -la hello.txt
-rw-r--r-- 1 geeko users 0 2007-04-06 12:40 hello.txt
```

The first 10 columns have the following significance:

- **1.** File type (such as –: normal file, d: directory, and l: link).

- **2-4.** File permissions of the user (u) who owns the file (**r**ead, **w**rite, and e**x**ecute).

- **5-7.** File permissions of the owning group (g) of the file (**r**ead, **w**rite, and e**x**ecute).

- **8-10.** File permissions of others (o) (not the owner and not a member of the group) (**r**ead, **w**rite, and e**x**ecute).

For files and directories the significance of the r, w, and x permission is slightly different, as shown in Table 7-2.

**Table 7-2**

| Permission | File | Directory |
|---|---|---|
| r | Read the content of the file | List the directory contents |
| w | Change the content of the file | Create and delete files within the directory |
| x | Execute the file | Change into the directory |

You can change the current values associated with ownership and permissions by knowing how to:

- Change the File Permissions with chmod
- Change the File Ownership with chown and chgrp
- Modify Default Access Permissions
- Configure Special File Permissions

## Change the File Permissions with chmod

You can use the command chmod to add (**+**) or remove (**-**) permissions. Both the owner of a file and root can use this command.

Table 7-3 lists some examples of using the command chmod.

**Table 7-3**

| Example | Result |
|---|---|
| chmod u+x | The owner is given permission to execute the file. |
| chmod g=rw | All group members can read and write to the file. |
| chmod u=rwx | The owner receives all permissions. |
| chmod u=rwx,g=rw,o=r | All permissions for the owner, read and write for the group, and read for all other users. |
| chmod +x | All users (owner, group, others) receive executable permission (depending on umask). |
| chmod a+x | All users (owner, group, and others) receive executable permission (**a** for **all**). |

In the following example, the user geeko allows the other users in the group users to write to the file hello.txt by using chmod:

```
geeko@da10:~ > ls -la hello.txt
-rw-r--r-- 1 geeko users 0 2007-04-06 12:40 hello.txt
geeko@da10:~ > chmod g+w hello.txt
geeko@da10:~ > ls -la hello.txt
-rw-rw-r-- 1 geeko users 0 2007-04-06 12:40 hello.txt
```

With the option –R and a specified directory, you can change the access permissions of all files and subdirectories under the specified directory.

Besides using letters (**rwx**), you can also use the octal way of representing the permission letters with groups of numbers:

**Table 7-4**

| Owner | Group | Others |
|---|---|---|
| rwx | rwx | rwx |
| 421 | 421 | 421 |

By using number equivalents, you can add the numbers, as shown in Table 7-5.

**Table 7-5**

| Owner | Group | Others |
|---|---|---|
| rwx | rw- | r-x |
| 421 (4+2+1=7) | 42- (4+2=6) | 4-1 (4+1=5) |

7

Table 7-6 shows examples of using numbers instead of letters:

**Table 7-6**

| Example | Result |
|---|---|
| **chmod 754 hello.txt** | All permissions for the owner, read and execute for the group, and read for all other users. |
| **chmod 777 hello.txt** | All users (user, group, and others) receive all permissions. |

Depending on what you want to do, either method has its advantages. Which one you prefer is up to you, of course, but you have to know them both.

If you want to add write permissions to the group, no matter the current permission, use **g+w**, like in the following example:

```
da10:/tmp # ls -l hello.txt
-rw-r--r-- 1 geeko users 0 2007-04-06 12:43 hello.txt
da10:/tmp # chmod g+w hello.txt
da10:/tmp # ls -la hello.txt
-rw-rw-r-- 1 geeko users 0 2007-04-06 12:43 hello.txt
```

If you have a certain set of permissions in mind that the file should have, the octal syntax is usually the most efficient.

Suppose you want to achieve rwx for the user, r for the group and no permissions for others. You could figure out what permissions to add and which to subtract, depending on the existing permissions. Another approach would be to use **o=rwx,g=r,o=**, which sets the permissions independently from the existing permissions. However, the octal syntax is much shorter, as the following example shows:

```
da10:/tmp # ls -l hello.sh
-rw-r--r-- 1 geeko users 0 2007-04-06 12:43 hello.txt
da10:/tmp # chmod 740 hello.sh
da10:/tmp # ls -la hello.sh
-rwxr----- 1 geeko users 0 2007-04-06 12:43 hello.txt
```

With a little practice you will get used to the octal syntax, even if it is not intuitive in the beginning.

## Change the File Ownership with chown and chgrp

The user root can use the command chown to change the user and group affiliation of a file by using the following syntax:

**chown** *new_user.new_group file*

To change only the owner, not the group, use the following command syntax:

**chown** *new_user file*

To change only the group, not the user, use the following command syntax:

**chown** *.new_group file*

As root, you can also change the group affiliation of a file by using the chgrp command. Use the following syntax:

**chgrp** *new_group file*

A normal user can use the command chown to allocate a file that she owns to a new group by using the following syntax:

**chown** *.new_group file*

The user can also do the same by using chgrp with the following syntax:

**chgrp** *new_group file*

The user can only change the group affiliation of the file that he owns if he is a member of the new group.

In the following example, root changes the ownership of the file hello.txt from geeko to the user newbie by using chown:

```
da10:/tmp # ls -la hello.txt
-rw-r--r-- 1 geeko users 0 2007-04-06 12:43 hello.txt
da10:/tmp # chown newbie.users hello.txt
da10:/tmp # ls -la hello.txt
-rw-r--r-- 1 newbie users 0 2007-04-06 12:43 hello.txt
da10:/tmp #
```

In the following example, chown is used to limit access to the file list.txt to members of the group advanced:

```
da10:/tmp # ls -la list.txt
-rw-r----- 1 geeko users 0 2007-04-06 12:43 list.txt
da10:/tmp # chown .advanced list.txt
da10:/tmp # ls -la list.txt
-rw-r----- 1 geeko advanced 0 2007-04-06 12:43 list.txt
da10:/tmp #
```

User root and the file owner continue to have rights to access the file.

Although the group has changed, the owner permissions remain the same.

## Modify Default Access Permissions

If the default settings are not changed, files are created with the access mode **666** and directories with **777** by default.

To modify (restrict) these default access mode settings, you can use the command **umask**. You use this command with a three-digit numerical value such as **022**.

How can you calculate the default setting for file and directory permissions from the umask value? The permissions set in the umask are removed from the default permissions.

Table 7-7 shows the permissions assigned to newly created directories and files after setting **umask 022**.

**Table 7-7**

|  | Directories | Files |
|---|---|---|
| **Default Permissions** | rwx  rwx  rwx<br>7    7    7 | rw-  rw-  rw-<br>6    6    6 |
| **umask** | ---  -w-  -w-<br>0    2    2 | ---  -w-  -w-<br>0    2    2 |
| **Result** | rwx  r-x  r-x<br>7    5    5 | rw-  r--  r--<br>6    4    4 |

Table 7-8 shows the permissions assigned to newly created directories and files after setting **umask 023**.

**Table 7-8**

|  | Directories | Files |
|---|---|---|
| **Default Permissions** | rwx  rwx  rwx<br>7    7    7 | rw-  rw-  rw-<br>6    6    6 |
| **umask** | ---  -w-  -wx<br>0    2    3 | ---  -w-  -wx<br>0    2    3 |
| **Result** | rwx  r-x  r--<br>7    5    4 | rw-  r--  r--<br>6    4    4 |

In the second example (umask 023), the **x** permission in the umask does not have any effect on the file permissions, as the x permission is missing in the default setting (rw- rw- rw-, 666).

By entering **umask 077** you restrict access to the owner and root only; the group and others do not have any access permissions.

To make the umask setting permanent, you can change the value of umask in the system-wide configuration file /etc/profile.

If you want the setting to be user-specific, enter the value of umask in the file .bashrc in the home directory of the respective user.

## Configure Special File Permissions

The three attributes in Table 7-9 are used for special circumstances (the uppercase letter is displayed in the output of ls -l in the absence of the execute bit).

**Table 7-9**

| Letter | Number | Name | Files | Directories |
|--------|--------|------|-------|-------------|
| t or T | 1 | Sticky bit | Not applicable | Users can only delete files when they are the owner, or when they are root or owner of the directory.<br><br>This is usually applied to the directory /tmp/. |
| s or S | 2 | SGID (set GroupID) | When a program is run, this sets the group ID of the process to that of the group of the file. | Files created in this directory belong to the group to which the directory belongs and not to the primary group of the user.<br><br>New directories created in this directory inherit the SGID bit. |
| s or S | 4 | SUID (set UserID) | Sets the user ID of the process to that of the owner of the file when the program is run. | Not applicable. |

You set the sticky bit with chmod, either via the permissions of others (such as **chmod o+t /tmp**) or numerically (such as **chmod 1777 /tmp**).

**CAUTION**

The sticky bit on older UNIX systems enabled the storing of an executable program in memory after it had been terminated, so it could be quickly restarted. However, with modern UNIX and Linux systems, this only affects directories.

The sticky bit is listed in the permissions for others (t), as in the following:

```
geeko@da10:~ > ls -ld /tmp
drwxrwxrwt 15 root root 608 2007-04-06 12:45 /tmp
```

The following is an example for SUID:

```
geeko@da10:~ > ls -l /usr/bin/passwd
-rwsr-xr-x 1 root shadow 79765 2007-03-24 12:19 /usr/bin/passwd
```

You can set this bit either by entering:

**chmod u+s /usr/bin/passwd**

or

**chmod 4755 /usr/bin/passwd**

The following is an example for SGID:

```
geeko@da10:~ > ls -l /usr/bin/wall
-rwxr-sr-x 1 root tty 10192 2007-03-22 05:24 /usr/bin/wall
```

You can set this bit either by entering:

**chmod g+s /usr/bin/wall**

or

**chmod 2755 /usr/bin/wall**

If the attributes SUID or SGID are set, the programs are carried out with the privileges the owner (in the example for SUID above: root) or the group (in the example for SGID above: tty) have.

If root is the owner of the program, the program is carried out with the permissions of root. Unfortunately, there is a certain security risk in doing this.

For example, it is possible for a user to take advantage of an error in the program, retaining root privileges after the process has been ended.

## Exercise 7-3    Manage File Permissions and Ownership

File permissions and ownership is a subject any user on a Linux system needs to understand. For a system administrator this understanding is of crucial importance, as faulty permissions can have serious impact on the system security.

To manage file permissions and ownership:

1. Open a terminal window as user geeko (do not su to root).
2. Create two files:

   **echo hello > perm_test1**

   **echo hello > perm_test2**

3. Allow only user geeko to read and write the file perm_test1 by entering:

   **chmod 600 perm_test1**

4. Verify that the change was made by entering:

   **ls -l**

   Notice that geeko is the owner of the file, and that the only permissions assigned to the file are rw for the file owner.

   Also notice that others can read (r) the contents of the file perm_test2.

5. Remove the read permission for others of the file perm_test2 by entering:

   **chmod o-r perm_test2**

6. Make sure that the permissions are correct by entering:

   **ls -l perm_test***

7. Su to root (**su -**) with a password of **novell**.

8. Create a file df by entering:

   **touch df**

9. Verify that the file was created by entering:

   **ls -l df**

   The owner of the file is root, and the file group is also root.

10. Change the owner of the file df to nobody by entering:

    **chown nobody df**

11. Change the group of the file df to nogroup by entering:

    **chgrp nogroup df**

12. Make sure that the settings are correct by entering:

    **ls -l df**

13. Log out as user root by entering:

    **exit**

14. Close the terminal window.

## OBJECTIVE 4   SET UP AND CONFIGURE DISK QUOTAS

Drive space continues to be a problem, especially when storing data such as user files, databases, and MP3 archives. Without imposing limits, a user can easily fill up 40 GB of hard drive space with pictures, software, and music.

Linux includes a quota system that lets you specify a specific amount of storage space for each user or group, and how many files that user or group can create.

In SUSE Linux Enterprise Server 9 (SLES 9) you can use the quota package to impose these limitations.

Figure 7-6 illustrates the quota architecture.

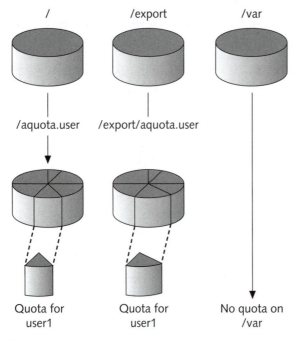

**Figure 7-6**

Disk quota support is already included in the kernel in SLES 9. You can implement disk quotas for partitions configured with the ext2, ext3, or ReiserFS file systems.

To set up and configure the disk quota service on your server, do the following tasks (in order):

1. Prepare the File System
2. Initialize the Quota System
3. Configure and Manage User and Group Quotas
4. Start and Activate the Quota Service

## Prepare the File System

When the system is started, the quotas for the file system must be activated. You can indicate for which file systems quotas are to be activated by configuring entries in the file /etc/fstab.

You enter the keyword **usrquota** for quotas on the user level and the keyword **grpquota** for group quotas, as in Figure 7-7.

```
/dev/hda2       /               reiserfs    acl,user_xattr,usrquota,grpquota      1 1
/dev/hda1       swap            swap        pri=42                 0 0
devpts          /dev/pts        devpts      mode=0620,gid=5        0 0
proc            /proc           proc        defaults               0 0
usbfs           /proc/bus/usb   usbfs       noauto                 0 0
sysfs           /sys            sysfs       noauto                 0 0
/dev/cdrom      /media/cdrom    subfs       fs=cdfss,ro,procuid,nosuid,nodev,exec,iocharset=utf8 0 0
/dev/fd0        /media/floppy   subfs       fs=floppyfss,procuid,nodev,nosuid,sync 0 0
```

**Figure 7-7**

In this example, quotas are configured for the file system **/** (root).

If you have configured /etc/fstab without rebooting your server, you need to remount the file systems in the root partition by entering the following:

**mount –o remount /**

## Initialize the Quota System

After remounting, you need to initialize the quota system. You can do this by using the command **quotacheck**, which is part of the package quota.

This command checks the partitions with quota keywords (in terms of already occupied data blocks and inodes) and stores the determined values in the files **aquota. user** (for user quotas) and **aquota. group** (for group quotas).

**NOTE**   Up to kernel version 2.4, these files were called quota.user and quota.group, and had to be created before quotacheck was run.

If you enter the command **quotacheck –avug**, all mounted file systems (**-a**) are checked for data blocks and inodes that are occupied by users (**-u**) and groups (**-g**). The option **-v** provides a detailed output.

When checking mounted file systems, you might need to use the option **-m** to force the check.

Assuming the quota entries exist for /, after running **quotacheck** the following files are created:

```
da10:~ # ls -l /aquota*
-rw-------   1 root root 9216 Aug 27 10:06 /aquota.group
-rw-------   1 root root 9216 Aug 27 10:06 /aquota.user
```

## Configure and Manage User and Group Quotas

To configure quotas for users and groups, you need to know how to do the following:

- Configure Soft and Hard Limits for Blocks and Inodes
- Configure Grace Periods for Blocks and Inodes
- Copy User Quotas
- Generate a Quota Report

### Configure Soft and Hard Limits for Blocks and Inodes

With the command **edquota** and the following options, you can edit the current quota settings for a user or group:

- **edquota -u** *user.* Set up user quotas.
- **edquota -g** *group.* Set up group quotas.

The current settings are displayed in the vi editor for you to edit. You can edit the soft and hard limits; however, the blocks and inodes values are for information only and cannot be edited.

For example, to configure quotas for the user geeko, enter:

**edquota -u geeko**

After entering the command, the following quota information appears in vi for geeko:

```
Disk quotas for user geeko (uid 1001):
  Filesystem       blocks     soft     hard     inodes     soft     hard
  /dev/sda2          7820    10000    20000        145        0        0
```

The following describes the settings:

- **Blocks.** How much hard disk space is currently used, with soft and hard limits listed.

  The values for blocks are given in blocks of 1 KB (independent of the block size of the underlying file system).

  For example, the value **7820** under Blocks indicates that the user geeko is currently using about 8 MB of hard drive space.

  The soft limit is set to **10** MB and the hard limit is set to **20** MB.

- **Inodes.** How many files belong to the user on the file system, with soft and hard limits listed.

  The soft and hard limits for geeko are set to **0**, which means that the user can create an unlimited number of files.

The soft limits indicate a quota that the user cannot permanently exceed. The hard limits indicate a boundary beyond which no more space or inodes can be used.

If users move beyond the soft limit, they have a fixed time available (a grace period) to free up space by deleting files or blocks.

If users exceed the grace period, they cannot create any new files until they delete enough files to move under the soft limit.

### Configure Grace Periods for Blocks and Inodes

You can use vi to edit the grace periods for blocks and inodes by entering **edquota -t**.

A screen similar to the following appears:

```
Grace period before enforcing soft limits for users:
Time units may be: days, hours, minutes, or seconds
  Filesystem                Block grace period      Inode grace period
  /dev/sda2                      7days                    7days
```

You can set the grace periods in days, hours, minutes, or seconds for a listed file system. However, you cannot specify a grace period for a specific user or group.

### Copy User Quotas

You can copy user quotas from one user to another by entering:

**edquota -p**

For example, to copy the user quotas for the user tux to the user geeko, enter:

**edquota -p tux geeko**

### Generate a Quota Report

The quota system files contain information in binary format about the space occupied by users and groups, and which quotas are set up. You can display this information by using the command **repquota**.

For example, entering **repquota -aug** displays a report similar to the following for all users and groups:

```
*** Report for user quotas on device /dev/sda2
Block grace time: 7days; Inode grace time: 7days
                          Block limits                    File limits
User            used     soft     hard  grace     used  soft  hard
grace
------------------------------------------------------------------
-----
root         -- 2646650       0        0            140161     0     0
geeko        +-   20000   10000    20000  7days        146     0     0
```

For additional details on using repquota, see **man 8 repquota**.

## Start and Activate the Quota Service

In order for the quota system to be initialized when the system is booted, the appropriate links must be made in the runlevel directories by entering:

**insserv quota** (**innserv quotad** for NFS)

You can then start the quota system by entering:

**/etc/init.d/quota start**

You can also start or stop the quota system by entering:

**/usr/sbin/quotaon** *filesystem*

**/usr/sbin/quotaoff** *filesystem*

You can use the option –a to activate and deactivate all automatically mounted file systems (except NFS) with quotas.

For additional information on quotaon options, enter **man quotaon**.

**NOTE**

## Exercise 7-4   Set Up and Configure Disk Quotas

Usually sooner or later the available storage space gets used up. While not a cure all, quotas are a means to prevent single users from using up the space, leaving too little for others to work effectively.

The purpose of this exercise is to practice setting and managing disk quotas.

To set up disk quotas, do the following:

1. From a terminal window, su to root (**su –**) with a password of **novell**.

2. Install the package qouta by entering **yast –i qouta** and inserting the SLES 9 DVD when prompted.

3. View the disk quota configuration for user geeko by entering:

   **quota –vu geeko**

   Notice that there are no quotas currently configured for geeko.

4. Add quota mount options to the partition /dev/hda2 (or the partition holding the directory / on your machine) by doing the following:

   a. Open the /etc/fstab file in the vi editor by entering:

   **vim /etc/fstab**

    b. Edit the /dev/hda2 entry to reflect the following:

       /dev/hda2 / reiserfs defaults,**usrquota,grpquota** 1 1

    c. When you finish, save the file and exit by entering :**wq**.

5. Remount the file system so it that reads the changes in file /etc/fstab by entering:

   **mount –o remount /**

**NOTE**  If you receive an error message / Not Mounted Already or Bad Option, check the contents of the /etc/fstab file. You might have misspelled the usrquota or grpquota option.

7

6. Run quotacheck to initialize the quota database by entering:

   **quotacheck –mavug**

   You receive several status messages about old quota files. These indicate that this is a new quota database with no previous quota database files on the system.

7. Verify that the files aquota.user and aquota.groups exist in the directory / by entering:

   **ls –l /**

8. Turn quotas on for all file systems that are mounted with these options by entering:

   **quotaon –av**

9. Make the quota system persistent after rebooting by entering:

   **chkconfig quota on**

10. View the quota report by entering:

   **repquota –av**

   The quotas are set by using the number of 1KB blocks.

   Notice that root is the only user listed.

11. Set a quota for geeko of a soft limit of 200 MB and a hard limit of 300 MB on /dev/hda2 by entering:

   **edquota –u geeko**

   The quota editor appears (the vi editor).

12. Enter the required *soft limit* and *hard limit* under the Soft and Hard columns for /dev/hda2 (press **Insert** twice to replace text).

13. When you finish, press **Esc**; then enter :**wq**.

14. Run repquota to view the quota information about all configured users by entering:

    **repquota -av**

    Notice that geeko is now listed with the soft limit and hard limit values you entered.

15. (Optional) If you finish early, you can set a quota for the users group of 500 MB for the soft limit, and 750 MB for the hard limit.

16. Close all open windows.

# OBJECTIVE 5   DECIDE WHICH FILE SYSTEM FORMAT TO USE

Even with quotas in use, usually after some time storage space needs to be added. This objective covers the criteria to choose the right file system and the next objective covers how to integrate additional hard disks or partitions into the system.

It is very important to understand that no single file system is best for all applications. Each file system has its particular strengths and weaknesses, which have to be taken into account.

And even the most sophisticated file system in the world will never substitute for a reasonable backup strategy.

SLES 9 supports a variety of file systems. These file systems can be grouped into two types:

- Non-journaling file systems (such as Ext2 and VFAT)

- Journaling file systems (such as Ext3, ReiserFS, JFS, and XFS)

In case of a system crash or a power outage, non-journaling file systems have a significant disadvantage compared with journaling file systems because the complete structure of the file system has to be checked to ensure integrity.

**CAUTION**

The terms *data integrity* or *data consistency*, when used in this section, do not refer to the consistency of the user space data (the data your application writes to its files). The consistency of user space data is controlled by the application itself.

Journaling file systems treat file system operations as transactions, just like database transactions. The journaling file system tracks changes to file system metadata or user data.

The transaction guarantees that either all or none of the file system updates are processed.

In the event of a system failure, the file system is restored to a consistent state by replaying the journal.

Rather than examine all metadata, the file system inspects only those portions of the metadata that have recently changed. Recovery is much faster and is usually complete in a matter of seconds.

This objective introduces the following file systems:

- Ext2
- Ext3
- ReiserFS
- JFS
- XFS

## Ext2

The origins of Ext2 go back to the early days of Linux history. Its predecessor, the Extended File System, was implemented in 1992 and integrated in Linux 0.96c.

Extended File System underwent a number of modifications and, as Ext2, became the most popular Linux file system for years. With the creation of journaling file systems and their astonishingly short recovery times, Ext2 became less important.

A brief summary of the strengths of Ext2 might help you understand why it was, and in some areas still is, the favorite Linux file system of many Linux users.

Ext2 underwent many improvements and was heavily tested. This might be the reason why people often refer to it as rock solid.

After a system outage, when the file system was not cleanly unmounted, **e2fsck** starts to analyze the file system data. Metadata is brought into a consistent state and non-allocated files or data blocks are written to a designated directory (called lost+found).

Unlike most journaling file systems, **e2fsck** analyzes the whole file system and not just the recently modified bits of metadata.

This takes significantly longer than checking the log data of a journaling file system. Depending on file system size, this procedure can take half an hour or more.

Therefore, you would not choose an Ext2 file system for any server that needs to be highly available. But it is also important to note that Ext2 is sometimes faster than other file systems, because it does not maintain a journal and uses significantly less memory.

## Ext3

Unlike other next generation file systems, Ext3 does not follow a completely new design principle—it is based on Ext2.

The code of Ext2 is the strong foundation on which Ext3 could become a highly acclaimed next generation file system. Its reliability and solidity were elegantly combined with some of the advantages of a journaling file system.

These two file systems are very closely related. An Ext3 file system can be easily built on top of an Ext2 file system. The most important difference between Ext2 and Ext3 is that Ext3 supports journaling.

Ext3 has the following advantages:

- Easy and Highly Reliable File System Upgrades from Ext2
- Reliability and Performance

## Easy and Highly Reliable File System Upgrades from Ext2

Because Ext3 is based on the Ext2 code and shares its on-disk format as well as its metadata format, upgrades from Ext2 to Ext3 are easy. They can even be performed while Ext2 file systems are mounted.

Unlike transitions to other journaling file systems (such as ReiserFS, JFS, or XFS) which can be quite tedious (making backups of the whole file system and recreating it from scratch), a transition to Ext3 takes a few minutes and is also very safe.

Considering the number of existing Ext2 systems that await an upgrade to a journaling file system, you can easily figure out why Ext3 might be of importance to many system administrators.

Downgrading from Ext3 to Ext2 is as easy as the upgrade. Just perform a clean unmount of the Ext3 file system and remount it as an Ext2 file system.

## Reliability and Performance

Other journaling file systems follow the metadata-only journaling approach. This means metadata will always be kept in a consistent state but consistency cannot be automatically guaranteed for the file system data itself.

Ext3 is designed to take care of both metadata and data. You can customize the degree of care.

- Enabling Ext3 in the data=journal mode offers maximum security (data integrity) but can slow down the system as both metadata and data are journaled.
- A relatively new approach is to use the data=ordered mode, which ensures both data and metadata integrity, but uses journaling only for metadata.

   The file system driver collects all data blocks that correspond to one metadata update. These blocks are grouped as a transaction and will be written to disk before the metadata is updated.

   As a result, consistency is achieved for metadata and data without sacrificing performance.

- A third option to use is data=writeback, which allows data to be written into the main file system after its metadata has been committed to the journal.

  This option is often considered to offer the best performance. It can, however, allow old data to reappear in files after crash and recovery while internal file system integrity is maintained.

Unless you specify something else, Ext3 is run with the data=ordered by default.

# ReiserFS

The Reiser File System (ReiserFS) was the first journaling file system available for Linux. The ReiserFS developer, Hans Reiser, used an approach that is completely different from Ext2 and Ext3.

ReiserFS's strengths are:

- Better Disk Space Utilization
- Better Space Usage by Dynamic Inode Allocation
- Better Disk Access Performance
- Fast Crash Recovery

### Better Disk Space Utilization

In ReiserFS, all data is organized in a structure called B tree (B stands for balanced).

The tree structure contributes to better disk space utilization because small files can be stored directly in the B tree leaf nodes instead of being stored elsewhere and just maintaining a pointer to the actual disk location.

In addition to that, storage is not allocated in chunks of 1 KB or 4 KB, but in portions of the exact size that is needed.

### Better Space Usage by Dynamic Inode Allocation

Another benefit of ReiserFS is the dynamic allocation of inodes. This keeps the file system more flexible in contrast to traditional file systems, like Ext2, where the inode density has to be specified at file system creation time.

### Better Disk Access Performance

For small files, both file data and stat_data (inode) information are often stored next to each other. They can be read with a single disk I/O operation, meaning that only one access to the disk is required to retrieve all the information needed.

### Fast Crash Recovery

Using a journal to keep track of recent metadata changes allows a file system check in a matter of seconds, even for huge file systems.

# JFS

JFS (Journaling File System) was developed by IBM for its AIX systems.

The first beta version of the JFS Linux port reached the Linux community in 2000. Version 1.0.0 was released in 2001.

JFS is tailored to suit the needs of high throughput server environments where performance is the ultimate goal.

JFS is a full 64-bit file system, which means it supports both large files and partitions. This also speaks positively for its use in server environments.

There are several reasons why this file system might be a good choice for your Linux server:

- Efficient Journaling
- Efficient Directory Organization
- Better Space Usage by Dynamic Inode Allocation

## Efficient Journaling

JFS follows a metadata-only approach like ReiserFS. Instead of an extensive check, only metadata changes generated by recent file system activity get checked, which saves a great amount of time in recovery.

Concurrent operations requiring multiple concurrent log entries can be combined into one group commit, greatly reducing performance loss of the file system through multiple write operations.

## Efficient Directory Organization

JFS supports two different directory organizations:

- For small directories, it allows the directory's content to be stored directly in its inode.
- For larger directories, it uses B+ trees, which greatly facilitate directory management.

## Better Space Usage by Dynamic Inode Allocation

For Ext2, you have to define the inode density (the space occupied by management information) in advance, which restricts the maximum number of files or directories of your file system.

With JFS, you do not have to worry about the number of inodes to create as it dynamically allocates inode space and frees it when it is no longer needed.

# XFS

SGI started XFS development in the early 1990s. XFS was originally intended as file system for SGI's IRIX OS.

The idea behind XFS was to create a high performance 64-bit journaling file system to meet today's extreme computing challenges.

XFS is very good at manipulating large files and performs well on high-end hardware. However, like ReiserFS, XFS takes a great deal of care with metadata integrity, but pays less attention to data integrity.

There are several reasons why XFS might prove to be a strong competitor for other journaling file systems in high-end computing:

- High Scalability by Using Allocation Groups
- High Performance by Efficient Management of Disk Space
- Preallocation to Avoid File System Fragmentation

## High Scalability by Using Allocation Groups

When an XFS file system is created, the block device underlying the file system is divided into eight or more linear regions of equal size. Those are referred to as *allocation groups*.

Each allocation group manages its own inodes and free disk space.

For practical purposes, allocation groups can be seen as file systems inside a file system. Because allocation groups are rather independent of each other, more than one of them can be addressed by the kernel simultaneously.

This feature is the key to XFS's great scalability. Naturally, the concept of independent allocation groups suits the needs of multiprocessor systems.

## High Performance by Efficient Management of Disk Space

Free space and inodes are handled by B+ trees inside the allocation groups. The use of B+ trees greatly contributes to XFS's performance and scalability.

There are also additional features that contribute to performance.

A feature unique to XFS is delayed allocation. XFS handles allocation by breaking the process into two pieces:

- A pending transaction is stored in RAM and the appropriate amount of space is reserved. XFS still does not decide where exactly (speaking of file system blocks) the data should be stored.
- This decision is delayed until the last possible moment. Some short-lived temporary data might never make its way to disk since it might be obsolete at the time XFS decides where to actually save it.

Thus, XFS increases write performance and reduces file system fragmentation. However, since delayed allocation results in less frequent write events than in other file systems, data loss after a crash during a write might be more severe.

### Preallocation to Avoid File System Fragmentation

Before writing the data to the file system, XFS reserves (preallocates) the free space needed for a file. This greatly reduces file system fragmentation.

Performance is increased since the contents of a file will not be distributed all over the file system.

---

## OBJECTIVE 6    MANAGE LOCAL STORAGE DEVICES AND FILE SYSTEMS

To manage local storage devices and file systems, for instance, when integrating an additional hard disk into the Linux system you need to understand how to:

- Partition a Hard Disk with the fdisk Command
- Use File System Management Commands
- Use File System Mount Commands

## Partition a Hard Disk with the fdisk Command

The program **fdisk** is used for partitioning hard disks.

When starting **fdisk**, you enter the device of the hard disk as a parameter.

To do this, you have to know which hard drive is involved (IDE or SCSI) and which rank it has (the first IDE hard disk in the system, the second IDE hard disk in the system, etc.).

This results in devices such as:

- **/dev/hda.** IDE hard disk, master on the first IDE controller.
- **/dev/hdb.** IDE hard disk, slave on the first IDE controller.
- **/dev/hdc.** IDE hard disk, master on the second IDE controller.
- **/dev/sda.** First SCSI hard disk.
- **/dev/sdb.** Second SCSI hard disk.

To run fdisk, enter:

```
da10:~ # fdisk /dev/hdb
```

fdisk is used with the keyboard: a letter, followed by **Enter**, carries out an action. Table 7–10 lists the keys you can use.

**Table 7-10**

| Letter | Action |
|---|---|
| d | Deletes a partition |
| m | Gives a short summary of the fdisk commands |
| n | Creates a new partition |
| p | Shows a list of partitions that are currently available on the hard disk specified |
| q | Ends the program fdisk without saving changes |
| t | Changes a partition's system ID |
| w | Saves the changes made to the hard disk and ends fdisk |

7

A maximum of four primary partitions can be set up on a hard disk.

CAUTION

The various architectures (Intel, SUN, Alpha, PowerPC) use different partitioning types.

If you need more partitions, declare one of these four as an extended partition. Then you can create further logical partitions in it (the maximum number of all partitions is 15 for SCSI and 64 for IDE drives).

To partition an empty hard disk, do the following:

1. Enter **fdisk** *hard_disk*, for example, **fdisk /dev/hdb**.

2. Enter **p**.

   For an empty hard disk, the following is displayed:

   ```
   Command (m for help): p

   Disk /dev/hdb: 32 heads, 63 sectors, 528 cylinders
   Units = cylinders of 2016 * 512 bytes

       Device Boot    Start      End   Blocks   Id  System

   Command (m for help):
   ```

3. To create a primary partition, enter **n**; then enter **p** as shown in the following:
   ```
   Command (m for help): n
   Command action
      e    extended
      p    primary partition (1-4)
   p
   Partition number (1-4): 1
   ```

```
First cylinder (1-528): 1
Last cylinder or +size or +sizeM or +sizeK (1-
528, default 528): +128M

Command (m for help):
```

4. To display the partition table with the current settings, enter **p**.

The following is displayed:

```
Command (m for help): p

Disk /dev/hdb: 32 heads, 63 sectors, 528 cylinders
Units = cylinders of 2016 * 512 bytes

   Device Boot    Start      End    Blocks   Id  System
/dev/hdb1                 1      131   132016+  83  Linux

Command (m for help):
```

This partition table contains all the relevant information on the partition created:

- This is the first partition of this hard disk (Device hdb1).

- It begins at cylinder 1 (Start) and ends at cylinder 131 (End).

- It consists of 132016 blocks (Blocks).

- Its Hex code (Id) is 83.

- Its type is Linux (System).

5. To set up an extended partition, enter **n**; then enter **e** as shown in the following:

```
Command (m for help): n
Command action
   e    extended
   p    primary partition (1-4)
e
Partition number (1-4): 2
First cylinder (132-528): 132
Last cylinder or +size or +sizeM or +sizeK (132-
528, default 528): 528

Command (m for help):
```

6. To display the partition table with the current settings, enter **p**.

The following is displayed:

```
Command (m for help): p

Disk /dev/hdb: 32 heads, 63 sectors, 528 cylinders
Units = cylinders of 2016 * 512 bytes
```

```
    Device Boot      Start      End     Blocks    Id   System
/dev/hdb1                 1      131    132016+   83   Linux
/dev/hdb2               132      528    400176     5   Extended

Command (m for help):
```

7. If an extended partition has been created, you can set up logical partitions by entering **n**; then enter **l** as shown in the following:

```
Command (m for help): n
Command action
    l    logical (5 or over)
    p    primary partition (1-4)
l
First cylinder (132-528, default 132): 132
Last cylinder or +size or +sizeM or +sizeK (132-
528, default 528): +128M

Command (m for help):
```

8. To display the partition table with the current settings, enter **p**.

   The following is displayed:

```
Command (m for help): p

Disk /dev/hda: 32 heads, 63 sectors, 528 cylinders
Units = cylinders of 2016 * 512 bytes

    Device Boot      Start      End     Blocks    Id   System
/dev/hdb1                 1      131    132016+   83   Linux
/dev/hdb2               132      528    400176     5   Extended
/dev/hdb5               132      262    132016+   83   Linux

Command (m for help):
```

   The standard type for these partitions is Linux.

9. To create a swap partition, change the type by doing the following:

   a. Enter **t**.

   b. Enter the partition number.

7

   c. Enter **L** or **l** to get the Hex Code list for changing the partition type.

   The following is displayed:

```
0  Empty              1b Hidden Win95 FA   63 GNU HURD or Sys   b7 BSDI fs
1  FAT12              1c Hidden Win95 FA   64 Novell Netware    b8 BSDI swap
2  XENIX root         1e Hidden Win95 FA   65 Novell Netware    c1 DRDOS/sec (FAT-
3  XENIX usr          24 NEC DOS           70 DiskSecure Mult   c4 DRDOS/sec (FAT-
4  FAT16 <32M         39 Plan 9            75 PC/IX             c6 DRDOS/sec (FAT-
5  Extended           3c PartitionMagic    80 Old Minix         c7 Syrinx
6  FAT16              40 Venix 80286       81 Minix / old Lin   da Non-FS data
7  HPFS/NTFS          41 PPC PReP Boot     82 Linux swap        db CP/M / CTOS / .
8  AIX                42 SFS               83 Linux             de Dell Utility
9  AIX bootable       4d QNX4.x            84 OS/2 hidden C:    e1 DOS access
a  OS/2 Boot Manag    4e QNX4.x 2nd part   85 Linux extended    e3 DOS R/O
b  Win95 FAT32        4f QNX4.x 3rd part   86 NTFS volume set   e4 SpeedStor
c  Win95 FAT32 (LB    50 OnTrack DM        87 NTFS volume set   eb BeOS fs
e  Win95 FAT16 (LB    51 OnTrack DM6 Aux   8e Linux LVM         ee EFI GPT
f  Win95 Ext'd (LB    52 CP/M             93 Amoeba            ef EFI (FAT-12/16/
10 OPUS               53 OnTrack DM6 Aux   94 Amoeba BBT        f1 SpeedStor
11 Hidden FAT12       54 OnTrackDM6        9f BSD/OS            f4 SpeedStor
12 Compaq diagnost    55 EZ-Drive          a0 IBM Thinkpad hi   f2 DOS secondary
14 Hidden FAT16 <3    56 Golden Bow        a5 BSD/386           fd Linux raid auto
16 Hidden FAT16       5c Priam Edisk       a6 OpenBSD           fe LANstep
17 Hidden HPFS/NTF    61 SpeedStor         a7 NeXTSTEP          ff BBT
18 AST Windows swa
```

   d. Enter the hex code.

   The following shows this procedure:

```
Command (m for help): t
Partition number (1-5): 5
Hex code (type L to list codes): 82
Changed system type of partition 5 to 82 (Linux swap)

Command (m for help):
```

10. To display the partition table with the current settings, enter **p**.

   The following is displayed:

```
Command (m for help): p

Disk /dev/hdb: 32 heads, 63 sectors, 528 cylinders
Units = cylinders of 2016 * 512 bytes

    Device Boot    Start      End    Blocks   Id  System
/dev/hdb1              1      131    132016+   83  Linux
/dev/hdb2            132      528    400176     5  Extended
/dev/hdb5            132      262    132016+   82  Linux swap

Command (m for help):
```

11. To finish the procedure, enter **w**.

The changes are written to the table.

**CAUTION**

When the new table is written, you are not asked for confirmation if you really want to do this.

# Use File System Management Commands

**7**

You must understand how to use the command-line to

- Create a File System from the Command-Line
- Check and Repair Any File System (fsck)
- Check and Repair ext2/ext3 and ReiserFS (e2fsck and reiserfsck)

## Create a File System from the Command-Line

You can use the following commands to create a file system from the command-line:

- mkfs
- mkreiserfs

**mkfs**   File systems (such as ext2, ext3, MS–DOS, MINIX, XFS, JFS) are created using the command **mkfs** (make file system).

This command is a frontend for the commands actually used to create file systems (such as **mkfs.ext2**, **mkfs.ext3**, and **mkfs.msdos**). You need to use the option -t with mkfs to indicate the file system type you want to create, or you call the file system specific command directly.

If no file system type is indicated, **mkfs** automatically creates an ext2 file system.

If you create an ext2 or ext3 file system with mkfs, you can use the options listed in Table 7-11.

**Table 7-11**

| Option | Description |
|---|---|
| -b *blocksize* | You can use this option to indicate the size of the data blocks in the file system. Values of 1024, 2048, . . . , 16384 are allowed for the block size. |
| -i *bytes_per_inode* | You can use this option to indicate how many inodes are created on the file system.<br><br>For *bytes_per_inode* you can use the same values available for the block size.<br><br>You should choose a larger value for the block size. However, it makes little sense to have a larger number of inodes than data blocks. |
| -j | You can use this option to create an ext3 journal on the file system. |

If you do not include options –b and –i, the data block sizes and the number of inodes is set by mkfs, depending on the size of the partitions.

The following is an example of creating a partition with an ext2 file system:

```
da10:~ # mkfs -t ext2 /dev/hdb1
mke2fs 1.34 (25-Jul-2003)
Filesystem label=
OS type: Linux
Block size=1024 (log=0)
Fragment size=1024 (log=0)
25688 inodes, 102400 blocks
5120 blocks (5.00%) reserved for the super user
First data block=1
13 block groups
8192 blocks per group, 8192 fragments per group
1976 inodes per group
Superblock backups stored on blocks:
8193, 16385, 24577, 32769, 40961, 49153, 57345, 65537,
73729, 81921, 90113, 98305
Writing inode tables: done
Writing superblocks and filesystem accounting information: done
This filesystem will be automatically checked every 31 mounts or
180 days, whichever comes first. Use tune2fs -c or -i to override.
da10:~ #
```

This mkfs example creates a 100 MB partition formatted with the following standard values:

- **Block size=1024 (log=0)**

  The block size is 1 KB.

- **25,688 inodes, 102,400 blocks**

  The maximum number of files and directories is 25688. The total number of blocks is 102400.

- **5120 blocks (5 percent) reserved for the super user**

  5 percent of the entire space is reserved for the system administrator. If the hard disk is 95 percent full, then a normal user cannot use any more space.

**NOTE**

You can also use the command mke2fs (which corresponds to mkfs.ext2 and mkfs.ext3) to create an ext2 or ext3 file system (see **man mke2fs**).

**mkreiserfs**   To create a Reiser file system, use the command **mkreiserfs**.

Table 7-12 lists commonly used parameters and options for mkreiserfs.

**Table 7-12**

| Option | Description |
|---|---|
| *number_of_blocks* | This parameter represents the size of the partition in number of blocks. If you do not include this parameter, mkreiserfs automatically determines the numbers of blocks. |
| --format *format* | You can use this option to specify the format of the Reiser file system (**3.5** or **3.6**). |

Other file system types, such as vfat and xfs are created similarily, using mkfs.vfat, mkfs.xfs, etc. The manual pages list the possible options for the respective type.

**NOTE**

The program parted allows you to create partitions with an ext2/3, FAT, or FAT32 file system at one time.

## Check and Repair Any File System (fsck)

The command **fsck** lets you check and optionally repair one or more Linux file systems. Normally, fsck tries to run file systems on different physical disk drives in parallel to reduce total amount time to check all of the file systems.

If you do not specify a file system on the command-line, and the -A option is not included, fsck defaults to checking file systems in /etc/fstab.

After checking, an exit code is returned that lists one or more of the conditions listed in Table 7-13.

**Table 7-13**

| Exit Code | Description |
|-----------|-------------|
| 0 | No errors |
| 1 | File system errors corrected |
| 2 | System should be rebooted |
| 4 | File system errors left uncorrected |
| 8 | Operational error |
| 16 | Usage or syntax error |
| 32 | Fsck canceled by user request |
| 128 | Shared library error |

In reality, fsck is simply a frontend for the various file system checkers (**fsck.fstype**) available in the system. The fsck utility looks for the system-specific checker in /sbin/ first, then in /etc/fs/ and /etc/, and finally in the directories listed in the PATH environment variable.

To check a specific file system, using the following syntax:

**fsck *filesystem***

For example if you want to check the file system on /dev/hda2, enter **fsck /dev/hda2**.

Some options that are available with fsck include **-A** (walk through the /etc/fstab file and try to check all the file systems in one pass), **-N** (don't execute, just show what would be done), and **-V** (verbose output).

## Check and Repair ext2/ext3 and ReiserFS (e2fsck and reiserfsck)

Switching off the Linux system without unmounting partitions (for example, when a power outage occurs) can lead to errors in the file system.

The next time the system is booted, the fact that the computer was not shut down correctly is detected and a file system check is performed.

Depending on the kind of errors found in the file system, the rescue system might need to be used. Depending on the file system type, you use either /sbin/e2fsck or /sbin/reiserfsck.

These tools check the file system for a correct superblock (the block at the beginning of the partition containing information on the structure of the file system), faulty data blocks, or faulty allocation of data blocks.

A possible problem in the ext2 (or ext3) file system is damage to the superblock. You can first view the location of all copies of the superblock in the file system using dumpe2fs.

Then, with e2fsck, you can copy one of the backup copies to the beginning of the file system, as shown in the following:

```
da10:~ # e2fsck -f -b 32768 /dev/hda1
```

In this example, the superblock located at data block 32768 in the ext2 file system of the partition /dev/hda1 is copied to the beginning of the file system.

 **CAUTION**     Normally a backup copy of the superblock is stored every 32,768 blocks.

With reiserfsck, the file system is subjected to a consistency check. The journal is checked to see if certain transactions need to be repeated. With the option **--fix-fixable**, errors such as wrong file sizes are fixed as soon as the file system is checked.

With an error in the binary tree, it is possible to have this rebuilt by entering **reiserfsck --rebuild-tree**.

## Use File System Mount Commands

To understand how to manage mounting (and unmounting) file systems, you need to know the following:

- Mount and Unmount a File System
- View Currently Mounted File Systems: the File /etc/mtab
- Configuration Files for Mounting

### Mount and Unmount a File System

Instead of using separate drive letters to represent different partitions in the file system (like it is done in MS-DOS and Windows® 9*x*), Linux mounts partitions in directories in the file system.

A directory used for this purpose is called a **mount point**.

To mount or unmount a file system, you need to know the following commands:

- mount
- umount

**mount**     To add a new hard disk to a Linux system, first you partition and format the drive. You then create a directory (such as /data/) in the file system and mount the drive in that directory using the command mount.

```
da10:~ #  mount -t ext2 /dev/hdb1 /data
```

Or, for a partition with ReiserFS, enter:

```
da10:~ # mount -t reiserfs /dev/hdb2 /data
```

The mount command can also be run without giving details of the file system type (-t option).

In this case the file system type is automatically detected and the partition is mounted accordingly.

 You can also mount remote file systems that are shared via the Network File System (NFS) to directories you create in your file system.

**NOTE**

The following are some of the options you can use when mounting a file system with the command mount or by entering them in /etc/fstab:

- **remount.** This option causes file systems that are already mounted to be mounted again.

  When you make a change to the options in /etc/fstab, you can use remount instead of rebooting the system to incorporate the changes.

- **rw, ro.** These options indicate whether a file system should be writable (**rw**) or only readable (**ro**).

- **sync, async.** These options set synchronous (**sync**) or asynchronous (**async**) input and output in a file system. The default setting is async.

- **atime, noatime.** These options set whether the access time of a file is updated in the inode (**atime**) or not (**noatime**). The option noatime should improve the performance.

- **nodev, dev.** The **nodev** option prevents device files from being interpreted as such in the file system.

- **noexec, exec.** You can prohibit the execution of programs on a file system with the option **noexec**.

- **nosuid, suid.** The **nosuid** option ensures that the suid and sgid bits in the file system are ignored.

Some options only make sense in the file /etc/fstab. These options include the following:

- **auto, noauto.** File systems set with the option **noauto** in the file /etc/fstab are not mounted automatically when the system is booted. These are usually floppy disk drives or CD-ROM drives.

- **user, nouser.** This option lets users mount the file system. Normally, this is a privilege of the user root.
- **defaults.** This option causes the default options rw, suid, dev, exec, auto, nouser, and async to be used.

The options **noauto** and **user** are usually combined for exchangeable media such as floppy disk or CD-ROM drives.

 **CAUTION**    Removable storage media like USB sticks usually appear in the system as SCSI devices. Enter **tail -f /var/log/messages** as root before plugging in the USB stick. The messages appearing in /var/log/messages will help you know which device to use in the mount command, like **/dev/sda1**.

**7**

**umount**    To unmount the file system, use the command umount:

```
da10:~ # umount /data
```

When you attempt to unmount file systems, Linux will refuse to unmount any partitions that are currently in use.

A common challenge faced by system administrators is figuring out just why a file system they need to unmount is still considered to be busy by the kernel.

The **fuser** utility can help you figure out why the file system is busy by listing all processes accessing a file or directory.

If all else fails, the Linux 2.4 kernel has support for forced unmounts. Entering **umount –f** lets you unmount file systems that the kernel thinks are busy.

This option should be used only as a last resort, because if the kernel thinks the file system is in use, it probably is in use.

## View Currently Mounted File Systems: the File /etc/mtab

You can view the file systems currently mounted in SUSE LINUX by entering the command mount. Information similar to the following appears:

```
da10:~ # mount
/dev/hda2 on / type reiserfs (rw,acl,user_xattr)
proc on /proc type proc (rw)
tmpfs on /dev/shm type tmpfs (rw)
devpts on /dev/pts type devpts (rw,mode=0620,gid=5)
/dev/hdc on /media/cdrom type subfs (ro,nosuid,nodev,fs=cdfss,
procuid, iocharset=utf8)
/dev/fd0 on /media/floppy type subfs (rw,nosuid,nodev,sync,
fs=floppyfss, procuid)
usbfs on /proc/bus/usb type usbfs (rw)
```

This information is stored in the file **/etc/mtab**, which is changed when a file system is mounted or unmounted.

You can also view this information in the file /proc/mounts, which is more accurate, because the file /etc/mtab cannot be updated sometimes; for instance, when the root file system is mounted read-only.

## Configuration Files for Mounting

If you want the file system to be automatically mounted the next time the system boots, a corresponding entry must be made in the file **/etc/fstab**.

The file /etc/fstab specifies which device files are mounted to the file system, with which file system type and with which options, and when the system is booted.

Each line stands for one device file and is divided into six fields, for example:

```
/dev/hdb1   /reallynew          ext2     usrquota,grpquota 1    2
```

The following describes the fields:

- **Field 1 (/dev/hdb1).** Name of the device file.
- **Field 2 (/reallynew).** The mount point (the directory where the file system is to be mounted).

  The directory specified here has to already exist.
- **Field 3 (ext2).** Type of file system (such as ext2 or reiserfs).
- **Field 4 (usrquota,grpquota).** Mounting options.

  Multiple options are separated by commas.

  The option user implies that even normal users (such as tux) are authorized to mount the device file in the Linux system.

  This usually affects the CD-ROM drive (/dev/cdrom) and the floppy disk drive (/dev/fd0).
- **Field 5 (1).** This determines whether the file system will be backed up by the data backup program dump.

  0 stands for do not process.
- **Field 6 (2).** This specifies in which order the file system check (by the fsck program) should run when rebooting:
  - **0.** For file systems that should not be checked.
  - **1.** For root directory.
  - **2.** For all other file systems that can be modified.

  In this file the order is also defined in which individual file systems are mounted (first /var/, then /var/tmp/).

In this example, the first partition of the second IDE hard disk is linked to the directory /reallynew, when the system boots, and can be reached via this path.

The options usrquota,grpquota ensure that these limitations are supported by the file system (quotas must be activated separately, however).

All removable devices are mounted by default to /media/, such as the following:

- A CD-ROM on /dev/cdrom is mounted by default to /media/cdrom.
- A floppy disk on /dev/floppy is mounted by default to /media/floppy.

When using SLES 9 from a desktop environment such as KDE, media such as floppy disks and CDs are automatically mounted and unmounted using the defaults in /etc/fstab and the feature submount/subfs.

subfs is a feature in kernel 2.6.*x*. that allows dynamic mounting and unmounting of removable media. With this feature, it is no longer necessary to manually mount and unmount a CD-ROM like in earlier Linux systems.

The file systems that automatically mount and unmount contain a subfs parameter in /etc/fstab, as in the following:

```
. . .
/dev/cdrom /media/cdrom    subfs    fs=cdfss,ro,procuid,nosuid,nodev,exec,
/dev/fd0   /media/floppy  subfs    fs=floppyfss,procuid,nodev,nosuid,sync
```

After the media is mounted to the directory in the file system, you can access the content on the media by changing to that directory.

The directory /mnt/ is used by default for mounting local and remote file systems manually.

# OBJECTIVE 7   EXECUTE RPM PACKAGE-RELATED OPERATIONS

The software included on the SLES 9 distribution is available in the form of RPM Package Manager (RPM) packages. These packages use the filename extension **.rpm**.

RPM packages to distribute software come in a special binary format. They contain, apart from the executable programs, configuration files and documentation, as well as additional information about the software, like information about dependencies on other packages, for instance, shared libraries.

The distribution also includes source packages, called source RPMs, which have the filename extension .src.rpm (.spm or .srpm are also possible) and contain the source code of the respective software.

When a package is to be installed, the RPM database is checked to see if all dependencies are fulfilled. The package is only installed if this is the case. (Source packages, however, are not included in this database.)

Any missing packages are listed in an error message. The database contains precise details on what packages are installed in which version. In addition, the database lists every file belonging to the packages. The files of the RPM database itself are stored in the directory /var/lib/rpm/.

When you install an RPM package, the executable programs, documentation files, configuration files, and start scripts are copied to the appropriate points in the file system.

To manage software using RPM you need to understand how to *Use the rpm Command*.

# Use the rpm Command

RPM is used to

- Build rpm packages from the source code.
- Manage software packages on the host.

Building packages is usually done by the distributor and is beyond the scope of this course.

To manage software using rpm, you need to know the following:

- Install Software Packages
- Query the rpm Database
- Remove Software Packages
- Verify File Integrity

## Install Software Packages

To install an RPM-package on a host, use the option **-i** (install):

```
da10:~ # rpm -i rsync-2.6.2-8.9.i586.rpm
```

If an earlier version of the package is already installed, you get error messages.

In this case, use the option **-U** (update, installs the package if there is no or an earlier version) or **-F** (freshen, installs the package only if there is an earlier version of it).

The option **-v** (verbose) is used to get more information, and the option **-h** produces a progress bar.

```
da10:~ # rpm -i rsync-2.6.2-8.9.i586.rpm
        file /usr/bin/rsync from install of rsync-2.6.2-8.9
conflicts with file from package rsync-2.6.2-8.6
        file /usr/sbin/rsyncd from install of rsync-2.6.2-8.9
conflicts with file from package rsync-2.6.2-8.6
        file /usr/share/man/man1/rsync.1.gz from install of rsync-2.6.2-8.9
conflicts with file  from package rsync-2.6.2-8.6
```

```
      file /usr/share/man/man5/rsyncd.conf.5.gz from install of rsync-2.6.2-8.9
conflicts with file from package rsync-2.6.2-8.6

da10:~ # rpm -Uvh rsync-2.6.2-8.9.i586.rpm
Preparing...  ######################################## [100%]
   1:rsync    ######################################## [100%]
```

Another error that could occur is that the package you want to install needs other packages to function properly, but they are not installed.

In this case you have to install the missing packages first.

```
da10:~ # rpm -Uvh imlib-1.9.14-180.11.i586.rpm
error: Failed dependencies:
        libpng.so.3 is needed by imlib-1.9.14-180.11
da10:~ # rpm -ivh libpng-1.2.5-182.10.i586.rpm
Preparing...   ######################################## [100%]
   1:libpng     ######################################## [100%]
da10:~ # rpm -Uvh imlib-1.9.14-180.11.i586.rpm
Preparing...   ######################################## [100%]
   1:imlib      ######################################## [100%]
```

You can install software in the RPM format by using YaST or by using the command **rpm**. YaST ensures the automatic resolution of dependencies, while rpm only controls them. Resolution must be performed by hand when using rpm directly.

## Query the rpm Database

Various information about the installed software packages is stored in the rpm database.

Use **rpm –q** to display this information:

- **rpm –qa.** Lists all installed packages.

- **rpm –qi** *package.* Shows information about *package*; for example:
  ```
  da10:~ # rpm -qi howto-2007.3.21-1
  Name       : howto             Relocations: (not relocatable)
  Version    : 2007.3.21            Vendor: SuSE Linux AG, Nuernberg, Germany
  Release    : 1               Build Date: Thurs Mar 22 14:35:05 2007
  Install date: Thurs Apr 5 16:20:55 2007  Build Host: giles.suse.de
  Group      : Documentation/Howto    Source RPM: howto-2007.3.21-1.nosrc.rpm
  Size       : 9101523             License: Unknown, GPL
  Signature  : DSA/SHA1, Thurs Mar 22 14:44:14 2007, Key ID a84edae89c800aca
  Packager   : http://www.suse.de/feedback
  Summary    : Collection of HOWTOs
  Description :
  ```

```
Documentation on many tasks relating to the setup and operation of
Linux software. English version, ASCII format

These documents will be installed in /usr/share/doc/howto. You can read
it with 'less <filename>'.
Distribution: SuSE SLES-9 (i586)
da10:~ #
```

- **rpm -qf** */path/file.* Finds the package which *file* belongs to.

- **rpm -ql** *package.* List the files contained in *package*. Entering **rpm -qpl** */software/package*.**rpm** lists all the files in package.rpm, as shown in the following example:

```
da10:~ # rpm -qpl /media/cdrom/suse/src/samba-3.0.2a-37.
src.rpm
ldapsmb-1.3.tar.bz2
libsmbclient-fixes.diff
nmbstatus
samba-3.0.2a.files.tar.bz2
samba-3.0.2a.tar.bz2
samba-com_err.diff
samba-ia64.diff
samba-s390.diff
samba-vscan-0.3.4.tar.bz2
samba.reg
samba.spec
smbprngenpdf
syscall.diff
da10:~ #
```

## Remove Software Packages

If you uninstall a package, all files except modified configuration files are removed from the system with the help of the RPM database. This ensures a clean uninstall.

To remove software, use the option **-e**:

```
da10:~ # rpm -e rsync
```

If there is no message, the package has been removed successfully.

Packages that are needed by other packages cannot be removed with the -e option only; an error message will tell you what packages need the package you are trying to remove.

Using additional options, like **--nodeps**, a package can be removed anyway, but you should only use this when you are absolutely sure of what you are doing.

## Verify File Integrity

Under certain circumstances, you might want to check if a file has been modified since it was installed.

To do this, use the **-V** option.

Additional options allow you to fine tune the verification.

In the following example, a file has been modified from the apache2 package:

```
da10:~ # rpm -V apache2
S.5....T c /etc/apache2/default-server.conf
```

In this case, a configuration file has been modified, changing the size, md5sum and the modification time.

**NOTE**

See the manual page **man rpm** for additional possible letters instead of the dots in the output and their significance.

If some files have been damaged or modified, you could reinstall the package to correct the error.

However, first find out if more basic correction is needed. If a hacker has modified the file, the whole machine needs to be installed from scratch after forensic analysis. If the file corruption is due to some hardware failure, the hardware needs to be repaired or replaced.

Another matter is the damage of the files of the rpm database itself in /var/lib/rpm/. This could happen, for example, by a loss of power while running rpm. In this case you should back up the files in the directory /var/lib/rpm/ and try to rebuild the database by using

**rpm --rebuilddb**

Table 7-14 gives a brief overview on frequently used options of the command rpm.

**Table 7-14**

| Option | Description |
|---|---|
| --checksig | Makes sure a package is complete and correct (PGP signature check) |
| -e or --erase | Uninstalls a package |
| -F or --freshen | Updates a package only if the package is already installed in an older version |
| --help | Lists options for the rpm command |
| -i or --install | Installs a package |
| -i --force | Installs a package even if rpm says that the package is already installed |
| -i --nodeps | Installs a package regardless of unresolved dependencies |

**Table 7-14**   (continued)

| Option | Description |
|---|---|
| -qa | Lists all installed packages |
| -qf | Displays which package a file belongs to |
| -qi | Gives brief information about the given package |
| -ql | Lists all files that belong to a package |
| -qpl | Lists all files of a package that is not installed |
| -U or --upgrade | Updates a package (in contrast to -f the package is installed even if there is no older version of the package installed) |
| --oldpackage | Installs an older version, even if the newer version is already installed (downgrade) |
| -V or --verify | Compares information about the installed files in the package with information about the files taken from the original package and stored in the rpm database.

Among other things, verifying compares the size, permissions, type, owner, and group of each file. Any discrepancies are displayed. |

A complete summary of all options can be found in the manual page (**man rpm**).

In general, it is simpler to install software in RPM format and, above all, to remove it again cleanly from the system than to use software that is not organized in packages.

The global RPM configuration file of the rpm command is /usr/lib/rpm/rpmrc. However, when the rpm command is updated, all changes to this file are lost.

To prevent the changes from being lost, write your individual configuration to **/etc/rpmrc** (for system configuration) or to a file **~/.rpmrc** (for user configuration). This is mainly relevant when you are building packages yourself.

## Exercise 7-5   Execute RPM Package-Related Operations

The standard tool to install and remove software in SLES 9 is YaST. YaST is a front end to the RPM package manager that is responsible for the actual installation of the software.

The purpose of this exercise is to show you how you can use RPM directly to install and remove software.

To execute RPM package-related operations, do the following:

1. From a terminal window, su to root (**su -**) with a password of **novell**.

2. Insert the **SLES 9 DVD** in your DVD drive.

3. List all files included in the uninstalled package gcal by entering:

   **rpm -qpl /media/dvd/suse/i586/gcal-3.01–581.1.i586.rpm**

4. Install the package gcal by entering:

   **rpm –ihv /media/dvd/suse/i586/gcal-3.01–581.1.i586.rpm**

5. Remove the DVD from your drive.

6. (Conditional) If the DVD drive does not open, enter:

   **umount /media/dvd**

   Then try again.

7. Test the installation of the software package by entering:

   **gcal**

8. List all files included in the installed package gcal by entering:

   **rpm –ql gcal**

9. Remove the package gcal by entering:

   **rpm –e gcal**

10. Verify that the package is no longer installed by entering:

    **rpm –ql gcal**

11. Log out as root by entering:

    **exit**

12. Close the terminal window.

---

# Objective 8    Perform a Standard Software Build from Source

In most cases programs use more than one source code file. In order to structure the source, developers tend to spread the code over multiple files.

It would be very difficult to compile a program with multiple source code files manually on the command-line. Fortunately, some tools are available to manage the compilation process.

In this objective, you learn how to do the following to perform a standard build process:

- Use configure to Prepare the Build Process
- Use make to Compile the Source Code
- Use make install to Install the Compiled Program
- Install the Required Packages for a Build Environment

## Use configure to Prepare the Build Process

Before the actual compilation process can be started, you must prepare the source code with a configure script. This needs to be done for the following reasons:

- Many applications can be compiled on different UNIX systems, Linux distributions, and hardware platforms. To make this possible, the build process needs to be prepared for the actual environment.

- The build process itself is controlled by a program called **make**. The instructions for how to compile the different source files are read from makefiles. The **configure** script generates these makefiles depending on the system environment.

- You can use **configure** to enable or disable certain features of an application.

To run the configure script, you need to use the following command at the top of the source directory:

**./configure**

To enable or disable certain features of an application, configure takes additional arguments. The available arguments depend on the application that will be compiled.

You can use the following command to list all available configure options:

**./configure --help**

## Use make to Compile the Source Code

You use the tool **make** to compile multiple source files in the correct order. Make is controlled by makefiles. Normally, these makefiles are generated by the configure script, but you can also create them manually.

You can also use **make** to install and uninstall the program to or from the right location on the hard disk.

The following is a simple makefile that shows how **make** works:

```
# Makefile for my_name

all: my_name

my_name: my_name.c
   gcc my_name.c -o my_name

install: my_name
   install -m 755 my_name /usr/local/bin/my_name

uninstall: /usr/local/bin/my_name
   rm -f /usr/local/bin/my_name
```

```
clean:
    rm -f my_name
```

This makefile can perform the following tasks:

- Compile the program from source
- Install the program
- Uninstall the program
- Clean up the directory where the compilation is performed

Every makefile consists of targets, dependencies, and commands for the targets. Targets and dependencies are separated by a colon. The commands must be placed under the target, indented with one tab space. A **#** introduces comments.

If you execute the command make while you are in the respective directory, the program make will search this directory for the files GNUMakefile, Makefile, or makefile.

If make is executed without any parameters, the first target of a makefile is used. In the example above, this is all. This target is associated with the target my_name, which specifies the step to take: compile the file my_name.c with gcc.

The command make can also be used with individual targets. For example, the command make install (as root) installs the binary file at the specified location and make uninstall removes the binary file.

Large software projects are created in the same way, but the makefiles are much more extensive and complex. If the software will be compiled to a functional program on multiple architectures, things are even more complicated.

For this reason, the makefile is usually generated by the configure script.

## Use make install to Install the Compiled Program

The last step when installing a program from source is to install the binary file and additional files belonging to the application.

This step is usually done with **make** and an **install** target in the corresponding makefile.

You can perform the installation by using the following command:

**make install**

You must enter this comment as root at the top level of the source directory.

## Install the Required Packages for a Build Environment

A lot of different software packages are required to perform the described build process. The easiest way to install all required packages is to select the selection C/C++ Compiler and Tools in the YaST package manager.

7

To access the predefined selections, select **Selections** from the Filter drop-down list, as shown in Figure 7-8.

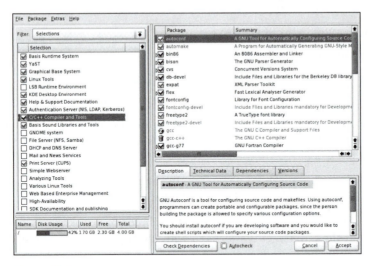

**Figure 7-8**

Selecting **Accept** will install the packages needed for successful software compilations.

---

## OBJECTIVE 9    UNDERSTAND AND CONFIGURE A BOOT MANAGER

To configure a boot manager, you need to know the following:

- What Is a Boot Manager?
- The Boot Manager GRUB
- The GRUB Shell
- The Boot Manager LILO
- The Boot Manager ELILO
- Additional Information

## What Is a Boot Manager?

To boot the system, a program that can boot the respective operating system is needed. This program—the boot loader—loads the operating system kernel which then loads the system.

In SUSE LINUX, this task is handled by the boot manager GRUB (**Gr**and **U**nified **B**ootloader, the default boot manager) or the boot manager LILO (Linux Loader). Almost all known EFI/IA-64 and EFI/IA-32 based systems use the boot manager ELILO.

A boot manager can:

- Boot various operating systems.
- Specify parameters for the kernel.

The general structure of a boot manager is as follows:

- **Stage 1**. The first stage of a boot manager is usually installed in the Master Boot Record (MBR) of the hard disk (first stage boot loader).

  Because the space in the MBR is limited to 446 bytes, this program code merely contains the information for loading the next stage.

  Stage 1 can not only be installed in the MBR but also in the boot sectors of partitions or on a floppy disk.

- **Stage 2**. This stage usually contains the actual boot manager.

  The files of the boot manager are located in the directory /boot/.

## The Boot Manager GRUB

GRUB is the standard boot manager in SLES 9. It features the following characteristics:

- Stage 2 includes file system drivers for ReiserFS, ext2, ext3, Minix, JFS, XFS, FAT, and FFS (BSD). Thus, the boot manager can be used to access files by means of filenames even before the operating system is loaded. For example, this feature is useful for searching for the kernel and loading it if the boot manager configuration is faulty.

- The boot manager GRUB has its own shell that enables the interactive control of the boot manager.

The boot manager GRUB is configured by means of the file /boot/grub/menu.lst.

**CAUTION**

In other Linux distributions, the configuration file for GRUB is now stored as /boot/grub/grub.conf.

The general structure of this file is as follows:

- First, the general options such as the background color of the boot manager menu are listed:

```
color white/blue black/light-gray
```

- This is followed by options for the various operating systems that can be booted with the boot manager. Each entry for an operating system begins with the command title; for example:

```
title linux
    kernel (hd0,0)/boot/vmlinuz root=/dev/hda1
    initrd (hd0,0)/boot/initrd
```

The following example shows a simple configuration file /boot/grub/menu.lst:

```
default 0
timeout 8

title linux
    kernel (hd0,0)/boot/vmlinuz root=/dev/hda1
    initrd (hd0,0)/boot/initrd
```

The following describes the lines:

- **default 0.** The first entry (numbering from 0) is the default boot entry that starts automatically if no other entry is selected with the keyboard.

- **timeout 8.** The default boot entry starts automatically after 8 seconds.

- **title linux.** This is the first entry in the boot menu. By default, this entry is started.

- **kernel (hd0,0)/boot/vmlinuz.** This entry describes the kernel location: first partition of the first hard disk. Please note the following regarding the designations for hard disks and partitions:

  - GRUB does not distinguish between IDE and SCSI hard disks. The hard disk that is recognized by the BIOS as the first hard disk is designated as hd0, the second hard disk as hd1 etc.

  - The first partition on the first hard disk is called hd0,0, the second partition hd0,1, etc.

- **root=/dev/hda1.** root= serves the specification of the root partition. This is followed by other kernel parameters.

- **initrd (hd0,0)/boot/initrd.** Specifies the location of the initial ramdisk (initrd).

Another important file is /etc/grub.conf. It contains information on how and where the components of the GRUB boot manager are supposed to be installed (such as whether GRUB should reside in the MBR or in the partition and so on.).

This file is usually read only when the boot manager is installed.

## The GRUB Shell

As mentioned above, the boot manager GRUB has its own shell. The advantage: if the Linux system does not start due to an error in the boot manager, this built-in shell can be used to boot the system manually.

You can start the GRUB shell in two different ways:

- Start the GRUB Shell in the Running System
- Start the GRUB Shell at the Boot Prompt

## Start the GRUB Shell in the Running System

In order to start the GRUB shell during operation, for example to generate an MD5 hash value for a grub password, enter **grub** as root:

```
GRUB  version 0.94  (640K lower / 3072K upper memory)

 [ Minimal BASH-like line editing is supported.  For the first word, TAB
   lists possible command completions.  Anywhere else TAB lists the
   possible completions of a device/filename. ]

grub>
```

Like in bash, GRUB shell commands can also be completed with the Tab key. In order to find out which partition contains the kernel, use the command find:

```
grub> find /boot/vmlinuz
 hd(0,2)

grub>
```

The kernel (/boot/vmlinuz) is located in the third partition of the first hard disk (hd0,2).

Close the GRUB shell by entering **quit** or pressing **Ctrl+d**.

## Start the GRUB Shell at the Boot Prompt

To start the GRUB shell at the boot prompt, do the following:

1. In the graphical boot selection menu, press **Esc**.

   You will be taken to a text-based menu.

2. Start the GRUB shell (command-line) by pressing **c** (with US keyboard layout).

# The Boot Manager LILO

LILO stands for Linux Loader. As LILO is not the default boot manager of SLES 9.

The LILO boot mechanism consists of the following components:

- The beginning—or first stage—of the LILO code in a boot sector that activates the system boot.
- The heart of the LILO code, located in /boot/boot-menu.b.
- A map file, normally /boot/map, where LILO enters the location of Linux kernels and other data during its installation.
- (Optional) The message file /boot/message, which displays the graphical boot menu from which the operating system can be selected.
- Different Linux kernels and boot sectors.

To understand the boot manager LILO, you need to know the following:

- Confiure LILO
- Understand the Structure of /etc/lilo.conf
- Update after Changing the Configuration
- Error Codes of LILO

## Configure LILO

LILO is a flexible boot manager that offers many ways of adapting a configuration to your needs. LILO is configured in the file /etc/lilo.conf. The most important options within this file are described below.

If you are installing LILO for the first time, use YaST to configure LILO. Fine-tune by editing /etc/lilo.conf later.

We recommend that you keep a backup of the previous lilo.conf file. Your settings only take effect when you run **lilo** after changing /etc/lilo.conf.

## Understand the Structure of /etc/lilo.conf

/etc/lilo.conf starts with a global section followed by one or more system sections for each operating system LILO should start.

A new section is started by a line beginning with either **image** or **other**.

The order of entries in /etc/lilo.conf matters only insofar as the first one in the list is booted by default unless the option **default** is used. A timeout can be set to allow the user to select another entry than the default.

A sample configuration for a computer with both Windows and Linux is shown in the following:

```
### LILO global section
boot = /dev/hda # LILO installation target: MBR
backup = /boot/MBR.hda.990428 # backup file for the old MBR
vga = normal # normal text mode (80x25 chars)
read-only
menu-scheme = Wg:kw:Wg:Wg
lba32 # Use BIOS to ignore
prompt
password = novell
timeout = 80 # Wait at prompt for 8 s before
message = /boot/message # LILO's greeting

### LILO Linux section (default)
image = /boot/vmlinuz # Default
label = linux
root = /dev/hda7 # Root partition for the kernel
initrd = /boot/initrd
```

```
### LILO Linux section (fallback)
image = /boot/vmlinuz.shipped
label = Failsafe
root = /dev/hda7
initrd = /boot/initrd.shipped
optional

### LILO other system section (Windows)
other = /dev/hda1 # Windows partition
label = windows

### LILO memory test section (memtest)
image = /boot/memtest.bin
label = memtest86
```

There is a Linux kernel (**/boot/vmlinuz**) and a fallback kernel (**/boot/vmlinuz.shipped**) and Windows on **/dev/hda1**. The program MemTest86 (**/boot/memtest.bin**) is also available.

Anything between **#** and the end of a line is regarded as a comment. Spaces and comments are ignored by LILO and can be used to improve readability.

The following explains only the mandatory entries:

- **Global section (Parameter part)**

  - **boot=***bootdevice.* The device on whose first sector LILO should be installed. *bootdevice* can be a floppy disk drive (/dev/fd0), a partition (e. g., /dev/hdb3), or an entire disk (such as /dev/hda). The last means installing LILO in the MBR.

    Default: If this option is missing, LILO is installed on the current root partition.

  - **lba32.** Ignore the 1024-cylinder limit of LILO if the BIOS supports this.

  - **prompt.** Forces the LILO prompt to be displayed. The default is no prompt.

    We recommend this if LILO needs to manage more than one system. **timeout** should be set to guarantee booting if nothing is entered at the prompt.

  - **timeout=***tenth-seconds.* Sets a timeout for an operating system to boot. If the user does not select another entry, then the default system is booted.

    Specify the time-out in tenth-seconds (0.1 second increments). Pressing **Shift** or the arrow keys disables the timeout option and LILO waits for orders.

    Default: 80.

- **Linux section**

  - **image=*kernelimage*.** Enter the name of the kernel image to boot, including its directory location.

    With a new system, this is most likely /boot/vmlinuz.

  - **label=*name*.** This name must be unique in /etc/lilo.conf. Otherwise, choose any name for the system (such as Linux).

    Maximum length is 15 characters. Use only letters, numbers, and underscore in names—no blanks or special characters.

    The default is the filename of the kernel image (such as /boot/vmlinuz).

    Use this name to select the system to boot from the menu. If several systems are installed, we recommend you use a message file displaying the possible selections.

  - **root=*rootdevice*.** This gives the kernel the name of the root partition (such as /dev/hda2) of your Linux system.

    We recommend this for security reasons.

    If this option is omitted, the kernel tries to use the root partition that is set in the kernel image.

- **Linux part (Linux – Safe Settings)**

  Even if you installed a customized kernel, you can still boot the SUSE Linux Enterprise Server default kernel.

  - **optional.** If you decide to delete /boot/vmlinuz.shipped (not recommended), this section will be skipped without an error message during LILO installation.

- **Other systems**

  - **other=*partition*.** Tells LILO to load the content of the bootrecord of that partition (such as /dev/hda1).

  - **label=*name*.** Select a name for the operating system. This is recommended, because the default—the raw device name—is not very informative.

- **Memory Test**

  Entry for the memory test program memtest86.

## Update after Changing the Configuration

If any of the LILO components have changed or you have modified your configuration in /etc/lilo.conf, update LILO.

This is easily done by launching the Map Installer **/sbin/lilo** as root.

LILO creates a backup of the target boot sector, writes its first stage into it, and generates a new map file.

LILO issues a report on each installed system, as shown in the following:

```
Added linux *
Added Failsafe
Added windows
Added memtest86
```

When the installation is completed, the machine can be rebooted by entering:

**shutdown -r now**

While rebooting, the BIOS first performs its system test.

Immediately afterward, you see LILO and its command prompt, where you can enter parameters and select a boot image from the recently installed configurations.

Press **Tab** to see a list of all installed systems.

### Error Codes of LILO

If you have problems with the LILO configuration, you can locate the problem at the LILO prompt:

- **L.** First module loaded, but cannot load second stage.
- **LI.** Loading correct. Failed to execute.
- **LIL.** Loading and execution OK. Descriptor table not loaded.
- **LIL?.** Second module loaded at incorrect address.
- **LIL-.** The descriptor table is corrupt.

## The Boot Manager ELILO

ELILO is a boot manager for EFI/IA-64 and EFI/IA-32 based platforms.

ELILO is configured by editing the file /etc/boot/elilo.conf. The syntax is similar to the syntax of LILO.

## Additional Information

Refer to the following sources for additional information on the boot managers GRUB and LILO:

- In electronic form in the Linux system:
  - Manual pages and info files:
    - info grub
    - man grub

- man grub-install

- man grub-md5-crypt

- man lilo

- man 5 lilo.conf

- README files:

  - In the directory /usr/share/doc/packages/grub/

  - In the directory /usr/share/doc/packages/lilo/

- On the Internet:

  - www.gnu.org/software/grub/

## CHAPTER SUMMARY

- User and password information is stored in the /etc/passwd file on older Linux systems. Newer Linux systems store user information in /etc/passwd and password information in /etc/shadow. You can use the **pwck** command to check these files. The **pwconv** and **pwunconv** commands can be used to configure the use of the /etc/shadow file.

- Group information is stored in the /etc/group file on Linux systems.

- You may use the **useradd**, **usermod**, and **userdel** commands to add, modify, and remove user accounts on your system, respectively. Similarly, you may use the **groupadd**, **groupmod**, and **groupdel commands** to add, modify, and remove group accounts on your system, respectively.

- You can change user account passwords using the **passwd** command.

- You set system user limits for system resource usage by using the **ulimit** command. Default limits are stored in the /etc/profile and /etc/security/limits.conf files.

- You can assign read, write, and execute permissions to files and directories. Their effect on files is different than on directories. In addition, there are three special permissions: SUID, SGID, and Sticky bit.

- Permissions can be set on the owner of a file (user), members of the group of the file (group), as well as everyone else on the system (other) using the **chmod** command. Similarly, you can change the owner and group owner for a file using the **chown** and **chgrp** commands.

- New files and directories receive default permissions from the system determined by the umask variable.

- You can use disk quotas on a filesystem to restrict the number of files and directories that individual users can create as well as the amount of disk space users can occupy. Quota entries are made using the **edquota** command. Each quota entry has a hard limit that cannot be exceeded as well as a soft limit that can be exceeded for a period of time.

❏ Different filesystems have different features. As a result, the filesystem type should be selected carefully when planning your physical disk structure.

❏ Journaling filesystems maintains a transaction log that is used to track changes to files and check for filesystem errors. Some common journaling Linux filesystems include Ext3, ReiserFS, JFS, and XFS. Nonjournaling Linux filesystems include Ext2 and VFAT. You can create these filesystems using the **mkfs** and **mkreiserfs** commands.

❏ Each filesystem contains a superblock that stores the structure of the filesystem, an inode section that contains file and directory information, and data blocks for file information. You can use the **fsck** and **reiserfsck** commands to check these areas of the filesystem for errors.

❏ Filesystems on a hard disk must reside in a partition. Each hard disk can contain up to four primary partitions, or three primary partitions and an extended partition that contains logical partitions within. You can create hard disk partitions using the **fdisk** utility in Linux.

❏ The **mount** command may be used to mount filesystems to mount point directories using a variety of options. Similarly, the **umount** command may be used to unmount filesystems. No user can be using the mount point directory when the **mount** and **umount** commands are used. The **fuser** command can be used to list the users that are using a mount point directory.

❏ Linux uses the /etc/fstab to automatically mount media as well as mount media at boot time.

❏ Most software in SLES is in Red Hat Package Manager (RPM) format. You can install, remove, verify, and find information about RPM software packages using the **rpm** command.

❏ Alternatively, you can compile source code into a program. This typically involves running a configuration program to create a makefile script, the **make** command to compile the source code, and the **make install** command to install the compiled program to the correct location on the filesystem.

❏ A boot manager (also called a boot loader) is used to load the Linux kernel at system initialization. The three most common boot managers in Linux are LILO, ELILO, and GRUB. GRUB is the default boot manger in SLES.

# KEY TERMS

**/boot/grub/grub.conf** — The GRUB configuration file in most Linux distributions.

**/boot/grub/menu.lst** — The GRUB configuration file in SLES.

**/etc/default/passwd** — A file that contains default values used when changing passwords such as encryption algorithm.

**/etc/default/useradd** — A file that contains default values used when creating user accounts.

**/etc/fstab** — A file used to store information used to mount filesystems.

**/etc/group** — The file that contains system groups and their members.

**/etc/grub.conf** — The file that contains information about GRUB components.

**/etc/gshadow** — A file that is typically used on older Linux computers. It can contain encrypted group passwords.

**/etc/lilo.conf** — The LILO configuration file.

**/etc/login.defs** — A file that contains default values used when creating user accounts.

**/etc/mtab** — A file that lists currently mounted filesystems.

**/etc/passwd** — The file that contains user account information such as name, UID, primary group, home directory, and shell.

**/etc/security/limits.conf** — A file that lists user resource limits.

**/etc/shadow** — The file that typically contains encrypted passwords and password expiry information for user accounts on the system.

**/etc/shells** — A file that lists valid system shells such as /bin/bash.

**/etc/skel** — A directory that contains files and directories that are copied to all new users' home directories when they are created.

**allocation groups** — Sections of a block within an XFS filesystem.

**aquota.group** — A file that stores group quota information for a filesystem.

**aquota.user** — A file that stores user quota information for a filesystem.

**B+ tree** — A structure used to organize files on a filesystem for fast access.

**block** — The unit of data commonly used by a filesystem.

**boot loader** — See **boot manager**.

**boot manager** — The program used to load and start the operating system kernel at system startup.

**chgrp (change group) command** — Used to change the group owner of a file or directory.

**chkconfig command** — Used to set the startup status of a service in Linux.

**chmod (change mode) command** — Used to change the mode (permissions) of a file or directory.

**chown (change owner) command** — Used to change the owner and group owner of a file or directory.

**dumpe2fs command** — Used to obtain filesystem information from Ext2 and Ext3 filesystems.

**edquota command** — Used to specify quota limits for users and groups.

**Ext2** — The traditional filesystem used on older Linux systems.

**Ext3** — A journaling version of the Ext2 filesystem.

**fdisk command** — Used to create, delete, and modify hard disk partitions.

**filesystem** — A structure used to organize blocks on a device such that they can be used by the operating system to store data.

**fsck command** — Used to check and repair filesystems.

**fuser command** — Used to identify users and processes using a particular file or directory.

**grace period** — The amount of time a user can exceed a quota limit.

**Grand Unified Boot Loader (GRUB)** — The default boot manager in SLES.

**group** — When referring to a long file or directory listing, it represents the group ownership of a file or directory.

**Group Identifier (GID)** — A number that uniquely identifies system groups.

**groupadd command** — Used to add a group to the system.

**groupdel command** — Used to delete a group from the system.

**groupmod command** — Used to modify the name, membership, or GID of a group on the system.

**hard limit** — A quota limit that cannot be exceeded.

**inode** — The section of a file or directory that stores all information about it except the filename.

**JFS** — A journaling filesystem that supports large filesystem sizes.

**journaling** — A filesystem feature that records all filesystem transactions in a small transaction log on the filesystem for tracking and troubleshooting purposes.

**lilo command** — Used to reinstall the LILO boot manager after configuration changes.

**Linux Loader (LILO)** — The traditional boot manager used on Linux systems. The 64-bit version of this boot loader is called ELILO.

**make command** — Used to compile source code into programs according to a makefile.

**make install command** — Used to copy a compiled program to the correct location on the filesystem.

**makefile** — A file created by a configuration script that contains settings used when compiling source code.

**metadata** — The section of a filesystem that is not used to store user data.

**mkfs command** — Used to create most filesystems in Linux.

**mkpasswd command** — Used to create an encrypted password string.

**mkreiserfs command** — Used to create ReiserFS filesystems.

**mount command** — Used to mount filesystems on devices to mount point directories.

**mount point** — A directory to which a device is mounted.

**other** — When referring to a long file or directory listing, it represents all users on the Linux system that are not the owner or a member of the group on the file or directory.

**owner** — The user whose name appears in a long listing of a file or directory and who typically has the most permissions to that file or directory.

**partition** — A physical division of a hard disk drive.

**passwd command** — Used to modify user passwords and expiry information as well as lock and unlock user accounts.

**Pluggable Authentication Modules (PAM)** — A set of components that allow programs to access user account information.

**primary group** — The group specified for a user in the /etc/passwd file that becomes the group owner on newly created files and directories.

**pwck command** — Used to check the validity of the /etc/passwd and /etc/shadow files.

**pwconv command** — Used to enable the use of the /etc/shadow file.

**pwunconv command** — Used to disable the use of the /etc/shadow file.

**quotacheck command** — Used to update the quota database files.

7

**quotaoff command** — Used to deactivate disk quotas.

**quotaon command** — Used to activate disk quotas.

**quotas** — Filesystem usage limits that may be imposed upon users and groups.

**Red Hat Package Manager (RPM)** — A format used to distribute software packages on most Linux systems.

**ReiserFS** — A journaling filesystem that uses B+ tree structures and has fast data access.

**reiserfsck command** — Used to check and repair ReiserFS filesystems.

**repquota command** — Used to produce a report on quotas for a particular filesystem.

**rpm command** — Used to install, remove, and find information on RPM software packages.

**Set Group ID (SGID)** — A special permission set on executable files and directories. When you run an executable program that has the SUID permission set, you become the group owner of the executable file for the duration of the program. On a directory, the SGID sets the group that gets attached to newly created files.

**Set User ID (SUID)** — A special permission set on executable files. When you run an executable program that has the SUID permission set, you become the owner of the executable file for the duration of the program.

**soft limit** — A quota limit that can be exceeded for a certain period of time.

**Sticky bit** — A special permission that is set on directories that prevents users from removing files that they do not own.

**superblock** — The section of a filesystem that stores the filesystem structure.

**ulimit command** — Used to set resource limits for user accounts.

**umask** — A system variable that sets permissions for newly created files.

**umask command** — Used to view and change the system umask.

**umount command** — Used to unmount a device from a mount point directory.

**user** — When referring to a long file or directory listing, it represents the owner of that file or directory.

**User Identifier (UID)** — A number that uniquely identifies each system user account.

**useradd command** — Used to add a user account to the system.

**userdel command** — Used to remove a user account from the system.

**usermod command** — Used to modify the properties of a user account on the system.

**VFAT** — A Linux version of the Microsoft FAT filesystem.

**XFS** — A journaling filesystem that uses allocation groups to manage data.

# REVIEW QUESTIONS

1. Which of the following are always stored in the /etc/passwd file? (Choose all that apply.)

   a. encrypted user passwords

   b. user home directory locations

   c. the default shell that each user uses

   d. primary groups for each user

2. When you check the /etc/shadow file on your system, you notice that the date of the last password change is 12907. What does this number represent?

   a. The number of days since installation of the operating system

   b. December 9$^{th}$ 2007

   c. The number of days since January 1$^{st}$ 1970

   d. February 29$^{th}$ 2001

3. You currently use both /etc/passwd and /etc/shadow files to store user account information. What command can you use to consolidate this information into the /etc/passwd file only? _____

4. Which of the following files could you edit to create groups and add members to those groups?

   a. /etc/passwd

   b. /etc/shadow

   c. /etc/groups

   d. /etc/group

5. Which of the following files are used to obtain default user account settings when you create a user with the **useradd** command? (Choose all that apply.)

   a. /etc/login.defs

   b. /etc/useradd.default

   c. /etc/default/useradd

   d. /etc/skel

6. You have a file called "Policies&Procedures.txt" that you wish to place in the home directories of all newly created user accounts. Where should you place these files? _____

7. What command can you use to add the user **bob** to your system, create a home directory for him, set his primary group to **acctg**, and give his account an expiry date of May 11, 2006? _____

8. After creating the user in Question 7, what must you do to allow the user to log in to the system? _____

9. What command can be used to change the UID of the user in Question 7 to **741**?
_____

10. What two commands below can be used to create the group **acctg** and add the user **bob** to it?

    a. groupadd –p acctg

    b. groupadd acctg

    c. groupmod –A bob acctg

    d. groupmod –A acctg bob

11. Which of the following commands may be used to see the current user resource limits for your system?

    a. ulimit –a

    b. ulimit –view

    c. ulimit –u

    d. ulimit –c

12. Which of the following file permissions gives the group owner the ability to edit the file contents? (Choose all that apply.)

    a. rw–rw–r–x

    b. rw–r–x–r–x

    c. rw–r––r–x

    d. r––rw–r–x

13. Which of the following directory permissions gives the owner the ability to list the contents of the directory? (Choose all that apply.)

    a. rwxr–x–r–x

    b. rwxr––r–x

    c. r–xrw–r–x

    d. –w–rw–r–x

14. What command could you use to change the owner to **bob** and the group owner to **acctg** for the file **/etc/yearend**? _____

15. What command could you use change the permissions on the file **/etc/yearend** to rw–rw–r–– using octal notation? _____

16. What permissions does the system give to new files and directories by default prior to applying the umask?

    a. Files receive 666 and directories receive 666.

    b. Files receive 666 and directories receive 777.

    c. Files receive 777 and directories receive 666.

    d. Files receive 777 and directories receive 777.

17. What will the permission be on a new directory if the umask is set to 027?
    _____

18. Which of the following commands will set the Sticky bit special permission on the directory **/public**?
    a. chmod 1777 /public
    b. chmod 2777 /public
    c. chmod 4777 /public
    d. chmod 7777 /public

19. You have enabled user and group quotas on the filesystem that is mounted to the /var directory. Which files contain the quota limits? (Choose two answers.)
    a. /var/aquota.group
    b. /var/aquota.user
    c. /aquota.group
    d. /aquota.user

20. What command can you use to modify the grace period for quota soft limits?
    _____

21. Which of the following are journaling filesystems that can be created using the **mkfs** command? (Choose all that apply.)
    a. Ext2
    b. Ext3
    c. ReiserFS
    d. JFS

22. How many partitions can be made on a single IDE hard disk using the **fdisk** program?
    a. 3
    b. 4
    c. 15
    d. 64

23. Which option to the **fsck** command would you use to check all filesystems listed in /etc/fstab? _____

24. What command would you use to check a ReiserFS filesystem for errors?
    _____

25. You cannot unmount a filesystem that you had previously mounted to the /mnt directory. What command can show you which users are still using the /mnt directory? _____

26. What command can you use to list the package in the RPM database that the /etc/hosts file belongs to? _____

7

27. You have downloaded the source code for a program that you wish to compile. Which command can you use in the source code directory to create a makefile?

    a. ./configure

    b. make

    c. make file

    d. make install

28. What is the first area on your hard disk that typically contains a Linux boot loader?

    a. MBR

    b. Boot sector on the first partition

    c. Superblock

    d. Inode table

29. Which of the following boot managers contain an interactive shell?

    a. GRUB

    b. LILO

    c. ELILO

    d. All of the above

30. You have modified the /etc/lilo.conf file, but your changes have not taken effect. What command must you run? _____

---

## Discovery Exercises

### Managing User Accounts

Log in to tty1 as the root user and create a user account called **bozo** that has a home directory of **/home/bozo** and a UID of **600**. Next, perform a long listing of all files in /etc/skel (including hidden files). Then perform a long listing of all files in the /home/bozo directory. Why are the lists identical? Who is the owner of the files in /home/bozo?

Next, delete the user **bozo** from the system without removing the home directory. Then perform another long listing of the files in the /home/bozo directory. Who is the owner? Why?

Create a new user called **bozoette** that has a home directory of **/home/bozoette** and a UID of **600**. Perform long listings of all files in the /home/bozoette and /home/bozo directories. Who is the owner and why? How could the steps in this Discovery Exercise be used in real world environments? When finished, log out of tty1.

## Managing User Accounts

Log in to tty1 as the root user and use the **tail** command to view the last ten lines of the /etc/shadow file. How many characters are used to store the password for the geeko user? What algorithm is used? Next, use the **vi** editor to change the line that reads **CRYPT=des** to **CRYPT=blowfish** in the file **/etc/default/passwd**. Following this, use the **passwd** command to change the password for the geeko user and enter the same password that was used previously for the geeko account. Next, use the **tail** command to view the last ten lines of the /etc/shadow file. Can you tell whether a new crypt algorithm was used to store geeko's password?

7

## Changing Groups

Log in to tty1 as the root user and type the **id** command to list the groups that the root user is a member of. How many groups are there? Which one is the primary group? Next, create a new file using the **touch** command and perform a long listing of the file. Who is the group owner of the file? Then run the **newgrp sys** command to temporarily change your primary group for this session to the sys group. Create another new file using the **touch** command and perform a long listing of the file. Who is the group owner of the file now? When finished, log out of tty1.

## Setting File Ownership and Permissions

Log in to tty1 as the root user and perform the following actions in order. For each action, write the command(s) that you used. When finished, log out of tty1.

1.  Create a new file in the root directory called **permtest** and perform a long listing of the file. What are the default permissions assigned to this file and why?

2.  Change your umask to 157, create a new file in the root directory called **permtest2**, and perform a long listing of the file. What are the default permissions assigned to this file and why?

3.  Change the owner of the /permtest file to **geeko** and group owner to **sys**.

4.  Change the permissions on the /permtest file such that the **geeko** user can open and edit it, members of the group **sys** can read and execute it, and everyone else can read it.

5.  Change the permissions on the /permtest2 file such that the user, group, and other have no permissions.

6.  Try to open the /permtest2 file using the **vi** editor, then add a line and save your changes using **:w!** in the **vi** editor. Were you successful? Why?

## Creating Partitions and Filesystems

Provided that you have free space on your hard disk that is not used by a Linux partition, log in to tty1 as the root user and use **fdisk** to create an additional partition and **mkfs** to place the Ext2 filesystem on it. Next, use the **tune2fs** command to convert the Ext2 filesystem to Ext3 (use the manual pages to identify the appropriate option required). Then reformat the partition to use the ReiserFS filesystem, create a /data directory, and add a line to /etc/fstab that will mount the filesystem automatically at boot time to the /data directory. Reboot your computer, log into tty1 as the root user, and verify that the mount was successful. Finally, unmount and check the /data filesystem for errors. When finished, remount the /data filesystem and log out of tty1.

## Installing RPM Software Packages

Use the Internet to find an RPM package that has been compiled for use on SLES (Some common Internet resources include *http://rpmfind.net* and *http://rpm.pbone.com*). Next, use the appropriate command to verify that the package has not already been installed. Then download the RPM package, install it on your system, and use the appropriate commands to view the files installed and version information. When finished, use the appropriate commands to remove the software package from your system.

## Installing Software Packages from Source

Use the Internet to find the source code for a program that you do not have installed on your system. (The best Internet resource for source code is *http://sourceforge.net*.) Next, download the source code tarball, extract the tarball, and use the appropriate commands within the souce code directory to compile and install the program. How can you determine which directory the program was installed in? How can you remove the software from your system?

## Using the GRUB Shell

One of the most useful features of the GRUB boot loader over other boot loaders is its interactive shell, which can run several functions and search files on the filesystem. The GRUB shell can also be run after the Linux kernel has been executed and your system is in full functional mode. Log in to tty1 as the root user and type **grub** to start the GRUB shell. Next, run the **help** command to see a list of commands that are available to you in this shell. Which command can display memory statistics? Execute this command. Next, type **find /boot/vmlinuz** to determine which drive and partition your kernel resides on. Explain the results. Then, type **cat hd(0,0)/boot/grub/menu.lst** to list the contents of the GRUB configuration file. (If your kernel is not on **hd(0,0)**, supply the appropriate hard disk and partition instead.) Finally, run the **quit** command to exit the GRUB shell and log out of tty1.

# PROCESSES, JOBS, AND RUNLEVELS

**This section introduces basic process management, including runlevels and multitasking, in Linux.**

◆ Understand Processes and Jobs

◆ View Processes from the GUI and the Command-Line Interface

◆ Manage Jobs and Processes

◆ Understand Runlevel

◆ Schedule Tasks

## OBJECTIVE 1    UNDERSTAND PROCESSES AND JOBS

To understand processes and jobs, you need to know the following:

- Process Definitions
- Jobs and Processes

## Process Definitions

The following terms are used to describe Linux processes:

- *Program.* A structured set of commands stored in an executable file on a Linux file system. A program can be executed to create a process.
- *Process.* A program that is running in memory and on the CPU.
- *User process.* A process launched by a user that runs from a terminal.
- *Daemon process.* A system process that is not associated with a terminal.

    In a multitasking system, the kernel allocates computer time to individual processes in fractions of a second, one after the other.

    This slows down the processes slightly, but it means that a process does not have to wait until another one is completely finished before it can start or continue running itself.

    In this way, several processes seem to run simultaneously without any noticeable interruption.

Figure 8-1 illustrates the relationship between daemon processes and user processes.

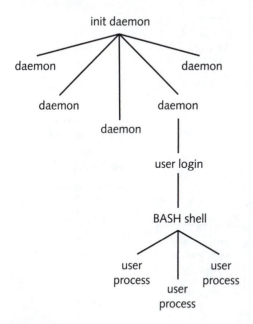

**Figure 8-1**

In this example, during the boot process of a Linux system, the init daemon launches several other daemons (called *daemon processes*), including a daemon for user login.

After the user logs in, she can start a terminal window or virtual terminal with a BASH shell that lets her start user processes manually.

- *Process ID (PID).* A unique identifier assigned to every process as it begins.

- *Child process.* A process that is started by another process (the parent process).

- *Parent process.* A process that starts other processes (child processes).

- *Parent Process ID (PPID).* The PID of the parent process that created the current process.

Figure 8-2 illustrates the relationship between parent and child process ID numbers.

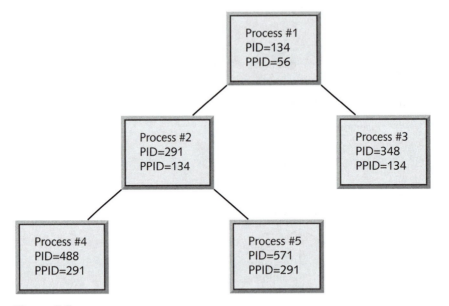

**Figure 8-2**

For example, Process #1 is assigned a PID of 134. This process also launches Process #2 with a PID of 291 and Process #3 with a PID of 348.

Because Process #1 launched Process #2 and Process #3, the second and third processes are considered child processes of Process #1 (the parent process). However, the PPID of Process #2 and #3 is the PID of Process #1–134.

## Jobs and Processes

Each process (no matter how it is started) is identified using a process ID (PID) that is unique across the entire system.

In Linux, you use a job identifier (commonly called a *job ID*) to refer to processes started from an interactive shell. The job identifier is a shell-specific numeric value that identifies programs started from and running within that shell.

Processes started from an interactive shell can be administered through that shell. In bash, the command *jobs* returns all processes that have been started from that shell and run in the background. The shell works as a controlling terminal for these processes.

Processes running in the background (daemons), which are either started automatically when the system is booted or started manually via a start script, cannot, in principle, be influenced by this, because they are not allocated to any controlling terminal.

All jobs have a PID, but not all processes have a usable job ID.

PID 1 always belongs to the init process. This is the first process started on the system and it creates a number of other processes, which in turn can generate additional processes. Each one is assigned a PID of its own.

When the maximum process number has been reached, the next process is allocated the lowest available number (such as PID 7494). Processes run for different lengths of time. After one process has ended, its number again becomes available.

When performing tasks such as changing the priority level of a running program, you use the PID instead of the job ID.

When you want to switch a process from the background to the foreground (and the process was started from a terminal), you use the job ID.

You learn more switching jobs and processes in Objective 3, Manage Jobs and Processes.

8

## OBJECTIVE 2    VIEW PROCESSES FROM THE GUI AND THE COMMAND-LINE INTERFACE

In this objective, you learn how to do the following:

- View Processes from the GUI
- View Processes from the Command-Line Interface

## View Processes from the GUI

To display currently running processes, use KDE System Guard, which can be found in the KDE menu under

**System > Monitor > KDE System Guard**

After the KDE System Guard starts, you can view the system load (the load on the processor and the memory) on the right side of the window. To see the process table, select the **Process Table** tab, as shown in Figure 8-3.

| | | | | | | | | |
|---|---|---|---|---|---|---|---|---|
| Process Table [modified] - KDE System Guard | | | | | | | | _ □ × |
| File  Edit  Settings  Help | | | | | | | | |

| Sensor Browser | Sensor Typ | System Load | Process Table |
|---|---|---|---|

| Name | PID | User% | System% | Nice | VmSize | VmRss |
|---|---|---|---|---|---|---|
| aio/0 | 34 | 0.00 | 0.00 | -10 | 0 | 1 |
| artsd | 26904 | 0.00 | 0.00 | 0 | 9,260 | 6,21 |
| bash | 26819 | 0.00 | 0.00 | 0 | 3,840 | 1,70 |
| cardmgr | 1832 | 0.00 | 0.00 | 0 | 1,524 | 73 |
| cron | 3194 | 0.00 | 0.00 | 0 | 1,584 | 71 |
| cupsd | 2864 | 0.00 | 0.00 | 0 | 6,496 | 3,39 |
| dcopserver | 19214 | 0.00 | 0.00 | 0 | 22,144 | 8,52 |

☐ Tree    All Processes ▾    ⟳ Refresh    Kill

| 91 Processes | Memory: 405,120 KB used, 631,628 KB free | Swap: 0 KB used, 1,048,312 KB free |
|---|---|---|

**Figure 8-3**

The information in Table 8-1 is displayed in columns in the Process table.

**Table 8-1**

| Column | Description |
|---|---|
| Name | Name of the process |
| PID | Number of the process (process ID) |
| User% | Processor load caused by the process |
| System% | Processor load caused by system processes required for the process |
| Nice | Priority of the process when allocated computer time by the kernel |
| VmSize | Virtual size of the process |
| VmRSS | Actual memory occupied |
| Login | Login name of the owner |
| Command | The start command for this process |

By default, the list is sorted by the name of the process. By selecting the head of a column, you can sort the list according to that column.

To end a process, select the corresponding line and then select **Kill**.

CAUTION

Every user (except for the system administrator root) can kill only his own processes.

## View Processes from the Command-Line Interface

To view processes, you can use the following programs:

- ps
- pstree
- lsof
- top

### ps

To see running processes, use the command **ps** (process status), as in the following:

```
tux@da10:~> ps
 PID  TTY     TIME CMD
 1301 tty2  00:00:00 -bash
 1349 tty2  00:00:00 ps
tux@da10:~>
```

If you include the option **x**, terminal-independent processes are also shown, as in the following (the 1344 process):

```
tux@da10:~> ps x
 PID  TTY   STAT TIME COMMAND
 1301 tty2    R  0:00 -bash
 1344  ?      S  0:00 sleep 99
 1348 tty2    R  0:00 ps x
tux@da10:~>
```

**NOTE**     The command **ps** uses options with and without a hyphen (-).

Table 8-2 lists ps command options.

**Table 8-2**

| Option | Description |
|--------|-------------|
| x | Lists terminal-independent processes |
| a | Lists all terminal-independent processes, including those of other users |
| w | (Wrap) Provides detailed output; long lines are not truncated, but spread over several lines |
| l | (Long) Provides more information about processes |
| u | (User) Lists processes ordered according to their owners |
| f | Lists processes hierarchically (in the form of a tree) |

8

For example, entering **ps axl** displays information similar to the following:

```
tux@da10:~> ps axl
  F   UID   PID  PPID  PRI NI   VSZ  RSS  WCHAN STAT TTY    TIME COMMAND
000 10376 1800 10035  11   0  5488 3512 do_sel S   ?      0:00 xterm
000 10376 1801 1672   14   0  2716 1532  wait4 S   pts/2  0:00 bash
000 10376 1859 1672    9   0  1452  500 nanosl S   pts/2  0:00 sleep 99
000 10376 1860 1858   17   0  2892 1924        - R pts/2  0:00 ps axl
```

However, entering **ps aux** displays the following:

```
tux@da10:~> ps aux
USER   PID %CPU %MEM VSZ  RSS   TTY   STAT START  TIME COMMAND
tux   1800 0.0   1.3 5488 3512 ?      S   14:35  0:00 xterm
tux   1801 0.0   0.6 2716 1532 pts/2  S   14:35  0:00 bash
tux   1859 0.0   0.1 1452  500 pts/2  S   14:43  0:00 sleep 99
tux   1860 0.0   0.6 2584 1652 pts/2  R   14:44  0:00 ps aux
```

The essential difference between these examples is that with option **l**, you see the PID of the parent process (PPID), the process priority (PRI), and the nice value (NI) of the individual processes. With the option **u**, you see the load percentage (%CPU, %MEM).

You can include formatting instructions with ps to present a customized display of the information, as in the following:

```
tux@da10:~ > ps ax --format "cputime %C, nice %n, name %c"
cputime %CPU, nice NI, name COMMAND
cputime  0.0, nice  0, name bash
cputime  0.0, nice  0, name sleep
cputime  0.0, nice  0, name ps
```

You can see a detailed summary of how to use ps by entering:

**man ps**

The output of ps includes the information in Table 8-3.

**Table 8-3**

| Column | Description |
|--------|-------------|
| UID | User ID |
| PID | Process ID |
| PPID | Parent process ID |
| TTY | Number of the controlling terminal |
| PRI | Priority; the lower it is, the more computer time is allocated to the process |
| NI | (Nice) Influences the dynamic priority adjustment |

**Table 8-3**   (continued)

| Column | Description |
|---|---|
| SIZE | Overall memory usage of the program |
| STAT | Current process status |
| TIME | Computer time used |
| COMMAND | Name of the command |

The process state in the STAT column uses the codes listed in Table 8-4.

**Table 8-4**

| Code | Description |
|---|---|
| R | (Runnable) Process can be run. |
| S | (Sleeping) Process is waiting for an external event (such as data arriving). |
| D | (Uninterruptable sleep) Comparable to S. The process cannot be terminated at the moment. |
| T | (Traced or stopped) Process is suspended. |
| x | Process is dead. |
| Z | (Zombie) Process has terminated itself, but its return value has not yet been requested. |

## pstree

You can use the command **pstree** to display a list of processes in the form of a tree structure. This gives an overview of the hierarchy of a process. To end a series of processes, find the appropriate parent process in the tree and end that instead.

You can use the option **–p** to display the PID of the processes, and the option **–u** to display the user ID (if the owner has changed).

Because the list of processes is often long, we recommended using **less** to display information, as in the following:

**pstree –up | less**

## lsof

You can use the command **lsof** (/usr/bin/lsof; list open files) to see which files are opened by processes.

You can view a description of the command and possible options by entering **man lsof**.

## top

You can use the command **top** to find out how much computing time processes use, as shown in the following:

```
top - 16:21:13 up 7 days, 1:11, 3 users, load average: 0.01, 0.03, 0.00
Tasks: 49 total,  1 running, 47 sleeping,  1 stopped,  0 zombie
Cpu(s): 0.7% us, 0.3% sy, 0.0% ni, 98.3% id, 0.7% wa, 0.0% hi, 0.0% si
Mem:  126508k total,  112568k used,  13940k free,  8452k buffers
Swap: 265064k total,   3252k used,  261812k free,  46820k cached

  PID  USER  PR  NI VIRT RES  SHR  S %CPU %MEM   TIME+  COMMAND
11677   tux  17   0 1760 900 1544  R  0.3  0.7  0:00.13 top
    1  root  16   0  588 108  444  S  0.0  0.1  0:09.62 init
    2  root  34  19    0   0    0  S  0.0  0.0  0:00.04 ksoftirqd/0
    3  root   5 -10    0   0    0  S  0.0  0.0  0:01.01 events/0
    4  root   5 -10    0   0    0  S  0.0  0.0  0:00.23 kblockd/0
   25  root  15   0    0   0    0  S  0.0  0.0  0:00.00 kapmd
   27  root   5 -10    0   0    0  S  0.0  0.0  0:02.67 pdflush
   30  root  15 -10    0   0    0  S  0.0  0.0  0:00.00 aio/0
   29  root  15   0    0   0    0  S  0.0  0.0  0:02.94 kswapd0
  177  root  25   0    0   0    0  S  0.0  0.0  0:00.00 kseriod
  216  root  20   0    0   0    0  S  0.0  0.0  0:00.00 scsi_eh_0
  217  root  15   0    0   0    0  S  0.0  0.0  0:00.00 ahc_dv_0
  242  root   5 -10    0   0    0  S  0.0  0.0  0:03.13 reiserfs/0
  491  root   6 -10    0   0    0  S  0.0  0.0  0:00.00 kcopyd/0
17689  root  15   0    0   0    0  S  0.0  0.0  0:00.00 khubd
18025  root  16   0 1524 676 1348  S  0.0  0.5  0:00.08 syslogd
...
```

The command top displays a list of the running processes, sorted by computing time. The display is updated every three seconds. You can terminate top by typing **q**.

Table 8-5 describes the default columns.

**Table 8-5**

| Command | Description |
|---------|-------------|
| **PID** | Process ID |
| **USER** | User name |
| **PR** | Priority |
| **NI** | Nice value |
| **VIRT** | Virtual image (in KB) |
| **RES** | Resident size (in KB) |
| **SHR** | Shared memory size (in KB) |
| **S** | Process status |
| **%CPU** | CPU usage |

**Table 8-5**   (continued)

| Command | Description |
|---------|-------------|
| %MEM | Memory usage (RES) |
| TIME+ | CPU time |
| COMMAND | Command name/line |

You can view the process management commands available in top by entering **?** or **h**.

Table 8-6 lists the following are some of the more commonly used commands.

**Table 8-6**

| Command | Description |
|---------|-------------|
| r | Assign a new nice value to a running process. |
| k | Send a running process a signal. |
| N | Sort by process ID. |
| P | Sort by CPU load. |

**8**

---

## OBJECTIVE 3   MANAGE JOBS AND PROCESSES

To control jobs and processes, you have to understand how to

- Control Jobs from the Shell
- Control Processes

## Control Jobs from the Shell

Commands in a shell can be started in the foreground or in the background. If you start a process in the background, the shell is available for further input of commands. Processes in the foreground can receive transmitted signals directly.

For example, to start xeyes in the foreground, enter:

```
tux@da10:~> xeyes
```

Entering further commands in the same shell is not possible.

To stop a process (such as xeyes), press **Ctrl+z**.

The following is displayed:

```
[1]+ Stopped          xeyes
tux@da10:~>
```

To continue operating a stopped program in the background, enter **bg**.

In the following, the stopped program xeyes begins running in the background by entering bg:

```
tux@da10:~> bg
[1]+ xeyes &
tux@da10:~>
```

In this example, the ampersand character **&** in the output mean that the process is now running in the background.

Append an ampersand character to a command to start it in the background directly, as in the following:

```
tux@da10:~> xeyes &
[2] 10982
tux@da10:~>
```

While the process is running in the background, you are returned to the shell prompt to continue entering commands. Notice that both the job ID (2) and the PID of the program (10982) are returned.

 Processes that require input within the terminal can be moved to the background as well, but when input is requested, the process will be suspended until it is brought to the foreground and the requested input is provided.

**CAUTION**

Each process started from the shell is assigned a job ID by the job control of the shell. The command **jobs** lists the contents of job control, as in the following:

```
tux@da10:~> jobs
[1]+ Stopped          xeyes
[2]  Running          xeyes &
[4]- Running          sleep 99 &
tux@da10:~>
```

In this example, the process with job ID 3 is already terminated. Processes 2 and 4 are running in the background (indicated by a trailing ampersand (&) character).

Notice that Process 1 is stopped. The next process started in the background will be assigned the job ID 5 (the highest current number +1). Gaps are not filled.

Besides using **bg** to restart a stopped process and switch it to the background, you can switch a process running in the background to the foreground by using the command **fg** with the job ID, as in the following:

```
tux@da10:~> fg 1
xeyes
```

The shell also informs you about the termination of a process running in the background:

```
[4]- Done            sleep 99
```

In this example, the job ID is displayed in brackets.

*Done* means the process terminated properly.

*Terminated* would indicate that the process was asked to terminate instead.

*Killed* would indicate a forceful termination of the process.

# Control Processes

To control processes, you have to know how to:

- Control Processes Using Signals
- Prioritize Processes
- Manage a Daemon Process

8

## Control Processes Using Signals

Processes can be controlled by signals.

If a process has no connection to a controlling terminal, it cannot be influenced by keyboard signals.

Externally generated signals are needed to terminate it.

Such signals are generated by the commands **kill** and **killall**.

**NOTE**

System processes that start automatically when the system boots are examples of processes that are not controlled from a terminal.

A process can do one of the following when it receives a signal:

- Capture the signal and react to it (if it has a corresponding function available). For example, an editor can close a file properly before it is terminated.

    *or*

- Ignore the signal if no function exists for handling that signal.

However, the process does not have control over the following two signals as they are handled by the kernel:

- **kill –SIGKILL** or **kill –9**
- **kill –STOP** or **kill –19**

These signals cause the process to end immediately (**SIGKILL**) or to be stopped (**STOP**).

**NOTE**    To see a list of all available signals, enter **kill -l** (list).

Table 8-7 lists the more commonly used signals.

**Table 8-7**

| Number | Name | Description |
|--------|------|-------------|
| 1 | SIGHUP | Reload the configuration file. |
| 2 | SIGINT | Interrupt the process from the keyboard (**Ctrl+C**). |
| 9 | SIGKILL | Kill the process. |
| 15 | SIGTERM | End the process immediately (terminate the process in a controlled manner so clean-up is possible). |
| 18 | SIGCONT | Continue the process stopped with STOP. |
| 19 | STOP | Stop the process (this is also the signal sent by the shell when pressing **Ctrl + z**). |

For the kernel to forward the signal to the process, it must be sent by the owner of the process or by root. By default (without options), kill and killall send signal 15 (SIGTERM).

The command kill requires the PID of the process (use ps or top to find the PID). The command killall needs the command name of the process. The signal to end the process can also be sent in top (using **k**).

For example, if you enter **xeyes** at the command line to start the xeyes program and the PID is 18734, enter:

**kill 18734**

*or*

**killall xeyes**

to end the process.

The following is the recommended way to end an unwanted process:

Send SIGTERM by entering one of the following:

- **kill –SIGTERM** *PID*

  *or*

- **kill –15** *PID*

  *or*

- **kill** *PID*

You can use killall instead of kill and the command name of the process instead of the PID.

Wait a few moments for the process to be cleaned up.

If the process is still there, send a SIGKILL signal by entering one of the following:

- **kill -SIGKILL** *PID*

 *or*

- **kill -9** *PID*

 You can use killall and the command name of the process instead of kill and the PID.

 If a process has been started from the bash shell, you can also use the job ID instead of the process number (such as **kill %4**).

## Exercise 8-1    Control Processes from the GUI and the Command Line Interface

In case the system seems to react sluggishly it is helpful to be able to find out what the likely cause of this might be. There are various commands available for this purpose, graphical as well as based on the command line.

The purpose of this exercise is to familiarize you with some of the available tools.

To control processes from the GUI and the command line interface, do the following:

1. Start KDE System Guard from the KDE menu by selecting:

 **System > Monitor > KDE System Guard**

2. Display the process table by selecting the **Process Table** tab.

3. Change the order of the process list by selecting the **System%** column heading.

 The processes that require the most processor load are now at the bottom of the list.

4. Scroll to the bottom of the list.

5. Open a terminal window.

6. Position the KDE System Guard window and the terminal window so you can view the entire Process Table.

7. In the terminal window, enter:

 **find / -name novell**

 Notice that the processes with the names **konsole** and **find** move to the bottom of the list.

**NOTE**

You might need to repeat the find command more than once for the processes konsole and find to move to the bottom of the list.

8.  From the process table, select the **Name** column heading; then find and select the **Konsole** line.

9.  Select **Kill**.

10. Confirm that you want to kill the process by selecting **Kill**.

    The Konsole terminal window disappears.

11. Close the KDE System Guard window.

12. Open a terminal window.

13. Start the program xeyes by entering **xeyes**.

14. Stop the process by pressing **Ctrl + z**.

15. Move the xeyes process into the background by entering **bg**.

16. Verify that the process is running by entering **jobs**.

17. Kill xeyes by entering:

    **killall xeyes**

18. Display all running processes by entering:

    **ps aux | less**

19. Scroll through the output by pressing **Down-Arrow** and **Up-Arrow**.

20. Return to the command line by typing **q**.

21. Close the terminal window by entering **exit**.

## Prioritize Processes

You can assign priorities to processes by using the following tools:

- nice and renice
- top

## nice and renice

Linux tries to distribute the available computing time equitably to all processes. However, you might want to assign a process more or less computing time.

You can do this with the command nice, as in the following:

**nice -n +5 sleep 99**

This command assigns a process a specific nice value that affects the calculation of the process priority (which is increased or decreased). If you do not enter a nice value, the process is started with the value +10.

The NI column in the top list (see top) contains the nice value of the process. The default value 0 is regarded as neutral. You can assign the nice level using a numeric value of –20 to 19.

The lower the value of the nice level, the higher the priority of the process. A process with a nice level of –20 runs at the highest priority; a process with a nice level of 19 runs at the lowest priority.

The nice level is used by the scheduler to determine how frequently to service a running process.

Only root can start a process with a negative nice value (such as **nice -n –3 sleep 99**). If a normal user attempts to do this, an error message is returned.

You can use the command renice to change the nice value of a running process, increasing or reducing its priority, such as

**renice 5 1712**

In this example, the command assigns the process with the PID 1712 the new nice value 5. This can also be done in top by entering **r**.

Only root can reduce the nice value of a running process (such as from 10 to 9 or from 3 to –2). All other users can only increase the nice value (such as from 10 to 11).

For example, if the user geeko attempts to assign a process that currently has a nice value of 3 to a new nice value of 1, a Permission Denied message is returned.

## top

The top command combines the functionality of the command ps and the command renice in a single utility that provides a real-time view of a running system.

The information displayed in top can be filtered by a specific user and can be sorted on any displayed field. By typing **r**, you can adjust the priority of a process, if you have sufficient privileges to do so.

**CAUTION**

As with the command renice, the same restrictions apply when changing process nice levels using top. Non-root users can lower the nice level, but they cannot raise it.

## Manage a Daemon Process

On a Linux system, the terms *process* and *service* are used to describe different kinds of software that run on the system.

A *service*, also called a ***daemon*** (disk and execution monitor), is a process or collection of processes that wait for an external event to trigger an action on the part of the program.

Daemons make a number of services available. Examples of common services are cron, atd, the Apache Web Server, the OpenLDAP server, and xinetd.

Daemons run in the background and are usually started when the system is booted. For this reason, daemons are terminal-independent processes, and are indicated in the **ps x** TTY column by a question mark (?).

In most cases, you can recognize a daemon by the ending "d" (such as syslogd or sshd). However, there are also a number of services where this is not the case (such as cron or portmap).

Two types of daemons are available:

- **Signal-controlled daemons.** These are always activated when a corresponding task exists (such as cupsd).

- **Interval-controlled daemons.** These are always activated at certain intervals (such as cron or atd).

For each daemon, there is a script in /etc/init.d/. Each script can be controlled and run with the parameters shown in Table 8-8.

**Table 8-8**

| Parameter | Description |
|---|---|
| start | Starts the service |
| stop | Stops the service |
| reload (or restart) | Reloads the configuration file of the service, or stops the service and starts it again |

For many scripts, there is a symbolic link in the directory /usr/sbin/ or in the directory /sbin/, such as the following:

```
da10:~ # ls -l /usr/sbin/rcsshd
lrwxrwxrwx  1 root root 16 Jul 16 17:26 /usr/sbin/rcsshd ->
/etc/init.d/sshd
```

You can start the service from the directory /etc/init.d/ (such as **/etc/init.d/sshd start**).

If a link exists in the /usr/sbin/ or /sbin/, you can use rc*service* (such as **rcsshd start**).

You can find configuration files for daemons in the directory /etc/ or in a subdirectory of /etc/.

The executable programs (the actual daemons) are located either in the directory /sbin/ or in the directory /usr/sbin/.

For more information on most daemons, see /usr/share/doc/packages/.

Some important daemons include the following:

- **cron.** Starts other processes at specified times.

  System-wide files are /etc/crontab and files in the directories /etc/cron.*.

  User-specific files are in /var/spool/cron/tabs/.

- **cupsd.** The printing daemon.

  When the system is booted, printing is started by the script /etc/init.d/cups.

- **httpd.** The daemon of the Apache2 Web server.

  The start script is /etc/init.d/apache2.

  The configuration files are in /etc/apache2/.

  The main configuration file is /etc/apache2/httpd.conf.

  The log files are in /var/log/apache2/.

- **sshd.** Enables secure communication within insecure networks (secure shell).

  The start script is /etc/init.d/sshd.

- **syslogd.** Logs system messages in the directory /var/log/.

  The start script is /etc/init.d/syslog.

  The configuration file is /etc/syslog.conf.

## Exercise 8-2   Manage Linux Processes and Services

Processes can run with different priorities, leaving more (or less) resources for other processes. And, independently from their priority, processes can run in the foreground or in the background.

The purpose of this exercise is to show you how you can influence the priorities of different processes.

In this exercise, you do the following:

- Part I: Move Processes to the Background
- Part II: Modify Process Priorities

### Part I: Move Processes to the Background

Do the following:

1. Make sure you are logged in as **geeko** on the KDE desktop.

2. Open a terminal window.

3. From the command line, display the processes that are currently owned by geeko by entering:

   **ps -lU geeko**

4. Display the processes that are currently owned by root by entering:

   **ps -lU root**

5. Start the program Xosview by entering **xosview**.

   The terminal is not available to receive new commands (no command is line displayed) because the Xosview program is running in the foreground.

6. Select the **Konsole** window to activate it.

7. Suspend the Xosview program by pressing **Ctl + z**.

   The data is no longer being updated in Xosview.

8. View the job in the background by entering **jobs**.

9. View the Xosview process running from the current terminal by entering **ps -l**.

   The process shows a status of T, which means that it is being traced or stopped.

10. Resume the Xosview program, running it in the background by entering **bg % 1**.

    The program Xosview is running again (notice the data being updated).

    Because it is running in the background, you can use the terminal window to enter other commands.

11. Verify that the job status is running by entering **jobs**.

12. View the Xosview branch in the process tree by entering:

    **pstree -p | grep xosview**

    Xosview is listed as part of the tree.

13. Bring the Xosview process into the foreground by entering:

    **fg %1**

14. Close the terminal window.

    The Xosview program ends as well.

15. Open a new terminal window.

16. Start Xosview in the background so that it runs when the terminal window closes by entering:

    **nohup xosview&**

17. Close the terminal window.

    The Xosview program is still running.

18. Open a new terminal window.

19. Start the top program by entering **top**.

20. View only the processes started by geeko by typing **u**; then enter **geeko**.

21. Check for the Xosview program (**xosview.bin**) listed in top.

22. (Conditional) If you cannot find the Xosview program, try maximizing the Konsole window.

23. Record the PID of the Xosview process:

24. Exit top by typing **q**.

25. View information about the Xosview process by entering:

    **ps *PID_of_xosview_process***

26. Stop the Xosview program and check the status by entering the following commands:

    **kill *PID_of_xosview_process***

    **ps aux | grep xosview**

27. Start the program xeyes in the background by entering:

    **xeyes&**

28. Kill the program xeyes by entering:

    **killall xeyes**

## Part II: Modify Process Priorities

Do the following:

1. Start the program Xosview in the background by entering:

   **xosview&**

2. Record the PID for Xosview (displayed in the terminal window):

3. View the process running by entering **ps lf**.

   Notice that the nice value (NI) is currently 0.

4. Increase the priority of the process to a nice value of –5 by entering:

   **renice –5 -p** *PID_of_xosview_process*

   A regular user cannot change the nice value below 0, only 0–20.

5. Su to root (**su -**) with a password of **novell**.

6. Try setting the nice value to –5 again by entering:

   **renice –5 -p** *PID_of_xosview_process*

7. Check that the setting is effective by entering **ps lf**.

   The process is not displayed because ps lf only displays processes started by the current user. The program Xosview was started by geeko, not root.

8. View all processes by entering **ps alf**.

   The Xosview process is now displayed.

9. Change the nice value for the Xosview process to a higher priority by entering:

   **renice –10 -p** *PID_of_xosview_process*

10. Verify that the Xosview process nice value is set to –10 by entering **ps alf**.

11. Exit the shell running as root by entering **exit**.

   You should now be user geeko again.

12. Start the program xeyes in the background with the nice value of +10 by entering:

   **nice xeyes&**

13. Verify that the xeyes process nice value is set to +10 by entering:

   **ps lf**

14. Kill the xosview and xeyes processes by entering the following commands:

   **kill** *PID_of_xosview_process*

   **killall xeyes**

---

## OBJECTIVE 4    UNDERSTAND RUNLEVEL

In this objective, you learn the following about runlevels:

- The init Program
- The Runlevels
- init Configuration File (/etc/inittab)
- init Directories and Scripts

## The init Program

The system is initialized by **/sbin/init**, which is started by the kernel as the first process of the system.

This process, or one of its child processes, starts all additional processes. In addition, because **init** is the last process running, it ensures that all other processes are correctly ended. This means that init controls the booting up and shutting down of the system.

Because of this position of priority, signal 9 (SIGKILL), with which all processes can normally be ended, has no effect on init.

The main configuration file of init is **/etc/inittab**. This file determines what happens in the individual runlevels. Various scripts are started by init, depending on these entries. In SLES 9, all these scripts are located in the directory /etc/init.d/.

In other Linux distributions, the init scripts are found in /etc/rc.d/init.d/.

Also, in other Linux distributions, the file /etc/rc.d/rc.local script (or some equivalent script) is run by the init command at boot time, or when changing runlevels, after all other initialization is complete. You can use this file to add additional commands necessary for your environment. For instance, you can start additional daemons or initialize a printer.

## The Runlevels

You need to understand the following:

- Runlevel Basics
- Change the Runlevel at Boot
- Manage Runlevels from the Command Line
- Shut down or Halt the System

### Runlevel Basics

In Linux, the runlevel defines the state of the system. The entry **initdefault** in the file /etc/inittab defines which runlevel is normally used by the system. (initdef is explained in detail in *init* Configuration File (/etc/inittab))

Table 8-9 shows the available runlevels.

**Table 8-9**

| Command | Description |
|---------|-------------|
| 0 | Halt |
| 1 | Single-user mode (no login for normal users, only root can log in on one local console) |
| 2 | Multiuser mode without network server services |
| 3 | Multiuser mode with network |

**Table 8-9**   (continued)

| Command | Description |
|---------|-------------|
| 4 | Not used |
| 5 | Multiuser mode with network and display manager |
| 6 | Reboot |

You can change a runlevel by entering:

**init** *runlevel*

The command **runlevel** displays the runlevel you are currently in (second number) and the previous runlevel (first number), as in the following:

```
da10:~ # runlevel
N 5
da10:~ #
```

## Change the Runlevel at Boot

The default runlevel is normally 3 or 5. However, you can boot to another runlevel. By default, the boot manager GRUB offers the following choices at system startup:

- Linux
- Floppy
- Failsafe

When you select one of these, the respective options are displayed in the Boot Options field. For example, an option for Linux might be **root=/dev/hdx,** which tells the kernel the location of the root partition of the system.

The option **vga=x**, which indicates the resolution for the frame buffer device, is often specified. At this point, the runlevel to which the system should boot can be added. This parameter is passed to init.

The following is an example entry in boot options:

```
root=/dev/hda4 vga=791 1
```

In this example, the root partition parameter of /dev/hda4 is sent to the kernel. The frame buffer is configured (vga=791), and the system boots to runlevel 1 (single user mode for administration).

## Manage Runlevels from the Command Line

After the system boots, you can switch to another runlevel by using the command **init**, as in the following:

**init 3**

In the same way, you can change back to the standard runlevel (such as **init 5**), in which all programs needed for operation are run and where individual users can log in to the system.

If the partition /usr of a system is mounted through NFS, you should not use runlevel 2 because NFS file systems are not available in this runlevel.

Many servers operate without a graphical user interface and must be booted in a runlevel without X windows (such as runlevel 3).

Runlevels are useful if you encounter problems caused by a particular service (X or network) in a higher runlevel. In this case, you can switch the system to a lower runlevel to repair the service.

If the graphical user interface freezes at any time, press **Ctrl + Alt + Backspace** to restart the X Window System.

**8**

You can also restart the X Window System by switching to a text console (press **Ctrl + Alt + F1**), logging in as root, and using the command **init 3** to switch to runlevel 3.

When the keyboard is nonfunctional, you must see a remote login to enter **init 3**.

This shuts down your X Window System, leaving you with a text console. To restart the graphical system, enter **init 5**.

## Shut down or Halt the System

Like most operating systems, Linux reacts sensitively to being switched off without warning. If this happens, the file systems need to be checked and corrected before the system can be used again.

For this reason, the system should always be shut down properly. With the appropriate hardware, Linux can also power off the machine as the last stage of shutting down.

You can shutdown the system by entering the following:

**init 0**

You can reboot (restart) the system by entering the following:

**init 6**

Although you can halt the system by changing to runlevel 0 and restarting in runlevel 6, Table 8-10 provides some other useful commands for properly shutting down the system or restarting it.

**Table 8-10**

| Command | Description |
|---|---|
| halt | This command ensures an immediate, controlled system halt. All processes are stopped and the system no longer reacts to any input.<br><br>You can now switch off the computer, if it is not configured to switch off automatically. |
| poweroff | This command has the same effect as halt, except that the machine is switched off automatically (if the hardware allows it). |
| reboot | This command reboots the system. |
| shutdown -h *time* | This command shuts down the system after the specified *time*: +m (number of minutes from now), hh:mm (time in hours: minutes, when Linux should shut down), and now (system is stopped immediately).<br><br>If you use the option -r instead of -h, the system is rebooted (runlevel 6). Without options, it changes to runlevel 1 (single user mode). |

The command shutdown shuts down the system in a special way, compared with the other stop commands. The command informs all users that the system will be shut down and does not allow other users to log in before it shuts down.

The command shutdown can also be used with a warning message, such as the following:

**shutdown +5 The new hard drive has arrived**

If a shutdown scheduled for a later time should not be carried out after all, you can revoke the shutdown by entering:

**shutdown -c**

You can change the standard runlevel (defined in /etc/inittab in the line initdefault) with the YaST Runlevel Editor (select **yast2** > **System** > **Runlevel Editor** > **Expert Mode**):

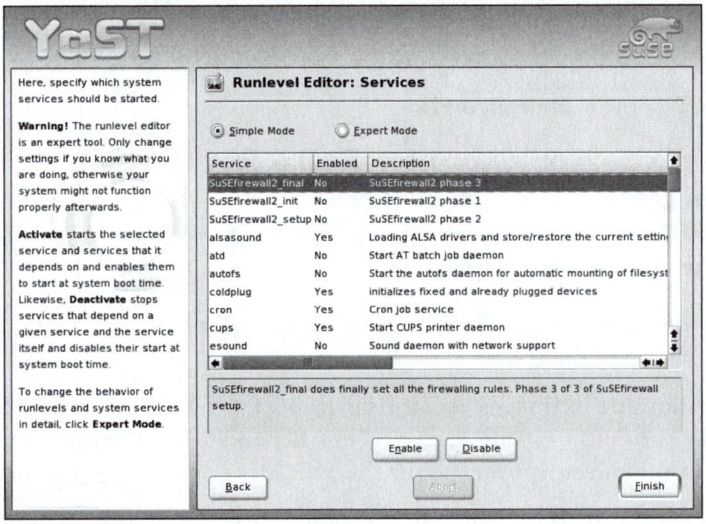

**Figure 8-4**

If the standard runlevel is 5, users can log in through the GUI login screen. If it is set to 3, no graphical login is available.

> **NOTE** If you want to look again later at the messages displayed during booting and initial starting of services, you can look at the log file **/var/log/boot.msg** with less.

## Exercise 8-3   Work with Runlevels

Usually there is rarely a reason to change the runlevel. The main reason is usually some maintenance work. The purpose of this exercise is to teach you how to change runlevels.

To understand how to work with runlevels, do the following:

1. Log out from KDE from the KDE menu by selecting **Logout** > **Logout.**

2. Switch to the first virtual terminal by pressing **Ctrl + Alt + F1.**

3. Log in as **root** with a password of **novell**.

4. Reboot by entering **init 6**.

5. When the Boot menu is displayed, press **Spacebar** to stop the timer.

6. In the Boot Options field type **3**; then press **Enter** to boot to runlevel 3.

7. When the login prompt appears, log in as **root** with a password of **novell**.

8. Display the current runlevel by entering **runlevel**.

9. Switch to runlevel 5 by entering **init 5**.

10. Switch back to the virtual terminal by pressing **Ctrl + Alt + F1.**

11. Log out as root by entering **exit**.

12. Switch back to the graphical user interface by pressing **Ctrl + Alt + F7.**

13. Log in as **geeko** with a password of **N0v3ll**.

# init Configuration File (/etc/inittab)

As mentioned previously, the system is initialized by **/sbin/init**, which is started by the kernel as the first process of the system.

The basic configuration file of init is **/etc/inittab**. This file determines what happens on individual runlevels. Various scripts are started by init, depending on these entries. All these scripts are located in the directory /etc/init.d/.

The main script is **/etc/init.d/rc**, which in turn controls other scripts.

To understand the contents of the file /etc/inittab, you need to know the following:

- inittab Syntax
- inittab Standard Entries

## inittab Syntax

The following is the syntax of each line in the file /etc/inittab:

*id:rl:action:process*

The following describes the parameters:

- *id.* A unique name for the entry in /etc/inittab. It can be up to four characters long.
- *rl.* Refers to one or more runlevels in which this entry should be evaluated.
- *action.* Describes what init will do.
- *process.* Is the process connected to this entry.

## inittab Standard Entries

The first entry in the file /etc/inittab contains the following parameters:

```
id:5:initdefault:
```

The parameter **initdefault** signals to the init process which level it will bring the system to. This can be overwritten at the boot prompt by entering a different level.

The following is the next entry:

```
si:bootwait:/etc/init.d/boot
```

The parameter **bootwait** indicates to carry out this command while booting and wait until it has finished.

The next few entries describe the actions for runlevels 0–6:

```
l0:0:wait:/etc/init.d/rc 0
l1:1:wait:/etc/init.d/rc 1
l2:2:wait:/etc/init.d/rc 2
l3:3:wait:/etc/init.d/rc 3
#l4:4:wait:/etc/init.d/rc 4
l5:5:wait:/etc/init.d/rc 5
l6:6:wait:/etc/init.d/rc 6
```

8

The parameter **wait** means that when the system changes to the indicated runlevel, init waits until the action indicated after the third colon has been completed. The parameter also means that further entries for the level are only performed after this process is completed.

This action carried out by init is to call the script **/etc/init.d/rc** with the runlevel as parameter.

The single user mode is a special case:

```
ls:S:wait:/etc/init.d/rc S
~~:S:respawn:/sbin/sulogin
```

First, the command to initialize the level is performed. Runlevel S is used by the scripts that are run when changing to runlevel 1.

Then the command **sulogin** is started. sulogin is intended only for the system administrator login.

The parameter respawn indicates to init to wait for the end of the process then restart it.

For those accustomed to PCs, /etc/inittab also defines the Ctrl+Alt+Del key combination for restarting:

```
ca::ctrlaltdel:/sbin/shutdown -r -t 4 now
```

The action ctrlaltdel is carried out by the init process only if these keys are pressed. If you do not want to allow this action, comment out (#) or remove the line.

The final large block of entries describe in which runlevels getty processes (login processes) are started:

```
1:2345:respawn:/sbin/mingetty --noclear tty1
2:2345:respawn:/sbin/mingetty tty2
3:2345:respawn:/sbin/mingetty tty3
4:2345:respawn:/sbin/mingetty tty4
5:2345:respawn:/sbin/mingetty tty5
6:2345:respawn:/sbin/mingetty tty6
```

The getty processes provide the login prompt and in return expect a user name as input. They are started in runlevels 2, 3, and 5.

Runlevel 4 in the above example is ignored because the line that defines the actions for the runlevel is commented out earlier in the file (#I4:4:wait:/etc/init.d/rc 4).

If a session ends, the processes are started again by init. If a line is disabled here, no further login is possible at the corresponding virtual console.

If /etc/inittab is damaged, the system might not boot properly. For this reason, you need to be extremely careful while editing /etc/inittab and always keep a backup of an intact version.

If an error does occur, you can still boot the system. To do so, insert **init=/bin/bash** in the GRUB boot menu after the other options; for example:

**root=/dev/hda1 vga=791 init=/bin/bash**

In this way, the init process is replaced by a shell (so inittab is not read) and you can then repair the system manually or replace /etc/inittab with your backup version using the command cp.

## init Directories and Scripts

In addition to /etc/inittab, you need to understand the following essential parts of the system startup mechanism:

- init Directories
- Runlevel Symbolic Links
- Startup Script Structure
- How init Determines Which Services to Stop and Start
- Activate and Deactivate Services for a Runlevel

## init Directories

All the scripts used by init to start and stop services are located in the directory /etc/init.d/, as in Figure 8-5.

```
DA50:/etc/init.d # ls -l
total 955
drwxr-xr-x  11 root root  4896 Jul  9 08:05 .
drwxr-xr-x  92 root root  8736 Aug  6 13:05 ..
-rw-r--r--   1 root root  7000 Jun 30 12:37 README
-rwxr-xr-x   1 root root  1640 Jun 30 12:24 SuSEfirewall2_final
-rwxr-xr-x   1 root root  1628 Jun 30 12:24 SuSEfirewall2_init
-rwxr-xr-x   1 root root  1856 Jun 30 12:24 SuSEfirewall2_setup
-rwxr-xr-x   1 root root  3702 Jun 30 12:07 acct
-rwxr--r--   1 root root  4153 Jun 30 12:23 acpid
-rwxr-xr-x   1 root root  2151 Jun 30 13:04 adsl
-rwxr-xr-x   1 root root  6537 Jun 30 16:26 alsasound
-rwxr-xr-x   1 root root  2391 Jun 30 16:40 amavis
-rwxr--r--   1 root root  8630 Jun 30 16:40 apache2
-rwxr-xr-x   1 root root  3638 Jun 30 15:17 argus
-rwxr-xr-x   1 root root  3849 Jun 30 16:22 arpwatch
-rwxr-xr-x   1 root root  2792 Jun 30 13:30 atalk
-rwxr-xr-x   1 root root  3689 Jun 30 16:23 atd
-rwxr--r--   1 root root  8946 Jun 30 16:10 autofs
-rwxr-xr-x   1 root root  2954 May 26 13:22 autoyast
-rwxr-xr-x   1 root root  2694 Jun 30 12:08 avgate
-rwxr-xr-x   1 root root  3523 Jun 30 13:43 bgpd
-rwxr-xr-x   1 root root  7096 Mar 26 07:07 boot
-rwxr-xr-x   1 root root  2494 Mar  8 03:44 boot.clock
```

**Figure 8-5**

These scripts can be called up in the following ways:

- Directly by init when you boot the system, when the system is shut down, when you stop the system with **Ctrl+Alt+Del**, or when there is a signal from an uninterruptable power supply (UPS) that there is a power failure.

- Indirectly by init when you change the runlevel. In this case, it is the script /etc/init.d/rc that runs the necessary scripts in the correct order during the runlevel change.

- Directly by /etc/init.d/*script* start or stop commands.

  You can also enter **rcscript start** or **stop** if corresponding links are set in /sbin/ or /usr/sbin/.

The following describes some of the more important scripts stored in /etc/init.d/:

- **boot.** This script is started directly by init when the system starts.

  It runs one time only.

  It evaluates the directory /etc/init.d/boot.d/ and starts all the scripts linked to filenames with an "S" at the beginning of their names (see Runlevel Symbolic Links).

  These scripts perform the following tasks:

  - Start the kernel daemon, which takes over the automatic loading of kernel modules.

- Check the file systems.

- Delete unnecessary files in /var/lock/.

- Set the system time.

- Configure PnP hardware with the isapnp tools.

  System extensions are activated from the script /etc/init.d/boot.local (you can add your own system extensions to this script).

- **boot.local.** This script includes additional commands to execute at boot before changing into a runlevel.

  It can be compared with AUTOEXEC.BAT on a DOS system.

- **boot.setup.** This script is run when changing from single user mode to any other runlevel and is responsible for a number of basic settings, such the keyboard layout and initialization of the virtual consoles.

- **halt.** This script is run if runlevel 0 or 6 is entered.

  It is called up either with the command halt (the system is completely shut down) or with the command reboot (the system is shut down and then rebooted).

- **rc.** This script is responsible for the correct change from one runlevel to another.

  It runs the stop scripts for the current runlevel, and then it runs the start scripts for the new one.

To create your own scripts, you can use the file /etc/init.d/skeleton as a template.

## Runlevel Symbolic Links

For each runlevel, there is a corresponding subdirectory in /etc/init.d/. For runlevel 1 it is /etc/init.d/rc1.d/, for runlevel 2 it is /etc/init.d/rc2.d/, and so on.

When you view the files in a directory such as /etc/init.d/rc3.d/, you see two kinds of files—those that start with a "K" and those that start with an "S" (see Figure 8-6).

| | | | | | |
|---|---|---|---|---|---|
| K10sshd | 3.6 KB | Shell Script | 2003-03-18 06:15 | rwxr-xr-x | root |
| K12nfs | 2.5 KB | Shell Script | 2004-06-21 09:10 | rwxr-xr-x | root |
| K12nfsboot | 1.1 KB | Shell Script | 2004-06-30 12:59 | rwx------ | root |
| K14portmap | 3.5 KB | Shell Script | 2004-06-30 12:49 | rwxr--r-- | root |
| K14resmgr | 3.4 KB | Shell Script | 2004-06-30 11:56 | rwxr-xr-x | root |
| K14smbfs | 4.5 KB | Shell Script | 2004-06-01 08:53 | rwxr-xr-x | root |
| K14splash_early | 617 B | Shell Script | 2004-06-30 12:45 | rwxr-xr-x | root |
| K16syslog | 2.8 KB | Shell Script | 2004-06-30 12:24 | rwxr-xr-- | root |
| K17network | 15.9 KB | Shell Script | 2004-07-01 06:36 | rwxr-xr-x | root |
| K20coldplug | 2.9 KB | Shell Script | 2004-06-30 12:03 | rwxr-xr-x | root |
| K21hotplug | 2.0 KB | Shell Script | 2004-06-30 12:03 | rwxr-xr-x | root |
| K21isdn | 5.4 KB | Shell Script | 2004-05-03 10:24 | rwxr-xr-x | root |
| K21random | 1.7 KB | Shell Script | 2003-09-01 05:11 | rwxr-xr-x | root |
| S01hotplug | 2.0 KB | Shell Script | 2004-06-30 12:03 | rwxr-xr-x | root |
| S01isdn | 5.4 KB | Shell Script | 2004-05-03 10:24 | rwxr-xr-x | root |
| S01random | 1.7 KB | Shell Script | 2003-09-01 05:11 | rwxr-xr-x | root |
| S02coldplug | 2.9 KB | Shell Script | 2004-06-30 12:03 | rwxr-xr-x | root |
| S05network | 15.9 KB | Shell Script | 2004-07-01 06:36 | rwxr-xr-x | root |
| S06syslog | 2.8 KB | Shell Script | 2004-06-30 12:24 | rwxr-xr-- | root |
| S08portmap | 3.5 KB | Shell Script | 2004-06-30 12:49 | rwxr--r-- | root |
| S08resmgr | 3.4 KB | Shell Script | 2004-06-30 11:56 | rwxr-xr-x | root |
| S08smbfs | 4.5 KB | Shell Script | 2004-06-01 08:53 | rwxr-xr-x | root |
| S08splash_early | 617 B | Shell Script | 2004-06-30 12:45 | rwxr-xr-x | root |

**Figure 8-6**

The first letter is always followed by two digits and the name of a service. Whether a service is started in a specific runlevel depends on whether there are **S***xxservice* and **K***xxservice* files in the **/etc/init.d/rc***x*.**d/** directory.

Entering **ls –l** in an /etc/init.d/rc*x*.d/ directory indicates that these files are actually symbolic links pointing to service scripts in /etc/init.d/ (as in Figure 8-7).

```
DA50:~ # cd /etc/init.d/rc3.d
DA50:/etc/init.d/rc3.d # ls -l
total 6
drwxr-xr-x    2 root root 1864 Aug  4 13:35 .
drwxr-xr-x   11 root root 4896 Jul  9 08:05 ..
lrwxrwxrwx    1 root root   14 Jul  9 07:59 K02splash_late -> ../splash_
late
lrwxrwxrwx    1 root root    7 Jul  9 07:59 K03cron -> ../cron
lrwxrwxrwx    1 root root    9 Jul 20 18:27 K03xinetd -> ../xinetd
lrwxrwxrwx    1 root root   10 Aug  4 13:35 K04apache2 -> ../apache2
lrwxrwxrwx    1 root root   12 Jul 21 13:00 K05nfsserver -> ../nfsserver
lrwxrwxrwx    1 root root   10 Jul  9 07:59 K05postfix -> ../postfix
lrwxrwxrwx    1 root root    7 Jul  9 07:59 K06nscd -> ../nscd
lrwxrwxrwx    1 root root    7 Jul  9 07:59 K07cups -> ../cups
lrwxrwxrwx    1 root root    9 Jul  9 07:59 K08hwscan -> ../hwscan
lrwxrwxrwx    1 root root    7 Jul  9 07:59 K08slpd -> ../slpd
lrwxrwxrwx    1 root root   13 Jul  9 07:51 K09powersaved -> ../powersav
ed
lrwxrwxrwx    1 root root    9 Jul  9 07:51 K09splash -> ../splash
lrwxrwxrwx    1 root root   12 Jul  9 08:26 K10alsasound -> ../alsasound
lrwxrwxrwx    1 root root    8 Jul  9 07:51 K10fbset -> ../fbset
lrwxrwxrwx    1 root root   14 Aug  3 16:45 K10powertweakd -> ../powertw
eakd
lrwxrwxrwx    1 root root   17 Jul  9 07:58 K10running-kernel -> ../runn
```

**Figure 8-7**

Usually two links point to the same script. For example, if you enter **ls –l *network** in the /etc/init.d/rc3.d/ directory, you see that two links point to the script /etc/init.d/network (see Figure 8-8).

```
DA50:/etc/init.d/rc3.d # ls -l *network
lrwxrwxrwx  1 root root 10 Jul  9 08:20 K17network -> ../network
lrwxrwxrwx  1 root root 10 Jul  9 08:20 S05network -> ../network
DA50:/etc/init.d/rc3.d #
```

**Figure 8-8**

By using symbolic links in subdirectories, only the script in /etc/init.d/ needs to be modified.

**NOTE**  Sometimes K*xx* links are referred to as *kill scripts*, while S*xx* links are referred to as *start scripts*. In fact there are no separate scripts for starting and stopping services—the script is just called with the parameters stop or start.

## Startup Script Structure

Each of the scripts in /etc/init.d is run both as a start script and a stop script. For this reason, you must understand the parameters listed in Table 8-11.

**Table 8-11**

| Parameter | Description |
|---|---|
| start | Starts a service that is not running |
| restart | Stops a running service and restarts it |
| stop | Stops a running service |
| reload | Rereads the configuration of the service without stopping and restarting the service itself |
| force-reload | Reloads the configuration if the service supports this; otherwise, it does the same thing as restart |
| status | Displays the current status of the service |

The following shows the beginning of the file skeleton stored in /etc/init.d/. There is a section in this script for each of the above parameters. You can use skeleton to create your own startup scripts, such as the following:

```
#! /bin/sh
# Copyright (c) 1995-2004 SUSE Linux AG, Nuernberg, Germany.
# All rights reserved.
#
# Author: Kurt Garloff
# Please send feedback to http://www.suse.de/feedback/
#
```

```
# /etc/init.d/FOO
#    and its symbolic link
# /(usr/)sbin/rcFOO
#
# Template system startup script for some example service/daemon FOO
#
# LSB compatible service control script;
# see http://www.linuxbase.org/spec/
#
# Note: This template uses functions rc_XXX defined in /etc/rc.status on
# UnitedLinux (UL) based Linux distributions. If you want to base your
# script on this template and ensure that it works on non UL based LSB
# compliant Linux distributions, you either have to provide the rc.status
# functions from UL or change the script to work without them.
#
### BEGIN INIT INFO
# Provides:          FOO
# Required-Start:    $syslog $remote_fs
# Should-Start:      $time ypbind sendmail
```

You can view the contents of this file (which is several pages long) by entering **less /etc/init.d/skeleton**. To create a start script for a service yourself, copy this file and edit it according to your needs in any text editor.

Each section has informative comments and helps you understand the general structure of the start scripts used for services.

## How init Determines Which Services to Start and Stop

You already know that a service is started with the parameter start and stopped with the parameter stop. The same parameters are also used when changing from one runlevel to another.

The script /etc/init.d/rc examines the directories /etc/init.d/rc*currentrl*.d/ and /etc/init.d/rc*newrl*.d/ and determines what to do. The following are three possibilities:

- There is a **K*xx*** link for a certain service in /etc/init.d/rc*currentrl*.d/ and there is an **S*xx*** link in /etc/init.d/rc*newrl*.d/ for the same service.

  In this case, the service is not started or stopped; the corresponding script in /etc/init.d/ is not called at all.

- There is a **K*xx*** link for a certain service in /etc/init.d/rc*currentrl*.d/ and there is no corresponding **S*xx*** link in /etc/init.d/rc*newrl*.d/.

  In this case, the script in /etc/init.d/service is called with the parameter stop and the service is stopped.

- There is an **S***xx* link in /etc/init.d/rc*newrl*.d/ and there is no corresponding **K***xx* link for the service in /etc/init.d/rc*currentrl*.d/.

  In this case, the script in /etc/init.d/service is called with the parameter start and the service is started.

The number after the K or S determines the sequence in which the scripts are called.

For example, script K10serviceA is called before script K20serviceB, which means that serviceA is shut down before serviceB.

Script S15serviceC is called before S23serviceD, which means that serviceC starts before serviceD. This is important if serviceD depends on a running serviceC.

For example the following happens when you change from runlevel 3 to runlevel 5:

1. You tell init to change to a different runlevel by entering (as root) **init 5**.

2. init checks its configuration file (/etc/inittab) and determines it should start /etc/init.d/rc with the new runlevel (**5**) as a parameter.

3. rc calls the stop scripts (**K***xx*) of the current runlevel for those services for which there is no start script (**S***xx*) in the new runlevel.

4. The start scripts in the new runlevel for those services for which there was no kill script in the old runlevel are launched.

When changing to the same runlevel as the current runlevel, init only checks /etc/inittab for changes and starts the appropriate steps (such as starting a getty on another interface).

## Activate and Deactivate Services for a Runlevel

The services in a runlevel can be activated and deactivated from the command line with the command insserv or by using YaST.

Although you could create symbolic create links in the runlevel subdirectories yourself to modify services that are stopped and started, an easier way is to edit the header of a script.

The INIT INFO block at the beginning of the script determines in which runlevel the service that the script controls should start or stop:

```
### BEGIN INIT INFO
# Provides: syslog
# Required-Start: network
# Required-Stop: network
# Default-Start: 2 3 5
# Default-Stop:
# Description: Start the system logging daemons
### END INIT INFO
```

The INIT INFO block is used by the program insserv to determine in which runlevel subdirectory links need to be placed and what numbers need to be put after K and S.

For more information on the program insserv, enter **man 8 insserv**.

**NOTE**

The entry Default–Start determines in which runlevel directory links are to be placed. The entry Required–Start determines which services have to be started before the one being considered.

After editing the INIT INFO block, enter **insserv** to create the needed links and renumber the existing ones as needed.

To remove all links for a service (disabling the service), stop the service (if it is running) by entering:

**/etc/init.d/***service* **stop**

then enter:

**insserv –r** *service*

You can also use the YaST Runlevel Editor to set these links. We recommend that you choose one method or the other. Switching between methods can lead to errors.

Another program to set and remove links in runlevel directories is **chkconfig**. It is available on other distributions too, but its syntax might be slightly different depending on the distribution.

**NOTE**

For more information, see **man chkconfig**.

chkconfig can also be used, to list which services are activated in which runlevel, using the option **–l**, as shown in the following example:

```
da10:~ # chkconfig -l
Makefile                0:off  1:off  2:off  3:off  4:off  5:off  6:off
SuSEfirewall2_final     0:off  1:off  2:off  3:off  4:off  5:off  6:off
SuSEfirewall2_init      0:off  1:off  2:off  3:off  4:off  5:off  6:off
SuSEfirewall2_setup     0:off  1:off  2:off  3:off  4:off  5:off  6:off
acpid                   0:off  1:off  2:off  3:off  4:off  5:off  6:off
alsasound               0:off  1:off  2:on   3:on   4:off  5:on   6:off
...
```

8

## Exercise 8-4  Enable Services

Depending on the purpose of the machines, certain services have to be available, whereas others have to be turned off.

There are convenient ways to activate or deactivate services in SLES 9 and the purpose of this exercise is to familiarize you with them.

In this exercise, do the following:

- Part I: Enable Services Using chkconfig and insserv
- Part II: Use YaST to Enable Services

Please note that when administering SLES 9 after completion of this course you should make up your mind as to which method to use and stick with that. Mixing chkconfig/ insserv and YaST to administer services is not advisable.

### Part I: Enable Services Using chkconfig and insserv

In this part of the exercise, you enable the system service **atd** to run at system boot at runlevels 2, 3, and 5.

**at** allows you to schedule commands to run at a future point in time. You use it later in this section.

Do the following:

1. From the terminal window, su to root (**su -**) with a password of **novell**.
2. View the current runlevel configuration for atd by entering:

   **chkconfig atd -l**

   The configuration is off for all runlevels.
3. Install the service to its predefined runlevels by entering:

   **insserv -d atd**
4. Check the modified runlevel configuration for atd by entering:

   **chkconfig atd -l**

   The default configuration for atd sets runlevels 2, 3, and 5 to on.
5. Change to the directory /etc/rc.d/rc3.d by entering:

   **cd /etc/rc.d/rc3.d**
6. List the atd files in the directory by entering:

   **ls -l \*atd**

   There are two atd links—one is used to start and one is used to kill the service atd.

7. Start the service atd by entering:

   **rcatd start**

8. Verify that the service is running by entering:

   **rcatd status**

9. Switch to virtual terminal 1 by pressing:

   **Ctrl + Alt + F1**

10. Log in as **root**.

11. Switch to runlevel 1 by entering **init 1**.

12. Enter a root password of **novell**.

13. Check to see if the service is running by entering:

    **rcatd status**

    The service is listed as unused because it is not configured to start at runlevel 1.

14. Switch back to your previous runlevel (5) by entering **init 5**.

    The GUI login screen appears.

15. Log in as **geeko** with a password of **N0v3ll**.

16. From the KDE desktop, open a terminal window and su to root (**su –**) with a password of **novell**.

17. From the command line, remove the service atd from system startup runlevels by entering:

    **chkconfig atd off**

18. View the current runlevel configuration for atd by entering:

    **chkconfig atd –l**

    The service is off for all runlevels.

19. Re-enable the service to start at the default runlevels by entering:

    **chkconfig atd on**

## Part II: Use YaST to Enable Services

Do the following:

1. From the KDE desktop, select the **YaST** icon; then enter a password of **novell** and select **OK**.

   The YaST Control Center appears.

2. Select **System > Runlevel Editor**.

   The Runlevel Editor: Services dialog box appears.

3. Switch to a more detailed view (with additional options) by selecting **Expert Mode**.

4. Scroll down the Services list and select **rsyncd**.

5. Below the list, configure this service to start at runlevels 3 and 5 by selecting **3** and **5**.

6. From the Set/Reset drop-down list select **Enable the Service**.

7. Start the service rsyncd from the Start/Stop/Refresh drop-down list by selecting **Start Now**.

   A status message appears indicating that the service started successfully.

8. Close the status message by selecting **OK**.

9. Stop the service rsyncd from the Start/Stop/Refresh drop-down list by selecting **Stop Now**.

   A status message appears indicating that the service stopped successfully.

10. Close the status message by selecting **OK**.

11. Change the configuration so that rsyncd does not run at any runlevel from the Set/Reset drop-down list by selecting:

    **Disable the service**

12. Save the changes by selecting **Finish**; then select **Yes**.

13. Close the YaST Control Center and the terminal window.

---

## Objective 5    Schedule Tasks

Most SLES 9 administrators and regular users find that they need to complete certain tasks regularly on a running system (such as updating a database or backing up data).

You can automate these jobs in Linux by doing the following:

- Schedule a Job (cron)
- Run a Job One Time Only (at)

### Schedule a Job (cron)

You can schedule jobs to be run on a regular basis by using the service **cron** (/usr/sbin/cron).

The service runs as a daemon and checks once a minute to see if jobs have been defined for the current time. By default, the service should be activated.

The file that contains the list of jobs is called a *crontab*. A crontab exists for the entire system as well as for each user defined on the system.

The file /etc/sysconfig/cron contains variables for the configuration of some scripts started by cron.

You can define two types of jobs with cron:

- System Jobs
- User Jobs

## System Jobs

You control system jobs with the file /etc/crontab. The cron jobs that are defined here after installation run the scripts contained in Table 8-12.

**Table 8-12**

| Directory | Interval |
|---|---|
| /etc/cron.hourly | Jobs are run on an hourly basis. |
| /etc/cron.daily | Jobs are run on a daily basis. |
| /etc/cron.weekly | Jobs are run on a weekly basis. |
| /etc/cron.monthly | Jobs are run on a monthly basis. |

You can add lines to /etc/crontab, but you should not delete the lines added at installation.

**NOTE**

For more information on the syntax for /etc/crontab, enter **man 5 crontab**.

The scripts called from the file /etc/crontab not only ensure that the scripts in the above mentioned directories are run at the prescribed intervals (handled by the script /usr/lib/cron/run-crons), but also that jobs are run later if they could not be run at the specified time.

For example, if a script could not be run at the specified time because the computer was turned off, the script is automatically run later using the settings in /etc/crontab.

This is only valid for jobs defined in a script in cron.hourly, cron.daily, cron.weekly, or cron.monthly.

Information about the last time the jobs were run is kept in the directory /var/spool/cron/lastrun/ in a file such as cron.daily.

The time stamp of the file is evaluated by the script /usr/lib/cron/run-crons to determine if scripts have to be run or not.

In a standard installation, only the directory /etc/cron.daily/ contains scripts, such as the following:

```
da10:~ # ls /etc/cron.daily
.              logrotate              suse.de-clean-tmp
```

```
..                  suse.de-backup-rc.config   suse.de-clean-vi
clean_catman        suse.de-backup-rpmdb       suse.de-cron-local
do_mandb            suse.de-check-battery
da10:~ #
```

These scripts are standard shell scripts set up to use a designated shell. These scripts are overwritten when you update your system.

For this reason, you should store any modifications to these scripts in the script /root/bin/cron.daily.local, because this script is not overwritten when you update your system.

Other files for system jobs can be stored in the directory /etc/cron.d/. These files must have the same format as /etc/crontab. Jobs defined in /etc/cron.d/ are not run automatically at a later time.

## User Jobs

You can set up cron to allow individual users (including root) to configure their own cron jobs by using the following two files:

- **/var/spool/cron/allow** (users entered here can define jobs)
- **/var/spool/cron/deny** (users who are not listed in this file can define jobs)

These files are text files you can modify or create.

By default, the file /var/spool/cron/deny already exists with its own entries, such as the following:

```
guest
gast
```

If the file /var/spool/cron/allow exists, only this file is evaluated. If neither of these files exist, only the user root can define jobs.

The jobs of individual users are stored in the directory /var/spool/cron/tabs/ in files matching the user names. These files always belong to the user root. You can use the command **crontab** to edit them.

Table 8-13 shows options for the command crontab.

**Table 8-13**

| Option | Description |
|---|---|
| crontab -e | Creates or edits jobs. The vi editor is used. |
| crontab *file* | The specified *file* contains a list of jobs. |
| crontab -l | Displays current jobs. |
| crontab -r | Deletes all jobs. |

Each line in a file defines a job. There are six fields in a line.

The first five fields define the time; the final field contains the command to run. This can be any type of command or shell script. However, no user interaction is available when the command or shell script is run.

The first five fields have the format shown in Table 8-14.

**Table 8-14**

| Field | Range |
|---|---|
| Minutes | 0–59 |
| Hours | 0–23 |
| Day of the month | 1–31 |
| Month | 1–12 |
| Weekday | 0–7 |

The following are guidelines for configuring these fields:

- If you want a job to run on every date, enter an asterisk (*) in the corresponding field.
- You can include several entries in a field, separated by commas.
- You can specify a range with start and end values separated by a hyphen.
- You can configure time steps with **/n** (where **n** stands for the size of the step).
- You can specify months and weekdays by their first three letters (not case sensitive). However, when you use letters, you cannot use ranges or lists.
- Numbers representing the weekdays start a 0 for Sunday and run through the entire week consecutively, with 7 representing Sunday again.

    For example, 3 is Wednesday and 6 is Saturday.

The following is an example of a cron job entry:

```
*/10 8-17 * * 1-5 fetchmail mailserver
```

In this example, from Monday to Friday (**1–5**) every 10 minutes (**\*/10**) between 8:00 A.M. to 5:00 P.M. (**8–17**), the command **fetchmail** is run to fetch incoming e-mails from the computer **mailserver**.

For system jobs, the user who has the permissions to run the command must be specified in the file /etc/crontab, by entering the user name between the time details (the first five fields) and the name of the command (which now becomes the seventh field).

## Run a Job One Time Only (at)

If you want to run a job one time only (instead of scheduling it on a regular basis with cron) you can use the command **at**. To use at, you must make sure the service atd is started.

Two files determine which users can run this command (in the same way as cron):

- **/etc/at.allow** (users entered here can define jobs)
- **/etc/at.deny** (users who are not listed in this file can define jobs)

These files are text files you can modify or create.

By default, the file /etc/at.deny already exists with its own entries, such as the following:

```
alias
backup
bin
daemon
ftp
games
...
```

If the file /etc/at.allow exists, only the file is evaluated. If neither of these files exist, only the user root can define jobs with at.

You define a job from a command prompt by entering:

**at** *launch_time* (where *launch_time* is when you want the job to begin).

At this point you are placed in a special environment where you enter commands, each on a line of its own. When you finish entering commands, you save the job by pressing **Ctrl+D**.

The following is an example of creating a job with the command at:

```
geeko@da10:~> at 21:00
warning: commands will be executed using /bin/sh
at> /home/geeko/bin/doit
at> mail -s "Results file of geeko" geeko@da10 < /home/geeko/results
at> <EOT>
job 4 at 2007-08-27 21:00
```

If the commands you want executed are contained in a text file, you need to enter **at –f** *file launch_time* (where *file* is the pathname of the file).

The following are some other commonly used commands and options for at:

**Table 8-15**

| Command | Description |
| --- | --- |
| atq | Displays defined jobs (including job numbers, which are needed to delete a job) |
| atrm *job_number* | Deletes a job (using the job number) |

## Exercise 8-5    Schedule Jobs with cron and at

Scheduling jobs with cron is a very common task. It can make system administration much easier to have certain regular tasks, like for instance backups, run automatically outside working hours.

at comes in very handy for one-time tasks.

The purpose of this exercise is for you to use the available tools for scheduling tasks.

In this exercise, you do the following:

- Part I: Schedule Jobs with at
- Part II: Schedule Jobs with cron

### Part I: Schedule Jobs with at

Do the following:

1. From a terminal window on your KDE desktop, su to root (**su –**) with a password of **novell**.

2. Verify that the service at is running by entering:

   **rcatd status**

3. (Conditional) If the at service is not running, start the service by entering:

   **rcatd start**

4. Display the current date and time by entering **date**.

5. Three minutes from now, log to /var/log/messages who is logged in by entering the following commands:

   **at *hh:mm***

   **finger >> /var/log/messages**

6. Exit the at editor by pressing **Ctrl + d**.

7. View the scheduled at jobs by entering **atq** (or **at –l**).

   Notice that the job number is listed as 1.

8. Wait for the three minutes to pass; then check the file /var/log/messages for the finger information by entering:

   **tail /var/log/messages**

   Login information for geeko is listed at the end of the file.

9. Schedule the same job to run tomorrow at noon by entering:

   **at noon tomorrow**

   **finger >> /var/log/messages**

   **Ctrl + d**

10. Schedule the date to be logged tomorrow at 2:00 P.M. to the file /var/log/ messages by entering:

    **at 14:00 tomorrow**

    **date >> /var/log/messages**

    **Ctrl + d**

11. View the scheduled at jobs by entering **atq** (or **at –l**).

    The two jobs are listed, each with an individual job number.

12. Remove the job scheduled for tomorrow at 2:00 P.M. by entering:

    **atrm *job_number***

13. View the scheduled at jobs by entering **atq** (or **at –l**).

    Only the job scheduled for 12:00 P.M. is still listed.

## Part II: Schedule Jobs with cron

Do the following:

1. Change to the Level 2 (Networked Workstation) security level:

   Before using cron as a normal user, you need to make sure that the security settings on your server are set to the correct level, or you cannot use the utility.

   a. From the KDE desktop, select the **YaST** icon; then enter a password of **novell** and select **OK**.

   The YaST Control Center appears.

   b. From the YaST Control Center, select:

   **Security and Users > Security Settings**

   c. Select **Level 2 (Networked Workstation)**; then select **Finish**.

2. Open a terminal window.

3. Schedule a cron job as geeko:

   a. Enter **crontab –e**.

   The vi editor is displayed for a cron table file (such as /tmp/crontab.11743).

   b. Press **Insert**.

c. Add a job that runs at 2:00 A.M. every Tuesday and creates a tarball of /etc that is saved in /tmp by entering:

**0 2 * * 2 tar czvf /tmp/etc.tgz /etc**

d. Press **Esc**.

e. Save the file and exit the vi editor by entering **:wq**.

f. Verify that the job is in the crontab file for geeko by entering:

**crontab -l**

4. Schedule a cron job as root:

a. Su to root (**su -**) with a password of **novell**.

b. Enter **crontab -e**.

c. Schedule a job to run every minute that uses finger to record to the file ~/users.log users who are logged in by pressing **Insert** and entering:

**\* \* \* \* \* finger >> ~/users.log**

d. Press **Esc**.

e. Save the file and exit the vi editor by entering **:wq**.

f. Watch the file users.log for a few minutes to make sure that it is being updated by entering:

**tail -f /root/users.log**

g. When you finish watching the file update, press **Ctrl + c**.

5. Remove root's crontab file by entering **crontab -r**.

6. Verify that the crontab file no longer exists by entering:

**crontab -l**

7. Verify that the crontab file is no longer active by entering:

**tail -f ~/users.log**

Entries to users.log are no longer being added.

8. Press **Ctrl + c**.

9. Log out as root by entering **exit**.

10. Remove geeko's crontab file by entering:

**crontab -r**

11. Verify that the crontab file no longer exists by entering:

**crontab -l**

8

12. Change to the security level back to Level 3 (Network Server):

   a. From the YaST Control Center, select:

   **Security and Users > Security Settings**

   b. Select **Level 3 (Network Server)**; then select **Finish**.

13. Close all open windows.

---

## CHAPTER SUMMARY

□ Processes are programs that are executing on the system. User processes run in a terminal and are executed by users, whereas daemon processes are system services that do not run on a terminal.

□ Every process has a PID, a PPID, and can possibly start an unlimited number of child processes.

□ The first process loaded by the kernel during system initialization is the init daemon, which always has a PID of 1.

□ In addition to a PID, background processes have a job ID that you can use to control their execution. You can start any program in the background by appending the & character to the program command.

□ You can view processes within a desktop environment using the KDE System Guard, or at a command prompt by using the **ps**, **pstree**, **lsof,** and **top** commands.

□ The KDE System Guard as well as the **kill**, **killall**, and **top** commands can be used to stop processes by sending them signals. Although there are many available signals, the default signal used by these commands is SIGTERM. The init daemon cannot be terminated by signals.

□ You can affect the priority of a process by changing its nice value. All processes are started with a 0 nice value, which can be decreased to -20 (high priority) or increased to +19 (low priority). Only the root user may increase the priority of a process.

□ You can use the **nice** command to set the priority of a program and run it. You must use the **renice** command to change the priority of a process that is already running.

□ Daemons may be started by running the appropriate script in the /etc/init.d directory with the **start** argument, or by using the **rcdaemonname start** command.

□ A Linux system is categorized using runlevels. There are seven standard runlevels based on the number and type of daemons loaded in memory.

□ The init daemon is responsible for loading and unloading daemons, using its configuration file /etc/inittab.

❑ The /etc/inittab file runs scripts that start with S (start) or K (kill) in the /etc/init.d/rc*.d when changing runlevels; these scripts are shortcuts to the scripts in the /etc/init.d directory used to start and stop daemons. You may edit these files to control the daemons that start and stop in a particular runlevel. Alternatively, you can use the YaST Runlevel Editor or **chkconfig** command to edit the appropriate runlevel files.

❑ You can view your current runlevel using the **runlevel** command, and force the init daemon to change runlevels using the **init** command.

❑ Commands may be scheduled to run at a later time using the at daemon.

❑ To schedule tasks to occur regularly in the future, you must use the cron daemon to create a crontab (cron table). System tasks are scheduled to run using the /etc/crontab file. User tasks may be scheduled using the **crontab** command and are stored in the /var/spool/cron/tabs directory.

**8**

# KEY TERMS

**&** — A special character used to start a program in the background.

**/etc/at.allow** — A file that lists users who can use the **at** command.

**/etc/at.deny** — A file that lists users who cannot use the **at** command.

**/etc/cron.d** — A directory that contains additional system cron tables.

**/etc/crontab** — The system cron table.

**/etc/init.d** — The directory that contains the scripts used to start most daemons.

**/etc/init.d/skeleton** — A sample script that may be copied to create scripts used to start a daemon.

**/etc/inittab** — The configuration file for the init daemon.

**/etc/rc.d/rc** — The script that executes files in the /etc/rc.d/rc*.d directories.

**/etc/rc.d/rc*.d** — The directories used by the init daemon to start and kill daemons in each runlevel.

**/var/log/boot.msg** — The log file that stores information about daemon startup at system initialization.

**/var/spool/cron/allow** — A file that lists users who can use the **crontab** command.

**/var/spool/cron/deny** — A file that lists users who cannot use the **crontab** command.

**/var/spool/cron/tabs** — The directory used to store user crontabs.

**at command** — Used to schedule commands to run at a certain time in the future.

**atq command** — Used to view scheduled at jobs.

**atrm command** — Used to remove a scheduled at job.

**background process** — A process that runs unnoticed in your terminal and does not interfere with your command line interface.

**bg command** — Used to start a process in the background.

**child process** — A process that is started by another process.

**chkconfig** — Used to configure the daemons that start in a runlevel.

**cron** — The system service that executes commands regularly in the future based on information in crontabs.

**crontab (cron table)** — A file specifying the commands to be run by the cron daemon and the schedule to run them.

**crontab command** — Used to view and edit user cron tables.

**daemon process** — A system process that is not associated with a terminal.

**fg command** — Used to force a background process to run in the foreground.

**foreground process** — A process that runs in your terminal and must finish execution before you receive your shell prompt.

**getty** — A program used to display a login prompt on a character-based terminal.

**halt command** — Used to quickly bring a system to runlevel 0.

**init** — The first daemon started by the Linux kernel; it is responsible for starting and stopping other daemons.

**init command** — Used to change the system runlevel.

**insserv command** — Used to enable scripts that are used to start daemons.

**Interval-controlled daemon** — A daemon that is started at a certain time on a regular basis.

**job** — See **background process**.

**job ID** — The ID given to a background process that may be used in commands that manipulate the process during execution.

**jobs command** — Used to view background processes in your terminal.

**KDE System Guard** — A graphical utility that may be used to view and control processes.

**kill command** — Used to send a signal to a process by PID or job ID.

**killall command** — Used to send a signal to a process by name.

**lsof command** — Used to list processes and the files that they have opened on the filesystem.

**nice command** — Used to change the priority of a process as it is started.

**nice value** — Represents the priority of a process. A higher nice value reduces the priority of the process.

**nohup command** — Used to prevent a process from stopping when the shell that started it has exited.

**parent process** — A process that has started another process.

**Parent Process ID (PPID)** — The PID of the parent process.

**poweroff command** — Used to quickly bring a system to runlevel 0 and power off the system.

**process** — A program currently loaded into memory and running on the CPU.

**Process ID (PID)** — A unique identifier assigned to every process.

**program** — A file that may be executed to create a process.

**ps command** — Used to list processes that are running on the system.

**pstree command** — Used to list processes that are running on the system as well as their parent and child relationships.

**reboot command** — Used to quickly bring a system to runlevel 6.

**renice command** — Used to change the priority of a running process.

**runlevel** — A category that describes the number and type of daemons on a Linux system.

**runlevel command** — Used to display the current and most recent runlevel.

**shutdown command** — Used to change to runlevel 0 at a certain time.

**signal** — A termination request that is sent to a process.

**Signal-controlled daemon** — A daemon that is started when an event occurs on the system.

**sulogin** — A program used to display a login prompt on a character-based terminal for the root user only in runlevel 1.

**top command** — Used to view, renice, and kill the processes on the system that are using the most CPU time.

**user process** — A process that is begun by a user and runs on a terminal.

**YaST Runlevel Editor** — A graphical program that may be used to configure the daemons that start in each runlevel.

8

## REVIEW QUESTIONS

1. Which of the following terms refers to a system service that does not run on a terminal?

   a. Program

   b. User Process

   c. Daemon Process

   d. Child Process

2. What is the PID of init? _____

3. Which of the following statements are true? (Choose all that apply.)

   a. A parent process may only have one child process.

   b. Each process is given a PPID that is used to uniquely identify it on the system.

   c. A child process may only have one parent process.

   d. All background processes have a PID and a job ID.

4. Which of the following commands can quickly identify the child processes started by a particular daemon?

   a. top

   b. lsof

   c. ps

   d. pstree

5. To what processes are regular users allowed to send kill signals?

   _____

6. You have just run the **ps aux** command and notice that most daemons have an S in the STAT column. What does this mean? _____

7. What key can you press in the **top** command to send the process a signal?

    a. s

    b. k

    c. R

    d. N

8. What can you type at a command prompt to run the **updatedb** command in the background? _____

9. Which of the following key combinations can you use to pause a foreground process, such that it may be send to the background with the **bg** command?

    a. Ctrl+c

    b. Ctrl+p

    c. Ctrl+z

    d. Ctrl+r

10. Which of the following kill commands may be used to send the second background job a SIGINT?

    a. kill -2 %2

    b. kill -1 −b 2

    c. kill -9 %2

    d. kill -15 2

11. If you do not specify the type of signal when using the **kill** or **killall** commands, which signal is used by default?

    a. SIGHUP

    b. SIGINT

    c. SIGKILL

    d. SIGTERM

12. What command could you use to change the priority of a process (PID=592) to run with the highest priority? _____

13. What action in the /etc/inittab file is used to determine the default runlevel at system initialization? _____

14. What is the default runlevel in SLES? _____

15. What runlevel loads all networking daemons (including NFS) but does not start a display manager?

    a. 1

    b. 2

    c. 3

    d. 5

16. What command can you type to change your runlevel to Single User Mode?

    _____

17. Which of the following commands will force your system to reboot? (Choose all that apply.)

    a. init 0

    b. reboot

    c. powerwait

    d. init 6

18. Which of the following commands may be used to stop the SSH daemon (sshd)? (Choose all that apply.)

    a. rcsshd stop

    b. kstopsys sshd

    c. /etc/init.d/sshd stop

    d. /etc/rc/stopsshd

19. What template can you copy to create a script that is used to start or stop daemons in the /etc/init.d directory _____

20. Which of the following methods can you use to start the SSH daemon (sshd) upon entering runlevel 3? (Choose all that apply.)

    a. Create a shortcut to the /etc/init.d/sshd script called /etc/init.d/rc3.d/S88sshd

    b. Create a shortcut to the /etc/init.d/sshd script called /etc/init.d/rc3.d/K88sshd

    c. Change the INIT INFO section of the /etc/init.d/sshd script and run the **insserv** command

    d. Run the YaST Runlevel Editor Ext3

21. You have a script that is used to remove temporary files and would like this script to run on a daily basis. What directory could you place this script in to have the cron daemon execute it each day? _____

22. What command could a regular user use to edit their crontab?

    _____

23. What lines would you add to your crontab to schedule the /bin/false command to run at 10:30 a.m. and 2:50 p.m. from Monday to Friday? _____

24. What command can you use to run the contents of the file **cleanup** at noon?

    _____

25. Which command can you use to view **at** jobs that have been scheduled on your system?

    a. at --view

    b. atq

    c. atrm

    d. cron --view

---

## DISCOVERY EXERCISES

### Viewing Processes Using ps

There are two main types of options that are used with the **ps** command: those that require a dash and those that do not. We have examined options that do not require a dash in this chapter (e.g., **ps aux**); these options have traditionally been used on BSD UNIX systems. Options that require a dash are taken from AT&T System V UNIX systems. Using the man or info pages, research four more options to the ps command that require a dash character. What processes does each option display? What information is given about each process?

### Using Kill Signals

Log in to tty1 as the root user and perform the following actions in order. For each action, write the command(s) that you used.

1. Run the **ps** command to view processes in your current shell. Record the PID for your bash shell.

2. Send the PID of your bash shell as SIGINT. What happened and why?

3. Send the PID of your bash shell as SIGTERM. What happened and why?

4. Send the PID of your bash shell as SIGCONT. What happened and why?

5. Send the PID of your bash shell as SIGKILL. What happened and why?

### Process Priorities

Log in to tty1 as the root user and perform the following actions in order. For each action, write the command(s) that you used. When finished, log out of tty1.

1. Start the **ps –l** command with the default nice value. What nice value is shown in the output?

2. Start the **ps –l** command with a nice value of –20, and verify the correct nice value in the output. Did this command run with high or low priority? Which users can run this command?

3. Start the **ps –l** command with a nice value of –19, and verify the correct nice value in the output. Did this command run with high or low priority? Which users can run this command?

DISCOVERY

## Manipulating Background Processes

Log in to tty1 as the root user and perform the following actions in order. For each action, write the command(s) that you used. When finished, log out of tty1.

8

1. Start the **sleep 50000** command in the background (this command simply waits for 50000 seconds). Repeat this command four more times.

2. View the background jobs.

3. Run the third background process in the foreground. Press Ctrl+z to stop the foreground process and view the background jobs. What is the status of the third background job?

4. Start the third background process in the background again. Verify that is it running in the background.

5. Send the fifth background process a SIGTERM and verify that it has stopped.

6. Kill all other sleep processes using a SIGINT.

DISCOVERY

## Starting a Daemon in a Runlevel

Log in to tty1 as the root user and create a file called /etc/init.d/sampledaemon that has the permissions 755. Next, edit this file with the **vi** editor and add a line that reads **echo My daemon has started**. Then, create a soft link to this file called /etc/init.d/rc3.d/ S90sampledaemon. In which runlevel will this script be run? Finally, change to runlevel 3 (press Enter to receive your prompt). Did your daemon start in this runlevel? When finished, log out of tty1.

DISCOVERY

## Scheduling Processes Using the at Daemon

The **at** command is versatile in that it can understand nearly any time format. Log in to tty1 as the root user, ensure that the **at** daemon is running, and schedule the **date** and **who** commands to run at teatime (use the **at teatime** command). When you have finished scheduling the at job, note the time that the two commands will be scheduled. Next, remove your at job and use the manual or info pages to research other time formats that may be used with the **at** command. When finished, log out of tty1.

## Cron Tables

Write the lines that you could use in your crontab to schedule the /bin/sample command to run:

1. every Friday at 1:30 a.m.

2. at 4:30 p.m. on May 15th only

3. at 4:00 p.m. and 4:30 p.m. on the first Sunday of every month

4. every 10 minutes from 9:00 a.m. to 5:00 p.m. on Monday

5. at 8:15 a.m. and 6:30 p.m. Monday to Friday

# MANAGE THE NETWORK CONFIGURATION

Linux is designed to work in a network environment. This section explains how to configure network settings with YaST and from the command line. It also introduces some basic commands that you can use to test the network connection.

♦ TCP/IP Fundamentals

♦ Manage the Network Configuration Using YaST

♦ Modify the Configuration of a Network Card from the Command Line

♦ Get to Know Network-Related Command-Line Commands

## OBJECTIVE 1    TCP/IP FUNDAMENTALS

In order to connect your SLES 9 server to a network that uses Transmission Control Protocol/Internet Protocol (TCP/IP), you need to understand the following:

- TCP/IP Network Components
- IP Address Structure
- Network Classes and IP Addresses
- Special IP Addresses

## TCP/IP Network Components

The following are the basic components used to build the Internet delivery architecture:

- **Host.** Any computer (client or server) on the Internet. If the host acts as a server it receives requests for information from the Internet and passes them to installed server applications (such as a Web server).

    After a server application fulfills the request the host sends the data back to the Internet.

    A host is also referred to as a *node* or *station*.

- **TCP/IP.** This protocol suite defines how packets of information should be structured for successful transmission over a TCP/IP network (such as an intranet or the Internet).

    TCP allows two hosts (or a host and a client) to establish a connection and exchange packets of data. TCP guarantees the delivery of data and guarantees that packets are delivered in the same order in which they were sent.

- **IP packet.** An electronic package of data sent over the Internet. The packet is labeled with information such as the sender's address, the receiver's address, and the type of packet.

    Packet types include TCP packets for delivering requests and content, and Internet Control Message Protocol (ICMP) Ping packets for testing an Internet connection between computers.

- **Router.** A hardware or software device that forwards an IP packet to the next network point on its way to a destination. A router is often included as part of a network switch.

    A packet normally travels through a number of network points with routers before arriving at its destination.

- **Firewall.** A set of related programs (often installed on a network gateway server or other hardware) that protects the resources of a private intranet or network from unauthorized access by users from other networks.

A company with an intranet that allows its employees to access the Internet can install a firewall to prevent outsiders from accessing its own private data resources and to control what outside resources its employees can access.

There are several firewall filtering (screening) methods. A simple one is to filter requests to make sure they come from acceptable (previously identified) domain name and IP addresses.

A firewall can also enforce company policies that prevent access to specific Internet sites (such as streaming media or pornographic sites).

## IP Address Structure

Every protocol suite defines some type of addressing that identifies computers and networks. An Internet address uses 32 bits and includes both a network ID and a host ID.

Routers locate hosts on the Internet based on their assigned IP addresses.

An IP address of a host consists of 4 bytes divided into 2 parts:

- A network address (from 1 to 3 bytes)
- A node or station address (from 1 to 3 bytes)

The **netmask** is used to determine where the network address ends and where the host address begins.

The netmask looks similar to a "normal" IP address and determines which bits of the IP address should be used for the network address. Those bits within the IP address that correspond to the bits set to 1 in the network mask are part of the network IP address.

If for example the netmask is 255.0.0.0, then the first byte/the first eight bits of the IP address are the network address. The remaining three bytes are the node address.

Another way to describe the netmask is just to count the bits that make up the netmask and append it to the IP address with a slash. Another way of describing an IP address of 10.0.0.1 with netmask 255.0.0.0 is therefore 10.0.0.1/8.

The IPv6 addressing scheme allows IP addresses to be 16 bytes long.

As shown in Figure 9-1, an IP network has been assigned the network address of 132.132 (netmask 255.255.0.0).

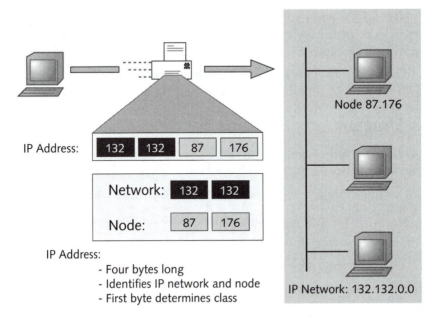

**Figure 9-1**

The 132.132 network address uniquely identifies the network from all other networks within the Internet.

Each host or node on this network must have an IP address such as 132.132.*x.x*, where the last two bytes of the address need to be unique on the network.

In the above example, a node that is assigned the last two octets of 87.176 is uniquely identified within the Internet by the IP address of 132.132.87.176.

Each byte of a node address falls in the range of 0 to 255, but 0 and 255 are usually not used in addressing. Not all systems support a node address of 0, and 255 is reserved for broadcast packets.

IP addresses take the form of a dotted octet; that is, each byte (8 bits in an octet) is separated by a dot. In binary format, an IP address looks like Figure 9-2, with each *x* representing a binary bit with the value of 0 or 1.

**Figure 9-2**

A complete IP address in binary format looks like the following:

`10101100.00010000.00000100.00000010`

When you convert the binary bits to decimal numbers, an IP address takes a readable form. Converting the binary example above to decimal numbers results in the IP address 172.16.4.2.

One easy way to convert from binary to decimal numbers is to create a binary table such as shown in Figure 9–3, with columns for each power of 2 with its decimal equivalent.

| Binary | $2^7$ | $2^6$ | $2^5$ | $2^4$ | $2^3$ | $2^2$ | $2^1$ | $2^0$ | Decimal Equivalent |
|---|---|---|---|---|---|---|---|---|---|
| Decimal | 128 | 64 | 32 | 16 | 8 | 4 | 2 | 1 | |
| | 1 | 0 | 1 | 0 | 1 | 1 | 0 | 0 | (1x128)+ (1x32)+ (1x8)+ (1x4)=172 |
| | 0 | 0 | 0 | 1 | 0 | 0 | 0 | 0 | (1x16)=16 |
| | 0 | 0 | 0 | 0 | 0 | 1 | 0 | 0 | (1x4)=4 |
| | 0 | 0 | 0 | 0 | 0 | 0 | 1 | 0 | (1x2)=2 |

**Figure 9-3**

Correspond each of the 8 bits in a byte to a column and add the decimal values for each bit with a value of 1 in a single row. The result is the decimal equivalent of the byte.

## Network Classes and IP Addresses

Figure 9-4 illustrates the five address classes that exist in the IP addressing scheme, classes A through E.

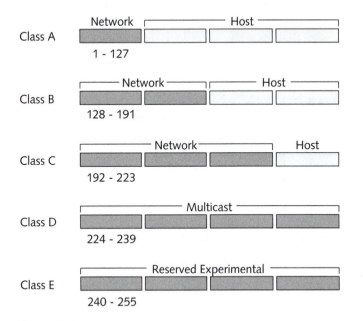

**Figure 9-4**

Classes A through C can be assigned; classes D and E are reserved for specific uses and are not assigned to hosts.

Your network class determines how the 4-byte IP address is divided between network and node portion, as shown in Figure 9-5.

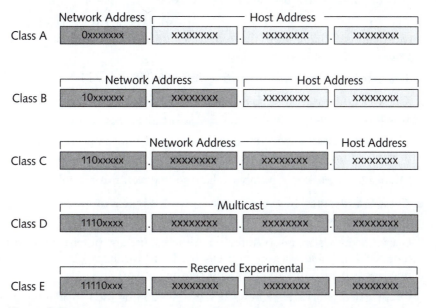

Figure 9-5

Notice that the first bits of the first byte in the address identify the network class.

The following describes the addresses available in each class:

- **Class A addresses.** In a class A address, the first byte is in the 0 to 127 range and also identifies the network; the final three bytes identify the node. The first bit must be zero.

  There are 126 possible class A networks (with 0.*x.x.x* not being used and 127.*x.x.x* being reserved for the local host), each having up to 16,777,216 hosts. Virtually all class A addresses have been assigned.

  The netmask in a class A network is 255.0.0.0 or /8.

- **Class B addresses.** In a class B address, the first byte is in the 128 to 191 range (the first two bits of the first byte are 1 and 0). The first two bytes identify the network, and the last two bytes identify the node on the network.

  There are 16,384 possible class B networks. Each class B network can have up to 65,534 hosts. Relatively few class B addresses remain available.

  The netmask in a class B network is 255.255.0.0 or /16.

- **Class C addresses.** In a class C address, the first byte is in the 192 to 223 range (the first three bits of the first byte are 1, 1, and 0). The first three bytes identify the network and the last byte identifies the node.

  There are 2,097,152 possible class C networks. Each class C network can have up to 255 hosts. Organizations that request a registered class B address can receive one or more class C addresses instead.

  The netmask in a class C network is 255.255.255.0 or /24.

- **Class D addresses.** In a class D address, the first byte is in the 224 to 239 range (the first four bits of the first byte are 1, 1, 1, and 0).

  Class D addresses are used for multicast packets. Multicast packets are used by a host to transmit messages to a specified group of hosts on the network.

  Multicasts are packets typically exchanged between routers only.

- **Class E addresses.** In a class E address, the first byte is in the 240 to 255 range (the first five bits of the byte are 1,1,1,1, and 0).

  Class E addresses are reserved for experimental use and potential future addressing modes. Class E addresses are typically used for broadcasts. (A broadcast message is one that is transmitted to every host on the network.)

  One particular class E address, 255.255.255.255, is used to identify a broadcast message. When the destination IP address is 255.255.255.255, the message is directed to all hosts on the network from which the broadcast originated.

  Routers do not typically forward broadcast messages to other networks.

- **CIDR (Classless Inter-Domain Routing) and Subnets.** In the class A, B, and C nets the netmask is 255.0.0.0, 255.255.0.0, and 255.255.255.0, respectively. However it is not mandatory that the network address part is exactly 1, 2 or 3 bytes long.

  A class C network can be divided into two smaller networks by extending the netmask into the last byte: 255.255.255.128 (/25). Even smaller networks are possible.

  Bigger networks can be achieved by combining for instance two class C networks into one network, using the netmask 255.255.254.0 (/23).

## Special IP Addresses

The addresses shown in Table 9-1 have special meaning within the TCP/IP protocol suite and should not be used when assigning IP addresses to hosts that are directly connected to the Internet.

**Table 9-1**

| IP Address | Purpose |
|---|---|
| Network 0.0.0.0 | Refers to the default route. This route is used to simplify routing tables used by IP.<br><br>On some older (BSD 4.2) networks the 0.0.0.0 address is used for broadcasts. |
| Network 127.0.0.0 | Reserved for loopback. The address 127.0.0.1 often is used to refer to the local host.<br><br>Using this address, applications can address a local host as if it were a remote host without relying on any configuration information. |
| 255.255.255.255 | Refers to a limited broadcast meant for hosts on this network only. |
| Class A network 10.x.x.x<br><br>Class B networks 172.16.x.x - 172.31.x.x<br><br>Class C networks 192.168.x.x | IP addresses within these networks are not used in the Internet and can be used within local area networks. |

**9**

**IPv6**  Since the address space within the current standard IPv4 is no longer considered adequate for future needs, IPv6 was developed some time ago.

It has been designed to overcome the address shortage and improve on various aspects of IPv4. Some of its features are:

- Longer addresses—128 bits instead of 32, allowing you to address a vastly increased number of hosts.

- Optimized header format to simplify routing.

- Support of service types, to improve transmission of certain kind of data, such as audio and video.

- Improved security (authentication and encryption).

Linux supports IPv6, as do the current versions of Windows. However, in general there has not been a big push to move the Internet infrastructure to IPv6.

Reasons for this are, amongst other things, that some of the improvements of IPv6 have been backported into IPv4, like IPSec, and the shortage of addresses has been circumvented to some degree with network address translation.

## OBJECTIVE 2    MANAGE THE NETWORK CONFIGURATION USING YaST

In order to allow your SLES system to participate on a network, you must first configure a network interface with protocol information. This section discusses:

- Network Interfaces in Linux
- Configuring a Network Card Using YaST

## Network Interfaces in Linux

In Linux, network interfaces are always referred to with a fixed name. The name depends on the type and position of the network card in the computer.

The first card is called eth0, the second is eth1, and so on. Similarly, the designations for token ring cards are tr0, tr1, and so on.

Linux supports a range of network cards and supports all well-known network protocols. This support is in the form of corresponding drivers, which must be available for the interfaces on the Linux computer.

SLES 9 already contains the drivers for all common network cards. These drivers are kernel modules that can be loaded if and when required.

## Configuring a Network Card Using YaST

You can access the YaST module for configuring network cards and the network connection from the YaST Control Center by selecting **Network Devices > Network Card**, as shown in Figure 9-6.

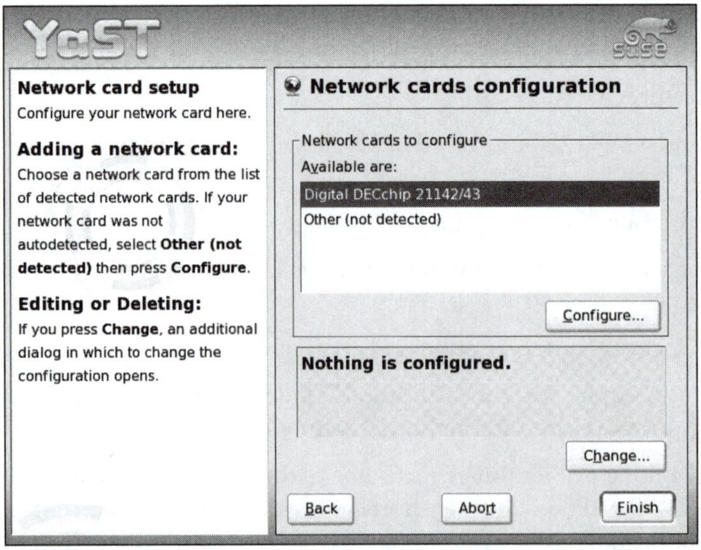

Figure 9-6

Any unconfigured network cards are listed in the top frame. The bottom frame displays configured network cards.

Select the card you want to configure; then select **Configure** (if the card is being set up for the first time) or **Change** (if you want to modify an existing configuration).

Usually the card is autodetected by YaST, and the correct kernel module is used.

If the card is not recognized by YaST, the required module must be entered manually. Select **Other** (not detected) and then select **Configure**.

A Manual Card Setup dialog box appears, and shown in Figure 9-7.

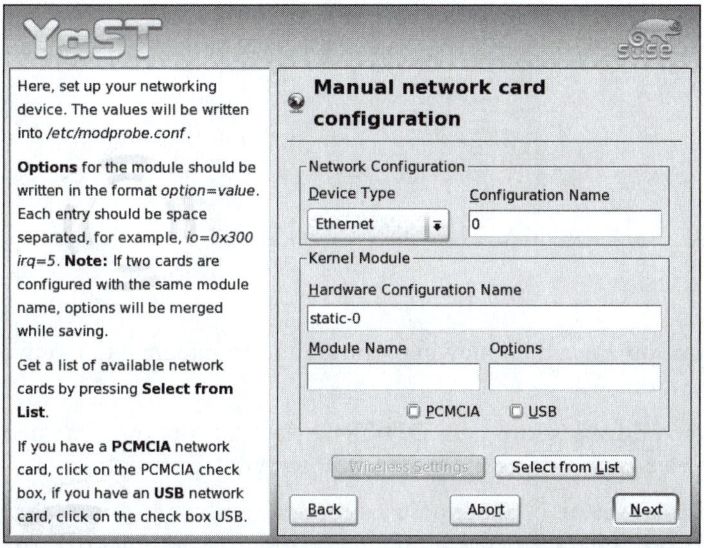

**Figure 9-7**

From this dialog box, you enter details of the interface to configure such settings as Network Device Type (**Ethernet**) and Configuration Name (**0**). Under Kernel module, enter the name of the module to load. You can select your card from a list of network cards.

Some kernel modules can be configured more precisely by adding options or parameters for the kernel. Details about parameters for specific modules can be found in the kernel documentation.

After selecting **Next**, the dialog box shown in Figure 9-8 appears.

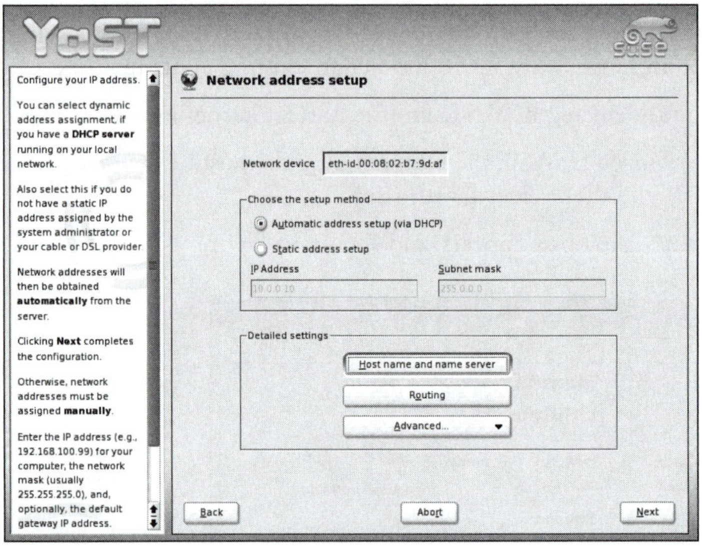

**Figure 9-8**

From this dialog box you enter the following information to integrate the network device into an existing network:

- **Automatic address setup (via DHCP).** Select this option if the network card should receive an IP address from a DHCP server.

- **Static address setup.** If you choose this option, you need to enter the IP address of the network interface of the computer in the network under **IP Address**.

  Each computer in the network has at least one address for each network interface, which must be unique in the entire network. According to the currently valid standard (IPv4), this address consists of a sequence of 4 bytes, separated by dots (such as 10.10.0.69).

  When choosing the IP address, you need to know if the computer will be directly connected to the Internet. In this case, an assigned official IP address must be used. Otherwise, use an address from a private address space.

- **Network mask.** The network mask (referred to as the *subnet mask* in YaST) determines in which network an IP address is located.

  The mask divides the IP address into a network section and a host section, thus defining the size of a network. All computers within the network can reach each other directly without a router in between.

- **Host name and name server.** Computers in the network can be addressed directly using their IP addresses or with a unique name. A name server (DNS) must exist for the resolution of names into IP addresses and vice versa.

  After selecting **Host name and name server**, the dialog box shown in Figure 9-9 appears.

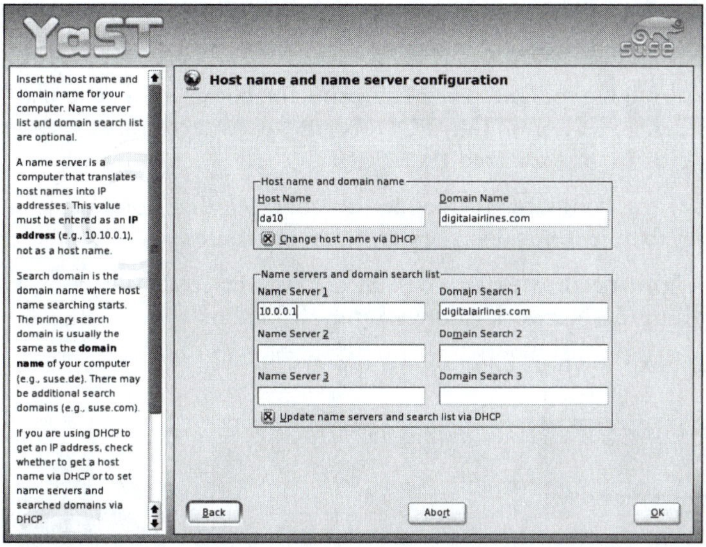

**Figure 9-9**

This dialog box lets you enter the following:

- **Host name.** Enter a name with which the computer can be addressed. This name should be unique within the network.

- **Domain name.** This is the name of the DNS domain to which the computer belongs. Domains help to divide networks. All computers in a defined organizational area normally belong to the same domain.

  A computer can be addressed uniquely by giving its FQDN (Fully Qualified Domain Name). The FQDN consists of the host name and the name of the domain, such as **da10.digitalairlines.com**. In this case, the domain would be digitalairlines.com.

- **List of name servers.** To address other computers in the network with their host names, identify the name server responsible for the conversion of computer names to IP addresses and vice versa.

  You can specify a maximum of three name servers.

- **Domain search list.** In the local network, it is more appropriate to address other hosts not with their FQDN, but with their host names. The domain search list specifies up to three domains with which the system can expand the host name to the FQDN.

  This complete name is then passed to the name server to be resolved. For example, **da2** is expanded with the search list **digitalairlines.com** to the FQDN **da2.digitalairlines.com**. This name is then passed to the name server to be resolved.

  If the search list contains several domains, the completion takes place one after the other, and the resulting FQDNs are passed to the name server until an entry returns an associated IP address.

- **Routing.** If the computer is intended to contact other computers in the same subnet only, then it is not necessary to enter any routes.

  However, if you need to enter a default gateway or create a routing table, select **Routing** from the Network Address Setup dialog box.

  The dialog box shown in Figure 9-10 appears.

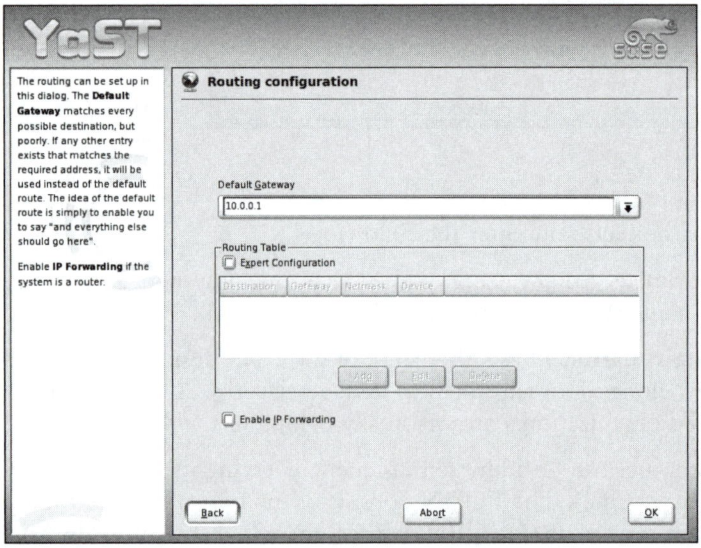

**Figure 9-10**

You can define the following:

- **Default Gateway.** If the network has a gateway (a computer that forwards information from a network to other networks), its address can be specified in the network configuration.

All data not addressed to the local network is then forwarded directly to the gateway.

- **Routing Table.** You can create entries in the routing table of the system after selecting **Expert Configuration**.

- **Advanced settings.** From the **Advanced** drop-down list, you can configure the following:

  - **Hardware Details.** From this dialog box you can configure kernel module settings such as hardware configuration name and module name. These settings are saved in the file corresponding to the interface in /etc/sysconfig/hardware/.

  - **DHCP Client Options.** From this dialog box you can configure client options such as request broadcast response and DHCP client identifier.

  - **Detailed Settings.** From this dialog box you can configure settings such as the maximum transfer unit (MTU) and when the device should be activated (such as at boot time).

  - **Virtual Aliases.** From this dialog box you can add, edit, or delete virtual aliases.

All the necessary information is now available to activate the network card. Save the configuration by selecting **Next** and then **Finish**.

After you save the configuration with YaST, the ethernet card should be available in the computer. You can verify this with the command **ifconfig** or **ip**.

If you run this command as a user other than root, you must enter the absolute path to the command:

**/sbin/ifconfig**

In the output of the command some information on the interface just configured should be visible.

Details on ifconfig are covered in the next objective, Modify the Configuration of a Network Card from the Command Line

## Exercise 9-1   Manage the Network Configuration Information from YaST

Configuring the network card using YaST is an easy task. In most of the cases it will work without any problems. The configuration is stored in files below /etc/sysconfig/network/.

To manage the network configuration information from YaST, do the following:

1.  Open a terminal window and su to root (**su –**) with a password of **novell**.

2. Use the **ifconfig eth0** and **hostname** commands to record the following information for your SLES 9 server:

   ■ IP address:

   ■ Host name:

3. Close the terminal window.

4. From the KDE Desktop, select the **YaST** icon; then enter a password of **novell** and select **OK**.

   The YaST Control Center appears.

5. Start the network card module by selecting:

   **Network Devices > Network Card**

   Your network card is listed under Already Configured Devices.

6. Change the configuration of your network card by selecting **Change**.

   Your network card is displayed in a list of configured cards.

7. Make sure *your network card* is selected; then select **Edit**.

8. Switch to the setup by selecting **Static Address Setup**.

9. In the IP Address field, enter the *IP address* from Step 2.

10. In the Subnet Mask field, enter **255.255.255.0**.

11. Select **Host name and name server**.

12. (Conditional) If a dialog box appears indicating that the **resolv.conf** files has been temporarily modified, continue by selecting **Modify**.

13. In the Host Name field, enter the *hostname* from Step 2.

14. In the Domain Name field, enter **digitalairlines.com**.

15. In the Name Server 1 field, enter the IP address of your DNS server (**10.0.0.254**).

16. If there are values in the other Name Server text fields, remove them.

17. In the Domain Search 1 field, enter **digitalairlines.com**.

18. If there are values in the other Domain Search text fields, remove them.

19. Select **OK**.

20. Select **Routing**.

21. In the Default Gateway field, enter the IP address of your Internet gateway (**10.0.0.254**).

22. Select **OK**.

23. Select **Next**.

24. Select **Finish**.

25. Close the YaST Control Center.

## OBJECTIVE 3    MODIFY THE CONFIGURATION OF A NETWORK CARD FROM THE COMMAND LINE

You can make temporary modifications to network card settings from the command line at any time by using the command **ifconfig** or the command **ip**. This type of modification is especially useful for testing purposes.

To make permanent configuration changes, you need to modify and save the configuration file manually, or use YaST to make the modifications.

To manually modify network card settings you need to how to do the following:

- Configure the Network Interface with ifconfig
- Configure IP Aliases with ifconfig
- Modify Network Interface Configuration Files
- Configure Host and Domain Names
- Configure and Manage Routes

## Configure the Network Interface with ifconfig

You can use the command **ifconfig** (/sbin/ifconfig) to manually configure network card interfaces. You can also view all information about the status of network interfaces.

The command also displays the MAC address (hardware address), which is unique for every network card.

For this reason, you should be familiar with the basic syntax of the command, even though it has now been replaced in the network scripts of SUSE Linux Enterprise Server (SLES) by the command **ip**.

If you change a configuration setting with ifconfig, the change is temporary. The new data is not written to any configuration file, so the original configuration is used again when the network is restarted.

The following is the syntax for the command ifconfig:

**ifconfig [*interface*] [*address*] [*options*]**

*interface* is the symbolic name of the network device to configure (such as eth0). *address* is the IP address to assign to the network card. The most commonly used *options* are listed in Table 9–2.

**Table 9-2**

| Option | Description |
|---|---|
| netmask *mask* | Assigns *mask* as the subnet mask. |
| broadcast *address* | Sets the broadcast address. |
| pointtopoint *address* | Sets the IP address of the other end for a ppp (point-to-point) connection. |
| mtu *bytes* | Sets the maximum transfer unit (MTU). This is the maximum size for a data packet in bytes. |
| up or down | Activates or deactivates the network card interface. |
| hw ether *MAC_address* | Sets the MAC address of an Ethernet network card to *MAC_address.* |

For example, if you enter **ifconfig eth0 192.168.0.1**, the network card eth0 is assigned IP address 192.168.0.1.

If the netmask and the broadcast address are not specified, they are set according to the network class for the IP address (see Network Classes and IP Addresses).

When an IP address is allocated, the interface is also activated (UP in the output of ifconfig).

If you enter:

**ifconfig eth0 down**

eth0 is deactivated.

If you enter:

**ifconfig eth0 up**

eth0 is activated again with the previous values.

This works only if values have previously been assigned to the interface, because ifconfig does not read any values from configuration files, but only from memory. If an interface has not yet been activated after a reboot, it cannot be activated directly by the option up.

Initial setup of the interface works only by assigning explicit values with the commands ifconfig or ip (as in the startup scripts). The same applies after the respective kernel module for the card has been unloaded with the command rmmod.

Entering **ifconfig** without options lists all defined network interfaces with their corresponding parameters, as in the following:

```
eth0      Link encap:Ethernet  HWaddr 00:11:25:82:D7:F9
          inet addr:10.0.0.10  Bcast:10.0.0.255  Mask:255.255.255.0
          inet6 addr: fe80::211:25ff:fe82:d7f9/64 Scope:Link
```

```
              UP BROADCAST NOTRAILERS RUNNING MULTICAST  MTU:1500  Metric:1
              RX packets:2986 errors:0 dropped:0 overruns:0 frame:0
              TX packets:458 errors:0 dropped:0 overruns:0 carrier:0
              collisions:0 txqueuelen:1000
              RX bytes:474080 (462.9 Kb)  TX bytes:72474 (70.7 Kb)
              Base address:0x8000 Memory:c0220000-c0240000
lo            Link encap:Local Loopback
              inet addr:127.0.0.1  Mask:255.0.0.0
              inet6 addr: ::1/128 Scope:Host
              UP LOOPBACK RUNNING  MTU:16436  Metric:1
              RX packets:8192 errors:0 dropped:0 overruns:0 frame:0
              TX packets:8192 errors:0 dropped:0 overruns:0 carrier:0
              collisions:0 txqueuelen:0
              RX bytes:809934 (790.9 Kb)  TX bytes:809934 (790.9 Kb)
```

This includes information such as address and network masks, packages received (RX, received) and sent (TX, transmitted), and collisions that might have occurred.

You can also display network device configuration information with the command **ip**, as in the following:

```
da10:~ # ip address show
1: lo: <LOOPBACK,UP> mtu 16436 qdisc noqueue
    link/loopback 00:00:00:00:00:00 brd 00:00:00:00:00:00
    inet 127.0.0.1/8 brd 127.255.255.255 scope host lo
    inet6 ::1/128 scope host
       valid_lft forever preferred_lft forever
2: eth0: <BROADCAST,MULTICAST,UP> mtu 1500 qdisc pfifo_fast qlen 1000
    link/ether 00:11:25:82:d7:f9 brd ff:ff:ff:ff:ff:ff
    inet 10.0.0.10/24 brd 10.0.0.255 scope global eth0
    inet6 fe80::211:25ff:fe82:d7f9/64 scope link
       valid_lft 2591994sec preferred_lft 604794sec
3: sit0@NONE: <NOARP> mtu 1480 qdisc noop
    link/sit 0.0.0.0 brd 0.0.0.0
```

In addition to any configured network device, two network devices are always set up by default: The loopback device (lo) and the device sit0@NONE, which is needed for integrating cards in networks with IPv6.

However, the command ifconfig does not display this network interface information by default.

Entering **ifconfig –a** (as in the following) lists all network interfaces including those that have not been configured:

```
da10:~ # ifconfig -a
eth0     Link encap:Ethernet  HWaddr 00:11:25:82:D7:F9
         inet addr:10.0.0.10  Bcast:10.0.0.255  Mask:255.255.255.0
         inet6 addr: fe80::211:25ff:fe82:d7f9/64 Scope:Link
         UP BROADCAST NOTRAILERS RUNNING MULTICAST  MTU:1500  Metric:1
         RX packets:2986 errors:0 dropped:0 overruns:0 frame:0
```

**9**

```
                    TX packets:458 errors:0 dropped:0 overruns:0 carrier:0
                    collisions:0 txqueuelen:1000
                    RX bytes:474080 (462.9 Kb)  TX bytes:72474 (70.7 Kb)
                    Base address:0x8000 Memory:c0220000-c0240000
eth1        Link encap:Ethernet  HWaddr 00:00:1C:B5:58:94
                    BROADCAST MULTICAST  MTU:1500  Metric:1
                    RX packets:0 errors:0 dropped:0 overruns:0 frame:0
                    TX packets:0 errors:0 dropped:0 overruns:0 carrier:0
                    collisions:0 txqueuelen:1000
                    RX bytes:0 (0.0 b)  TX bytes:0 (0.0 b)
                    Interrupt:16 Base address:0xb000
...
```

# Configure IP Aliases with ifconfig

With ifconfig, you can define more than one IP address for a network card by using *IP aliases*. There is virtually no limit for the number of possible IP aliases you can define.

For example, if a host only has one network card but needs to be addressed directly from several different subnets, you can use IP aliases to interface with these subnets.

However, it is always better to use a number of interfaces with genuine addresses (instead of IP aliases). This is because a host can only send or receive packets via one address on an interface at any given time.

You can configure an IP alias by using ifconfig, ip, or YaST.

The following is an example of configuring an IP alias by using ifconfig:

```
da10:~ # ifconfig eth0:1 192.168.0.10
da10:~ # ifconfig
eth0        Link encap:Ethernet  HWaddr 00:11:25:82:D7:F9
                    inet addr:10.0.0.10  Bcast:10.0.0.255  Mask:255.255.255.0
                    inet6 addr: fe80::211:25ff:fe82:d7f9/64 Scope:Link
                    UP BROADCAST RUNNING MULTICAST  MTU:1500  Metric:1
                    RX packets:3374 errors:0 dropped:0 overruns:0 frame:0
                    TX packets:536 errors:0 dropped:0 overruns:0 carrier:0
                    collisions:0 txqueuelen:1000
                    RX bytes:522857 (510.6 Kb)  TX bytes:83946 (81.9 Kb)
                    Base address:0x8000 Memory:c0220000-c0240000

eth0:1      Link encap:Ethernet  HWaddr 00:11:25:82:D7:F9
                    inet addr:192.168.0.10  Bcast:192.168.0.255  Mask:255.255.255.0
                    UP BROADCAST RUNNING MULTICAST  MTU:1500  Metric:1
                    Base address:0x8000 Memory:c0220000-c0240000
...
```

You can use both letters and numbers for IP aliases (such as **eth0:100**, **eth0:a1**, or **eth1:B42**). Remember that IP alias letters are case sensitive.

To view IP aliases, you can also enter **ip address show**.

## Modify Network Interface Configuration Files

In order to save the network configuration settings permanently, you need to manually edit and save the appropriate configuration files.

You can find all relevant network configuration files in the directory /etc/sysconfig/ network/. This directory contains a configuration file for each configured network adapter including details of the device.

For example, /etc/sysconfig/network/ifcfg-eth-id-00:00:1c:b5:55:74 is the configuration file for the network card with the hardware address 00:00:1c:b5:55:74, and /etc/sysconfig/ network/ifcfg-lo is the configuration file for the loopback device.

To understand the structure of the configuration files, you need to know something about the activation of the network device when booting.

All network interfaces (as well as configured routes) are activated at boot by the script /etc/init.d/network, which is run in runlevels 2, 3, and 5.

By accessing the settings of the existing configuration files in /etc/sysconfig/network/, the script knows which interfaces need to be activated at boot or deactivated when the computer is shut down.

The file /etc/sysconfig/network/config contains a number of general variables that influence the behavior of the script, such as whether a search should be made for existing connections when the interface is deactivated and if these should be automatically terminated.

The directory /etc/sysconfig/network/scripts/ contains additional scripts that are run by /etc/init.d/network (depending on the type of interface).

Activating or deactivating network interfaces is performed by running the script /sbin/ifup from the script /etc/init.d/network. With this script, the configuration files for the interface are evaluated and the network cards are activated with the command ip.

The scripts /sbin/ifdown (deactivating network interfaces) and /sbin/ifstatus (displaying the status of network interfaces) are only symbolic links to the script /etc/sbin/ifup.

If the start script /etc/init.d/network is used, all configured network interfaces are activated or deactivated, or the status of all configured network interfaces is given.

To activate just a single interface with the preconfigured values, or to find out the status of the single interface, or to deactivate only one interface, you have to add the interface name after start, stop, or status (such as **/etc/init.d/network stop eth0** or **/etc/init.d/ network start ippp0**).

9

You can also enter the commands ifup, ifstatus, and ifdown directly from the command line.

For example, entering:

**ifup eth0**

activates the first Ethernet network card, and entering:

**ifup eth1**

activates the second Ethernet network card or network device.

Entering **ifstatus eth0** displays information similar to the following:

```
da10:~ # ifstatus eth0
    eth0  device: Digital Equipment Corporation DECchip 21142/43 (rev 41)
    eth0  configuration: eth-id-00:11:25:82:d7:f9
eth0 is up
2: eth0: <BROADCAST,MULTICAST,UP> mtu 1500 qdisc pfifo_fast qlen 1000
link/ether 00:11:25:82:d7:f9 brd ff:ff:ff:ff:ff:ff
    inet 10.0.0.10/24 brd 10.0.0.255 scope global eth0
    inet6 fe80::211:25ff:fe82:d7f9/64 scope link
valid_lft forever preferred_lft forever
    eth0      IP address: 10.0.0.10/24
Configured routes for interface eth0:
  default 10.0.0.254 - -
  169.254.0.0 - 255.255.0.0 eth0
Active routes for interface eth0:
  10.0.0.0/24  proto kernel  scope link  src 10.0.0.10
  default via 10.0.0.254
1 of 2 configured routes for interface eth0 up
```

When the interfaces are activated through the script /etc/init.d/network or ifup, the settings are read from the configuration file for that particular network adapter.

The following are example settings in the configuration file /etc/sysconfig/network/ifcfg-eth-id-00:00:1c:b5:55:74:

```
BOOTPROTO='static'
BROADCAST='10.0.0.255'
IPADDR='10.0.0.10'
MTU=''
NETMASK='255.255.255.0'
NETWORK='10.0.0.0'
REMOTE_IPADDR=''
STARTMODE='onboot'
UNIQUE='gZD2.+xOL8ZCSAQC'
_nm_name='bus-pci-0000:00:0b.0'
```

These settings are evaluated by /sbin/ifup (enter **man 8 ifup** for a detailed description). The script calls up /sbin/ip with the evaluated settings in order to assign settings such as the address and network mask for that particular network interface and to set routes.

The parameter UNIQUE contains a unique hash value that is required by YaST to identify the network card to activate.

In the example, a static address is assigned (BOOTPROTO='static'). In a configuration for DHCP, the value dhcp would appear.

The STARTMODE='onboot' setting specifies that this interface should be activated when the script /etc/init.d/network is run.

The values IPADDR='10.0.0.10', NETMASK='255.255.255.0', and NETWORK='10.0.0.0' specify the IP address, network mask, and network address for the network card.

If the configuration is implemented through DHCP, these entries remain empty or are deleted entirely.

9

**NOTE**

For more information about network configuration, see /usr/share/doc/packages/sysconfig/ or refer to the man pages for the individual commands.

To configure IP aliases permanently, you need to enter them in the respective configuration file of the network card. For an example, see the template file /etc/sysconfig/network/ifcfg.template.

When the network script /etc/init.d/network is executed, this alias will also be activated.

## Configure Host and Domain Names

In order to provide a host name and domain name for a server whose network settings are configured manually, you need to modify the following two files:

- **/etc/HOSTNAME.** The entry for the FQDN of the host is located in this file and looks like the following:

```
da10.digitalairlines.com
```

- **/etc/resolv.conf.** The information about the name servers to query and the domain search list are stored in this file, and look like the following:

```
nameserver 10.0.0.254
nameserver 10.0.0.253
search digitalairlines.com
```

You can list a maximum of three name server entries. To enter several domains in the search list, keep them in the same line separated by blank spaces.

Also check /etc/hosts to see if the entries there match your configuration.

## Configure and Manage Routes

For IP packets to reach their destination, TCP/IP networks use routes. For packets that are not addressed to a host in the local network, routes show the way to a router that forwards the packets to their respective destinations.

In a running system, the routes are read from the kernel routing table. This table does not exist as an actual file but is generated in memory by the kernel.

If you need to configure routes permanently, you need to create a corresponding configuration file. This file is read by the script /etc/init.d/network and the routes listed are activated (they are inserted in the kernel routing table).

To configure and manage routes, you need to know the following:

- Route Types
- Manage Routes with route
- Modify Route Configuration Files
- Activate Routing
- Manage the Network Interface and Routes with ip

### Route Types

There are three basic types of routes:

- Host Routes
- Network and Gateway Routes
- Default Route

**Host Routes**    A host route defines the path that a data packet can take for exactly one destination host. For example, you need host routes when using ISDN cards to define the point-to-point connection on the provider connection.

The following from a routing table shows typical host routes:

```
Kernel IP routing table
Destination   Gateway       Genmask           Flags Metric Ref   Use Iface
[...]
192.168.1.2   0.0.0.0       255.255.255.255   UH    0      0       0 ippp0
192.168.15.7  10.0.0.3      255.255.255.255   UGH   0      0       0 eth0
```

The defined target with the IP address **192.168.1.2** appears, which represents one host. The corresponding netmask **255.255.255.255** is always set for host routes.

The set flags **U** and **H** specify that the route is up (U) and that this involves a host route (H).

The name of the network interface tells a correspondingly addressed data packet through which interface the packet should leave the Linux computer.

In this case, an outgoing data packet is leaving through the network interface **ippp0** (the first ISDN interface) toward 192.168.1.2. The gateway address **0.0.0.0** indicates that no routing gateway is needed to reach the destination. This represents a point-to-point connection to the provider's dial-in server.

In the second line, a host route is defined for the host **192.168.15.7**. This host can only be accessed by way of the router (gateway) **10.0.0.3**, which is marked with the flag **G** (Gateway).

**Network and Gateway Routes**    A network route defines the path a data packet can take for an entire destination network. Network routes are most frequently used because they define the path into your own network and into remote networks.

The following from a routing table shows two typical network routes:

```
Kernel IP routing table
Destination    Gateway         Genmask        Flags Metric Ref   Use Iface
10.0.0.0       0.0.0.0         255.255.255.0  U     0      0       0 eth0
192.168.15.0   10.0.0.253      255.255.255.0  UG    0      0       0 eth0
```

In the above example, the network route for your own network appears first (**eth0**).

The network address for your own network is **10.0.0.0** with a netmask of **255.255.255.0**. This results in a total addressable range of 256 IP addresses (10.0.0.0–10.0.0.255).

All data packets from this Linux computer addressed to an address in this range leave the Linux computer via the interface eth0.

The route to network **192.168.15.0** also addresses a total of 256 IP addresses (192.168.15. 0–192.168.15.255). The set flag **G** indicates that this network is a special case.

This route represents a gateway route—a route to the destination network via a defined gateway.

The corresponding gateway is defined with the IP address **10.0.0.253** and must be located in a network directly connected to the Linux machine.

Data packets to the defined destination network 192.168.15.0 are forwarded directly by the Linux machine to the specified gateway.

The gateway in turn has its own routes and forwards the data packets received depending on the rules defined in its own routing table.

**Default Route**    A default route is a special gateway route. It defines the route a data packet can take if no previous host, network, or gateway route matched the destination of the packet.

9

The following from a routing table shows a typical default route in the last line:

```
Kernel IP routing table
Destination    Gateway       Genmask          Flags Metric Ref    Use Iface
10.0.0.0       0.0.0.0       255.255.255.0    U     0      0        0 eth0
192.168.15.0   10.0.0.253    255.255.255.0    UG    0      0        0 eth0
0.0.0.0        10.0.0.254    0.0.0.0          UG    0      0        0 eth0
```

The destination of the default route is defined by the IP address **0.0.0.0** and the network mask **0.0.0.0**. This definition includes all existing IP addresses in the range 0.0.0.0–255.255.255.255.

If a data packet is generated on the Linux computer that cannot be delivered to the networks **10.0.0.0** and **192.168.15.0** over one of the first two routes, the data packet will always be delivered over the default route to the configured default gateway.

A Linux computer that is connected to an Internet service provider through an ISDN point-to-point connection will always have a default route defined on the IP address of the opposite point of the provider (on the provider's gateway) so all computers on the Internet can be reached via this gateway.

A corresponding routing table with just one installed network interface could be configured as follows:

```
Kernel IP routing table
Destination    Gateway       Genmask           Flags Metric Ref    Use Iface
192.168.1.2    0.0.0.0       255.255.255.255 UH    0      0        0 ippp0
0.0.0.0        192.168.1.2   0.0.0.0          UG    0      0        0 ippp0
```

## Manage Routes with route

You can use the command route (/sbin/route) to check and edit the routing table.

For example, the command **route -n** returns a table of activated routes with the listed addresses in numerical form (no name server query).

Although the functions of the command route are covered by the command ip in the script for starting the network, it is important that you are familiar with the command route, because it is a standard tool in all Linux distributions.

**CAUTION** Routes defined with the command **route** are entered directly in the kernel routing table and no longer exist after you restart the server. To define permanent routes, you need to modify the respective configuration files.

To manage routes with the command route, you need to know how to do the following:

- **Create a route.** The following is the syntax for creating new routes (on one line):

  **route add [-net | -host *destination*] [netmask *mask*] [gw *gateway*] [metric *n*] [dev *interface*]**

  For example, to set up a new route for the directly connected network 10.0.0.0/255.255.255.0 on the network interface eth0, enter

  **route add -net 10.0.0.0 netmask 255.255.255.0 dev eth0**

  Routes for the directly connected network are set automatically when bringing up the interface, as covered in *Modify Route Configuration Files*.

  To set up a new network route for a network lying behind the gateway with the IP address 10.0.0.253 using the address range 192.168.3.0/255.255.255.240, enter on one line

  **route add -net 192.168.3.0 netmask 255.255.255.240 gw 10.0.0.253 dev eth0**

  Static routing is set up by default. You can implement dynamic routing by installing and configuring a routing daemon.

  If you want to use dynamic routing, you need to add the option **metric *n***, where ***n*** is a value greater than or equal to zero and is used to define the distance to the destination host or network.

  The higher the value, the more costly the connection to the destination network is estimated to be by the routing daemon. In this way, several routes to a destination network can be defined.

  When a data packet is sent, the system will first try to deliver it over the most convenient route. The system will deliver the data packet through the next most favorable route only if the path is closed due to overload or failure of the targeted transmission route.

- **Delete a route.** You can also remove an existing route from the routing table with the command **route**. The following is the syntax for deleting a route (on one line):

  **route del [-net | -host *destination*] [gw *gateway*] [netmask *mask*] [dev *interface*]**

  For example, to remove the previously configured routes from the routing table, enter:

  **route del -net 192.168.3.0 netmask 255.255.255.240**

  To delete the default route, enter:

  **route del default**

9

To delete a network route, you need to specify the target address and the network mask.

**NOTE**

- **Reject a route.** You can also block the routing to certain networks:

**route add –net 172.16.0.0 netmask 255.255.0.0 reject**

## Modify Route Configuration Files

An entry is generated in the kernel routing table for all active network interfaces. This means that all hosts in the local network can be addressed without defining any further routes.

For example, if you assign the following parameters to the network interface eth0

```
da10:~ # ifconfig eth0 10.0.0.10 netmask 255.255.255.0
```

the output of the existing routes is as follows:

```
da10:~ # route -n
Kernel IP routing table
Destination    Gateway        Genmask         Flags Metric Ref    Use Iface
10.0.0.0       0.0.0.0        255.255.255.0   U     0      0        0 eth0
```

Notice that a route was generated to the local network, which is defined by the network mask.

Additional static routes are defined by entries in the respective configuration files and activated when the network is started.

As long as the system is up, these routes will not be modified by any dynamic processes and will be kept until they are deleted. For this reason, they are referred to as *static routes*.

All static routes are configured in the files

- /etc/sysconfig/network/routes
- /etc/sysconfig/network/ifroute-Interface

These files are read when the network is started, and the routes are written to the routing table.

The script /etc/init.d/network is responsible for transferring the entries from /etc/sysconfig/network/routes to the routing table and is executed automatically when the machine is booted to runlevels 2, 3, or 5.

When you use the YaST module Network Services Routing, the entries in these files are automatically updated. You can also define your own static routes in these files with any editor.

The structure of the files is largely based on the output of **route –n**. The entries include the following fields (in the order of their appearance):

- The destination network/destination host

- The gateway to use

- The network mask

- The network interface over which the packets are to be sent (this field can remain empty)

The following is an example of typical entries in the file /etc/sysconfig/network/routes:

```
10.0.0.0          0.0.0.0         255.255.255.0
192.168.15.0      10.0.0.253      255.255.255.0
192.168.17.12     10.0.0.251      255.255.255.255
default           10.0.0.254      0.0.0.0              eth0
```

A typical example for a routing file for a special interface is /etc/sysconfig/network/ifroute-ippp0. This route is only set when a dial-in connection is established with the provider by way of the ISDN card. Normally, the default route is set (such as

**default 192.168.1.2 0.0.0.0 ippp0**).

For the default route, do not enter **0.0.0.0** as a destination in the file; instead, use the keyword **default**.

## Activate Routing

A Linux host can also serve as a router. However, this setting is deactivated by default. An entry in the process file system activates routing in the kernel:

**echo 1 > /proc/sys/net/ipv4/ip_forward**

If a 0 is entered in this file, routing will be deactivated. To activate routing permanently, set the following variable in the file /etc/sysconfig/sysctl:

**IP_FORWARD="yes"**

## Manage the Network Interface and Routes with ip

In SLES, the commands ifconfig and route have been replaced (as far as possible) in the scripts for network configuration by the command **ip**.

You can use the command ip to perform the following common administrative tasks:

- Assign addresses to network interfaces

- Assign parameters to network interfaces

- Set routes

- Define simple filter rules

- Display the current configuration

Because there are so many tasks you can perform with ip, the command syntax is relatively complex. The following is the general syntax for the command:

**ip [*options*] *object* [*command* [*parameters*]]**

*object* specifies what should be changed with the command. Table 9–3 lists some possible values for *object*.

**Table 9-3**

| Object | Description |
|---|---|
| link | Allocates parameters for a network interface |
| addr or address | Determines an address for a network device |
| route | Configures routes |

Depending on the objects, various options and commands are available. You can also significantly abbreviate command parameters (such as entering **ip a s** instead of **ip address show**).

As with ifconfig, all modifications made with the command ip are temporary and are no longer valid after restarting the network script /etc/init.d/network.

For configuration changes to be permanent, you need to make them with YaST or directly edit the appropriate configuration files.

You can perform the following common tasks with the command ip:

- Assign Parameters for Network Interfaces (ip link)
- Assign IP Addresses (ip address)
- Set up Routes (ip route)

**NOTE**

Many other configuration options are available for the command ip, such as setting simple filter rules or adding other types of routes.

For more information on the command ip, see /usr/share/doc/packages/iproute2/ip-cref.pdf.

**Assign Parameters for Network Interfaces (ip link)**   The only commands you can use when you assign parameters to network devices with ip are set (to set values) and show (to display set parameters).

Table 9-4 lists some commonly used parameters for set.

**Table 9-4**

| Parameter | Description |
|---|---|
| dev *interface* | Name of the interface to address (standard parameter) |
| up or down | Activates or deactivates the interface |

**Table 9-4**   (continued)

| Parameter | Description |
|---|---|
| mtu | Sets the maximum transfer unit (MTU) which is the maximum size of a data packet in bytes |
| address *MAC_address* | Overwrites the MAC address of the interfaces |

For example, entering **ip link set eth0 mtu 1492** sets the MTU value for the network card eth0 to 1492 bytes.

The parameter dev (normally in front of eth0) does not have to be given, since this is the default parameter.

Entering **ip link set eth0 down** deactivates network card eth0.

Entering **ip link show** displays parameters for all configured network interfaces, as in the following:

```
da10:~ # ip link show
1: lo: <LOOPBACK,UP> mtu 16436 qdisc noqueue
    link/loopback 00:00:00:00:00:00 brd 00:00:00:00:00:00
2: eth0: <BROADCAST,MULTICAST,UP> mtu 1500 qdisc pfifo_fast qlen 1000
    link/ether 00:00:1c:b0:a2:85 brd ff:ff:ff:ff:ff:ff
3: eth1: <BROADCAST,MULTICAST> mtu 1500 qdisc noop qlen 1000
    link/ether 00:00:1c:b5:58:94 brd ff:ff:ff:ff:ff:ff
4: sit0: <NOARP> mtu 1480 qdisc noqueue
    link/sit 0.0.0.0 brd 0.0.0.0
```

**Assign IP Addresses (ip address)**    When configuring IP addresses, the most important commands are

- **add**. Assign an address
- **del**. Delete an address
- **show**. Display addresses

Table 9-5 lists some commonly used parameters for add.

**Table 9-5**

| Parameter | Description |
|---|---|
| dev *interface* | Name of the interface to address |
| local *address/mask* | IP address and netmask of the interface (default parameter) |
| peer *address* | IP address of the other end of a PPP connection |
| broadcast *address* | Broadcast address (must be given explicitly) |
| label *name* | Generates an IP alias with the *name* |

The following is an example of use of the parameter dev:

```
da10:~ # ip address add 10.0.0.10/24 dev eth0 broadcast +
```

In this example, the network card eth0 is given the IP address 10.0.0.10. In contrast to the command ifconfig, you need to specify a netmask when using ip; otherwise, the netmask is set to 255.255.255.255 by default.

For the same reason, you need to specify a broadcast address. In this example, entering broadcast + sets a broadcast address calculated from the given net mask.

You do not need to enter the parameter local (before the IP address) because this is the default parameter for ip. You can also abbreviate the parameter broadcast to brd.

The following example uses parameters dev and label:

```
da10:~ # ip address add 192.168.1.1/24 broadcast 192.168.1.
255 dev eth0 \ label eth0:1
```

In this example, the IP alias eth0:1 is activated with the given values. Assigned IP aliases are listed with the network interface, as in the following:

```
da10:~ # ip address show
1: lo: <LOOPBACK,UP> mtu 16436 qdisc noqueue
    link/loopback 00:00:00:00:00:00 brd 00:00:00:00:00:00
    inet 127.0.0.1/8 brd 127.255.255.255 scope host lo
    inet6 ::1/128 scope host
       valid_lft forever preferred_lft forever
2: eth0: <BROADCAST,MULTICAST,UP> mtu 1500 qdisc pfifo_fast qlen 1000
    link/ether 00:00:1c:b0:a2:85 brd ff:ff:ff:ff:ff:ff
    inet 10.0.0.10/24 brd 10.0.0.255 scope global eth0
    inet 192.168.1.1/24 brd 192.168.1.255 scope global eth0:1
    inet6 fe80::211:25ff:fe82:d7f9/64 scope link
       valid_lft forever preferred_lft forever
3: eth1: <BROADCAST,MULTICAST> mtu 1500 qdisc noop qlen 1000
    link/ether 00:00:1c:b5:58:94 brd ff:ff:ff:ff:ff:ff
4: sit0: <NOARP> mtu 1480 qdisc noqueue
    link/sit 0.0.0.0 brd 0.0.0.0
```

In the following example, the IP alias with the address 192.168.1.1 is deleted:

```
da10:~ # ip address delete 192.168.1.1 dev eth0
```

**Set up Routes (ip route)**    When you set up routes using ip route, you can add routes (add), modify routes (change), delete routes (delete), and display routes (show).

Table 9-6 lists some commonly used parameters for adding routes.

**Table 9-6**

| Parameter | Description |
|---|---|
| default | Adds a default route |
| via *address* | Specifies the IP address of a gateway |
| dev *interface* | Specifies the name of the interface to which packets should be sent |

The following is an example of using the parameter via:

```
da10:~ # ip route add 192.168.1.0/24 via 10.0.0.253
```

The route to the network 192.168.1.0/24 is added through the gateway host 10.0.0.253.

The following is an example of how to delete the default route:

```
da10:~ # ip route delete default
```

**9**

## OBJECTIVE 4   GET TO KNOW NETWORK-RELATED COMMAND-LINE COMMANDS

A large network usually includes exchange network components (such as routers, hubs, and switches) that ensure the correct forwarding of data traffic.

As the number of components installed in a network increases, so does the number of possible sources of error.

To be able to analyze and correct errors, you need suitable diagnosis tools. This objective introduces the most important diagnostic tools needed for daily work in a TCP/IP-based network:

- Determine Connectivity Between Hosts Using ping
- Display the Route Between Hosts with traceroute
- Check for Service Availability with netcat
- List Currently Active Network Connections with netstat
- Analyze Network Traffic (tcpdump and ethereal)

## Determine Connectivity Between Hosts Using ping

The command /bin/ping is a simple diagnosis tool you can use to check network connections. It is normally available on all hosts which contain a TCP/IP stack and should always be the first tool you use to diagnose network errors.

To effectively use ping, you need to understand the following:

- Common Use of ping
- Command Options
- Problem Analysis

## Common Use of ping

The command ping lets you check network connections in a simple way between two hosts. The hosts can be located in the same or in remote networks.

If the ping command works, then both the physical and logical connections are correctly set up between the two hosts.

In the simplest scenario, you enter **ping** *host*, which causes the host to send an ICMP datagram to the target host with the message echo request.

If this ICMP datagram can be received by the target host, it will answer the initiating host with an ICMP datagram, (the message echo reply).

When the message is sent using the ICMP protocol, no higher-level protocols, such as TCP or UDP, are used. This means that incorrect configurations within the higher protocols do not automatically lead to a reply failing.

A typical output of the ping command looks like the following:

```
da1:~ # ping da2
PING da2.digitalairlines.com (10.0.0.2) from 10.0.0.254 :
 56(84) bytes of data.
64 bytes from da2.digitalairlines.com (10.0.0.2): icmp_
seq=1 ttl=255 time=0.309 ms
64 bytes from da2.digitalairlines.com (10.0.0.2): icmp_
seq=2 ttl=255 time=0.191 ms
64 bytes from da2.digitalairlines.com (10.0.0.2): icmp_
seq=3 ttl=255 time=0.194 ms

-- da2.digitalairlines.com ping statistics ---
3 packets transmitted, 3 received, 0% loss, time 2010ms
rtt min/avg/max/mdev = 0.191/0.231/0.309/0.056 ms
```

A total of three ICMP datagrams (echo requests) were sent to the host da2.digitalairlines. com. The datagrams were answered with the message echo reply. The output shows the following details:

- The IP address of the target host (da2 is resolved to da2.digitalairlines.com, and da2.digitalairlines.com is resolved to 10.0.0.2).
- The size of an ICMP datagram (data, ICMP header and IP header): 56(84) bytes of data.

- The sequence number of each reply datagram (icmp_seq, starting with 1 and increasing by 1 each time).

- The TTL (ttl, or time to live) of the datagram.

  When the datagram is sent, it has the value 255 in Linux. Each time it passes through a router in the Internet, it is decreased by 1. If the TTL reaches the value 0, then the packet is discarded.

  You can often deduce how many routers a datagram has passed through from the destination host by using the TTL value.

- The time (time) each round-trip needs.

  In other words, the amount of time needed to transmit an echo request datagram and receive the corresponding echo reply datagram.

- A statistical output of the round-trip times: min/avg/max/mdev (minimum/average/maximum/median deviation).

If a network connection fails, a typical output of the ping command looks like the following:

```
da1:~ # ping da2
PING da2.digitalairlines.com (10.0.0.2) from 10.0.0.254 :
 56(84) bytes of data.
From da1.digitalairlines.com (10.0.0.254): icmp_
seq=1 Destination Host Unreachable
From da1.digitalairlines.com (10.0.0.254) icmp_
seq=1 Destination Host Unreachable
--- 10.0.0.2 ping statistics ---
2 packets transmitted, 0 received, +2 errors, 100% loss, time
2010ms, pipe 3
```

In the above output, the ping command tried to send a total of two ICMP (echo request) datagrams to the target host da2.digitalairlines.com, but the sending host received no answer from the target host within a given period of time.

## Command Options

The command ping provides a variety of options for checking a network connection. Table 9-7 lists some of the more commonly used options.

**Table 9-7**

| Parameter | Description |
|---|---|
| -c *count* | Specifies how many echo request datagrams are sent before ping terminates. |
| -I *interface_addr* | Specifies the interface to be used on a server with several network interfaces. |
| -i *wait* | Specifies the number of seconds (*wait*) between individual datagrams (default: 1 second). |

**Table 9-7** (continued)

| Parameter | Description |
|---|---|
| -f (flood ping) | Datagrams are sent one after another at the same rate as the respective replies arrive, or one hundred times per second (whichever is greater).<br><br>Only root can use this option. For normal users, the minimum time is 200 milliseconds. |
| -l *preload* | This parameter causes ping to send *preload* datagrams without waiting for a reply |
| -n | Forces a numerical output of the IP address. Address resolutions to hostnames are not carried out. |
| -t *ttl* | Specifies the TTL value for echo request datagrams. |
| -w *maxwait* | Specifies a timeout (in seconds) before ping exits regardless of how many packets have been sent or received. |
| -b | Sends echo request datagrams to the broadcast address of the network. |

**NOTE**

For more information on all parameters available for the command ping, enter **man 8 ping**.

## Problem Analysis

If you want to examine communication between two hosts, then you should start by checking the internal host network (**ping localhost**). Then you should check the network interface connected to your own host (**ping** *interface_addr*).

If these checks of the host internal network and the connected network interface are successful, then you should check the network segment associated with the next closest network element (such as the default gateway router) in the direction of the target host. You should then check the network section containing the next but one segment, and so on, until the check ends at the target host.

If, during this check, no reply datagram is returned at a certain point, you can assume that at least one error is located in the last segment (such as cables, hub, switch, and router configuration). As a rule, using such a procedure can help you narrow down the source of the error.

# Display the Route Between Hosts with traceroute

You can use the command /usr/sbin/traceroute to help you follow the route taken by an IP datagram to the given target host.

This tool is primarily used to check routings between different networks and to illustrate the routings involved between the various TCP/IP-based networks.

To effectively use the traceroute command, you need to understand the following:

- Common Use of traceroute
- Command Options
- Problem Analysis

## Common Use of traceroute

The command **traceroute** is primarily used to check routings between different networks and to illustrate the routings involved between the various TCP/IP-based networks.

To achieve this task, traceroute sends datagrams with an increasing TTL (Time To Live) value to the destination host. First, three packets with a TTL=1 are sent to the host, then three packets with a TTL=2, and so on.

Since the TTL is reduced by one when the UDP datagram passes through a router (hop) and this datagram is discarded at TTL=0, a gateway at TTL=0 sends an ICMP datagram with the message Time To Live exceeded back to the sender.

If the UDP datagram reaches the target host, it will reply with an ICMP datagram port unreachable, since the target port for the UDP datagrams is set to values for which no services from the target host are normally offered.

From the ICMP message port unreachable, the sender recognizes that the target host has now been reached. Traceroute evaluates the information collected and also provides some statistical information on the standard output.

In the simplest scenario, you can perform a check of routing to the target host by entering:

**traceroute** *host*

A typical output of traceroute looks like the following:

```
da1: # traceroute pluto
traceroute to pluto.digitalairlines.com (192.168.2.1), 30 hops max,
40 byte packets
 1 da1.digitalairlines.com (10.0.0.254) 0 ms 0 ms 0 ms
 2 antares.digitalairlines.com (192.168.1.254) 14 ms 18 ms 14 ms
 3 pluto.digitalairlines.com (192.168.2.1) 19 ms * 26 ms
```

In the example, a total of three nodes were detected in the network across which the datagrams were routed to the target host. The output shows the following details:

- The IP address of the target host, Pluto, is resolved to pluto.digitalairlines.com; and pluto.digitalairlines.com is resolved to 192.168.2.1.

- The maximum TTL of a UDP packet is 30 (30 hops), which means that a maximum of 30 steps over routers and gateways can be detected on the path to the destination host.

- A UDP datagram has a length of 40 bytes.

- The time for a round trip for a total of three packets sent in succession by each router or recipient is displayed in milliseconds (ms).
- The second UDP datagram to reach pluto.digitalairlines.com directly was not answered within the given timeout of three seconds (indicated by *).

## Command Options

The command **traceroute** provides a variety of options for tracing a route over a network. Table 9-8 lists some of the more commonly used options.

**Table 9-8**

| Parameter | Description |
|---|---|
| -m *max_ttl* | Sets the TTL (maximum number of hops) to *max_ttl*. (Default: 30) |
| -n | Only outputs the IP addresses of the hops being surveyed (does not resolve any addresses). |
| -p *port* | Sets the target port for the UDP datagrams to *port*. This is increased by 1 for each datagram. (Default: port 33434) |
| -q *nqueries* | Sets the number of UDP datagrams for each hop to *nqueries*. (Default: 3) |
| -r | Sends a UDP datagram directly to a host in the local network without taking the routing table into account. |
| -S *src_addr* | Sets the sender address to *src_addr* if the sending host has multiple interfaces. The parameter *src_addr* must be valid for this host. |
| -w *waittime* | Sets the time (in seconds) to wait for a response to a probe. |

For more information on all parameters available for the command traceroute, enter **man traceroute**.

**NOTE**

## Problem Analysis

If communication between two networks is defective, the transport path between these two networks might contain errors. traceroute is an ideal tool to check routers that are located on this transport path.

It provides detailed information about the path that a datagram must take to the target network. It also provides information on the availability of the routers installed on this path.

If you enter **traceroute** with the parameter *target host*, you can see at a glance at which hop a data package can move along the transport path without a problem and at which point the transport path is faulty.

## Check for Service Availability with netcat

The command /usr/bin/netcat (called *nc* on other systems) is a UNIX tool that uses the TCP and UDP protocols to read and write data through network connections.

You can use netcat for establishing connections of any kind and can control it with scripts.

To use the command effectively, you need to know the following:

- Use netcat
- Advanced Use of netcat
- Command Options

### Use netcat

You can establish a connection to another host with netcat by entering:

**netcat** *host port*

as in the following:

```
da10:~ # netcat da50 80
GET /
<html>
<head>
<title>Web server on da50.digitalairlines.com</title>
</head>
<frameset cols=21%,79%>
<frame src="content.html" name="content">
<frame src="start.html" name="main">
</frameset>
</html>
```

In the above example, all entries to the standard input (GET /) are sent to the specified host and all responses from that host are displayed in the standard output (the <html> lines).

You can also use a telnet client to establish a connection to another host. However, netcat offers more possibilities, such as using the UDP protocol or deploying as a server waiting for a connection.

For example, entering:

**netcat –v –l –p 2000**

means that if a client connects to port 2000 (possibly also using netcat), everything that is entered in the associated terminal window will be transmitted to the client. The same takes place in the opposite direction.

## Advanced Use of netcat

You can use netcat to query a number of ports and display the responses of the services, as in the following examples:

```
geeko@da10:~> netcat -v -w 2 -z da50 20-80
da50.digitalairlines.com [10.0.0.50] 80 (http) open
da50.digitalairlines.com [10.0.0.50] 22 (ssh) open

geeko@da10:~> echo QUIT | netcat -v 10.0.0.50 22
da50.digitalairlines.com [10.0.0.50] 22 (ssh) open
SSH-1.99-OpenSSH_3.8p1
Protocol mismatch.
```

For a simple port scan, the program nmap is more suitable. However, you can enter the command (in the second part of the example) to quickly obtain information about a service.

The command shown in the first part of the example (on port 80) can also be used to check a connection to a host that does not respond to ping queries (possibly because they are blocked by a packet filter).

If a response similar to the one shown in the above example is received, the host is accessible.

Another use of netcat is to transmit files between hosts. For example, if no FTP server is available, start netcat on the server side by entering:

**netcat –l –p 2000 < this_file**

On the client side, fetch the file by entering:

**netcat host 2000 > that_file**

This connection remains intact until you terminate it by pressing **Ctrl + c**.

## Command Options

There is no man page for netcat. However, you can display a list of available options by using the command:

**netcat –h**

Table 9-9 lists some commonly used netcat options.

**Table 9-9**

| Option | Description |
|--------|-------------|
| -l | netcat starts in listen mode; this option can only be used with the option -p. |
| -p | Specifies the local port netcat should use. |
| -u | Prompts netcat to use the UDP protocol. |
| -v | Controls the verbosity level of the output of netcat. |
| -vv | Produces even more information that -v. |

**Table 9-9** (continued)

| Option | Description |
|--------|-------------|
| -w | Limits the time spent trying to make a connection. |
| -z | Shows which ports are open. |

**NOTE**

For more information about netcat, see /usr/share/doc/packages/netcat/ README.

This file describes additional usage possibilities and security issues that netcat can cause when used by malicious individuals.

# List Currently Active Network Connections with netstat

You can use the **/bin/netstat** command to determine the status of all network connections, routes, and interfaces on a host.

To effectively use the command, you need to understand the following:

- Common Use of netstat
- Command Options
- Problem Analysis

## Common Use of netstat

The command **netstat** displays the status of all open sockets (network connections) and analyzes all network connections on the host.

In the simplest scenario, you can enter **netstat** without options to display information similar to the following:

```
da1:/ # netstat
Active Internet connections (w/o servers)
Proto Recv-Q Send-Q Local Address          Foreign Address
State
tcp    0    0 da1.digitalairlines.com:604  da10.digitalairlines.
com:966 TIME_WAIT
tcp    0    0 da1.digitalairlines.com:1023 da10.digitalairlines.
com:ssh ESTABLISHED
Active UNIX domain sockets (w/o servers)
Proto RefCnt Flags  Type       State I-Node Path
unix   8     [ ]    DGRAM            746  /dev/log
unix   2     [ ]    DGRAM            748  /var/lib/dhcp/dev/log
unix   2     [ ]    DGRAM            81109
unix   3     [ ]    STREAM  CONNECTED 8214  /tmp/.X11-unix/X0
unix   3     [ ]    STREAM  CONNECTED 8213
unix   3     [ ]    STREAM  CONNECTED 8199  /tmp/.X11-unix/X0
unix   3     [ ]    STREAM  CONNECTED 8191
...
```

netstat provides information on all active network connections (sockets). This output displays two blocks with the following information:

- In the first block, each socket is listed on a separate line:

  - The first line involves a socket between the hosts da1.digitalairlines.com (Local Address) and da10.digitalairlines.com (Foreign Address) via the TCP protocol (Proto).

    The connection was established between the ports 604 (da1) and 966 (da10).

  - The information below Recv-Q and Send-Q shows that no data is waiting to be collected by the process in the receive queue for this host and that no data is waiting for the host da10.digitalairlines.com in the send queue. All available data until now has already been processed.

  - Finally, the information under State provides details of the socket's current condition. TIME_WAIT signals that the socket still needs to be "cleared up" but is almost closed. An active socket is referred to as ESTABLISHED.

- The second block provides information on the UNIX domain sockets active on this host. Each line stands for one socket:

  - The protocol (Proto) is always unix.

  - The reference counter (RefCnt) shows the number of active processes that are connected to the matching socket.

  - Special flags (Flags) are not set (possible flags: SO_ACCEPTION = ACC, SO_WAITDATA = W, SO_NOSPACE = N).

**NOTE**

For more information, see **man netstat**.

- The type of the sockets listed is DGRAM, or STREAM for connection-oriented sockets.

- All listed STREAM sockets are connected (State, CONNECTED).

- Finally, the inodes (I-Node) of the sockets and the pathname (Path) of the process connected to them are listed.

## Command Options

netstat has a variety of options for viewing the connection status of all open sockets. Table 9-10 lists some of the more commonly used options.

Table 9-10

| Parameter | Description |
|-----------|-------------|
| -a | Lists all active and passive sockets. |
| -e | Displays additional information. |
| -i *interface* | Displays information for *interface*. Without a specified interface, a table of all network interfaces is displayed. |
| -p | Shows the PID and name of the program to which each socket belongs. |
| -rn | Lists the entries of the routing table. There is no resolution of addresses to names. |
| -t | Lists only sockets for TCP packets. |
| -u | Lists only sockets for UDP datagrams. |

**NOTE**

For more information on all parameters available for netstat, enter **man 8 netstat**.

9

### Problem Analysis

You can use netstat to monitor the use of resources for network sockets on a host.

If a number of clients access a server simultaneously, it is possible that the number of sockets available or the resources for these are no longer sufficient.

In these cases, netstat provides detailed information on existing and available network sockets or resources.

## Analyze Network Traffic (tcpdump and ethereal)

You can use the tools tcpdump and ethereal in networks for troubleshooting a variety of problems, from analyzing the causes of simple broadcasts to analyzing complex data connections between two or more hosts.

To effectively use **tcpdump** and ethereal, you need to know the following:

- Use tcpdump
- tcpdump Command Options
- Use ethereal
- Troubleshooting Suggestions

### Use tcpdump

The command tcpdump (/usr/sbin/tcpdump) is a diagnosis tool that lets you analyze data packets through a network interface connected to the network.

The simplest way to use tcpdump is to enter:

**tcpdump −i** *interface*

This command puts the network interface into promiscuous mode (the interface evaluates all data packets received) and displays some information about the data reaching the network interface.

When you enter this command, information similar to the following is displayed:

```
da10:~ # tcpdump -i eth0
tcpdump: listening on eth0

12:15:43.666301 da10.digitalairlines.com.1023 > da50.
digitalairlines.com.ssh:
 S 4057372301:4057372301 (0)
win 32120 <mss 1460,sackOK,timestamp 359463 0,nop,wscale 0> (DF)

12:15:43.666836 da50.digitalairlines.com.ssh > da10.
digitalairlines.com.1023:
 S 4047727479:4947727479 (0)
ack 4057372302 win 32120 <mss 1460,sackOK,timestamp 327365500 359
nop,wsacle 0> (DF)

12:15:43.666943 da10.digitalairlines.com.1023 > da50.
digitalairlines.com.ssh:
. 1:
1(0) ack 1 win 32120 <nop,nop,timestamp 359463 327365500> (DF)

. . .
```

In the above example, the following information is displayed:

- The network interface over which the information is collected (listening on eth0)
- Each of the information blocks represents one sent packet and contains the following data:
  - The time for each datagram (such as 12:15:43.666301)
  - The sender, sender port, destination, and destination port (such as da10. digitalairlines.com.1023 > da50.digitalairlines.com.ssh)
- The flags set in the protocol header (possible flags are S (SYN), F (FIN), P (PUSH), R (RST))
- The data sequence number (such as 4057372301:4057372301(0)).
- An ACK bit that might have been set with the sequence number of the next data packet to be expected (such as ack 4057372302)

- The size of the receive buffer for data packets in the opposite direction (such as win 32120)

- Additional TCP options (such as mss 1460,sackOK,timestamp 3594630,nop, wscale 0)

## tcpdump Command Options

tcpdump has many options for analyzing data packets. Table 9-11 lists some of the more commonly used options.

**Table 9-11**

| Parameter | Description |
| --- | --- |
| -l | Buffers the output to the standard output. |
| -e | Prints the link-level header on each dump line. |
| -n | Does not convert addresses (host or port) to names. |
| -q | Displays a brief output with less information (less verbose). |
| -v, -vv, or -vvv | Displays more detailed information. |
| -x | Displays the output in hexadecimal format. |
| -c *count* | Ends when the number of packets specified in *count* have been received. |
| -i *interface* | Uses the network interface (specified in *interface*). If unspecified, tcpdump searches the system interface list for the lowest-numbered interface (such as eth0). |
| -r *file* | Reads the data packets from the specified *file*. |
| -w *file* | Writes data packets to the specified *file*. |
| *expression* | A filter for the packets you want to display. If you do not specify a filter, all packets in the network are displayed. The options for *expression* are described in the man pages of tcpdump (enter **man tcpdump**). |

The following are examples of using tcpdump:

- **tcpdump –nv –i eth0 –c 64 –w /tmp/tcpdump.net192 net 192**

  64 packets are written to the file /tmp/tcpdump.net192 (–w). Addresses are not converted to names (–n) and the output contains detailed information (–v).

  This information is gathered by the interface eth0 (–i eth0) and is shown only if the sender or recipient addresses are located in the network 192.0.0.0/255.0.0.0 (net 192).

- **tcpdump –r /tmp/tcpdump.net192**

  tcpdump gathers data from the file /tmp/tcpdump.net192 and displays this to the standard output.

- **tcpdump –e –i eth0 src 192.168.0.1 and dst 192.168.0.2 \**
- **or host 192.168.0.3**

All packets sent from the IP address 192.168.0.1 to the IP address 192.168.0.2 are shown. In addition, all data packets that contain the IP address 192.168.0.3 as sender or recipient are shown.

**NOTE**

For more information about all parameters available for the command tcpdump, enter **man tcpdump**.

## Use ethereal

The program ethereal is a graphical tool that provides the same functionality as tcpdump. It can be configured entirely through menus and provides a direct way of displaying all data at once, which is sent over a TCP connection.

The ethereal utility is located in the ethereal package and must first be installed with YaST. The dialog box shown in Figure 9-11 appears when you select **Capture > Start**.

```
Ethereal: Capture Options
┌─ Capture ──────────────────────────────────────────────────────┐
│ Interface:  eth0                                            ▼   │
│ Link-layer header type: [↕]                                     │
│ ☑ Capture packets in promiscuous mode                           │
│ ☐ Limit each packet to 68 [↕] bytes                             │
│ [🔧 Capture Filter:] [                                      ]   │
├─ Capture File(s) ──────────────────┬─ Display Options ──────────┤
│ File: [              ] [📁]         │                            │
│ ☐ Use multiple files               │ ☐ Update list of packets in│
│ ☐ Next file every 1 [↕] megabyte(s)│   real time                │
│ ☐ Next file every 1 [↕] minute(s)  │ ☐ Automatic scrolling in   │
│ ☑ Ring buffer with 2 [↕] files     │   live capture             │
│ ☐ Stop capture after 1 [↕] file(s) ├─ Name Resolution ──────────┤
├─ Stop Capture ... ─────────────────┤ ☑ Enable MAC name resolution│
│ ☐ ... after 1 [↕] packet(s)        │ ☐ Enable network name      │
│ ☐ ... after 1 [↕] megabyte(s)      │   resolution               │
│ ☐ ... after 1 [↕] minute(s)        │ ☑ Enable transport name    │
│                                    │   resolution               │
├────────────────────────────────────┴────────────────────────────┤
│ [Help]                              [✗ Cancel] [OK]             │
└──────────────────────────────────────────────────────────────────┘
```

**Figure 9-11**

You can configure settings for monitoring the network traffic such as the following:

- **Interface.** Enter or select the interface on which you want to listen.
- **Capture limits.** Enter the scope and duration of the data capture.
- **Name resolution.** Specify whether to perform name resolutions.

When you finish, you can start monitoring network traffic by selecting **OK**.

Your screen will look similar to Figure 9-12.

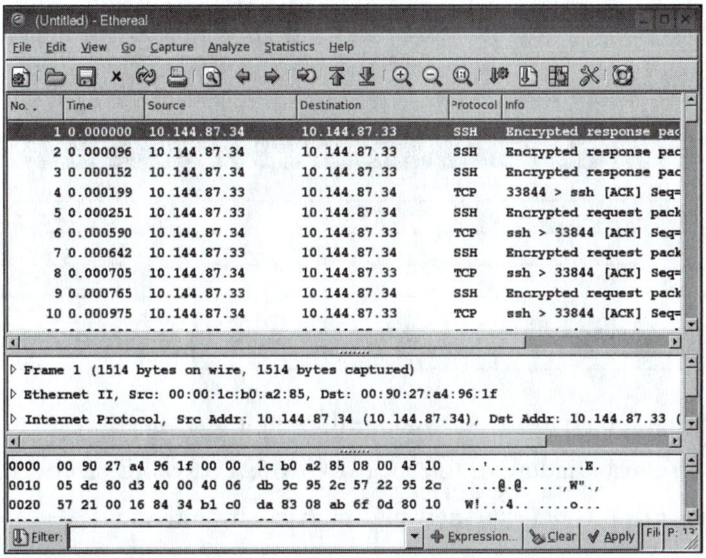

**Figure 9-12**

Individual packets are listed in the upper large window. You can select a packet to view details and contents of the packet in the two lower windows.

You can right-click a TCP packet to access a context menu. If you select **Follow TCP Stream**, the entire content of the TCP connection is displayed in a new window.

## Troubleshooting Suggestions

If communication in the network is faulty or nontransparent and you have used tools such as ping and traceroute without success, try using tcpdump or ethereal to analyze details of network traffic.

These tools can help you find which packets are exchanged by which applications in the network. They are also very useful when networks are frequently overloaded and no physical errors are detected.

tcpdump and ethereal are highly recommended for security-critical environments (such as firewalls) to more precisely analyze data traffic passing through and design a more secure environment.

## Exercise 9-2   Configure and Test Your Network Connection

The purpose of this exercise is to show you where to find information on the network configuration and how to troubleshoot networking problems.

- Part I: View and Record Network Configuration
- Part II: Test the Network Card Configuration

### Part I: View and Record Network Configuration

In this part of the exercise, you fill in the right column of Table 9-12 by entering commands at a shell prompt.

**Table 9-12**

| Item | Network Setting |
|------|-----------------|
| Host Name | |
| Domain Name | |
| IP Address | |
| Subnet Mask | |
| Default Gateway | |
| DNS Server | |

Do the following to find the information you need to fill in the table:

1. From a terminal window, su to root (**su –**) with a password of **novell**.

2. View information about the network interfaces by entering:

   **ifconfi g –a**

3. View information about the loopback network interface by entering:

   **ifstatus lo**

4. View information about the eth0 network interface by entering:

   **ifstatus eth0**

5. Change to the directory /etc/sysconfig/network by entering:

   **cd /etc/sysconfig/network**

6. List the configuration file for the eth0 network interface by entering:

   **ls –l ifcfg–eth–id\***

   Note the ID number associated with the filename.

7. View the contents of the configuration file by entering:

   **cat ifcfg–eth–id–*number***

8. View network interface statistics by entering:

   **netstat –i**

9. View the routing in numeric format by entering:

   **netstat –nr**

10. Remove the default route by entering:

    **route del default**

11. View the routing in numeric format by entering:

    **route –n**

12. Add a default route with a gateway of 10.0.0.254 by entering:

    **route add default gw 10.0.0.254 dev eth0**

13. View the routing in numeric format by entering:

    **route –n**

14. Shut down eth0 by entering:

    **ifdown eth0**

15. Bring up eth0 by entering:

    **ifup eth0**

16. View the system host name by entering:

    **hostname**

17. View the system DNS domain name by entering:

    **dnsdomainname**

18. View the DNS configuration by entering:

    **cat /etc/resolv.conf**

19. Verify that the default route is accessible by pinging the default gateway (**ping –c 3 10.0.0.254**).

## Part II: Test the Network Card Configuration

Do the following:

1. Test the connection to DA1 by entering:

   **ping 10.0.0.254**

2. Stop the ping process by pressing **Ctrl + c**.

3. Test the connection to the host www.novell.com by entering:

   **ping 130.57.4.27**

4. Test the name resolution and the connection to the host www.novell.com by entering:

**ping www.novell.com**

5. Test the connection to the host www.novell.com by entering:

**traceroute 130.57.4.27**

6. Verify that the file /etc/HOSTNAME contains the correct hostname by entering:

**cat /etc/HOSTNAME**

7. Check the listening sockets on your server, and the PID and name of the program to which each socket belongs by entering:

**netstat –lp**

8. Query the ports 20–80 on DA1 to display the service responses by entering:

**netcat –v –w 2 –z DA1 20-80**

9. Try querying another student's computer with the same netcat command and compare the results.

10. In the original terminal window, capture packets by entering:

**tcpdump –i eth0**

11. Open a Konqueror browser window; then enter:

**www.novell.com**

12. When you are finished viewing the traffic from the tcpdump screen, press **Ctrl + c** to kill the trace.

13. When you finish, close all open windows.

---

## CHAPTER SUMMARY

❑ Each host that communicates on a TCP/IP network has an IP address and subnet mask (or netmask) that identifies the network that the host is on as well as the host itself. The 127.0.0.0 network is used for testing the local computer.

❑ Three classes of IP networks are used for IP addressing: Class A, Class B, and Class C. Each class contains a reserved network range and can be subdivided into smaller networks (subnets) using CIDR.

❑ Different TCP/IP networks are connected to one another via routers. A host has a routing table that typically contains a default gateway route that identifies the router on the local network that is used to relay messages to remote TCP/IP networks. You can view and change the routing table using the **route** and **ip** commands.

❑ Each host contains a host name that is stored in the /etc/HOSTNAME file.

❏ To connect to network resources by host name, a host typically contains the address of up to three DNS servers in the /etc/resolv.conf file. Hosts contact these DNS servers to resolve remote host names to their respective IP addresses.

❏ You can view and change your TCP/IP configuration using the **ipconfig** and **ip** commands; you can also create IP aliases. Alternatively, you can manage your TCP/IP configuration in a desktop environment using the Network Card utility of YaST.

❏ Network interface and TCP/IP information is stored in the /etc/sysconfig/network directory and started by the /etc/init.d/network script at system initialization. After system initialization, you can use the **netstat** command to view network interface statistics, or the **ip**, **ifup**, **ifdown**, and **ifstatus** commands to manage the status of your network interfaces.

❏ The **ping** and **traceroute** commands can be used to test network communication and routing respectively. Similarly, the **netcat** command may be used to test TCP and UDP connections to other computers.

❏ To capture and analyze network traffic, you can use the **tcpdump** and **ethereal** utilities.

9

---

# KEY TERMS

**/etc/HOSTNAME** — A file that contains the name of the host.

**/etc/hosts** — A local file that contains host names and their respective IP addresses.

**/etc/init.d/network** — The script that activates network interfaces at system initialization.

**/etc/resolv.conf** — A file that lists up to three DNS servers and which may be contacted to resolve a remote host name to an IP address.

**/etc/sysconfig/network** — The directory that contains most network configuration information.

**/etc/sysconfig/network/ifcfg-template** — A template file that may be used to create the TCP/IP configuration for a network interface.

**/etc/sysconfig/network/ifroute-*interface*** — A file that stores static routes for a specific *interface*.

**/etc/sysconfig/network/routes** — A file that stores static routes for use on the system.

**/proc/sys/net/ipv4/ip_forward** — A file that is used to enable routing on a router.

**broadcast** — A message destined for all computers on a TCP/IP network.

**Class A address** — An IP address that uses the first byte to identify the TCP/IP network.

**Class B address** — An IP address that uses the first two bytes to identify the TCP/IP network.

**Class C address** — An IP address that uses the first three bytes to identify the TCP/IP network.

**Class D address** — An IP address that is used for communicating to several hosts simultaneously, using multicast packets.

**Class E address** — An IP address that cannot be used on a TCP/IP network and is intended for research purposes only.

**Classless Inter-Domain Routing (CIDR)** — A standard that allows the subdivision of traditional Class A, B, and C networks into subnets.

**default gateway** — The router that connects a network to other networks. Packets whose destination networks are not included in the routing table are sent to the default gateway.

**default route** — See **default gateway**.

**DNS server** — A server that contains records for hosts on a network. It may be queried to resolve a host name to an IP address.

**dnsdomainname command** — Used to display the domain name of a host.

**domain** — A portion of DNS.

**Domain Name System (DNS)** — The naming system used on the Internet. Each host is identified by a host name and domain name.

**Dynamic Host Configuration Protocol (DHCP)** — A protocol that is used to assign TCP/IP configuration information to a host on the network.

**Ethereal** — A graphical program used to capture and examine packets on the network.

**Ethernet** — The standard method used to access network media today. Most network adapters on networks use Ethernet.

**firewall** — A software feature that allows a host to drop IP packets that meet a certain criteria.

**host** — A computer or device that can communicate on a network.

**host ID** — The part of an IP address that uniquely identifies a host on a network.

**hostname command** — Used to display and set the host name of the computer.

**ifconfig command** — Used to view, configure, and manage IP addresses on a network interface.

**ifdown command** — Used to deactivate a network interface.

**ifstatus command** — Used to display the status of a network interface.

**ifup command** — Used to activate a network interface.

**Internet Control Message Protocol (ICMP)** — A part of the TCP/IP protocol suite that is used to relay information about network communications.

**Internet Protocol (IP) address** — A unique address used to identify a computer on a TCP/IP network.

**Internet Protocol (IP) packet** — A unit of information sent on a TCP/IP network.

**IP aliases** — Additional IP addresses that are assigned to a network interface.

**ip command** — Used to view, configure, and manage network interfaces and the routing table.

**IPv4** — The current version of the TCP/IP protocol suite.

**IPv6** — A new version of the TCP/IP protocol suite that contains a larger address space and improvements to routing and security.

**loopback** — An IP address that is used to test the local host.

**name server** — See **DNS server**.

**netcat command** — Used to test communication among hosts using TCP or UDP.

**netmask (network mask)** — See **subnet mask**.

**network ID** — The part of an IP address that identifies the network a host is on.

**node** — See **host**.

**ping command** — Used to test network connectivity using ICMP.

**route command** — Used to view and modify the routing table.

**router** — A device that is used to relay packets from one network to another.

**routing** — The process of sending IP packets from one IP network to another.

**routing table** — A table that is stored on each host and which contains a list of local and remote networks and routers.

**socket** — An established network connection between two hosts. TCP uses STREAM sockets, whereas UDP uses DGRAM sockets.

**static route** — Identifies a remote network and the router that must be used to forward packets to it.

**subnet (sub-network)** — A division of a Class A, B, or C network.

**subnet mask** — A number used to determine which portions of an IP address are the network ID and host ID.

**tcpdump command** — Used to capture and examine IP packets on the network.

**traceroute command** — Used to identify the route an IP packet takes to a remote host.

**Transport Control Protocol (TCP)** — A part of the TCP/IP protocol suite that provides reliable communication between hosts on a network.

**Transport Control Protocol / Internet Protocol (TCP/IP)** — A suite of protocols that are used to communicate with other computers on a network.

**User Datagram Protocol (UDP)** — A part of the TCP/IP protocol suite that provides fast but unreliable communication between hosts on a network.

---

## REVIEW QUESTIONS

1. What must each computer have in order to participate on a TCP/IP network as well as contact hosts on remote networks by name? (Choose all that apply.)

   a. IP address

   b. netmask

   c. DNS server

   d. default gateway

2. How long is the host ID by default in a Class A network?

   a. 1 byte

   b. 2 bytes

   c. 3 bytes

   d. 4 bytes

3. Which of the following are Class B IP addresses? (Choose all that apply.)
   a. 192.168.1.1
   b. 177.16.41.10
   c. 127.0.0.1
   d. 133.1.1.2

4. What network address is reserved for loopback? _____

5. What name is used to identify the first Ethernet network interface in Linux?
   _____

6. What file stores the list of DNS servers that your computer can contact to resolve hostnames into IP addresses?
   a. /etc/resolv.conf
   b. /etc/sysconfig/network/scripts
   c. /etc/dns.sysconfig
   d. /etc/sysconfig/network/ifcfg-dns

7. What command can you use to configure the IP address 192.168.1.1 and default subnet mask on your first Ethernet network interface? _____

8. What command can you use to configure an additional IP address of 192.168.1.2 and default subnet mask on the same network interface configured in Question 7?
   _____

9. Which of the following commands may be used to view IP configuration? (Choose all that apply.)
   a. ifshow eth0
   b. ip address show
   c. ifconfig –a
   d. ifstatus eth0

10. What file contains the information used to configure your second Ethernet network interface at boot time? _____

11. What line would you configure in the file described in Question 10 to obtain an IP configuration from a DHCP server? _____

12. How many DNS servers may be listed in /etc/resolv.conf?
    a. one
    b. three
    c. ten
    d. unlimited

13. Which two commands could you type at a command prompt to add a route to the 188.16.0.0 network via the router 192.168.1.254?

   a. ip route add 188.16.0.0/16 via 192.168.1.254

   b. route add 188.16.0.0 via 192.168.1.254

   c. ip route add gw 192.168.1.254 via 188.16.0.0/16

   d. route add —net 188.16.0.0 netmask 255.255.0.0 gw 192.168.1.254

14. What file could you use to configure the static route configured in Question 13 for use with all network interfaces on your system? _____

15. What command could you use to send five ICMP requests to the host 192.168.1.254? _____

16. What command could you use to listen to all traffic sent to port 1433 on your computer? _____

17. What option(s) to the **netstat** command could you use to display the routing table? _____

18. What command could you use to listen to all packets received on your first Ethernet network inteface? _____

9

## DISCOVERY EXERCISES

### Network Interface Commands

Log in to tty1 as the root user and perform the following actions in order. For each action, write the command(s) that you used. When finished, log out of tty1.

1. Configure your first Ethernet adapter such that your IP address is 10.10.10.x (where x is a unique student number assigned by your instructor).

2. View your IP configuration.

3. Deactivate and reactivate your first Ethernet adapter.

4. View your IP configuration. What file does this configuration come from?

### Configuring IP Aliases

Log in to tty1 as the root user and perform the following actions in order. For each action, write the command(s) that you used. When finished, log out of tty1.

1. Configure an IP alias for your first Ethernet adapter such that your first virtual IP address is 10.10.10.x (where x is a unique student number assigned by your instructor).

2. View your IP configuration.

3. Use the **ping** command to verify both virtual IP addresses.

4. Deactivate and reactivate your first Ethernet adapter.

**DISCOVERY**

## Routing Commands

Log in to tty1 as the root user and perform the following actions in order. For each action, write the command(s) that you used. When finished, log out of tty1.

1. Create a route to the 42.0.0.0 network via the gateway 10.18.11.88 using the **route** command.

2. Create a route to the 43.0.0.0 network via the gateway 10.68.1.9 using the **ip** command.

3. View the routing table.

4. Remove all routes from your system.

# 10

# MANAGE NETWORK SERVICES: DNS, AND FILE AND PRINT SERVICES

**SUSE Linux Enterprise Server 9 (SLES 9) comes with a large variety of network services. This section covers DNS as well as file and print services.**

- ◆ Configure a DNS Server Using BIND
- ◆ Configure Network File Systems
- ◆ Configure and Manage Network Printing Services

## OBJECTIVE 1    CONFIGURE A DNS SERVER USING BIND

The Domain Name System (DNS) is one of the most important network services. Without DNS, it would be difficult, if not impossible, to work with networked computers.

To configure a DNS server (also called a *name server*) using BIND (Berkeley Internet Name Domain) the most popular software you need to:

- Understand the Domain Name System
- Install and Configure the BIND Server Software
- Configure a Caching-Only DNS Server
- Configure a Master Server for Your Domain
- Configure the Client Computers to Use the DNS Server
- Use Command-Line Tools to Query DNS Servers
- Find More Information about DNS

## Understand the Domain Name System

To understand the basics of name resolution with DNS, you need to know the following:

- How Name Resolution Worked in the Early Days of the Internet
- The Internet Domain Concept
- How Name Servers Work
- How to Query DNS

### How Name Resolution Worked in the Early Days of the Internet

Computers communicate with each other by using IP addresses, but for humans it is more simple to address a computer by using its name. This requires some kind of conversion that provides computers with IP addresses when a user enters a computer name.

In ARPANET, when there were relatively few computers connected to each other, a file was maintained at the Network Information Center (NIC) of the Stanford Research Institute (SRI) in California that provided exactly this conversion.

Whenever system administrators added a new computer to the Internet or changed the name of an already connected computer, these changes were sent by e-mail to SRI-NIC where they were written to a file called hosts.txt.

Every system administrator worldwide had to copy this file by FTP and distribute it to all computers for which he was responsible.

In 1984, Paul Mockapetris created a powerful solution: the Domain Name System (DNS). DNS is a distributed database system that allows local administration of areas and guarantees unique computer names worldwide. Its hierarchical structure is very similar to the tree structure of the Linux file system.

## The Internet Domain Concept

DNS consists of several domains that can be divided into subdomains. The top level of this structure is the root domain. It is represented simply by a dot (.).

There are over 13 computers worldwide that act as root name servers. In the first layer beneath the root domain contains the top level domains (TLDs).

In the early days of DNS there were seven TLDs:

- **.com** for commercial institutions (such as novell.com and suse.com)

- **.edu** for educational institutions and research institutes (such as harvard.edu and stsci.edu)

- **.gov** for institutions of the U.S. government (such as nasa.gov and whitehouse.gov)

- **.int** for international institutions (such as un.int and ecb.int)

- **.mil** for U.S. military institutions (such as army.mil and navy.mil)

- **.net** for institutions that provide and manage network infrastructure (such as internic.net and att.net)

- **.org** for noncommercial institutions (such as eso.org andeff.org)

.arpa was used as a TLD while the ARPANET transferred from host files to DNS. All computers from the ARPANET were later put into the other TLDs. The arpa TLD still has a special meaning that will be explained later in this section.

These TLDs are also known as generic TLDs. Other TLDs for individual countries were defined, such as .de for Germany, .uk for the United Kingdom, and .ch for Switzerland.

Recently, TLDs such as .info or .biz have become operational. Each of these TLDs is administered by its own institution.

10

Part of the Internet namespace is shown in the Figure 10-1.

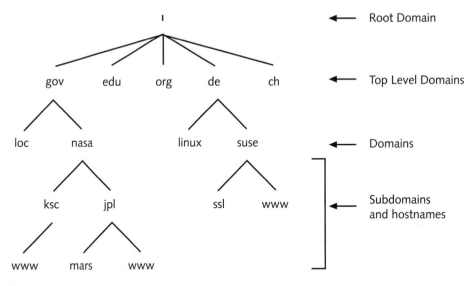

**Figure 10-1**

The complete computer name, or fully qualified domain name (FQDN), is made from the actual computer name, the domain name, and the name of the TLD (one or more subdomains might be included).

Examples of FQDNs are

- ns. suse.de
- www.astro.physik.uni–goettingen.de
- mail.novell.com

To be precise, all these names end with a dot (such as ns. suse.de.) indicating the root domain. But as a rule the dot normally is not used.

## How Name Servers Work

Domains are administered locally instead of using a global authority. Each domain has its own administration point (in practice, many domains are administered from one location).

For each domain there is one DNS server (or name server) defined as being "in charge" of its domain. This server is known as the *master server*, and it is the authority for this domain (providing authoritative answers).

This authoritative information is important because DNS servers also temporarily store information on other domains in a cache and can pass this information on, with the note that it is a nonauthoritative answer.

Other DNS servers called *slave servers* distribute the load and serve as backups. Slave servers keep a copy of the information on the master server and update this information at regular intervals. This update is called *zone transfer*.

Table 10-1 describes the DNS server types available.

**Table 10-1**

| Server Type | Description |
|---|---|
| Master server | Has the main responsibility for a domain. Gets its data from local files. |
| Slave server | Gets its data from the master server using zone transfer. |
| Caching-only server | Queries data from other DNS servers and stores the information in the cache until its expiration date. All replies are nonauthoritative. |
| Forwarding server | All queries the server cannot answer authoritatively are forwarded to other DNS servers. |

## How to Query DNS

Various programs are involved in processing a request to the DNS database. The first is the resolver, which is a set of library routines used by various programs.

The resolver makes a request to a DNS server, interprets the answer (real information or error message), and sends back this information to the program that called it up.

If the DNS server receives a request from a resolver, one of two things happens:

- If the DNS server is the authority for the requested domain, the DNS server provides the required information to the resolver (the authoritative answer).

    *or*

- If the DNS server is not the authority for the required domain, the DNS server queries the responsible authority for the requested domain and gives the result to the resolver.

    The data is stored in the cache of the DNS server. If there is another request for this data later, the DNS server can provide it immediately (a nonauthoritative answer). All data has a time stamp, and information is deleted from the cache after a certain time.

Assume that your DNS server wants to find the IP address of the computer *www.suse.de*. To do this, the following happens:

1. The DNS server first makes a request to one of the DNS servers of the root domain.

   Each DNS server knows the authorities responsible for the TLDs. The address for each authority required is passed on to the requesting DNS server. For *www.suse.de*, this is a DNS server for the TLD .de, that is, the computer dns2.denic.de.

2. Your DNS server then asks this for the authority for the domain suse.de and as an answer is given the computer ns. suse.de.

3. The DNS server is queried and (as an answer) gives the IP address of the SUSE Web server. This answer is returned by your DNS server to the request-ing resolver.

This procedure is illustrated in the Figure 10-2.

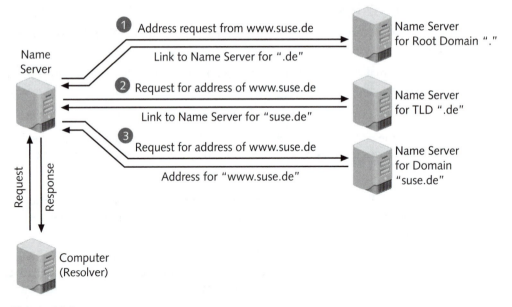

**Figure 10-2**

The DNS servers for the root domain play a very important role in name resolution. In order to reduce the server load due to queries, every DNS server stores the information received from other name servers in its cache.

When queries are made, this information is sent without querying the root DNS server again. However, root DNS servers are very busy despite this caching mechanism. Several thousand queries per second are nothing unusual.

## Install and Configure the BIND Server Software

To run a DNS server, you need to install the following packages:

- **bind.** The BIND server software (version 9 in SLES 9)
- **bind-utils.** Utilities that query and test BIND (included in standard installation)

Before starting the DNS server, you have to make some basic configuration changes.

After finishing your configuration, start the DNS server by entering:

**rcnamed start**

To stop a running DNS server, enter:

**rcnamed stop**

To have the DNS server start automatically at boot time, enter:

**insserv named**

This creates the necessary links in the runlevel directories.

## Configure a Caching-Only DNS Server

A caching-only DNS server does not manage its own databases but merely accepts queries and forwards them to other DNS servers. The supplied replies are saved in the cache.

A caching-only DNS server can be used on a workstation or a gateway that has access to an external DNS server.

The DNS server configuration is defined in the file /etc/named.conf. You can use the example file that is installed with the DNS package as a configuration file for a caching-only server.

The following example shows a simple configuration:

```
#
# /etc/named.conf: Configuration of the name server (BIND9)
#
# Global options
#
options
{
#
# In which directory are the database files?
#
        directory "/var/lib/named";
};
```

The global options are defined in the options block at the beginning of the file. The directory containing the database files (or zone files) is listed. Normally, this is /var/lib/named/.

All filenames further down in the file named.conf are relative to the directory /var/lib/named. The directory is created when the server package is installed. It contains several preconfigured files. Other options can also be defined in this file.

The Global options section is followed by the definition of the database files for the domains managed by the DNS server. Several entries are needed for basic DNS server functions such as those provided by a caching-only server.

Three entries are needed for every DNS server:

- The entry for root DNS servers (not needed for BIND 9 because it has the list of root DNS servers compiled into the software).

- The forward resolution for localhost

- The reverse resolution for the network 127.0.0.0 (localhost)

The following are examples of these entries:

```
## entry for root nameservers#
zone "." in {          type hint;
        file "root.hint";
};


#
# forward resolution for localhost
#
zone "localhost" in {
        type master;
        file "localhost. zone";
};


#
# reverse resolution for localhost
#
zone "0.0.127.in-addr.arpa" in {
        type master;
        file "127.0.0. zone";
};
```

The zone entry for the root DNS servers contains a reference to a file containing the addresses of the root DNS servers. This file (root.hint) is generated in the directory /var/lib/named/ during the BIND installation.

The two files that resolve localhost are also generated during the BIND installation. The structure of these files is explained later.

The root.hint entry refers queries to the responsible DNS servers as shown in . However, this resolution method can be very slow. This problem can be solved by using forwarders.

Forwarders are other DNS servers that are queried in case the DNS server cannot resolve a host name itself. You might be able to use the DNS servers of an Internet service provider for this purpose, because they usually have a lot of information in their cache.

You can define these DNS servers in the options block in the file

/etc/named.conf, as in the following:

```
options
{
        directory "/var/lib/named";

        forwarders
        {
                10.0.0.254;
        };
};
```

You can enter up to three DNS server addresses. Queries that cannot be resolved by the local DNS server are forwarded to one of the specified DNS servers.

If these DNS servers cannot be reached, the queries are sent directly to the root DNS servers.

## Configure a Master Server for Your Domain

The following are the tasks you need to do to configure a master DNS server for your domain:

- Adapt the Main Server Configuration File
- Create the Zone Files
- Create Additional Resource Records
- Slave Servers

### Adapt the Main Server Configuration File

You can adapt the configuration for the caching-only DNS server to configure a DNS server containing its own information files.

This configuration already contains the global entries for the directory and the forwarders entries (which can be omitted) in the options block. The file also contains the mandatory entries for the root servers and the resolution of localhost.

The global options are followed by definitions for the database files (or zone files) for the domains this DNS server serves. At least two files are necessary for each domain:

- A file for forward resolution (allocating an IP address to a computer name)
- A file for reverse resolution (allocating a computer name to an IP address)

If several subnets belong to a domain, then one file for each of these networks must be created for reverse resolution.

Each definition begins with the instruction *zone* (this is why the database files are also known as zone files), followed by the name of this zone.

For forward resolution, this is always the domain name. For reverse resolution, the network prefix of the IP address must be given in reverse order (10.0.0.0 becomes 0.0.10.) to which the suffix in-addr.arpa is added (0.0.10.in-addr.arpa).

The zone name is always followed by an "in" for Internet. (DNS servers can administer information on different name spaces, not only that of the Internet. However, other name spaces are practically never used.)

The text in curly brackets defines the type of DNS server this is for the corresponding zone (here it is always the type master; other types are introduced later).

Finally, there is the name of the file in which the entries for this zone are located.

The entries for the Digital Airlines configuration look like the following:

```
#
# forward resolution for the domain digitalairlines.com
#
zone "digitalairlines.com" in
{
        type master;
        file "master/digitalairlines.com. zone";
};
#
# reverse resolution for the network 10.0.0.0
#
zone "0.0.10.in-addr.arpa" in
{
        type master;
        file "master/10.0.0. zone";
};
```

## Create the Zone Files

The two files for the domain localhost and the file for the root DNS servers are always included in the installation. You do not need to change these files; however, you must create the files required for the actual domain.

The subdirectory /var/lib/named/master/ is used for the database files of a master server.

You need to know the following to manually create the zone files:

- Structure of the File
- The File /var/lib/named/master/digitalairlines.com.zone
- The File /var/lib/named/master/10.0.0.zone

- The File /var/lib/named/master/localhost.zone
- The File /var/lib/named/master/127.0.0.zone

**NOTE**

In these files, the semicolon is used as a comment sign.

**Structure of the Files**    Each of the database files consists of a series of entries, or resource records. The syntax of these records is always as follows:

*reference* **[TTL]** *class type value*

The following describes each part of a record:

- *reference.* The reference to which the record refers. This can be a domain (or subdomain) or a standalone computer (name or IP address).
- *TTL.* The Time To Live value for the record. If this expires, a default TTL value is used.
- *class.* The class of the record. For TCP/IP networks, this is always IN (internet).
- *type.* The type of the record. The most important types are listed in the table below.
- *value.* The value of the record. The value depends on the type of record as listed in Table 10-2.

**10**

**Table 10-2**

| Record Type | Meaning | Value |
|---|---|---|
| SOA | Start of Authority (term for the authority) | Parameter for the domain |
| NS | DNS server | Name of one of the DNS servers for this domain |
| MX | Mail exchanger | Name and priority of a mail server for this domain |
| A | Address | IP address of a computer |
| PTR | Pointer | Name of a computer |
| CNAME | Canonical name | Alias name for a computer |

Individual entries must always start in the first column with the reference. If an entry does not start in the first column, the reference is taken from the previous entry.

**CAUTION**

**The File /var/lib/named/master/digitalairlines.com.zone** Unlike earlier versions of BIND, BIND 9 requires you to specify a default TTL for all information at the beginning. This value is used whenever the TTL has not been explicitly given for an entry.

You define the TTL with the following instruction:

```
;
; definition of a standard time to live, here: two days
;
$TTL 172800
```

In this example, the TTL is given in seconds. But it can be given in other units, such as 2D for two days. Other units are M (minutes), H (hours), and W (weeks).

This is followed by the definition of the SOA (Source of Authority) entry, which specifies which DNS server has the authority for this domain:

```
;
; SOA Entry
;
digitalairlines.com. IN SOA da1.digitalairlines.com.
adm.digitalairlines.com. (
                2004092601 ; serial number
                1D         ; refresh (one day)
                2H         ; retry (two hours)
                1W         ; expiry time (one week)
                3H         ; "negative" validity (three hours)
                )
```

The domain to which this entry refers (here, **digitalairlines.com**) is listed first. The domain name must end with a dot. If a name does not have a dot at the end, the name of the domain is appended, which could lead to an error here.

After the SOA entry the name of the DNS server is listed (in this example, **da1.digitalairlines.com** with a dot at the end). Alternatively, you could write da1, and the domain name digitalairlines.com would be added after the name.

Next comes the e-mail address of the person who is responsible for the administration of the DNS server. The @ symbol usually used in e-mail addresses must be replaced by a dot (so the e-mail address in this example is *adm.digitalairlines.com*). This is necessary because @ has a special meaning as an abbreviation.

After this information, there is a serial number. Any number can be used, but normally the date and a version number are used here. After any change to the data in this file, the serial number has to be increased.

Slave servers use this number to detect if they need to copy this zone file or not. If the serial number on the master server is greater than that on the slave server, the file is copied.

This is followed by the following time information (the first three entries listed here are only important for slave servers):

- The first entry causes a slave server to query a master server after this length of time, to see if there is a new version of the files (in the example, this is 1D, or one day).

- If the slave server cannot reach the master server, the next time entry specifies at what intervals new attempts should be made (in the example, this is 2H, or two hours).

- If the master server is not reached for a longer period of time, the first time entry specifies when the slave server should discard its information on this zone (in the example, this is 1W, or a week).

  The basic idea here is that it is better not to pass on any information than to pass on outdated information.

- The fourth entry defines for how long negative responses from the DNS server are valid. Each requesting server stores responses in its cache, even if a computer name could not be resolved (in the example, this is 3H, or 3 hours).

These time definitions are followed by the name of the computer that is responsible for this domain as the DNS server. In all cases, the master server must be entered here. If slave servers are used, they should also be entered, as in the following:

```
;
; entry for the name server
;
digitalairlines.com.          IN NS    da1.digitalairlines.com.
```

The name of the domain can be omitted at this point. Then the name from the previous entry is taken (the SOA entry).

At the end of this file are the IP addresses that are allocated to computer names. This is done with A (address) entries, as in the following:

```
;
; Allocation of IP addresses to host names
;
da10              IN A      10.0.0.10
da11              IN A      10.0.0.11
da12              IN A      10.0.0.12
```

**The File /var/lib/named/master/10.0.0.zone**    The file for reverse resolution contains entries similar to those in the file for forward resolution. The definition of a default TTL and an SOA entry is at the beginning of the file.

In the SOA and NS entries, the IP address of the network is written in reverse order:

```
; Database file for the domain digitalairlines.com:
; reverse resolution for the network
; 10.0.0.0
;
; Definition  of a default TTL,here: two days
;
$TTL 172800
;
; SOA entry
;
0.0.10.in-addr.arpa. IN SOA da1.digitalairlines.com.
adm.digitalairlines.com. (
                    2004092601 ; serial number
                    1D          ; refresh (one day)
                    2H          ; retry (two hours)
                    1W          ; expiry time (one week)
                    3H          ; "negative" validity (three hours)
                    )
;; Entry for the name server
;
                    IN NS    da1.digitalairlines.com.
```

At the end of this file are the IP addresses that are allocated to computer names, this time with the PTR (Pointer) entry, as in the following:

```
;
; Allocation of host names to IP addresses
;
10              IN PTR   da10.digitalairlines.com.
11              IN PTR   da11.digitalairlines.com.
12              IN PTR   da12.digitalairlines.com.
13              IN PTR   da13.digitalairlines.com.
```

The following two files must exist for the local computer. These are created automatically during installation and should not be modified.

**The File /var/lib/named/master/localhost.zone**    The following is an example of the file /var/lib/named/master/localhost. zone:

```
$TTL 1W
@           IN SOA       @                root (
                         42               ; serial (d. adams)
                         2D               ; refresh
                         4H               ; retry
```

```
                      6W                      ; expiry
                      1W )                    ; minimum

         IN NS        @
         IN A         127.0.0.1
```

In this example, the @ character is used as an abbreviation (for this reason, it must be replaced by a dot in the e-mail address in the database files).

Using @ instead of the domain name causes the file /etc/named.conf to be read to see for which domain this file is responsible.

In this case, it is localhost, which is also used for the name of the DNS server (this is why @ appears several times in the file).

**The File /var/lib/named/master/127.0.0.zone**    In this file, the abbreviation @ is also used. But here the computer name must be given explicitly with localhost (remember the dot at the end):

```
$TTL 1W
@         IN SOA        localhost.      root.localhost. (
                        42              ; serial (d. adams)
                        2D              ; refresh
                        4H              ; retry
                        6W              ; expiry
                        1W )            ; minimum

          IN NS         localhost.
1         IN PTR        localhost.
```

## Create Additional Resource Records

Apart from the resource records already discussed (SOA, NS, A, PTR), there are MX and CNAME resource records, which are used to do the following:

- Define Mail Servers for the Domain

- Assign Aliases for Computer

**Define Mail Servers for the Domain**    To be able to use e-mail addresses in the form geeko@digitalairlines.com, the e-mail server responsible for the domain must be defined (the e-mail cannot be sent directly to the domain, but must be sent to a mail server).

To achieve this, an MX (Mail Exchange) entry must be made in the database file for forward resolution, after the DNS server entry:

```
digitalairlines.com.          IN MX   0 mail
                              IN MX   10 da1
                              IN MX   10 da5
```

If an e-mail is now sent to the address geeko@digitalairlines.com, the computer sending the mail asks the DNS server which computer is the mail server and is sent the list of the MX entries in return.

Several mail servers can be given. On the basis of their priorities, it is then decided to which computer the e-mail is sent. The priority of mail servers is defined by the number in front of the computer name; the lower this number, the higher the priority.

In this example the computer mail.digitalairlines.com has the highest priority (and is therefore the primary mail server). da1.digitalairlines.com and da5.digitalairlines.com both have the same priority.

If the mail server with the highest priority cannot be reached, the mail server with the second highest priority is used. If several mail servers have the same priority, then one of them is chosen at random. An address entry must be made for each mail server.

**Assign Aliases for Computers**    If you want a computer to be reached by more than one name (such as addressing one computer as da30.digitalairlines.com and www.digitalairlines.com), then corresponding aliases must be given.

These are the CNAME (canonical name) entries in the database file for forward resolution:

```
da30              IN A      10.0.0.30
www               IN CNAME  da30
```

The names of the mail servers for the domain (MX entry) cannot be alias names, since some mail servers cannot handle this correctly.

### Slave Servers

To guarantee reliable operation, at least one more DNS server besides the master server is required. It receives the zone information from the DNS master server and can take over part of the load from the master. But it is especially important in case the DNS master server is not available. The configuration of a slave server is not covered in this course.

## Configure the Client Computers to Use the DNS Server

You can use YaST to configure a client computer to use the DNS server during installation or later. You simply have to enter the IP address of the DNS server and possibly add some information about your domain.

This information is written to the file **/etc/resolv.conf**, as in the following:

```
search digitalairlines.com
nameserver 10.0.0.254
```

Normally, this file has the following two types of entries:

- **search.** A list of names of domains (or subdomains) is provided after this keyword. Several domain names are entered on one line. This allows only the host name to be used to resolve to the correct IP address.

  The host name is expanded by the domain names specified here until a matching IP address is found.

  For example, if you provide digitalairlines.com and atl.digitalairlines.com as domain names, the host "server" is expanded to server.digitalairlines.com and server.atl.digitalairlines.com when looking for the corresponding IP address of "server." The first matching IP address is returned.

  If both of these host names exist, you have to specify the FQDN to resolve the IP address.

- **nameserver.** The keyword nameserver specifies the IP address of a DNS server to use. You can have up to three entries, but each of them must only contain one server address. If several entries of this type exist, the DNS servers are queried in this order.

There is another important file for the clients:

**/etc/nsswitch.conf**. This file applies to all programs that use the resolver functions of the current GNU C Library (libc6). (The predecessor of this file is /etc/host.conf, which applies to older versions of the GNU C Library.)

This file configures the name service switch, which is responsible for resolving host names, network names, users, and groups.

The relevant part for resolving host names looks like the following:

```
#
# /etc/nsswitch.conf
#
...
hosts:          files dns
networks:       files dns
...
```

Both entries shown here define that the first attempt to resolve a host name is done using the file /etc/hosts. If this fails, a DNS server resolves the name. The same applies to the resolution of network names, using /etc/networks first.

## Use Command-Line Tools to Query DNS Servers

Several command-line tools are available to query a DNS server. These include the following:

- host Command
- dig Command
- nslookup Command

### host Command

The most important command-line tool for querying a DNS server is called **host**. The general syntax is as follows:

**host** *computer nameserver*

The following example shows how it is used:

```
da10:~ # host da50
da50.digitalairlines.com has address 10.0.0.50
da10:~ # host 10.0.0.49
49.0.0.10.in-addr.arpa domain name pointer da49.digitalairlines.com.
...
```

If a DNS server address is not provided, host contacts the servers listed in /etc/resolv.conf. If you want to use another DNS server, you have to provide its IP address with the command.

By default, host returns the IP address or the host name, depending on which information is given. If you want to query domain information, you need to use the option -t with the type of information required, as in the following:

```
da10:~ # host -t ns novell.com
novell.com name server ns.novell.com.
novell.com name server ns1.westnet.net.
novell.com name server ns.utah.edu.
```

In this example, the host names of the DNS servers for the domain novell.com are requested.

### dig Command

A more verbose command is **dig**, which is normally used to troubleshoot DNS problems. The general syntax is as follows:

**dig** *@nameserver computer type query_options*

The options are listed in Table 10–3.

**Table 10-3**

| Option | Description |
|---|---|
| *nameserver* | The IP address or name of the DNS server that should be queried. If not specified, dig checks all DNS servers listed in /etc/resolv.conf. |
| *computer* | The resource record to query about (such as a host name, an IP address, or a domain name). |
| *type* | The type of resource record to be returned, such as A (IP address), NS (DNS server), MX (mail exchanger), -x (pointer), or ANY (all information). |
| *query_options* | Defines how the query is done and how the results are displayed. Each query option starts with a plus sign (+). |

The most important difference between host and dig is that dig does not use the domain list from /etc/resolv.conf by default to expand the host name. This means that the FQDN or IP address of the host must be specified. If the domain list should be used, you need to use the query option +search.

The following example demonstrates the application:

```
da10:~ # dig ripe.net ns

; <<>> DiG 9.2.3 <<>> ripe.net ns
;; global options:  printcmd
;; Got answer:
;; ->>HEADER<<- opcode: QUERY, status: NOERROR, id: 1315
;; flags: qr rd ra; QUERY: 1, ANSWER: 5, AUTHORITY: 0,
ADDITIONAL: 9

;; QUESTION SECTION:
;ripe.net.                       IN      NS

;; ANSWER SECTION:
ripe.net.            158814  IN      NS      ns2.nic.fr.
ripe.net.            158814  IN      NS      sunic.sunet.se.
ripe.net.            158814  IN      NS      auth03.ns.uu.net.
ripe.net.            158814  IN      NS      munnari.oz.au.
ripe.net.            158814  IN      NS      ns.ripe.net.

;; ADDITIONAL SECTION:
ns.ripe.net.         171939  IN      A       193.0.0.193
ns.ripe.net.         171939  IN      AAAA    2001:610:240:0:53::193
ns2.nic.fr.          344302  IN      A       192.93.0.4
ns2.nic.fr.          344302  IN      AAAA    2001:660:3005:1::1:2
sunic.sunet.se.      172586  IN      A       192.36.125.2
auth03.ns.uu.net.170436  IN      A       198.6.1.83
```

**10**

```
munnari.oz.au.    170107   IN      A        128.250.22.2
munnari.oz.au.    170107   IN      A        128.250.1.21
munnari.oz.au.    21410    IN      AAAA     2001:388:c02:4000::1:21
```

```
;; Query time: 51 msec
;; SERVER: 10.0.0.254#53(10.0.0.254)
;; WHEN: Thurs Sep 27 15:27:01 2007
;; MSG SIZE  rcvd: 329
```

The QUESTION SECTION shows what was queried and the ANSWER SECTION shows the response: a list of DNS servers of the domain ripe.net.

The IP addresses of certain DNS servers are listed under ADDITIONAL SECTION. The address in the last line is an IPv6 address (**2001:388:c02:4000::1:21**).

Data about the query, such as the duration of the query (**Query time**), the server that answered the query (**SERVER**), and the date of the query (**WHEN**) are listed at the end of the output.

### nslookup Command

The **nslookup** (name service lookup) command is older than the dig and host commands. It might be removed from future releases of the BIND utilities. But it can be used in current releases to query the DNS database for the IP address or name of a server on the network.

The basic syntax for the nslookup command is:

**nslookup** *<servername>* *or* *<ipaddress>*

For example, entering **nslookup da1.digitalairlines.com** would return information showing the IP address of the server answering the query and the name and address of the server being looked up, as shown in the following:

```
da10:~ # nslookup da1.digitalairlines.com
Note:  nslookup is deprecated and may be removed from future releases.
Consider using the 'dig' or 'host' programs instead. Run nslookup with
the '-sil[ent]' option to prevent this message from appearing.
Server:        10.0.0.254
Address:       10.0.0.254#53

Name:   da1.digitalairlines.com
Address: 10.0.0.254
```

## Find More Information about DNS

If there are syntax errors in one of the configuration or zone files, BIND writes verbose messages to the file /var/log/messages. These messages also contain information on the filename and the line in which the error occurs.

If there is an error, the processing of the file is interrupted at this point (that is, errors later in the file are not detected now).

**NOTE**

For more information about BIND and DNS, see ***DNS and BIND*** by Paul Albitz and Cricket Liu and the BIND homepage at www.isc.org/sw/bind/.

## Exercise 10-1   Configure a DNS Caching-Only Server

A caching only DNS Server queries other servers and keeps the answers in its cache. If the same query comes again later, it is answered out of the cache without contacting servers in the Internet.

Such a DNS server acts as a proxy and makes direct connections from the clients in the LAN to DNS servers in the Internet unnecessary.

To configure a caching-only DNS server, do the following:

- Part I: Install BIND
- Part II: Configure a DNS Caching-Only Server

### Part I: Install BIND

Do the following:

1. From the KDE menu, select **System > YaST**.

2. Enter the root password and select **OK**.

3. From the YaST Control Center, select

   **Software > Install and Remove Software**

4. From the Filter drop-down menu, select **Search**.

5. In the Search field, enter **bind**; then select **Search**.

6. On the right, select the **bind** package.

7. Select **Accept**; then insert the SLES 9 DVD.

8. When installation is complete, remove the DVD and close the YaST Control Center.

### Part II: Configure a DNS Caching-Only Server

1. Open a terminal window and su to **root**.

2. Open the file **/etc/named.conf** in a text editor.

**10**

3. Configure the forwarders line to match the following:

**forwarders { 10.0.0.254; };**

Make sure that you delete the comment character from the beginning of the forwarders line.

4. Save and close the file.

5. Open a second terminal window and **su** to root.

6. Enter the following command:

**tail –f /var/log/messages**

7. Switch to the first terminal window and start BIND with the following command:

**rcnamed start**

**CAUTION**

If there are errors in the file /etc/named, they are noted in the output (with specific references and line numbers). The named daemon will not start until these errors are fixed.

8. From the second terminal window, watch the log output of bind for any messages such as **Unknown RR Type** or **File Not Found**.

9. (If there are no such error messages, then your server is most probably configured correctly.)

10. If any errors occur, try to fix them and restart BIND.

11. From the first terminal window, start BIND automatically when the system is booted by entering the following:

**insserv named**

12. Open the file **/etc/resolv.conf** in a text editor.

13. Delete all existing **nameserver** entries.

14. Add the following entry:

**nameserver** *your_ip_address*

15. Save and close the file.

16. Verify that your DNS server works, querying the nameserver running on da1. digitalairlines.com, by entering:

**host da20.digitalairlines.com**

## OBJECTIVE 2    CONFIGURE NETWORK FILE SYSTEMS

UNIX/Linux networks, NFS, is usually used to access files over the network; in Windows-based networks SMB/CIFS is used.

Linux can access and share files in both systems.

To configure network file systems on SUSE Linux Enterprise Server, you need to understand:

- Network File System (NFS)
- Samba (CIFS)

## Network File System (NFS)

Network File System (NFS) lets you configure an NFS file server to give users transparent access to programs, files, or storage space on the server.

To configure NFS for your network, you need to know the following:

- Network File System Basics
- How NFS Works
- NFS Configuration Overview
- Configure an NFS Server with YaST
- Configure an NFS Server Manually
- Export a Directory Temporarily
- Configure NFS Client Access with YaST
- Configure NFS Client Access Manually
- Temporarily Import Directories Manually from an NFS Server
- Monitor the NFS System

### Network File System Basics

NFS is designed for sharing files and directories over a network. NFS requires configuration of an NFS server (where the files and directories are located) and NFS clients (user computers that access the files and directories remotely).

File systems are exported by an NFS server and appear and behave on a NFS client as if they are located on a local machine.

For example, with NFS each user's home directory can be exported by an NFS server and imported to a client, so the same home directories are accessible from every workstation on the network.

Directories like /home/, /opt/, /usr/, and /var/spool/mail/ are good candidates for export via NFS. However, others, including /bin/, /boot/, /dev/, /etc/, /lib/, /root/, /sbin/, /tmp/, and (parts of) /var/, should be available on the local disk only.

NFS is frequently used together with Network Information Service (NIS) to provide centralized user management on a network.

Figure 10-3 shows an example of mounting the directory /home/ (exported by the NFS Server *sun*) on the host computer *earth*.

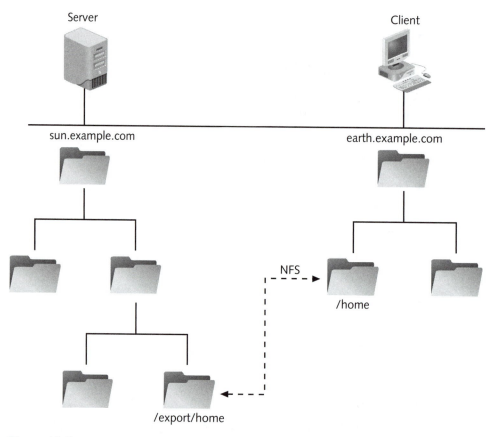

**Figure 10-3**

A computer can be both an NFS server and an NFS client. It can supply file systems over the network (export) and mount file systems from other hosts (import).

A computer that hosts an NFS server generally has a very large hard disk capacity. Its file systems are mounted by other clients.

The NFS daemon is part of the kernel and only needs to be configured, then activated. The start script is /etc/init.d/nfsserver.

A number of additional tools are included in the package nfs-utils, which is part of the standard installation.

The kernel NFS daemon includes file locking, which means that only one user at a time has write access to files.

## How NFS Works

Both NFS and NIS are Remote Procedure Call (RPC) services. An essential component for RPC services is the *portmapper* that manages these services. Portmapper must be started before NFS and NIS.

When an RPC service starts up, it binds to a port in the system (as any other network service), but also communicates this port and the service it offers (such as NFS) to the portmapper.

Because every RPC program must be registered by the portmapper when it is started, RPC programs must be restarted each time you restart the portmapper.

Table 10-4 lists the services required on an NFS server.

**Table 10-4**

| Service | Program (daemon) | Start Script |
|---|---|---|
| Port mapper | /sbin/portmap | /etc/init.d/portmap |
| NFS locking daemon | /sbin/rpc.lockd | /etc/init.d/nfslock (started automatically with nfsserver) |
| NFS server | /usr/sbin/rpc.nfsd  /usr/sbin/rpc.mountd | /etc/init.d/nfsserver |

File locking is activated through the script /etc/init.d/nfslock. The script controls the daemon /sbin/rpc.lockd.

You can use the command /etc/init.d/nfsserver to start the NFS server. The script nfsserver passes the list of exported directories to the kernel, and then starts or stops the daemons rpc.nfsd and rpc.mountd.

The NFS service daemon (/usr/sbin/rpc.nfsd) starts the required kernel threads.

The mount daemon (/usr/sbin/rpc.mountd) accepts each mount request and compares it with the entries in the configuration file /etc/exports. If access is allowed, the data is delivered to the client.

Because daemon rpc.nfsd can be started directly with several kernel threads, the start script interprets the variable USE_KERNEL_NFSD_NUMBER in the file /etc/sysconfig/nfs.

This variable determines the number of threads to start. By default, four server threads are started.

## NFS Configuration Overview

All configuration settings for the NFS server are stored in the file /etc/exports (enter **man 5 exports**). These settings include information such as which directories should be exported over the network with which options and which computers can access them.

Client-side configuration takes place using the file /etc/fstab (enter **man 5 nfs**).

Both the NFS server and the clients can be configured with YaST modules. You can also modify the configuration files directly.

For the NFS server to start automatically when the computer is booted, the corresponding soft links in the runlevel directories must first be generated.

If you configure the NFS server with YaST, this is done automatically; otherwise, you need to generate the soft links with insserv.

## Configure an NFS Server with YaST

To use YaST to configure the NFS server, do the following:

1. From the KDE desktop, start the YaST NFS Server module by doing one of the following:

   - Select the **YaST** icon, enter the root password *novell*, and select **OK**; then select **Network Services > NFS Server**.

     *or*

   - Open a terminal window and enter **sux –** and the root password *novell*; then enter **yast2 nfs_server**.

Figure 10-4 appears.

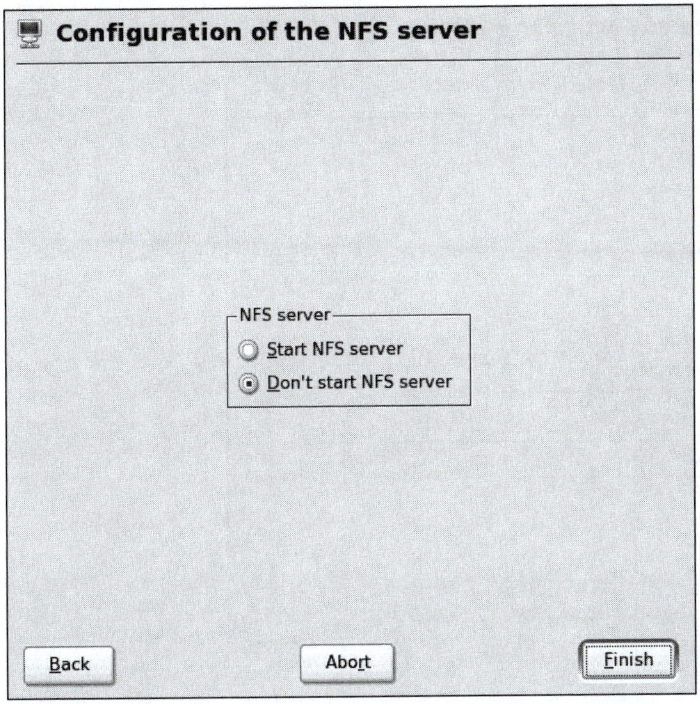

**Configuration of the NFS server**

NFS server
- ○ Start NFS server
- ● Don't start NFS server

Back     Abort     Finish

**Figure 10-4**

2. Select **Start NFS Server**; then select **Next**.

A Directories to export to the others dialog box, shown in Figure 10-5, appears.

**Figure 10-5**

3. Add a directory for export by selecting **Add Directory**; then enter or browse to and select a *directory*.

The dialog box shown in Figure 10-6 appears.

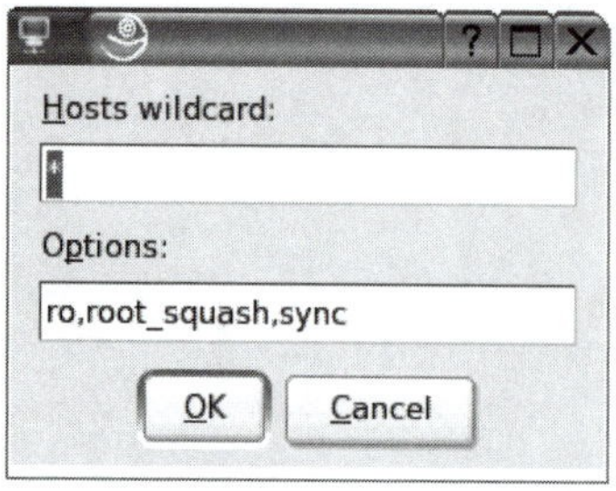

**Figure 10-6**

This dialog box lets you configure the hosts that should have access to the directory. There are four options that can be set: single host, netgroups, wildcards, and IP networks.

For details on configuring the host settings, see *Configure an NFS Server Manually*.

4. Add other directories by again selecting **Add Directory**.

   You can also edit a directory or delete it by selecting the directory and selecting **Edit** or **Delete**.

5. Add, edit, or delete a host for a directory by selecting the directory; then select **Add Host**, **Edit**, or **Delete**.

6. When you finish, save the configuration by selecting **Finish**.

## Configure an NFS Server Manually

If you do not want to use YaST to set up an NFS server, you can configure the server from the command line by doing the following:

- **Check for service (daemon) availability.** Make sure the following are available on your NFS server:

  - RPC portmapper (portmap)

  - RPC mount daemon (rpc.mountd)

  - RPC NFS daemon (rpc.nfsd)

- **Configure the services to be available at bootup.** For these services to be started by the scripts /etc/init.d/portmap and /etc/init.d/nfsserver when the system is booted, enter the following commands:

  **insserv /etc/init.d/nfsserver**

  **insserv /etc/init.d/portmap**

- **Define exported directories (file systems) in /etc/exports.** You need to define which file systems should be exported to which host in the configuration file /etc/exports.

  For each directory to export, 0ne line is needed to set which computers can access that directory with what permissions. All subdirectories of this directory are automatically exported as well.

  The following is the general syntax of the file /etc/exports:

  *directory* **[*host*[(*option1,option2,option3,...*)]]** ...

  Do not put any spaces between the host name, the parentheses enclosing the options, and the option strings themselves.

**10**

A *host* can be one of the following:

- A standalone computer with its name in short form (it must be possible to resolve this with name resolution), with its Fully Qualified Domain Name (FQDN), or with its IP address.

- A network, specified by an address with a netmask or by the domain name with a prefixed placeholder (such as *****.example.com**).

Authorized computers are usually specified with their full names (including domain name), but you can use wildcards like * or ?.

If you do not specify a host, any computer can import the file system with the given permissions.

- **Set permissions for exported directories (file systems) in /etc/exports.** You need to set permission options for the file system to export in brackets after the computer name. The most commonly used options include those shown in Table 10-5.

**Table 10-5**

| Option | Meaning |
|---|---|
| ro | File system is exported with read-only permission (default). |
| rw | File system is exported with read-write permission. |
| root_squash | This ensures that the user root of the given machine does not have root permissions on this file system. This is achieved by assigning user ID 65534 to users with user ID 0 (root). This user ID should be set to nobody (which is the default). |
| no_root_squash | Does not assign user ID 65534 to user ID 0, keeping the root permissions valid. |
| link_relative | Converts absolute links (those beginning with /) to a sequence of ../. This is only useful if the entire file system of a machine is mounted (default). |
| link_absolute | Symbolic links remain untouched. |
| map_identity | User IDs are exactly the same on both the client and server (default). |
| map_daemon | Client and the server do not have matching user IDs. This tells nfsd to create a conversion table for user IDs. The ugidd daemon is required for this to work. |

The following is an example of an edited /etc/exports file that includes permissions:

```
#
# /etc/exports
#
/home           da20(rw)  da30(rw)
/usr/X11        da20(ro)  da30(ro)
/usr/lib/texmf  da20(ro)  da30(rw)
/               da40(ro,root_squash)
```

```
/home/ftp        +(ro,sync)
# End of exports
```

Whenever you want an additional directory (such as /home/geeko/pictures/) exported to form part of an already exported directory (such as /home/geeko/), the additional directory needs its own separate entry in /etc/exports, as shown in the following:

```
/home/geeko/pictures da30(rw,all_squash,anonuid=150,
anongid=100,sync)
```

■ **Restart mountd and nfsd.** The /etc/exports is read by mountd and nfsd. If you change anything in this file, you need to restart mountd and nfsd for your changes to take effect. You can do this by entering **rcnfsserver restart**.

## Export a Directory Temporarily

You can export a directory temporarily (without editing the file /etc/exports) by using the command **exportfs**.

For example, to export the directory /software to all hosts in the network 10.0.0.0/24, enter:

**exportfs –o ro,root_squash,sync 10.0.0.0/24:/ software**

To restore the original state, enter:

**exportfs –r**

The file /etc/exports is reloaded and the directory /software is no longer exported.

The directories that are currently exported are listed in the file /var/lib/nfs/etab. The content of this file is updated when you use the command exportfs.

## Configure NFS Client Access with YaST

Users authorized to do so can mount NFS directories from an NFS server into their own file system tree. The easiest way to do this is to use the YaST NFS Client module.

Do the following:

1. Start the YaST NFS Client module by doing one of the following:

   ■ From the desktop, start the YaST Control Center by selecting **Start Applications > System > YaST**; then enter the root password *novell* and select **Network Services > NFS Client**.

   *or*

   ■ From a terminal window, enter **sux –** and enter a password of *novell*; then enter **yast2 nfs–client**.

**10**

The Configuration of the NFS client dialog box appears, as shown in Figure 10-7.

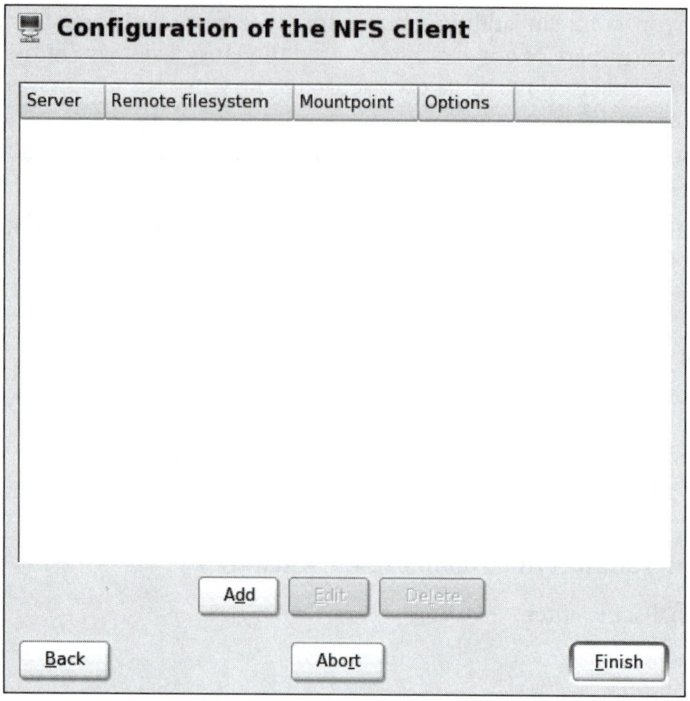

**Figure 10-7**

A list in the dialog box lets you add, edit, or delete NFS server directories in your file tree.

2. Add a directory to the list by selecting **Add**.

A screen similar to Figure 10-8 appears.

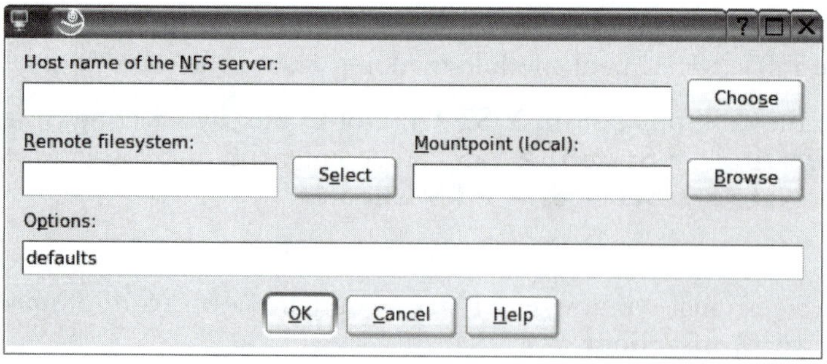

**Figure 10-8**

From this dialog box, you can configure the directory to mount in your file tree.

3. Configure the directory by doing the following:

a. In the ***Host Name*** of the NFS Server field, enter the host's name or find and select the NFS server from a list of NFS servers on your network by selecting **Choose**.

b. In the Remote Filesystem field, enter the ***exported directory*** on the NFS server you want to mount, or find and select the available directory by selecting **Select**.

c. In the Mountpoint (Local) field, enter the ***mountpoint*** in your local file tree to mount the exported directory, or browse to and select the mount point by selecting **Browse**.

d. In the Options field, enter any ***options*** you would normally use with the mount command.

**NOTE**

For a list of these options, enter **man mount**.

10

e. When you finish configuring the directory, select **OK**.

You are returned to the Configuration of the NFS Client dialog box.

4. Save the NFS client settings by selecting **Finish**.

The settings are saved, services are restarted, and the exported directories are mounted in your local file system tree.

5. (Optional) If you started YaST from the desktop, close the **YaST Control Center**.

## Configure NFS Client Access Manually

To mount directories automatically when booting (such as the home directories of a server), you need to make corresponding entries in the file /etc/fstab.

When the system is booted, the start script /etc/init.d/nfs loads the file /etc/fstab, which indicates where file systems are mounted and with what options.

The following is an example of an entry for an NFS mount point in the file /etc/fstab:

```
da1:/training/home   /home   nfs   soft,rsize=8192,wsize=8192   0   0
```

The parts of this entry mean are described in the following:

- **da1:/training/home.** This indicates the host name of the NFS server (da1) and the directory it exports (/training/home/).

- **/home.** This indicates the mount point, which is the directory in the local file system where the exported directory should be attached.

- **nfs.** This indicates the file system type.

- **soft,rsize=8192,wsize=8192.** These comma-separated values provide NFS-specific mounting options.

- **0 0.** These two numbers indicate whether to back up the file system with the help of dump (first number) and whether to perform a file system check on the mounted volume with fsck (second number).

  In the example, the system does neither, as both options are set to 0.

After modifying the file /etc/fstab, you can have the system read the changes by entering **mount –a**. All new entries that do not contain the option noauto are evaluated and the corresponding directories or partitions are mounted.

You also need to activate the start script of the NFS client by entering **insserv nfs** (which sets the symbolic links in the respective runlevel directories).

## Temporarily Import Directories Manually from an NFS Server

You can import a directory (file system) manually from an NFS server by using the command mount. The only prerequisite is a running RPC port mapper, which you can start by entering (as root) the command **rcportmap start**.

The command mount automatically tries to recognize the file system (such as ext2, ext3, or ReiserFS). However, if that recognition fails, you must use the mount option –t to indicate the file system type, as shown in the following:

**mount –t** *filesystemtype* **–o** *options device directory*

If you do not want to mount a directory permanently or if it should not be imported automatically when the computer is booted, you can mount a directory exported by NFS like a local partition with the mount option **–o**.

The following is an example:

**mount –t nfs –o soft da1:/training/home /home**

Instead of a device file used for local file systems, you pass the name of the NFS server together with the directories to import to the mount command.

The following are the most important –o options:

- **soft (opposite: hard).** If the attempt to access the NFS server extends beyond the preset time frame (the major timeout is 60 seconds), the mount attempt will be aborted.

  Otherwise, the client attempts to mount the exported directory until it receives feedback from the server that the attempt was successful.

  This can cause the boot process to hang because the process will stop at this point when it attempts to mount the NFS directory.

For directories that are not essential for the system to function, you can use the option soft. For directories that must be mounted (such as home directories), you can use the option hard.

- **bg (default: fg).** If you use this option, and the first attempt is unsuccessful, all further mount attempts are run in the background.

  This prevents the boot process from hanging when NFS exports are automatically mounted, with attempts to mount the directories continuing in the background.

- **rsize=$n$.** This option lets you set the number of bytes ($n$) that NFS reads from the NFS server at one time.

  Because older NFS versions have a limitation of 1024 bytes, this is the default value. The current version (NFSv3) can process larger amounts of data.

  For quicker access, we recommend resetting the rsize to **8192**.

- **wsize=$n$.** This option lets you set the number of bytes ($n$) that can be written to the NFS server.

  The default value is set to 1024. For faster write access, we recommend setting wsize to **8192**.

- **retry=$n$.** This option lets you set the number of minutes (**n**) an attempt can take to mount a directory through NFS. The default value is **10000** minutes (approximately one week).

- **nosuid.** This option lets you disable any evaluation of the SUID and SGID bits on the corresponding file system.

  For security reasons, always use this option for any file system that might be susceptible to tampering.

  If you do not use this option, there is a possibility that a user can obtain root access to the local file system by putting an SUID root executable on the imported file system.

- **nodev.** This option lets you disable any interpretation of device files in the imported file system. We recommend that you use this option for security reasons.

  If you do not set this option, someone could create a device such as /dev/hda on the NFS export, then use it to obtain write permissions for the hard disk as soon as the file can be accessed from the client side.

You can use the command umount (enter **man umount**) to unmount a file system. However, you can only do this if the file system is currently not being accessed.

When attempting to unmount file systems, Linux will refuse to unmount any partitions that are currently in use.

**10**

A common challenge faced by system administrators is figuring out just why a file system they need to unmount is still considered to be busy by the kernel.

The **fuser** utility can help you figure out why the file system is busy by listing all processes accessing a file or directory.

If all else fails, the Linux 2.4 kernel has support for forced unmounts.

To unmount file systems that the kernel thinks are busy, enter:

**umount -f**

This option should be used only as a last resort, because if the kernel thinks the file system is in use, it probably is in use.

 For more information about nfs, mount options and on the file /etc/fstab, enter **man 5 nfs**, **man 8 mount**, or **man 5 fstab**.

**NOTE**

## Monitor the NFS System

Some tools are available to help you monitor the NFS system.

For example, you can enter **rpcinfo -p** to display information about the portmapper. The option **-p** displays all the programs registered with the portmapper, similar to the following:

```
da10:~ # rpcinfo -p
   program vers proto    port
    100000    2   tcp     111   portmapper
    100000    2   udp     111   portmapper
    100003    2   udp    2049   nfs
    100003    3   udp    2049   nfs
    100227    3   udp    2049   nfs_acl
    100003    2   tcp    2049   nfs
    100003    3   tcp    2049   nfs
    100227    3   tcp    2049   nfs_acl
    100021    1   udp   32773   nlockmgr
    100021    3   udp   32773   nlockmgr
    100021    4   udp   32773   nlockmgr
    100024    1   udp   32773   status
    100021    1   tcp   32872   nlockmgr
    100021    3   tcp   32872   nlockmgr
    100021    4   tcp   32872   nlockmgr
    100024    1   tcp   32872   status
    100005    1   udp     693   mountd
 . . .
```

The NFS server daemon registers itself to the port mapper with the name nfs. The NFS mount daemon uses the name mountd.

You can use the command **showmount** to display information about the exported directories of an NFS server.

For example, **showmount –e da20** displays the exported directories of the machine da20. The option –a shows which computers have mounted which directories.

## Exercise 10-2    Set up and Manage Network File System (NFS)

Today it is more the rule than the exception that files on some file server are exported to client workstations. In a purely Unix/Linux environment this is usually accomplished using NFS.

The purpose of this exercise is to walk you through the necessary steps to export and import such directories.

In this exercise, you use NFS as a server and a client to share files between Linux hosts.

Do the following:

- Part I: Add a Remote File System to the NFS Client
- Part II: Set up an NFS Server

### Part I: Add a Remote File System to the NFS Client

In this part of the exercise you access a remote file system (/export/sles9) on the instructor's server.

Do the following:

1. From your KDE desktop, open a terminal window and su to root (**su –**) with a password of **novell**.

2. Create a mount point named /mnt/sles9 for the instructor's remote file system to be mounted on your server by entering the following:

   **mkdir –p /mnt/sles9**

3. Add a remote file system to the NFS client configuration:

   a. From your KDE desktop, select the **YaST** icon; then enter a password of **novell** and select **OK**.

   The YaST Control Center appears.

   b. Select **Network Services > NFS Client**.

   The Configuration of the NFS Client dialog box appears.

   c. Mount a remote file system by selecting **Add**.

   A dialog box appears for adding the remote file system.

10

d. Enter the following:

- Hostname of the NFS Server: **10.0.0.254** (this is the address of the instructor's server)

- Remote filesystem: **/export/sles9/**

- Mountpoint (local): **/mnt/sles9/**

- Options: **defaults,rsize=8192,wsize=8192,soft**

e. Save the configuration by selecting **OK**.

You are returned to the Configuration of the NFS client dialog box where the remote file system is listed.

4. Save the changes to the system by selecting **Finish**.

5. From the terminal window, verify that the file system is mounted by entering **mount**.

You see the remote host mounted on /mnt/sles9.

6. List the files in the mounted file system by entering:

**ls -l /mnt/sles9**

7. Check the entry entered by YaST in the file /etc/fstab by entering:

**cat /etc/fstab**

This entry ensures that the file system is mounted each time the server boots.

8. Check for any other exports on the instructor's SLES 9 server by entering:

**showmount -e 10.0.0.254**

## Part II: Set up an NFS Server

Do the following:

1. From your KDE desktop, open a terminal window and su to root (**su -**) with a password of **novell**.

2. Create the directory /export/data if it does not exist by entering:

**mkdir -p /export/data**

3. Create a file in that directory by entering:

**echo hello > /export/data/hallo.txt**

4. From the YaST Control Center, configure an NFS server on your computer by selecting **Network Services > NFS Server**.

A Configuration of the NFS Server dialog box appears.

5. Select **Start NFS Server**; then continue by selecting **Next**.

   A Directories to Export to the others dialog box appears.

6. Add the directory /export/data to the list for export:

   a. Select **Add Directory**.

      A dialog box appears, requesting the directory to export.

   b. Enter **/export/data/**; then select **OK**.

      A dialog box appears with fields for entering a wild card and options.

   c. Enter the following:

      ■ Hosts wild card: **\***

      ■ Options: **rw,no_root_squash,sync** (make sure you replace "ro" with "rw")

   d. Continue by selecting **OK**.

      The directory is added to the list.

7. Save the changes to the system by selecting **Finish**.

8. From the terminal window, verify that the file system was exported by entering the following:

   **showmount -e localhost**

9. View the entry made by YaST to the file /etc/exports by entering:

   **cat /etc/exports**

   These are the settings you entered in YaST.

10. Work with a partner to access the directory /export/data directly from the partner's server by doing the following:

    a. Create a mountpoint /mnt/share on your server by entering:

       **mkdir -p /mnt/share**

    b. Mount your partner's directory doing one of the following:

       ■ Enter

       ■ **mount -t nfs** *partner_IP*:**/ export/data /mnt/share**

       *or*

       ■ Use the YaST NFS Client module to mount the directory.

11. Verify that your partner's directory is mounted by entering:

    **mount**

12. Start Konqueror in the Super User Mode by pressing **Alt + F2** and entering **kdesu konqueror**; then select **Run**.

**10**

13. Enter a password of **novell** and select **OK**.

14. View your NFS export by entering the following URL:

    **nfs://localhost**

15. View your partner's NFS export by entering the following URL:

    **nfs://*partner_server_IP_address***

16. (Optional) If you finish early, try changing the entry in the **/etc/exports** file so that only you or your partner can write to the file system, and only one of you can read from it.

17. When you finish, close all open windows and dialog boxes.

## Samba (CIFS)

Samba is a software package that implements the following Microsoft networking protocols on Linux:

- **Server Message Block (SMB).** SMB is a protocol for sharing resources between networked computers. SMB can be implemented over a number of protocols including TCP/IP, NetBEUI (often called NetBIOS), or IPX/SPX.

**NOTE**

For more information about SMB, see www.samba.org/cifs/docs/what-is-smb.html.

- **Common Internet File System (CIFS).** CIFS is an implementation of SMB over native TCP/IP that does not require NetBIOS.

    CIFS is a client/server protocol and is used by Windows operating systems. It is also implemented on many other platforms (such as DOS, NetWare, UNIX, Linux, and VMSTM).

With Samba installed, a Linux computer can function as the following:

- **Microsoft Windows server.** Samba enables a server to provide Windows file and print services to users.

- **Microsoft Windows client.** Samba enables a workstation to access and use Windows file and print services, whether they originate on a Windows server or on a Linux server with Samba installed.

To configure Samba on your SUSE Linux Enterprise server, you need to know the following:

- Samba Features and Version
- Samba Client Support on Linux

- Start and Stop Samba Services
- Configure a Samba Server with YaST
- Configure a Samba Client with YaST
- Monitor and Test Samba

**NOTE**

For more information about Samba, enter **man samba** at the command line or browse the directory /usr/share/doc/packages/samba/. If the documentation is not installed, use the YaST Install and Remove Software module to install the documents.

## Samba Features and Version

SLES 9 includes version 3 of the Samba suite, which includes the following new important features:

- Improved Unicode support
- Complete revision of the internal authentication mechanisms
- Improved support for the Windows 200*x*/XP printing system
- The ability to set up servers as member servers in Active Directory domains
- Adoption of a Windows NT 4 domain, enabling the migration from an NT 4 domain to a Samba domain

## Samba Client Support on Linux

All common operating systems, such as Mac OS X, Windows, and OS/2, support the SMB protocol. For the SMB protocol to operate, the TCP/IP protocol must be installed on all computers.

**CAUTION**

Clients can only access the Samba server via TCP/IP. NetBEUI and NetBIOS via IPX cannot be used with Samba.

Samba provides a client for the different UNIX versions. For Linux, there is a file system kernel module for SMB that allows for the integration of SMB resources on the Linux system level.

SMB servers use shares to provide hard disk space to their clients. A share includes a directory and its subdirectories on the server. It is exported by means of a name and can be accessed by its name.

The share name can be set to any name—it does not have to be the name of the export directory.

A printer is also assigned a name. Clients can access the printer by its name.

## Start and Stop Samba Services

To start the services required for Samba, enter:

**rcnmb start && rcsmb start**

To stop the Samba services, enter:

**rcsmb stop && rcnmb stop**

**Samba Configuration File**  The main configuration file of Samba is /etc/samba/smb.conf.

This file can be divided into two logical sections:

- **[global] section.** Contains the central and global settings
- **[share] sections.** Contain the individual file and printer shares

By using two logical sections, you can set the configuration of shares individually or by using global settings included in the [global] section.

The following helps you understand how the smb.conf file is configured:

- [global] Section Configuration
- [cdrom] and [homes] Shares Configuration Examples
- Share Password Protection

You can configure the file manually or by using the YaST Samba Server module.

**NOTE**

You can find a commented example configuration file in /usr/share/doc/packages/samba/examples/smb.conf. SuSE.

**[global] Section Configuration**  The following parameters of the [global] section need to be adjusted to match the requirements of your network setup (manually or through YaST) so other machines can access your Samba server via SMB in a Windows environment:

- **workgroup = TUX-NET.** This line assigns the Samba server to a workgroup. Replace TUX-NET with an appropriate workgroup of your networking environment.
- **netbiosname = MYNAME.** Your Samba server appears under its DNS name unless this name has been assigned to another computer in the network. If the DNS name is not available, set the server name using netbiosname=MYNAME.

For more details about this parameter, see **man smb.conf**.

- **os level = 2.** This parameter triggers whether your Samba server tries to become LMB (Local Master Browser) for its work group.

  Choose a very low value to protect the existing Windows network from any disturbances caused by a misconfigured Samba server.

For more information about this important topic, see the file /usr/share/doc/packages/samba/htmldocs/howto/NetworkBrowsing.html.

**10**

- **wins support and wins server.** To integrate your Samba server into an existing Windows network with an active WINS server, enable the **wins server** option and set its value to the IP address of that WINS server.

  If your Windows computers are connected to separate subnets and need to be aware of each other, you need to set up a WINS server.

  To turn a Samba server into a WINS server, set the wins support option to **Yes** (**wins support = Yes**). Make sure that only one Samba server on the network has this setting enabled.

  The options **wins server** and **wins support** must never be enabled at the same time in the file smb.conf.

**[cdrom] and [homes] Shares Configuration Examples**   The following examples illustrate how a CD-ROM drive and user directories (homes) can be made available to SMB clients by configuring shares in the file smb.conf:

- **[cdrom].** The following lines make the CD-ROM drive on your Linux server available to the clients:

```
[cdrom]
        comment = Linux CD-ROM
        path    = /media/cdrom
        locking = No
```

You can configure the following:

  - **[cdrom].** This is the name of the share that can be seen by all SMB clients on the network.

  - **comment.** Use this to add an additional comment that describes the share.

  - **path.** This is the path for exporting the cdrom directory (such as **path = /media/cdrom**).

By means of a very restrictive default configuration, this kind of share is only made available to the users present on this system.

If this share should be made available to everybody, add a **guest ok = yes** line to the configuration. This setting gives read permissions to anyone on the network.

You need to handle this parameter with great care, especially when using it in the [global] section.

- **[homes].** If a user has a valid account and password for the Linux file server and her own home directory, she can be connected to it through the [homes] share.

The following is an example of a configured [homes] share:

```
[homes]
        comment = Home Directories
        valid users = %S
        browseable = No
        read only = No
        create mask = 0640
        directory mask = 750
        inherit permissions = Yes
```

Configure the following:

- **[homes].** As long as there is no other share using the share name of the user connecting to the SMB server, a share is dynamically generated using the [homes] share directives.

  The resulting name of the share is identical to the user name.

- **valid users = %S.** %S is replaced with the actual name of the share as soon as a connection has been successfully established.

  For a [homes] share, this is always identical to the user's name. As a consequence, access rights to a user's share are restricted exclusively to the user.

- **browseable = No.** This setting enables the share to be invisible in the network environment.

- **read only = No.** By default, Samba prohibits write access to any exported share by means of this parameter.

  To make a share writable, set the value **read only = No**, which is equivalent to **writeable = Yes**.

- **create mask = 0640.** Systems that are based on Windows NT do not understand the concept of UNIX permissions, so they cannot assign permissions when creating a file.

  This parameter defines the access permissions assigned to newly created files. This only applies to writable shares.

  In this example, the owner has read and write permissions and the members of the owner's primary group have read permissions.

**CAUTION**

The parameter **valid users = %S** prevents read access even if the group has read permissions. If you want the group to have read or write access, you need to deactivate the line valid users = %S.

**Share Password Protection**   The SMB protocol comes from the DOS and Windows environment and directly considers the problem of security.

Each share access can be protected with a password. SMB has three possible ways of checking the permissions:

- **Share Level Security (security = share).** A password is firmly assigned to a share. Everyone who knows this password has access to that share.

- **User Level Security (security = user).** All users must register with the server with their own password. After registering, the server can grant access to individual exported shares dependent on user names.

- **Server Level Security (security = server).** To its clients, Samba pretends to be working in User Level Mode.

  However, it passes all password queries to another User Level Mode Server, which takes care of authentication. This setting expects an additional parameter (**password server =**).

Setting share, user, and server level security applies to the entire server. It is not possible to offer individual shares of a server configuration with share level security and others with user level security. However, you can run a separate Samba server for each configured IP address on a system.

**NOTE**

For more information about password security, check the Samba HOWTO Collection.

**10**

### Configure a Samba Server with YaST

To configure a Samba server with YaST, do the following:

1. From the KDE desktop, start the YaST Samba Server module by doing one of the following:

   - Select the **YaST** icon, enter the root password *novell*, and select **OK**; then select **Network Services > Samba Server**.

   *or*

   - Open a terminal window and enter **sux –** and the root password *novell*; then enter **yast2 samba-server**.

   A screen similar to Figure 10-9 appears.

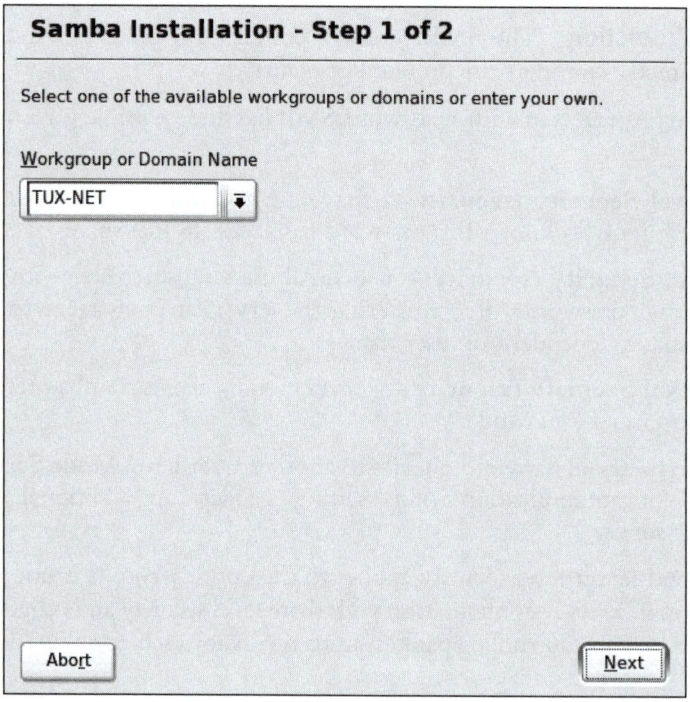

---

**Samba Installation - Step 1 of 2**

Select one of the available workgroups or domains or enter your own.

Workgroup or Domain Name

| TUX-NET | ⬇ |

Abort                                                                 Next

---

**Figure 10-9**

2. From the drop-down list, select an available *workgroup* or *domain* on the network (detected by YaST), or enter a name.

3. Continue by selecting **Next**.

A screen similar to Figure 10-10 appears.

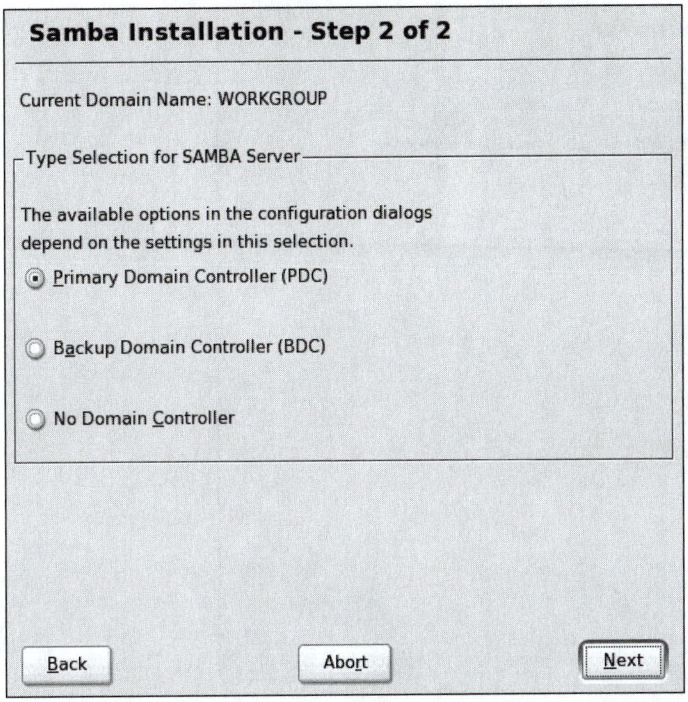

**Samba Installation - Step 2 of 2**

Current Domain Name: WORKGROUP

┌Type Selection for SAMBA Server───────────────────────

The available options in the configuration dialogs
depend on the settings in this selection.

◉ Primary Domain Controller (PDC)

○ Backup Domain Controller (BDC)

○ No Domain Controller

Back          Abort          Next

**Figure 10-10**

4. Select a *domain controller* type for your Samba server; then select **Next**.

   Normally, you will want to select **Primary Domain Controller** to use the locally defined users and passwords for security purposes.

The dialog box shown in Figure 10-11 appears.

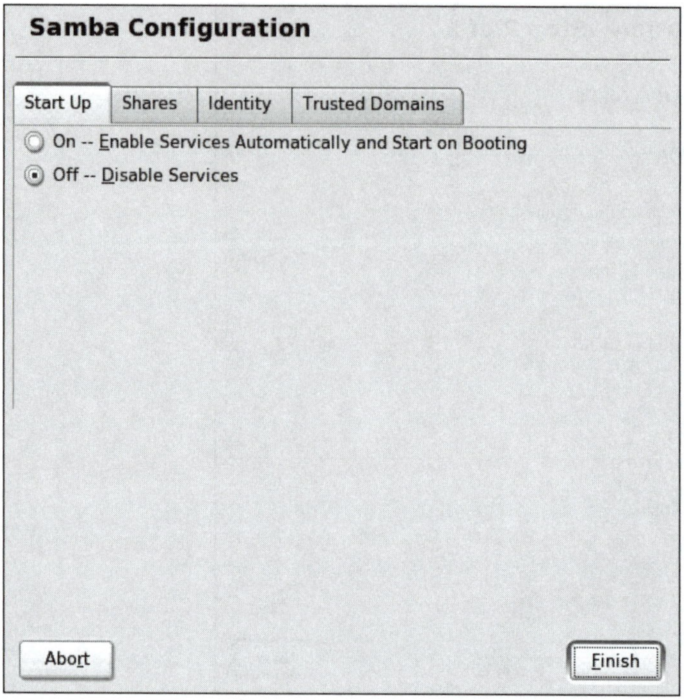

**Samba Configuration**

| Start Up | Shares | Identity | Trusted Domains |
|---|---|---|---|

○ On -- Enable Services Automatically and Start on Booting
◉ Off -- Disable Services

Abort                                                Finish

**Figure 10-11**

The four tabs on the dialog box let you configure startup, shares, identity, and trusted domains for your Samba server.

5. Configure the system services to start on bootup by selecting **On**.

6. Display a list of configured shares by selecting **Shares**.

The dialog box shown in Figure 10-12 appears.

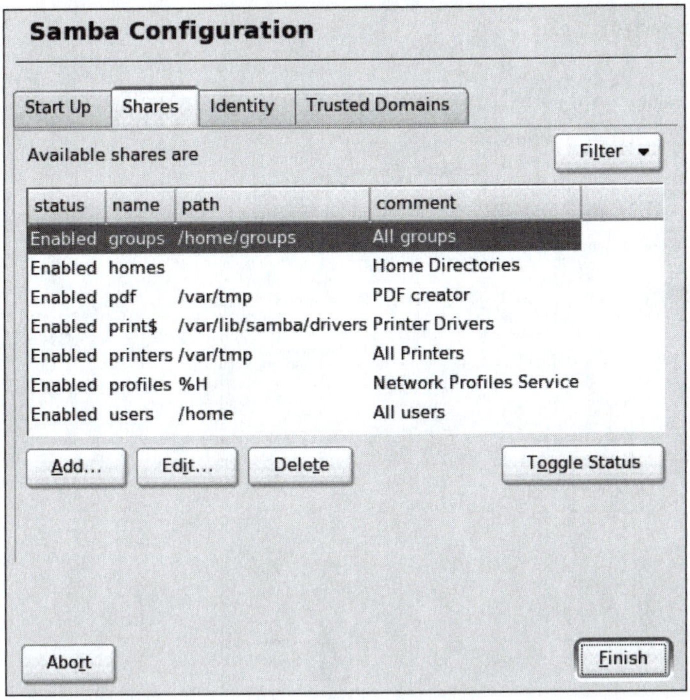

**Samba Configuration**

| Start Up | Shares | Identity | Trusted Domains |

Available shares are                                    Filter ▼

| status | name | path | comment |
|--------|------|------|---------|
| Enabled | groups | /home/groups | All groups |
| Enabled | homes | | Home Directories |
| Enabled | pdf | /var/tmp | PDF creator |
| Enabled | print$ | /var/lib/samba/drivers | Printer Drivers |
| Enabled | printers | /var/tmp | All Printers |
| Enabled | profiles | %H | Network Profiles Service |
| Enabled | users | /home | All users |

Add...    Edit...    Delete                    Toggle Status

Abort                                          Finish

**Figure 10-12**

You can manage the available shares list by adding (**Add**), editing (**Edit**), or deleting (**Delete**) shares.

You can also enable or disable a selected share by selecting **Toggle Status**. Disabled indicates that the share will not be activated when you boot the server.

7. You can display options for configuring the Samba server identity by selecting **Identity**.

The dialog box shown in Figure 10-13 appears.

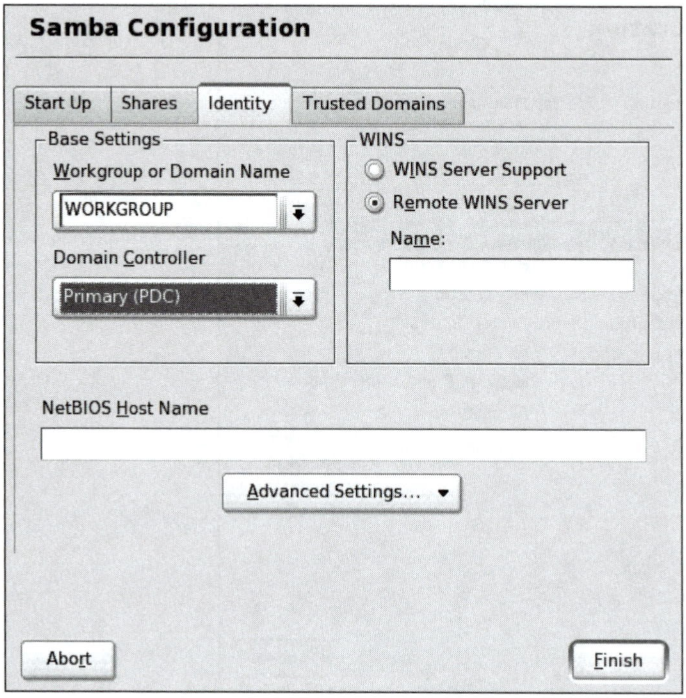

**Figure 10-13**

You can change the base settings you configured during installation (select **Workgroup or Domain Name** and **Domain Controller**).

You can also configure the host as a WINS server, or enter the IP address of a WINS server on the network. If you enter an asterisk (*), YaST will automatically find the WINS server.

In addition, you can determine whether to use an alternative host name in the network by entering the name in the **NetBIOS Host Name** field.

8. Display a list of trusted domains by selecting Trusted Domains.

The dialog box shown in Figure 10-14 appears.

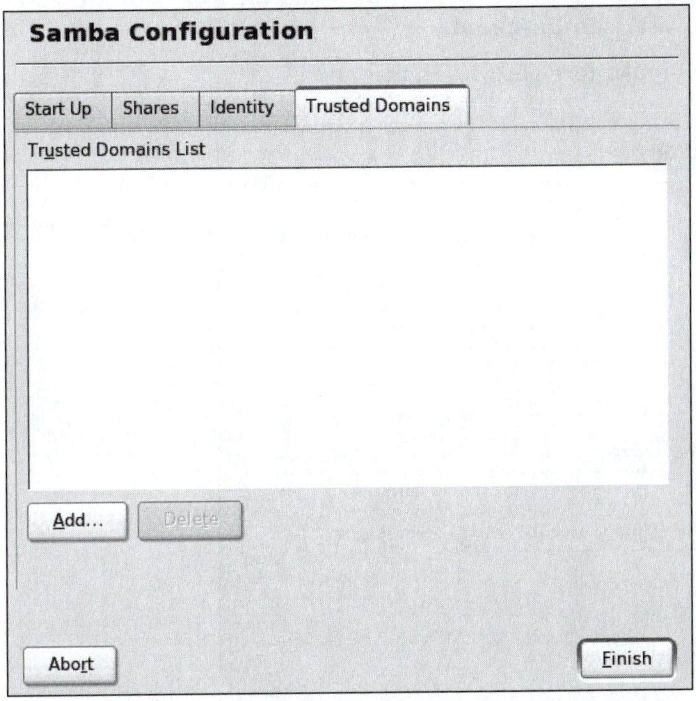

**Figure 10-14**

You can manage the list of which domains the host can trust by adding (**Add**) or deleting (**Delete**) domains.

Remember that adding a trusted domain means that you adopt the respective settings of that domain.

9. When you finish configuring the Samba server, save the settings by selecting **Finish**.

10. (Optional) If you started YaST from the desktop, close the **YaST Control Center**.

## Configure a Samba Client with YaST

To configure a Samba client with YaST, do the following:

1. Start the YaST Samba Client module by doing one of the following:

   - From the desktop, start the YaST Control Center by selecting **Start Applications > System > YaST**; enter the root password *novell*, and select **OK**; then select:

     **Network Services > Samba Client**

*or*

- From a terminal window, enter **sux –** and the root password *novell*, then enter **yast2 samba–client**.

A screen similar to Figure 10-15 appears.

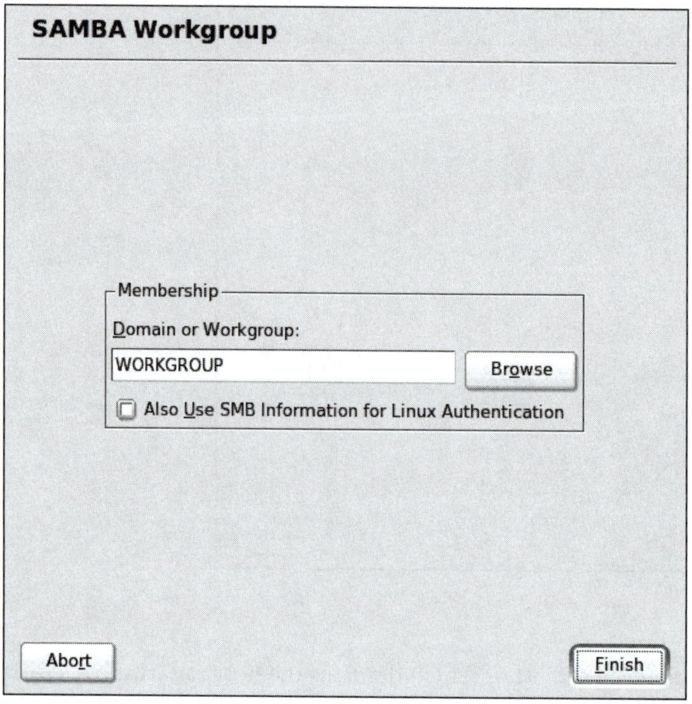

**SAMBA Workgroup**

Membership

Domain or Workgroup:

WORKGROUP    Browse

☐ Also Use SMB Information for Linux Authentication

Abort    Finish

**Figure 10-15**

2. Enter the name of a *workgroup* or NT *domain* for the Samba client member-ship, or find and select an available workgroup or domain by selecting **Browse**.

3. Allow for verification of passwords against an NT server by selecting **Also Use SMB Information for Linux Authentication**.

4. When you finish, save the Samba client configuration settings by selecting **Finish**.

5. (Optional) If you started YaST from the desktop, close the **YaST Control Center**.

## Monitor and Test Samba

After configuring Samba, you need to know the following to monitor and test your configuration:

- Diagnosis Tools
- How to Start and Test Samba
- Use smbclient to Access SMB Shares
- Mount SMB Shares into the Linux File System

**Diagnosis Tools**     The following are commands you can use to check your Samba configuration:

- **/usr/bin/testparm.** You can enter this command to perform a syntax check of the file /etc/samba/smb.conf.

   A list is displayed of all set parameters. However, only the output following the last listed section (which interrupts the cursor) is important for your initial check of the configuration.

   Look for the following:
   ```
   Loaded services file OK.
   ```
   If you see this message, everything is okay so far. If you press **Enter**, a long list is displayed. You only need to evaluate this list if you are doing advanced debugging.

   If a service has a syntax error, testparm usually displays this immediately. The file /etc/samba/smb.conf has become much less susceptible to syntax errors compared with earlier versions.

   However, you should avoid writing options and comments on the same line. If the option line contains a faulty expression (such as **security = purchase**), Samba reverts to the default **security = user**.

   Although this is more reliable, it is easy to overlook in practice.

- **/usr/bin/nmblookup.** You can enter this command to display the registered local or remote names of a host, regardless of the operating system with which NetBIOS is run. (The Microsoft counterpart is nbtstat.)

   You can review the variety of features available with this command by entering **nmblookup -help**.

   The command nmblookup is a bit more verbose with the options -A and -S. When you use the option -S, nmblookup first displays the IP number of the queried host, then all names under which they are registered, including all aliases.

   However, using the option -A limits the output to the unique entries bearing the same name and the group entries. Both options display the status of the registrations.

**10**

When you use the option –M, you can display the local master browser of each workgroup.

- **/usr/bin/smbclient.** This is explained in more detail in Use smbclient to Access SMB Shares.

- **/usr/bin/smbstatus.** You can use this command to list all currently existing connections to the Samba server.

**How to Start and Test Samba**   All the Samba server really needs is the file /etc/samba/smb.conf with an entry about the workgroup. Entering the following lines in the configuration file is enough to start the server:

```
[global]

workgroup = TUX-NET
encrypt passwords = yes
guest account = nobody
```

Entering **rcsmb start** at the command line is enough to make the host visible with its host name in a Windows environment.

You can use nmblookup to see whether the new Samba host is already visible in the network environment (such as **nmblookup da10**).

**CAUTION**

If nmb does not run, nmblookup does not seem to come up with a sensible response. Try entering **rcnmb start && rcsmb start** instead of rcsmb start.

**Use smbclient to Access SMB Shares**   With the smbclient tool, you can access SMB shares on the network. It's also a very useful tool to test a Samba server configuration.

You can perform three basic tasks with smbclient.

- Browse the Shares Provided by a Server

- Access Files Provided by an SMB Server

- Print on Printers Provided by an SMB Server

**Browse the Shares Provided by a Server**   To display the shares offered by an SMB server, enter:

**smbclient –L //Fileserver**

When smbclient asks for a password, press **Enter** to proceed.

The output of smbclient looks like the following:

```
Domain=[DigitalAirlines] OS=[Unix] Server=[Samba 3.0.4-SUSE]
        Sharename       Type        Comment
        ---------       ----        -------
        data            Disk        Data
        IPC$            IPC         IPC Service
        ADMIN$          IPC         IPC Service
Domain=[DigitalAirlines] OS=[Unix] Server=[Samba 3.0.4-SUSE]
        Server                  Comment
        ---------               -------
        Workgroup               Master
        ---------               -------
        DigitalAirlines         Fileserver
```

smbclient first displays all available shares of the SMB server.

Beside the shares you have configured in the smb.conf file, an SMB server always offers at least two other shares:

- **IPC$.** This share provides information about the other shares available on the SMB server.

- **ADMIN$.** On a Windows computer this share points to the directory where Windows itself is installed.

    This can be useful for administrative tasks. When Samba tries to emulate a Windows server, it also offers this share.

    However, it is not needed to administer a Linux server.

The lower part of the smbclient output gives some information about the workgroup of the system.

This command can also very be valuable for testing purposes.

After you have set up a share, you can check the availability of the share with smbclient.

The following is a recommended command syntax:

**smbclient –L //** *hostname* **[–I** *IP_address* **–U** *username*]

This provides a list of all shares on the specific host as well as the member and group names of the host.

To specify the host address of the target host, enter:

**–I** *IP_address*

If there are special shares linked to a user authentication, include the login name by entering:

**–U** *username*

Some shares are not browseable without authentication.

In this case, pass a user name to smbclient by entering:

**smbclient –L //Fileserver –U tux**

In this example, smbclient connects to the server with the user name tux and prompt for the corresponding password.

**Access Files Provided by an SMB Server**     The command to access a share on a server is similar to the command used to browse for available shares, but instead of supplying just the server name, the full path to the share needs to be supplied without the –L option.

To connect to the share data on the server Fileserver, enter:

**smbclient //Fileserver/data**

If the share data is not configured with the guest ok = yes option, a user name can be supplied with the –U option.

After smbclient has connected to a share, it displays the following prompt:

Smb: \>

smbclient can be used like a command-line FTP client.

The most important commands are the following:

- **ls.** Displays the content of the current directory.
- **cd.** Changes to a directory.
- **get.** Copies a file from the share to the current working directory.
- **put.** Copies a file to the share. The share must be writable to use this command.

**Print on Printers Provided by an SMB Server**     You can use smbclient to print on shared network printers.

The basic syntax of a print command is:

**smbclient //Printserver/laser –c 'print letter.ps'**

In this example, the file letter.ps is printed on a network printer accessed through the share laser of the SMB server Printserver.

You can also use the command print on the smbclient command line after you have connected to the server.

The –c option performs the given command automatically after the connection to the server has been established.

**Mount SMB Shares into the Linux File System**     Instead of accessing shared files with smbclient, you can mount a share into the file system like a hard disk partition or a CD-ROM drive.

The basic mount command is:

**mount –t smbfs //Fileserver/data /mnt**

In this example, the share data of the SMB server Fileserver is mounted into the directory /mnt.

The option –t smbfs is necessary to specify that the resource to be mounted is an SMB share.

If the share requires authentication, you can supply a username:

**mount –t smbfs –o username=tux //Fileserver/data /mnt**

You are prompted for the password. You can also supply the password in the command line directly with the following syntax (on one line):

**mount –t smbfs –o username=tux,password=novell**

**//Fileserver/data /mnt**

## Exercise 10-3   Configure a Basic Samba Server

NFS clients for Windows machines exist, but it is far more common to use the SMB protocol instead of NFS when Windows machines are involved in sharing resources (files, printers) over the network.

Samba offers a large variety of configuration options. Only the most common ones are covered in this exercise. Its purpose is to help you set up a simple Samba service.

In this exercise, you do the following:

- Part I: Configure the Samba Client
- Part II: Configure the Samba Server

### Part I: Configure the Samba Client

In this part of the exercise, you connect to the instructor's Samba server by doing the following:

1. From the KDE desktop, select the **YaST** icon; then enter a password of *novell* and select **OK**.

   The YaST Control Center appears.

2. Select **Network Services > Samba Client**.

   A Samba Workgroup dialog box appears.

3. In the Domain or Workgroup field, browse to and select or enter **SUSE-CLASS**.

4. Save the changes by selecting **Finish**.

5. Open a terminal window and su to root (**su –**) with a password of **novell**.

6. Connect to the instructor's Samba server by entering:

   **smbclient //10.0.0.254/sles9 –U geeko**

7. Enter a password of **N0v3ll**.

   You are logged in to an smbclient session.

8. View the files on the share by entering **dir**.

9. Copy the file manual.pdf to the local directory /tmp by entering:

   **lcd /tmp**

   **cd SUSE-SLES-Version-9/CD1/docu/en**

   **get manual.pdf**

10. End the smbclient session by entering **quit**.

11. Create the directory /mnt/sles9-2 by entering:

    **mkdir –p /mnt/sles9-2**

12. Mount the remote CIFS file system to the local host by entering (in one line):

    **mount –t smbfs –o username=geeko,password=N0v3ll //10.0.0.254/ sles9 /mnt/sles9-2**

    Now the files on the instructor's system are accessible through the NFS and CIFS protocols.

13. Verify that the file system mounted by entering **mount**.

14. View the files in the directory by entering:

    **ls –l /mnt/sles9-2**

## Part II: Configure the Samba Server

In this part of the exercise you configure a basic CIFS server using YaST to configure Samba.

Do the following:

1. Open a terminal window and **su –** to root with a password of **novell**.

2. From the terminal window, create the user account geeko for the Samba server by entering:

   **smbpasswd –a geeko**

3. Enter a password of **N0v3ll** twice.

4. Verify that the user geeko was added to the Samba user database by entering:

   **cat /etc/samba/smbpasswd**

5. Check with **ls /export/** whether the directory /export/data exists. If not, create it with **mkdir –p /export/data**.

6. From the YaST Control Center, select:

   **Network Services > Samba Server**

   A Samba Configuration dialog box appears.

7. Select the **Startup** tab; then select:

   **On – Enable Service Automatically and Start on Booting**

8. Select the **Shares** tab.

9. Add a share by selecting **Add**.

   An Add New Share dialog box appears.

10. Enter the following:

    - Share Name: **data**
    - Description: **Data**
    - Share Type: **Directory**
    - Share Path: **/export/data/**

11. When you finish, select **OK**.

    You are returned to the Samba Configuration dialog box, and the share data is added to the list.

12. Save the changes to the system by selecting **Finish**.

    A dialog box appears requesting a root password.

13. Enter **novell** twice; then select **OK**.

14. From the terminal window, view the CIFS shares enabled in the Samba configuration by entering:

    **smbclient –L localhost –U geeko**

15. Enter a password of **N0v3ll**.

16. Open a Konqueror browser window; then enter the following URI:

    **smb://geeko@*your_IP_address*/data**

    An authentication dialog box appears.

17. Authenticate as **geeko** with a password of **N0v3ll**; then select **OK**.

18. From Konqueror, access a partner's /export/data directory by entering:

    **smb://geeko:N0v3ll@*your_partner's_IP_address*/data**

    An authentication dialog box appears.

19. When you finish, close all open windows.

**10**

## OBJECTIVE 3    CONFIGURE AND MANAGE NETWORK PRINTING SERVICES

To configure network printing services in SUSE Linux Enterprise Server, you need to understand the following:

- Printers and Linux Support
- CUPS and SUSE Linux Enterprise Server
- Configure a Network Printer
- Modify a SUSE Linux Enterprise Server Network Printer
- Manage Printing from the Command Line
- Restrict Printer Access
- Access the CUPS Web Administration Tools
- Troubleshoot the CUPS Printing System

## Printers and Linux Support

If you want to find out if a printer is supported by Linux, check the following sources:

- http://cdb. suse.de/ or http://hardwaredb. suse.de/. This is the SUSE Linux Enterprise Server printer database.
- http://www.linuxprinting.org/. This contains the printer database on linuxprinting.org.
- http://www.cs.wisc.edu/~ghost/. This is the Ghostscript Web page.
- file:/usr/share/doc/packages/ghostscript/catalog.devices. This lists included drivers.

The online databases always show the latest Linux printing support status. However, a Linux distribution can only integrate the drivers available at the production time.

For this reason, a printer currently rated as Perfectly Supported might not have had this status when the latest SUSE Linux Enterprise Server version was released.

## CUPS and SUSE Linux Enterprise Server

CUPS (Common Unix Printing System) is the default printing system of SUSE Linux Enterprise Server.

To understand how CUPS works with SUSE Linux Enterprise Server, you need to know the following:

- How CUPS Handles Print Jobs
- How the cupsd Printer Daemon Works

## How CUPS Handles Print Jobs

The following is the sequence of events that happens between submitting a print job and getting the actual printout on the printer:

1. The print job is created by a user or a program.

2. The file to print is saved in a queue.

   This creates two files for the print job in the directory /var/spool/cups/. One of the files contains the data to print and the other contains information about the print job (such as who submitted the print job and which printer is addressed).

3. The printer daemon cupsd collects the file to print from the queue, determines the type of the data to print, and converts it to the printer-specific format.

4. The printer receives the data and prints it.

5. When the print job has been transmitted completely to the printer, it is removed from the queue.

This sequence of events ensures that you can submit print jobs at any time. It also ensures that the print jobs are processed one after the other without losing any print jobs.

## How the cupsd Printer Daemon Works

The printer daemon cupsd is a background process and is launched at system start-up by the script /etc/init.d/cups. Its configuration file is /etc/cups/cupsd.conf.

The cupsd daemon administers the local queues and filters or converts data to print to a printer-specific format.

The following describes how cupsd handles print jobs:

1. cupsd gets the submitted print jobs from the queue and sends them to the printer.

2. cupsd then executes the print jobs in the queue in order.

   It controls the state of the queues and displays information about it, if queried.

**10**

Figure 10-16 illustrates and describes how cupsd filters or converts data to print.

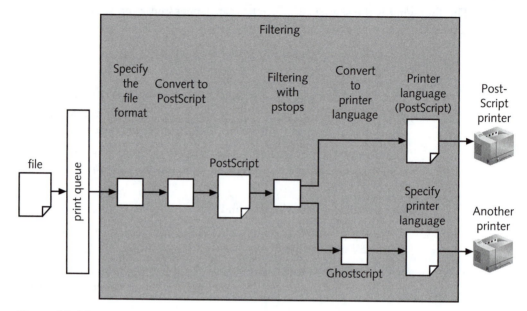

**Figure 10-16**

a. First, the data type is determined with the help of /etc/cups/mime.types.

b. Next, the data is converted to PostScript by using the tool specified in /etc/cups/mime.convs.

c. After that, the number of pages is determined with the tool pstops (/usr/lib/cups/filter/pstops). The number of pages is written into the file /var/log/cups/page_log.

d. If necessary, further pstops filtering functions are enabled, depending on which options were chosen for the printing. These include options such as selected pages (the psselect option of pstops) or multiple pages should on one sheet of paper (the ps-n-up option of pstops).

e. If data is printed on a non–PostScript printer, a filter that converts the data into the printer-specific format starts (such as /usr/lib/cups/filter/cupsomatic which calls Ghostscript).

f. The filter processes all device-dependent print options, such as resolution and paper size.

g. To print the data on the printer itself, an additional filter (stored in /usr/lib/cups/backend) is started, depending on how the printer is connected.

3. After the conversion, the data is transmitted to the printer.

As the root user, you can start or stop cupsd manually by using:

- **/etc/init.d/cups start** *or* **rccups start**
- **/etc/init.d/cups stop** *or* **rccups stop**

If you make changes manually to the file /etc/cups/cupsd.conf, you need to restart the daemon by entering **/etc/init.d/cups restart** or **rccups restart**.

## Configure a Network Printer

After connecting a printer to the network and installing the software, you need to install the printer in the SUSE Linux Enterprise Server operating system.

If at all possible, you should use the command line and YaST tools that are included with SUSE Linux Enterprise Server. Because SUSE Linux puts great emphasis on security, third-party tools often have difficulties with the security restrictions and end up causing more problems than solutions or benefits.

To configure a network printer for SUSE Linux Enterprise Server, you need to know the following:

- SUSE Linux Enterprise Server and Supported Printing Protocols
- SUSE Linux Enterprise Server and PostScript Printers
- Configure a Network Printer with YaST
- Configure a Network Printer from the Command Line

### SUSE Linux Enterprise Server and Supported Printing Protocols

A network printer can support various protocols.

Although most of the supported protocols are standardized, some manufacturers modify the standard protocol to test systems that have not implemented the standard correctly or to provide certain functions that are not available in the standard protocol.

In addition, some manufacturers believe that they can integrate these extensions and test them on Windows only, assuming they will not cause any difficulties for other operating systems.

Unfortunately, these extensions that run well on Windows can causes problems in Linux. For this reason, you cannot assume that every protocol works properly in Linux. You might have to experiment with various options to achieve a functional configuration.

CUPS supports the socket, LPD, IPP, and smb protocols. The following describes these protocols:

- **socket.** This refers to a connection in which data is sent to an Internet socket without first performing a data handshake. Some of the socket port numbers that are commonly used are 9100 or 35.

  Device URI example: **socket://*host-printer*:9100/**

- **LPD (Line Printer Daemon).** The LPD protocol is described in RFC 1179. Under this protocol, some job-related data such as the printer queue is sent before the actual print data.

  This means that a printer queue must be specified when configuring the LPD protocol for the data transmission.

  The implementations of most printer manufacturers are flexible enough to accept any name as the printer queue. If necessary, the printer manual might indicate which name to use (such as LPT, LPT1, or LP1).

  Of course, an LPD queue can also be configured on a different Linux or UNIX host in a network that uses the CUPS system. The port number for an LPD service is 515.

  Device URI example: **lpd://*host-printer*/LPT1**

- **IPP (Internet Printing Protocol).** IPP is a relatively new protocol (since 1999) that is based on the HTTP protocol. Under IPP, much more job-related data can be transmitted than in the other protocols.

  CUPS uses IPP for the internal data transmission. This is the preferred protocol for a forwarding queue between CUPS servers.

  You need the name of the printer queue to configure IPP correctly. The port number for IPP is 631.

  Examples of Device URI's are:

  **ipp://*host-printer*/ps** :

  **ipp://host-cupsserver/printers/ps**

- **SMB (Standard Message Block).** CUPS also supports printing on printers connected to Windows shares. The protocol used for this purpose is SMB.

  SMB uses port numbers 137, 138, and 139.

  Some examples of Device URI's are:

  **smb://*user:password@workgroup/server/printer***

  **smb://*user:password@host/printer***

  **smb://*server/printer***

The protocol supported by the printer must be determined prior to the configuration. If the manufacturer does not provide the needed information, you can use the command **nmap** (package nmap) to guess the protocol. The command checks a host for open ports.

An example is, **nmap -p 35,137–139,515,631,9100–10000.**

## SUSE Linux Enterprise Server and PostScript Printers

PPD (PostScript Printer Description) is the computer language that describes the properties (such as resolution) and options (such as duplex unit) of PostScript printers.

These descriptions are necessary to use the various printer options in CUPS. Without a PPD file, the print data would be forwarded to the printer in a raw state, which is usually not desired.

During the installation of SUSE Linux Enterprise Server, a lot of PPD files are preinstalled. In this way, even printers that do not have built-in PostScript support can be used.

If a PostScript printer is configured, the best approach is to get a suitable PPD file and store it in the directory /usr/share/cups/model/ or add it to the print system with YaST (preferred approach). You can then select the PPD file during the installation.

Be cautious if a printer manufacturer wants you to install entire software packages. This kind of installation results in the loss of the support provided by SUSE Linux.

In addition, print commands might work in a different way than before and the system might not be able to address devices from other manufacturers.

## Configure a Network Printer with YaST

The following are the basic steps for configuring a network printer with YaST:

1. From the KDE desktop, start the YaST Printer module by doing one of the following:

   - Select the **YaST** icon, enter the root password *novell*, and select **OK**; then select **Hardware > Printer**.

     *or*

   - Open a terminal window and enter **sux –** and the root password *novell*; then enter **yast2 printer**.

**10**

The dialog box shown in Figure 10-17 appears.

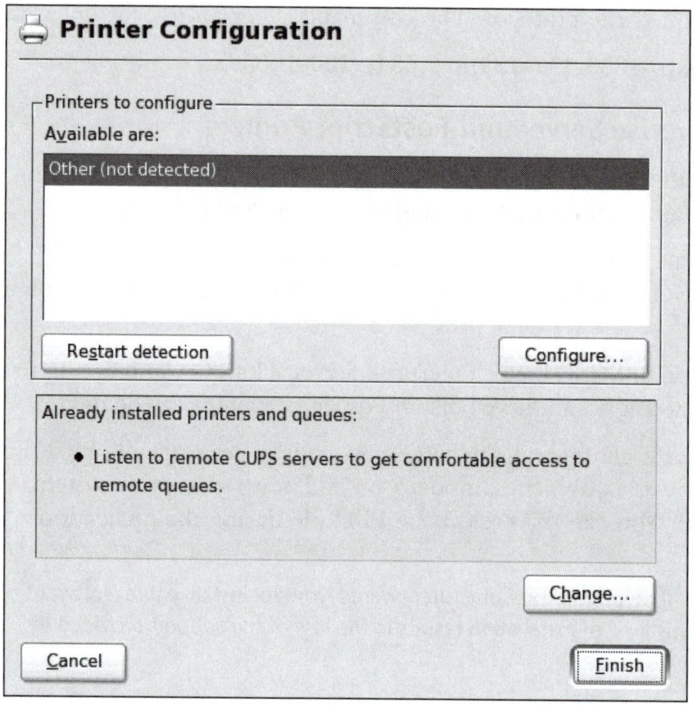

**Figure 10-17**

You can do one of three basic tasks:

- If your printer was detected and is listed, create a configuration for the printer by selecting it from the list; then select **Configure**.

  *or*

- If your printer was *not* detected, set up a printer configuration manually by selecting **Other**; then select **Configure**.

  You can try automatically detecting your printer by selecting **Restart Detection**.

  *or*

- Edit a configured printer queue by selecting **Change**.

  To add a printer manually, continue with Step 2.

2. To add a new printer manually to the system, select **Other**; then select **Configure**.

A list of printer types appears, as shown in Figure 10-18.

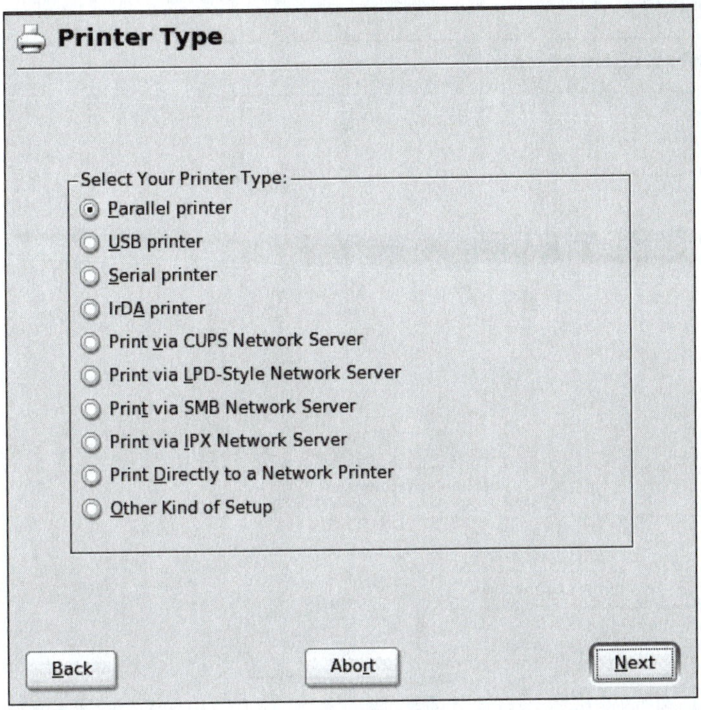

**Figure 10-18**

3. Select the *printer type* you want to configure (such as **Parallel Printer**); then select **Next**.

The configuration screens that appear depend on the type of printer you select.

For example, if you select **Parallel Printer**, the dialog box shown in Figure 10-19 appears.

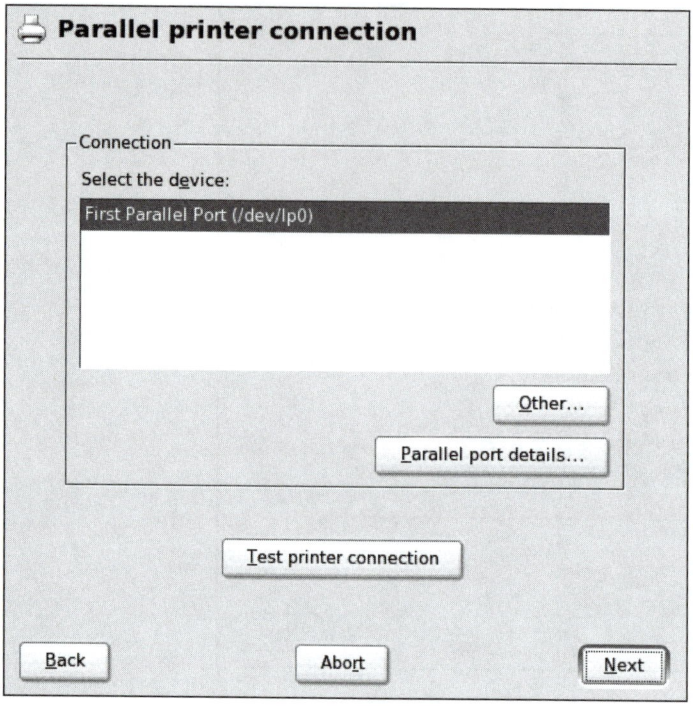

**Figure 10-19**

From this dialog box, you can configure the parallel port (one or more ports). By selecting **Next**, you move through a series of configuration screens that let you enter printer information such as the queue name and printer manufacturer and model.

If you select a printer type such as **Print via CUPS Network Server**, the dialog box shown in Figure 10-20 appears.

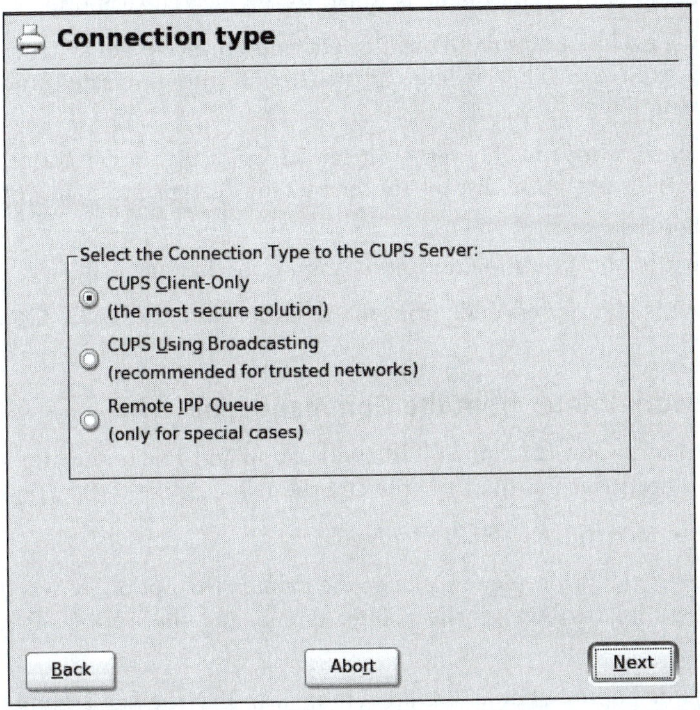

---

🖨 **Connection type**

---

Select the Connection Type to the CUPS Server:

◉ CUPS Client-Only
   (the most secure solution)

○ CUPS Using Broadcasting
   (recommended for trusted networks)

○ Remote IPP Queue
   (only for special cases)

[ Back ]          [ Abort ]          [ Next ]

**Figure 10-20**

From this dialog box, you can select one of three connection types for CUPS printing. What you configure next depends on the type of connection you select.

**NOTE**

For additional information about configuring a printer type, use the Help screens available with each configuration screen.

4. When you finish selecting a printer type and configuring it, save the configuration by selecting **Finish**.

   You are returned to the YaST Control Center.

   After configuring the printer (print queue), the following happens:

   ■ The print queue is added to the file /etc/cups/printers.conf with default queue settings.

- A ppd file for the printer is created in /etc/cups/ppd which includes settings such as paper size and paper type.

- The name of the print queue is added to the file /etc/printcap.

  This file is a link pointing to the file /etc/cups/printcap which is generated by cupsd from the file /etc/cups/printers.conf, and is created and updated automatically.

  The entries in this file are critical to particular applications (such as OpenOffice.org) that display the entries of /etc/printcap in your printer dialog box.

  For that reason, you should avoid changing the file manually.

5. (Optional) If you started YaST from the desktop, close the **YaST Control Center**.

## Configure a Network Printer from the Command Line

Besides using YaST, you can also configure CUPS with command-line tools. After collecting the information you need (such as the PPD file and the name of the device), enter:

**lpadmin -p** *queue* **-v** *device-URI* **-P** *PPD-file* **-E**

The option **-p** specifies the print queue name of the printer, the option **-v** sets the device URI (such as a filename) attribute of the printer queue, and the option **-P** specifies a PostScript printer.

Do not use **-E** as the first option. For all CUPS commands, –E as the first argument implies the use of an encrypted connection and –E at the end enables the printer to accept print jobs.

For example, to enable a parallel printer, enter a command similar to the following:

**lpadmin -p ps -v parallel:/dev/lp0 -P \\**

**/usr/share/cups/model/Postscript.ppd.gz -E**

To enable a network printer, enter a command similar to the following:

**lpadmin -p ps -v socket://10.0.1.0:9100/ -P \\**

**/usr/share/cups/model/Postscript-level1.ppd.gz -E**

## Modify a SUSE Linux Enterprise Server Network Printer

During the installation of SUSE Linux Enterprise Server, YaST allows certain print options to be activated by default. You can modify these options for every print job (depending on the print tool that is used) or modify them later with YaST or from the command line.

To modify the network printer options, you need to know the following:

- Modify a Network Printer with YaST
- Modify a Network Printer from the Command Line
- Modify Printer Settings from KDE

## Modify a Network Printer with YaST

The following are the basic steps for modifying a network printer with YaST:

1. From the KDE desktop, start the YaST Printer module by doing one of the following:

   - Select the **YaST** icon, enter the root password *novell*, and select **OK**; then select **Hardware > Printer**.

     *or*

   - Open a terminal window and enter **sux –** and the root password *novell*; then enter **yast2 printer**.

   The Printer Configuration dialog box appears.

2. Select **Change**.

**10**

A Printer administration for CUPS dialog box appears with a list of configured printers, as shown in Figure 10-21.

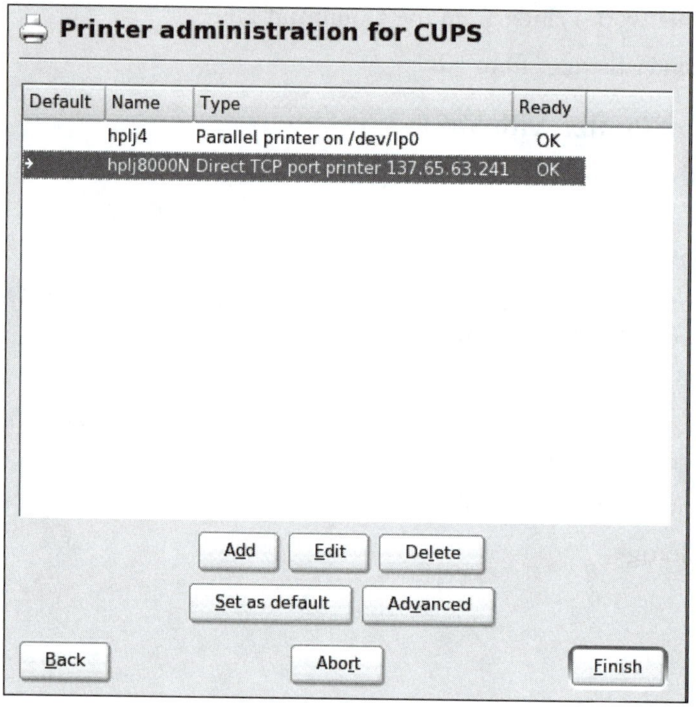

**Figure 10-21**

From this dialog box you can perform the following tasks:

- Create a printer configuration by selecting **Add**.

  This is the same as adding a printer configuration from the main Printer Configuration screen by selecting **Configure**.

- Edit configuration settings for a printer in the list by selecting **Edit**.

- Delete a printer in the list by selecting **Delete**.

- Select a printer and make it the default printer by selecting **Set as Default**.

- Perform additional configuration (such as switching from a CUPS server installation to a CUPS client configuration) by selecting **Advanced**.

3. Edit an existing network printer configuration by selecting the *network printer* from the list; then select **Edit**.

A screen similar to Figure 10-22 appears.

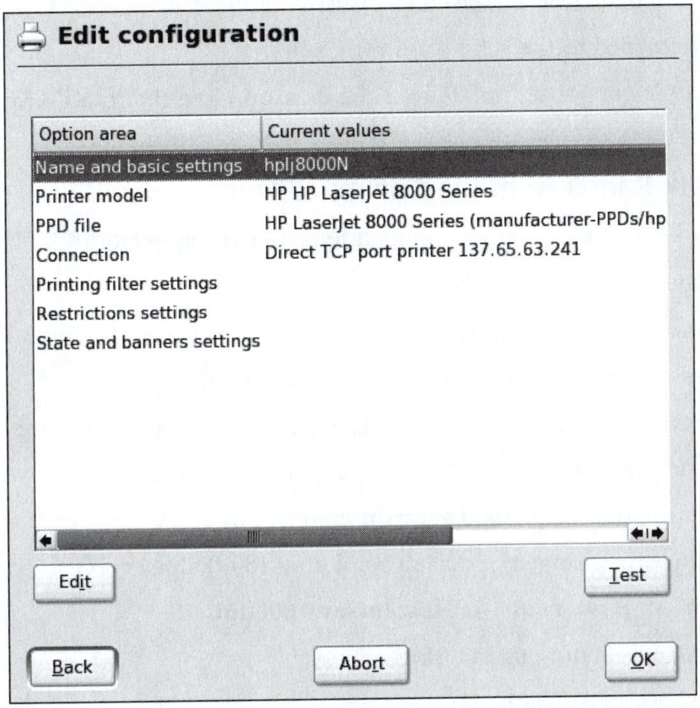

**Figure 10-22**

From this list you can modify settings such as the PPD file, filter settings, and restriction settings.

These settings are stored in the file /etc/cups/printers.conf which contains the printing queues that have been configured by YaST.

4. Select an *option area*; then select **Edit**.

A configuration dialog box appears.

You can use the Help information on the left to complete or select settings that meet your needs.

5. When you finish making configuration changes, select **Next**.

You are returned to the Edit Configuration dialog box.

6. Do one of the following:

  ■ Select another *option area* to configure; then select **Edit**.

    *or*

  ■ Finish the configuration by selecting **OK**.

You are returned to the Printer Administration for CUPS dialog box.

7. Save the configuration by selecting **Finish**.

   You are returned to the YaST Control Center.

8. (Optional) If you started YaST from the desktop, close the **YaST Control Center**.

## Modify a Network Printer from the Command Line

To modify a network printer from the command line, do the following:

1. List all options for a printer by entering:

   **lpoptions -p** *queue-name* **-l**

   Information similar to the following is displayed:

   ```
   Resolution/Output Resolution: 150dpi *300dpi 600dpi 1200dpi
   ```

   The default option is marked with an asterisk (*).

2. Change an option using the **lpadmin** command.

   For example, to change the default resolution to 600dpi, enter:

   **lpadmin -p** *queue-name* **-o Resolution=600dpi**

3. Check the new setting by entering:

   **lpoptions -p** *queue-name* **-l**

## Modify Printer Settings from KDE

The KDE desktop environment provides a *kprinter* utility for changing the properties of a printer (print queue) stored in its ppd file (/etc/cups/ppd/ directory).

This kprinter dialog box is available when you print from a desktop application, or you can start it from the command line.

To change print queue settings using kprinter, do the following:

1. Start kprinter from an application (by selecting a menu option such as **Print**), or from the command line by entering **kprinter**.

The dialog box shown in Figure 10-23 appears.

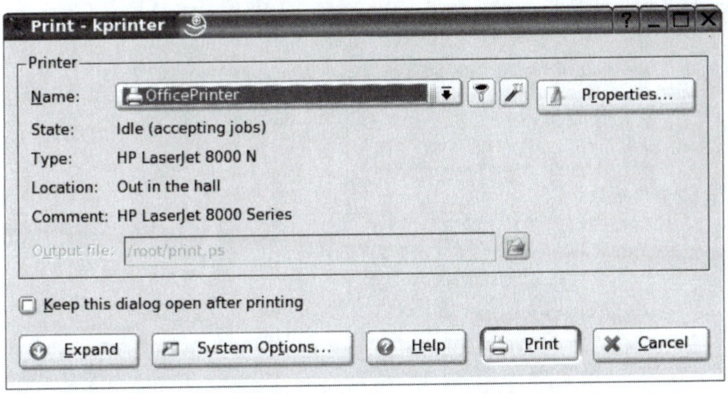

**Figure 10-23**

**10**

2. From the Name drop-down list, select the *printer* (print queue) you want to modify; then select **Properties**.

The dialog box shown in Figure 10-24 appears.

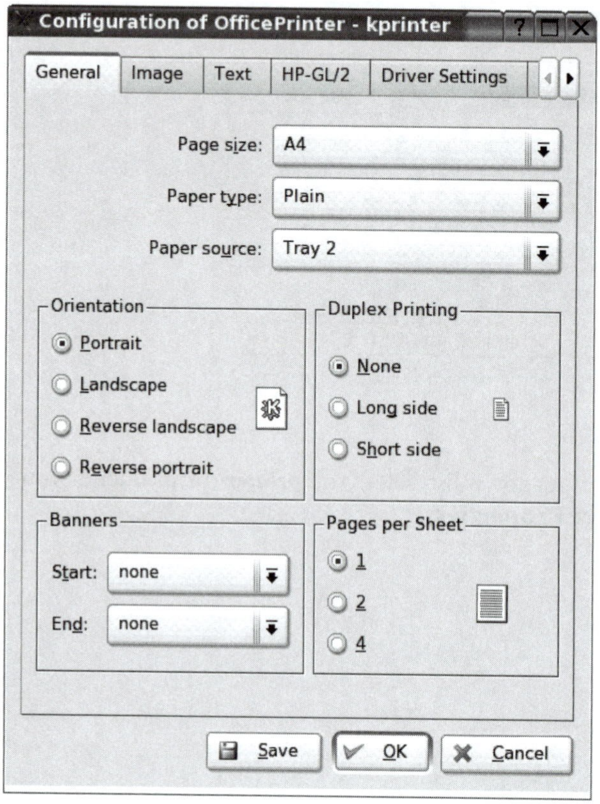

**Figure 10-24**

From this dialog box you can change settings such as page size and paper type.

3. When you finish modifying the settings, select **Save**.

   If you start kprinter as root, the changes are saved to the file /etc/cups/lpoptions and affect all users.

   If you start kprinter as a normal user, the changes are saved to the user's home directory in .lpoptions and affect only the print jobs for that user.

## Manage Printing from the Command Line

To manage print jobs from the command line, you need to know the following:

- Basic Printer Management
- CUPS Printer Commands

## Basic Printer Management

You can use the following commands to perform basic printer management tasks:

- **/usr/bin/enable** *printer.* You can use this command to start a printer queue for the indicated *printer.*

    If there are any queued print jobs, they are printed after the printer is enabled.

    You need to enter the path with the queue name, because enable is also a bash built-in command.

- **/usr/bin/disable** *printer.* You can use this command to stop a printer queue for the indicated *printer.*

    Disabling a printer is useful if the printer malfunctions and you need time to correct the problem.

    Printers that are disabled can still accept jobs for printing but won't actually print any files until they are restarted.

- **/usr/sbin/reject** *printer.* You can use this command to reject print jobs for the indicated *printer.*

    While the command /usr/sbin/stop stops the printer from printing, the print queue continues to accept submitted print jobs.

    With the command /usr/sbin/reject, the printer finishes the print jobs in the queue but rejects any new print jobs.

    This command is useful when you need to perform maintenance on a printer and the printer will not be available for a significant period of time.

- **/usr/sbin/accept** *printer.* You can use this command to accept print jobs for the indicated *printer.*

    By using this command, you can reset the print queue to begin accepting and printing new print jobs.

## CUPS Printer Commands

CUPS provides two kinds of commands: Berkeley3 and System V. You can also use the System V commands to configure queues.

The following are print management tasks you can perform using CUPS printer commands:

- **Submit a print job (lpr, lp).** The following is the syntax for these commands:

    - Berkeley: **lpr –P** *queue file*
    - System V: **lp –d** *queue file*

    The following are examples:

    **lpr –P color chart.ps**

**10**

*or*

**lp -d color chart.ps**

In this example, the file **chart.ps** is printed over the queue color.

You can use the **-o** option to specify options regarding the printout, such as the following:

**lpr -P lp -o duplex=none order.ps**

*or*

**lp -d lp -o duplex=none order.ps**

In this example, the file **order.ps** is submitted to the queue lp and the duplex function of the printer is disabled for the printout (duplex=none).

**NOTE**

For more information about these commands, enter **man lpr** or **man lp**, or enter http://localhost:631 in a Web browser and select **On-Line Help**.

- **Display print jobs (lpq, lpstat).** The following is the syntax for these commands:
  - Berkeley: **lpq -P** *queue*
  - System V: **lpstat -o** *queue* **-p** *queue*

If you do not specify a queue, all queues are displayed. lpstat -o displays the active print jobs in the following format:

*queue-jobnumber*

To display more information, enter:

**lpstat -l -o** *queue* **-p** *queue*

To display all available information, enter:

**lpstat -t** or **lpstat -l -t**

**NOTE**

For additional information about these commands, enter **man lpq** or **man lpstat**, or enter http://localhost:631 in a Web browser and select **On-Line Help**.

- **Cancel print jobs (lprm, cancel).** The following is the syntax for these commands:
  - Berkeley: **lprm -P** *queue jobnumber*
  - System V: **cancel** *queue-jobnumber*

For more information about these commands, enter **man lprm** or **man cancel**, or enter http://localhost:631 in a Web browser and select **On-Line Help**.

- **Configure a queue (lpoptions).** You can find the printer-specific options to determine the kind of printout for a printer in the PPD file (/etc/cups/ppd/ directory) that belongs to a queue.

All users can display the options by entering:

**lpoptions -p** *queue* **-l**

The following are some examples of what might be displayed:

```
PageSize/Page Size: A3 *A4 A5 Legal Letter
Resolution/Resolution: 150 *300 600
```

The asterisk (*) in front of an option indicates the current setting. In the example above, the paper format is set to A4 and the resolution to 300 dpi.

You can change the options of a queue with the following command:

**lpoptions -p** *queue* **-o option=***value*

For example, to change the paper format for the queue lp to letter, enter:

**lpoptions -p lp -o PageSize=Letter**

The affect of these new settings depends on the following:

- If a normal user (such as **geeko**) enters the command, the change affects only that user. The setting is saved in the file **.lpoptions** in the user's home directory.

- If **root** enters the command, the settings become preferences for every user on the local computer and are saved in the file /etc/cups/lpoptions. The corresponding PPD file will remain unchanged.

For information about hardware-independent standard options for printout types, read the file /usr/share/doc/packages/cups/sum.html#USING_SYSTEM.

For information about saving options, read the file /usr/share/doc/packages/cups/sum.html#SAVING_OPTIONS.

## Restrict Printer Access

The access to various CUPS resources can be restricted.

The resources are displayed as directories (/printers or /jobs}).

Normally, the following resources are available on the CUPS server:

- **/(root).** The access restrictions for this resource apply to all following resources, provided no other restrictions are specified there.

- **/printers.** All printers or queues.

- **/classes.** Available printer classes, such as all color printers.

- **/jobs.** Print jobs on the CUPS server.

- **/admin.** These settings concern the access to the server configuration.

These resources can be accessed in various ways, such as with a Web browser, as shown in the following:

- http://localhost:631/printers

  *or*

- http://localhost:631/admin

The following topics describe how to:

- Configure Access Restrictions with YaST

- Configure Access Restrictions for Users and Groups

- Con

## Configure Access Restrictions with YaST

Under **YaST > Hardware > Printer > Change > Advanced CUPS Server Settings > Change Permissions**, you can define the order in which access directives are applied (whether to apply the Allow rules first and then the Deny rules, or vice versa) and the default directive.

Under **Permissions**, define the entities to which the access rules should be applied in line with the previously specified order.

Access settings are stored in the **/etc/cups/cupsd.conf** configuration file.

Here is an example:

```
<Location />
Order Deny,Allow
Allow From 127.0.0.1
</Location>

...

<Location /admin>
...
Order Deny,Allow
Deny From All
Allow From 127.0.0.1
```

```
</Location>
...
<Location /printers>
Deny From All
Allow From 10.10.0.0/24
Allow From 10.10.1.2
Order Deny,Allow
</Location>

<Location /classes>
Deny From All
Allow From 10.0.0.2
Allow From 10.0.0.4
Allow From 10.0.1.2
Order Deny,Allow
```

The configuration directives are explained in the following:

- **Order.** Defines the order of the rules and the default directive.

  Order Deny, Allow interprets the Deny directives first, then the Allow directives. Deny from All allows requests only from those listed in an Allow directive

  The default directive is Deny (access denied).

- **Deny from All.** All access to the resource is prohibited.

- **Allow from.** Access to the resource is permitted.

Access directives for all printers and queues are stored in the file **/etc/cups/printers.conf.**

Optionally, they can be kept in the file /etc/cups/cupsd.conf.

Such a section could look like the following:

```
<Location /printers/lp>
Deny From All
Allow From 10.10.0.0/24
Order Deny;Allow
</Location>
```

If you read this sample together with the sample on 10-110, all clients belonging to network 10.0.0.0 and host 10.0.1.2 can print on all queues available in the network.

An exception is the lp queue, which can be accessed only by clients in network 10.0.0.0.

The syntax to specify clients that should have printer access is described in the file **/etc/cups/cupsd.conf**

See the following:

```
# Order: the order of Allow/Deny processing.
#
# Allow: allows access from the specified hostname, domain,
# IP address, network, or interface.
```

```
#
# Deny: denies access from the specified hostname, domain,
# IP address, network, or interface.
#
# Both "Allow" and "Deny" accept the following notations for addresses:
#
#    All
#    None
#    *.domain.com
#    .domain.com
#    host.domain.com
#    nnn.*
#    nnn.nnn.*
#    nnn.nnn.nnn.*
#    nnn.nnn.nnn.nnn
#    nnn.nnn.nnn.nnn/mm
#    nnn.nnn.nnn.nnn/mmm.mmm.mmm.mmm
#    @LOCAL
#    @IF(name)
```

**Configure Access Restrictions for Users and Groups**    You can also restrict access to the printers on the user and group level.

To configure access restrictions for user and groups, use YaST or the lpadmin command, as described in the following:

- To permit printing for individual users, enter:

  **lpadmin -p** *queue* **-u allow:tux,geeko**

- To permit printing for a group, enter:

  **lpadmin -p** *queue* **-u allow:@users**

- To prohibit printing for users or groups, enter:

  **lpadmin -p** *queue* **-u deny:joe@guests**

- To permit printing for all, enter:

  **lpadmin -p** *queue* **-u allow:all**

These access restrictions are written to the file **/etc/cups/printers.conf.**

**Configure User Authentication**    You can use passwords to protect resources such as the administration interface.

The configuration entry in /etc/cups/cupsd.conf looks like the following:

```
<Location /admin>
AuthType BasicDigest
AuthClass Group
AuthGroupName sys
Order Deny,Allow
```

```
Deny From All
Allow From 127.0.0.1
</Location>
```

The relevant directives are:

- **AuthType BasicDigest.** A special CUPS user database (/etc/cups/passwd.md5) is used for the authentication.

- **AuthClass Group.** Permits access only for valid users who are members of the system group.

- **AuthGroupName.** Name of the system group (here: sys).

With this configuration, CUPS accesses the user database /etc/cups/passwd.md5.

However, this database is still empty at this stage.

To generate user entries (for example, to create the user admin in the group sys), enter:

```
da10:~ # lppasswd -a admin -g sys
Enter password:
Enter password again:
```

To use the normal Linux user data for the authentication, change the entry AuthType from BasicDigest to Basic.

## Access the CUPS Web Administration Tools

CUPS provides a Web page for administering printers. You can access this interface by entering the following:

**http://localhost:631**

**10**

The Web page shown in Figure 10-25 appears.

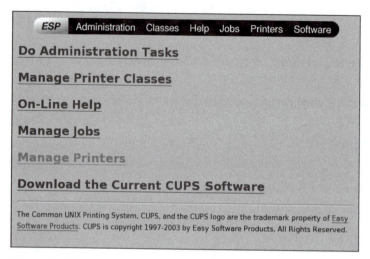

**Figure 10-25**

From this Web page you can perform tasks such as managing printer classes, jobs, and printers.

To use the management options on this Web page (or the printer administration tool in KDE), **root** must be set up as a CUPS administrator with the CUPS administration group sys and a CUPS password.

You can do this as the root user by entering the following command:

**lppasswd –g sys –a root**

**NOTE**

For information on setting up another user as a CUPS administrator, see Section 13.6.2 in the *SLES 9 Installation and Administration manual*.

## Troubleshoot the CUPS Printing System

The following are basic tasks for troubleshooting the CUPS print system:

- Set the Log Level to Record Errors
- Check the Access Log
- Perform Basic Troubleshooting

## Set the Log Level to Record Errors

Messages from cupsd are written to the file /var/log/cups/error_log. By default, only inquiries and status changes are logged to the file.

If you want errors recorded, you need to change the LogLevel option in the cupsd configuration file /etc/cups/cupsd.conf:

```
# LogLevel: controls the number of messages logged to the ErrorLog
# file and can be one of the following:
#
#     debug2    Log everything.
#     debug     Log almost everything.
#     info      Log all requests and state changes.
#     warn      Log errors and warnings.
#     error     Log only errors.
#     none      Log nothing.
#
```

```
LogLevel debug2
```

For debugging and troubleshooting, set the log level to **debug2**. After changing the configuration, restart CUPS by entering **rccups restart**.

## Check the Access Log

The file /var/log/cups/access_log logs every access to the CUPS daemon from a browser or a CUPS/IPP client. Each line includes the fields shown in Table 10-6.

**Table 10-6**

| Field | Description |
|---|---|
| host | DNS name or IP number |
| group | The group name (always "–" for CUPS) |
| user | User name if the user identified himself with a login and password (otherwise "–") |
| date | The current date |
| method | The HTTP method (such as GET or POST) |
| resource | The requested resource |
| version | The HTTP version (with CUPS, always HTTP/1.1) |
| status | The HTTP result status (normally 200, but other codes are also possible) |
| bytes | The number of transmitted bytes |

## Perform Basic Troubleshooting

To perform basic troubleshooting of CUPS, do the following:

1. Set the LogLevel to **debug** in the **/etc/cups/cupsd.conf** file.

2. Stop cupsd by entering **rccupsd stop**.

3. Avoid searching through large log files by renaming the file /var/log/cups/ error_log (such as the following, on one line):

   **mv /var/log/cups/error_log /var/log/cups/error_log-*yyyymmdd***

4. Start cupsd by entering **rccupsd start**.

5. Repeat the action that led to the problem.

6. Check the messages in **/var/log/cups/error_log** to identify the cause of the problem.

# Exercise 10-4    Configure CUPS Network Printing Services

It is usually more economical to have one larger printer within a department than to equip each workstation with a printer of its own. This printer is then used by several persons via the network.

There are various protocol possible to address such a printer. Cups uses primarily the Internet Printing Protocol (IPP).

In this exercise you set up and manage a CUPS printing environment on your SLES 9 server by doing the following:

- Part I: Manage the Printer from the Command Line
- Part II: Manage the Printer with YaST
- Part III: Provide Access to the CUPS Administrator
- Part IV: Print to a Remote CUPS Printer

 You have to set up a printer in Exercise 4.4 to complete this exercise.

**CAUTION**

## Part I: Manage the Printer from the Command Line

Do the following:

1. Open a terminal window.

2. Send a print job to the HP LaserJet 4 printer using the Berkeley printer commands:

   a. Send the file /etc/hosts to be printed by entering:

      **lpr -P hplj4 /etc/hosts**

   b. View the print queue for hplj4 by entering:

      **lpq -P hplj4**

      The jobs to print the hosts file is listed. Note the job number.

3. Send a print job to the HP LaserJet 4 printer using the System V printer commands:

   a. Send the file **/etc/hosts** to the printer by entering:

      **lp -d hplj4 /etc/hosts**

   b. View the print queue for hplj4 by entering:

      **lpstat hplj4**

      There are two jobs listed—the two hosts file jobs.

4. In a Konqueror window view http://localhost:631/ and view the CUPS job page by selecting **Jobs** to see the new jobs in the Web interface.

5. From a terminal window, cancel the test page job (the job number shown in Step 2b) by entering:

   **lprm -P hplj4 *x***

6. Enter **lpstat hplj4**.

   The print job has been deleted.

7. Check the status of the printer by entering **lpc status**.

8. Reload the CUPS jobs page to verify that the job *x* has been removed.

9. From the terminal window, view the contents of the file /etc/printcap by entering **cat /etc/printcap**.

## Part II: Manage the Printer with YaST

In this part of the exercise, you perform some basic printer management tasks with YaST.

Do the following:

1. Change basic settings for the HP LaserJet 4 printer:

   a. From the YaST Control Center select **Hardware > Printer**.

      The Printer Configuration dialog box appears.

   b. Modify an existing printer by selecting **Change**.

**10**

c. Make sure the **hplj4** printer is selected; then select **Edit**.

A list of option areas to edit appears.

d. Make sure **Name and Basic Settings** is selected; then select **Edit**.

e. Enter the following:

- Description of Printer: **LaserJet 4 on DA*xx*** (where ***xx*** is your host number)

- Location of Printer: **DA*xx* computer**

f. Return to the Edit configuration dialog box by selecting **Next**.

g. Save the changes and close the YaST module by selecting **OK**; then select **Finish**.

h. From the Konqueror browser, view the changes by selecting **Printers**.

2. Change the filter settings for the HP LaserJet 4 printer:

a. From the YaST Control Center select **Hardware > Printer**.

The Printer Configuration dialog box appears.

b. Modify the existing printers by selecting **Change**.

c. Make sure the **hplj4** printer is selected; then select **Edit**.

A list of option areas to edit appears.

d. Select **Printing Filter Settings**; then select **Edit**.

A list of options appears at the top of the screen with a list of values for each option at the bottom of the screen.

e. Scroll down the list of options and select **Page Size**.

Notice that the page size is set to **A4**.

f. Change the page size to US Letter by selecting **Letter**; then select **Next**.

g. Save the changes and close the YaST module by selecting **OK**; then select **Finish**.

h. From the terminal window, verify that the new default page size is set to US Letter by entering:

**grep DefaultPageSize /etc/cups/ppd/hplj4.ppd**

## Part III: Provide Access to the CUPS Administrator

Before printers can be administered through a Web browser, you need to create a CUPS password for each authorized user.

Do the following:

1. Make sure you are su'd to root in the terminal window.

2. Enter the following to create a CUPS digest password for the root user:

    **lppasswd –a root**

3. Enter a password of **N0v3ll** twice.

4. From the Konqueror Web browser, enter the following URL:

    **http://localhost:631/admin**

5. Log in by entering the following:

    ▪ Username: **root**

    ▪ Password: **N0v3ll**

    The CUPS administrator page appears.

## Part IV: Print to a Remote CUPS Printer

The HP LaserJet 4 printer is configured to print locally through your parallel port. However, a CUPS network printer is also available on the Digital Airlines office network that you would like to access.

**NOTE**  In a classroom environment, this printer has already been set up for students on the DA1 server. If there is no CUPS printer configured on another server, you can use your own server and print queue for this part of the exercise.

Do the following:

1. From the YaST Control Center select **Hardware > Printer**.

    The Printer Configuration dialog box appears.

2. Add a new CUPS printer by selecting **Configure**.

3. Select **Print via CUPS Network Server**; then select **Next**.

4. Select **Remote IPP Queue**; then select **Next**.

5. Next to the Host Name of the Printer Server field, select **Lookup**; then select **Scan for IPP Servers**.

6. From the drop-down list, select **da1.digitalairlines.com**.

    If da1.digitalairlines.com does not appear in the drop-down list, enter **da1.digitalairlines.com** in the field.

7. Next to the Name of the Remote Queue field, select **Lookup** to select the default queue configured on da1.

8. Test connectivity to the printer server by selecting:

    **Test Remote IPP Access**

9.  When a success message appears, select **OK**.

10. Continue by selecting **Next**.

    A Queue Name dialog box appears.

    Local Filtering is not selected because filtering is being done on the remote CUPS printer server.

11. From the Name for printing field, record the name of the printer queue on the instructor's server:

12. Accept the default settings by selecting **Next**.

13. Save the configuration changes by selecting **Finish**.

14. From the terminal window, test printing to the instructor's server by entering:

    **lpr –P** *queue_name* **/etc/hosts**

    (where *queue_name* is the name instructor's printer)

15. From the Konqueror Web browser, check your print job on the instructor's computer by selecting **jobs**.

16. The job is displayed in the Jobs list.

17. Try monitoring your print job from the instructor server by entering:

    **http://10.0.0.254:631/printers**

18. Select the *printer link* for the instructor's printer or select **Jobs**.

19. (Conditional) If you do not see your print job, try selecting **Show Completed Jobs**.

20. When you finish, close all windows.

---

## CHAPTER SUMMARY

❏ DNS consists of a hierarchical name space that consists of a root domain (.) followed by top-level domains, domains, and subdomains. Each host that uses DNS has an FQDN that identifies its host name and domain name.

❏ FQDNs and their associated IP addresses are stored on authoritative DNS servers in a zone file. Master DNS servers hold a read-write copy of the zone file and transfer this to Slave DNS servers as read-only. Caching-only or forwarding DNS servers simply forward requests to a Master or Slave DNS server and cache the results for future reference.

❏ Clients can query a DNS server listed in /etc/resolv.conf to resolve an FQDN to an IP address (forward lookup), or to resolve an IP address to an FQDN (reverse lookup). Name resolution requests are stored in a cache on the client computer for a certain period of time determined by the TTL.

❑ To become a DNS server, you must install the BIND server software, edit the /etc/named.conf configuration file, create zone files in the /var/lib/named directory and create resource records. This can be done manually or using YaST.

❑ The **host**, **dig**, and **nslookup** commands may be used to test DNS name resolution.

❑ On TCP/IP networks, NFS is typically used to share files between Linux and UNIX computers using RPCs, whereas Samba is used to share files among Linux, UNIX, and Windows computers using the SMB/CIFS protocol.

❑ An NFS server shares directories to NFS clients using the **exportfs** command or entries in the /etc/exports file. NFS clients mount shared NFS directories on remote computers to local directories using the **mount** command or entries in the /etc/fstab file. YaST may also be used to configure an NFS server or client.

❑ The **showmount** and **rpcinfo** commands may be used to troubleshoot NFS servers and clients.

❑ To become a Samba server, you must start the Samba and NetBIOS daemons, configure entries in the /etc/samba/smb.conf file, and configure Samba user accounts. YaST may be used to configure a Samba server. In addition, the **testparm**, **nmblookup**, and **smbstatus** commands may be used to troubleshoot a Samba server.

❑ You can connect to a Windows or Samba file server using the **mount** and **smbclient** commands.

❑ SLES uses the CUPS printing system, which supports the socket, LPD, IPP, and SMB printing protocols.

❑ You can configure CUPS using YaST, the **lpadmin** command-line utility, the CUPS Web Administration Tool (http://hostname:631), or by editing the appropriate configuration files in the /etc/cups directory and restarting the CUPS daemon.

❑ The CUPS daemon writes logging information to the /var/log/cups/error_log and /var/log/cups/access_log files. You can control the level of logging by editing the /etc/cups/cupsd.conf file.

❑ Print jobs are sent to a queue directory before being sent to the printer itself. You can use the **enable**, **disable**, **accept**, and **reject** commands to control this process.

❑ The **lp** and **lpr** commands may be used to create print jobs within a command-line terminal. Similarly, the kprinter utility may be used to print from graphical applications.

❑ You can view print jobs in the print queue using the **lpstat** or **lpq** commands, and remove print jobs from the print queue using the **cancel** or **lprm** commands.

❑ Users can modify print options using the **lpoptions** command or by using the kprinter utility in a desktop environment. System-wide print options are stored in the /etc/cups/lpoptions file and user-specific print options are stored in the ~/.lpoptions file.

**10**

## KEY TERMS

**. (root domain)** — The root domain of DNS.

**/etc/cups/cupsd.conf** — The main CUPS configuration file.

**/etc/cups/lpoptions** — The file that stores system-wide print options set by the root user.

**/etc/cups/ppd** — The directory that stores the active PPD files used for a particular printer.

**/etc/cups/printers.conf** — Contains CUPS printer definitions.

**/etc/exports** — The file that lists exported directories on an NFS server.

**/etc/hosts** — A file used for local name resolution.

**/etc/named.conf** — A file that lists the type of zones hosted on the DNS server and the location of the zone files.

**/etc/networks** — A file used for local network name resolution.

**/etc/resolv.conf** — A file on a resolver that lists up to three DNS servers which may be used to perform name resolution.

**/etc/samba/smb.conf** — The main Samba configuration file.

**/usr/share/cups/model** — The directory that stores sample PPD files used for a particular printer.

**/var/lib/named** — The directory that stores zone files in SLES.

**/var/lib/nfs/etab** — A file that lists currently exported directories on an NFS server.

**/var/log/cups/access_log** — A CUPS log file that stores information about network print requests.

**/var/log/cups/error_log** — A CUPS log file that stores information about the CUPS daemon.

**/var/log/messages** — The default log file for the DNS daemon.

**/var/spool/cups** — The default print queue directory in SLES.

**~/.lpoptions** — The file that stores user-defined print options.

**accept command** — Allows print jobs to enter the print queue.

**Address record (A)** — A DNS record that identifies hosts within a domain.

**ARPANET** — The network that led to the development of the Internet. It stands for Advanced Research Projects Agency Network.

**authoritative answer** — A name resolution response from a DNS server where the DNS server contained the appropriate record in its zone database.

**Berkeley Internet Name Domain (BIND)** — The reference implementation for DNS.

**cache** — An area of memory that stores information obtained from resolving DNS names. Entries are kept in the cache for the time period specified by the TTL.

**caching-only server** — A DNS server that is not authoritative for any zones. It only answers DNS queries where the answers come from other DNS servers.

**cancel command** — Used to remove a print job from the print queue.

**Canonical NAME (CNAME)** — An alias for an A record in DNS.

**Common Internet File System (CIFS)** — A file- and printer-sharing protocol used by Windows systems.

**Common Unix Printing System (CUPS)** — The default printing system in SLES.

**CUPS Web Administration Tools** — A series of CUPS administration utilities that may be accessed using a Web browser on port 631.

**dig command** — Used to perform and test name resolution using a variety of options.

**disable command** — Prevents print jobs in the print queue from being sent to the printer.

**DNS server** — A server that hosts the BIND service and responds to client (resolver) queries for name resolution.

**domain** — The name in DNS that identifies the organization and which exists under the TLD.

**Domain Name System (DNS)** — The naming system used on the Internet. Each host is identified by a host name and domain name.

**enable command** — Allows print jobs in the print queue to be sent to the printer.

**exportfs command** — Used to temporarily export directories on an NFS server.

**forward resolution** — A name resolution request that desires the IP address for a particular FQDN.

**forwarding server** — A DNS server that forwards any DNS queries it cannot resolve to another DNS server on the network.

**Fully Qualified Domain Name (FQDN)** — A complete name that identifies a host computer in DNS. It consists of a host name (or computer name) followed by subdomain/domain names and a TLD (e.g., www.west.africa.com).

**fuser command** — Displays the users and processes that are accessing a certain directory.

**host command** — Used to perform and test name resolution.

**Internet Printing Protocol (IPP)** — A printing protocol that allows print jobs to be sent across the Internet using a Web browser.

**kprinter** — A graphical utility that is invoked when a graphical application creates a print job. It may also be used to change printing options, such as resolution.

**Line Printer Daemon (LPD)** — A common printing protocol used on older Linux and UNIX computers.

**lp command** — Used to create a print job.

**lpadmin command** — Used to create and manage CUPS printers.

**lpoptions command** — Used to create or change printing options, such as resolution.

**lppasswd** — Used to create CUPS passwords and access to the CUPS Web Administration Tools.

**lpq command** — Used to view print jobs in the print queue.

**lpr command** — Used to create a print job.

**lprm command** — Used to remove a print job from the print queue.

**lpstat command** — Used to view print jobs in the print queue.

**Mail eXchanger (MX)** — A DNS record that identifies the e-mail servers for a domain.

**master server** — A DNS server that contains a read-write copy of the zone database.

**name resolution** — The process where an FQDN is associated with its IP address.

**name server** — See **DNS server**.

**10**

**Name Server (NS)** — A DNS record that identifies a DNS server that is authoritative for the zone.

**named** — The DNS/BIND daemon in Linux.

**NetBIOS** — A Windows protocol that uses unique, 15-character computer names to identify network hosts.

**Network File System (NFS)** — A file-sharing protocol used by UNIX and Linux systems.

**Network Information Service (NIS)** — A service that allows the centralization of Linux and UNIX configuration.

**NFS client** — A computer that accesses exported files on an NFS server using the NFS protocol.

**NFS server** — A computer that hosts (exports) files using the NFS protocol.

**nmblookup command** — Displays NetBIOS computer names for hosts.

**nonauthoritative answer** — A name resolution response from a DNS server where the DNS server had to query other DNS servers in order to find the appropriate record.

**nslookup command** — Used to perform and test name resolution using a variety of options.

**PoinTeR (PTR)** — A DNS record that identifies the FQDN associated with an IP address for reverse resolution.

**portmapper** — The service that provides for RPCs in Linux.

**PostScript Printer Description (PPD)** — A printing format that is widely used by many printers and printing systems.

**queue** — A directory used to store print jobs before they are sent to the physical printer.

**reject command** — Prevents print jobs from entering the print queue.

**Remote Procedure Call (RPC)** — A routine that is executed on a remote computer.

**resolver** — A host that requests name resolution using DNS.

**reverse resolution** — A name resolution request that desires the FQDN for a particular IP address.

**rpcinfo command** — Displays information regarding the RPM portmapper daemon.

**Samba** — A set of services in Linux that provides the SMB and CIFS protocols for file and printer sharing with Windows computers.

**Server Level Security** — A Samba share security level that requires a valid login to another server in order to access a shared directory.

**Server Message Block (SMB)** — A file- and printer-sharing protocol used by Windows systems.

**Share Level Security** — A Samba share security level that requires a password in order to access a shared directory.

**showmount command** — Displays exported directories on an NFS server.

**slave server** — A DNS server that contains a read-only copy of the zone database obtained from a master server via a zone transfer.

**smbclient command** — Used to view and access Windows file and printer shares.

**smbpasswd command** — Sets a Windows-formatted password for Linux user accounts.

**smbstatus command** — Displays current Samba server connections.

**socket** — An established network connection between two hosts. CUPS can use sockets to print to a remote system and vice versa.

**Start Of Authority (SOA)** — A DNS record that identifies zone-specific information and zone transfer settings.

**subdomain** — The name in DNS that identifies a division of an organization and which exists under the domain and TLD.

**testparm command** — Checks the syntax of /etc/samba/smb.conf.

**Time To Live (TTL)** — The amount of time a name resolution result is cached on the computer. The default TTL is set in the SOA in the zone file on the DNS server.

**Top Level Domain (TLD)** — The first level of names underneath the root domain in DNS.

**User Level Security** — A Samba share security level that requires a valid Linux login in order to access a shared directory.

**workgroup** — A name that identifies a group of computers in a Windows network that are not part of a domain.

**zone** — A specific domain in DNS that is represented by file on a DNS server that contains the records used for name resolution.

**zone transfer** — The process whereby a master DNS server sends zone information to a slave DNS server.

# REVIEW QUESTIONS

1. What is the TLD for www.sample.domain.com? _____

2. What determines the default length of time that a name resolution result is cached on your computer?

   a. The resolver settings in IP properties

   b. The search line in /etc/resolv.conf

   c. The TTL in the SOA record on the DNS server

   d. The NS record on the DNS server in the TLD

3. Which two packages must you have installed for your computer to function as a DNS server?

   a. bind

   b. dns

   c. bind–utils

   d. named

4. What line in the /etc/named.conf file can be used to forward name resolution requests that cannot be resolved locally to a DNS server with an IP address of 192.168.1.242? _____

5. What record in a DNS zone file is used to map names to IP addresses for hosts on the network?

   a. SOA

   b. NS

   c. MX

   d. A

6. How does a slave DNS server know that changes have been made on the master DNS server?

   a. By broadcasting to the master DNS server

   b. By querying the serial number in the SOA on the master DNS server

   c. By receiving a zone notification from the master DNS server

   d. By obtaining an NS record from the master DNS server

7. How many other DNS servers can a single DNS server be configured to forward name resolution requests to? _____

8. What three commands could you use to test name resolution?

   _____

9. What line in the /etc/exports file will export the /home directory to the host **arfa** as read-write, while ensuring that the root user does not have administrative rights to the exported directory? _____

10. What three services need to be started on an NFS server?

    a. RPC mount daemon

    b. RPC portmapper

    c. RPC NFS daemon

    d. RPC exporter

11. What command may be used to mount the /home directory on a remote computer called **server2** using the NFS protocol to the local /mnt directory?

    _____

12. What command may be used to display the NFS ports registered by the RPM port-mapper daemon? _____

13. What two commands can you run to activate changes made to the /etc/samba/smb. conf file?

   a. smbclient --restart

   b. rcsmb restart

   c. nmbclient --restart

   d. rcnmb restart

14. What command can you use to check the /etc/samba/smb.conf file for errors?
   _____

15. What command may be used to mount the **acctg** shared directory on the server **arfa** to the local /mnt directory using SMB? _____

16. Which command may be used to create printers?

   a. cupsadmin

   b. lpadmin

   c. lpstat

   d. cupsd

17. When you try to send a print job to the printer **p1**, you receive an error message stating that the print queue is unavailable. What command can you use to allow print jobs to enter the print queue for **p1**? _____

18. What address would you use in your Web browser to administer your local CUPS server? _____

19. When you save print options in the kprinter utility as the root user, what file are these options saved to? _____

20. What CUPS log stores remote printing requests? _____

## DISCOVERY EXERCISES

### Configuring a Local DNS Server

Using the information in this chapter, install and configure a DNS server on your computer that is authoritative for the **sample.com** domain. Add the appropriate zone files to your system and create A, NS, MX, and CNAME records that resolve to your IP address. Ensure that you forward any queries to 10.0.0.254. When finished, configure the /etc/resolve.conf file to use your own IP as a DNS server, and use the **nslookup, dig**, and **host** commands to ensure that you can resolve names for the sample.com domain and other domains hosted by 10.0.0.254.

## Configuring a Samba Domain Controller

Use the Internet to research the steps required to use your Samba server as a Windows domain controller. Next, log in to tty1 as the root user and configure your Samba service as a domain controller by editing your /etc/samba/smb.conf file. The minimum lines required in this file are:

[global]

        domain logons = yes

        security = user

        encrypt passwords = yes

        wins support = yes

        netbios name = _____

        workgroup = _____ (put your domain name here)

[netlogon]

        path=/netlogon (create this directory with permissions 777)

        public = no

        writable = no

        locking = no

Next, create a new user on the system (**useradd −m testuser**) and give the user an encrypted password in the samba database (**smbpasswd testuser**). Then, add computer accounts for each Windows XP computer that will be joining the domain on your Linux computer by adding a line to /etc/passwd and /etc/shadow that lists the computer name followed by a $ character, as shown below:

/etc/passwd sample line:

        clientcomputername$:x:5000:5000::/dev/null:/bin/false

/etc/shadow sample line:

        clientcomputername$:*:6445::::::

When finished, test your configuration by joining a Windows client to the domain and testing domain logon. Log out of tty1 on your Samba server when finished.

## Researching File- and Printer-Sharing Protocols

Use the Internet to find three organizations that use SLES. Summarize the file- and printer-sharing protocols that each company uses in their network infrastructure and their configuration. For each organization, provide a rationale for the use of each technology.

SECTION

# 11

# MANAGE NETWORK SERVICES: NIS, MAIL, AND XINETD

**SUSE Linux Enterprise Server 9 (SLES 9) comes with a large variety of network services. In this section NIS, LDAP, Mail, xinetd, DHCP, and others are covered.**

♦ Manage Resources on the Network

♦ Manage Electronic Mail

♦ Enable the Extended Internet Daemon (xinetd)

♦ Further Services

---

## OBJECTIVE 1    MANAGE RESOURCES ON THE NETWORK

To manage resources on the network, you need to understand the following:

- Network Information Service (NIS)
- LDAP

## Network Information Service (NIS)

When multiple Linux/UNIX systems in a network are configured to access common resources, it becomes important that all user and group identities are the same for all computers in that network.

In other words, the network should be transparent to the user. No matter which computer a user logs in to, that user should always see exactly the same environment.

You can make sure this happens by using Network Information Service (NIS) and Network File System (NFS) services. NFS is discussed in *Network File System (NFS)*.

To configure NIS for your network, you need to know the following:

- Network Information Service Basics
- NIS Domain Components
- NIS Configuration Overview
- Configure a NIS Master Server with YaST
- Configure a NIS Master Server Manually
- Configure Maps Manually
- Configure a Slave Server
- Configure a NIS Client with YaST
- Configure NIS Users with YaST
- NIS Security Considerations
- NIS Utilities

### Network Information Service Basics

NIS is a database system that allows the centralized administration of configuration files. NIS enables centralized user management and printer administration as well.

In addition, NIS makes it easier to administer large networks by distributing configuration files to individual workstations. NIS is usually installed with the network file system (NFS)—the user's configuration files and home directories are administered centrally on one or more servers.

Linux administrators originally referred to NIS as "YP," which simply stands for the idea of the network's "yellow pages." The names of specific components of NIS still use the YP (such as ypbind, ypserv, and yppaswd).

The NIS server stores the files to distribute over the whole network in maps. The files are stored in a special database format with the corresponding keys.

For example, the file /etc/passwd can be converted to a database using the UID or user name as the key. The respective database files are then called passwd.byuid or passwd.byname.

Other files that are often converted to map databases for distribution across a network include /etc/passwd, /etc/shadow, /etc/group, /etc/hosts, and /etc/services.

## NIS Domain Components

In a NIS domain, there are three types of computers:

- **Master server.** All important configuration files distributed across the network are stored on the master server. These configuration files are converted to NIS maps (files in DBM format) and distributed to slave servers.

  Daemons run on the master server and are responsible for processing the NIS clients' requests. The NIS server program is ypserv.

- **Slave servers.** Slave servers help the master server process requests. For example, they can process NIS requests if the master server cannot be accessed.

  After the maps on the master server have been updated, they are automatically passed to the slave servers. Either a master server or a slave server can respond to requests. The first response that arrives is used.

- **NIS clients.** NIS clients retrieve the configuration files (stored as maps) from the NIS server. You can configure a client to completely ignore local configuration files and to use only the NIS maps.

  You can also configure a client to use both local configuration files and NIS maps in any order. This is done in the file /etc/nsswitch.conf. The NIS client program is ypbind.

**11**

The NIS servers, together with their clients, form a NIS domain, which works as illustrated in Figure 11-1.

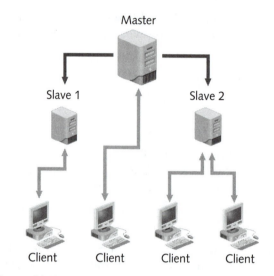

Figure 11-1

You can configure these components with YaST or manually.

## NIS Configuration Overview

The name of the NIS domain is stored in the file /etc/defaultdomain and the server to address is written to the file /etc/yp.conf.

If several NIS servers are in the domain (such as a master server and a number of slave servers), it makes sense to enter the slave servers before the master server in yp.conf.

On a slave server, the local NIS server should be addressed first, then any other existing slave servers, and finally the master server.

The following is an example of addressing the servers:

```
da10:~ # cat /etc/yp.conf
ypserver 127.0.0.1
ypserver 10.0.0.2
ypserver 10.0.0.254
```

On the slave server, first the local host is queried (127.0.0.1). If this is not available, another slave server (10.0.0.2) is queried. If this does not respond, the master server (10.0.0.254) is contacted.

The NIS client must be configured to use the NIS maps instead of or in addition to the local configuration files. The configuration file you need to modify is /etc/nsswitch.conf.

The order of queries is also determined by this configuration file. This file contains an entry for almost every configuration file that can be administered across the network.

The following is an example of setting the order of queries:

```
passwd:          compat
group:           compat

hosts:           files nis dns
services:        files
protocols:       files
```

In this example, the entry for name resolution (**hosts: files nis dns**) means that first the local file /etc/hosts is queried, then the corresponding NIS map, and finally the DNS server.

The entry **compat** for passwd and group means that a compatibility mode should be used for programs linked to older versions of the GNU C Library.

To achieve this, an entry is added automatically by YaST as a last entry in the files /etc/passwd and /etc/group.

This entry specifies that the contents of the NIS maps should be regarded as an extension of the files and should be evaluated after the local files.

If only the NIS maps should be used, you need to modify the entries for passwd and shadow in the file /etc/nsswitch.conf as follows:

```
passwd: nis
group: nis
```

For more information about nsswitch.conf, enter **man nsswitch.conf**.

**NOTE**

## Configure a NIS Master Server with YaST

To use YaST to configure your host as a NIS server, do the following:

1. From the KDE desktop, start the YaST NIS Server module by doing one of the following:

   - Select the **YaST** icon, enter the root password *novell*, and select **OK**; then select **Network Services > NIS Server**.

     *or*

   - Open a terminal window and enter **sux –** and the root password *novell*; then enter **yast2 nis_server**.

The dialog box shown in Figure 11-2 appears.

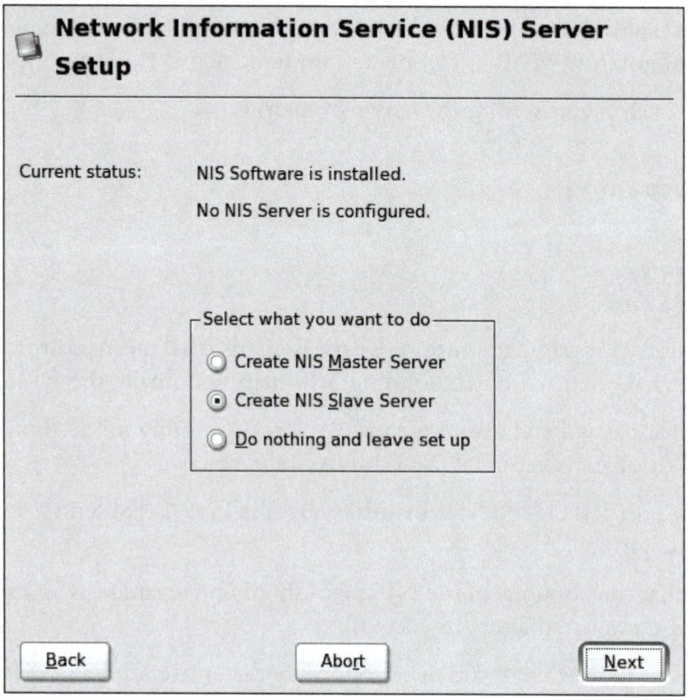

**Network Information Service (NIS) Server Setup**

Current status:    NIS Software is installed.

                   No NIS Server is configured.

Select what you want to do

○ Create NIS Master Server

⊙ Create NIS Slave Server

○ Do nothing and leave set up

Back          Abort          Next

**Figure 11-2**

This initial configuration dialog box lets you create a master NIS server or a slave NIS server.

2. Do one of the following:

   ■ If no NIS server exists in your network, select **Create NIS Master Server**.

   ■ If you already have a NIS master server in the network, you can add a NIS slave server by selecting **Create NIS Slave Server**.

      For example, you might want to create a slave server if you want to configure a new subnetwork.

   ■ If you want to quit the NIS server setup, select **Do Nothing and Leave Set Up**.

3. Create a NIS master server by doing the following:

   a. Select **Create NIS Master Server**.

The dialog box shown in Figure 11-3 appears.

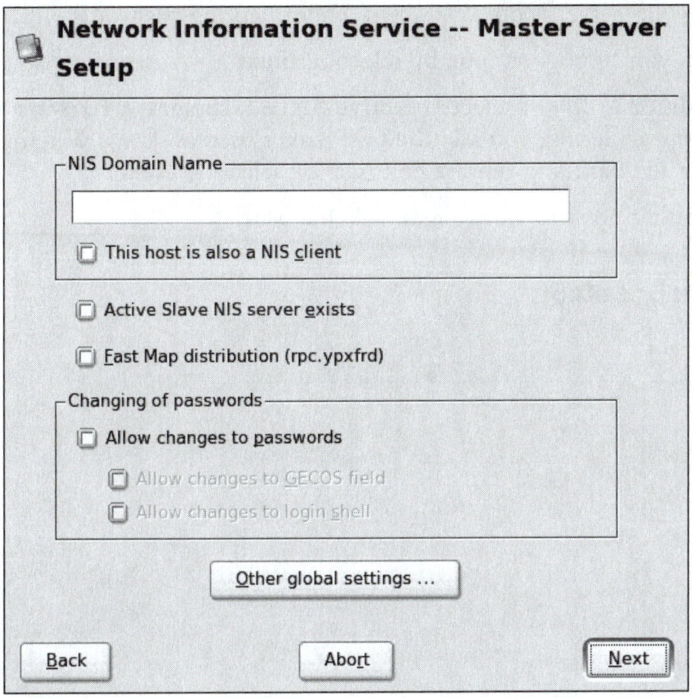

**Network Information Service -- Master Server Setup**

┌─ NIS Domain Name ─────────────────────────────────┐
│  ┌──────────────────────────────────────────────┐  │
│  │                                              │  │
│  └──────────────────────────────────────────────┘  │
│  ☐ This host is also a NIS client                 │
└───────────────────────────────────────────────────┘

☐ Active Slave NIS server exists

☐ Fast Map distribution (rpc.ypxfrd)

┌─ Changing of passwords ───────────────────────────┐
│  ☐ Allow changes to passwords                     │
│     ☐ Allow changes to GECOS field                │
│     ☐ Allow changes to login shell                │
└───────────────────────────────────────────────────┘

[ Other global settings ... ]

[ Back ]          [ Abort ]          [ Next ]

**Figure 11-3**

b. Enter the NIS server *domain name* in the **NIS Domain Name** field.

c. Select from the following options:

- **This Host Is Also a NIS Client.** Select this option to indicate that the host should also be a NIS client, enabling users to log in and access data from the NIS server.

- **Active Slave NIS Server Exists.** Select this option to configure additional NIS servers (slave servers) in your network later.

- **Fast Map Distribution.** Select this option to set fast transfer of the database entries from the master to the slave server.

- **Allow Changes to Passwords.** Select this option to let users in your network (both local users and those managed through the NIS server) to change their passwords on the NIS server (with the command **yppasswd**).

- **Allow Changes to GECOS Field** and **Allow Changes To Login Shell.** Selecting Allow Changes to Passwords makes these options available. Selecting *GECOS* means that the users can also change their names and address settings with the command **ypchfn**. Selecting *SHELL* allows users to change their default shells with the command **ypchsh** (such as switching from bash to csh).

- **Other Global Settings.** Select this option to open a dialog box that lets you perform configuration tasks such as changing the source directory of the NIS server (**/etc/** by default) and merging passwords.

d. When you finish, continue by selecting **Next**.

e. (Conditional) If you selected **Active Slave NIS server Exists**, a dialog box appears letting you add the host names used as slaves. When you finish adding the names to the list, continue by selecting **Next**.

The dialog box shown in Figure 11-4 appears.

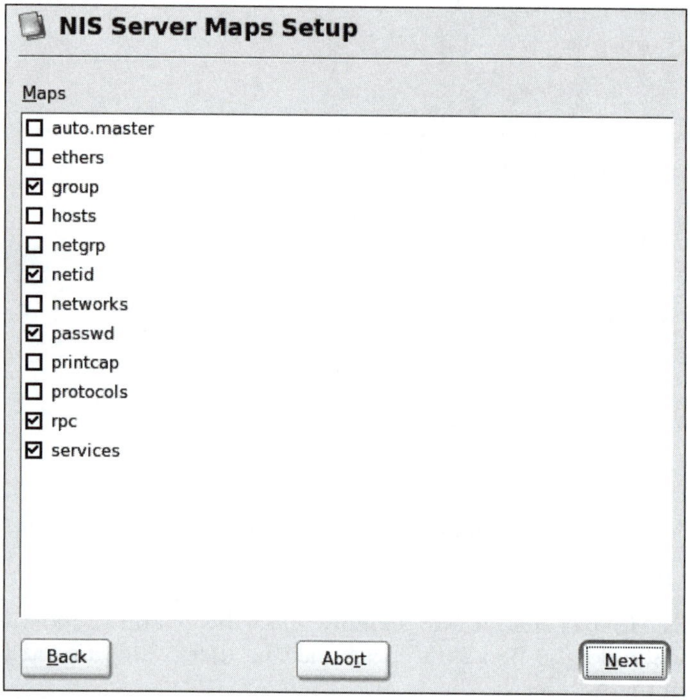

---

**NIS Server Maps Setup**

Maps

- ☐ auto.master
- ☐ ethers
- ☑ group
- ☐ hosts
- ☐ netgrp
- ☑ netid
- ☐ networks
- ☑ passwd
- ☐ printcap
- ☐ protocols
- ☑ rpc
- ☑ services

[ Back ]   [ Abort ]   [ Next ]

---

**Figure 11-4**

f. Select the maps (the partial databases) to transfer from the NIS server to the client; then continue by selecting **Next**.

The default settings are usually adequate, so you should normally leave them unchanged.

**CAUTION**

The dialog box shown in Figure 11-5 appears.

**NIS Server Query Hosts Setup**

| Netmask | Network |
|---------|---------|
| 255.0.0.0 | 127.0.0.0 |
| 0.0.0.0 | 0.0.0.0 |

Add    Edit    Delete

Back          Abort          Finish

**Figure 11-5**

This is the last dialog box in the NIS server configuration. It lets you specify from which networks requests can be sent to the NIS server. You can add, edit, or delete networks from the list.

Normally, requests will be sent from your internal network. For example, if this is the case, and your network is **10.0.0.0/24**, you only need the following two entries:

**255.0.0.0 127.0.0.0**

**255.255.255.0 10.0.0.0**

The entry 127.0.0.0 enables connections from your own host, which is the NIS server. The entry 10.0.0.0 allows all hosts from the network 10.0.0.0/24 to send requests to the server.

g. (Optional) If you need to change the entry 0.0.0.0, highlight the entry, select **Edit**, make the appropriate changes, and then select **OK**.

h. Add all networks you want to honor requests from; then save the NIS server configuration settings by selecting **Finish**.

i. (Optional) If you started YaST from the desktop, close the **YaST Control Center**.

## Configure a NIS Master Server Manually

If you want to configure a NIS server manually, do the following:

- Make sure that the following software packages are installed on the NIS server:

  - **ypserv** (on the NIS server)

  - **ypbind** (on the clients and server)

  - **yp-tools** (contains the NIS utilities)

  - **portmap** (RPC port mapper)

  Because NIS is an RPC service, the port mapper must be started on the server and on the clients. This is done by default in the standard installation of SUSE Linux Enterprise Server.

  You can display the RPC services registered with the port mapper by entering:

  **rpcinfo -p**

- If you want the NIS server to be started automatically when the system is booted, you need to generate the symbolic links in the respective runlevel directories by entering:

  **insserv portmap**

  **insserv yppasswdd**

  **insserv ypserv**

- You also need to set the NIS domain name by using the command ypdomain-name, similar to the following:

  **ypdomainname digi-air**

  To make sure the domain name is set correctly the next time the system is booted, you need to include it in the file /etc/defaultdomain.

- Most configuration files for the NIS server are located in the directory /var/yp/. In addition, a number of variables are set in /etc/sysconfig/ypserv.

  Check the following configuration files:

  - **/etc/yp.conf.** This file only exists on the server if it has also been configured as a client. It contains the NIS server for the client to address.

  - **/etc/ypserv.conf.** This file is involved with security aspects of the NIS server daemon ypserv and the transfer daemon ypxfrd.

  - **/etc/sysconfig/ypserv.** The following values are stored in this file:

    - **YPPWD_SRCDIR.** The NIS source directory.

    - **YPPWD_CHFN.** Indicates if users can change the GECOS field (Yes or No).

    - **YPPWD_CHSH.** Indicates if users can change their login shell (Yes or No).

- Information about the YP source directory is required to generate the NIS maps.

  You create the NIS maps with the command make, which creates the database files based on information in the makefile (/var/yp/Makefile).

  You need to edit the following options in the makefile /var/yp/Makefile:

  - **NOPUSH.** If you are using slave servers, you must set this option to **FALSE**. This makes sure that after NIS maps are generated, they are transferred (pushed) to the slaves.

  - **MINUID and MINGID.** With these options, you can set the lowest UID and GID numbers that are accepted by the NIS maps (such as **MINUID=500** and **MINGID=100**).

  - **all.** After the keyword all, list all the configuration files that should be presented by the NIS server as maps (such as **all: group netid passwd rpc services**).

- There are additional configuration files in the directory /var/yp/ that include the following:

  - **securenets.** This file contains the networks from which the server can be queried.

  - **ypservers.** This file lists the slave servers to which the maps should be transferred if they are modified.

  - **nicknames.** This is a preconfigured file providing an allocation of "nicknames" to existing NIS maps. For example, it is evaluated by ypcat.

## Configure Maps Manually

To create NIS maps, the makefile (/var/yp/Makefile) is evaluated. To generate maps using the makefile, the NIS domain name must be set.

You can display the domain name by entering **ypdomainname**; you can set the domain name by entering:

**ypdomainname** *domain_name*.

Once you set the NIS domain name, you can create the NIS maps with the command **make**.

You can run the command from the directory where the Makefile is located, or use the option –C followed by the directory where the makefile is located (such as **make –C /var/yp**).

If the daemon ypserv is not running or if slave servers were entered that are not yet active, the command make gives a series of error messages that you can safely ignore.

11

The makefile evaluates the NIS domain name and creates a directory in /var/yp/ with the name of the NIS domain. All NIS maps are stored in DBM format in this directory.

If you want to set up a cron job to regularly regenerate the NIS maps, the option –s (silent) is useful. It ensures that make does not generate any output.

If you make changes to the server configuration with YaST, the NIS maps are regenerated automatically. Changing password data with yppasswd also causes the NIS maps to be updated immediately.

After creating a new user account, you need to run the command make (such as **make –C /var/yp –s**) to include the new user in the NIS maps (see the steps in Conf).

## Configure a Slave Server

Theoretically, one master server and an unlimited number of slave servers can run in a NIS domain. To spread the load evenly, we recommend using slave servers in networks with a large number of NIS clients.

Only copies of the NIS maps exist on the slave server. The copies are automatically updated if changes are made to the maps on the master server.

To copy the maps from the master server to the slave server, you use the program /usr/sbin/yppush.

To configure a slave server, you need to know how to do the following:

- Inform a Master Server of Existing Slave Servers
- Configure a Slave Server

**Inform a Master Server of Existing Slave Servers**    You can inform a master server of existing slave servers when you configure the master server with YaST.

By selecting **Active Slave NIS server exists**, the entry for pushing the maps is activated in the Makefile on the server (the option NOPUSH is set to false).

By selecting **Fast Map Distribution** on the master, rpc.ypxfrd (the YP transfer daemon) is started, which ensures a quicker transfer of the NIS maps to the slave servers.

The slave servers entered in YaST are written to the file /var/yp/ypservers. Only the slave servers listed there are sent the NIS maps by the master server.

**Configure a Slave Server**    You can also configure a slave server with YaST.

After starting the NIS Server module (**Network Services > NIS Server**), select the option **Create NIS Slave Server > Next** and follow the prompts.

As with the master server, the package ypserv is needed on the slave server (installed by default). The symbolic links for starting in the corresponding runlevels are also set automatically by YaST.

The slave server is given the name of the NIS domain for which it should be responsible as well as the IP address of the NIS master server. You also need to decide if the slave server should function as a NIS client and which access permission should be configured.

The makefile (/var/yp/Makefile) on a slave server does not need to be adjusted, because the maps are only collected from the server and are never generated on the slave server.

When the configuration with YaST is finished, the command **/usr/lib/yp/ypinit -s** *master-server* is run once in the background. This causes the slave server to request the maps from the master server.

On the slave server, the maps are also stored in the directory **/var/yp/NIS-domain-name**. As soon as the maps have been generated on the master server, the slave will automatically receive the new files.

### Configure a NIS Client with YaST

To use YaST to configure your host as a NIS client, do the following:

1. From the KDE desktop, start the YaST NIS Client module by doing one of the following:

   - Select the **YaST** icon, enter the root password *novell*, and select **OK**; then select **Network Services > NIS Client**.

     *or*

   - Open a terminal window and enter **sux –** and the root password *novell*; then enter **yast2 nis-client**.

**11**

The dialog box shown in Figure 11-6 appears.

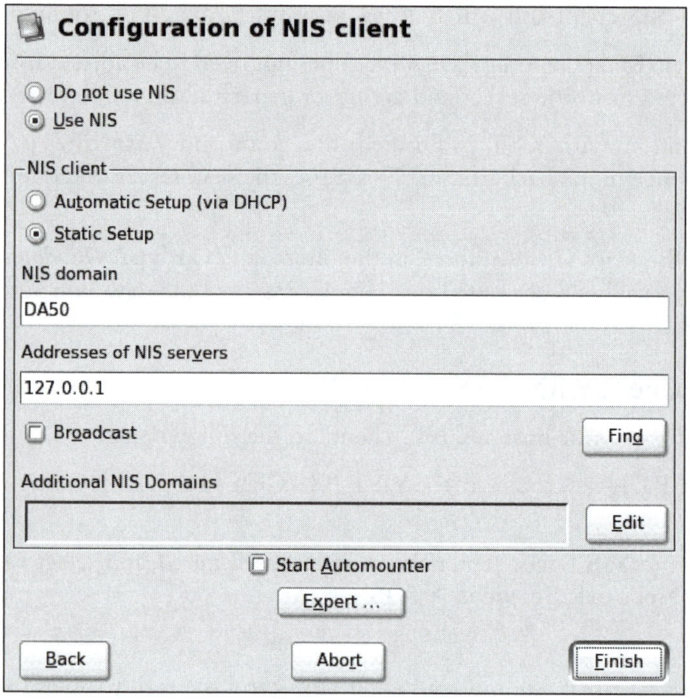

**Figure 11-6**

2. Make sure **Use NIS** is selected.

3. Do one of the following:

   ■ If the host gets an IP address through DHCP, select **Automatic Setup (via DHCP)**.

   *or*

   ■ If the host has a static (fixed) IP address, select **Static Setup**.

4. (Conditional) If you select Static Setup, do the following:

   a. In the **NIS Domain** field, enter the *NIS domain name*.

   b. In the **Addresses of NIS Servers** field, enter the *NIS server IP address*.

   You can also search for and select NIS servers broadcasting in the network by selecting **Find**. Multiple servers in the field need to be separated with spaces.

   c. If you want NIS to search for additional servers in the local network when the configured servers fail to respond, select **Broadcast**.

We do not recommend selecting this option due to security risks.

    d. Add additional NIS domains (and set a default domain) for the NIS client by selecting **Edit**.

5. (Conditional) If you have configured auto.* files to automatically mount directories (such as user home directories) with the Automounter daemon, select **Start Automounter**.

6. Access additional configuration options (such as **Answer to Local Host Only**) by selecting **Expert**.

7. When you finish configuring the NIS client, save the configuration settings by selecting **Finish**.

8. (Optional) If you started YaST from the desktop, close the **YaST Control Center**.

## Configure NIS Users with YaST

In order for users to be recognized by NIS, they need to have a NIS user account created on the NIS server host machine. In addition, you need to create a home directory for the NIS network users.

To configure NIS users on the NIS server host machine, do the following:

1. Create a directory for NIS network users.

   For example, enter the following:

   **mkdir -p /export/nis-*hostname*/home**

2. From the KDE desktop, start the YaST Edit and create users module by doing one of the following:

   ■ Select the **YaST** icon, enter the root password *novell*, and select **OK**; then select **Security and Users > Edit and create users**.

   *or*

   ■ Open a terminal window and enter **sux –** and the root password *novell*; then enter **yast2 users**.

The dialog box shown in Figure 11-7 appears.

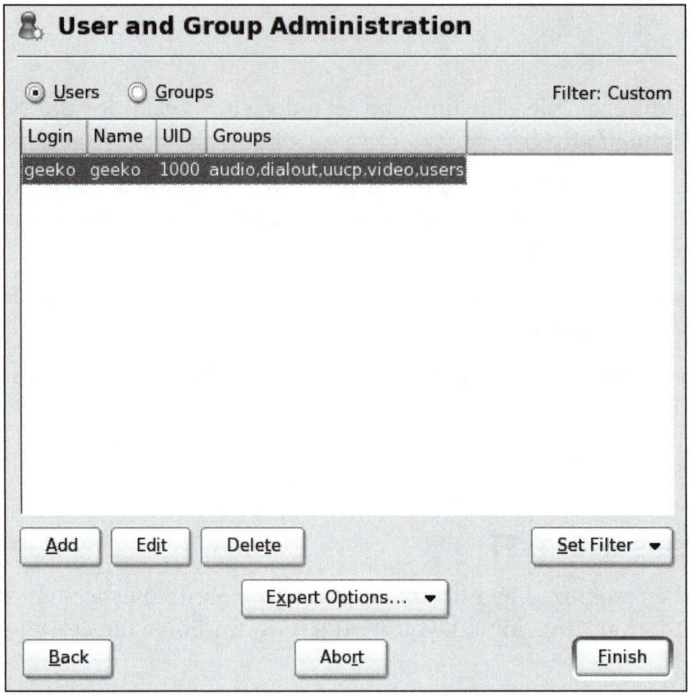

**Figure 11-7**

3. Select **Set Filter**; then select **Local Users**.
4. Create a new user by selecting **Add**.

The dialog box shown in Figure 11-8 appears.

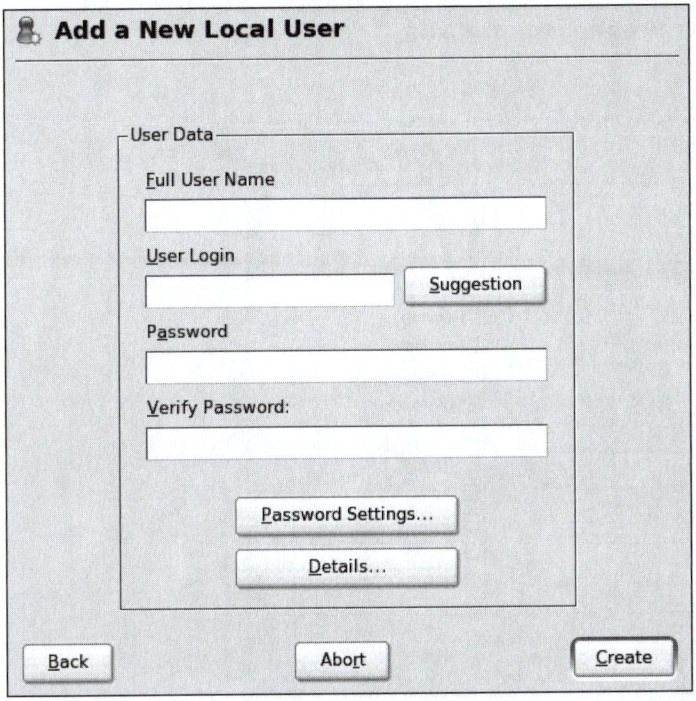

**Figure 11-8**

5. Enter a *full user name*, *user login ID*, and *password* (twice).

6. Select **Details**.

The dialog box shown in Figure 11-9 appears.

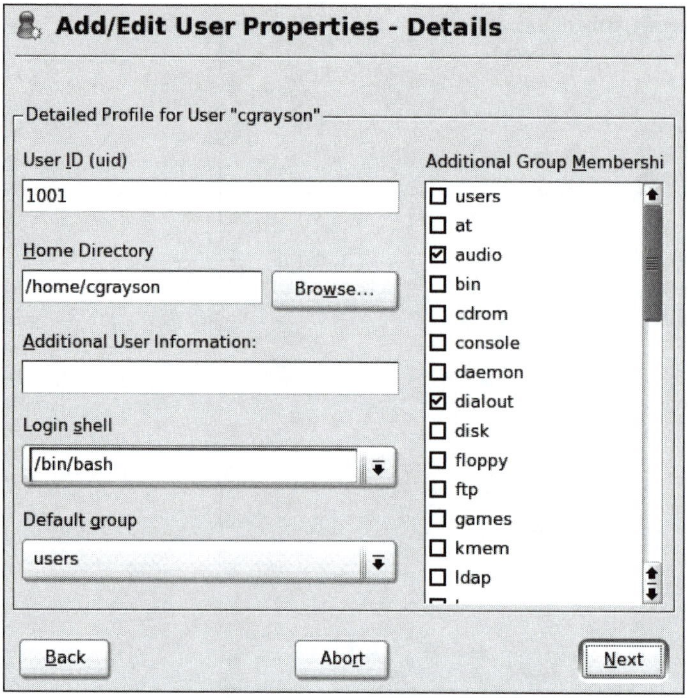

**Figure 11-9**

7. In the **Home Directory** field, enter the *home directory* for the user based on the directory you created for the NIS network users (such as **/export/nis-hostname/home/joe/**).

   You can also edit user properties such as the default login shell and the default group (see the Help information in the dialog box).

8. When you finish configuring the additional user properties, continue by selecting **Next**.

   You are returned to the Add a New Local User dialog box.

9. Add the user by selecting **Create**.

   You are returned to the User and Group Administration dialog box.

10. With the *new user* selected in the list, select **Set Filter**; then select **NIS Users**.

    The user has not been added as a NIS account.

11. Save the changes by selecting **Finish**.

Although you have created the user account, users do not show up in NIS until the maps are updated. Accounts need to be created in the file /etc/passwd and then ported to NIS.

12. Open a terminal window; su to root with **sux –** and a password of *novell.*

13. Change to the directory /var/yp/ by entering **cd /var/yp**.

14. Update the NIS maps by entering **make**.

15. From the Yast Control Center, select:

    **Security and Users > Edit and Create Users**

    or in the terminal window, enter:

    **yast2 users**

16. Select **Set Filter > NIS Users**.

    The new user account is now displayed.

17. Close the **User and Group Administration** dialog box and the **YaST Control Center**.

## NIS Security Considerations

An important question when implementing NIS is that of access protection. How can you restrict access to a NIS domain and the information stored there?

You can configure this type of restriction in the file /var/yp/securenets. All networks that require access to the NIS server must be listed in this file.

For example, the following securenets file provides for the NIS server to be accessible from the network 10.0.0.0/24, from the computer 10.0.1.1, and from itself (with access refused to all other computers):

```
255.0.0.0 127.0.0.0
255.255.255.0 10.0.0.0
255.255.255.255 10.0.1.1
```

Entries for individual computers can also be made with the keyword host (such as **host 10.0.1.1**). Although not accepted by YaST, you can use this option when editing the file manually.

**NOTE**

For more information about the structure of the file /var/yp/securenets, enter **man 8 ypserv**.

Only IP addresses are valid in /var/yp/securenets; you cannot use host or network names.

**CAUTION**    If you are using a version of ypserv in which TCP wrapper support is still included, the files /etc/hosts.allow and /etc/hosts.deny must be modified accordingly.

For more information, enter **man 5 hosts_access** or **man 5 hosts_options**.

## NIS Utilities

There are many utilities available for NIS. Some are for diagnostic purposes, but others are normal user programs (such as **yppasswd** for changing the NIS password).

These utilities are in the package yp-tools. The following are some of the more commonly-used utilities:

- **/bin/ypdomainname.** If you enter **ypdomainname** without options, the command displays the name of the current NIS domain.

  To set a new domain name, use the command ypdomainname. For example, to set the current NIS domain name to digi-air, enter **ypdomainname digi-air**.

- **/usr/bin/ypwhich.** You can use this utility to display the NIS server used by the client.

  You can also query the NIS client on other machines for the server addressed by it, as shown in the following:

  ```
  da10:~ # ypwhich
  da1.digitalairlines.com
  da10:~ # ypwhich da1.digitalairlines.com
  localhost
  ```

  In this example, entering ypwhich displays the NIS server the local computer is using (**da1.digitalairlines.com**). By entering ypwhich da1.digitalairlines.com you find out which NIS server da1.digitalairlines.com is using (**localhost**).

  By using the option -m, you can display all NIS maps with the NIS master server to which they belong, as shown in the following:

  ```
  da10:~ # ypwhich -m
  passwd.byname da1.digitalairlines.com
  passwd.byuid da1.digitalairlines.com
  services.byname da1.digitalairlines.com
  services.byservicename da1.digitalairlines.com
  rpc.byname da1.digitalairlines.com
  rpc.bynumber da1.digitalairlines.com
  group.byname da1.digitalairlines.com
  group.bygid da1.digitalairlines.com
  ypservers da1.digitalairlines.com
  netid.byname da1.digitalairlines.com
  ```

- **/usr/bin/ypcat.** You can use this utility to display the contents of a NIS map. Include either the nickname (such as passwd) or the name of the map itself (such as passwd.byuid).

- **/usr/bin/ypmatch.** You can use this utility to query the key field of a NIS map such as passwd.byname or passwd.byuid, and have the corresponding entry for the field displayed.

  For example, to search in the map passwd.byuid for the user with a UID of 500, you would enter **ypmatch 500 passwd.byuid**.

- **/usr/bin/yppasswd.** You can use this utility to change the password of the user on the NIS server.

  This command requires that rpc.yppasswdd (the YP password daemon) is running on the NIS master server.

  When you use this command, the password in the file /etc/shadow on the NIS server is changed and the corresponding NIS maps are automatically regenerated.

  If slave servers exist, the modified maps are also transferred to them automatically.

  The same applies for the commands ypchfn and ypchsh, which users can use to change their description field and their standard shell.

  If the user has changed her password, it is valid immediately. However, if she logs in again immediately, the old password might nevertheless still be expected.

  This is because the nscd (Name Service Cache Daemon) saves various information in its cache for a certain length of time. What information is stored and for how long is defined in the configuration file /etc/nscd.conf.

  The contents of the file passwd are stored for 10 minutes (600seconds) by default.

  You can shorten the time for which the old password is still valid by changing this value, or you can turn off nscd by entering **rcnscd stop** or restart it by entering **rcnscd restart**.

- **/usr/sbin/yppoll.** You can use this utility to display the ID number of a NIS map used by the NIS server.

  This ID number is assigned by the system. It changes whenever a map is updated. Use the command whenever you want to make sure your servers are using the most current version of a NIS map.

  The syntax of yppoll is:

  **yppoll [-h** *host*] [-d *domain*] *mapname*

  Replace ***mapname*** with the full name of the NIS map. The command cannot handle nicknames. Table 11-1 describes the options.

**11**

Table 11-1

| Option | Description |
|---|---|
| -h *host* | This option enables you to specify a server other than the default server. To find out which server the command defaults to, use the command ypwhich.<br><br>If a host is not specified, the server polled is the default server. |
| -d *domain* | This option enables you to specify a domain other than the default domain. To find out which domain the command defaults to, use the command ypdomainname.<br><br>If domain is not specified, the domain polled is the default domain. |

## Exercise 11-1 Enable Network Information Service (NIS) on Your Network

Within a network of any size it is not possible to keep the user accounts locally. This is just not manageable, as it means one has to add and delete users on every single workstation.

NIS is a solution for this that exists already for some time. While it is still workable, it should be replaced by LDAP where possible to avoid certain security issues inherent in NIS.

The purpose of this exercise is to walk you through the steps necessary to set up NIS.

In this exercise, you do the following:

- Part I: Configure a NIS Server with YaST
- Part II: Create a NIS User
- Part III: Update the NIS Maps
- Part IV: Verify a Local NIS Configuration
- Part V: Prepare for NIS Network Users
- Part VI: Configure the NIS Client Using YaST

In this exercise, you work with a partner with one of your computers acting as the NIS server and the other as the NIS client.

For this exercise to work properly, all the steps need to be done in sequence. For example, in Part V complete the steps on the NFS server computer before completing the steps on the NFS client computer.

**CAUTION**

## Part I: Configure a NIS Server with YaST

From the NIS server computer, do the following:

1. From the KDE desktop, select the **YaST** icon; then enter a password of **novell** and select **OK**.

   The YaST Control Center appears.

2. Select **Network Services > NIS Server**.

   The Network Information Service (NIS) Server Setup dialog box appears.

3. Select **Create NIS Master Server**; then continue by selecting **Next**.

   The Master Server Setup dialog box appears.

4. In the NIS Domain Name field enter **NIS-DA***xx* (where *xx* is the host number of your server).

   For example, if your server hostname is DA50, you would enter **NIS-DA50**.

5. Select the following options:

   - **This Host Is Also a NIS client**
   - **Fast Map Distribution (rpc.ypxfrd)**
   - **Allow Changes to Passwords**
   - **Allow Changes to GECOS Field**
   - **Allow Changes to Login Shell**

6. Continue by selecting **Next**.

   A NIS Server Maps Setup dialog box appears.

7. From the list of server maps, deselect **netid**; then make sure that **group**, **passwd**, **rpc**, and **services** are selected.

8. Continue by selecting **Next**.

   The NIS Server Query Hosts Setup dialog box appears.

9. Accept the default settings and complete the NIS server setup by selecting **Finish**.

## Part II: Create a NIS User

Before testing the NIS configuration, you need to create a NIS user on the computer where the NIS server is configured.

**11**

From the NIS server computer, do the following:

1. From a terminal window, su to root (**su -**) with a password of **novell**.

2. Create the directory /export/nis-xx/home for NIS network users by entering the following:

   **mkdir -p /export/nis-*xx*/home**

   (where *xx* is the host number of your server)

3. From the YaST Control Center, select:

   **Security and Users > Edit and Create Users**

   The User and Group Administration dialog box appears.

4. Select **Set Filter**; then select **NIS Users**.

   Notice that when you create new users they are added as NIS users by default.

5. Select **Set Filter**; then select **Local Users**.

6. Create a new user by selecting **Add**.

   The Add a New Local User dialog box appears.

7. Enter the following (where *xx* is the host number of your server):

   - Full User Name: **dba*xx***

   - User Login: **dba*xx***

   - Password: **N0v3ll**

   - Verify Password: **N0v3ll**

8. Select **Details**.

   A Details dialog box appears.

9. In the Home Directory field, enter:

   **/export/nis-*xx*/home/dba*xx***

   Then select **Next**.

10. Continue by selecting **Create**.

    User dba*xx* is listed with the other users.

11. Select **Set Filter**; then select **NIS Users**.

    The maps have not been updated, so the user dba*xx* is not listed as a NIS user.

12. Save the changes by selecting **Finish**.

13. From the terminal window, enter:

    **ls -l /export/nis-*xx*/home/**

    Check to make sure that the owner of the directory **dba*xx*** is user dba*xx*.

14. (Conditional) If dba*xx* is not the owner, then enter:

    **chown −R dba*xx*.users /export/nis−*xx*/home/dba*xx***

## Part III: Update the NIS Maps

From the NIS server computer, update the NIS maps by doing the following:

1. From the terminal window, make sure that the yp services are running by entering:

    **rcypserv restart**

2. Change to the directory /var/yp by entering **cd /var/yp**.

3. Update the NIS maps by entering **make**.

## Part IV: Verify a Local NIS Configuration

From the NIS server computer, do the following:

1. Switch to a virtual console by entering **Ctrl + Alt + F2**.

2. Log in as **dba*xx*** with a password of **N0v3ll**.

    You are now ready to test the configuration.

3. Check the NIS domain by entering **domainname**.

    You see NIS-DA*xx* listed.

4. Change the GECOS field by entering **chfn**; then enter a password of **N0v3ll**.

5. Enter the following values:

    - Room Number: **Classroom**

    - Work Phone: **555–1212**

    - Home Phone: **444–1212**

6. Su to root (**su −**) with a password of **novell**.

7. Update the NIS maps by changing to the directory /var/yp (**cd /var/yp**) and entering **make**.

8. Verify that the NIS map was updated by entering:

    **ypcat passwd**

9. Return to the KDE desktop by pressing **Ctrl + Alt + F7**.

## Part V: Prepare for NIS Network Users

A NIS user needs a home directory on the NIS client computer.

In this part of the exercise, you work with a partner to create an NFS export of the NIS home directory path and then mount this exported file system on the NIS client computer.

11

On the NIS server computer, do the following:

1. Configure the directory /export/nis-*xx* as an NFS export:

   a. From the YaST Control Center, configure the NFS server by selecting **Network Services > NFS Server**.

      A Configuration of the NFS Server dialog box appears.

   b. Make sure **Start NFS Server** is selected; then continue by selecting **Next**.

      A Directories to Export to the Others dialog box appears.

   c. Select **Add Directory**.

      A dialog box appears requesting the directory to export.

   d. Browse to and select or enter **/export/nis-*xx*/**; then select **OK**.

      A dialog box appears with fields for entering a wild card and options.

   e. Enter the following:

      ■ Hosts Wildcard: **\***

      ■ Options: **rw,no_root_squash,sync**

      Make sure you replace the ro with rw or you will not be able to log in remotely to the KDE desktop as dba*xx*.

   f. Continue by selecting **OK**.

      The directory is added to the list.

   g. Save the changes to the system by selecting **Finish**.

   h. From the terminal window, verify that the file system was exported by entering:

      **showmount -e localhost**

   i. View the entry made by YaST to the file /etc/exports by entering **cat /etc/exports**.

2. On the NIS client computer, do the following:

   a. From a terminal window, su to root (**su -**) with a password of **novell**.

   b. Create a directory /export/nis-*xx* (where *xx* is the host number of the NIS server computer) by entering:

      **mkdi -p /export/nis-*xx***

      For example, if your NIS server is DA50, you would enter

      **mkdir -p /export/nis-50**

   c. From the KDE desktop, select the **YaST** icon; then enter a password of **novell** and select **OK**.

      The YaST Control Center appears.

    d.  From the YaST Control Center, select:

    **Network Services > NFS Client**

    The Configuration of the NFS Client dialog box appears.

    e.  Mount a remote file system by selecting **Add**.

    A dialog box appears for adding the remote file system.

    f.  Enter the following:

- Host Name of the NFS Server: **10.0.0.*rr*** (where **rr** is the host number of the NIS server computer)

- Remote Filesystem: **/export/nis-*xx***

- Mountpoint (Local): **/export/nis-*xx*/** (where **rr** is the host number of the remote NFS server)

- Options Field: **defaults,rsize=8192,wsize=8192,soft**

    g.  Save the configuration by selecting **OK**.

    You are returned to the Configuration of the NFS Client dialog box where the remote file system is listed.

    h.  Save the changes to the system by selecting **Finish**.

    i.  From the terminal window, verify that the file system is mounted by entering **mount**.

    j.  Verify that an entry exists in /etc/fstab by entering:

    **cat /etc/fstab**

## Part VI: Configure the NIS Client Using YaST

From the NIS client computer, do the following:

1. From the YaST Control Center, select:

    **Network Services > NIS Client**

    The Configuration of NIS Client dialog box appears.

2. Make sure **Use NIS** is selected.

3. In the NIS domain field, enter **NIS-DA*rr*** (where **rr** is the host number of your NIS server computer).

4. In the Addresses of NIS Servers field, enter **10.0.0.*rr*** (where **rr** is the host number of your NIS server computer).

5. Save the changes to the system by selecting **Finish**.

**11**

6. Test the NIS remote access:

a. Log out of the KDE desktop by selecting:

**KDE Menu > Logout > Logout**

The GUI login screen appears.

Scroll through the list of users and notice that the **dbaxx** user appears, even though it is not a local user account.

b. Log in as the user **dbaxx** with a password of **N0v3ll**.

c. When you finish, log out as **dbaxx**; then log back in as **geeko**.

# LDAP

It is crucial within a networked environment to keep important information structured and quickly available. In the ideal case, a central server keeps the data in a directory and distributes it to all clients using a certain protocol.

An open and standardized protocol like LDAP (Lightweight Directory Access Protocol) ensures that as many different client applications as possible can access such information.

LDAP is an Internet communications protocol that lets client applications access Directory information. It is based on the X.500 Directory Access Protocol (DAP) but is less complex and can be used with any directory service later than X.500.

The use of TCP/IP by LDAP makes it easy to establish interfaces between an application and the LDAP service.

The OpenLDAP package (openldap2) included in SLES 9 consists of the following:

- **slapd.** A standalone LDAPv3 server that administers object information in a BerkeleyDB-based database.

- **slurpd.** This program enables the replication of modifications to data on the local LDAP server to other LDAP servers installed on the network.

- **slapcat, slapadd, slapindex.** These are additional tools for system maintenance.

One of the most common uses of LDAP is user authentication. To set up OpenLDAP for user authentication, you need to know the following:

- LDAP vs. NIS
- Structure of an LDAP Directory Tree
- Configure an LDAP Server with YaST
- Configure an LDAP Client with YaST
- Configure Users for LDAP Authentication

## LDAP vs. NIS

System administrators for Linux/UNIX have traditionally used NIS service for authentication, name resolution, and data distribution in a network. The configuration data contained in various files in /etc/ (group, hosts, netgroup, networks, passwd, printcap, protocols, rpc, and services) are distributed to clients all over the network.

However, NIS is designed for Linux/UNIX platforms only, which limits its use in a multiplatform network.

Unlike NIS, the LDAP service is not restricted to pure Linux/UNIX networks. Windows servers (Windows 2000 and later) support LDAP as a directory service. Novell NetWare also offers an LDAP service. Application tasks mentioned above are also supported in non-Linux/UNIX systems.

LDAP can be applied to any data structure that should be centrally administered, including:

- Replacement for NIS
- Mail routing (postfix, sendmail)
- Address books for mail clients like Mozilla, Evolution, and Outlook
- Administration of zone descriptions for a BIND9 name server

This list can be extended because LDAP is extensible as opposed to NIS. In addition, the hierarchical structure of LDAP helps when performing administrative tasks such as searching through large amounts of data.

## Structure of an LDAP Directory Tree

An LDAP directory has a tree structure. All entries (called *objects*) of the directory have a defined position within the tree. This hierarchy is called the *directory information tree* (DIT).

A complete path to a certain entry is called the *distinguished name* (DN). The single nodes along the path to this entry are called the *relative distinguished name* (RDN).

You can generally assign objects to one of two types:

- **container.** These objects can contain other objects. Such object classes are *root* (the root element of the directory tree, which does not really exist), *c* (country), *ou* (organizational unit), and *dc* (domain component).

  This model is similar to the directories (folders) in a file system.

- **leaf.** These objects sit at the end of a branch and have no subordinate objects. Examples are *person*, *InetOrgPerson*, or *groupofNames*.

**11**

Figure 11-10 shows an example of an LDAP tree hierarchy.

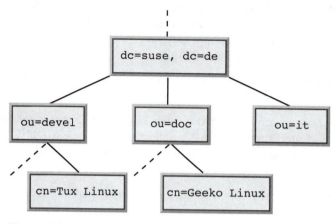

**Figure 11-10**

In this example, the complete, valid DN for the SUSE employee Geeko Linux is:

cn=Geeko Linux,ou=doc,dc=suse,dc=de

It is created by adding the RDN **cn=Geeko Linux** to the DN **ou=doc,dc=suse,dc=de**.

The definition of which types of objects can be stored in the DIT is called the *schema*, which includes object classes. An *object class* defines what attributes the object must or can be assigned.

While there are a few common schemas (see RFC 2252 and 2256). it is possible to create custom schemas or to use multiple schemas complementing each other if this is required by the environment in which the LDAP server operates.

**NOTE**    For a good introduction in the use of schemes see the OpenLDAP documentation in /usr/share/doc/packages/openldap2/admin-guide/index.html. You might need to install the documentation.

## Configure an LDAP Server with YaST

Typically, an LDAP server handles user account data, but with SUSE Linux Enterprise Server it can also be used for mail, DHCP, and DNS-related data. By default, an LDAP server is set up during installation.

To set up an LDAP server for user authentication, you can use YaST. Do the following:

1. From the KDE desktop, start the YaST LDAP Server module by doing one of the following:

   - Select the **YaST** icon, enter the root password *novell*, and select **OK**; then select **Network Services > LDAP Server**.

   *or*

   - Open a terminal window and enter **sux –** and the root password *novell*; then enter **yast2 ldap–server**.

   The dialog box shown in Figure 11–11 appears.

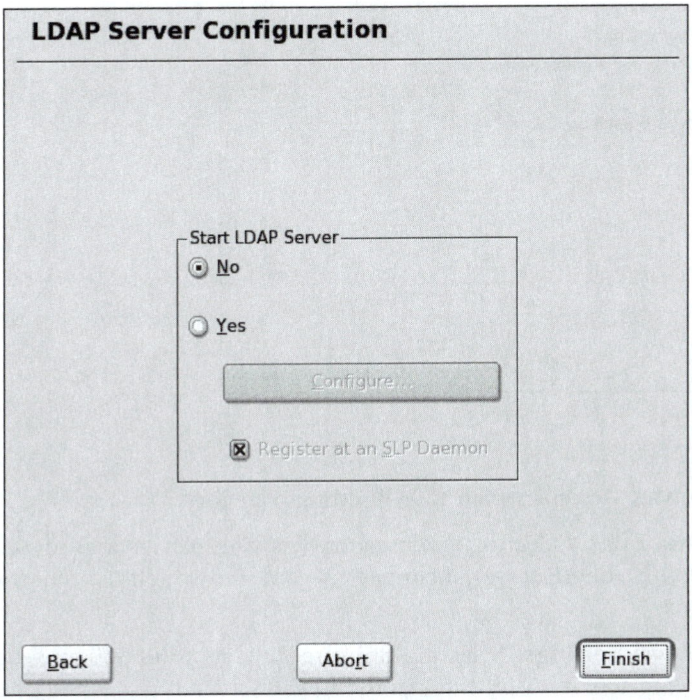

**LDAP Server Configuration**

Start LDAP Server
- ◉ No
- ○ Yes

Configure...

☒ Register at an SLP Daemon

Back      Abort      Finish

**Figure 11-11**

2. Start the LDAP server by selecting **Yes**.

3. Configure the LDAP server by selecting **Configure**.

4. At the left, view the configuration settings by expanding **Global Settings**; then select a *category*.

For example, if you select **Log Level Settings**, the dialog box shown in Figure 11-12 appears.

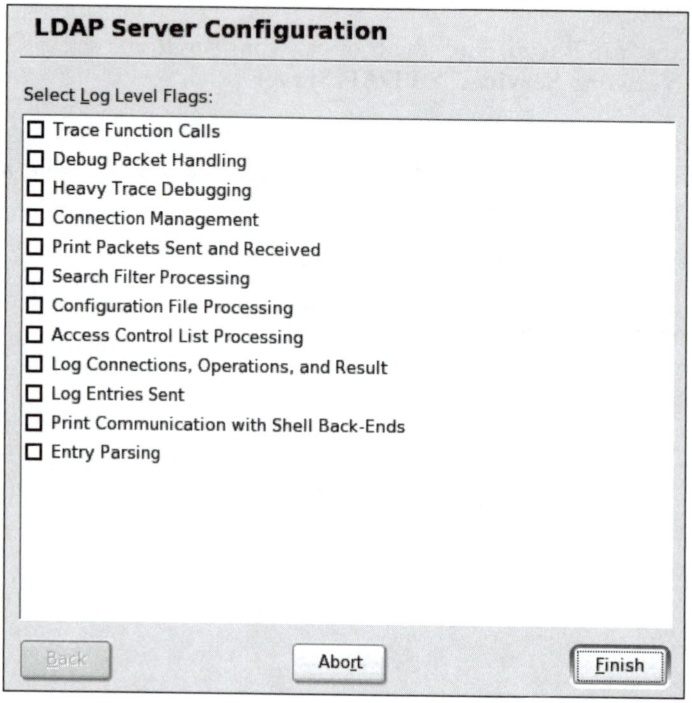

**LDAP Server Configuration**

Select Log Level Flags:
- ☐ Trace Function Calls
- ☐ Debug Packet Handling
- ☐ Heavy Trace Debugging
- ☐ Connection Management
- ☐ Print Packets Sent and Received
- ☐ Search Filter Processing
- ☐ Configuration File Processing
- ☐ Access Control List Processing
- ☐ Log Connections, Operations, and Result
- ☐ Log Entries Sent
- ☐ Print Communication with Shell Back-Ends
- ☐ Entry Parsing

Back     Abort     Finish

**Figure 11-12**

5. The following describes each LDAP settings category:

- **Schema Files.** Selecting this category lets you manage a list of schema files used by the LDAP server, including the order in which the schema files are accessed.

- **Log Level Settings.** Selecting this category lets you configure the degree of logging activity (verbosity) of the LDAP server.

  From the predefined list, select or deselect logging options. The more options you enable, the larger your log files will grow.

- **Allow Settings.** Selecting this category lets you define which connection types should be allowed by the LDAP server.

- **TLS Settings.** Selecting this category lets you define how the data traffic between server and client should be secured.

- **Databases.** Selecting this option lets you select the databases to be managed by the server by selecting **Add Database**.

For more information about configuring the LDAP server from the LDAP Server Configuration dialog box, see Section 21.8.5 in the *SLES 9 Installation and Administration Manual*.

6. When you finish the configuration, save the LDAP server setting by selecting **Finish**.

7. (Optional) If you started YaST from the desktop, close the **YaST Control Center**.

## Configure an LDAP Client with YaST

YaST includes an LDAP Client module to set up LDAP-based user management. If you did not enable this feature during installation, you can configure the LDAP client by doing the following:

1. From the KDE desktop, start the YaST LDAP Client module by doing one of the following:

   ■ Select the **YaST** icon, enter the root password *novell*, and select **OK**; then select **Network Services > LDAP Client**.

   *or*

   ■ Open a terminal window and enter **sux –** and the root password *novell*; then enter **yast2 ldap–client**.

   YaST automatically enables any PAM and NSS-related changes as required by LDAP and installs the necessary files.

**11**

The dialog box shown in Figure 11-13 appears.

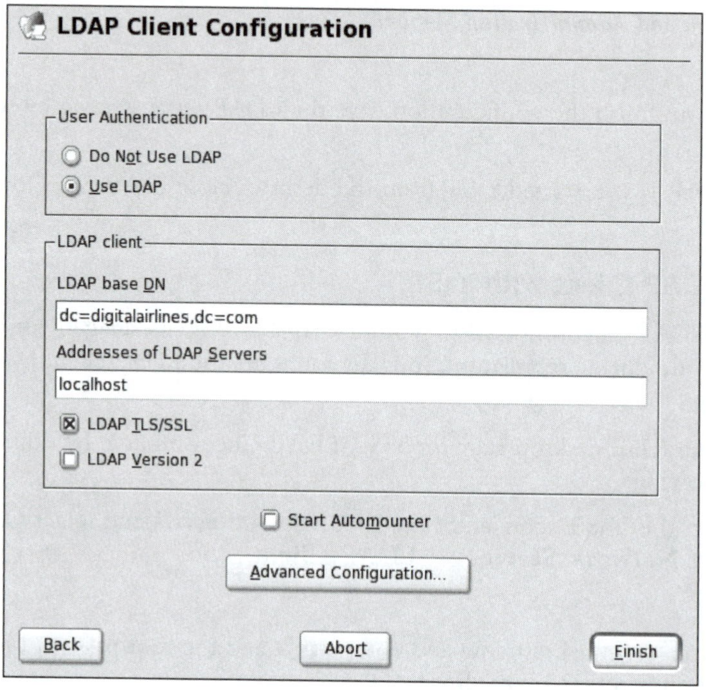

## LDAP Client Configuration

┌─ User Authentication ──────────────────────────────────────────────┐
│   ○ Do Not Use LDAP                                                 │
│   ⊙ Use LDAP                                                        │
└─────────────────────────────────────────────────────────────────────┘

┌─ LDAP client ──────────────────────────────────────────────────────┐
│   LDAP base DN                                                      │
│   ┌───────────────────────────────────────────────────────────────┐ │
│   │ dc=digitalairlines,dc=com                                     │ │
│   └───────────────────────────────────────────────────────────────┘ │
│   Addresses of LDAP Servers                                         │
│   ┌───────────────────────────────────────────────────────────────┐ │
│   │ localhost                                                     │ │
│   └───────────────────────────────────────────────────────────────┘ │
│   ☒ LDAP TLS/SSL                                                    │
│   ☐ LDAP Version 2                                                  │
└─────────────────────────────────────────────────────────────────────┘

                    ☐ Start Automounter

              [ Advanced Configuration... ]

[ Back ]              [ Abort ]                      [ Finish ]

**Figure 11-13**

2. Enable user authentication with an LDAP server by selecting **Use LDAP**.

3. In the **LDAP Base DN** field, enter the DN of the search base.

4. In the **Addresses of LDAP Servers**, enter the *IP address* of the LDAP server.

   You can enter multiple IP addresses by separating them with spaces. You can also specify the port on which the LDAP service is running (*IP address*: *port*)

5. (Conditional) Select **LDAP TLS/SSL** if your LDAP server supports TLS/SSL.

6. (Conditional) If the LDAP server is using version 2 protocol, select **LDAP Version 2**.

7. Configure advanced LDAP settings by selecting **Advanced Configuration**.

**NOTE**

For details on configuring advanced LDAP client settings, see Section 21.8.6 in the *SLES 9 Installation and Administration Manual*.

8. Automatically mount directories on remote hosts by selecting **Start Automounter**.

9. When you finish configuring the LDAP client, save the settings by selecting **Finish**.

10. (Optional) If you started YaST from the desktop, close the **YaST Control Center**.

## Configure Users for LDAP Authentication

To configure user accounts for LDAP authentication, do the following:

1. From the KDE desktop, start the YaST Edit and Create Users module by doing one of the following:

   - Select the **YaST** icon, enter the root password *novell*, and select **OK**; then select **Security and User > Edit and create users**.

     *or*

   - Open a terminal window and enter **sux –** and the root password *novell*; then enter **yast2 users**.

2. Select **Set Filter > Local Users**.

3. From the User list, select a *user*; then select **Edit**.

   The Edit an Existing Local User dialog box appears.

4. Select **Details**.

**11**

The dialog box shown in Figure 11-14 appears.

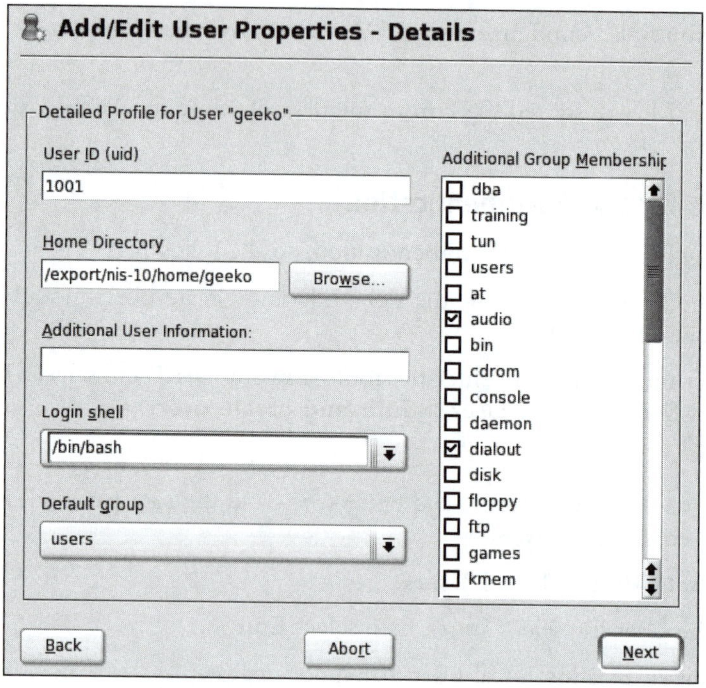

**Figure 11-14**

From this dialog box you can configure settings such as group membership, login shell, and the home directory.

5. Continue by selecting **Next**.

If LDAP authentication has been configured, the dialog box shown in Figure 11-15 appears.

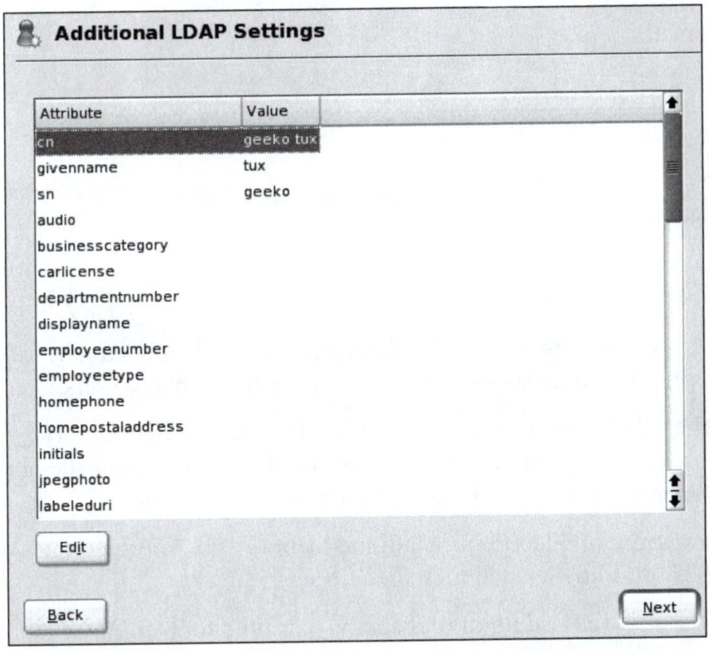

---

**Additional LDAP Settings**

| Attribute | Value |
|---|---|
| cn | geeko tux |
| givenname | tux |
| sn | geeko |
| audio | |
| businesscategory | |
| carlicense | |
| departmentnumber | |
| displayname | |
| employeenumber | |
| employeetype | |
| homephone | |
| homepostaladdress | |
| initials | |
| jpegphoto | |
| labeleduri | |

    Edit

    Back          Next

**Figure 11-15**

A list of attributes appears with values for each attribute.

6. Edit an attribute value by selecting the attribute; then select **Edit**.

7. When you finish, continue by selecting **Next**.

You are returned to the User and Group Administration dialog box.

**NOTE**

For more information on OpenLDAP, see Section 21.8.7 in the *SLES 9 Installation and Administration Manual*.

Users are now authenticated against the information stored in the LDAP directory when they log in.

## OBJECTIVE 2    MANAGE ELECTRONIC MAIL

In this objective, the following topics are described:

- About E-mail
- Postfix
- Sendmail
- Procmail
- Mail Clients

## About E-mail

Since the Internet was established, e-mail (Electronic Mail) has been one of the most important services offered—doubtlessly the most important for many users.

Until the end of the 1980s, it was mainly scientists who used e-mail to share their latest research results. However, the growing popularity of the Internet in the general public was accompanied by a substantial increase in e-mail traffic.

E-mail is an abbreviation of Electronic Mail and denotes the Internet message format (defined in RFC 822) and how e-mail messages are sent.

In the early days of e-mail, the coding of messages was limited to 7-bit ASCII and therefore offered only rudimentary options for the message layout.

Since then, e-mail has expanded to include special characters, such as accents or German umlauts, HTML text, and file attachments with arbitrary contents.

You can exchange all types of files using e-mail. The MIME format (Multipurpose Internet Mail Extensions), defined in RFC 1341, regulates the correct exchange of arbitrary file types.

E-mail clients also know how to display certain MIME formats; for example, an HTML text sent by e-mail can be passed to a browser for display or a PNG graphics file can be displayed in a graphics display program.

To understand e-mail, you need to know about:

- Simple Mail Transfer Protocol (SMTP)
- The Three Mail Agents
- The Mail Cycle

### Simple Mail Transfer Protocol (SMTP)

Sending e-mail is controlled uniformly in the Internet by SMTP (Simple Mail Transfer Protocol).

SMTP is defined in RFC 821.

Since its creation in 1982, it has undergone numerous extensions, such as MIME format (RFC 2045) and SMTP Service Extensions (RFC 1869).

SMTP has the following characteristics:

- There is a direct TCP connection between the sending and receiving computers and the processes involved.
- The task of SMTP is only transmission, not receiving or storing messages.
- Every message is confirmed.
- Messages can be forwarded; for example, if an address has changed.
- The client and the server communicate through readable plain text commands.

  The commands are:

  - **HELO.** (hello) Is used by the SMTP sender to open a connection to an SMTP recipient and followed by the full host name.
  - **MAIL FROM:.** Initializes transmission of an e-mail message.

    In the simplest case, the MAIL command takes the sender's e-mail address (reverse-path) as an argument.

  - **RCPT TO:.** (recipient) Sets the recipient's address (forward-path) for an item of mail.

    If the mail should be sent to several recipients at the same time, this command is repeated for each recipient.

  - **DATA.** Tells the SMTP mailer that anything that follows is the content of the mail.

    The end of the mail content is indicated by line feed and a single dot on a separate line.

  - **VRFY.** (verify) Verifies a user ID.

    This causes the SMTP recipient to check the validity of the address given as an argument.

  - **EXPN.** (expand) Instructs the SMTP recipient to treat the argument as a mailing list.

  - **RSET.** (reset) Resets all the information previously stored about the SMTP recipient.

  - **HELP.** Takes as its argument any other SMTP command.

    A page of tips about how to use the corresponding instruction will be displayed.

  - **NOOP.** (no operation) Causes the SMTP recipient to answer with an **OK**.

  - **QUIT.** Ends the connection between the SMTP sender and recipient.

**11**

Commands can be written in lowercase or uppercase; SMTP commands are not case sensitive. Not all mail servers implement all commands.

During communication between the SMTP sender and SMTP recipient, the sender transmits various commands to the recipient and controls the course of the communication as a whole.

The recipient acknowledges the messages and gives the status of command processing with a corresponding reply code.

It start transmitting the next command only when the sender has received a confirmation for the previous command.

The text below shows a typical example of an SMTP session. It can easily be reproduced by using telnet to connect to port 25 (standard mail server port):

```
tux@da10:~ > telnet da2.digitalairlines.com 25
Trying 10.0.0.2...
Connected to da2.digitalairlines.com.
Escape character is '^]'.
220 da2.digitalairlines.com ESMTP Postfix
HELO da10.digitalairlines.com
250 digitalairlines.com
MAIL FROM:<tux@da10.digitalairlines.com>
250 OK
RCPT TO:<information@digitalairlines.com>: Recipient address
rejected: \
User unknown in local recipient table
RCPt TO:<info@digitalairlines.com>
250 OK
DATA
354 Start mail input; end with <CR><LF>.<CR><LF>
Hallo,
from today I will no longer be sending e-mails with KMail, but
only with the program Telnet.
Tux
.
250 OK: queued as AD86A16199
QUIT
221 Bye
Connection closed by foreign host.
tux@da1:~ >
```

## The Three Mail Agents

Programs that process Internet messages are called *agents*.

There are three types of agents:

- MTA (Mail Transfer Agent)
- MDA (Mail Delivery Agent)
- MUA (Mail User Agent)

**MTA (Mail Transfer Agent)**   E-mails are passed by the e-mail software of the user to the MTA. It sends them to a recipient MTA, which checks to see if the address exists locally. If this is the case, the recipient MTA passes the mail to an MDA.

If the address does not exist locally, the recipient MTA sends the message back to the sending MTA. However, chains are also possible: an MTA sends a message to another one and this passes it to others.

Each recipient MTA leaves a "received" entry in the header of the message sent.

Some well-known MTAs are the programs Sendmail, Postfix, Exim, and Qmail.

**MDA (Mail Delivery Agent)**   The MTA specifies for which local user the message is intended and passes it to an MDA, which stores it in the right location.

A well-known MDA is the program Procmail.

**MUA (Mail User Agent)**   The MUA reads saved messages and passes new messages to the MTA.

It is the interface between the MDA and the user.

The MUA can receive saved messages in three different ways:

- By mail access protocols (such as IMAP or POP)
- Remotely by file access protocols, such as NFS
- Through access to local files

When mail is accessed using IMAP or POP, an IMAP or POP server is involved as an additional component. This server is contacted by the MUA to pick up the mail from where it is stored.

**11**

## The Mail Cycle

Figure 11-16 shows the mail cycle.

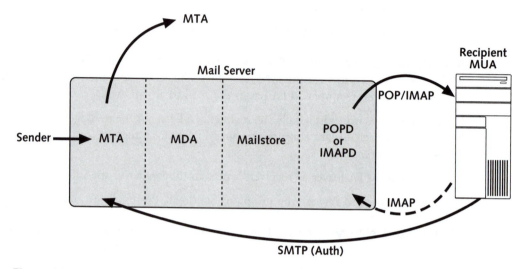

**Figure 11-16**

When an MTA receives an e-mail, it checks to see if this is for a local user. If this is not the case, it sends it to another MTA.

If the mail is intended for a local user, the MTA passes it to the MDA, which then saves it.

From there, the recipient can retrieve the mail via the POP or IMAP protocol, or by remote or local file access.

When the POP protocol is used, e-mails are transferred to the MUA.

If IMAP is used, mails are kept on the mail server and the MUA looks for the mails on the server using the IMAP protocol.

A mail written on the MUA is passed to the MTA, which sends it on to the MTA that is responsible for the recipient's e-mail. Unlike in the past, MTAs today usually require authentication of the user sending mail to avoid the relay of spam mails.

# Postfix

To understand Postfix, you need to know the following:

- Basics
- Components of the Postfix Program Package
- The Postfix Master Daemon
- Global Settings

- Lookup Tables
- Postfix Tools

## Basics

The standard mail server in SUSE Linux Enterprise Server is Postfix.

Postfix was written as an alternative to the widely known Mail Transfer Agent (MTA) Sendmail.

The author of Postfix, Wietse Venema, had various objectives in the development of Postfix, the most important of which were the following:

- Postfix should be a fast mailer.
- Postfix should be easy to administer.
- Postfix should be secure.
- Postfix should behave as far as possible in a manner compatible with Sendmail.

## Components of the Postfix Program Package

**11**

During the installation of Postfix, files with similar functions are grouped in various locations:

- **/etc/postfix/.** All the configuration files defining Postfix mail processing are located in this directory.

  Normally, the Postfix administrator is the only one allowed to make changes to these files.

- **/etc/aliases.** This is the only file saved directly under /etc/. It has the same format as the aliases file for the MTA Sendmail and contains local address aliases.

- **/usr/lib/postfix/.** This directory contains all the programs needed directly by Postfix.

  To be more precise, these are the Postfix binaries. These programs are not accessed directly by the system administrator.

- **/usr/sbin/.** This directory contains the administration programs for maintaining and manually controlling Postfix.

  An administrator uses these programs during maintenance work.

- **/usr/bin/.** Symbolic links with the names **mailq** and **newaliases** are found here.

  Both links point to the program /usr/sbin/sendmail, which provides a Sendmail-compatible administration interface for Postfix.

- **/var/spool/postfix/.** This directory contains the queue directories for Postfix; for example, its own directory etc/ and lib/ for Postfix processes that run in a chroot environment.

- **/usr/share/man/man[1|5|8]/.** This directory contains the manual pages for the Postfix binaries, for the configuration files, and for the administration programs.

- **/usr/share/doc/packages/postfix/.** This directory contains the documentation for Postfix.

   The subdirectory html/ contains a detailed HTML description of Postfix and a very useful FAQ.

## The Postfix Master Daemon

The Postfix master daemon /usr/lib/postfix/master is started directly by Postfix when the system is booted and is only terminated when the system is down or when Postfix is ended.

Its task is to monitor the entire mail system. It consists of the following individual tasks:

- Controlling and monitoring individual Postfix processes.

- Adhering to configured resource limits, which were defined in the file master.cf.

- Restarting killed Postfix processes.

Each line in the file /usr/lib/postfix/master contains an entry for one Postfix process.

The behavior of each process is defined by the configuration in the respective line.

## Global Settings

All further configuration definitions (besides the configuration of processing rules in lookup tables) are undertaken in the file:

**/etc/postfix/main.cf**

On a SUSE Linux Enterprise Server system, the most frequently needed parameters of this file can be modified by means of the files

**/etc/sysconfig/mail**

and

**/etc/sysconfig/postfix**

For the MTA (no matter whether you use Sendmail or Postfix) to operate correctly, two settings must be made in the file /etc/sysconfig/mail:

- The Fully Qualified Domain Name (FQDN) must be entered in the variable **FROM_HEADER**.

- The variable **SMTPD_LISTEN_REMOTE** should be set to Yes, as otherwise only e-mail from the local host will be accepted.

By means of the /sbin/SuSEconfig script, both settings and the entries in the file /etc/sysconfig/postfix are translated into suitable parameters in the file /etc/postfix/main.cf.

## Lookup Tables

Lookup tables contain rules for processing e-mails within the overall Postfix system.

These tables are activated via variables in the file **/etc/postfix/main.cf** and then defined in **/etc/postfix/*lookup-table*.**

After a lookup table has been defined, it needs to be converted to the required format (usually in the form of a hash table) using the **postmap** command.

For example, for the table sender_canonical this is done by entering the command:

```
postmap hash:/etc/Postfix/sender_canonical
```

The structure of lookup tables is subject to the following general rules.

- Blank lines or lines that begin with a # are not interpreted as command lines.
- Lines that begin with a space are regarded as a continuation of the previous line.

A manual page exists for every lookup table: **man 5 *lookup-table*.**

The following lookup tables are described:

- The access Lookup Table
- The canonical Lookup Table
- The recipient_canonical Lookup Table
- The sender_canonical Lookup Table
- The relocated Lookup Table
- The transport Lookup Table
- The virtual Lookup Table
- The aliases Lookup Table

**The access Lookup Table**    The /etc/postfix/access lookup table can be used to reject or allow e-mails from defined senders. The smtpd daemon evaluates this table when e-mails arrive.

**The canonical Lookup Table**    The lookup table /etc/postfix/canonical can be used to rewrite sender and recipient addresses of incoming and outgoing e-mails.

Both the header and the envelope are rewritten. The cleanup daemon reads this table when an e-mail arrives.

**The recipient_canonical Lookup Table**    The /etc/postfix/recipient_canonical lookup table can be used to convert recipient addresses of incoming and outgoing e-mails.

The cleanup daemon evaluates this table when an e-mail arrives before the generic lookup table /etc/postfix/canonical is evaluated.

11

**The sender_canonical Lookup Table**   The /etc/postfix/sender_canonical lookup table can be used to rewrite sender addresses of incoming and outgoing e-mails (for example, for outgoing e-mails: *login@mycompany*.com to *firstname.surname@*digitalairlines.com).

The cleanup daemon reads this table when an e-mail arrives before the generic lookup table /etc/postfix/canonical is read.

**The relocated Lookup Table**   If the server receives an e-mail for an address that is not used anymore, you can configure the /etc/postfix/relocated lookup table to inform the sender.

**The transport Lookup Table**   The /etc/postfix/transport lookup table can be used to define e-mail routing for special e-mail address ranges.

**The virtual Lookup Table**   The /etc/postfix/virtual lookup table can be used to set up e-mails for a number of domains with separate user names.

**The aliases Lookup Table**   The /etc/aliases lookup table can be used to define e-mail aliases for delivering e-mails.

## Postfix Tools

Postfix also has a whole range of other useful administration tools that can make life considerably easier for a postmaster when it comes to analyzing problems.

This section briefly introduces the administration tools for Postfix.

- **newaliases.** Converts the ASCII file /etc/aliases to the hash table /etc/aliases.db.

- **mailq.** Lists all e-mails in the mail queues that have not yet been sent.

- **postalias.** See newaliases.

- **postcat.** Displays the contents of a file from the queue directories in a readable form.

- **postconf.** Without any parameter, this tool displays the values of all variables defined in the file /etc/postfix/main.cf, as well as the default values of all other variables used by postfix that are not modified in /etc/postfix/main.cf.

  Enter **postconf -e** *key=value* to modify variables directly.

  These changes are automatically integrated into the file main.cf.

- **postdrop.** This is run automatically via the command sendmail, if sendmail cannot, because of missing world-writeable permissions, write any files to the maildrop directory, and saves those e-mails as **sgid maildrop**.

- **postfix.** Helps to find configuration errors (postfix check), forces e-mails from the deferred queue to be delivered immediately (postfix flush), or rereads the Postfix configuration files (postfix reload).

- **postmap.** Generates the hash tables for the lookup tables in the directory /etc/postfix/.

- **postsuper.** Checks the file structure in the queue directories and removes unneeded files and directories (**postsuper –s**) or deletes files and directories that have been left after a system crash and are useless (**postsuper –p**).

  Individual e-mail messages can be removed from the mail queues with **postsuper –d *ID***.

  In general, postsuper removes all files that are not normal files or directories (such as symbolic links).

  We recommend that you run the command **postsuper –s** immediately before starting the Postfix system.

**NOTE**

For more information about these tools, see the manual page **man 1 Postfix-Tool**.

11

# Sendmail

The best known MTA (Mail Transport Agent) is Eric Allman's Sendmail.

Sendmail has the reputation of being one of the most complex, if not *the* most complex, programs to administer.

It is therefore no surprise that there are only a handful of experts in the world who understand how to configure all of its options and features.

To understand Sendmail, you need to know the following:

- Installation and Start
- Further Useful Programs for Sendmail
- Configuration Files for Sendmail

## Installation and Start

In SUSE Linux Enterprise Server, Sendmail is installed using YaST.

To do this, select the **sendmail** package and confirm that the installation should proceed.

To start Sendmail automatically the next time the system is booted, enter:

```
da10:~ # insserv /etc/init.d/sendmail
```

In addition, the FQDN should be entered in the file /etc/sysconfig/mail in the line **FROM_HEADER**.

To start Sendmail manually in SUSE Linux, enter:

```
da10:~ # rcsendmail start
```

To stop the Sendmail server, enter:

```
da10:~ # rcsendmail stop
```

As with Postfix, all activities of Sendmail are logged in the file **/var/log/mail**.

## Further Useful Programs for Sendmail

Useful programs for Sendmail are the following:

- **mailq.** Reports the contents of the e-mails waiting in the mail queue to be delivered.
- **newaliases.** Produces a hash table for the /etc/aliases file.
- **mailstats.** Produces statistics on e-mails received and delivered.
- **makemap.** Produces hash tables important for Sendmail, such as the one for the access table.

## Configuration Files for Sendmail

Sendmail's main configuration file is **/etc/sendmail.cf**.

This file configures almost every aspect of Sendmail's behavior.

The file comprises behavior rules, arranged into classes.

For example, the local host name is defined by the **Cw** macro in the **C** class.

The macro **Cwlocalhost da10.digitalairlines.com** defines Sendmail's host name as da10.

The /etc/sendmail.cf file contains further macro definitions and also ruleset definitions.

Rulesets provide the means to modify e-mails in Sendmail while they are being processed before delivery (such as changes to the header or checking for spam addresses.).

The following is an example for defining rulesets:

```
# check sender address: user@address, user@, address
R<$+> $+ < @ $* > $: @<$1> <$2 < @ $3 >> $| <F:$2@$3> <U:$2@> <H:$3>
R<$+> $+ $: @<$1> <$2> $| <U:$2@>
R@ <$+> <$*> $| <$+> $: <@> <$1> <$2> $| $>SearchList <+From> $| <$3>
R<@> <$+> <$*> $| <$*> $: <$3> <$1> <$2> reverse result
```

This ruleset defines how incomplete addresses in the mail header should be processed.

Fortunately, there are a few other configuration files that, unlike /etc/sendmail.cf, are relatively easy to understand and configure, such as the files found in the /etc/mail/ directory since Sendmail version 8.9.

In practice, these files almost always meet all the configuration needs and enable a simple but adequate configuration of Sendmail.

The following files contain the most important Sendmail configuration options:

- **/etc/mail/access.** Definition of hosts, domains, and networks whose mails can be delivered, forwarded, or rejected.
- **/etc/mail/genericstable.** Definitions of sender addresses.
- **/etc/mail/virtusertable.** Definitions of recipient addresses.
- **/etc/mail/mailertable.** Routing table for outgoing mail.
- **/etc/aliases.** E-mail alias addresses.

These files are readable with a text editor, but they need to be converted to a hash table so Sendmail can also understand them.

The hash tables are located in the same directory as the configuration files and have the same names, but with the ending **.db**.

The procedure for converting a single configuration file to a hash table is always described at the end in the following sections.

In SUSE Linux Enterprise Server, all of these configuration files can also be converted to the corresponding hash table by entering:

```
da10:~ # SuSEconfig --module sendmail
```

or

```
da10:~ # /sbin/conf.d/SuSEconfig.sendmail
```

The following topics are described below:

- General MTA Settings
- The /etc/mail/access Configuration File
- The /etc/mail/genericstable Configuration File
- The /etc/mail/virtusertable Configuration File
- The /etc/mail/mailertable Configuration File
- The /etc/aliases Configuration File
- The /etc/sysconfig/sendmail Configuration File

**General MTA Settings**  In the file /etc/sysconfig/mail, two settings must be performed for the MTA (no matter whether Sendmail or Postfix) to function correctly.

- The FQDN should be entered in the variable **FROM_HEADER**.
- The variable **SMTPD_LISTEN_REMOTE** should be set to Yes, otherwise, only e-mails from the local host will be accepted.

**The /etc/mail/access Configuration File**   /etc/mail/access defines the hosts, networks, and domains that are relayed via this server.

Each line of the file contains a rule for the forwarding of e-mails.

The first column contains an e-mail address, a domain name, or a network address.

The second column is separated from the first by a tab and contains a keyword or an SMTP reply code that defines the action for this line.

If an SMTP reply code is used, an extra optional message text can be given that will be sent to the e-mail sender when this rule is activated.

The e-mail address, domain name, or network address, in conjunction with one of the following keywords or an SMTP code, defines the action for all e-mails that match the entry in the first column:

- **OK.** Mails are accepted, even if a reject rule exists.
- **REJECT.** Mails are rejected. The sender receives an error message.
- **RELAY.** Mails are forwarded if no other reject rules exist.
- **DISCARD.** Mails are discarded. The sender is not informed.
- **ERROR:"*Reply-Code text-message*".** The defined text is sent back to the sender of an e-mail if a specific reply code occurs.

The configuration file /etc/mail/access needs to be converted to a hash table, which can then be evaluated by the mail server.

To convert the file to the hash table, enter (as the user root):

```
da10:/ # makemap hash -f /etc/mail/access.db < /etc/mail/access
```

**The /etc/mail/genericstable Configuration File**   /etc/mail/genericstable modifies the sender address for outgoing e-mail.

This is most commonly needed at a mail gateway between a local network and the Internet, where the local e-mail addresses are not the same as the official Internet e-mail addresses.

Each line of the file contains a rule for an e-mail address. The value in the first column defines the original sender address and the value in the second column is the address that is supposed to appear on outgoing mails. The two columns are separated by tabs.

After changing the /etc/mail/genericstable file, enter:

```
da10:/ # makemap hash -f /etc/mail/genericstable.db < /etc/mail/genericstable
```

to create the required hash table.

**The /etc/mail/virtusertable Configuration File**   /etc/mail/virtusertable allows the recipient address to be changed for incoming mails.

Each line of this file contains a conversion rule for an e-mail recipient address.

The first column contains a complete e-mail address (user@domain) or just the recipient domain. The second column contains the value that should replace the corresponding recipient address.

/etc/mail/virtusertable enables Sendmail to host the same e-mail addresses for different domains in that it readdresses e-mails to different local or remote e-mail addresses.

After changing /etc/mail/virtusertable, enter:

```
da10:/ # makemap hash -f /etc/mail/virtusertable.db < /etc/mail/virtuserstable
```

to translate it to the hash table.

**The /etc/mail/mailertable Configuration File**     /etc/mail/mailertable defines the routing for outgoing mails. Each line contains the definition of a route for an address range.

The first column contains a target host or a target domain.

All e-mails that fall within this range are sent via the route defined in the second column.

The routing can be defined UUCP, SMTP, or local delivery.

The columns are separated by tabs.

After changing /etc/mail/mailertable, enter:

```
da10:/ # makemap hash -f /etc/mail/mailertable.db < /etc/mail/mailertable
```

to convert to the necessary hash table.

**The /etc/aliases Configuration File**     The file /etc/aliases (the alias database) allows the definition of e-mail aliases.

It is a plain-text file that defines a new e-mail address with each line.

This e-mail alias can be totally fictitious, but must point to a real existing e-mail address or at least another already known e-mail alias.

The file is constructed in two columns:

- The first column contains the new e-mail alias, followed by a colon (such as maillist:).
- The second column is separated from the first by one or more tabs and contains a list, separated by commas, of real e-mail recipient addresses on which the new alias is based.

You can edit /etc/aliases in a text editor. To translate it into the required hash table, run the command newaliases as the user root.

11

**The /etc/sysconfig/sendmail Configuration File**    The file /etc/sysconfig/sendmail in SUSE Linux Enterprise Server offers additional parameters. Each parameter is described with a comment.

After changing parameters, you must run SuSEconfig to translate the entries in /etc/sysconfig/sendmail to entries in the appropriate configuration files used by sendmail.

# Procmail

Procmail is currently the most widely used MDA (Mail Delivery Agent) under Linux.

Procmail is installed in a standard SUSE Linux Enterprise Server installation. Sendmail and Postfix integrate Procmail as an MDA.

Procmail is a highly flexible MDA. It is capable of sorting e-mails into mailboxes, forwarding them to other recipients, or deleting them according to almost any arbitrary criteria a user specifies.

In particular, Procmail is extremely good at sorting large quantities of mail and automatically disposing of unwanted e-mail (spam).

The following topics are described below:

- Installation
- Configuration

## Installation

Procmail (package procmail) is automatically installed during the installation of Sendmail or Postfix.

## Configuration

If Postfix is used as the MTA, the following entry is required in /etc/postfix/main.cf:

```
mailbox_command = /usr/bin/procmail
```

Postfix then passes received e-mail to Procmail for local delivery.

If Sendmail is used, the configuration does not need to be modified, because Sendmail is already preconfigured for the use of Procmail.

If, however, Procmail should be used as the MDA for an MTA other than Sendmail, you have two options:

- The configuration of the MTA must be changed so it accepts Procmail as the local MDA.

    The configuration depends on the MTA.

- In general, all common MTAs use the ~/.forward file on receipt of a mail for local delivery.

Every e-mail is passed to Procmail if the following entry is made to the following file

```
|exec /usr/bin/procmail
```

It is not necessary to take any further configuration steps to get Procmail to deliver e-mail to the mailbox of the respective user.

Further information about all possible Procmail options is in the manual pages (**man 1 procmail** and **man 1 procmailrc**).

The following topics are described below:

- Filter and Distribute Incoming E-mail
- An Example File for Procmail

**Filter and Distribute Incoming E-mail**    The most interesting aspect of using Procmail is the prefiltering and distributing of e-mail based on the information in the mail header or the e-mail body.

This is Procmail's great strength—it offers more filtering options than any other MDA.

It is possible to set up separate filters for each mail recipient. Each e-mail recipient can place a ~/.procmailrc file in her home directory and install her own desired settings.

Where these configuration files do not yet exist or contain no commands for Procmail, all mail is delivered to the /var/spool/mail/*username* mailbox.

**CAUTION**

If incoming e-mails should be distributed by Procmail to several different mailboxes, the directories containing the mailboxes must exist.

**An Example File for Procmail**    A typical configuration file for Procmail is similar to the following:

```
PATH=/bin:/usr/bin
MAILDIR=$HOME/Mail
LOGFILE=$MAILDIR/mail.log
:0
* ^From.*novell
$MAILDIR/Novell
:0
*
$MAILDIR/Inbox
```

This configuration file causes Procmail to respond to e-mail as follows:

- The $PATH environment variable is set to **/bin:/usr/bin**.
- The $MAILDIR environment variable is set to **$HOME/Mail**.

Procmail interprets any further entries with a relative path in the configuration file relative to this directory.

- The $LOGFILE environment variable is set to **$MAILDIR/mail.log.**

This is where log information is placed.

- The next three lines build a rule comprising of a key, a filter, and an action.

  a. The line containing **:0** (the key) specifies that data from the e-mail header will be compared with the filter expression in the following line.

  When a match is found, the e-mail will be processed in accordance with the last line.

  Procmail will not process the mail further, even when it matches further rules.

  b. The line **\* ^From.\*novell** now compares all lines in the e-mail header with the given regular expression **^From.\*novell**. The comparison here is not case sensitive.

  All e-mails that contain **novell** in the From line match this filter.

  c. The line containing **$MAILDIR/Novell** instructs Procmail to place the corresponding e-mails in this mail folder.

- The last three lines build a further rule just like the first one.

All e-mails that pass through this last rule are in turn checked by the filter expression **\***.

Since no filter is given here, the rule matches all remaining e-mails and these are placed in the corresponding mail folder, in accordance with the last line (**$MAILDIR/Inbox**).

**NOTE**

For more information about the ~/.procmailrc configuration file, see the manual page (**man 5 procmailrc**).

There is also a good collection of useful configuration examples in the manual page of ~/.procmailrc examples (**man 5 procmailex**).

## Mail Clients

To work with mail clients, you need to know the following:

- Read Status Mail
- Use the Simple Mail Client
- Further Mail Clients

## Read Status Mail

Some programs send status mail messages or notes to the user root. If you log in at a virtual terminal, you get a notification if there are mail messages for you, as shown in the following:

```
da10 login: root
Password:
You have new mail in /var/mail/root.
Last login: FRI Jul 18 13:23:51 from 10.0.0.6
da10:~ #
```

To read these messages, use the command **mail,** as shown in the following:

```
da10:~ # mail
mailx version nail 10.6 11/15/03. Type ? for help.
"/var/mail/root": 3 messages 3 new
>N 1 root@da1  Wed Jul 9 15:02 28/894   SuSEconfig: xntp.caveats
 N 2 root@da1  Wed Jul 9 15:02 43/1836  SuSEconfig: SuSEfirewall2
 N 3 root@da1  Wed Jul 9 15:02 151/5888 SuSEconfig: openssh-chang
?
```

The prompt for mail is a ?.

At the prompt, use the commands listed in Table 11-2.

**Table 11-2**

| Command | Purpose |
|---|---|
| t *message_list* | Type messages. |
| n | Go to and type the next message. |
| e *message_list* | Edit messages. |
| f *message_list* | Give headlines of messages. |
| d *message_list* | Delete messages. |
| u *message_list* | Undelete messages. |
| R *message_list* | Reply to message senders. |
| r *message_list* | Reply to message senders and all recipients. |
| m *user_list* | Send mail to specific users. |
| q | Quit and save unresolved messages in mbox. |
| x | Quit and do not remove system mailbox. |

A *message_list* consists of integers, ranges of integers, or user names separated by spaces. If omitted, mail uses the last message typed.

A *user_list* consists of user names or aliases separated by spaces. Aliases are defined in .mailrc in your home directory.

## Use the Simple Mail Client

You can use the program mail as a normal mail client on the command line.

11

The simplest form of using mail is:

**mail** *mail_address*

Instead of *mail_address* you can enter a username of someone on your local machine. (For sending messages to other users than the local users you need to configure a mail server on your local host.)

mail first asks you for the subject of the mail and after this you can enter the body of your message.

To finish the text, enter a single full stop in the last line, as shown in the following:

```
tux@da10:~ > mail root
Subject: A simple Mail
This is just a test mail.
The body of the text ends with an single full stop.
.
```

mail confirms the end of the text body with EOT (end of text) and sends the mail immediately.

Table 11-3 lists the most important options of mail.

**Table 11-3**

| Option | Description |
|---|---|
| -a *file* | Attach the given *file* to the message. |
| -b *list* | Send blind carbon copies to *list*. List should be a comma-separated list of names. |
| -c *list* | Send carbon copies to *list* of users. |
| -q *file* | Start the message with the contents of the specified *file*. Can be given in send mode only. |
| -s *subject* | Specify *subject* on command line (only the first argument after the -s flag is used as a subject; be careful to quote subjects containing spaces). |
| -R *address* | Specify reply-to *address* on command line. Only the first argument after the -R flag is used as the address. |
| -F | Read e-mails that are stored in the file ~/mbox. With -F mail opens this file to read these old e-mail messages. |

# Exercise 11-2   Send Mail to root

Sometimes a very simple mail client is all you need. The purpose of this exercise is to introduce you to the program mail for this purpose.

To send mail to root, do the following:

1. Open a terminal window.

2. Enter **mail root**.

3. Enter the subject **My first e-mail with mail**.

4. Enter the following three lines of text (press **Enter** after each line):

   **I have just installed SLES 9**

   **on my computer and I'm ready**

   **for administration training.**

5. To finish, enter a single dot in a new line and press **Enter**.

6. Su to root by entering **su –**; then enter a password of **novell**.

7. Enter **mail**.

   In the last line of the list you should find the mail message you just sent to root.

8. To read the message, enter the *number* in the second column of the table.

9. Delete the message by entering **d** and the *number* of the message (such as **d 4**).

10. Quit mail by entering **q**.

11. Verify that the message was deleted by entering **mail**; then exit mail by entering **q**.

12. Log out as root by entering **exit**.

13. Close the terminal window.

## Further Mail Clients

There are more intuitive mail clients than **mail** available for Linux.

Generally you can distinguish between

- Graphical mail clients
- Text-based mail clients for the console

**11**

The most common graphical mail clients for Linux are

- Novell Evolution, shown in Figure 11-17.

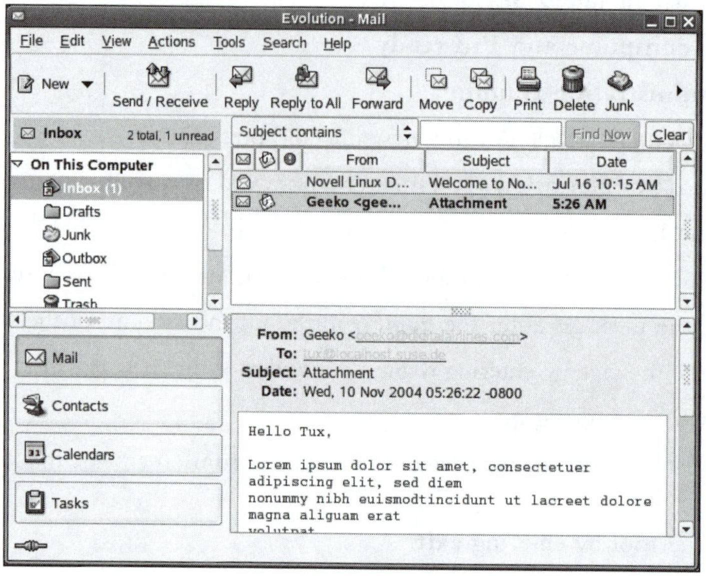

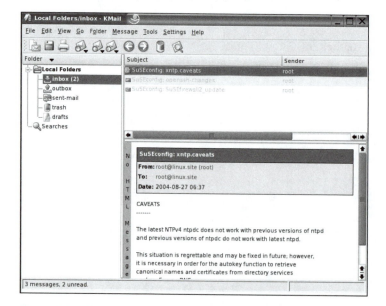

**Figure 11-17**

- KMail, shown in Figure 11-18.

**Figure 11-18**

- Mozilla Thunderbird, shown in Figure 11-19.

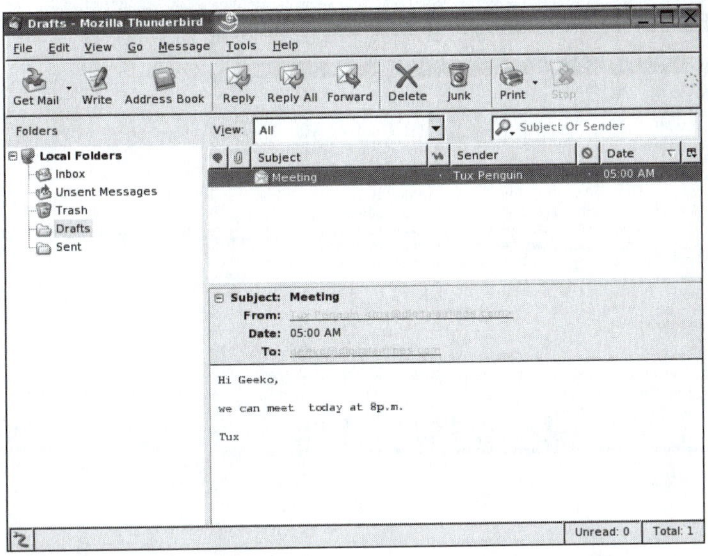

**Figure 11-19**

Mail clients for the console are not less powerful than graphical clients. The most important console clients are:

- Mutt, shown in Figure 11-20.

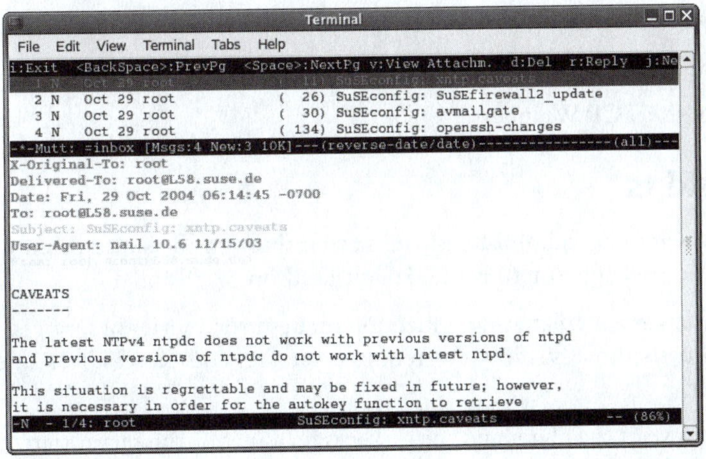

**Figure 11-20**

- Pine, shown in Figure 11-21.

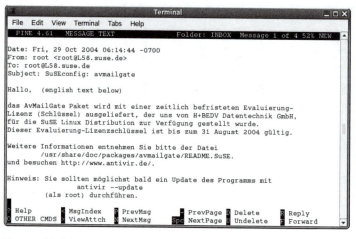

**Figure 11-21**

## OBJECTIVE 3    ENABLE THE EXTENDED INTERNET DAEMON (XINETD)

In this objective you learn how to enable the extended Internet daemon (xinetd) by reviewing the following:

- What inetd/xinetd Is
- Configure xinetd with YaST
- Manage xinetd Manually
- Enable the Internet Daemon (inetd)
- Configure the TCP Wrapper

### What inetd/xinetd *Is*

Many services on a server are administered and started through the super daemon package inetd, or xinetd. The package xinetd is the default used on SLES 9.

The super daemon acts as a mediator of connection requests for a series of services. It accepts the connection requests directly, starts the required service, and passes the request to the newly started server.

If the connection between the client and the server is terminated, the server started by inetd is removed from memory.

Starting services through inetd has both advantages and disadvantages. The most significant advantage is saving resources (especially memory), since a server is only started when it is needed. A disadvantage, however, is that a delay occurs while the required service is loaded, started, and connected.

As a rule, you only want to use inetd for services that are occasionally (not permanently) needed on the server. Some of the services run traditionally by inetd include Telnet and FTP.

## Configure xinetd with YaST

To configure the services mediated by xinetd, you can use the YaST Network Services (inetd) module.

Do the following:

1. From the KDE desktop, start the YaST Network Services (inetd) module by doing one of the following:

   ■ Select the **YaST** icon, enter the root password *novell*, and select **OK**; then select **Network Services > Network Services (inetd)**.

   *or*

   ■ Open a terminal window and enter **sux –** and the root password *novell*; then enter **yast2 inetd**.

**11**

The dialog box shown in Figure 11-22 appears.

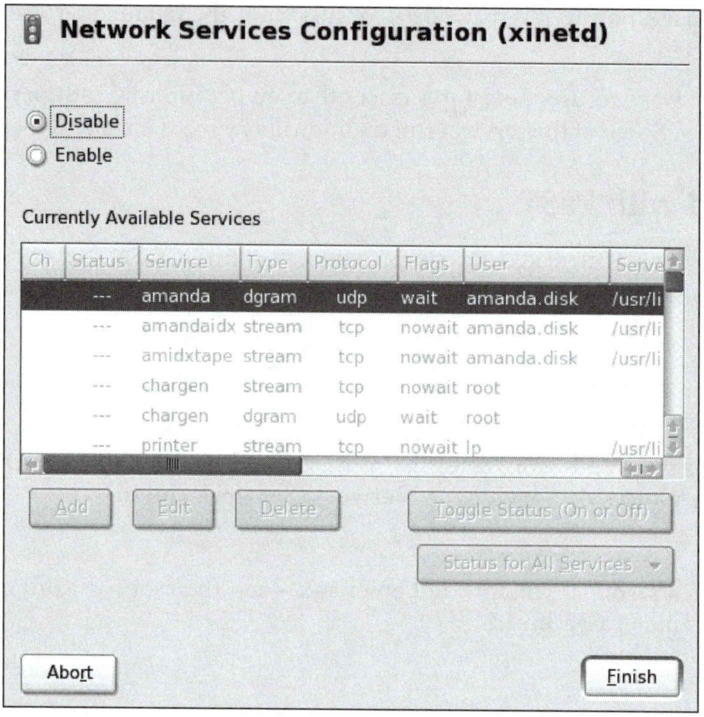

**Network Services Configuration (xinetd)**

- ◉ Di̲sable
- ○ Enab̲le

Currently Available Services

| Ch | Status | Service | Type | Protocol | Flags | User | Serve |
|----|--------|---------|------|----------|-------|------|-------|
| --- | | amanda | dgram | udp | wait | amanda.disk | /usr/li |
| --- | | amandaidx | stream | tcp | nowait | amanda.disk | /usr/li |
| --- | | amidxtape | stream | tcp | nowait | amanda.disk | /usr/li |
| --- | | chargen | stream | tcp | nowait | root | |
| --- | | chargen | dgram | udp | wait | root | |
| --- | | printer | stream | tcp | nowait | lp | /usr/li |

[ Add ]  [ Edit ]  [ Delete ]    [ Toggle Status (On or Off) ]

[ Status for All Services ▼ ]

[ Abo̲rt ]                                    [ F̲inish ]

**Figure 11-22**

2. Enable the inetd super daemon by selecting **Enable**.

   This enables inetd or xinetd, depending on what you have installed (the default for SLES 9 is xinetd).

   The Currently Available Services list is activated. You can add, edit, or delete services in the list.

**NOTE**

To manage the services available through inetd (except for enabling services such as Telnet or FTP) requires a skill set beyond the objectives of this course. This is especially true of configuring services with **Edit**.

   Notice that some services are off (---), while others are not installed (NI) and cannot be configured.

3. Configure a service to be administered by inetd by selecting the service; then select **Toggle Status (On or Off)**.

The word On appears in the Status column. An X appears in the Changed (Ch) column to indicate that the service has been edited and will be changed in the system configuration.

4. (Optional) Change the status of all installed services to On or Off by selecting:

   **Status for All Services > Activate All Services**

   *or*

   **Status for All Services > Deactivate All Services**

5. When you finish configuring the services, save the configuration setting and start the inetd (or xinetd) daemon by selecting **Finish**.

6. (Optional) If you started YaST from the desktop, close the **YaST Control Center**.

## Manage xinetd Manually

To manage xinetd manually, you need to know how to do the following:

- Start, Stop, and Restart xinetd
- Configure xinetd
- Configure Access Control
- Configure Log Files

### Start, Stop, and Restart xinetd

**rcxinetd** is a link to the script (/etc/init.d/xinetd) that starts xinetd. To provide services through xinetd, you need to install and start the daemon on your SUSE Linux Enterprise Server.

To have the daemon automatically activated at boot, enter **insserv xinetd**. You can find out whether the daemon is activated or not by entering **rcxinetd status**. You can also start and stop the daemon by entering **rcxinetd start** or **rcxinetd stop**. A restart of xinetd is achieved with **rcxinetd restart**.

### Configure xinetd

To configure xinetd, you need to know the following:

- Edit the File xinetd.conf
- The Directory /etc/xinetd.d/
- Internal Services

**Edit the File xinetd.conf**   You can configure xinetd manually by editing the configuration file /etc/xinetd.conf. With more than two dozen keywords recognized by /etc/xinetd.conf, it can be difficult to modify the file (despite the good documentation).

The following is the syntax of /etc/xinetd.conf for the default configuration parameters of xinetd:

```
defaults
      {
            key operator parameter parameter. . .
      }
```

The following is the syntax for configuring each network service in the file:

```
service service_name
      {
            key operator parameter parameter. . .
      }
```

Operators include **=**, **-=**, and **+=**. Most attributes (keys) only support the operator **=**, but you can include additional values to some attributes by entering **+=** or remove them by entering **-=**.

The first entry in the configuration file is optional and sets default configuration values such as the following:

```
defaults
{
            log_type          = FILE /var/log/xinetd.log
            log_on_success    = HOST EXIT DURATION
            log_on_failure    = HOST ATTEMPT
#            only_from         = localhost
            instances         = 30
            cps               = 50 10
```

The configurations for log_type and instances will be overwritten if something else has been defined in the individual service entries. For all other attributes, the default configurations are combined with the values set in the services.

The **log_type** statement can define whether the output is written directly to a log file (/var/log/xinetd.log in the example) or forwarded to the daemon syslog (such as **log_type = SYSLOG authpriv**).

If there are high security demands, you might want to consider leaving logging up to the syslog daemon in order to prevent potential unwanted access to the xinetd log file.

The keywords **log_on_success** and **log_on_failure** configure what should be recorded in the log file, depending on whether the network service runs successfully or fails.

The value for **instances** can be used to limit the maximum possible number of daemons for each service, which protects the computer from either intentional or accidental overload due to too many simultaneous connections (denial of service attempts).

**cps** stands for connections per second. The first value (50) sets the maximum number of connections per second that can be handled. The second value (10) is the wait period before accepting new connections after the maximum has been exceed, which is helpful in preventing denial of service attacks.

All other entries look similar to the default entry but only contain the configuration for the respective network service, such as the following example for finger:

```
# default: off
# description: The finger server answers finger requests. Finger is \
#       a protocol that allows remote users to see information such \
#       as login name and login time for currently logged in users.
service finger
{
        socket_type     = stream
        protocol        = tcp
        wait            = no
        user            = nobody
        server          = /usr/sbin/in.fingerd
        server_args     = -w
#        disable        = yes
}
```

Table 11-4 describes the keywords in the example.

**Table 11-4**

| Keyword | Description |
|---|---|
| socket_type | Refers to the type of socket (stream, dgram, raw, or seqpacket). |
| protocol | Refers to the protocol (usually tcp or udp) used by the corresponding network service. The protocol must be entered in the file /etc/protocols. |
| wait | Specifies whether xinetd must wait for the daemon to release the port before it can process further connection requests for the same port (Yes: single-threaded; No: multithreaded). |
| user | Indicates under which user ID the daemon will start. The user name must be listed in the file /etc/passwd. |
| server | Specifies the absolute path name of the daemon to start. |
| server_args | Specifies which parameters to pass to the daemon when it starts. |

**NOTE**

For a description of all possible parameters, enter **man xinetd.conf**.

11

**The Directory /etc/xinetd.d/**    Besides the configuration of services in the file /etc/ xinetd.conf, you can create a separate configuration file for every service in the directory **/etc/xinetd.d/**.

The directive **includedir /etc/xinetd.d** in the file /etc/xinetd.conf prompts xinetd to interpret all files in the directory /etc/xinetd.d/ for the configuration of the services. The same attributes and the same syntax can be used as in xinetd.conf.

The main advantage of splitting the configuration into several files is improved transparency.

**Internal Services**    The daemon xinetd contains internal services (such as echo, time, daytime, chargen, and discard) that can be labeled in the configuration as follows:

```
type = INTERNAL
```

Otherwise, xinetd assumes that external services are involved. With services such as echo, which are both TCP and UDP-based services, you not only have to specify the respective socket_type, but you also need to identify the service in the id field in such a way that it is properly distinguished from other services.

The following is an example for echo:

```
# /etc/xinet.d/echo
# default: off
# description: An echo server. This is the tcp version.

service echo
{
        type                = INTERNAL
        id                  = echo-stream
        socket_type         = stream
        protocol            = tcp
        user                = root
        wait                = no
        disable             = yes
}
# /etc/xinet.d/echo-udp
# default: off
# description: An echo server. This is the udp version.
service echo
{
        type                = INTERNAL UNLISTED
        id                  = echo-dgram
        socket_type         = dgram
        protocol            = udp
        user                = root
        wait                = yes
        disable             = yes
        port                = 7
}
```

Table 11-5 lists signals for checking xinetd.

**Table 11-5**

| Signal | Number | Description |
|---|---|---|
| SIGUSR1 | 10 | Causes an internal state dump (the default dump file is /var/run/xinetd.dump) |
| SIGQUIT | 3 | Causes xinetd termination |
| SIGTERM | 15 | Terminates all running services before terminating xinetd |
| SIGHUP | 1 | xinetd re-reads the configuration file and terminates the servers for services that are no longer available |
| SIGIO | 29 | Causes an internal consistency check to verify that the data structures used by the program have not been corrupted |

## Configure Access Control

The daemon xinetd recognizes the following four parameters used to control access monitoring:

- **only_from.** With this parameter, you define which hosts can use which service. You can specify complete IP addresses from hosts or networks or just the network or host names.

  You can define this parameter in the defaults section or in the service section.

- **no_access.** With this parameter, you define which hosts can be excluded from access. You can specify complete IP addresses from hosts or networks or just the network or host names.

  You can define this parameter in the defaults section or in the service section.

- **access_time.** You can use this parameter to define at which times the service is available (in 24-hour format).

  You can define this parameter in the defaults section or in the service section.

- **disabled.** You can use this parameter to completely shut off a server, even if there is a service entry for it in the configuration file. This also applies to logging access attempts.

  This parameter can only be used in the defaults section.

The following is an example for the Telnet service:

```
# default: off
# description: Telnet is the old login server which is INSECURE and should
#   therefore not be used. Use secure shell (openssh).
#   If you need telnetd not to "keep-alives" (e.g. if it runs over a ISDN \
#   uplink), add "-n".  See 'man telnetd' for more details.
```

**11**

```
service telnet
{
        socket_type     = stream
        protocol        = tcp
        wait            = no
        user            = root
        server          = /usr/sbin/in.telnetd
        server_args     = -n
        only-from       = 10.0.0.3  10.0.0.7  10.0.0.9
        only-from      += 10.0.0.10 10.0.0.12
        no_access       = 10.0.1.0
        flags           = IDONLY
        access_times    = 07:00-21:00
#          disable = yes
}
```

These settings result in the following:

- Access is permitted for machines with the following IP addresses:

  10.0.0.3

  10.0.0.7

  10.0.0.9

  10.0.0.10,

  10.0.0.12

- Access is denied to the network with the IP address 10.0.1.0.

- The service is available from 7:00 A.M. to 9:00 P.M.

The following is an example for the parameter disabled:

```
disabled = finger
```

With this setting, the service finger is switched off completely. If a computer tries to access the service, the attempt is not even logged.

If you place high demands on access monitoring, you can tighten the security level even more by using the parameters INTERCEPT and IDONLY in the flags entry.

If the parameter USERID was set in the log_on_access and log_on_failure entries, IDONLY then makes sure that a connection to the network service is permitted only when the user identification service (such as identd) of the host requesting the network service issues the user ID.

If the parameter INTERCEPT has been entered as well, xinetd also attempts to make sure that an authorized host is on the other end of already existing connections—that the connection has not been intercepted.

However, connection monitoring only functions if no multithreaded or no internal xinetd service is involved. In addition, it puts a heavy burden on the network connection and the performance of the network service.

### Configure Log Files

Almost every hacker has to make several attempts and needs some time before breaking in to a system. To protect your server, you not only need hacker-resistant software, but you need log files written by the software to detect unauthorized login attempts.

Because of this, it does not make sense to deter only unauthorized access attempts. To maintain optimal system security, you need to record failed and unauthorized connection attempts as well.

To shut off a service but still retain its logging functions, configure only_from without using any additional parameters (such as the following):

```
only_from       =
```

Logging through xinetd is controlled by the log_type statement along with the attributes log_on_success and log_on_failure.

These let you record from which host and for how long an access attempt was made, and which user was using the service (if the remote host supports this feature).

In addition, you can also log the circumstances of how and why the network service was used. However, even the best log does not mean much if you do not check it on a regular basis for failed connection attempts.

 For more information about xinetd, enter **man 8 xinetd**.

## Enable the Internet Daemon (inetd)

The **inetd** can be used as an alternative to xinetd to start Internet services.

In this objective you learn how to enable the internet daemon (inetd) by reviewing the following:

- Configure inetd
- Start, Stop, and Restart inetd

## Configure inetd

To configure inetd, you need to know the following:

- Edit the File inetd.conf
- Describe Internal Services

**Edit the File inetd.conf** You can configure inetd manually by editing the configuration file **/etc/inetd.conf**.

Empty lines and lines beginning with # are ignored.

Each line of this configuration file describes a service to be maintained and is put together as follows (see Table 11-6):

```
service_name socket_type protocol flags user server_path
arguments
```

**Table 11-6**

| Parameter | Description |
|---|---|
| service_name | A valid symbolic service name, corresponding to an entry from the file /etc/services or, for RPC based services, to an entry from the file /etc/rpc.<br><br>If you want a service to be accessible only over a specific IP address (not all interfaces), enter:<br><br>**IP:**service_name<br><br>e.g., **10.0.0.254:ftp** |
| socket_type | Describes the type of network socket; usually **stream** or **dgram**. Further possible entries are **raw**, **rdm**, or **seqpacket**. |
| protocol | A valid symbolic entry of the protocol used in the file /etc/protocols (usually tcp or udp).<br><br>For RPC services, rpc/tcp or rpc/udp is entered here. |
| flags | Valid entries are **wait** and **nowait**.<br><br>For TCP-based services, the value nowait is always used.<br><br>UDP-based services can be configured here with the value wait, if they are capable of processing all incoming datagrams via one socket (single-threaded server).<br><br>One option is to give a number (nowait.number), which defines the maximum number of connection requests that can be processed in one minute.<br><br>The default for this value is 40. |

Table 11-6   (continued)

| Parameter | Description |
|---|---|
| user | This entry should contain the name of the user with whose permission the service is run.<br><br>It is also possible to specify a group here (*user.group*). |
| server_path | This entry specifies the complete path and file name of the program that inetd starts when a connection request is made.<br><br>For a number of internal services of inetd (echo, discard, chargen, daytime, and time), the value *internal* must be entered. |
| arguments | The entry **arguments** contains all arguments (including the name of the server: argv[0]), which are passed to the server when it starts. |

NOTE

For more information about the syntax of the file /etc/inetd.conf, see the manual page (**man 8 inetd.conf**).

**11**

As an example, here is an extract from the file /etc/inetd.conf, containing typical entries:

```
...
# These are standard services.
#
# ftp stream tcp nowait root /usr/sbin/tcpd in.ftpd
ftp stream tcp nowait root /usr/sbin/tcpd vsftpd
...
# swat is the Samba Web Administration Tool
swat stream tcp nowait.400 root /usr/sbin/swat swat
...
```

- The ftp service awaits an existing connection (stream) via the TCP protocol.

  The service is started with permission of the user root and, after a request has been connected to the ftp service (vsftpd), inetd immediately waits for further requests (nowait).

  The ftp service in this case is called up via the TCP wrapper (/usr/sbin/tcpd).

- Calling up the swat service differs in only a few details from calling up the ftp service.

  Specifying nowait.400 guarantees that inetd starts a maximum of 400 instances of the service in the course of sixty seconds.

  The service itself is started with the path /usr/sbin/swat and with argv[0] as an argument for swat.

**Describe Internal Services** The inetd daemon comprises a number of internal services:

- echo
- discard
- chargen
- daytime
- time

All of these internal services are TCP-based and mainly serve diagnostic purposes. The functions of the internal services are described in Table 11-7.

**Table 11-7**

| Internal Service | Function |
|---|---|
| echo | Returns the transmitted character string (see RFC 862) |
| chargen | (character generator) Continuously generates character strings (see RFC 864) |
| discard | Discards all received data (see RFC 863) |
| daytime | Delivers the date in readable format (see RFC 867) |
| time | Delivers the time since January 1, 1900, in seconds (see RFC 868) |

To test an internal service, connect to the respective port using **telnet**:

```
da10:~ # telnet localhost chargen
```

## Start, Stop, and Restart inetd

**rcinetd** is a link to the script (/etc/init.d/inetd) that starts inetd.

To provide services through inetd, you need to install and start the daemon on your SUSE Linux Enterprise Server.

To have the daemon automatically activated at startup, enter:

**insserv inetd**

To find out whether the daemon is activated or not, enter:

**rcinetd status**

To start, stop, or restart the daemon, enter:

**rcinetd start**

or

**rcinetd stop**

or

**rcinetd restart**

## Configure the TCP Wrapper

Every computer connected to a network can be accessed from the network as long as the connection exists.

If the computer is not protected by software (such as a firewall), anyone on the Internet can attempt to use the network services on an unprotected computer without being noticed.

You can use the ***TCP wrapper*** to restrict access to individual network services.

For standalone services, TCP wrapper support must be compiled into the daemon, service, or application. For services started via inetd, TCP wrapper support is controlled by inetd.conf.

To configure TCP wrappers, you need to understand the following:

- The Role of the tcpd Daemon
- Configure Access Controls
- Check the TCP Wrapper

### The Role of the tcpd Daemon

The standard inetd does not let you regulate access to the services on your own computer. inetd uses a separate application, the TCP wrapper **/usr/sbin/tcpd**, to regulate that access.

The TCP wrapper acts as a filter, and is placed between inetd and the service daemons. Inetd starts the wrapper instead of directly starting the service.

The wrapper writes the name and address of the host requesting the connection to a log file, verifies that the request is permitted, then starts the corresponding daemon.

This is reflected in /etc/inetd.conf, which uses /usr/sbin/tcpd instead of the service daemon (such as /usr/sbin/vsftpd for FTP) to start the service.

The following is an example:

```
ftp      stream  tcp    nowait  root    /usr/sbin/tcpd  vsftpd
telnet   stream  tcp    nowait  root    /usr/sbin/tcpd  in.telnetd
finger   stream  tcp    nowait  nobody  /usr/sbin/tcpd  in.fingerd -w
```

Because the wrapper is not integrated with the client or with the server program, its existence cannot be perceived from the outside. This also guarantees that the wrapper can remain independent of the programs it is supposed to monitor.

When the connection between the client and the server program is established, the wrapper is deleted from memory and does not create any additional load for the current connection.

However, after an authorized server has started, it can accept additional connections on its own without consulting the wrapper about whether additional connections should take place.

For example, some UDP services remain in memory for a while after the connection has already been closed in order to receive additional connection requests.

You can recognize these UDP-based services in inetd.conf because they include the wait option.

## Configure Access Controls

You can configure access controls for the TCP wrapper by editing /etc/hosts.allow (to permit requests) and /etc/hosts.deny (to deny requests).

When receiving a request, tcpd first reads /etc/hosts.allow. If no matching pattern is found, then tcpd reads /etc/hosts.deny.

**CAUTION**
If you allow access in /etc/hosts.allow, it cannot be restricted again in /etc/hosts.deny.

If tcpd does not find a pattern that matches the request in either of the configuration files, the connection is permitted. The same is true if one or both configuration files are empty or do not exist.

The syntax of both configuration files is the same and consists of the following three fields:

*daemon*: *host* [: *option* : *option* ...]

- *daemon*. A list of services from /etc/inetd.conf.

- *host*. A list of host names or IP addresses separated by commas.

- *option*. A list of options.

In addition, tcpd recognizes the keywords ALL and EXCEPT for the first two fields and LOCAL, KNOWN, UNKNOWN, and PARANOID for the host field.

Table 11-8 provides a description of these keywords.

**Table 11-8**

| Keyword | Description |
|---------|-------------|
| **ALL** | All services and all hosts from which exceptions can be defined by EXCEPT |
| **LOCAL** | All host names that do not have a dot in the name; usually all the host names defined in /etc/hosts |
| **UNKNOWN** | All hosts whose names tcpd cannot distinguish |
| **KNOWN** | All hosts in which the host name matches the given IP address and vice versa |
| **PARANOID** | All hosts in which the host name does not match the given IP address and vice versa |

The following examples show configurations for hosts.allow and hosts.deny that permit the use of all network services in the local network but deny external computers access to telnet, finger, and FTP:

- **/etc/hosts.allow:**
  ```
  ALL: LOCAL
  ```

- **/etc/hosts.deny:**
  ```
  in.telnetd, in.fingerd, vsftpd: ALL
  ```

The following is an example of a more complex configuration:

- **/etc/hosts.allow:**
  ```
  ALL: da10.digitalairlines.com
  ALL EXCEPT vsftpd: da20.digitalairlines.com
  vsftpd: da30.digitalairlines.com
  ```

- **/etc/hosts.deny:**
  ```
  ALL: ALL
  ```

The first line in /etc/hosts.allow ensures that all network services can be accessed from da10.digitalairlines.com. In the second line, all network services other than FTP are made available for da20.digitalairlines.com.

The third line ensures that only FTP transfers are possible from the host da30.digitalairlines.com.

In /etc/hosts.deny, all other hosts are denied all services. "All services" also includes services that are not started via inetd, but run as independent services, and whose access control is also implemented via the files /etc/hosts.allow and /etc/hosts.deny.

Since this might apply to the portmapper, NFS would also be affected by the above configuration—a possibly unwanted effect, which, if you do not take it into consideration, could lead to a long search for the cause of errors.

Table 11-9 lists some of the more commonly used keywords for monitoring access.

**Table 11-9**

| Keyword | Description |
|---------|-------------|
| **ALLOW** and **DENY** | You can use these keywords to summarize all the access rules in the file /etc/hosts.allow. These options either allow or refuse access. |
| **spawn** | This executes the given shell script after the placeholders shown in Table are replaced. |
| **twist** | The given command is started instead of the running process. Existing placeholders are replaced first. |

**Table 11-9**   (continued)

| Keyword | Description |
|---|---|
| rfc931 [*timeout*] | This option identifies users attempting to establish a connection. For this, a client-side RFC93-compatible daemon is required. If the daemon is not present, it can lead to delays in setting up the connection. If no value is given for *timeout*, the default value (10 seconds.) is used. |
| banners /*directory* | Searches in /*directory* for a file whose name matches the daemon to be started. If such a file is found, its contents will be sent to the client after the placeholders have been expanded. |
| nice [*number*] | The server process is started with the corresponding nice value. This makes more resources available to other server processes. |
| setenv *name value* | This option defines environment variables for the server process. Here, too, a placeholder expansion is executed. |

The following example in /etc/hosts.allow allows Telnet access from anywhere:

```
in.telnetd: ALL: banners /etc/tcpd: ALLOW
```

If a file in.telnetd is located in the /etc/tcpd directory, its contents will be sent to the client before the Telnet service is started.

In the following example, finger is only allowed in the local network:

```
in.fingerd: ALL EXCEPT LOCAL: banners /etc/tcpd: spawn ( echo
"finger request from %h"| mail -s "finger!!" root ) & : DENY
```

Clients outside the local network can obtain information from the /etc/tcpd/in.fingerd file. An e-mail to root is generated that contains the host name or IP address of the machine making this request.

The following example starts the FTP daemons with a nice value of 15:

```
vsftpd: ALL: nice 15
```

This allows you to influence the load on a server, for instance, to allocate more resources to other services.

In the following example, the command **echo "No one logged in"** is started instead of the finger daemon:

```
in.fingerd: ALL: twist ( echo "No one logged in" )
```

The client is informed that no one is logged in.

**NOTE**    For more information about these and other options, enter **man hosts_options**.

In addition to the files **/etc/hosts.allow** and **/etc/hosts.deny** it is possible for FTP to define in the file **/etc/ftpusers** which users may not connect to the ftp server. The file lists root and various system accounts.

## Check the TCP Wrapper

Since a command's flexibility can easily lead to configuration errors, you cannot just hope that your network services are secure without reviewing them first.

Fortunately, the TCP wrapper package offers some tools for troubleshooting as well as for error analysis.

You can review the configuration of tcpd using the **tcpdchk** command. This program reports a multitude of possible problems; these can be network services listed in /etc/inetd. conf that do not really exist, syntax errors in the configuration files, or unknown host names.

However, there are some configurations in which tcpdchk does not find any errors, but where tcpd still does not act as expected. In such cases, you can use **tcpdmatch** to provide information about how tcpd would handle various types of access attempts.

You can enter shell commands in the configuration files, which will be executed when the request matches one of the patterns defined in the daemon and host fields.

Because tcpd recognizes the placeholders shown in Table 11-10 that can be used in shell scripts, you can monitor attempts at accessing certain services.

**Table 11-10**

| Placeholder | Description |
|---|---|
| %a | Address of the host making the request |
| %c | Information about the host making the request (such as user@host and user@address) depending on the information available |
| %d | Name of the daemon |
| %h | Name of the host making the request or the address, if the name cannot be ascertained |
| %n | Name of the host making the request, unknown, or paranoid |
| %p | The process ID of the daemon |
| %s | Information about the server (such as daemon@host and daemon@ address) depending on the information available |
| %u | User name on the host making the request or unknown if the remote host does not possess a user ID as recognized by RFC 931 |

The following example shows a script in the configuration file /etc/hosts.allow that records all successful access attempts to the network services in a log file:

```
ALL: ALL: spawn echo "Access of %u@%h to %d" >> /var/log/net.log
```

A finger client (/usr/sbin/safe_finger) is also included in the TCP wrapper package to provide better protection against defense measures that other machines might have in store when their finger daemons are queried.

The idea behind safe_finger is to entrap (using simple methods) possible intruders by uncovering their identities with a **fingerd** query.

In the following example, all query results of access attempts to any network service taking place outside the network, other than finger, are stored in a log file:

```
ALL EXCEPT in.fingerd : ALL EXCEPT LOCAL : \
twist /usr/sbin/safe_finger -l @%h >> /var/log/unknown.net.log
```

Excluding finger itself from this screening process is a measure of caution. If such a trap including finger were set up remotely, an endless loop could result, where the finger query of one machine would respond with a finger query of the other in an endless cycle.

## Exercise 11-3    Configure the Internet Daemon (xinetd) and TCP Wrapper

Various services can be offered via inetd/xinetd. In both cases additional fine tuning of access restrictions is possible using the TCP wrapper and the files /etc/hosts.allow and /etc/hosts.deny.

The purpose of this exercise is to show you the basic configuration steps necessary to offer services using xinetd.

In this exercise, you will work with a partner to do the following:

- Part I: Enable xinetd Services with YaST
- Part II: Enable xinetd Services Manually
- Part III: Configure a TCP Wrapper

### Part I: Enable xinetd Services with YaST

Do the following:

1. From your KDE desktop, select the **YaST** icon; then enter a password of **novell** and select **OK**.

   The YaST Control Center appears.

2. Select **Network Services > Network Services (inetd)**.

   The Network Services Configuration (xinetd) dialog box appears.

3. Select **Enable**.

   A list of currently available services becomes active.

4. Scroll down and select the service **Telnet**; then set the service to On by selecting **Toggle Status (On or Off)**.

5. Save the configuration to the system by selecting **Finish**.

6. Test the configuration:

   a. Open a terminal window and su to root (**su -**) with a password of **novell**.

   b. Telnet to localhost by entering **telnet localhost**.

   c. Log in as **geeko** with a password of **N0v3ll**.

   d. Log out by entering **exit**.

   e. Log in to a partner's server as geeko by entering:

      **telnet *partner_server_IP_address***

      You'll need to wait until the neighbor completes enabling inetd and Telnet.

   f. Log out by entering **exit**.

## Part II: Enable xinetd Services Manually

Enable the FTP server by doing the following:

1. From the terminal window, edit the file /etc/xinetd.d/vsftpd by entering:

   **vim /etc/xinetd.d/vsftpd**

2. At the bottom of the file, change the disable = yes setting to the following:

   disable = **no**

3. Exit vi and save the changes by entering :**wq**.

4. Restart the service xinetd by entering **rcxinetd restart**.

5. Test the FTP service by doing the following:

   a. Enter **ftp localhost**.

   b. Log in anonymously by entering the following:

      ■ Name: **ftp**

      ■ Password: *your e-mail address*

   c. Exit FTP by entering **exit**.

   d. Log in to a partner's server anonymously by entering:

      **ftp *partner_server_IP_address***

   e. Log out by entering **exit**.

11

## Part III: Configure a TCP Wrapper

Do the following:

   1. Secure the Telnet service so that everyone in the classroom except your part-
      ner can Telnet to your system:

      a. Edit the file /etc/hosts.deny by entering:

         **vim  /etc/hosts.deny**

      b. Add the following to the end of the file:

         **in.telnetd : *partner_server_IP_address***

         Make sure there is an empty line at the end of the file or the configuration will
         not work.

      c. Exit vi and save the file by entering **:wq**.

      d. Have your partner attempt to Telnet to your host; then have another stu-
         dent in the classroom attempt to Telnet to your host.

         The connection for your partner is closed. However, others can Telnet to your
         server.

**NOTE**

If the results are not what you expect, check the file /var/log/messages by
entering **tail -f /var/log/messages**.

      e. Edit the file /etc/hosts.deny again by entering:

         **vim  /etc/hosts.deny**

      f. Place a comment character (#) in front of the line you just added to the file
         /etc/hosts.deny; then add the following line.

         **ALL ALL**

      g. Exit vi and save the file by entering **:wq**.

         Apply the same security restriction by editing the file /etc/hosts.allow.

      h. Edit the file /etc/hosts.allow by entering:

         **vim  /etc/hosts.allow**

      i. Add the following to the end of the file:

         **in.telnetd : ALL EXCEPT *partner_server_IP_address***

      j. Exit vi and save the file by entering **:wq**.

      k. Have your partner attempt to Telnet to the system; then have another stu-
         dent in the classroom attempt to Telnet to your host.

         The results are the same as with the file hosts.deny.

2. Perform a twist by editing ALL : ALL in the file /etc/hosts.deny:

   a. Edit the file /etc/hosts.deny by entering:

      **vim /etc/hosts.deny**

   b. Edit the ALL:ALL line to reflect the following (in one line):

      **ALL: ALL: twist echo "This service is not accessible from %a!"**

   c. Exit vi and save the file by entering :**wq**.

   d. Have your partner attempt to Telnet to the system to verify that the message is sent.

   e. When you finish testing the twist, edit the file /etc/hosts.deny by entering:

      **vim /etc/hosts.deny**

   f. Comment out (#) the ALL: ALL: ... line.

   g. Exit vi and save the file by entering :**wq**.

      Commenting out the line makes sure that exercises later in the course work properly.

3. Make sure that all users that Telnet or FTP to your server are logged by IP address to the file /tmp/service-access.log:

   a. Edit the file /etc/hosts.allow by entering:

      **vim /etc/hosts.allow**

   b. At the bottom of the file, change the line in.telnetd to reflect the following (on one line):

      **in.telnetd,vsftpd : ALL EXCEPT** *partner_server_IP_address* **: spawn (echo "%a accessed %s" >> /tmp/service-access.log)**

   c. Exit vi and save the file by entering :**wq**.

   d. Have someone in the class other than your partner attempt to Telnet to your system to verify that the entry is logged.

   e. Verify that all of the activity to the services under xinetd have been logged in /var/log/xinetd.log by entering:

      **cat /var/log/xinetd.log**

**11**

4. Disable the vsftpd service:

   a. Edit the file /etc/xinetd.d/vsftpd by entering:

      **vim /etc/xinetd.d/vsftpd**

      disable = **yes**

   b. Exit vi and save the file by entering **:wq**.

   c. Restart the service xinetd by entering **rcxinetd restart**.

5. Close all open windows.

---

## OBJECTIVE 4    FURTHER SERVICES

SUSE Linux Enterprise Server 9 comes with various services that cannot all be covered extensively here. Some of the more common ones are:

- Secure Shell SSH

- DHCP

- HTTP Daemon: Apache2

## Secure Shell SSH

SSH is a replacement for the various r-tools: rsh, rlogin, rcp.

Unlike the r-tools, SSH uses strong encryption, protecting the authentication password as well as the transmitted content from any sniffer on the network.

The configuration file for the server is **/etc/ssh/sshd_config**.

Table 11-11 lists some of the more commonly used options.

**Table 11-11**

| Option | Description |
| --- | --- |
| **AllowUsers** | Allows an SSH login for selected users |
| **DenyUsers** | Denies an SSH login for selected users |
| **Protocol** | Specifies the protocol versions supported. (Default: 2,1 ) |

To log in from one server to another, use **ssh**:

```
da10:~ # ssh da20
The authenticity of host 'da20 (10.0.0.20)' can't be established.
RSA key fingerprint is 23:0c:77:9a:09:75:fe:2b:af:5e:61:c6:3f:10:2d:f5.
Are you sure you want to continue connecting (yes/no)? yes
Warning: Permanently added 'da20' (RSA) to the list of  known hosts.
```

```
Password:
Last login: Tue Mar 15 13:44:25 2005 from 10.0.0.1
da20:~ #
```

If this is the first connection, there is a message regarding the authenticity. You could contact the system administrator of the server (in this case da20) to find out if the fingerprint of da20 matches what you see on your screen. If it does, you can be sure that you are really connecting to the server you want to connect to.

Without an option, the login name on the remote machine is the same as the local one. If you want to log in as a different user, use a command like the following:

```
da10:~ # ssh geeko@da20
Password:
Last login: Tue Mar 15 13:46:30 2005 from 10.0.0.10
geeko@da20:~>
```

If you want to start graphical programs on the remote machine, add the option **-X**.

You can also copy files from one machine to another using **scp**:

```
da10:~ # scp /etc/motd geeko@da20:.
Password:
motd                                    100%    0     0.0KB/s   00:00
da10:~ #
```

The SSH client can be configured system wide using **/etc/ssh/ssh_config**.

User-specific configurations are stored in ~/.ssh/config.

The directory ~/.ssh/ also contains any keys the user might have generated, as well as information on hosts contacted in the past.

For more information on SSH server configuration options, enter **man sshd**.

# DHCP

The Dynamic Host Configuration Protocol (DHCP) is used to provide hosts with IP addresses and other information on the network, like DNS servers to be used, routings, and domain names.

SLES 9 comes with the ISC DHCP server. The default DHCP client installed is dhcpcd (DHCP Client Daemon).

The following topics are discussed in the following:

- dhcpd
- DHC

## dhcpd

The main configuration file of the DHCP server is /etc/dhcpd.conf.

To configure the DHCP server, you can either:

- Use the YaST DHCP Server module and the wizard that comes with it.

  or

- Copy the file /usr/share/doc/packages/dhcp-server/examples/ simple_dhcpd. conf to /etc/dhcpd.conf and modify the configuration according to your needs.

**NOTE**

For more information on how to configure dhcpd see the manual page **man dhcpd.conf** and man **dhcp-options**.

With SLES 9 you also should have a look at /etc/sysconfig/dhcpd before actually starting the server.

The interface where the server listens for requests is configured here and you can also determine whether the server should run in a change-root environment.

Information such as which IP address was assigned to which MAC address and when it expires is kept in /var/lib/dhcp/db/dhcpd.leases.

### DHCP Client Daemon

When the network interface is configured to use DHCP to get the IP address, the scripts that set up the network interface start dhcpd.

Information on the lease is kept in /var/lib/dhcpcd/.

The file dhcpcd-eth*x*.info contains the information in human readable format.

To look at it, use:

**cat /var/lib/dhcpcd/dhcpcd-eth*x*.info**

# HTTP Daemon: Apache2

To run a basic Web service, you need to understand:

- Background Information on the World Wide Web
- Installing and Starting Apache2
- Configuration Files

## Background Information on the World Wide Web

The terms *Internet* and *World Wide Web* are often used synonymously. This is incorrect, however, because the Internet has been around since the end of the 1960s, while the World Wide Web was only developed in 1990.

The foundations of the World Wide Web were established in 1990, when two software developers, Tim Berners-Lee and Robert Cailliau, wanted to install an information system for researchers at the European Centre for Nuclear Research (CERN) in Geneva to enable the exchange of knowledge between the various research groups.

After a number of different names, the system was finally named the World Wide Web (WWW).

What was special about this system was the use of a hypertext format, making it possible to refer to other documents through links. Hypertext links are what footnotes and bibliographies are for a printed text—they are connections between different documents.

Server software is needed to make the published documents available on the Internet. The most frequently used software for this purpose is the Apache Web server.

The software used to view the documents is a Web browser. Various browsers are available on Linux, like Konqueror, Firefox, Mozilla, and Opera for the text console. Lynx and w3m are available.

The protocol used between a Web browser and a Web server is HTTP, the Hypertext Transfer Protocol. There is an encrypted variant, HTTPS, that uses Secure Sockets Layer (SSL) to protect the transmitted information from eavesdropping.

Documents are usually plain ASCII texts that are formatted by using HTML, the Hypertext Markup Language.

## Installing and Starting Apache2

To install version 2 of the Apache Web server on SLES 9, do the following:

1. From the KDE desktop, start the YaST module to install software by doing one of the following:

   - Select the **YaST** icon, enter the root password *novell*, and select **OK**; then select **Software > Install and Remove Software**.

     *or*

   - Open a terminal window and enter **sux –** and the root password *novell*; then enter **yast2 sw_single**.

2. Under Filter, select **Selections**.

3. Select **Simple Webserver >Accept**.

To start and stop Apache, do the following:

**rcapache2** is a link to the script (/etc/init.d/apache2) that is used to start the Web server. To start use **rcapache2 start**, to stop **rcapache2 stop**, and to view the status of Apache2 use **rcapache2 status**.

## Configuring Apache2

To present documents in the Web, you need to understand the following:

- Configuration Files
- Document Files

**Configuration Files**    The main configuration file for Apache2 is **/etc/apache2/httpd.conf**.

To prevent this file from becoming too big, it has been devided into several files that have been put in subdirectories, like /etc/apache2/sysconfig.d/, /etc/apache2/sysconfig.d/ and /etc/apache2/vhosts.d.

Files in these subdirectories are integrated into httpd.conf using include statements like the following:

```
...
# run under this user/group id
Include /etc/apache2/uid.conf
...
```

At the beginning of /etc/apache2/httpd.conf there is a section that shows in detail which files are included at which point.

On SLES 9 the configuration of Apache2 should not be done in httpd.conf directly, but in the appropriate file in the directory /etc/apache2 or its subdirectories.

In /etc/sysconfig/apache2, you can set certain parameters that are evaluated by the start-script /etc/init.d/apache2 when the server is started. These parameters are translated into configuration parameters that influence the behavior of Apache2.

This course does not cover the configuration of Apache, because this is a subject of its own, covering several days.

**NOTE**    To learn more about Apache, read the comments in the configuration files in /etc/apache2/, in /etc/sysconfig/apache2, and visit the Web site of the Apache project at *http://httpd.apache.org/docs-2.0/*

**Document Files**    The documents actually transmitted to the visitors of the Web site to be viewed in their browser are kept in the document root directory.

In SLES 9 this is the directory: /srv/www/htdocs/

# Chapter Summary

- NIS is unique to UNIX and Linux operating systems. It has traditionally been used to distribute data on a network, provide central authentication, and resolve names.

- NIS clients obtain information from a NIS master server or NIS slave servers for a particular NIS domain. NIS slave servers are additional NIS servers that may be used to aid in distributing data to NIS clients.

- To create a NIS server, you must create NIS maps of various system components and start the **ypserv, ypbind**, and RPM portmapper daemons. NIS clients need to start the **ypbind** daemon and typically forward information requests to NIS servers based on entries in the /etc/nsswitch.conf file. YaST may be used to configure a NIS master server, NIS slave server, or NIS client.

- The LDAP service provides the same functionality as NIS, but is supported by nearly all operating systems.

- LDAP resources are organized into a directory information tree. Each resource (leaf object) is stored in a series of container objects and can be accessed using a DN or RDN.

- YaST may be used to configure LDAP servers and clients as well as LDAP authentication for local user accounts.

- E-mail is relayed on the Internet by MTAs (e-mail servers) using the SMTP protocol. MDAs store these e-mails for use by MUAs (e-mail readers), which typically access their e-mail using the IMAP and POP protocols and send new e-mails using the SMTP protocol.

- Two common Linux MTAs include Postfix and Sendmail. Postfix is a modular, fast MTA that uses lookup tables to process incoming e-mails. Sendmail is a large MTA that uses a series of configuration files to store processing information.

- The most common MDA in Linux is Procmail. Procmail uses filters to process mail messages, and typically stores local mail in /var/spool/mail/*username*.

- Although you can use one of several graphical MUAs to read Internet e-mails, the **mail** command is typically used to view and send local e-mails on a Linux system.

- Some network daemons are started by the Internet Super Daemon (inetd) or Extended Internet Super Daemon (xinetd). SLES uses xinetd by default to start network daemons via entries in the /etc/xinetd.d directory.

- The TCP wrapper daemon (tcpd) may be used with inetd or xinetd to provide additional security for network daemons via lines in the /etc/hosts.allow and /etc/hosts.deny files.

- The SSH daemon (sshd) provides a secure remote login on most Linux computers and replaced the nonsecure r-tools used in earlier versions of Linux.

- You may start the DHCP daemon (dhcpd) to automate the assignment of IP addresses and IP options on your network. The dhcpd daemon uses entries in the /etc/dhcpd.conf file to configure client computers.

- The Apache Web server (httpd) is the most common Web server on Linux systems. By default, Apache uses the configuration file /etc/apache2/httpd.conf to distribute Web content in the /srv/www/htdocs directory to client Web browsers.

11

## KEY TERMS

**/etc/aliases** — Contains mail aliases for user accounts.

**/etc/apache2/httpd.conf** — The main Apache configuration file.

**/etc/defaultdomain** — A file that stores the default NIS domain name.

**/etc/dhcpd.conf** — The DHCP daemon configuration file.

**/etc/hosts.allow** — A text file used by tcpd listing hosts that are allowed to connect to network daemons.

**/etc/hosts.deny** — A text file used by tcpd listing hosts that are not allowed to connect to network daemons.

**/etc/inetd.conf** — The main configuration file for inetd.

**/etc/nsswitch.conf** — A file that determines when NIS maps are used to configure system information.

**/etc/sendmail.cf** — The main Sendmail configuration file.

**/etc/ssh/ssh_config** — The system-wide ssh client program configuration file.

**/etc/ssh/sshd_config** — The SSH daemon configuration file.

**/etc/sysconfig/ypserv** — Stores NIS server options.

**/etc/xinetd.conf** — The main configuration file for xinetd. It loads configuration files from the /etc/xinetd.d directory.

**/etc/xinetd.d** — The directory that stores most xinetd configurations.

**/etc/yp.conf** — A file that stores the location of NIS servers.

**/etc/ypserv.conf** — The main NIS server configuration file.

**/srv/www/htdocs** — The default location for Web site content in Apache.

**/var/lib/dhcp/db/dhcpd.leases** — The file that contains current DHCP leases on a DHCP server.

**/var/spool/mail** — The default location for local e-mails.

**/var/yp/Makefile** — A file whose settings are used to create NIS maps.

**/var/yp/nicknames** — A file that contains aliases for NIS maps.

**/var/yp/securenets** — A file on a NIS server that lists valid networks for NIS clients.

**/var/yp/ypservers** — A file on a NIS master server that lists NIS slave servers.

**~/.forward** — An MTA file used to configure e-mail handling options.

**~/.procmailrc** — A file that contains Procmail e-mail filtering criteria.

**~/.ssh/config** — The ssh client program configuration file.

**Apache** — The default Web server software in SLES.

**container** — An LDAP object used to organize leaf objects.

**dhcpd** — The DHCP server daemon.

**Directory Information Tree (DIT)** — The hierarchical structure of an LDAP database.

**Distinguished Name (DN)** — A full pathname to an LDAP leaf object.

**Dynamic Host Configuration Protocol (DHCP)** — A protocol that is used to assign TCP/IP configuration information to a host on the network.

**Evolution** — A common Linux MUA.

**Exim** — A common MTA on Linux systems.

**inetd** — The Internet Super Daemon used to start other network daemons on Linux systems.

**Internet Message Access Protocol (IMAP)** — A protocol used to obtain e-mails from an e-mail server.

**KMail** — A common Linux MUA.

**leaf** — An LDAP object that represents a network resource.

**Lightweight Directory Access Protocol (LDAP)** — A protocol used to provide central authentication and distribute information to network computers.

**lookup table** — A Postfix file used to process e-mails.

**mail command** — An MUA available on most Linux systems.

**Mail Delivery Agent (MDA)** — A program that stores e-mails for later access.

**Mail Transfer Agent (MTA)** — A server program that relays e-mail on the Internet. It is commonly called a mail server.

**Mail User Agent (MUA)** — An e-mail reader program.

**mailq command** — Lists mail in the Postfix/Sendmail mail queue.

**mailstats command** — Displays e-mail statistics.

**make command** — Used to generate NIS maps using the Makefile.

**makemap command** — Generates lookup tables for Sendmail information.

**maps** — NIS database files containing information that is central to the network, such as user accounts and host names.

**master server** — A NIS server that contains the maps used to configure NIS clients.

**Multipurpose Internet Mail Extensions (MIME)** — A standard used for attaching files to e-mails.

**Mutt** — A common Linux MUA.

**Network Information Service (NIS)** — A service that allows the centralization of Linux and UNIX configuration.

**newaliases command** — It converts the plain text /etc/aliases file into the /etc/aliases.db database file for use by the system.

**NIS client** — A computer that authenticates or obtains its configuration information from a master or slave NIS server.

**object** — A component of an LDAP database. The two main object types are container objects and leaf objects.

**object class** — A type of object within an LDAP database.

**Pine** — A common Linux MUA.

**Post Office Protocol (POP)** — A protocol used to obtain e-mails from an e-mail server. POP3 is the latest version of POP.

**postalias command** — A postfix program that performs the same function as the **newaliases** command.

**postcat command** — Displays contents of files in the Postfix mail queue.

**postconf command** — Displays and sets Postfix variables.

**postdrop command** — Creates files in the postdrop directory.

11

**Postfix** — A common MTA on Linux systems.

**postfix command** — Checks for Postfix configuration problems.

**postmap command** — Generates lookup tables for Postfix information.

**postsuper command** — Cleans up unused files in the Postfix queue directories.

**Procmail** — A common MDA on Linux systems.

**Qmail** — A common MTA on Linux systems.

**rcp** — Used to copy files to and from remote computers.

**Relative Distinguished Name (RDN)** — The simple name of an object in LDAP.

**rlogin** — Used to obtain a shell on a remote computer.

**rpcinfo command** — Displays RPC ports and their associated services.

**rsh** — Used to obtain a shell or run a program on a remote computer.

**r-tools** — The rsh, rlogin, and rcp programs.

**schema** — The list of object and object properties for an LDAP database.

**Secure SHell (SSH)** — A software service that provides an encrypted shell session to and from remote computers.

**Sendmail** — A common MTA on Linux systems.

**Simple Mail Transfer Protocol (SMTP)** — The protocol used to send e-mails to MTAs on the Internet.

**slave server** — A NIS server that contains a copy of the maps from the master server and uses them to configure NIS clients.

**ssh command** — Used to obtain a shell from a remote SSH server.

**TCP wrapper (tcpd)** — A small program that is used to start network daemons via inetd or xinetd. It provides additional security by using the /etc/hosts.allow and /etc/hosts.deny files to control access.

**tcpdchk command** — Reports on the configuration of the tcpd program.

**tcpdmatch command** — Used to test the behavior of the tcpd program.

**Thunderbird** — A common Linux MUA.

**World Wide Web (WWW)** — A naming convention for Internet services that may be queried using a Web browser.

**xinetd** — The Extended Internet Super Daemon used to start other network daemons on Linux systems. It is the default Internet Super Daemon used in SLES.

**ypbind** — The NIS client program. This program also runs on NIS servers.

**ypcat command** — Displays the contents of NIS maps.

**ypdomainname command** — Used to set the NIS domain name for a computer.

**ypinit command** — The NIS slave server program.

**ypmatch command** — Used to query NIS maps for specific information.

**yppasswd command** — Used to change a user password on a NIS server.

**yppoll command** — Displays NIS map ID numbers.

**yppush command** — Copies NIS maps from master servers to slave servers.

**ypserv** — The NIS server program.

**ypwhich command** — Displays the NIS server used by a host.

## REVIEW QUESTIONS

1. Which of the following daemons is started on a NIS server? (Choose all that apply.)

   a. ypbind

   b. ypwhich

   c. ypserv

   d. RPC portmapper

2. What command may be used to generate NIS maps on the command line using entries on the /var/yp/Makefile? _____

3. You have configured your system to authenticate to a NIS server. When you use the **passwd** command to change your password, it does not change as expected. What command must you use to change your NIS password for it to take effect on the NIS server? _____

4. Which of the following is a valid DN for an LDAP object?

   a. cn=joe

   b. cn=joe.ou=acctg.

   c. cn=joe.ou=acctg.dc=suse

   d. cn=joe.ou=acctg.dc=suse.dc=com

5. What package is used to implement LDAP in SLES 9? _____

6. Which of the following are common MTAs in Linux? (Choose all that apply.)

   a. Postfix

   b. Procmail

   c. mail

   d. Sendmail

7. What two protocols do MUAs typically use to retrieve e-mails from across the network? _____

8. What protocol does an MUA typically use to send e-mails to an MTA?

   _____

9. You have recently modified the /etc/aliases file. What command can you run to update your MTA with the changes?

   a. newaliases

   b. alias

   c. postsuper

   d. mailq

**11**

10. What file can you place in your home directory to create Procmail filters for your e-mail? _____

11. What xinetd file could you edit to configure the telnet daemon?

   a. /etc/telnet.d

   b. /etc/inetd

   c. /etc/xinetd.d/telnet

   d. /etc/xinetd

12. What lines could you add to the /etc/hosts.allow and /etc/hosts.deny files to allow only the host **arfa** the ability to use the **telnet** utility when connecting to your server? (Choose two answers.)

   a. /etc/hosts.allow: **in.telnetd: arfa**

   b. /etc/hosts.allow: **in.telnetd: ALL**

   c. /etc/hosts.deny: **in.telnetd: arfa**

   d. /etc/hosts.deny: **in.telnetd: ALL**

13. What command could you use to check the syntax of your TCP wrappers? _____

14. What option to the **ssh** command can be used to start graphical programs on the remote computer? _____

15. Where can you find a sample DHCP server configuration file to copy and modify for your own DHCP server? _____

16. What directory on an SLES system contains the default Web page for the Apache Web server? _____

## DISCOVERY EXERCISES

DISCOVERY

### Configuring LDAP

As the root user, configure your system to be an LDAP server using YaST. On a partner's computer, use YaST to configure their computer as an LDAP client and set the properties of user accounts on the system to authenticate to your LDAP server. Test your configuration. When finished, remove the LDAP configuration from both systems.

## Using the Apache Web Server

Use YaST to add the Apache Web Server (httpd) to your system. Then remove any files in the /srvr/www/htdocs directory and create a /srv/www/htdocs/index.html file. Ensure that the permissions on this file are rw-r--r-- (**chmod 644 /srv/www/htdocs/index.html**). Next, add the following lines to the file, using the **vi** editor:

<HTML>

<BODY>

<H1> My sample Web page! </H1>

</BODY>

</HTML>

Next, start your apache daemon (**rchttpd start**)and place the URL **http://127.0.0.1** in your Web browser to test your Web page.

## Creating and Testing a DHCP Server

Log in to the KDE desktop and install the DHCP server package using YaST. Next, log in to tty1 as the root user. Edit the /etc/dhcpd.conf file and add the following lines to the bottom of the file, using the **vi** editor:

default-lease-time 72000;

ddns-update-style ad-hoc;

option routers 10.0.0.254;

option domain-name-servers 10.0.0.254;

subnet 10.0.0.0 netmask 255.255.255.0 {

range 10.100.0.1 10.100.0.1;

}

When finished, save your changes and start the DHCP daemon (**rcdhcpd start**). Connect your computer to another computer using a crossover cable, then configure the second computer as a DHCP client and obtain an IP address. Check the /var/lib/dhcp/db/dhcpd.leases file to verify that the DHCP lease was successful. When finished, log out of tty1.

11

## MANAGE SECURITY

**The topic of Linux security is a broad subject capable of filling several books. The intent of this section is to give you a brief overview of the subject.**

- ◆ Manage and Secure the Linux User Environment
- ◆ Use System Logging Services
- ◆ Audit Log Files and Authentication
- ◆ Understand ipchains and iptables
- ◆ Security Vulnerabilities
- ◆ Understand Intrusion Detection

## OBJECTIVE 1    MANAGE AND SECURE THE LINUX USER ENVIRONMENT

This objective covers tasks in the area of user management and file permissions that go beyond creating, modifying and deleting individual user accounts or using chown or chmod on individual files.

The following topics are discussed:

- Configure Security Settings
- Set Defaults for New User Accounts
- Perform Administrative Tasks as root
- Use sudo to Delegate Administrative Tasks
- How Special File Permissions Affect the System's Security
- Configure File Permissions
- Additional Security Considerations

## Configure Security Settings

Yast provides a Security Settings module that lets you configure the following local security settings for your SUSE Linux Enterprise Server:

- Password settings
- Boot configuration
- Login settings
- User creation settings
- File permissions

You can select from (or modify) three preset levels of security, or create your own customized security settings to meet the requirements of your enterprise security policies and procedures.

To use the Security Settings module, do the following:

1. From the KDE desktop, start the YaST Security Settings module by doing one of the following:

   - Select the **YaST** icon, enter the root password *novell*, and select **OK**; then select

     **Security and Users > Security Settings**

     *or*

   - Open a terminal window and enter **sux –** and the root password *novell*; then enter **yast2 security**.

The dialog box shown in Figure 12-1 appears.

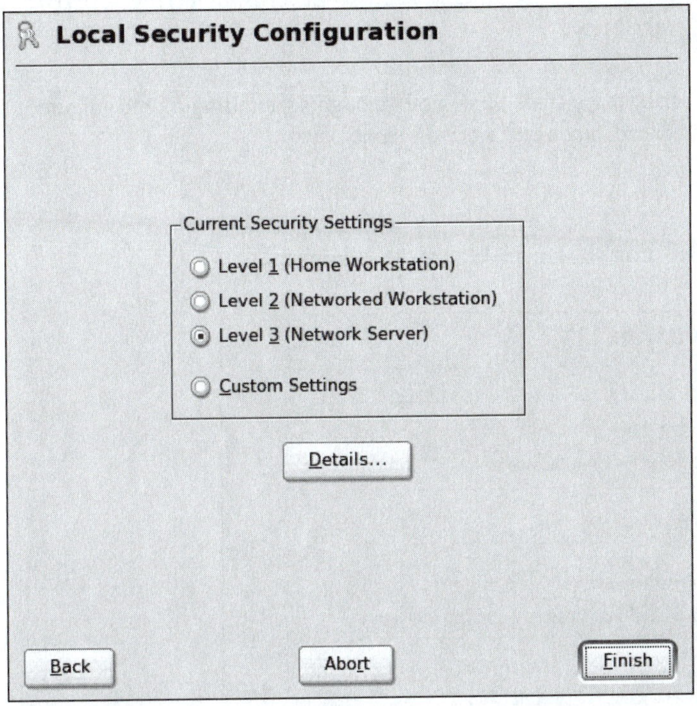

**Figure 12-1**

From this dialog box, you can select one of the following preset configurations:

- **Level 1 (Home Workstation).** Select for a home computer not connected to any type of a network.

- **Level 2 (Networked Workstation).** Select for a computer connected to any type of a network or the Internet.

- **Level 3 (Network Server).** Select for a computer that provides any type of service (network or otherwise).

You can also select **Details** or **Custom Settings** to modify an existing security level or create your own configuration.

2. Do one of the following:

- Select a preconfigured *security level* setting; then configure your server by selecting **Finish**.

  *or*

- Select a preconfigured **security level** setting; then customize the level by selecting **Details**.

*or*

- Create your own customized security level by selecting **Custom Settings**; then select **Next**.

**NOTE**

The remainder of these steps guide you through customizing a preconfigured security level or creating a customized security level.

The dialog box shown in Figure 12-2 appears.

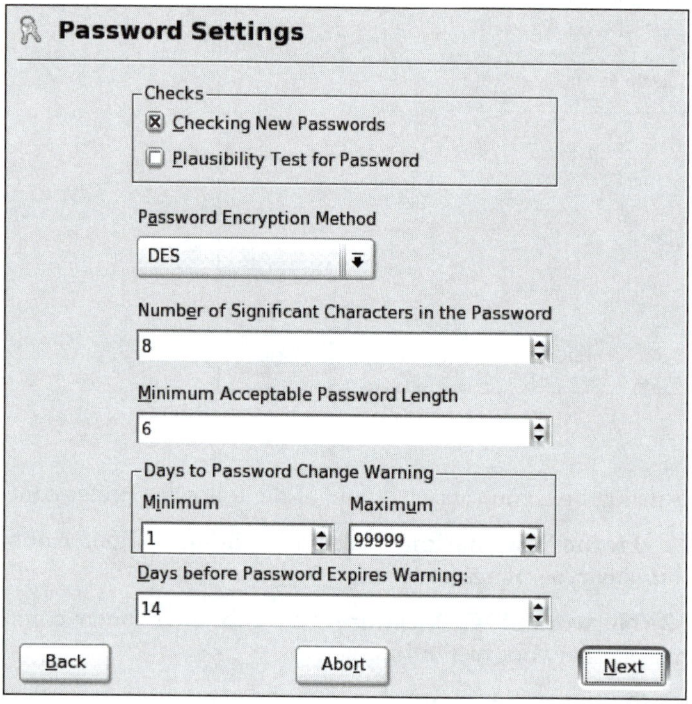

---

**Password Settings**

Checks
- [X] Checking New Passwords
- [ ] Plausibility Test for Password

Password Encryption Method

DES

Number of Significant Characters in the Password

8

Minimum Acceptable Password Length

6

Days to Password Change Warning
Minimum          Maximum
1                99999

Days before Password Expires Warning:

14

Back          Abort          Next

---

**Figure 12-2**

From this dialog box, you can select or enter the following password settings (mainly stored in /etc/login.defs):

- **Checking New Passwords.** It is important to choose a password that cannot be found in a dictionary and is not a name or other simple, common word. By selecting this option, you enforce password checking in regard to these rules.

- **Plausibility Test for Passwords.** Passwords should be constructed using a mixture of characters. This makes it very difficult to guess the password. Select this option to enable additional checks.

- **Password Encryption Method.** From the drop-down list, select one of the following encryption methods:

  - **DES.** This is the Linux default method. It works in all network environments, but it restricts you to passwords no longer than eight characters. If you need compatibility with other systems, select this method.

  - **MD5.** This encryption method allows longer passwords and is supported by all current Linux distributions, but not by other systems or older software.

  - **Blowfish.** This encryption method is similar to MD5, but uses a different algorithm to encrypt passwords. It is not yet supported by many systems. A lot of CPU power is needed to calculate the hash, which makes it difficult to crack passwords with the help of a dictionary.

- **Number of Significant Characters in the Password.** You can only set this number for DES encryption. The default is **8** characters.

  This option is ignored for the other encryption methods (MD5=**127**; Blowfish=**72**).

- **Minimum Acceptable Password Length.** Enter the minimum number of characters for an acceptable password. If a user enters fewer characters, the password is rejected.

  Entering **0** disables this check.

- **Days to Password Change Warning.** Minimum refers to the number of days that have to elapse before a password can be changed again. Maximum is the number of days after which a password expires and must be changed.

- **Days before Password Expires Warning.** This sets the number of days before his password expires a user receives a warning.

**NOTE**

Although root receives a warning when setting a password, she can still enter a bad password despite the above settings.

3. When you finish configuring password settings, continue by selecting **Next**.

**12**

The dialog box shown in Figure 12-3 appears.

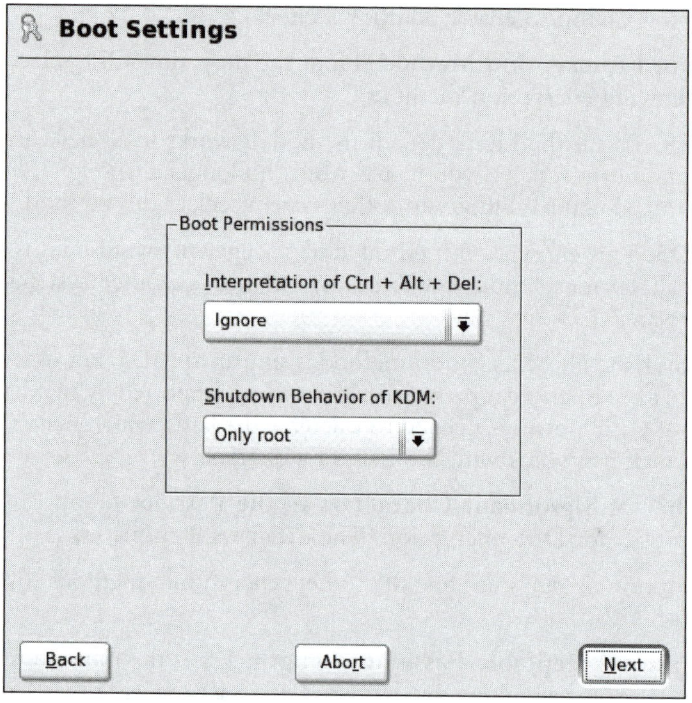

## Boot Settings

Boot Permissions

Interpretation of Ctrl + Alt + Del:

Ignore

Shutdown Behavior of KDM:

Only root

Back            Abort            Next

**Figure 12-3**

From this dialog box, you can select the following boot settings (which update the file /etc/inittab):

- **Interpretation of Ctrl + Alt + Del.** When someone at the console presses **Ctrl + Alt + Del**, the system usually reboots.

  Sometimes you want to have the system ignore this keystroke combination, especially when the system serves as both workstation and server.

  You can select from **Ignore**, **Reboot**, or **Halt**. If you select **Halt**, the system shuts down when this key combination is pressed.

- **Shutdown Behavior of KDM.** You use this option to set who is allowed to shut down the computer from KDM.

  You can select from **Only root**, **All users**, **Nobody**, **Local users**, and **Automatic**.

  If you select Nobody, you can only shut down the system from a text console.

4. When you finish configuring boot settings, continue by selecting **Next**.

The dialog box shown in Figure 12-4 appears.

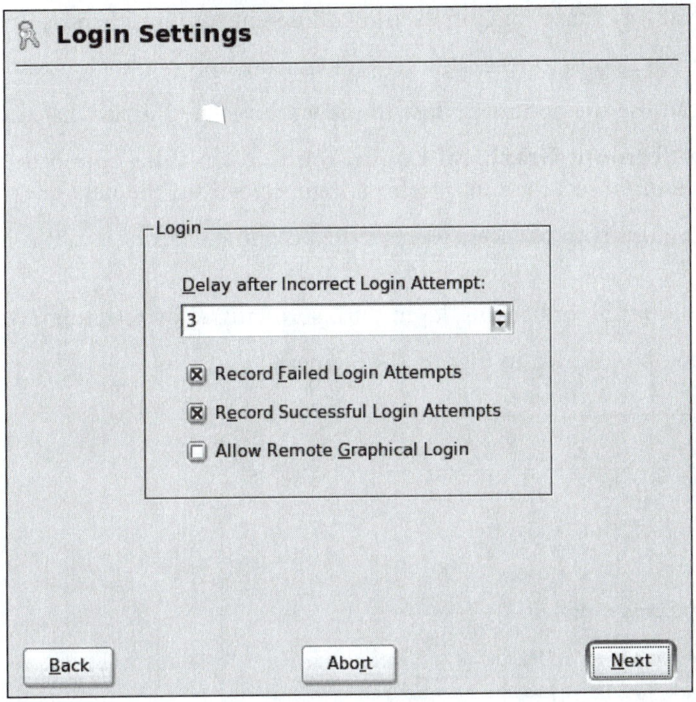

**Login Settings**

Login

Delay after Incorrect Login Attempt:

3

[X] Record Failed Login Attempts
[X] Record Successful Login Attempts
[ ] Allow Remote Graphical Login

Back          Abort          Next

**Figure 12-4**

From this dialog box, you can enter and select the following login settings (mainly stored in /etc/login.defs):

■ **Delay after Incorrect Login Attempt.** Following a failed login attempt, there is typically a waiting period of a few seconds before another login is possible. This makes it more difficult for password crackers to log in.

This option lets you adjust the time delay before another login attempt.

Make the time small enough so users do not need to wait too long to retry if a password is mistyped.

A reasonable value is **3** seconds.

■ **Record Failed Login Attempts.** It is useful for you to know if somebody tried to log in and failed, especially when that person is trying to guess other users' passwords.

Select this option to specify whether failed login attempts should be recorded in /var/log/faillog.

To view failed login attempts, enter the command **faillog**.

**12**

- **Record Successful Login Attempts.** Logging successful login attempts can be useful, especially in warning you of unauthorized access to the system (such as a user logging in from a different location than normal).

  Select this option to record successful login attempts in the file /var/log/wtmp.

  You can use the command **last** to view who logged in at what time.

- **Allow Remote Graphical Login.** You can select this option to allow other users access to your graphical login screen via the network.

  Because this type of access represents a potential security risk, it is inactive by default.

5. When you finish configuring login settings, continue by selecting **Next**.

   The dialog box shown in Figure 12-5 appears.

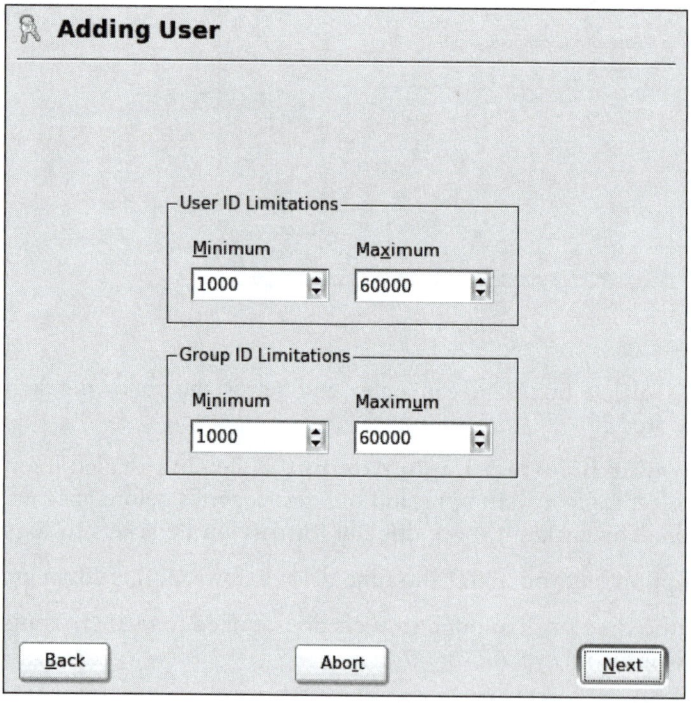

**Adding User**

User ID Limitations

Minimum
1000

Maximum
60000

Group ID Limitations

Minimum
1000

Maximum
60000

Back          Abort          Next

**Figure 12-5**

From this dialog box, you can enter the following ID settings:

- **User ID Limitations.** Enter a minimum and maximum value to configure a range of possible user ID numbers. A minimum of 500 is suitable for users.

- **Group ID Limitations.** Enter a minimum and maximum value to configure a range of possible group ID numbers.

6. When you finish configuring user and group ID limitations, continue by selecting **Next**.

The dialog box shown in Figure 12-6 appears.

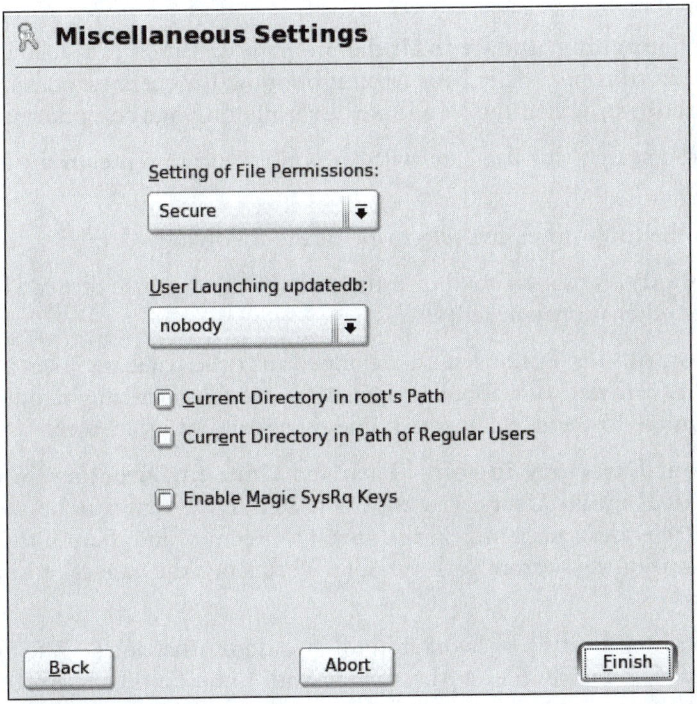

**Figure 12-6**

From this dialog box, you can select the following miscellaneous global settings:

- **Setting of File Permissions.** Settings for the permissions of certain system files are configured in **/etc/permissions.secure** or **/etc/permissions.easy**.

  From the drop-down list, select one of the following:

  - **Easy.** Select this option to allow read access to most of the system files by users other than root.

- **Secure.** Select this option to make sure that certain configuration files (such as /etc/ssh/sshd_config) can only be viewed by the user root. Some programs can only be launched by root or by daemons, not by an ordinary user.

- **Paranoid.** Select this option for an extremely secure system. All SUID/ SGID-Bits on programs have been cleared. Remember that some programs might not work or not work correctly, because users no longer have the permissions to access certain files.

Running SuSEconfig sets these permissions according to the settings in the /etc/permissions.* files.

This fixes files with incorrect permissions, whether this occurred accidentally or by intruders.

- **User Launching updatedb.** If the program updatedb is installed, it automatically runs on a daily basis or after booting. It generates a database (**locatedb**) in which the location of each file on your computer is stored.

You can search this database with the utility locate (enter **man locate** for details).

From the drop-down list, select one of the following:

- **nobody.** A user can find only the paths in the database that can be seen by any other (unprivileged) user.

- **root.** All files in the system are added into the database. This means that users can find out about the existence of files that might otherwise be invisible to them, e.g. in the home directories of other users.

- **Current Directory in root's Path** and **Current Directory in the Path of Regular Users.** On a DOS system, DOS first searches for executable files (programs) in the current directory, and then in the directories listed in the current path variable. This is not the case on a Linux system.

Some systems set up a "workaround" by adding the dot (".") to the search path, which enables files in the current path to be found and executed.

If you deselect these options, users must always launch programs in the current directory by adding "./" (such as *./* **configure**).

If you select these options, the dot (".") is appended to the end of the search path for root and users, allowing them to enter a command in the current directory without having to prefix it with "./".

Selecting these options can be very dangerous because users can accidentally launch unknown programs in the current directory.

In addition, selecting these options allows execution of Trojan Horses, which can exploit this weakness and intrude your system.

■ **Enable Magic SysRq Keys.** Selecting this option gives you some control over the system even if it crashes (such as during kernel debugging).

NOTE

For details, see /usr/src/linux/Documentation/sysrq.txt.

7. When you finish configuring the miscellaneous settings, save the settings and run SuSEconfig by selecting **Finish**.

## Set Defaults for New User Accounts

You can use YaST to select default settings to be applied to new user accounts by doing the following:

1. From the KDE desktop, start the YaST Edit and create users module by doing one of the following:

   ■ Select the **YaST** icon, enter the root password *novell*, and select **OK**; then select:

   **Security and Users > Edit and create users**

   *or*

   ■ Open a terminal window and enter **sux –** and the root password *novell*; then enter **yast2 users**.

2. Select **Expert Options > Defaults for New Users**.

12

The dialog box shown in Figure 12-7 appears.

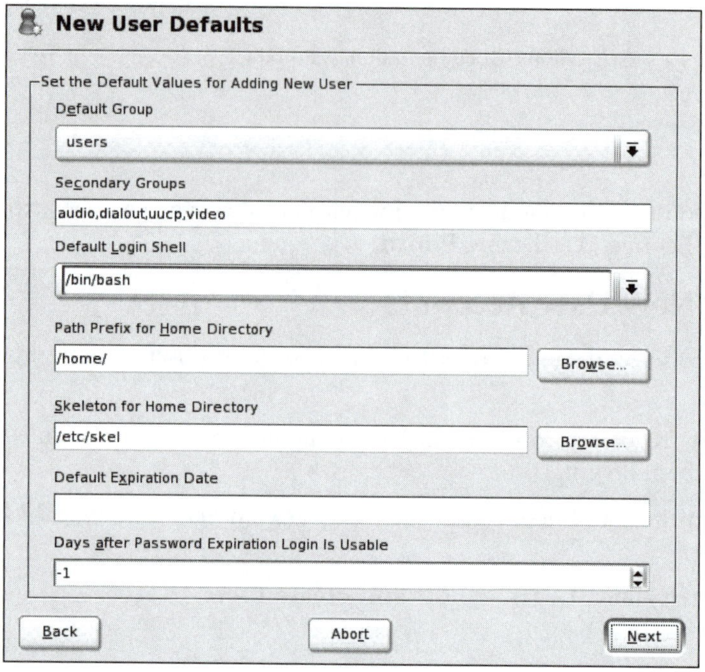

**Figure 12-7**

3. Enter or edit information in the following fields:

- **Default Group.** From the drop-down list select the primary (default) group.

- **Secondary Groups.** Enter a list of secondary groups (separated by commas) to assign to the user.

- **Default Login shell.** From the drop-down list select the default login shell (command interpreter) from the shells installed on your system, or enter your own path to the shell.

- **Default Home.** Enter or browse to the initial path prefix for a new user's home directory.

  The user's name will be appended to the end of this value to create the default name of the user's home directory.

- **Skeleton Directory.** Enter or browse to the skeleton directory.

  The contents of this directory will be copied to the user's home directory when you add a new user.

- **Default Expiration Date.** Enter the date on which the user account is disabled.

    The date must be in the format YYYY-MM-DD.

    Leave the field empty if this account never expires.

- **Days after Password Expiration Login Is Usable.** This setting enables users to log in after passwords expire.

    Set how many days after a password expires it is still allowed to log in.

    Enter **-1** for unlimited access.

4. Save the configuration settings by selecting **Next > Finish**.

# Perform Administrative Tasks as root

As a system administrator, you should log in as a normal user and only switch to root to perform tasks that require root permissions.

To switch between a normal user and root while performing administrative tasks, you can do the following:

- Use su to Switch to Another User
- Use newgrp to Switch to Another Group
- Start Programs as Another User from KDE

## Use su to Switch to Another User

You can use the su command (switch user) to assume the UID of root or of other users.

The following is the su syntax:

**su [*options*] ...[-] [*user*[*argument*]]**

For example, to change to the user geeko, enter:

**su geeko**

To change to the user root, enter:

**su root**

or

**su**

(without a user name).

Root can change to any user ID without knowing the password of the user.

To start a login shell when changing to the user root, enter:

**su –**

To change to the user root and execute a single command, use the –c option as shown in the following:

**su – –c "grep geeko /etc/shadow"**

For additional information on the command su, enter **su --help**.

## Use newgrp to Switch to Another Group

A user can be a member of many different groups, but only one GID is his *effective* (current) group at any one time. Normally this is the *primary group*, which is specified in the file /etc/passwd.

If a user creates directories or files, then they belong to the user and to the effective group.

You can change the effective group ID with the command **newgrp** or **sg** (such as **sg video**).

Only group members may perform this group change, unless a group password is defined. In this case, any user that knows the group password can make the change.

To undo the change (return to the original effective GID), enter **exit** or press **Ctrl + d**.

## Start Programs as Another User from KDE

In KDE you can start any program with a different UID (as long as you know the password) by doing the following:

1.  From the KDE desktop, open a command-line dialog box by pressing **Alt + F2**; then select **Options**.

The dialog box shown in Figure 12-8 appears.

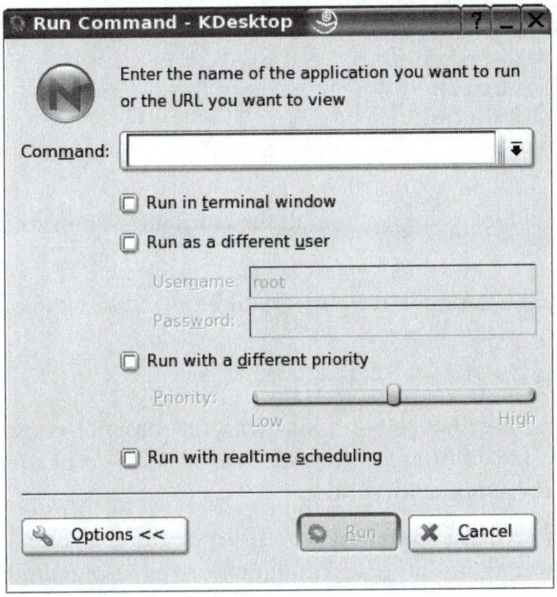

**Figure 12-8**

From this dialog box, you can enter a command that you want to run (or enter a URL to view).

There are also several options, including the option to run the command as a different user.

2. Select **Run as a Different User**: then enter the *username* (such as **root**) and the *password*.

3. Enter the command you want to run as another user; then select **Run**.

> **NOTE**
> You can also enter **kdesu** *program_name* to start a program as root. You are prompted for the root password before the program starts.

## Use sudo to Delegate Administrative Tasks

Sometimes it is necessary to allow a normal user access to a command usually reserved for root. For example, you might want a co-worker to take over tasks such as shutting down the computer and creating users while you are on vacation.

To enable a command to be run by a normal user, you can use the command **sudo**; as shown in the following:

```
geeko@da10:~ > sudo /sbin/shutdown -h now
We trust you have received the usual lecture from the local System
Administrator. It usually boils down to these two things:
#1) Respect the privacy of others.
#2) Think before you type.
Password:
```

You are prompted for a password, which is, depending on the configuration in /etc/sudoers, either the

- **user password.** This is the configuration used in SLES 8 and also the one needed for the vacation szenario given above.

- **root password.** This is the default configuration in SLES 9.

  To change this so that the user has to enter his own password, put comment signs (#) in front of the lines "Defaults targetpw" and "%users ALL=(ALL) ALL" in the file /etc/sudoers using the command visudo.

As administrator, you can specify which commands a user can or cannot enter by configuring the file /etc/sudoers. You can modify the configuration by using the command **visudo**.

The following is the general syntax of an entry in the configuration file:

*user/group host = command1, command2 ...*

For example:

**geeko ALL = /sbin/shutdown**

In this example, the user geeko is able to carry out the command **/sbin/shutdown** with the permissions of root on all computers (**ALL**).

Figure 12-9 shows a more complex example that illustrates the flexibility of sudo.

```
   User_Alias   ADMINS     = tux, geeko
 2 User_Alias   WEBMASTER  = john
   User_Alias   SUBSTITUTE = olli, klaas
 4
   # Cmnd alias specification
 6
   Cmnd_Alias   PRINTING = /usr/sbin/lpc, /usr/bin/lprm
 8 Cmnd_Alias   SHUTDOWN = /sbin/shutdown
   Cmnd_Alias   APACHE   = /etc/init.d/apache
10
12 # User privilege specification
   root    ALL=(ALL) ALL
14
   ADMINS       ALL = NOPASSWD: !/usr/bin/passwd, /usr/bin/passwd [A-z]*,
16 !/usr/bin/passwd root
   WEBMASTER  ALL = APACHE
18 SUBSTITUTE ALL = SHUTDOWN, PRINTING
```

**Figure 12-9**

Lines 1 to 9 define aliases. You can do this for the following:

- Users with User_Alias (lines 1–3)
- Commands with Cmnd_Alias (lines 7–9)
- Hosts with Host_Alias

Lines 14–17 in this example show how these aliases can be used in the actual rules:

- **ADMINS.** This is the User_Alias for the users tux and geeko (see line 1).

  The following are additional parameters:

  - **!/usr/bin/passwd, /usr/bin/passwd [A-z]\*.** This indicates that both users are allowed to run the command passwd with one single argument and change the passwords for user accounts.

  - **!/usr/bin/passwd root.** This indicates that both users are not allowed to change the password for root.

    However, they can change the passwords of other users.

With this configuration, tux and geeko could still lock out root by entering **sudo /usr/bin/passwd root -l**.

**12**

- **WEBMASTER.** This is the User_Alias for the user account john (see line 2).

  This user can start and stop the Web server (APACHE).

- **SUBSTITUTE.** This is the User_Alias for the user accounts olli and klaas (see line 3).

  These users can execute commands summarized in sections SHUTDOWN and PRINTING (see lines 7 and 8).

For additional documentation, caveat and configuration examples, enter **man 5 sudoers**.

## How Special File Permissions Affect the System's Security

There are three file system permissions that influence security in a special way:

- **The SUID bit.** If the SUID bit is set for an executable, the program is started under the user ID of the owner of the file. In most cases, this is used to allow normal users to run applications with the rights of the root user.

This bit should only be set for applications that are well tested and in cases where there is no other way to perform a specific task.

An attacker could get access to the root account by exploiting an application that runs under the UID of root.

- **The SGID bit.** If this bit is set, it lets a program run under the GID of the group the executable file belongs to. It should be used as carefully as the SUID bit.

- **The sticky bit.** The sticky bit can influence the security of a system in a positive way. In a globally writable directory, it prevents users from deleting each others files that are stored in these directories.

Typical application areas for the sticky bit include directories for temporary storage (such as /tmp and /var/tmp). Such a directory must be writable by all users of a system.

However, the write permissions for a directory do not only include the permission to create files and subdirectories, but also the permission to delete these, regardless of whether the user has access to the contents of these files and subdirectories.

If the sticky bit is set for such a writable directory, deleting or renaming files in this directory is only possible if one of the following conditions is fulfilled:

- The effective UID of the deleting or renaming process is that of the file owner.

- The effective UID of the deleting or renaming process is that of the owner of the writable directory marked with the sticky bit.

- The superuser root is allowed to do anything.

## Configure File Permissions

As a general rule, always work with the most restrictive privileges possible for a given task.

For example, it is definitely not necessary to be the user root to read or write e-mail. If the mail program has a bug, this bug could be exploited for an attack that acts with exactly the permissions of the program when it was started. By following the above general rule, you can minimize the possible damage.

The permissions of the more than 200,000 files included in a SUSE Linux distribution are carefully chosen. A system administrator who installs additional software or other files should take great care when doing so, especially when setting the permission bits.

Experienced and security-conscious system administrators always use the **-l** option with the command **ls** to get an extensive file list, which allows them to detect any incorrect file permissions immediately.

An incorrect file attribute not only means that files might be changed or deleted, but that the modified files might be executed by root or, in the case of configuration files, programs could use such files with the permissions of root.

This significantly increases the chances of an attacker. Attacks like this are called *cuckoo eggs*, because the program (the egg) is executed (hatched) by a different user (bird), just like a cuckoo tricks other birds into hatching its eggs.

A SUSE Linux system includes the files **permissions**, **permissions.easy**, **permissions.secure**, and **permissions.paranoid**, all in the directory /etc/.

The purpose of these files is to define special permissions, such as world-writable directories or, for files, the setuser ID bit (a program with the setuser ID bit set does not run with the permissions of the user that has launched it, but with the permissions of the file owner, in most cases, root).

An administrator can use the file /etc/permissions.local to add her own settings.

To learn more about the permissions topic, read the comments in the file /etc/permissions and refer to the man page of chmod (**man chmod**).

For additional details on types of security breaches (such as buffer overflows and viruses, see Section 26.7, "Security and Confidentiality" in the *SLES 9 Installation and Administration Manual*.

## Additional Security Considerations

In order to provide a secure environment for your users and data in a multiuser environment, you need to consider the following guidelines when implementing your enterprise security policies on SUSE Linux Enterprise Server:

- Local Security and User Accounts
- Linux Password Encryption
- Boot Procedure Protection
- Network Security and Local Security

### Local Security and User Accounts

The main goal of local security is to keep users separate from each other, so no user can assume the permissions or the identity of another.

However, the user root holds the ultimate power on the system and can log in as any other local user without a password and read and change any locally stored file.

Therefore the system administrator is required to have a very high level of integrity and loyalty.

## Linux Password Encryption

On a Linux system, passwords are, of course, not stored as plain text, and the text string entered is not simply matched with the saved pattern.

If this were the case, all accounts on your system would be compromised as soon as someone got access to the corresponding file.

Instead, the stored password is encrypted (or more exactly, hashed) and, each time it is entered, it is encrypted again with the two encrypted strings being compared.

 This only provides more security if the encrypted password cannot be reverse-computed into the original text string.

**CAUTION**

This encryption is actually achieved by a special kind of algorithm, also called *one way hash (trapdoor) algorithm*, because it only works in one direction. An attacker who has obtained the encrypted string is not able to get your password by simply applying some algorithm.

Instead, it is necessary to test all the possible character combinations until a combination is found that, when encrypted, looks like your encrypted password. With passwords 8 characters long, there are quite a number of possible combinations to calculate.

## Boot Procedure Protection

You should configure your Linux system so it cannot be booted from a floppy disk or from CD, either by removing the drives entirely or by setting a BIOS password and configuring the BIOS to allow booting from a hard disk only.

Normally, a Linux system is started by a boot loader, allowing you to pass additional options to the booted kernel. This has implications to your system's security.

Not only does the kernel itself run with root permissions, but it is also the first authority to grant root permissions at system start-up.

You can prevent others from using arbitrary parameters during boot by setting an additional password in /boot/grub/menu.lst (see **info grub** for details).

## Network Security and Local Security

Network security is important for protecting from an attack that is started outside. The typical login procedure requiring a user name and a password for user authentication is still a local security issue.

In the particular case of logging in over a network, you need to differentiate between the two security aspects. What happens up to the actual authentication is network security and anything that happens afterward is local security.

## OBJECTIVE 2    USE SYSTEM LOGGING SERVICES

In a Linux system, there are many logs that track various aspects of system operation. Many services log their activities to their own log files, and the level of detail can be set on a per-service basis. In addition, system logs in /var/log/ track system-level events.

The information logged in these log files is typically used to assist in troubleshooting and security auditing. However, you will probably want to review the logs from time to time as a preventative measure.

To use system logging services, you need to understand the following:

- The syslog Daemon
- Important Log Files
- Use YaST to View Log Files
- Archive Log Files (logrotate)
- Monitor Hard Drive Space

## The syslog Daemon

12

The syslog daemon **syslogd** is used by many services to log system events. The advantage in using a single service for logging is that all logging can be managed from one configuration file.

The daemon syslogd in Linux is based on the BSD syslogd service. While it conforms to standard behavior, it has been extended for use in Linux as well. This means that syslogd is compatible with non-Linux systems that conform to the documented BSD interfaces.

**NOTE**

The syslog daemon accepts messages from system services and logs them based on settings in the configuration file **/etc/syslog.conf**.

For details on the syslog.conf file, enter **man syslog.conf**.

**NOTE**

The following is an example of the syslogd configuration file:

```
# /etc/syslog.conf - Configuration file for syslogd(8)
#
# For info about the format of this file, see "man syslog.conf".
#

#
```

```
# print most on tty10 and on the xconsole pipe
#
kern.warning;*.err;authpriv.none          /dev/tty10
kern.warning;*.err;authpriv.none          |/dev/xconsole
*.emerg                                    *

# enable this, if you want that root is informed
# immediately, e.g. of logins
#*.alert                                   root
...
```

The file /etc/syslog.conf contains one rule per line. Each rule consists of two fields separated by spaces or tabs.

The category is given in the first field, which is always allocated a priority, separated by a dot (such as **kern.warn**). The second field specifies what should be done with the corresponding system messages (such as **/dev/xconsole**).

To understand how syslog.conf works, you need to know about the following components:

- Categories
- Priorities
- Second Field Options
- Additional Priority Parameters

## Categories

The category refers to the subsystem that provides the corresponding message. Each program that uses syslog for logging is assigned such a category. Table 12-1 describes these categories.

**Table 12-1**

| Category | Description |
|----------|-------------|
| authpriv | Used by all services that have anything to do with system security or authorization. All PAM messages use this category.<br><br>The ssh daemon uses the auth category. |
| cron | Accepts messages from the cron and at daemons. |
| daemon | Used by various daemons that do not have their own category, such as the ppp daemon. |
| kern | A category for all kernel messages. |
| lpr | This category handles messages from the printer system. |
| news | This category is for messages from the news system. As with the mail system, many messages might need to be logged in a short time. |
| mail | This category is for messages from the mail system. This is important because many messages can arrive very quickly. |

**Table 12-1**   (continued)

| Category | Description |
|---|---|
| syslog | This category is for internal messages of the syslog daemon. |
| user | This is a general category for messages on a user level. For example, It is used by login to log failed login attempts. |
| uucp | This category handles messages from the uucp system. |
| local0 – local7 | These 8 categories are available for your own configuration. All of the local categories can be used in your own programs.<br><br>By configuring one of these categories, messages from your own programs can be administered individually through entries in the file /etc/syslog.conf. |

## Priorities

The priority gives details about the urgency of the message. Table 12-2 shows the priorities available (listed in increasing degree of urgency).

**Table 12-2**

| Priority | Description |
|---|---|
| debug | This priority should only be used for debugging purposes, since all messages of this category and higher are logged. |
| info | This priority is for messages that are purely informative. |
| notice | This priority is for messages that describe normal system states that should be noted. |
| warning | This priority is for messages displaying deviations from the normal state. |
| err | This priority displays the occurrence of an error. |
| crit | This priority informs you of critical conditions for the specified program. |
| alert | This priority level informs the system administrator is required that immediate action is needed to keep the system functioning. |
| emerg | This priority warns you that the system is no longer usable. |

**12**

## Second Field Options

As already mentioned, the second field for each entry determines what will be done with the corresponding message.

The following options are available:

- **Output of a file.** Adding a - before the filename specifies that the file is not synchronized for each entry.

  The following is an example:
  ```
  mail.*          -/var/log/mail
  ```

- **Specifying the device file for a text console.** All corresponding messages are sent to the console specified.

  The following is an example:
  ```
  kern.warn;*.err;authpriv.none        /dev/tty10
  ```

- **Specifying a FIFO file (named pipe) by putting the pipe character (|) in front of the file name.** All corresponding messages are written into the FIFO file.

  The following is an example:
  ```
  kern.warn;*.err;authpriv.none        |/dev/xconsole
  ```

- **Specifying a user list.** All users mentioned who are logged in receive a message on their text terminal (this does not work on all terminal types).

  The following is an example:
  ```
  *.alert         root,geeko
  ```

- **Specifying a computer name with a prefixed @.** Messages are forwarded to the computer specified and logged there by syslog, depending on the configuration on that computer.

  The following is an example:
  ```
  *.*             @da2.digitalairlines.com
  ```

- **Using an asterisk (*).** All users logged in receive a message through the **wall** (write all) command.

  The following is an example:
  ```
  *.crit          *
  ```

## Additional Priority Parameters

The rules listed are always valid for the specified priority and all higher priorities. The following are additional parameters you can use for defining the priority in a rule:

- **An equal sign (=) before the priority.** By entering an equal sign, the rule is set only for messages of this priority.

  The following is an example:
  ```
  *.=warn;*.=err          -/var/log/warn
  ```

- **An exclamation mark (!) before the priority.** By entering an exclamation mark, this and all higher priorities are excluded from logging.

The following is an example

```
mail.*;mail.!=info              /var/adm/mail
```

- **Add an asterisk (\*).** If you enter an asterisk, it stands for "all categories" or "all priorities."

- **Set none as the priority.** You can exclude a category from logging by setting none as the priority.

The following is an example:

```
*.*;mail.none;news.none         -/var/log/messages
```

You can specify parameters for the syslog daemon in the file /etc/sysconfig/syslog.

The variable KERNEL_LOGLEVEL determines the logging level for the kernel log daemon (klogd). You can use the variable SYSLOGD_PARAMS to pass start parameters to the daemon.

For example, if you want a host to log messages of other hosts, the syslog daemon of the host that should accept the messages from a remote syslog must be started with the option **-r**.

In this case, the entry in the file /etc/sysconfig/syslog looks like the following:

```
## Type:              string
## Default:           ""
## Config:            ""
## ServiceRestart:    syslog
#
# if not empty: parameters for syslogd
# for example SYSLOGD_PARAMS="-r -s my.dom.ain"
#
SYSLOGD_PARAMS="-r"
```

## Important Log Files

The log file to which most messages are written is the file /var/log/messages. Often hints can be found here about problems such as why a service does not function properly when it starts.

The entry **-- MARK --** is written to the file by the syslog daemon every 20 minutes if no other messages to log exist. This makes it easy to check whether the syslog daemon has been running the entire time or if the daemon has been stopped (in this case the entries -- MARK -- are missing).

The best approach for reading the log files from the command line is to use the command tail (**tail /var/log/messages**). This displays the last 10 lines of the file, which are also the most current entries.

By using **tail -n** (such as **tail -n 30**) you can specify the number of lines to display.

If you want to have new messages displayed immediately, use the interactive mode with **tail -f**.

12

For example, entering:

**tail –20f /var/log/messages**

switches tail to interactive mode. The last 20 lines of the file /var/log/messages are displayed. If new messages are added these are displayed immediately.

You can close the display by pressing **Ctrl + c**.

Table 12-3 lists important log files stored in the directory /var/log/ or its subdirectories.

**Table 12-3**

| Log File | Description |
| --- | --- |
| **/var/log/cups/** | This directory stores the log files for the printing system CUPS. |
| **/var/log/news/** | This directory stores messages for the news system. |
| **/var/log/YaST2/** | This directory stores log files for YaST. |
| **/var/log/boot.msg** | When the system boots, all boot script messages are displayed on the first virtual console. This often happens so fast that you cannot read all the messages.<br><br>You can, however, read the boot messages including the output from start scripts of services in this file.<br><br>You can display the messages from the kernel during the boot procedure later with the command **dmesg** (/bin/dmesg). |
| **/var/log/mail** | Messages from the mail system are written to this file. Because this system often generates a lot of messages, there are additional log files:<br>• /var/log/mail.err<br>• /var/log/mail.info<br>• /var/log/mail.warn |
| **/var/log/wtmp** | This file contains information about which user was logged in from where and for how long (since the file was created).<br><br>The file contents are in binary form and can only be displayed with the command **last** (/usr/bin/last).<br><br>Because of the binary format, it is difficult to manipulate entries in this file. |
| **/var/log/lastlog** | This file contains information about user's last login, from where, and for how long.<br><br>You can only view the contents with the command **lastlog** (/usr/bin/lastlog). |

## Use YaST to View Log Files

You can view startup or system logs with YaST by doing the following:

1. From the KDE desktop, start the YaST View Start-up Log or View System Log module by doing one of the following:

   - Select the **YaST** icon, enter the root password *novell*, and select **OK**; then select:

     **Misc > View Start-up Log** or **Misc > View System Log**

     *or*

   - Open a terminal window and enter **sux –** and the root password *novell*; then enter **yast2 view_anymsg**.

   The dialog box shown in Figure 12-10 appears.

```
/var/log/messages                                    ↧

System log (/var/log/messages)
Jul 28 10:20:14 DA50 su: pam_unix2: session started for user root, service su
Jul 28 10:20:14 DA50 su: pam_unix2: session finished for user root, service su
Jul 28 10:20:14 DA50 su: (to root) geeko on /dev/pts/2
Jul 28 10:20:14 DA50 su: pam_unix2: session started for user root, service su
Jul 28 10:49:26 DA50 -- MARK --
Jul 28 10:59:00 DA50 /USR/SBIN/CRON[25580]: (root) CMD ( rm -f /var/spool/cron/lastrun/cron.hourly)
Jul 28 11:09:26 DA50 -- MARK --
Jul 28 11:29:26 DA50 -- MARK --
Jul 28 11:49:26 DA50 -- MARK --
Jul 28 11:59:00 DA50 /USR/SBIN/CRON[25671]: (root) CMD ( rm -f /var/spool/cron/lastrun/cron.hourly)
Jul 28 12:09:26 DA50 -- MARK --
Jul 28 12:29:26 DA50 -- MARK --
Jul 28 12:42:20 DA50 su: (to root) geeko on /dev/pts/3
Jul 28 12:42:20 DA50 su: pam_unix2: session started for user root, service su
Jul 28 12:59:00 DA50 /USR/SBIN/CRON[25798]: (root) CMD ( rm -f /var/spool/cron/lastrun/cron.hourly)
Jul 28 13:09:26 DA50 -- MARK --
Jul 28 13:29:26 DA50 -- MARK --
Jul 28 13:35:35 DA50 su: pam_unix2: session finished for user root, service su
Jul 28 13:40:42 DA50 su: (to root) geeko on /dev/pts/3
Jul 28 13:40:42 DA50 su: pam_unix2: session started for user root, service su
Jul 28 13:43:31 DA50 su: pam_unix2: session finished for user root, service su

                              OK
```

**Figure 12-10**   FiF

The same dialog box is used for both YaST modules; the only difference is the default log displayed (messages for System Log and boot.msg for Start-up Log).

2. Select a *log* to view from the drop-down list.

3. When you finish viewing logs, close the dialog box by selecting **OK**.

**NOTE**

To view log files in a console use **less** or **tail -f**.

## Archive Log Files (logrotate)

It is important to ensure that log files do not get too large or too complex, or require too much space inside the system. For this reason, size and age of log files are monitored automatically by the program logrotate (/usr/sbin/logrotate).

The program is run daily by the cron daemon (/etc/cron.daily/logrotate). The program checks all log files listed in its configuration files (based on the parameters given).

You can configure the settings in the files to indicate whether files should be compressed or deleted in regular intervals or when a determined size is reached.

You can also configure how many compressed versions of a log file are kept over a specified period of time, and the forwarding of log files through e-mail.

The configuration file of logrotate is /etc/logrotate.conf, which contains general configuration settings. The following is an example of logrotate.conf:

```
# see "man logrotate" for details
# rotate log files weekly
weekly

# keep 4 weeks worth of backlogs
rotate 4

# create new (empty) log files after rotating old ones
create

# uncomment this if you want your log files compressed
#compress

# uncomment these to switch compression to bzip2
#compresscmd /usr/bin/bzip2
#uncompresscmd /usr/bin/bunzip2

# RPM packages drop log rotation information into this directory
include /etc/logrotate.d
...
```

Table 12-4 describes the options in the file.

**Table 12-4**

| Option | Description |
|--------|-------------|
| weekly | The log files are created or replaced once a week. |
| rotate 4 | Unless the option rotate is specified, the old files are deleted.<br><br>In this example, the last 4 versions of the log file are kept (rotate 4). |
| create | The old file is saved under a new name and a new, empty log file is created. |
| compress | If the option compress is activated, the copies are stored in a compressed form. |

Many RPM packages contain preconfigured files for evaluation by logrotate, which are stored in /etc/logrotate.d/. The files contained in that directory are read by logrotate due to the entry **include /etc/logrotate.d** in /etc/logrotate.conf.

Any settings in the logrotate.d files supersede the general settings in logrotate.conf.

All the files to monitor must be listed. This is done through the entries in /etc/logrotate. conf (such as **/var/log/wtmp {[*options*]}**) or in separate configuration files.

The following is an example of the file syslogd in /etc/logrotate.d/:

```
/var/log/warn /var/log/messages /var/log/allmessages\
   /var/log/localmessages /var/log/firewall {
   compress
   dateext
   maxage 365
   rotate 99
   missingok
   notifempty
   size +4096k
   create 640 root root
   sharedscripts
   postrotate
       /etc/init.d/syslog reload
   endscript
}

/var/log/mail /var/log/mail.info /var/log/mail.warn /var/log/mail.err {
   compress
   dateext
   maxage 365
   rotate 99
   missingok
   notifempty
   size +4096k
```

**12**

```
create 640 root root
sharedscripts
postrotate
    /etc/init.d/syslog reload
endscript
}
```

The file syslogd contains settings configuring how the log files written by the daemon syslog will be treated.

Table 12-5 describes the options in the file.

**Table 12-5**

| Option | Description |
|---|---|
| size +4096k | Files will not be rotated weekly, but as soon as they reach a size of 4096 KB. |
| rotate 99 | Ninety-nine versions of each of the files will be kept. |
| compress | The old log files will be stored compressed. |
| maxage 365 | As soon as a compressed file is older than 365 days, it is deleted. |
| notifempty | If a log file is empty, no rotation takes place. |
| create 640 root root | New log files are created after the rotation and owner, group, and permissions are specified. |
| postrotate . . . endscript | Scripts can be called after the rotation. For example, some services have to be restarted after log files have been changed.<br><br>In this example, the syslog daemon will reread its configuration files after the rotation (/etc/init.d/syslog reload). |

Most of the services whose log files should be monitored come with preconfigured files, so normally only minor adjustments are needed.

 For a complete list of all possible options, enter **man logrotate**.

NOTE

## Monitor Hard Drive Space

There is no automatic warning generated when the system is about to run out of hard disk space. To receive a warning in such a case, the system administrator would need to set up an appropriate cron job.

To monitor hard drive space, there are the following programs:

- df (disk free)
- du (disk usage)
- KDE Info Center and KDiskFree

## df (disk free)

You can use the command **/bin/df** (disk free) to monitor hard drive space. For all mounted partitions, the command displays how much space is used and how much is still available.

With the option -h (for human-readable) the output is given in units of GB or MB, which is easier to interpret, as in the following:

```
da10:~ # df -h
Filesystem      Size  Used  Avail Use% Mounted on
/dev/hda1       500M  152M  348M   31% /
/dev/hda2       2.0G  551M  1.4G   27% /opt
/dev/hda3       7.0G  1.3G  5.7G   18% /misc
/dev/hda5       500M  141M  359M   29% /tmp
/dev/hda6       3.0G  2.5G  521M   84% /usr
/dev/hda7       2.0G  119M  1.8G    6% /var
tmpfs           374M     0  373M    1% /dev/shm
/dev/hda8      19:0G  5:4G   13G   29% /home
```

## du (disk usage)

To find out how large individual files or directories are, use the command **/usr/bin/du** (disk usage). Without any options, it displays, for each subdirectory and the current directory, how much space (in 1KB units) is used by the current directory and its subdirectories.

Table 12-6 lists some commonly used options with the command du.

**Table 12-6**

| Option | Description |
|---|---|
| -a | Displays the size of directories and files. |
| -c | Displays the total as the final value. This option is useful to determine how much space is taken up by all files with a specific extension (such as .tex) |
| -h | Displays the sizes (in KB and MB) in a human-readable format. |
| -s | Shows only the total amount. This option is useful to find out how much space is taken up by directories. |

12

The following are some examples of using the command du:

```
geeko@da10:~ > du
4          ./Letters
400        .
geeko@da10:~ > du -h
4.0k       ./Letters
400k       .
geeko@da10:~ > du -ha
4.0k       ./Letters
4.0k       ./file1
4.0k       ./file2
308k       ./file3
76k        ./file4
400k       .
```

If you enter a command such as:

**du -h -c /home/geeko**

first the size of the directories in the home directory of the user geeko is given, and then (with total), the total size of the directory (with the size of files included).

## KDE Info Center and KDiskFree

For a high-level view of disk space usage, you can run utilities from the KDE desktop such as Info Center (Storage Devices) or KDiskFree.

You can access the Info Center from the Start menu by selecting **System > Monitor > Info Center** or by entering **kinfocenter**.

You can access the KDiskFree from the Start menu by selecting **System > File System > KDiskFree** or by entering **kdf**.

Figure 12-11 shows an example of a KDiskFree display.

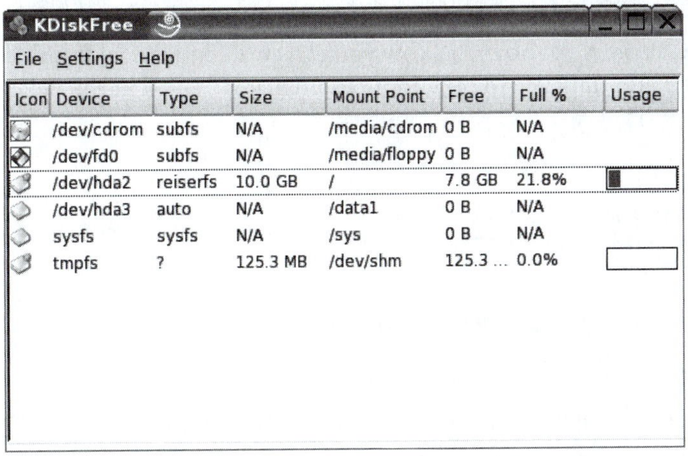

**Figure 12-11**

You can also monitor disk space usage by directory or file when using views such as Tree View or Detailed List View in Konqueror, as shown in Figure 12-2.

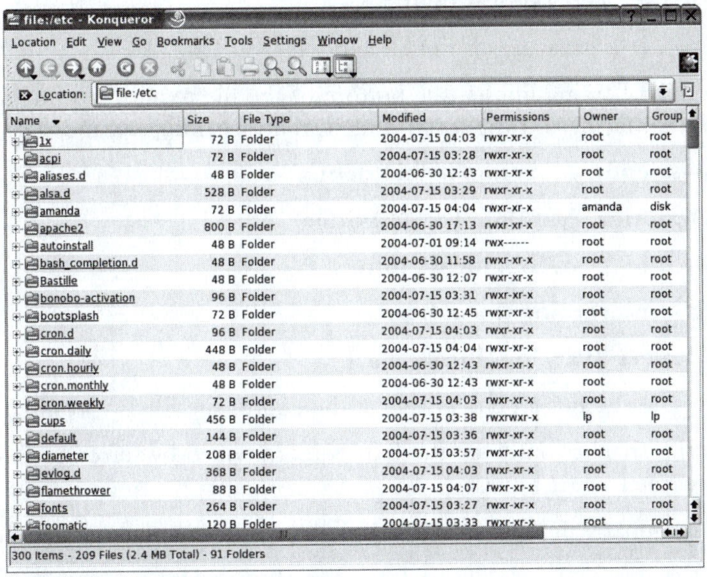

**12**

**Figure 12-12**

However, you can only view individual directory and file sizes. You cannot automatically determine total amounts for a group of files (such as all the files in a directory).

## Exercise 12-1   Manage System Logging

System logging is an essential part of system security.

The purpose of this exercise is to show you how you can create individual log files according to your needs You will also understand how to modify what is logged in the default log files and how to influence the way log files are archived.

In this exercise, you do the following:

- Part I: Modify the Syslog Configuration
- Part II: Configure logrotate

### Part I: Modify the Syslog Configuration

Do the following:

1. Make a backup copy of /etc/syslog.conf by entering:

   **cp /etc/syslog.conf /etc/syslog.conf.original**

2. Edit the file /etc/syslog.conf:

   a. Open the file /etc/syslog.conf in an editor by pressing **Alt + F2** and entering:

   **kdesu kate /etc/syslog.conf**

   Then enter a password of **novell** and select **OK**.

   b. Add the following lines at the bottom of the file to allow for logging of the local4 facility on the levels of debug, notice, info, err, and alert:

   **local4. debug /var/log/local4.debug**

   **local4.notice /var/log/local4.notice**

   **local4.info /var/log/local4.info**

   **local4.err /var/log/local4.err**

   **local4.alert /var/log/local4.alert**

   c. Make sure there is an empty line at the end of the file by pressing **Enter**.

   d. Save the changes but keep the Kate window open by selecting **File > Close**; then select **Save**.

3. From a terminal window, su to root (**su -**) with a password of **novell**.

4. Restart the syslog daemon by entering **rcsyslog restart**.

5. Check the configuration by logging an entry to the info level in the local4 facility:

   a. To monitor the activity of the log file, enter:

     **tail –f /var/log/local4.info**

   b. Open another terminal window (su to **root**) and log an entry to the info level in the local4 facility by entering:

     **logger –p local4.info "Info message 1"**

   c. Check the results in the second terminal window.

     The message is logged in the file /var/log/local4.info.

     The message should also be logged in the file /var/log/localmessages because of other entries in /etc/syslog.conf.

   d. In the terminal window where the log activity is being monitored with tail –f, stop the monitoring by pressing **Ctrl + c**.

6. Repeat step 4 to send a message at each of the log levels (such as **logger –p local4. debug "Info message 2"**) and monitor the messages with tail –f for the associated log file (such as **tail –f /var/log/local4. debug**).

   Notice that at certain levels messages from other levels are also recorded.

**CAUTION**

Only those log level files with entries will be compressed in Part II of the exercise during log rotation.

## Part II: Configure logrotate

Now that the local4 facility is being logged to separate files, you can use the program logrotate to manage the files for the system by creating a file /etc/logrotate.d/local4 that does the following:

- Compresses the old logs in gzip format
- Saves the old logs with a date extension
- Limits the oldest log to one day
- Limits the rotated logs saved to 5
- Limits the maximum size of the file to 20 bytes
- Proceeds without error if a log file is missing
- Logs the date in the local4.info file each time a new log file is generated

**12**

Do the following:

1. From the Kate window in a new document, enter:

   **/var/log/local4.err /var/log/local4.info**

   **/var/log/local4.alert /var/log/local4. debug /var/log/local4.notice**

   **{**

       **compress**

       **dateext**

       **maxage 1**

       **rotate 5**

       **size=20**

       **postrotate**

       **date >> /var/log/local4.info**

       **endscript**

   **}**

   Make sure the directories are written in one line and separated with spaces.

2. Save the file by selecting **File > Save**; then enter **/etc/logrotate.d/local4** and select **Save**.

3. Close the Kate window by selecting **File > Quit**.

4. Switch to virtual terminal 1 by pressing **Ctrl + Alt + F1**.

5. Log in as **root** with a password of **novell**.

6. Rotate the logs manually by entering:

   **logrotate /etc/logrotate.conf**

7. Check the directory /var/log for the zipped local4 log files by entering:

   **ls -l /var/log | less**

   You see files such as the following:

   - **local4.info-*current_date*.gz**

   - **local4.notice-*current_date*.gz**

   For example, if the current date is July 15, 2006, then the zipped file for local4.info would be **local4.info-20060715**.

**CAUTION**    Only those log files with entries are zipped.

8. Exit the list by typing **q**.

9. Check the contents of the local4.info zipped archive by entering:

   **less /var/log/local4.info-***current_date***.gz** or

   **zcat /var/log/local4.info-***current_date***.gz**

10. Log out as root by entering **exit**.

11. Return to the KDE desktop by pressing **Ctrl + Alt + F7**.

12. Close all open windows.

---

# OBJECTIVE 3   AUDIT LOG FILES AND AUTHENTICATION

Linux writes extensive log files via the syslog daemon.

To be of any use, these files have to be looked at regularly by the system administrator.

Depending on the services running on a machine and their activity, log files can grow several MB per day.

Without specific tools, it becomes very difficult for the administrator to find out about unusual acitivies or security violations.

Tools exist to

- Extract Information from Log Files
- Run Security Checks on the Machine

## Extract Information from Log Files

The following introduces two tools used to extract relevant information from log files:

- logcheck
- logsurfer

### logcheck

**logcheck** (http://logcheck.org/) parses system logs and generates e-mail reports based on anomalies.

In the beginning logcheck produces long reports. The system administrator has to modify the configuration of logcheck so that entries that are harmless do not turn up in the report anymore.

12

After that initial phase, the reports mailed by logcheck should contain only relevant information on security violations and unusual activities.

logcheck should be called regularly via cron to parse log files. As logcheck remembers the point to which a log file was scanned previously, only the new section is scanned on the next call.

### logsurfer

The simple parsing of log files line by line has the disadvantage that each line is independent of all other lines. However it could happen that a system administrator wants additional information when a certain entry is found in the log file.

**logsurfer** offers this functionality with so-called contexts: Several lines matching a pattern can be stored in memory as a context.

Depending on further patterns in the log file, such a context could be for example mailed to the system administrator for his inspection, or some other action, like starting a program, could be triggered.

If this further pattern is not found within a certain time or number of lines, the context could be deleted again.

Dynamic creation or deletion of matching rules depending on entries in the log file is also possible.

As logsurfer can be configured in great detail, the configuration is not trivial. However, the advantage is that the system administrator can configure very precisely what should happen under what circumstances.

## Run Security Checks on the Machine

In addition to checking configuration files, further checks are possible to find out about system configurations that could constitute a danger to security.

While such scripts can also detect a system compromise under certain circumstances, one should be aware that a successful cracker can modify such scripts to avoid detection.

The following is described:

- Monitor Login Activity from the Command Line
- Implement Security Rules and Tips
- SUSE Security Information Resources
- seccheck
- Custom Scripts

## Monitor Login Activity from the Command Line

One of the most critical tasks you have as an administrator is to make sure that there is no suspicious activity on your system that might compromise security.

Monitoring tasks include evaluating login activity for signs of a security breach, such as multiple failed logins.

**NOTE**

Reviewing files such as messages in /var/log/ also gives you information about login activity.

To monitor login activity, you can use the following commands:

- **who.** This command shows who is currently logged in to the system and information such as the time of the last login.

  You can use options such as **-H** (display column headings), **-r** (current runlevel), and **-a** (display information provided by most options).

  For example, entering **who -H** returns information similar to the following:

```
da10: ~ # who -H
NAME       LINE       TIME             Command
root       0          Aug 23 05:41     (console)
geeko      pts/2      Aug 24 02:32     (10.0.0.50)
da10:~ #
```

- **w.** This command displays information about the users currently on the machine and their processes.

  The first line includes information the current time, how long the system has been running, how many users are currently logged on, and the system load averages for the past 1, 5, and 15 minutes.

  Below the first line is an entry for each user that displays the login name, the tty name, the remote host, login time, idle time, JCPU, PCPU, and the command line of the user's current process.

  The JCPU time is the time used by all processes attached to the tty. It does not include past background jobs, but does include currently running background jobs.

  The PCPU time is the time used by the current process, named in the What field.

  You can use options such as –h (don't display the header), –s (don't display the login time, JCPU, and PCPU), and –V (display version information).

  For example, entering **w** returns information similar to the following:

```
da10: ~ # w
USER       TTY        LOGIN@           IDLE   JCPU   PCPU   WHAT
root       0          Mon05            ?xdm?  1:48   0.02s  -0
```

**12**

```
geeko      pts/2      02:32            0.00s  0.10s  0.02s  ssh: geeko [priv]
da10:~ #
```

- **finger.** This command displays information about local and remote system users. By default, the following information is displayed about each user currently logged in to the local host:

  - Login name

  - User's full name

  - Associated terminal name

  - Idle time

  - Login time (and from where)

You can use options such as -l (long format) and –s (short format).

For example, entering **finger –s** returns information similar to the following:

```
da10: ~ # finger -s
Login    Name                Tty       Idle  Login Time      Where
geeko    The SUSE Chameleon  pts/2      -        Tue 02:32    10.0.0.50
root     root                0         54d       Mon 05:41    console
da10:~ #
```

- **last.** This command displays a listing of the last logged in users.

Last searches back through the file /var/log/wtmp (or the file designated by the option -f) and displays a list of all users logged in (and out) since the file was created.

You can specify names of users and tty's to only show information for those entries.

You can use options such as *–num* (where *num* is the number of lines to display), **-a** (display the hostname in the last column), and **-x** (display system shutdown entries and runlevel changes).

For example, entering **last –ax** returns information similar to the following:

```
da10: ~ # last -ax
geeko        pts/2      Tue Aug 24 02:32    still logged in    10.0.0.50
geeko        pts/2      Tue Aug 24 02:29 - 02:30   (00:00)     10.0.0.50
geeko        pts/2      Tue Aug 24 02:29 - 02:28   (00:07)     10.0.0.50
geeko        pts/2      Tue Aug 24 02:29 - 00:39   (00:00)     10.0.0.50
geeko        pts/2      Tue Aug 24 02:29 - 08:20   (00:07)     10.0.0.50
root         0          Mon Aug 23 05:41    still logged in    console


wtmp begins Mon Aug  6 09:04:35 2007
da10:~ #
```

- **lastlog.** This command formats and prints the contents of the last login log file (/var/log/lastlog). The login-name, port, and last login time are displayed.

  Entering the command without options displays the entries sorted by numerical ID.

  You can use options such as **-u** *login_name* (display information for designated user only) and **-h** (display a one-line help message).

  If a user has never logged in the message **Never logged in** is displayed instead of the port and time.

  For example, entering **lastlog** returns information similar to the following:

```
da10: ~ # lastlog
Username       Port        From          Latest
root           0           console       Thurs Aug 23 05:41:50 -0600 2007
bin                                      **Never logged in**
daemon                                   **Never logged in**
lp                                       **Never logged in**
mail                                     **Never logged in**
...
```

- **faillog.** This command formats and displays the contents of the failure log (/var/log/faillog) and maintains failure counts and limits.

  You can use options such as **-u** *login_name* (display information for designated user only) and **-p** (display in UID order).

  The command faillog only prints out users with no successful login since the last failure. To print out a user who has had a successful login since his last failure, you must explicitly request the user with the **-u** option.

  Entering **faillog** returns information similar to the following:

```
da10: ~ # faillog
Username       Failures    Maximum    Latest
root           0           0          Mon Aug 20 07:20:11 -0600 2007 on tty1
geeko          0           0          Thurs Aug 16 16:48:34 -0600 2007 on tty3
da10:~ #
```

**12**

You can activate or deactivate logging activity in /var/log/lastlog and /var/log/faillog by setting options in the YaST Security settings module (see *Configure Security Settings*).

## Implement Security Rules and Tips

The following is a list of rules and tips you might find useful in dealing with basic security concerns:

- According to the rule of using the most restrictive set of permissions possible for every job, avoid doing your regular jobs when you are logged in as root.

    This reduces the risk of getting a cuckoo egg or a virus and protects you from your own mistakes.

- If possible, always try to use encrypted connections to work on a remote machine. Using SSH (secure shell) to replace telnet, ftp, rsh, and rlogin should be standard practice.

- Avoid using authentication methods based on IP addresses alone.

- Try to keep the most important network-related packages up-to-date and subscribe to the corresponding mailing lists to receive announcements on new versions of programs such as bind, postfix, and ssh.

    The same should apply to software relevant to local security.

- Disable any network services you do not absolutely require for your server to work properly. This will make your system safer.

    Open ports, with the socket in state LISTEN, can be found by using the netstat program.

    As for the options, we recommended that you use **netstat -ap** or **netstat -anp**.

    The -p option lets you see which process is occupying a port under which name.

- RPM packages from SUSE are digitally signed. You can verify the integrity of any SUSE RPM package by entering:

    **rpm -- checksig package.rpm**

    The needed public gpg-key is copied to the home directory of root upon installation.

- Check your backups of user and system files regularly. Remember that if you do not test whether the backup will work, it might actually be worthless.

- Check your log files. Whenever possible, write a small script to search for suspicious entries. Admittedly, this is not exactly a trivial task. In the end, only you can know which entries are unusual and which are not.

- Use SUSEfirewall to enhance the security provided by tcpd (tcp wrapper).

- Design your security measures to be redundant. A message seen twice is much better than no message at all.

## SUSE Security Information Resources

To handle security competently, it is important to keep up with new developments and to stay informed about the latest security issues.

One very good way to protect your systems against problems of all kinds is to install the updated packages recommended by security announcements as quickly as possible.

SUSE security announcements are published on a mailing list to which you can subscribe by using the following the link: *www. suse.de/security*.

The list **suse-security-announce@suse.de** is a first-hand source of information regarding updated packages and includes members of SUSE's security team among its active contributors.

The mailing list **suse-security@suse.de** is a good place to discuss any security issues of interest.

The list **bugtraq@securityfocus.com** is one of the best-known security mailing lists worldwide. We recommend that you read this list (which receives between 15 and 20 postings per day).

You can find more information at www.securityfocus.com.

**NOTE**

## seccheck

The package seccheck offers a series of scripts that check the machine regularly (daily, weekly, monthly) and send reports to the system administrator.

Items checked by the scripts are:

- Kernel modules loaded
- SUID files
- SGID files
- Bound sockets
- Users with accounts who never logged in
- Weak passwords
- etc

A mail is sent to the system administrator detailing what was found.

**12**

### Custom Scripts

There is no limit to what the system administrator could check or have sent to him using shell or perl scripts.

Some possibilities are:

- Output of **last**
- Output of **df**
- Output of **netstat**
- Output of **ps**
- /etc/passwd to check if another account than root has UID 0
- etc

## OBJECTIVE 4    UNDERSTAND IPCHAINS AND IPTABLES

The Linux kernel allows filtering of IP packets according to various rules. Packets can be accepted or dropped depending on various criteria. This makes it possible to include Linux machines as components of firewalls.

**iptables** is the program to control the packet filtering capabilities of the 2.4.x and 2.6.x Linux kernels. **ipchains** is the program used for this purpose with 2.2.x kernels.

Before implementing ipchains and iptables you need to:

- Understand Packet Filters
- Understand iptables Syntax
- Understand ipchains Peculiarities

## Understand Packet Filters

A TCP/IP connection between two computers is characterized by IP addresses, ports and the protocol used.

In the case of someone connecting to a Web server, this could look like this:

- Client computer:
  - IP address 217.83.16.7
  - Port 1054
  - Protocol TCP

- Web server:
    - IP address 130.57.4.27
    - Port 80
    - Protocol TCP

To view a Web page, the browser opens a socket (that is the combination of IP address and port) on the client and sends a request to the IP address of the Web server and its port 80, using the TCP protocol.

As part of the TCP protocol, the connection is established first using a specific sequence of IP packets. Once that is done, the Web server sends the data to the client.

The information is not transferred between the computers on a dedicated line like when using the phone, but in chunks of a certain size, called packets. These do not necessarily all need to take the same route from source to destination.

Each packet contains the IP addresses and ports of the involved computers and is independent of any other packet.

To control the flow of the packets to, from and through (if two network cards are present) the machine, filtering rules can be set up that allow packets to continue to their destination or discard them according to various criteria.

This can be used to prevent a machine to be contacted from other machines while still allowing it to contact others, or to only allow certain traffic across a gateway while denying everything else.

Such a mechanism is called a packet filter. In Linux the capability to filter packets is part of the kernel. The functionality is controlled by the **iptables** program.

**12**

## Understand iptables Syntax

You use the **iptables** program to set or delete the packet filter rules.

To understand a packet filter, you need to understand:

- Chains
- Policy
- Syntax
- Further Features
- Warning

### Chains

Rules are organized in so-called chains. Within a chain, the rules are checked one after the other until a rule matches.

If no rule matches, a default action is taken. This default action is referred to as the policy of the chain.

There are several chains, the built-in ones being:

- **INPUT**
- **OUTPUT**
- **FORWARD**

Figure 12-13 is from *www.netfilter.org/documentation/HOWTO/ packet-filtering-HOWTO-6.html*.

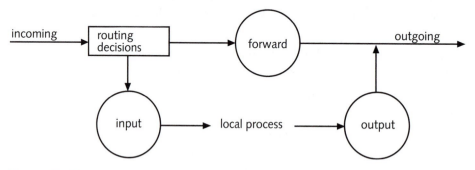

**Figure 12-13**

The following describes the process:

1. When a packet comes in (e.g., through the Ethernet card) the kernel first looks at the destination of the packet: this is called routing.

2. If it's destined for this box, the packet passes downwards in the diagram, to the INPUT chain.

   If it passes this, any processes waiting for that packet will receive it.

3. Otherwise, if the kernel does not have forwarding enabled, or it doesn't know how to forward the packet, the packet is dropped.

   If forwarding is enabled, and the packet is destined for another network interface (if you have another one), then the packet goes rightwards on our diagram to the FORWARD chain.

   If it is ACCEPTed, it will be sent out.

4. Finally, a program running on the box can send network packets.

   These packets pass through the OUTPUT chain immediately: if it says ACCEPT, then the packet continues out to whatever interface it is destined for.

## Policy

The policy decides what happens to a packet that did not match a rule in the chain. The policy could either be to accept the packet or to drop it. There are 2 approaches possible:

- Everything is forbidden, except if explicitly allowed.
- Everything is allowed, except if explicitly forbidden.

From a security viewpoint, only the first approach is valid.

## Syntax

iptables is called with various options to specify a rule. A chain consists of several rules that are checked one after the other until one matches.

If a rule matches, the target of the rule is executed, usually accepting or dropping the packet.

The options are used to accomplish the following:

- **Add and Delete Rules:** The following commands are possible:
  - **-A.** Add a rule to the end of the chain.
  - **-D.** Delete a rule.
  - **-R.** Replace a rule.
  - **-I.** Insert a rule.

  To insert a rule at position 3 of the chain, enter:

  **iptables -I INPUT 3 ...**

- **Manipulate Whole Chains:** The following commands are possible:
  - **-F.** Delete (flush) all rules from a chain.
  - **-Z.** Zero the byte counter of a chain.
  - **-L.** List the rules of a chain (add -v for more information).
  - **-N.** Create a user defined (new) chain.
  - **-E.** Rename a user defined chain.
  - **-X.** Delete an empty user defined chain.

- **Match Rules:** Not every option has to be given.

  If an option is not specified, for example, the destination port, the rule applies no matter the destination port.

  - Specify the interface: **-i** for input, **-o** for output
  - Specify the protocol: **-p TCP**, **-p UDP**
  - Specify source/destination IP: **-s 1.2.3.4**, **-d 192.168.0.0/24**
  - Specify source/destination port: **--sport 1024:65535**, **--dport 80**

**12**

- **Target:** The target specifies what happens to a packet that matches a rule.

  After a match, subsequent rules are not checked. The target is given after the option –j (jump). Possible targets are:

  - ACCEPT
  - REJECT
  - DROP
  - LOG
  - A user defined chain.

  LOG is different from the other targets as the packet continues through the chain after being logged.

Examples:

- To block all incoming packets on eth1 with a source IP of 10.x.x.x, enter:

  **iptables –A INPUT –i eth1 –s 10.0.0.0/8 –j DROP**

- To reject all incoming TCP packets on eth1 with a source IP of 10.x.x.x, enter:

  **iptables –A INPUT –i eth1 –p tcp –s 10.0.0.0/255.0.0.0 –j REJECT**

  The default for REJECT is to send an ICMP message "port unreachable", if applicable. (For example no ICMP messages are sent in response to certain ICMP messages.)

  It is possible to specify the ICMP message (or a TCP reset) to be sent:

  **–j REJECT --reject-with** *type*

  e.g. icmp-proto-unreachable, icmp-host-unreachable, tcp-reset, etc.

- To accept all incoming ICMP packets on eth1, enter:

  **iptables –A INPUT –i eth1 –p icmp –j ACCEPT**

- To accept all outgoing tcp packets to port 80, enter:

  **iptables –A OUTPUT –p tcp --dport 80 –j ACCEPT**

- To accept all incoming TCP packets from port 80 providing the syn–bit is not set (! is used to negate an option), enter:

  **iptables –A INPUT –p tcp ! --syn --sport 80 –j ACCEPT**

Usually a second rule is needed to take care of the packets received in answer.

The port you put in the rules depends on the service you want to access. /etc/services lists the ports and the service that usually can be found on that port.

While usually UDP and TCP have the same service on the same port, this is not necessarily so. Some of the more frequently used ports are the following:

- **20.** ftp-data
- **21.** ftp
- **22.** ssh
- **23.** telnet
- **25.** smtp
- **53.** domain (dns)
- **80.** www
- **110.** pop3
- **111.** sun-rpc
- **113.** ident
- **137–139.** netbios ports
- **143.** imap
- **443.** https

**12**

As rules defined on the command line are lost with the next reboot, the rules that make up the packet filter are written into a shell script that is executed during system start up.

To integrate the script into the startup mechanism, use /etc/init.d/skeleton as a guideline.

In addition to setting the rules (start) such a script should allow to delete the rules (stop) and to show the currently active rules (status).

There is no single right way to write such a script. Keep it as simple as possible so you don't inadvertently open security holes.

Use comments within the script liberally so you can still understand it when you have to modify it later.

## Further Features

The above is just a brief introduction to iptables. Some of the capabilities of iptables include:

- User defined chains
- Stateful packet filtering
- Network address translation (source and destination network address translation, with or without port address translation)
- Masquerading
- Limiting the number or certain packets or log entries
- Marking/modifying packets

## Warning

You need good understanding of TCP/IP to implement your own packet filter.

The above information is most likely not sufficient to achieve that.

There are various resources, books as well as Internet sites, you could consult, e.g.:

- FAQs and howtos: *www.faqs.org/docs/iptables/*
- iptables tutorial: *www.faqs.org/docs/iptables/*

In any event have someone else look at your final iptables script as cross check and, using nmap, test if your script denies connections as intended.

## Understand ipchains Peculiarities

With a 2.2.x kernel, the program to set packet filter rules is **ipchains**.

While there are similarities to iptables, there are also differences. One of the major differences is how packets traverse the chains. With the kernel 2.4.x and 2.6.x, a packet traverses either the input, the forward or the output chain.

With kernel 2.2.x, a forwarded packet goes through all three chains. Other differences concern for example:

- **Targets.** DENY in ipchains, DROP in iptables.
- **Capitalization.** input in ipchains, INPUT in iptables.
- **Syntax.** -y in ipchains, --syn in iptables.

Generally you will most likely not have to set up a packet filter using ipchains, as current installations usually use a 2.4.x or 2.6.x kernel.

---

## Objective 5     Security Vulnerabilities

As a system administrator it is usually not your task to find security vulnerabilities yourself. This is what the maintenance of SLES 9 is all about: To monitor any weaknesses found in the software that comes with SLES 9 and to provide you with fixed packages.

Even if you had the expertise, you probably would not have the time to find vulnerabilities while actively managing the machines and networks you are in charge of.

Part of the system administrator's job is to stay informed about vulnerabilities found and (hopefully) fixed by others, and to keep the software up to date accordingly.

To do this, you have to do the following:

- Define Information Resources
- Scan the Network for Existing Security Vulnerabilities

## Define Information Resources

An important resource on security issues are mailing lists.

Every major Linux distributor runs a security mailing list to inform users about security issues in his products.

For SUSE Linux, this list is **suse-security-announce** which can be subscribed to on *www.suse.com/us/private/support/online_help/mailinglists/ index.html.*

Registered customers using SLES 9 get informed about available updates independently of the above mailing list by Maintenance Support Information. There are various other lists and Web sites to stay informed about security issues, for example:

- BugTraq:

  *www.securityfocus.com/archive/*

- CERT Coordination Center:

  *www.cert.org/*

  There are national CERT centers in various countries.

- Packet Storm:

  *http://packetstormsecurity.org/alladvisories/*

- LinuxSecurity.com:

  *www.linuxsecurity.com*

**NOTE**

SLES 9 offers the possibility to install software updates using the YaST Online Update. This can be automated by using cron. This requires a valid maintenance contract with Novell.

## Scan the Network for Existing Security Vulnerabilities

With a series of different operating systems, different versions, and different service packs, it is not easy to maintain an overview of what fix has been installed where.

This is complicated by the fact that services might be running on a machine nobody really knows about.

One way to solve this is to scan the network for existing vulnerabilities. There are commercial tools to do this. One well know open source program for this purpose is **nessu**. nessus can be used to scan single hosts or whole networks in a highly configurable way to find out about existing vulnerabilities.

**nessusd** runs as a deamon on a machine and is controlled by **nessus** running on the same or another machine. It produces detailed reports on the security issues detected on the scanned hosts.

12

Vulnerabilities are detected using plugins which can be obtained from *www.nessus.org/*. They are available for free 7 days after their development. A subscription is required if you need them earlier.

A nessus scan can crash services or entire hosts under certain conditions. Don't scan without permission by the relevant authorities and coordinate with the system administrators in charge to avoid server downtimes and upsets.

Nessus comes with SLES 9. Information is available under www.nessus.org.

## Objective 6    Understand Intrusion Detection

Even if you keep all software updated continuously your machines might get compromised if you are unlucky enough to be the first to be hit by a new exploit that has not been published yet.

In this section you learn how to detect the fact that the machine has been compromised or that an attack is being prepared or in progress.

To do this, you need to:

- Understand Host Based Intrusion Detection
- Understand Network Based Intrusion Detection

## Understand Host Based Intrusion Detection

When someone gets access to a machine illegally he will usually try to

- Hide the fact of his intrusion.
- Install software to be able to come back to the machine even if the original vulnerability has been fixed.

Hiding the fact of his intrusion includes manipulating log files and replacing system programs by modified versions.

Manipulating log files could consist of deleting entries or trying to hide the relevant information by filling the log files with huge amounts of irrelevant entries.

Modified versions of for example ps, top and ls don't show certain processes and files the intruder uses in the course of his attack.

One way to prevent the manipulation of log files by deletion of entries is to not only log on the host itself but to send the log information across the network to another host.

Depending on the security needs, the loghost can even write the logs onto a worm- (write once, read many-) medium, making it impossible to change them even if the loghost gets compromised.

Once the intruder managed to get root access he can install any software he deems useful.

This can be anything from compilers, server software to run as a daemon to allow the intruder access to the machine later, to root kits manipulating the kernel, or any other software.

After a machine has been compromised the detection of manipulated or added files is only reliable if the machine is booted from a clean medium, like a rescue system from CD-ROM.

Inspecting the machine while it is up and running after an attack has some value. But it does not allow a definite statement whether files have been manipulated or not, as the tools, libraries, or the kernel involved in the check might have themselves been manipulated.

The following topics are described below:

- rpm
- tripwire and AIDE

## rpm

The integrity of files installed from rpm packages can be checked by using:

**rpm -V**

This check relies on the MD5 hash of the files, file size and modification time.

## tripwire and AIDE

Additional checks are offered by dedicated programs for host based intrusion detection.

Programs commonly used for this purpose are **tripwire** or **AIDE**. They work in two stages:

- Build a database of checksums (MD5 and others) and other information on files in the filesystem.
- At a later date, compare the database to the filesystem and note any differences.

The first step is to determine which files are to be monitored and to modify the respective configuration file accordingly.

Then after final installation and configuration, but before connecting to any network, have the program build the initial database.

To avoid manipulation of the database, it should be stored elsewhere, not on the machine itself, like on a CD-ROM together with the version of the program from the installation media.

This database has to be updated after each software installation or update to reflect the current state of the installation.

If at a later date the files are to be checked, the program is run against that database and any changes to programs and deleted or added files are shown.

# Understand Network Based Intrusion Detection

Even with patches available these are sometimes not applied – not necessarily due to neglect, but because of interoperability, support or legal issues of other software.

That causes a catch 22 situation: Not installing the patch might cause being vulnerable, installing the patch might mean loosing support.

One approach could be to put such machines into separate subnets protected by firewalls.

Another approach might be to install an intrusion detection system (IDS) that ideally detects an attack and alerts the system administrator before it can cause actual harm.

Intrusion detection involves monitoring the network traffic in various ways. It ranges from detecting new network cards in the network to monitoring the traffic running across the wire.

Each method has its strengths and weaknesses and none can guarantee to detect every attack.

The following topics are described below:

- snort
- arpwatch
- Argus
- scanlogd
- PortSentry

## snort

**snort** is an intrusion detection system based on attack signatures. It is the most sophisticated open source IDS available. It scans the network traffic for any pattern of a known attack via the network.

You need to connect the machine running snort to the network in a way that it can "see" the network traffic, like to the monitor port of a switch.

Depending on where you place the machine (outside or inside the firewall) you will get more or less alerts.

Primarily known attacks can be detected and the ability to detect new attacks is limited. Its advantage is that you can monitor a whole network with one host.

## arpwatch

**arpwatch** monitors the arp (Address Resolution Protocol) traffic and detects new mac addresses in the network and IP address changes.

When started, it builds up a database of MAC addresses and the IP addresses associated with them. Later changes are detected using this database.

arpwatch is useful to detect new hardware, for example a rogue notebook connected to the network in violation of the company's security policy.

However, if DHCP is used it produces a lot of alerts that probably have no significance.

## Argus

Argus (Audit Record Generation and Utilization System, *www.qosient.com/argus/*) is designed to track and report on the status and performance of all network transactions seen in a data network traffic stream.

It does not monitor the content of connections but what connections exist between various hosts.

While its purpose is comprehensive IP network traffic auditing in general, it can also be used for example to find out about connections that violate security policy.

Argus runs as a daemon and collects its information in a file that can become rather big depending on the amount of network traffic. It comes with a tool to generate reports from its database.

## scanlogd

If multiple packets to different ports originating from a single source are detected, an entry is made to /var/log/messages via syslog. No other action is taken.

To alert the system administrator to a scan, other tools that watch the log file need to be used, like logsurfer.

## PortSentry

PortSentry binds to configurable ports as if a service were running there and reports on scans of those ports. It has to run on each host that is being monitored.

It allows to block the traffic from an attacking host, offering the attacker an effective way to a denial of service attack by sending packets with a spoofed source IP.

It is not advisable to use this program, as its functionality is covered better by other programs.

**12**

## CHAPTER SUMMARY

◻ You can select an overall security level for your system using YaST to modify several configuration files that contain security-related information such as password encryption and system file permissions. In addition, you can use YaST to set the default parameters for user creation.

◻ To reduce the security risks associated with the root user, it is good form to log in as a nonroot user and switch to the root user status to perform administrative tasks only. The **su** command may be used to switch user accounts, and the **newgrp** command may be used to switch primary group accounts. Alternatively, you can use the Alt+F2 key combination to start a program as another user in a desktop environment. The **sudo** command may be used to execute commands as other users using the entries in the /etc/sudoers file.

◻ When using the SUID and SGID permissions to programs, test your program thoroughly to ensure that no security loopholes exist during execution. In addition, use the sticky bit on public directories to prevent data loss.

◻ Only assign the minimum permissions necessary to users. You can also edit the /etc/ permissions.* files to refine permissions allowed on system files.

◻ Ensure that users have passwords that are eight characters long or longer.

◻ Protect your servers by removing accessible drives, locking down the boot process, using encrypted communications, disabling unused network services, verifying the digital signatures on RPM packages, viewing the latest security information on the Internet, and using SUSEfirewall. The **seccheck** package contains scripts that may be used to check your system for security weaknesses, and the **nessus** daemon may be used to check network systems for security weaknesses.

◻ Monitor disk usage to prevent filesystems from filling up and causing system problems. The **df** command, **du** command, KDE Info Center, and KDiskFree utility can be used to monitor disk usage.

◻ Most system logging is performed centrally by the syslog daemon (syslogd) via entries in the /etc/syslog.conf file. Most log files are stored in the /var/log directory. The last entries of these files may be viewed using a text program such as **tail** or by using YaST.

◻ The **logrotate** program is run daily to archive log files, using entries in the /etc/logrotate. conf file and application-specific information in the /etc/logrotate.d directory.

◻ An effective Linux maintenance and security policy requires the auditing of log files and authentication. The **logcheck** and **logsurfer** programs may be used to monitor log file entries, whereas the **who**, **w**, **finger**, **last**, **lastlog**, and **faillog** commands can monitor user logins.

◻ To reduce network security breaches, you can use the **iptables** command to create packet filters on network interfaces that drop packets based on chains of rules.

❏ When a security breach occurs, system files are typically changed by the intruder. To detect a security breach, you can use HostBased Intrusion Detection systems such as **rpm**, **tripwire**, and **AIDE** to search for changes in system files.

❏ To monitor intruders that attempt to connect to your computer, you may use a Network Based Intrusion Detection system such as snort, arpwatch, Argus, **scanlogd**, and **PortSentry**. These utilities typically identify attack patterns in network traffic, caches, and log files.

## KEY TERMS

**/etc/login.defs** — A file that stores defaults for user logins and user account creation.

**/etc/logrotate.conf** — The configuration file for the **logrotate** command. Additional configuration files for **logrotate** may be in the /etc/logrotate.d directory.

**/etc/logrotate.d** — This directory contains additional configuration files for the **logrotate** command.

**/etc/permissions.easy** — A file that lists the least secure file permission restrictions for system files.

**/etc/permissions.local** — A file that lists user-defined file permission restrictions for system files.

**/etc/permissions.paranoid** — A file that lists the most secure file permission restrictions for system files.

**/etc/permissions.secure** — A file that lists secure file permission restrictions for system files.

**/etc/sudoers** — A file that lists the users who are allowed to run certain commands as other users.

**/etc/sysconfig/syslog** — A file that contains parameters for the syslogd daemon.

**/etc/syslog.conf** — The main configuration file for the syslogd daemon.

**/var/log/boot.msg** — A text file that lists system initialization messages.

**/var/log/faillog** — A data file that lists failed login attempts.

**/var/log/lastlog** — A data file that lists recent login attempts.

**/var/log/mail** — A text file that lists message from the mail system.

**/var/log/wtmp** — A data file that lists successful login attempts.

**Advanced Intrusion Detection Environment (AIDE)** — A common Host Based IDS used to monitor key system files.

**arpwatch** — A common Network Based IDS used to identify network attacks by monitoring the ARP cache.

**Audit Record Generation and Utilization System (Argus)** — A common Network Based IDS used to identify network attacks by monitoring network transactions.

**Blowfish** — An encryption method used to encrypt Linux passwords.

**chains** — Collections of firewall rules that may be used to match network traffic.

**Data Encryption Standard (DES)** — The default encryption method used in SLES for passwords.

**df command** — Displays disk usage by file system.

**dmesg command** — Used to view the contents of /var/log/boot.msg.

**du command** — Displays disk usage by directory.

**effective group** — See **primary group**.

**faillog command** — Displays the contents of /var/log/faillog.

**finger command** — Displays information about local user accounts.

**General Electric Comprehensive Operating System (GECOS)** — Represents a description of a user account stored in the comments field of /etc/passwd.

**Host Based IDS** — A software system that detects changes to key system files to identify a security breach.

**Intrusion Detection System (IDS)** — A software system designed to check for evidence of security threats and breaches.

**ipchains command** — Used to configure firewall rules on network interface in older versions of Linux.

**iptables command** — Used to configure firewall rules on network interface in SLES.

**KDE Info Center** — A graphical utility that displays system information.

**kdf command** — Starts the KDiskFree utility.

**KDiskFree** — A graphical utility that displays free space by filesystem.

**kinfocenter command** — Starts the KDE Info Center utility.

**last command** — Displays the most recent users who have logged in to the system from entries in /var/log/wtmp.

**lastlog command** — Displays the most recent users who have logged in to the system from entries in /var/log/lastlog.

**logcheck** — A utility that may be used to locate and extract anomalies in log files.

**logrotate command** — Used to archive log files using entries in the /etc/logrotate.conf file and other configuration files that may exist in the /etc/logrotate.d directory.

**logsurfer** — A utility that may be used to check log files for certain patterns and trigger actions.

**Message Digest 5 (MD5)** — An encryption method used to encrypt Linux passwords.

**Nessus** — A program that may be used to monitor security settings on network computers.

**netstat command** — Displays network statistics and open ports.

**Network Based IDS** — A software system that detects patterns in network traffic and log files to identify a security breach or attack.

**newgrp command** — Used to change the current primary group for a user account.

**one-way hash algorithm** — An algorithm that encrypts data but cannot be used to decrypt it. It is also called a trapdoor algorithm.

**policy** — The action that is applied for packets that do not match a chain rule.

**PortSentry** — A common Network Based IDS used to identify network attacks by listening to multiple TCP/IP ports.

**primary group** — The group specified for a user in the /etc/passwd file that becomes the group owner on newly created files and directories.

**Red Hat Package Manager (RPM)** — A format used to distribute software packages on many Linux systems.

**rpm command** — Used to install, remove, and find information on RPM software packages and to verify RPM packages and RPM digital signatures.

**scanlogd** — A common Network Based IDS used to identify network attacks by listening to traffic sent on multiple ports.

**seccheck** — A package that contains a series of scripts that may be used to check for security vulnerabilities on your system.

**Set Group ID (SGID)** — A special permission set on executable files and directories. When you run an executable program that has the SGID permission set, you become the group owner of the executable file for the duration of the program. On a directory, the SGID sets the group that gets attached to newly created files.

**Set User ID (SUID)** — A special permission set on executable files. When you run an executable program that has the SUID permission set, you become the owner of the executable file for the duration of the program.

**Snort** — A common Network Based IDS used to identify network traffic attacks.

**Sticky bit** — A special permission that is set on directories that prevents users from removing files they do not own.

**su (switch user) command** — Used to change the current user account.

**sudo command** — Used to run commands as another user via entries in /etc/sudoers.

**SUSEfirewall** — A graphical firewall utility in YaST.

**syslogd** — The daemon responsible for most logging on Linux systems. It stands for System Log Daemon.

**trapdoor algorithm** — See **one-way hash algorithm**.

**Tripwire** — A common Host Based IDS used to identify changes to key system files.

**w command** — Displays the users currently logged in to the system and their processes.

**who command** — Displays the users currently logged in to the system. It can also be used to display the contents of the /var/log/wtmp file.

12

---

# REVIEW QUESTIONS

1. Which YaST security level is recommended for a networked workstation?

   a. Level 1

   b. Level 2

   c. Level 3

   d. Level 4

2. What would you type at a command prompt to execute a program called **sampleprog** in your current directory, if the current directory is not in your path statement? _____

3. Which command(s) may be used to change to the root user and start a new shell? (Choose all that apply.)

   a. su – root

   b. su root

   c. su –

   d. su

4. What line in /etc/sudoers could you use to allow the user **dgrant** to execute the **/sbin/useradd** program as the root user on the computer **ARFA**? _____

5. What special permission should be set on public directories to prevent users from deleting files that other users have contributed? _____

6. What file should you modify to restrict files in the **/home** directory from running with the SUID bit?

   a. /etc/permissions.easy

   b. /etc/permissions.secure

   c. /etc/permissions.paranoid

   d. /etc/permissions.local

7. Which of the following are good security practices? (Choose all that apply.)

   a. Assigning only necessary filesystem permissions

   b. Using passwords that are four characters long or longer

   c. Disabling unused network services

   d. Updating network software

8. What line can you add to the **/etc/syslog.conf** file to log messages of priority **crit** from the Linux kernel to **/var/log/kernlog**?

   a. kern.crit /var/log/kernlog

   b. kern.=crit /var/log/kernlog

   c. kern.crit -/var/log/kernlog

   d. kern.crit |/var/log/kernlog

9. Which of the following commands may be used to display boot error messages? (Choose all that apply.)

    a. dmesg | less

    b. less /var/log/boot

    c. less /var/log/wtmp

    d. less /var/log/boot.log

10. You have added the following lines to the /etc/logrotate.d/mylog file:

    /var/log/mylog {

    maxage 44

    rotate 5

    notifempty

    compress

    }

    Which of the following statements are true about the rotation of the /var/log/mylog file? (Choose all that apply.)

    a. A maximum of five archive logs will be kept.

    b. A maximum of 44 archive logs will be kept.

    c. The log file will be rotated if the file is empty.

    d. The log file will be compressed after being rotated.

11. What command can you use to display the disk usage for mounted filesystems?

    _____

12. Which of the following may be used to check your system for weak passwords? (Choose all that apply.)

    a. nessus

    b. security --check

    c. seccheck scripts

    d. who -a

13. What command may be used to prevent packets from the 3.0.0.0/8 network from being routed through your Linux router?

    a. iptables −A INPUT −s 3.0.0.0/8 −m REJECT

    b. iptables −A FORWARD −s 3.0.0.0/8 −m REJECT

    c. iptables −A INPUT −s 3.0.0.0/8 −j REJECT

    d. iptables −A FORWARD −s 3.0.0.0/8 −j REJECT

**12**

14. What port could you restrict using **iptables** to reject telnet traffic? _____

15. Which of the following Linux Intrusion Detection Systems scans your system to detect changes to system files?

    a. Tripwire

    b. Snort

    c. Argus

    d. AIDE

16. What command can you use to display failed logins? _____

---

## Discovery Exercises

### Configuring Local Security

Log in to the KDE desktop as the geeko user and run the YaST program as the root user. Next, use the Security Settings module under Security and Users to set custom security settings for your computer to perform the following actions. Log out of your system when finished.

1. Require that passwords be a minimum of eight characters long, be checked against dictionary words, and be difficult to guess.

2. Store passwords using the Blowfish encryption algorithm.

3. Expire passwords every 42 days. Users should be warned five days before expiry.

4. Restrict the ability to shut down the system from the KDM to the root user.

5. Record failed login attempts, and set a delay after two invalid login attempts.

6. Set secure file permissions.

7. Allow the current directory in the path statement for all users.

### Configuring a Firewall

Log in to tty1 as the root user and run the command **iptables -L**. What firewall rules exist by default? Test your loopback adapter by running the **ping 127.0.0.1** command. Press Ctrl+C when finished. Next, run the command **iptables -A INPUT -j DROP** and repeat the ping command you used earlier. Were you successful? Why?

Run the command **iptables -L** to flush all firewall rules. Next, run the command **iptables -A INPUT -s 127.0.0.1 -j ACCEPT** followed by the command **iptables -A INPUT -j DROP** and repeat the ping command you used earlier. Were you successful? Why? Use the **iptables -L** command to verify your answer. Finally, remove all firewall rules with the **iptables -F** command and log out of tty1.

## Configuring syslogd

Log in to tty1 as the geeko user. Use the **vi** editor to add the following line to the /etc/syslog.conf file:

**\*.debug /var/log/mylog**

When finished, save your changes and quit the **vi** editor. What does this line do?

Restart the syslog daemon using the command **rcsyslog restart** and view the contents of /var/log/mylog. Are there entries? Log out of tty1.

## Configuring an Intrusion Detection System

Log in to the KDE desktop as the geeko user and download the latest version of Tripwire and Tripwire documentation from *http://sourceforge.net*. In a terminal run as the root user, extract the Tripwire file and follow the instructions in the documentation file to install and configure Tripwire on your system. When finished, perform a system scan using Tripwire to create a file checksum database. Use Tripwire again to check your system against this database to see if any files have changed. Log out of your system when finished.

## Using sudo

Log in to tty1 as the root user and edit the /etc/sudoers file (using **visudo**) and add the following line to the bottom of the file:

**geeko ALL = /usr/bin/killall**

When finished, save your changes and quit the **vi** editor. What does this line do?

Use the **su** command to switch the **geeko** user and run the **sudo killall –9 bash** command. Type geeko's password for confirmation. Why were you successful?

12

# 13

# HARDWARE BASICS

**The CompTIA Linux+ exam also covers general hardware topics, which are covered in this section. Their relationship to Linux is covered as well.**

♦ Describe Common Hardware Components and Resources

♦ Diagnose Hardware Problems

♦ Describe Multimedia Components

♦ Identify and Configure Removable System Hardware

♦ Access and Write Data to Recordable Media

♦ Configure Advanced Power Management and the ACPI Tool

♦ Understand Mass Storage

## OBJECTIVE 1    DESCRIBE COMMON HARDWARE COMPONENTS AND RESOURCES

The following topics are described:

- Understand Hardware Parameters
- Configure SCSI Devices
- Obtain Hardware Configuration Information from YaST
- Hardware Information (/proc/)

## Understand Hardware Parameters

When a certain piece of hardware is used in a computer, usually certain parameters come into play—like the number of the interrupt or the memory address used.

Depending on the hardware, these parameters are permanently fixed, can be set using jumpers or little switches, or are set automatically. For example, older ISA cards need to be configured manually, but modern PCI cards manage their parameters automatically.

To work with hardware, you need to understand the following:

- Mainboards
- Hardware Addresses
- The Interrupt System
- The DMA System
- Configure Hardware Parameters
- Card Memory

### Mainboards

The processor (central processing unit, or CPU) is the heart of the computer. It executes the commands it gets from programs. Another important part of the computer is the RAM (random access memory). It stores the data of currently running processes.

Other components are necessary to make up a functioning computer; hard disk, video card, interfaces to keyboard and other peripherals, etc.

The mainboard brings all these components together. It holds the CPU and the physical interfaces to the various components, such as memory, video card, hard disks, DVD drives, floppy drives, USB sockets, and serial interfaces.

When a program executes, it needs to access these hardware components. Bus systems enable communication between the processor and these components. Bus systems are integrated on the mainboard, together with the necessary hardware (the chip set) to coordinate and control them.

For example, to communicate with the working memory, the processor uses a dedicated bus system.

## Hardware Addresses

Every memory cell has its own number to address it.

If the processor wants to access a memory cell it must send the address number first on the address bus to open a channel to the memory cell.

After this it can access the memory cell using the data bus. For the processor, there is no difference between accessing memory or accessing another hardware component. Therefore, each component needs its own address.

The processor first sends the address to the address bus to open a channel to the hardware component. Then it can send or receive data on the data bus.

The processor only needs to know the hardware address. It does not need to know how the hardware component works internally.

The hardware address is called I/O (input/output) address or I/O port. The hardware address must be unique.

## The Interrupt System

The processor processes data according to the instructions of a program. Data and instructions are both kept in memory.

Sometimes it is necessary to interrupt these instructions and to do something different.

When new data are waiting to be processed, the respective piece of hardware has to inform the processor.

For example, if you press a key on your keyboard, the processor needs to be interrupted to read the information (in this case, which key was hit) from the I/O address of the keyboard.

Every hardware component that allows input needs a means to request the processor to interrupt its current task. This is achieved by sending an interrupt request (IRQ) on the interrupt channel.

The processor will stop its work and process the data from the input device. After this it can proceed with the things it did before.

The processor obviously needs to know which component is requesting an interrupt. Therefore, all possible interrupts are collected in a interrupt table.

13

By default, some IRQs are allocated for system hardware, as shown in Table 13-1.

**Table 13-1**

| IRQ | Hardware |
| --- | --- |
| 0 | Timer |
| 1 | Keyboard |
| 2 | Second IRQ controller |
| 3 | Second and fourth serial interface |
| 4 | First and third serial interface |
| 5 | Free (formerly the second parallel interface) |
| 6 | Floppy disk drive |
| 7 | Free (formerly the first parallel interface) |
| 8 | Real time clock |
| 9–11 | Free |
| 12 | Free (this is usually used by the PS/2 mouse) |
| 13 | Free |
| 14 | First IDE controller |
| 15 | Second IDE controller |

On older computers, if two devices share one interrupt channel, the possibility of errors increases. Most newer PCI cards allow to share IRQs.

## The DMA System

DMA (direct memory access) means the direct access from hardware to the memory without the detour to the processor.

Hardware that needs frequent fast memory access can decrease the processor load using DMA.

Each DMA channel can be used only by one hardware component.

A standard PC has eight DMA channels that allow direct memory access.

DMA channel 4 is used by the bus system.

The processor needs to know which hardware component can use which DMA channel.

## Configure Hardware Parameters

For each new hardware component you have to configure the following three parameters (unless the hardware takes care of it automatically):

- **IO address.** Every hardware needs an I/O address.
- **IRQ.** Hardware for input additionally needs an IRQ.
- **DMA channel.** Hardware that needs direct memory access needs a DMA channel.

These parameters need to be configured on the hardware and also in the software. The configuration needs to be the same on both sides.

Depending on the hardware, you can use the following configuration methods:

- **Hardware fixed on the mainboard.** The configuration needs to be done with the BIOS setup program.

- **Very old ISA cards.** These cards need to be configured by jumpers or DIP switches on the card.

- **Newer ISA cards.** The last generation of ISA cards had some memory (EEPROMS, Flash-EPROMS).

  You could store the configuration of the card in this memory.

- **ISA plug and play cards.** If the operating system is plug and play ready, these cards can communicate with the operating system to inform about the hardware configuration.

- **PCI extension cards.** Newer computers use PCI cards, which are able to negotiate the configuration parameters with the operating system. No manual configuration is needed.

### Card Memory

Some cards have their own memory built into the card. This can be RAM or EPROM.

To access this memory, the system needs to know the beginning address of this memory.

These address is called Memory Base or MemBase.

## Configure SCSI Devices

SCSI (Small Computer System Interface) is the most common and important bus system for hard disks drives, CD-ROM drives, scanners, and other external devices in enterprise environments.

Most servers have SCSI devices, not IDE devices.

IDE devices are cheaper, but there are features–such as hot plugging–that make SCSI irreplaceable.

To configure SCSI devices, you need to understand the following:

- Basics of SCSI Architecture
- Types of SCSI
- Addresses for the SCSI Bus
- The SCSI BIOS
- Boot from SCSI Devices

13

## Basics of SCSI Architecture

The device that connects the SCSI bus with the computer is called the ***host adapter***. (The name "SCSI controller" is common but incorrect.)

One SCSI host adapter can manage up to eight devices (16 devices for Wide SCSI). One of these devices is the SCSI host adapter itself.

The SCSI bus is a flat cable with 50 wires. Externally, a specially shielded cable is used. SCSI devices are connected to this bus.

Remember the following when you build a SCSI bus:

- A SCSI bus always has two ends. Branches are not possible.
- Each end has to have a terminator. (Newer SCSI devices can terminate themselves.)
- The distance between two SCSI devices has to be greater than 10 cm (4 inches).
- The maximum total length of the bus is 3 m (10 ft).
- There always has to be one device at the end of the bus.

## Types of SCSI

Various generations of SCSI have evolved over time:

- **SCSI (or SCSI1).** The classical SCSI.

  It can manage up to eight devices (seven plus the host adapter) and uses a cable with 50 wires.

  SCSI became standard in 1986.

- **SCSI2.** An extension to the classical SCSI command set to access other devices than hard disks.

  There are two variants of SCSI2:

  - Fast SCSI2 (faster than the original).
  - Wide SCSI2 (supports up to 16 devices).

- **SCSI3 (or Ultra SCSI).** Much faster than Fast SCSI2 and uses other cable types.

  To access more than eight devices, the wide SCSI variants use a cable with 68 wires (16 bit bus) instead of 50 (8 bit bus).

Table 13-2 gives an overview of the different SCSI variants, including their transfer rates.

**Table 13-2**

| Bus | Wires | Transfer Rate: Standard | Transfer Rate: Fast | Transfer Rate: Ultra |
|-----|-------|-------------------------|---------------------|----------------------|
| 8 bit | 50 | 5 MB/sec | 10 MB/sec | 20 MB/sec |
| 16 bit | 68 | 10 MB/sec | 20 MB/sec | 40 MB/sec |

## Addresses for the SCSI Bus

Every SCSI device needs a SCSI ID, a unique numeric address to access it. The numbering starts with 0.

Normally, the host adapter has ID 7. The higher the number the higher the priority.

The numbering is independent from the physical order of the bus.

You have to set the device IDs at the host adapter or via switches at the device.

If you address subdevices (such as, four hard disks in a disk rack), you use the LUN (Logical Unit Number). For the SCSI bus, the subdevices appear as one device.

Furthermore, you can connect more than one host adapter to the computer. The first bus is labeled with number 0.

With these three numbers you can address all SCSI devices in the following way:

**bus_number, SCSI-ID,LUN**

## The SCSI BIOS

SCSI does not know anything of the standard BIOS; accessing the SCSI devices is done by device drivers of the OS.

Therefore it is not possible to boot from a SCSI device if the host adapter has no BIOS of its own.

## Boot from SCSI Devices

If you want to boot from a SCSI device, you need to configure the SCSI ID and the transfer rate of the device in the SCSI BIOS.

Inside this BIOS, you can select the device you want to boot from.

You have to tell your system BIOS that you want to boot from a SCSI device. You cannot select a specific SCSI device there.

After booting the system, the system BIOS delegates the boot process to the SCSI BIOS.

**13**

## Obtain Hardware Configuration Information from *YaST*

To obtain information about the configuration of your hardware from the YaST Control Center select

**Hardware > Hardware Information**

After scanning the hardware for a few moments, YaST displays a dialog box similar to Figure 13-1 that summarizes the information about the detected hardware.

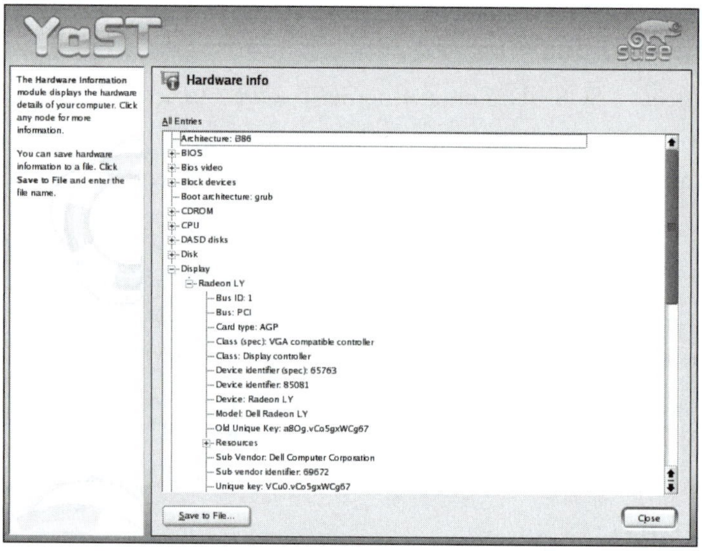

**Figure 13-1**

## Hardware Information (/proc/)

The directory /proc/ lets you view hardware information stored in the kernel memory space.

For example, if you enter:

**cat /proc/cpuinfo**

output is generated from data stored in kernel memory that gives you information such as the CPU model name and cache size.

You can view the available information by using commands such as cat, more, or less with a filename (such as **cat /proc/cpuinfo**).

The following are some of the commonly used filenames that generate information:

- **/proc/devices.** Shows the devices used on your Linux system.
- **/proc/cpuinfo.** Shows processor information.
- **/proc/ioports.** Shows the I/O ports on your server.
- **/proc/interrupts.** Shows the IRQ assignments for your Linux system.

- **/proc/dma.** Shows the DMA channels used on your Linux system.

- **/proc/bus/pci/devices.** Shows the PCI information on your Linux system.

- **/proc/scsi/scsi.** Shows a summary of the SCSI information on your Linux system.

- **/proc/bus/usb/devices.** Shows information about the USB (universal serial bus) devices on your Linux system.

- **/proc/bus/usb/drivers.** Shows information about the USB drivers on your Linux system.

**NOTE**    For a list of all the available filenames, enter **ls -al /proc**.

---

## OBJECTIVE 2   DIAGNOSE HARDWARE PROBLEMS

There are various approaches to diagnosing hardware problems, including:

- View Boot Messages
- Get Information about Installed Hardware
- List, Load, and Unload Kernel Modules
- Find Out about Current Configuration
- Hardware on Non-Linux Computers

**13**

## View Boot Messages

When the computer starts, a lot of messages scroll across the screen, often too fast to be read. Even if there was information regarding a hardware problem, you hardly have a chance to understand it.

These messages are stored in /var/log/boot.msg up to the point the default runlevel set in /etc/inittab has been reached.

Independently from that file, kernel messages are stored in memory in a ring buffer with a size of 16 KB.

Use **less /var/log/boot.msg** to view the log file written at boot up.

The command **dmesg** shows the content of the kernel ring buffer.

If there is a problem when the computer starts, both files can give invaluable hints on what is wrong.

# Get Information about Installed Hardware

Taking a screwdriver and opening up a machine is not always an option when you need information about the specific hardware installed in the machine. And in most cases it is not even necessary.

To get information about installed hardware, use the following:

- lspci
- hwinfo
- hdparm
- The /sys/ File System

## lspci

**lspci** gives a brief overview on devices connected to the PCI bus.

```
da10:~ # lspci
0000:00:00.0 Host bridge: Intel Corp. 440BX/ZX/DX - 82443BX/ZX/DX Host
bridge (rev 03)
0000:00:01.0 PCI bridge: Intel Corp. 440BX/ZX/DX - 82443BX/ZX/DX AGP bridge
(rev 03)
0000:00:04.0 ISA bridge: Intel Corp. 82371AB/EB/MB PIIX4 ISA (rev 02)
0000:00:04.1 IDE interface: Intel Corp. 82371AB/EB/MB PIIX4 IDE (rev 01)
0000:00:04.2 USB Controller: Intel Corp. 82371AB/EB/MB PIIX4 USB (rev 01)
0000:00:04.3 Bridge: Intel Corp. 82371AB/EB/MB PIIX4 ACPI (rev 02)
0000:00:06.0 SCSI storage controller: Adaptec AHA-2940U2/U2W / 7890/7891
0000:00:09.0 Multimedia audio controller: Ensoniq ES1371 [AudioPCI-97]
(rev 06)
0000:00:0a.0 Ethernet controller: Intel Corp. 82557/8/9 [Ethernet Pro 100]
(rev 05)
0000:00:0b.0 Ethernet controller: Realtek Semiconductor Co., Ltd.
RTL-8139/8139C/8139C+ (rev 10)
0000:01:00.0 VGA compatible controller: nVidia Corporation NV5 [RIVA
TNT2/TNT2 Pro] (rev 11)
```

## hwinfo

The output of lspci might be too terse sometimes.

**hwinfo** is the tool used by the installer to find out about available hardware during installation. It can also be called after installation when some information on the hardware is needed.

**hwinfo --help** shows the available options, as shown in the following:

```
da10:~ # hwinfo --help
Usage: hwinfo [options]
Probe for hardware.
  --short         just a short listing
  --log logfile   write info to logfile
  --debug level   set debuglevel
  --version       show libhd version
  --dump-db n     dump hardware data base, 0: external, 1: internal
  --hw_item       probe for hw_item
  hw_item is one of:
    cdrom, floppy, disk, network, gfxcard, framebuffer, monitor, camera,
    mouse, joystick, keyboard, chipcard, sound, isdn, modem, storage-ctrl,
    netcard, printer, tv, dvb, scanner, braille, sys, bios, cpu, partition,
    usb-ctrl, usb, pci, isapnp, ide, scsi, bridge, hub, memory, smp, pppoe,
    pcmcia, pcmcia-ctrl, wlan, zip, dsl, all, reallyall

  Note: debug info is shown only in the log file. (If you specify a
  log file the debug level is implicitly set to a reasonable value.)
```

When called without any parameters, hwinfo checks all categories. The result is a long list of devices. Specifying a hardware item results in a specific answer, as shown in the following:

```
da10:~ # hwinfo --netcard
18: PCI 0a.0: 0200 Ethernet controller
  [Created at pci.244]
  Unique ID: bSAa.ST_bb9LG_k7
  SysFS ID: /devices/pci0000:00/0000:00:0a.0
  SysFS BusID: 0000:00:0a.0
  Hardware Class: network
  Model: "IBM 82558B Ethernet Pro 10/100"
  Vendor: pci 0x8086 "Intel Corporation"
  Device: pci 0x1229 "82557/8/9 [Ethernet Pro 100]"
  SubVendor: pci 0x1014 "IBM"
  SubDevice: pci 0x005c "82558B Ethernet Pro 10/100"
  Revision: 0x05
  Driver: "e100"
  Memory Range: 0xe1000000-0xe1000fff (rw,prefetchable)
  I/O Ports: 0xb400-0xb41f (rw)
  Memory Range: 0xde000000-0xde0fffff (rw,non-prefetchable)
  Memory Range: 0x00000000-0x000fffff (ro,prefetchable,disabled)
  IRQ: 5 (122491 events)
  HW Address: 00:04:ac:d6:55:f4
  Driver Info #0:
    Driver Status: e100 is active
    Driver Activation Cmd: "modprobe e100"
  Driver Info #1:
    Driver Status: eepro100 is active
    Driver Activation Cmd: "modprobe eepro100"
  Config Status: cfg=no, avail=yes, need=no, active=unknown
```

## hdparm

You can use the utility **hdparm** to get and set drive parameters on IDE hard disks.

You can view the partitioning of the hard disks by entering:

**fdisk –l**

## The /sys/ File System

In the past it was difficult to determine which interface (software component) belonged to which device (physical object).

This changed with kernel version 2.6.*x* when the sysfs file system was introduced. sysfs is a virtual file system that is mounted under /sys/.

In a virtual file system, there is no physical device that holds the information. Instead, the file system is generated on the fly by the kernel.

sysfs represents all devices and interfaces of a Linux system.

In sysfs, there are four main directories:

- **/sys/bus** and **/sys/devices.** These directories contain different representations of system hardware. Devices are represented here.

  For example, the following represents a digital camera connected to the USB bus:
  ```
  /sys/bus/usb/devices/1-1/
  ```

  This directory contains several files that provide information about the device.

  The following is a listing of the files in this directory:

  ```
  1-1:1.0              bMaxPower           manufacturer
  bcdDevice            bNumConfigurations  maxchild
  bConfigurationValue  bNumInterfaces      power
  bDeviceClass         detach_state        product
  bDeviceProtocol      devnum              serial
  bDeviceSubClass      idProduct           speed
  bmAttributes         idVendor            version
  ```

  For example, by reading the content of the manufacturer file, you can determine the manufacturer of the device:

  ```
  cat manufacturer
  OLYMPUS
  ```

  In this case, an Olympus digital camera is connected to the system.

- **/sys/class** and **/sys/block.** The interfaces of the devices are represented under these two directories.

  For example, the interface belonging to the Olympus digital camera is represented by the following directory:
  ```
  /sys/block/sda/
  ```

  The directory named **sda** represents the digital camera accessed like a SCSI hard disk.

The following is the content of the sda directory:

```
dev       queue   removable  size
device    range   sda1       stat
```

The subdirectory **sda1** represents the interface to the first partition on the camera's memory card.

For example, by reading the content of sda1/size, you can determine the size of the partition:

```
cat sda1/size
31959
```

The partition has a size of 31959 512-byte blocks, which is about 16 MB.

To connect an interface with a device, file system links are used.

In the Olympus digital camera example, a link exists from the file /sys/block/sda/device to the corresponding device:

```
ll device
lrwxrwxrwx  1 root root 0 Aug 17 14:03 device -> ../../devices/
pci0000:00/0000:00:1d.0/usb1/1-1/1-1:1.0/host0/0:0:0:0
```

In this way, all interfaces of the system are linked with their corresponding devices.

Beside the representation in sysfs, there are also the device files in the /dev/ directory.

These files are needed for applications to access the interfaces of a device. The name *device file* is a bit misleading, as the name *interface file* would be more suitable.

## List, Load, and Unload Kernel Modules

Once the type of hardware is established using one of the above ways, the question arises if the module to control the device has been loaded.

You can check this by using the command **lsmod**.

```
da10:~ # lsmod
Module                 Size  Used by
raid5                 20736  1
xor                   15240  1 raid5
nvram                  8456  0
speedstep_lib          3712  0
freq_table             4612  0
snd_seq_oss           31232  0
snd_pcm_oss           57512  0
snd_mixer_oss         18944  1 snd_pcm_oss
...
```

Usually the kernel modules are loaded automatically during system startup or when hotpluggable hardware like a USB device is connected to the machine.

You can also load modules by hand, using:

**modprobe** *kernel_module*

You can unload unused kernel modules by using:

**rmmod**

# Find Out about Current Configuration

The configuration of hardware devices is stored in files in the directory /etc/.

These files are used as the devices are initialized upon startup.

In many instances, the configuration is done via files in the /proc file system.

Like the /sys file system, this is a virtual file system that is not stored on the hard disk but created at system startup.

You can use **cat** to read the current configuration, and in some cases it is also possible to change the runtime configuration.

The following is an example of /proc/sys/:

```
da10:~ # cat /proc/sys/net/ipv4/ip_forward
0
da10:~ # echo 1 > /proc/sys/net/ipv4/ip_forward
da10:~ # cat /proc/sys/net/ipv4/ip_forward
1
```

net/ipv4/ip_forward:

This file determines whether IP packets are routed from one network interface to another.

If the value in the file is set to 0, no routing takes place.

Writing a 1 into the file switches on routing.

Some other files with useful information in the /proc file system are:

- **/proc/cpuinfo.** Shows information about the processor.
- **/proc/filesystems.** Lists the supported file systems.
- **/proc/interrupts.** Lists interrupts and what hardware uses them.
- **/proc/ioports.** Lists I/O ports and what hardware uses them.
- **/proc/modules.** Lists the loaded modules.
- **/proc/mounts.** Lists the mounted file systems.
- **/proc/partitions**. Lists the available partitions.
- **/proc/pci**. Lists the detected PCI devices.
- **/proc/swaps**. Lists the swap partitions.

To read and set the IP configuration of the network interfaces the command ifconfig can be used:

```
da10:~ # ifconfig
eth0      Link encap:Ethernet  HWaddr 00:04:AC:D6:55:F4
          inet addr:10.0.0.10 Bcast:10.0.0.255  Mask:255.255.255.0
          inet6 addr: fe80::204:acff:fed6:55f4/64 Scope:Link
          UP BROADCAST NOTRAILERS RUNNING MULTICAST  MTU:1500  Metric:1
          RX packets:32488 errors:1 dropped:0 overruns:0 frame:1
          TX packets:30091 errors:0 dropped:0 overruns:0 carrier:0
          collisions:1431 txqueuelen:1000
          RX bytes:4999132 (4.7 Mb)  TX bytes:20609959 (19.6 Mb)

lo        Link encap:Local Loopback
          inet addr:127.0.0.1  Mask:255.0.0.0
          inet6 addr: ::1/128 Scope:Host
          UP LOOPBACK RUNNING  MTU:16436  Metric:1
          RX packets:38509 errors:0 dropped:0 overruns:0 frame:0
          TX packets:38509 errors:0 dropped:0 overruns:0 carrier:0
          collisions:0 txqueuelen:0
          RX bytes:21589144 (20.5 Mb)  TX bytes:21589144 (20.5 Mb)
```

For information about setting IP addresses, see the man page for **ifconfig**.

To view the routing table, use the commands:

**route**

*or*

**netstat -r**

Changing the routing table is possible by using the command:

**route**

**man route** gives the syntax.

Network configuration is covered extensively in *Manage the Network Configuration*.

**13**

## Hardware on Non-Linux Computers

On a computer running another operating system, the tools listed above are not available.

However, you can see this information without altering the installed system if it can be booted from CD-ROM.

In this case, use a Linux system that can start and run from a CD-ROM or DVD.

The *SLES 9 DVD* comes with a rescue system that can be used for this purpose.

There is also a live CD version of SUSE Linux Professional 9.2.

Various other projects exist that provide bootable ISO-images, a well known one being Knoppix.

Insert the DVD and boot the system. Once the system is started, it can check the hardware as described above. It usually reacts a bit slower than a system installed on the hard disk, because the DVD drive is not as fast as the hard disk.

To access files on the hard disk, you must mount the respective partitions.

The root file system of the Linux system running from DVD lies in a RAM disk. To access files on the hard disks, the file systems have to be mounted into that root filesystem, such as below /mnt.

---

## Objective 3    Describe Multimedia Components

Since SUSE Linux Enterprise Server is not designed for multimedia, this objective describes multimedia features of Linux in a more general way.

The following topics are described:

- Sound
- Video
- DVDs

## Sound

Linux offers a wide range of sound applications in various stages of development.

ALSA stands for the Advanced Linux Sound Architecture.

ALSA consists of a set of kernel drivers, an application programming interface (API) library, and utility programs for supporting sound in Linux.

ALSA consists of a series of kernel device drivers for many different sound cards, and it also provides an API library, libasound.

Application developers are encouraged to program using the library API and not the kernel interface. The library provides a higher-level and more developer-friendly programming interface along with a logical naming of devices.

ALSA uses plug-ins that allow extensions to new devices, including virtual devices implemented entirely in software. ALSA provides a number of command-line utilities, including a mixer, sound file player, and tools for controlling special features of specific sound cards.

The following topics are described in the following:

- The ALSA PCM Types
- Mixers
- Buffering and Latencies
- Direct Recording and Playback of WAV Files
- Compressing Audio Data
- ALSA and MIDI

## The ALSA PCM Types

PCM (Pulse Code Modulation) designates the digital output interfaces when relating to sound cards.

You can influence the way ALSA addresses the sound card by selecting a specific PCM type. The main PCM types are hw and plughw.

To understand the difference between the two types, consider how a PCM device is opened. It must be opened with specific settings for at least the following parameters:

- Sample format
- Sample frequency
- Number of channels
- Number of periods (previously referred to as fragments)
- Size of a period

For example, an application might try to play a WAV file with a sample frequency of 44.1 kHz although the sound card does not support this frequency.

In this case, ALSA can automatically convert the data in the plug-in layer to a format supported by the sound card.

The conversion affects the following parameters:

- Sample Format
- Sample Frequency
- Number of Channels

To activate the plug-in layer by selecting the PCM type, enter plughw.

If the PCM type **hw** is selected, ALSA tries to open the PCM devices directly with the parameters required by the application.

13

The complete designator for a PCM device consists of the PCM type followed by a colon, the card number, and the device number, for example:

**plughw:0,0**

The **dmix** output plug-in is a recent addition to the PCM types. It allows applications to share access to a PCM device on sound cards that do not support this natively.

The complete identifier is:

**plug:dmix**

For more information about dmix, see http://alsa.opensrc.org/index.php?page=DmixPlugin.

## Mixers

Mixers provide a convenient means of controlling the volume and balance of the sound output and input of computers.

The main difference between the various mixers consists in the appearance of the user interface.

However, there are a number of mixers that are designed for specific hardware.

**alsamixer** is part of the alsa package and can be run from the command line without the X environment, as shown in Figure 13-2.

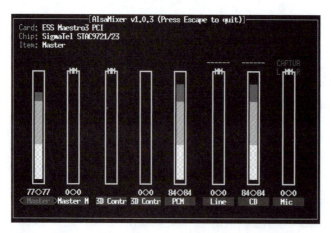

**Figure 13-2**

You control the application by using cursor keys.

Use Q, W, E, Y, X, and C to set different levels for the left and right channels.

M mutes single channels. In this case, **MM** appears above the muted controller.

To terminate alsamixer, press **Esc**.

The basic controls for sound output are:

- **Master.** Sets the master volume.
- **PCM and CD.** Control the respective weighting of the PCM and audio CD channels.

To determine the recording source, press **Spacebar**.

The **capture** controller regulates the input amplifier.

Whether the **Line** controller or the **MIC** controller is used depends on the recording source.

 For more information, enter **man alsamixer**.

**NOTE**

**alsamixergui** is a graphical version of alsamixer.

## Buffering and Latencies

A problem inherent in Linux and all other multitasking operating systems is ensuring uninterrupted audio playback.

In a multitasking operating system, several processes usually run concurrently.

Because the processor can only handle one process at a time, each process is assigned a certain amount of time by the operating system's scheduler.

The switching action between processes normally happens so quickly that the user does not notice it. However, during audio playback, even brief interruptions are noticeable in the form of clicks.

Therefore, audio programs use a buffer for the playback, enabling the audio data in the buffer to be emitted continuously by the sound card even when the audio program is interrupted by the scheduler.

Accordingly, the playback is click-free, providing the buffer is large enough to bridge the longest possible interruption.

However, the buffer size also determines the reaction time (latency) of the program.

13

Therefore, the buffer size is kept as small as possible especially for interactive applications, such as real-time synthesizers and DJ mixer consoles.

Basically, the length of the interruptions depends on the system load and the priority of the process.

Consequently, the size of the buffer required for click-free playback can be reduced by increasing the priority of the audio program or by switching to a real-time scheduler.

For this reason, many audio programs attempt to switch their processes to a real-time scheduler, but switching a process to another scheduler is only possible if you have root privileges.

### Direct Recording and Playback of WAV Files

**arecord** and **aplay** provide a simple and flexible interface to the PCM devices.

You can use arecord and aplay to record and play audio data in the WAV format, among other formats.

To records a WAV file of ten seconds in CD quality (16 bit, 44.1 kHz), enter:

```
arecord -d 10 -f cd -t wav mysong.wav
```

To list all options of arecord and aplay, use the **--help** option.

### Compressing Audio Data

Uncompressed audio data in CD quality consumes almost 10 MB per minute.

The MP3 procedure was developed by Fraunhofer IIS for the purpose of drastically compressing this data. Unfortunately, this procedure is patented. Therefore, companies that distribute MP3 encoders are required to pay license fees.

The powerful MP3 encoder Lame was developed for Linux. In some countries (including Germany and the United States), the use of Lame is permitted for research purposes only.

Although the source code of Lame is provided under the GPL, SUSE/Novell is not allowed to include this encoder in the SLES distribution. For more information about this, visit the project Web page at http://lame.sourceforge.net.

**NOTE**

OggVorbis (package vorbis-tools) is a free audio compression format that is now supported by the majority of audio players.

For more information, see www.xiph.org/ogg/vorbis.

**NOTE**

The latest version of the Ogg encoder even supports encoding with a variable bit rate. In this way, an even higher degree of compression can be achieved.

### ALSA and MIDI

Besides playing PCM data, many sound cards also offer MIDI functionality. The ALSA MIDI sequencer implements an efficient architecture for routing MIDI data.

Many sound cards have an external MIDI port for connecting MIDI devices, such as synthesizers, keyboards, and sound modules.

If the MIDI port of the card is supported by ALSA, use a sequencer application, such as **jazz**, to record and play MIDI files.

Some sound cards do not have a WaveTable synthesizer for playing MIDI files with the loaded sound font (or instrument patch). In this case, use a software WaveTable synthesizer like **fluidsynth** or **timidity++**.

## Video

Compressed video files consists of one data container.

This container consists of:

- A header with information about the content of the container
- One or more video streams
- One or more audio streams

The most famous containers are AVI and Quicktime.

Video and audio streams have their own formats. These formats are called *codecs*.

Known video codecs are the following:

- DivX
- MPEG4
- Sorenson

Audio codecs are the following:

- MP2
- MP3
- WMA

AVI files often include the video codecs DivX or MPEG 4. Quicktime usually includes the Sorenson codec.

In most cases, MP3 is used as an audio codec.

**13**

None of these codecs are open source; they are commercial. You can use them with Linux, but they are not free and open.

Two open source codecs are available:

- Xvid (video)
- Ogg Vorbis (audio)

Both produce quality as good as or better than the commercial codecs. The needed disk space is small.

You cannot include an Ogg Vorbis audio file in an AVI or Quicktime container. If you want to include it in a container, you can use the new container format OGM (Ogg Media).

OGM is not as popular as AVI. You need to determine whether your video player software is able to play OGM files.

## DVDs

The movie industry does not want to make it too easy to make copies of DVDs. Therefore, most movies on DVD are encrypted by an encoding mechanism, the Content Scrambling System (CSS).

The software needed to decode encrypted DVDs was sold to vendors of DVD players. Because there was no player available at all to play DVDs on Linux, a Norwegian student, Jon Lech Johansen programed one in 1999, breaking CSS. Years of legal struggles followed. And while Johansen was finally acquitted in Norway, in general the legal issues still exist.

There are three possible solutions in Linux:

1. Use a software DVD player that only plays unencrypted DVDs.

   This is a perfectly legal solution, but the problem is that only a very small number of DVDs are not encrypted, so not many people are really interested in this level of functionality.

   Possible programs to use for this purpose are Xine or Kaffeine.

2. Wait for a commercial manufacturer of DVD players to come out with a Linux DVD player.

3. Use a DVD player that uses software with questionable legality to decode the DVDs.

   It is up to you to find out whether using such software is legal in your country. In any event, you have to find the source code and compile it yourself.

## OBJECTIVE 4    IDENTIFY AND CONFIGURE REMOVABLE SYSTEM HARDWARE

The following is described:

- PCMCIA
- USB
- IEEE1394 (FireWire)
- The Hotplug System
- Dynamic Device Nodes with udev

## PCMCIA

This section covers special aspects of PCMCIA hardware and software in laptops.

PCMCIA (Personal Computer Memory Card International Association) is a collective term used for all related hardware and software.

You need to know the following about PCMCIA:

- Hardware
- Software
- Configuration

### Hardware

The most important component is the PCMCIA card. There are two types of PCMCIA cards:

- **PC Cards.** These cards have been around since the since of PCMCIA.

  They use a 16-bit bus for the data transmission and are usually quite inexpensive.

  Some modern PCMCIA bridges have difficulty detecting these cards. Nevertheless, once they are detected, they usually run smoothly and do not cause any problems.

- **CardBus cards.** This is a more recent standard.

  They use a 32-bit bus, which makes them faster but also more expensive. They are integrated in the system like PCI cards and also run smoothly.

If the PCMCIA service is active, the command:

**cardctl ident**

reveals the type of the inserted card.

A list of supported cards is available in the file /usr/share/doc/packages/pcmcia/SUPPORTED.CARDS. The latest version of the PCMCIA howto is also in the same directory.

The second important component is the PCMCIA controller or the PC Card or CardBus bridge, which establishes the connection between the card and the PCI bus. All common models are supported.

To determine the controller type, enter:

**pcic_probe**

If it is a PCI device, the command:

**lspci –vt**

provides further information.

## Software

There are two PCMCIA software components:

- Base Modules
- Card Manager

**Base Modules**    The required kernel modules are located in the kernel packages.

The following packages are also needed:

- pcmcia
- hotplug

When PCMCIA is started, the following modules are loaded:

- pcmcia_core
- yenta_socket

In very rare cases, the module tcic is needed instead of yenta_socket.

- ds

These modules initialize the existing PCMCIA controllers and provide the base functionality.

**Card Manager**    Because PCMCIA cards can be changed while the system is running, the activities in the slots have to be monitored.

This task is handled by the card services implemented in the base module.

The initialization of a card is handled by one of the following:

- **Card manager (for PC Cards).** The card manager is started by the PCMCIA start script after the base modules are loaded.

    *or*

- **The kernel's hotplug system (for Card Bus cards).** Hotplug is activated automatically.

If a card is inserted, the card manager or hotplug determines its type and function and loads the respective modules.

After the modules have been loaded successfully, the card manager or hotplug launches certain initialization scripts, depending on the function of the card.

The initialization scripts establish the network connection, mount partitions of external SCSI hard disks, or perform other hardware-specific actions.

The scripts of the card manager are located in the directory /etc/pcmcia/.

The scripts for hotplug are located in /etc/hotplug/.

When the card is removed, the card manager or hotplug terminates all card activities with the same scripts. Subsequently, the modules that are no longer needed are unloaded.

These actions are referred to as ***hotplug events***.

Whenever hard disks or partitions are added (***block events***), the hotplug scripts use subfs to make the new media available for immediate use in /media/. To mount media by means of the older PCMCIA scripts, subfs should be disabled in hotplug.

Both the PCMCIA start-up and the card events are logged in the system log file (/var/log/ messages). The modules that are loaded and the scripts that are executed are recorded in this log file.

Theoretically, you can remove a PCMCIA card without doing anything other than unplugging it.

This works for network, modem, and ISDN cards, provided there are no more active network connections.

However, this does not work for mounted partitions of an external hard disk or NFS directories. Such units must be synchronized and unmounted properly. Of course, this is not possible after the card has been taken out.

If you are not sure whether a card can be taken out safely, enter:

**cardctl eject**

to deactivate all cards that are still inserted in the laptop.

To deactivate only one of the cards, specify the slot number; for example:

**cardctl eject 0**

## Configuration

To determine whether PCMCIA should be started when the system is booted, use the YaST Runlevel Editor module.

To start this module, select:

**yast2 > System > Runlevel Editor**

The following three variables are defined in the file /etc/sysconfig/pcmcia:

- **PCMCIA_PCIC.** Contains the name of the module that controls the PCMCIA controller.

  Normally, the start script should determine the module automatically.

  If it does not, enter the module here.

  Otherwise, this variable should be left empty.

- **PCMCIA_CORE_OPTS.** This variable was designed for parameters for the pcmcia_core module.

  However, these parameters are rarely used.

**NOTE**

The options are described in the man page of pcmcia_core. Because this man page refers to the module from the pcmcia-cs package, it lists more parameters than the module from the kernel actually supports; namely, all parameters beginning with cb_ and pc_debug.

- **PCMCIA_BEEP.** Enables and disables the acoustic signals of the card manager.

The files /etc/pcmcia/config and /etc/pcmcia/*.conf contain the assignment of the drivers to PC Cards.

First, config is read and then *.conf in alphabetic order.

The last entry found for a card is used.

**NOTE**

For more information about the syntax of these files, see the man page of pcmcia.

The files **/etc/sysconfig/hardware/hwcfg-*configuration_name*** contain the assignment of drivers to CardBus cards.

These files are created by YaST when you configure a card.

**NOTE**

More information about the configuration names can be found in /usr/share/doc/packages/sysconfig/README and in the man page of getcfg.

The configuration of the following is described:

- Network Cards
- ISDN
- Modem
- SCSI and IDE

**Network Cards**    Ethernet, wireless LAN, and TokenRing network cards can be configured with YaST like normal network cards.

If your card was not detected, select the card type PCMCIA in the hardware settings.

**ISDN**    Like other ISDN cards, ISDN PC cards can also be configured with YaST.

It does not matter which of the listed PCMCIA ISDN cards is selected, as long as it is a PCMCIA card.

When configuring the hardware and selecting a provider, the operating mode must always be hotplug, not onboot.

ISDN modems also exist in the form of PCMCIA cards. These are modem cards or multifunction cards with an additional ISDN connection kit. They are treated like modems.

**Modem**    Normally, there are no PCMCIA-specific settings for modem PC cards. A soon as a modem is inserted, it is available under /dev/modem.

Some of the PCMCIA modem cards are soft modems that are not supported by Linux. If drivers are available for these cards, they must be installed in the system.

**SCSI and IDE**    The suitable driver module is loaded by the card manager or by hotplug.

As soon as a SCSI or IDE card is inserted, the connected devices can be used. The device names are determined dynamically.

Information about available SCSI and IDE devices can be found in /proc/scsi/ and /proc/ide/.

**NOTE**

External hard disks, CD-ROM drives, and similar devices must be switched on before the PCMCIA card is inserted in the slot.

Use active termination for SCSI devices.

Before a SCSI or IDE card is removed, all partitions of the connected devices must be unmounted by using umount. If you forget to do this, you will be able to access these devices again only after rebooting the system.

**CAUTION**

**13**

# USB

The following topics explain what you need to know about USB devices:

- Basics of the Universal Serial Bus
- Host Controllers
- USB Devices and Transfer Characteristics
- Hubs
- Data Flow Types

## Basics of the Universal Serial Bus

In 1994, an alliance of four industrial partners (Compaq, Intel, Microsoft and NEC) developed the specifications for the Universal Serial Bus (USB).

The USB bus was originally designed to:

- Connect the PC to the telephone
- Be easy-to-use
- Provide port expansion

Version 1.0 was first released in January 1996. Version 2.0 was announced in 1999.

USB is strictly hierarchical and it is controlled by one host. The host uses a master/slave protocol to communicate with connected USB devices.

Devices cannot establish any direct connection to other devices. This prevents problems like collision avoidance or distributed bus arbitration.

USB 1.1 allows 127 devices to be connected at the same time and the total communication bandwidth is limited to 12 Mbps.

However, using low speed devices, USB interrupts and other overhead mean that actual throughput cannot exceed about 8.5 Mbps under near ideal conditions, and typical performance may be around 2 Mbps.

With USB 2.0 bandwidth is much higher, in theory data rates up to 480 MBit/s are possible.

## Host Controllers

Most modern motherboard chipsets provide a USB host controller.

Older machines that are not equipped with a USB host controller can be upgraded using a PCI Card with a host controller built in.

Available USB host controllers are compatible with either:

- The Open Host Controller Interface (OHCI, by Compaq)

    *or*

- The Universal Host Controller Interface (UHCI, by Intel) standard

Both types have the same capabilities and USB devices work with both host controller types.

Basically the hardware of UHCI is simpler and cheaper, but the device driver is more complex and causes a higher CPU load.

### USB Devices and Transfer Characteristics

The implementation details can vary widely, because there are a lot of different devices available.

Even the maximum communication speed can differ for particular USB devices.

### Hubs

USB ports can be used to attach normal devices or a hub.

A hub is a USB device that extends the number of ports to connect other USB devices.

The maximum number of user devices is reduced by the number of hubs on the bus.

### Data Flow Types

The communication on USB is done in two directions and uses four different transfer types:

- Control transfers are used to request and send reliable short data packets.

  Control transfers are used to configure devices and are each required to support a minimum set of control commands.

- Bulk transfers are used to request or send reliable data packets up to the full bus bandwidth.

- Interrupt transfers are similar to bulk transfers that are polled periodically.

  If an interrupt transfer was submitted, the host controller driver will automatically repeat this request in a specified interval (1ms–127ms).

- Isochronous transfers send or receive data streams in realtime with guaranteed bus bandwidth but without any reliability.

## IEEE1394 (FireWire)

IEEE1394 is the standard for a high speed serial bus.

Different manufacturers have their own names for their own implementation of this standard.

The most common name is FireWire (which is what Apple names it), other names are i.link (Sony) and Lynx (not the Lynx browser).

The first standard, IEEE 1394a, is capable of speeds up to 400 Mbps while the newer standard IEEE 1394b (which uses a cable with more contacts) is capable of speeds up to 800 Mbps. IEEE1394a is the far more common of the two.

13

You can connect up to 64 devices (host adapter included) to one IEEE1394 bus.

Another feature that makes IEEE 1394 equipment interesting is its support for isochronous data, delivering data at a guaranteed speed, making it suitable for continuous data streams like video.

IEEE1394a is often compared to USB 2, because on paper they offer similar transfer speeds. In practice, IEEE1394a is typically faster.

IEEE1394 devices are much more independent than USB devices. In fact, the IEEE1394 protocol specifies how these devices are to interact without even the need for a host computer. For example, you should be able to plug in a FireWire video camera to a FireWire external hard disk and transfer files without even needing a computer.

Support for IEEE1394 in Linux depends on the used IEEE1394 chipset (either onboard or a PCI card) and the specific device.

All important kernel modules are in **/lib/modules/***kernel_version***/kernel/drivers /ie1394/**.

To enable IEEE1394, you must load the **ohci1394.ko** module.

The mechanism for using a IEEE1394 bus is similar to the USB mechanism; both use the hotplug system.

## The Hotplug System

The hotplug system is not only used for devices that can be inserted and removed during operation but for all devices that are only detected after the kernel has been booted.

These devices and their interfaces are entered in the sysfs file system, which is mounted under /sys/.

Until the kernel has been booted, only devices that are absolutely necessary, such as bus system, boot disks, and keyboard, are initialized.

Normally, devices are detected by a driver, which triggers a hotplug event that is handled by suitable scripts. For devices that cannot be detected automatically, coldplug uses static configurations.

Apart from a few historic exceptions, most devices are now initialized when the system is booted or when the devices are connected.

The initialization often results in the registration of an interface.

The registration of the interface, in turn, triggers hotplug events that cause an automatic configuration of the respective interface.

Formerly, a set of configuration data was used as the basis for initializing devices.

Now, the system searches for suitable configuration data on the basis of existing devices.

Thus, the initialization procedure has been reversed, enabling a more flexible use of hotplug devices.

The most important hotplug functions are configured in two files:

- **/etc/sysconfig/hotplug.** Contains variables that influence the behavior of hotplug and coldplug.
- **/proc/sys/kernel/hotplug.** Contains the name of the executable program called by the kernel.

Device configurations are located in /etc/sysconfig/hardware.

You need to understand the following:

- Devices and Interfaces
- Hotplug Events
- Hotplug Agents

## Devices and Interfaces

The hotplug system administers interfaces and devices. A device is linked to either a bus or an interface. An interface links devices to each other or to an application.

A device is always connected to an interface. A bus can be regarded as a multiple interface. There are also virtual devices, such as network tunnels. Every interface is connected to another device or to an application.

The distinction of devices or interfaces is important for understanding the overall concept.

Devices entered in sysfs are found in /sys/devices/. Interfaces are located in /sys/class/ or /sys/block/. All interfaces in sysfs should have a link to their devices.

However, there are still some drivers that do not automatically add this link.

Devices are addressed by means of either the device path in sysfs (/sys/devices/pci0000:00/0000:00:1e.0/0000:02:00.0), a description of the connection point (bus–pci–0000:02:00.0), an individual ID (id-32311AE03FB82538), or something similar.

In the past, interfaces were addressed by means of their names. However, these names represent a simple numbering of the existing devices and may change when devices are added or removed.

Therefore, interfaces can also be addressed by means of a description of the associated device.

Usually, the context indicates whether the description refers to the device itself or to its interface.

## Hotplug Events

Every device and every interface has an associated hotplug event, which is processed by the responsible hotplug agent.

Hotplug events are triggered by the kernel when a link is established to a device or when a driver registers an interface.

A hotplug event is a program call, usually /sbin/hotplug, if nothing else is specified in /proc/sys/kernel/hotplug.

/sbin/hotplug searches for a hotplug agent that matches the type of event. If no suitable agent is found, the program is terminated.

## Hotplug Agents

A hotplug agent is an executable program that performs suitable actions for an event.

The agents for device events are located in /etc/hotplug and are designated as *eventname*.agent.

For interface events, all programs in /etc/dev.d/ are executed by udev.

Usually, device agents load kernel modules, but occasionally they also call additional commands.

In SUSE Linux Enterprise Server, this is handled by:

- **/sbin/hwup**

    *or*

- **/sbin/hwdown**

These programs search for a configuration suitable for the device in the directory /etc/sysconfig/hardware/ and apply it.

To prevent a certain device from being initialized, create a suitable configuration file with the start mode set to Manual or Off.

If /sbin/hwup does not find any configuration, modules are automatically loaded by the agent.

**NOTE**

For more information about /sbin/hwup see /usr/share/doc/packages/ sysconfig/README and the man page of hwup.

Interface agents are started indirectly over udev. In this way, udev first generates a device node the system can access. udev enables the assignment of persistent names to interfaces. Subsequently, the individual agents set up the interfaces.

The procedures for some interfaces are described in the following:

- Activate Network Interfaces
- Activate Storage Devices
- Load Modules Automatically

**Activate Network Interfaces**     Network interfaces are initialized by using:

**/sbin/ifup**

and deactivated by using:

**/sbin/ifdown**

Because Linux does not use device nodes for network interfaces, these are not managed by udev.

If a computer has several network devices with different drivers, the designations of the interface can change if another driver is loaded faster after the system is booted.

For this reason, SUSE Linux Enterprise Server uses a queue to manage events for PCI network devices.

This feature can be disabled by the variable:

**HOTPLUG_PCI_QUEUE_NIC_EVENTS=no**

in the file /etc/sysconfig/hotplug.

The best way to achieve consistent interface designations is to specify the names of the individual interfaces in the configuration files.

**Activate Storage Devices**     Interfaces to storage devices must be mounted to be able to access the devices. Mounting can be fully automated or preconfigured.

The configuration takes place in the variables **HOTPLUG_DO_MOUNT, HOTPLUG_MOUNT_TYPE** and **HOTPLUG_MOUNT_SYNC** in /etc/sysconfig/hotplug and in the file /etc/fstab.

Fully automated operation can be activated by setting the variable:

**HOTPLUG_DO_MOUNT=yes**

Use the variable:

**HOTPLUG_MOUNT_TYPE**

to switch between two modes:

- **subfs**

    In the mode:

    **HOTPLUG_MOUNT_TYPE=subfs**

    a directory is created in the directory /media/. The name of the subdirectory is derived from the device properties.

    When the medium is accessed, it is automatically mounted and unmounted by submountd.

    You can remove devices in this mode when the access control light goes out.

**13**

- **fstab**

    In the mode:

    **HOTPLUG_MOUNT_TYPE=fstab**

    storage devices are mounted in the conventional way by means of a suitable entry in the file /etc/fstab.

You can set the variable:

**HOTPLUG_MOUNT_SYNC**

to enable access in synchronous or asynchronous mode.

In asynchronous mode, write access is faster, because the results are buffered. However, carelessly removing the data medium can result in incomplete writing of data.

In synchronous mode, all data is written immediately, but the access takes longer.

The device must be unmounted manually by using umount.

You can deactivate fully automated operation by setting the variable:

**HOTPLUG_DO_MOUNT=no**

In this case, the device must be manually mounted and unmounted.

When you use the two latter operating modes, we recommend that you use persistent device names because traditional device names might change depending on the initialization sequence.

**Load Modules Automatically**  If a device cannot be initialized by /sbin/hwup, the agent searches the module maps for a suitable driver.

First, it searches the maps contained in /etc/hotplug/*.handmap.

If it does not find the driver there, it also searches in /lib/modules/*kernelversion*/modules.*map.

To use a driver other than the standard driver for the kernel, enter the driver in /etc/hotplug/*.handmap, because this is the first file read.

The USB agent also searches for user-mode drivers in the files /etc/hotplug/usb.usermap and /etc/hotplug/usb/*.usermap.

User-mode drivers are programs that control access to a device instead of a kernel module. In this way, it is possible to call executable programs for particular devices.

In the case of PCI devices, pci.agent first queries hwinfo about driver modules. The agent looks in pci.handmap and the kernel map only if hwinfo does not know of any drivers.

Because hwinfo has already looked there, the inquiry must fail. hwinfo has an additional database for driver mappings. However, it also loads pci.handmap to make sure that any individual mapping in this file is applied.

If several suitable modules are found in a map file, only the first module is loaded. To load all modules, set the variable:

**HOTPLUG_LOAD_MULTIPLE_MODULES=yes**

However, it is better to create a separate device configuration /etc/sysconfig/hardware/ hwcfg-* for this device.

Modules loaded with hwup are not affected by this.

## Dynamic Device Nodes with udev

Traditionally, device nodes were stored in the /dev/ directory on Linux systems. There was a node for every possible type of device, regardless of whether it actually existed in the system. This directory took up a lot of space.

The command devfs has brought a significant improvement, because now only devices that really exist are given a device node in /dev/.

udev introduces a new way of creating device nodes. It compares the information made available by sysfs with data provided by the user in the form of rules.

sysfs is a new file system in kernel 2.6. It provides basic information about devices connected to the system. sysfs is mounted under /sys/.

It is not absolutely necessary to create rules. If a device is connected, the appropriate device node is created.

However, using rules allows you to change the names for the nodes. This offers the convenience of replacing a cryptic device name with a name that is easy to remember and also of having consistent device names where two devices of the same type have been connected.

Unless otherwise specified, two printers are given the designations /dev/lp0 and /dev/lp1.

Which device is given which device node depends on the order in which they are switched on.

Another example is external mass storage devices, such as USB hard disks.

The udev command allows exact device paths to be entered in /etc/fstab.

The following topics are described:

- Create Rules
- Use NAME and SYMLINK to Automate

### Create Rules

Before udev creates device nodes under /dev/, it reads the file:

**/etc/udev/udev.rules**

The first rule that applies to a device is used, even if other rules also apply.

Comments are introduced with a hash sign (#).

Rules take the following form:

**key, [key,...] NAME [, SYMLINK]**

At least one key must be specified, because rules are assigned to devices on the basis of these keys. It is also essential to specify a name.

The device node that is created in /dev/ bears this name. The optional SYMLINK parameter allows nodes to be created in other places.

A rule for a printer looks like the following:

```
BUS="usb", SYSFS{serial}="12345", NAME="lp_hp", SYMLINK="printers/hp"
```

In this example, there are two keys:

- BUS
- SYSFS{serial}

udev compares the serial number to the serial number of the device that is connected to the USB bus. To assign the name lp_hp to the device in /dev/, all the keys must agree.

In addition, a symbolic link /dev/printers/hp, which refers to the device node, is created. During this operation, the printers directory is automatically created.

Print jobs can then be sent to /dev/printers/hp or /dev/lp_hp.

## Use NAME and SYMLINK to Automate

The parameters NAME and SYMLINK allow the use of operators for automatic assignments.

These operators refer to kernel data on the corresponding device.

A simple example illustrates the procedure:

```
BUS="usb", SYSFS{vendor}="abc", SYSFS{model}="xyz", NAME="camera%n"
```

The operator %n in the name is replaced by the number of the camera device, such as camera0 or camera1.

Another useful operator is %k, which is replaced by the standard device name of the kernel, for example, hda1.

To see a list of all the operators, see the man page of udev.

**NOTE**

## OBJECTIVE 5    ACCESS AND WRITE DATA TO RECORDABLE MEDIA

To access and write data to recordable media, you need to know the following:

- Create CDs
- Mobile Hardware

## Create CDs

It takes two steps in Linux to burn CDs:

1. Create an image of the files in the file format especially for CDs.

2. Write the image on the CD.

The following is described:

- Create a CD Image
- Test the CD Image
- Write the CD Image to a CD

### Create a CD Image

**13**

Before you can use any storage medium (such as a floppy disk, hard disk, or CD), it must be formatted. During the formatting process, a file system is built on the medium.

The file system is responsible for organizing and incorporating the files that should be stored on the medium. For CDs, the file system is called ISO 9660.

On a hard disk you can create an empty file system. After creation, you can fill it with information (files).

Since a CD is only writable once, if you formatted a CD with an empty file system, you would not be able to write data on the CD any more.

Before writing files to a CD, you have to create an ISO 9660 image of the data you want to store.

To do this, use the **mkisofs** program.

The syntax of mkisofs is:

**mkisofs [*options*] *directory***

mkisofs has a lot of options, but the following are among the most important:

- **-o *file*.** Specifies the output file (the ISO image).
- **-V "*name*".** Specifies the label of the CD.
- **-R.** Enables RockRidge-extensions.
- **-r.** The same as –R but sets also the permissions of all files to public readable.
- **-J.** Generate MS Joilet directory records in addition to regular ISO 9660 file names.

Each file written to the ISO 9660 filesystem must have a filename in the 8.3 format (8 characters, dot, 3 characters). You might be familiar with this from DOS.

If you enable the Rock Ridge extensions you can use long filenames and the file information (such as permissions and filename) you know from Linux.

Microsoft Windows 95 and later allows filenames with more than 8.3 characters. Microsoft does not use Rock Ridge extensions but uses MS Joliet instead to use longfile names on CD-ROMs.

 To view more options, see the man page: **man 8 mkisofs**.

**NOTE**

## Test the CD Image

Linux can mount files as if they were disk partitions.

This feature is useful to check that the directory layout and file access permissions of the CD image.

To mount the ISO file created with mkisofs, enter:

**mount –t iso9660 –o ro,loop=/dev/loop0 image.iso /mnt**

After entering this command, you can change into the /mnt/ directory and inspect the files. They appear exactly as if they were on a real CD.

To umount the CD image, enter:

**umount /mnt**

## Write the CD Image to a CD

After creating an ISO image with mkisofs or downloading an ISO image from the Internet, you might want to write the image to CD.

Writing an CD can be done in two modes:

- TAO track at once
- DAO disk at once

To write CDs in TAO mode, use the **cdrecord** program.

To write CDs in DAO mode, use the **cdrdao** program.

Because TAO is used in the most cases, it is the only option explained in this topic.

**NOTE**

For more information about cdrdao, enter **man 1 cdrdao**.

Some time ago, you needed an SCSI CD Writer to write CDs with Linux. The next step in the development was a kernel module emulating SCSI for IDE devices. The writer appeared to be a SCSI device. Current kernels support IDE CD writers directly.

You often need to know to which SCSI device your SCSI CD writer is connected. The output of **cdrecord –scanbus** gives you this information.

cdrecord has many options; but the following are the most important:

- **–v.** Verbose mode.
- **–dummy.** The CD recorder will go through all steps of the recording process, but the laser is turned off during this procedure.
- **–dao.** Set DAO (disk at once) writing mode.
- **–sao.** Set SAO (session at once) mode which is usually called disk at once mode.

  This currently only works with MMC drives that support session at once mode.
- **–tao.** Set TAO (track at once) writing mode. (Default)
- **–raw.** Set RAW writing mode. You need to know the size of each track.

  Use this mode for burning ISO 9660 images.
- **–multi.** Allow multisession CDs to be made.
- **–fix.** The disk will only be fixated.
- **–nofix.** Do not fixate the disk after writing the tracks.
- **–eject.** Eject disk after doing the work.
- **speed=*integer*.** Set the speed factor of the writing process to *integer*.

  *integer.* represents a multiple of the audio speed.
- **blank=*type*.** Blank a CD-RW and exit or blank a CD-RW before writing.

  The most important types are:
  - **all.** Blank the entire disk.

    This might take a long time.
  - **fast.** Minimally blank the disk.

    This results in erasing the PMA, the TOC (table of contents) and the pregap.
  - **track.** Blank a track.
  - **unclose.** Unclose last session.
  - **session.** Blank the last session.

**13**

- **dev=***device***.** Sets the SCSI target for the CD recorder.

  Get the the device number by using the option –scanbus.

- **–overburn.** Allow cdrecord to write more than the official size of a medium.

- **–ignsize.** Ignore the known size of the medium.

- **–audio.** If this option is set, all subsequent tracks are written in CD-DA (similar to Red Book) audio format.

  The file with data for this tracks should contain stereo, 16-bit digital audio with 44100 samples per second.

- **–data.** If this option is set, all subsequent tracks are written in CD-ROM mode 1 (Yellow Book) format.

  The file with track data should contain an ISO 9660 or Rock Ridge file system image.

To burn an ISO image created previously to CD, enter:

```
da10:~ # cdrecord -v speed=4 dev=0,0,0 image.iso
```

To create an audio CD of some WAV files, enter:

```
da10:~ # cdrecord -v speed=4 dev=0,0,0 -audio track*.wav
```

For more information about cdrecord, see man page **man 1 cdrecord**.

**NOTE**

## Mobile Hardware

SUSE Linux supports the automatic detection of mobile storage devices over FireWire (IEEE 1394) or USB.

The term *mobile storage device* comprises any kind of FireWire or USB hard disk, USB flash drive, or digital camera. (They are usually treated as SCSI disks with devices sda*x*, sdb*x*, etc.)

These devices are automatically detected and configured via hotplug as soon as they are connected with the system over the corresponding interface.

Use the subfs and submount commands to ensure that the devices are mounted to the corresponding locations in the file system.

Manual mounting and unmounting (as in previous versions of SUSE Linux Enterprise Server) is no longer required. Devices can simply be disconnected as soon as no program accesses it.

- **External hard disks (USB and FireWire).** As soon as an external hard disk has been correctly recognized by the system, its icon appears in KDE or GNOME in the list of mounted drives.

  You can create folders and files here and edit or delete them.

  The descriptor by which the device is mounted in /media/usb-* or /media/ieee1394-* remains unaffected by this.

- **USB flash drives.** These devices are handled by the system just like external hard disks.

  The descriptor by which the device is mounted in /media/usb-*.

- **Digital cameras (USB and FireWire).** Digital cameras recognized by the system appear as external drives.

## Objective 6    Configure Advanced Power Management and the ACPI Tool

Unlike APM (Advanced Power Management), which was previously used on laptops for power management only, the hardware information and configuration tool ACPI (Advanced Configuration and Power Interface) is available on most computers, laptops, desktops, and servers.

On many types of hardware, the CPU frequency can be adapted to the load, which helps save valuable battery time especially on mobile devices (CPU frequency scaling).

All power management technologies require suitable hardware and BIOS routines. Most laptops and many modern desktops and servers meet these requirements.

APM is used on many older computers. Because APM largely consists of a function set implemented in the BIOS, the level of APM support varies depending on the hardware. This is also true of ACPI, which is even more complex. For this reason, it is virtually impossible to recommend one over the other. Simply test the various procedures on your hardware, then select the technology that is best supported in your environment.

In this chapter, the following topics are described:

- Power Saving Functions
- APM
- ACPI
- powersave
- The YaST Power Management Module

13

## Power Saving Functions

Although many of these functions are of general interest, they are especially important for mobile deployment. The following describes the functions and which systems offer them.

- **Standby.** This operating mode merely turns off the display. On some computers, the processor performance is throttled. This function is not available in all APM implementations. The corresponding ACPI state is S1.

- **Suspend (to memory).** This mode writes the entire system state to the RAM. Subsequently, the entire system except the RAM is put to sleep. Because the computer consumes very little power in this state, the battery can last anywhere from twelve hours to several days, depending on the device.

  The advantage of this state is that you can resume work at the same point within a few seconds without having to boot and restart applications.

  Most newer devices can be suspended by closing the lid and activated by opening it. The corresponding ACPI state is S3. Support of this state largely depends on the hardware.

- **Hibernation (suspend to disk).** This operating mode enables the computer to hibernate, because the entire system state is written to the hard disk and the system is powered off.

  The reactivation from the state of hibernation takes about 30–90 seconds. The state prior to the suspend state will be restored. Some manufacturers offer useful hybrid variants of this mode in their APM (such as RediSafe in IBM Thinkpads). The corresponding ACPI state is S4.

- **Battery monitor.** In addition to monitoring the battery charge level, something must be done when power reserves are low. This control function is handled by ACPI or APM.

- **Automatic power-off.** Following a shutdown, the computer is powered off. This is especially important when an automatic shutdown is performed shortly before the battery is empty.

- **Shutdown of system components.** The most important component for saving power is the hard disk. Depending on the reliability of the overall system, the hard disk can be put to sleep for some time.

  However, the risk of losing data increases with the duration of the sleep periods. Other components can be deactivated via ACPI (at least theoretically) or permanently in the BIOS setup.

- **Processor speed control.** AMD PowerNow! and Intel SpeedStep are two concepts designed for reducing the power consumption of the overall system.

In processor speed control, the power consumption of the most powerhungry component—the processor—is reduced. A pleasant side effect of the reduced processor speed is the reduced generation of heat, so adjustable fans also produce less noise.

This feature is controlled by the CPU frequency scaling functions of the Linux kernel.

Basically, three different processor speed levels are available:

- **Performance.** Maximum processor performance for AC operation.

- **Powersave.** Minimum processor performance for battery operation.

- **Dynamic.** Dynamic adaption of the processor performance to the current processor load. This is the recommended setting for battery operation and AC operation to save battery power, reduce noise, and achieve optimum performance. Switching between the speed levels usually takes place seamlessly, unnoticed by the user.

# APM

Some of the power saving functions are performed by the APM BIOS itself.

On many laptops, you can activate standby and suspend states with key combinations or by closing the lid, without any special operating system function. However, to activate these modes with a command, certain actions must be triggered before the system is suspended.

To view the battery charge level, you need a suitable kernel and the respective packages.

By default, APM support is integrated in the kernels shipped with SUSE Linux Enterprise Server. However, APM is only activated if no ACPI is implemented in the BIOS and an APM BIOS is detected.

To activate APM support, disable ACPI by entering:

**acpi=off**

at the boot prompt.

Enter:

**cat /proc/apm**

to check if APM is active. An output consisting of various numbers indicates that everything is OK.

You should now be able to shut down and turn off the computer by entering **shutdown -h**.

The following topics are described:

- Boot Parameters

- The APM Daemon (apmd)

- Further Commands

## Boot Parameters

Strange things might happen if the BIOS implementation does not fully comply with the standard.

Some problems can be avoided by using special boot parameters (formerly kernel configuration options).

Enter all parameters at the boot prompt in the form:

**apm=***parameter*

The following parameters are possible:

- **On or off.** Enables or disables APM support.
- **(no-)allow-ints.** Allows interrupts during the execution of BIOS functions.
- **(no-)broken-psr.** The Get Power Status function of the BIOS does not work properly.
- **(no-)realmode-power-off.** Resets processor to real mode prior to shutdown.
- **(no-)debug.** Logs APM events in system log.
- **(no-)power-off.** Powers system off after shutdown.
- **bounce-interval=***n.* Time in hundredths of a second after a suspend event during which additional suspend events are ignored.
- **idle-threshold=***n.* System inactivity percentage from which the BIOS function idle is executed (0=always, 100=never).
- **idle-period=***n.* Time in hundredths of a second after which the system activity is measured.

## The APM Daemon (apmd)

The apm daemon (package apmd) monitors the battery and can trigger certain actions when a standby or a suspend event occurs. Although it is not mandatory for operation, it can be useful for some problems.

apmd is not started automatically when the system is booted. If you want it started automatically, edit the settings for the system services with the YaST Runlevel Editor module. Alternatively, use the **chkconfig** utility.

You can start the daemon manually by entering:

**rcapmd start**

A number of configuration variables are available in /etc/sysconfig/powermanagement.

As the file is commented, only some information is provided:

- **APMD_ADJUST_DISK_PERF.** Adapts the disk performance to the power supply status.

This can be done with a number of additional variables beginning with:

- APMD_BATTERY (for battery operation)

  *or*

- APMD_AC (for AC operation)

- **APMD_BATTERY/AC_DISK_TIMEOUT.** Disk inactivity period after which the disk is spun down.

  The values are described in the man page for hdparm, option –S.

- **APMD_BATTERY/AC_KUPDATED_INTERVAL.** Interval between two cycles of the kernel update daemon.

- **APMD_BATTERY/AC_DATA_TIMEOUT.** Maximum age of buffered data.

- **APMD_BATTERY/AC_FILL_LEVEL.** Maximum fill level of the hard disk buffer.

- **APMD_PCMCIA_EJECT_ON_SUSPEND.** Although PCMCIA is implemented with APM support, difficulties might sometimes be encountered.

  Some card drivers do not resume correctly after a suspend (such as xirc2ps_cs). Therefore, apmd can deactivate the PCMCIA system prior to the suspend and reactivate it afterward.

  To do this, set this variable to **yes**.

- **APMD_INTERFACES_TO_STOP.** Sets network interfaces to stop prior to a suspend and restart afterward.

- **APMD_INTERFACES_TO_UNLOAD.** Use this variable if you also need to unload the driver modules of these interfaces.

- **APMD_TURN_OFF_IDEDMA_BEFORE_SUSPEND.** Sometimes, resuming after a suspend might not work if an IDE device (hard disk) is still in DMA mode.

Other options let you correct the key repeat rate or the clock after a suspend or shut down the laptop automatically when the APM BIOS sends a battery critical event.

To execute special actions, adapt the script /usr/sbin/apmd_proxy (performs the tasks listed above) to fit your needs.

## Further Commands

The package apmd contains a number of useful tools.

**apm** can be used to query the current battery charge level and to set the system to standby (**apm –S**) or suspend (**apm –s**).

**13**

For more information, see to the man page of apm.

The command **apmsleep** suspends the system for a specified time.

To watch a log file without keeping the hard disk spinning, use **tailf** instead of **tail –f**.

There are also tools for the X Window System. apmd contains the graphical **xapm** utility for displaying the battery charge level.

If you use the KDE desktop or at least kpanel, use **kbatmon** to view the battery charge level and suspend the system.

**xosview** is another interesting alternative.

# ACPI

ACPI was designed to enable the operating system to set up and control the individual hardware components.

ACPI supersedes both PnP and APM. It delivers information about the battery, AC adapter, temperature, fan, and system events, like Close Lid or Battery Low.

The BIOS provides tables containing information about the individual components and hardware access methods. The operating system uses this information for tasks like assigning interrupts or activating and deactivating components.

Because the operating system executes commands stored in the BIOS, the functionality depends on the BIOS implementation.

The tables ACPI is able to detect and load are reported in /var/log/boot.msg.

The following topics are described:

- ACPI in Action
- The ACPI Daemon (acpid)
- ACPI Tools
- Troubleshooting

## ACPI in Action

If the kernel detects an ACPI BIOS when the system is booted, ACPI is activated automatically (and APM is deactivated).

The boot parameter **acpi=on** might be necessary for some older machines. The computer has to support ACPI 2.0 or later.

Check the kernel boot messages in /var/log/boot.msg to see if ACPI was activated. If this is the case, there is a directory /proc/acpi/, which is described later.

After ACPI is activated, a number of modules must be loaded. This is done by the start script of the ACPI daemon.

If any of these modules causes problems, the respective module can be excluded from loading or unloading in /etc/sysconfig/powersave/common.

The system log (/var/log/messages) contains the messages of the modules, enabling you to see which components were detected.

In /proc/acpi/, you find a number of files that provide information about the system state or can be used to change some of the states actively.

However, many features do not work yet, either because they are still under development or because they have not been implemented by the manufacturer.

All files (except dsdt and fadt) can be read by **cat**.

In some files, settings can be modified by entering:

**echo X > *file***

to specify suitable values for X (the objects in /proc are not real files on the hard disks but interfaces to the kernel).

The most important files are the following:

- **/proc/acpi/info.** General information about ACPI.

- **/proc/acpi/alarm.** Specifies when the system should wake from a sleep state. Currently, this feature is not fully supported.

- **/proc/acpi/sleep.** Provides information about possible sleep states.

- **/proc/acpi/event.** All events are reported here and processed by a daemon like acpid or powersaved.

  If no daemon accesses this file, events, such as a brief click on the power button or closing the lid, can be read by entering:

  **cat /proc/acpi/event**

  (Press **Ctrl + c** to terminate the event.)

- **/proc/acpi/dsdt and /proc/acpi/fadt.** These files contain the ACPI tables DSDT (Differentiated System Description Table) and FADT (Fixed ACPI Description Table).

  They can be read by entering:

  - **acpidmp**

  - **acpidisasm**

  - **dmdecode**

**13**

These programs and their documentation are located in the package pmtools.

- **/proc/acpi/ac_adapter/AC/state.** Shows if the AC adapter is connected.

- **/proc/acpi/battery/BAT\*/{alarm,info,state}.** Shows detailed information about the battery state.

  The charge level is read by comparing the last full capacity from info with the remaining capacity from state.

  The charge level at which a battery event is triggered can be specified in alarm.

- **/proc/acpi/button.** Contains information about various switches.

- **/proc/acpi/fan/FAN/state.** Shows if the fan is currently active.

  The fan can be activated and deactivated manually by writing 0 (on) or 3 (off) into this file.

  However, both the ACPI code in the kernel and the hardware (or the BIOS) overwrite this setting when it gets too warm.

- **/proc/acpi/processor/CPU\*/info.** Shows information about the energy saving options of the processor.

- **/proc/acpi/processor/CPU\*/power.** Shows information about the current processor state.

  An asterisk next to C2 indicates that the processor is idle. This is the most frequent state, as can be seen from the usage figure.

- **/proc/acpi/processor/CPU\*/performance.** This interface is no longer used.

- **/proc/acpi/processor/CPU\*/throttling.** Enables further linear throttling of the processor.

  This interface is no longer used.

  Its function has been taken over by the settings in /etc/sysconfig/powersave/common.

- **/proc/acpi/processor/CPU\*/limit.** If the performance and the throttling are automatically controlled by a daemon, you can specify the maximum limits here.

  Some of the limits are determined by the system, some can be adjusted by the user.

  However, their function has been taken over by the settings in /etc/sysconfig/powersave/common.

- **/proc/acpi/thermal_zone/.** A separate subdirectory exists for every thermal zone.

  A thermal zone is an area with similar thermal properties whose number and names are designated by the hardware manufacturer.

  However, many of the possibilities offered by ACPI are rarely implemented. Instead, the temperature control is handled conventionally by the BIOS.

The operating system is not given much opportunity to intervene, as the life span of the hardware is at stake.

Therefore, some of the following descriptions only have a theoretical value.

- **/proc/acpi/thermal_zone/\*/temperature.** Shows current temperature of the thermal zone.

- **/proc/acpi/thermal_zone/\*/state.** The state indicates if everything is **OK** or if ACPI applies **active** or **passive** cooling.

  In the case of ACPI-independent fan control, this state will always be **OK**.

- **/proc/acpi/thermal_zone/\*/cooling_mode.** Enables the selection of the passive (less performance, very economical) or active (full performance, uninterrupted fan noise) cooling method for full ACPI control.

- **/proc/acpi/thermal_zone/\*/trip_points.** Enables the determination of temperature limits for triggering specific actions like passive or active cooling, suspension (hot), or a shutdown (critical).

- **/proc/acpi/thermal_zone/\*/polling_frequency.** If the value in temperature is not updated automatically when the temperature changes, the polling mode can be toggled here.

  To query the temperature every $x$ seconds, enter:

  **echo $x$ > /proc/acpi/thermal_zone/\*/polling_frequency**

  Set **x=0** to disable polling.

## The ACPI Daemon (acpid)

Like the APM daemon, the ACPI daemon processes certain events. Currently, the only supported events are the actuation of switches, such as the power button or the lid contact.

All events are logged in the system log.

Set the actions to perform in response to these events in the variables:

**ACPI_BUTTON_POWER** and **ACPI_BUTTON_LID**

in **/etc/sysconfig/powermanagement**.

For more options, modify the script:

**/usr/sbin/acpid_proxy**

or the acpid configuration in:

**/etc/acpi/**

Unlike apmd, little is preconfigured here, as ACPI in Linux is still in a very dynamic development stage.

If necessary, configure acpid according to your needs.

**13**

## ACPI Tools

The range of more or less comprehensive ACPI utilities includes:

- Tools that merely display information, like the battery charge level and the temperature (such as acpi, klaptopdaemon, and wmacpimon).

- Tools that facilitate the access to the structures in /proc/acpi.

- Tools that assist in monitoring changes (such as akpi, acpiw, and gtkacpiw).

- Tools for editing the ACPI tables in the BIOS (package pmtools).

## Troubleshooting

There are two different types of problems you might have when using ACPI. First, the ACPI code of the kernel may contain bugs that were not detected in time. In this case, a solution will be made available for download. More often, however, the problems are caused by the BIOS.

Sometimes, deviations from the ACPI specification are purposely integrated into the BIOS to circumvent errors in the ACPI implementation in other widespread operating systems.

Hardware components that have serious errors in the ACPI implementation are recorded in a blacklist that prevents the Linux kernel from using ACPI for these components.

The first thing to do when you have problems is to update the BIOS. This will solve many problems.

If the computer does not boot properly, it might be helpful to use one of the following boot parameters:

- **pci=noacpi.** Do not use ACPI for configuring the PCI devices.

- **acpi=oldboot.** Only perform a simple resource configuration. Do not use ACPI for other purposes.

- **acpi=off.** Disable ACPI.

Look at the boot messages by entering:

**dmesg | grep -2i acpi**

(You can also look at all messages after booting, as the problem might not be caused by ACPI.)

If an error occurs while parsing an ACPI table, the most important table—the DSDT—can be replaced with an improved version. In this case, the faulty DSDT of the BIOS will be ignored.

In the kernel configuration, there is a switch for activating ACPI debug messages. If a kernel with ACPI debugging is compiled and installed, experts searching for an error can be supported with detailed information.

## powersave

On laptops, the powersave package can be used to control the power saving function during battery operation.

Some of the features of this package can also be used on normal workstations and servers (suspend, standby, ACPI button functionality, and putting IDE hard disks to sleep).

This package comprises all power management features of your computer. It supports hardware using ACPI, APM, IDE hard disks, and PowerNow! and SpeedStep technologies.

The functionalities from the packages apmd, acpid, ospmd, and cpufreqd (now cpuspeed) have been consolidated in the powersave package.

For this reason, daemons from these packages should not be run together with the powersave daemon.

Even if your system does not have all hardware elements listed above (APM and ACPI are mutually exclusive), use the powersave daemon for controlling the power saving function.

The daemon automatically detects any changes in the hardware configuration.

The following topics are described:

- Configure powersave
- Configure APM and ACPI
- Additional ACPI Features
- Troubleshooting

**13**

### Configure powersave

The configuration of powersave is distributed to several files:

- **/etc/powersave.conf.** The powersave daemon needs this file for delegating system events to the powersave_proxy.

  Additionally, custom settings for the behavior of the daemon can be made in this file.

- **/etc/sysconfig/powersave/common.** This file provides the general configuration of the startup script (rcpowersave) and the proxy.

  Usually, the default settings can be used as they are.

- **/etc/sysconfig/powersave/scheme_*.** These are the various schemes or profiles that control the adaption of the power consumption to specific scenarios, some of which are already preconfigured and ready to use without any changes.

  Any custom profiles can be saved here.

## Configure APM and ACPI

To configure APM and ACPI, you need to know the following:

- Suspend and Standby
- Custom Battery States
- Adapt the Power Consumption to Various Conditions

**Suspend and Standby**    In the file /etc/sysconfig/powersave/common, specify any critical modules and services that need to be unloaded or stopped prior to a suspend or standby event.

When the system operation is resumed, these modules and services will be reloaded or restarted.

The default settings mainly affect USB and PCMCIA modules.

- **POWERSAVE_SUSPEND_RESTART_SERVICES="".** List the services to restart after a suspend.

- **POWERSAVE_STANDBY_RESTART_SERVICES="".** List the services to restart after a standby.

- **POWERSAVE_UNLOAD_MODULES_BEFORE_SUSPEND="".** List the modules to unload before a suspend.

- **POWERSAVE_UNLOAD_MODULES_BEFORE_STANDBY="".** List the modules to unload before a standby.

Make sure that the following standards for correct processing of suspend, standby, occurrence, and resume are set (normally, these are the default settings following the installation of SUSE Linux Enterprise Server), as shown in the following:

```
POWERSAVE_EVENT_GLOBAL_SUSPEND="prepare_suspend"
POWERSAVE_EVENT_GLOBAL_STANDBY="prepare_standby"
POWERSAVE_EVENT_GLOBAL_RESUME_SUSPEND="restore_after_suspend"
POWERSAVE_EVENT_GLOBAL_RESUME_STANDBY="restore_after_standby"
```

In /etc/powersave.conf (configuration file of the powersave daemon), these events are allocated to the powersave_proxy script.

This script is executed when these events occur (default setting following the installation), as shown in the following:

```
global.suspend=/usr/sbin/powersave_proxy
global.standby=/usr/sbin/powersave_proxy
global.resume.suspend=/usr/sbin/powersave_proxy
global.resume.standby=/usr/sbin/powersave_proxy
```

**Custom Battery States**    In the file /etc/powersave.conf, you can define three battery charge levels (in percent) that trigger system alerts or execute specific actions when they are reached, as shown in the following:

```
POWERSAVED_BATTERY_WARNING=20
POWERSAVED_BATTERY_LOW=10
POWERSAVED_BATTERY_CRITICAL=5
```

The actions or scripts to execute when the charge levels drops under the specified limits are defined in /etc/powersave.conf.

The action type is configured in /etc/sysconfig/powersave/common, as shown in the following:

```
POWERSAVE_EVENT_BATTERY_NORMAL="ignore"
POWERSAVE_EVENT_BATTERY_WARNING="notify"
POWERSAVE_EVENT_BATTERY_LOW="notify"
POWERSAVE_EVENT_BATTERY_CRITICAL="suspend"
```

Further options are explained in this configuration file.

**Adapt the Power Consumption to Various Conditions**    The system behavior can be adapted to the type of power supply.

Thus, the power consumption of the system should be reduced when the system is disconnected from the AC power supply and operated with the battery.

In the same way, the performance should automatically be increased as soon as the system is connected to the AC power supply.

You can modify the CPU frequency, the power saving function of IDE hard disks, and some other factors.

In /etc/powersave.conf, the execution of the actions triggered by the disconnection from or connection to the AC power supply is delegated to **powersave_proxy**.

Define the setting groups (called schemes or profiles) to apply in /etc/sysconfig/powersave/common, as shown in the following:

```
POWERSAVE_AC_SCHEME="performance"
POWERSAVE_BATTERY_SCHEME="powersave"
```

The schemes are located in files designated as:

**scheme_*name-of-the-scheme***

in /etc/sysconfig/powersave.

The example refers to two schemes:

- **scheme_performance**

    and

- **scheme_powersave**

The YaST Power Management module can be used to edit, create, and delete schemes or change their association with specific power supply states.

## Additional ACPI Features

If you use ACPI, you can control the response of your system to ACPI buttons (Power, Sleep, Lid Open, Lid Closed).

In /etc/powersave.conf, the execution of the respective actions is delegated to the **powersave_proxy**.

The action itself is defined in the file:

**/etc/sysconfig/powersave/common**

The individual options are explained in this configuration file.

- **POWERSAVE_EVENT_BUTTON_POWER="wm_shutdown".**    When the power button is pressed, the system responds by shutting down the respective window manager (such as KDE, GNOME, and fvwm).

- **POWERSAVE_EVENT_BUTTON_SLEEP="suspend".** When the sleep button is pressed, the system is set to the suspend mode.

- **POWERSAVE_EVENT_BUTTON_LID_OPEN="ignore".** Nothing happens when the lid is opened.

- **POWERSAVE_EVENT_BUTTON_LID_CLOSED="saver".** When the lid is closed, the screen saver is activated.

Further throttling of the CPU performance is possible if the CPU load does not exceed a specified limit for a specified time.

Specify the load limit in:

**POWERSAVED_CPU_LOW_LIMIT**

and the timeout in:

**POWERSAVED_CPU_IDLE_TIMEOUT**.

## Troubleshooting

All error messages and alerts are logged in /var/log/messages.

If you cannot find the needed information, use the DEBUG variable for powersave in the file /etc/sysconfig/powersave/common to increase the verbosity of the messages.

Increase the value of the variable to 7 or even 15 and restart the daemon.

The error messages in /var/log/messages will be more detailed, enabling you to identify the error.

## The YaST Power Management Module

The YaST Power Management module can configure all power management settings described above.

Do the following:

1. Ensure you are logged in to your server's GUI environment as **geeko** with the password of **N0v3ll**.

2. Start YaST from the main menu by selecting:

   **System > Configuration > YaST Control Center**

3. Enter the root password *novell*, and select **OK**.

   The YaST Control Center appears.

4. Select **System > Power Management**.

   The Power Management Settings dialog box appears, as shown in Figure 13-3.

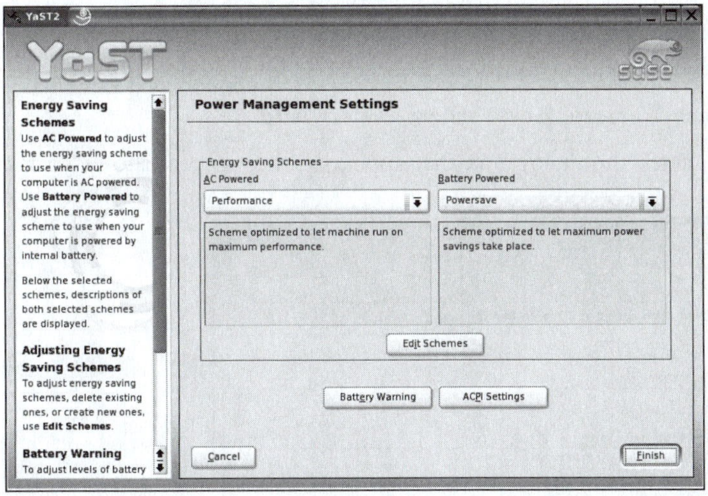

**Figure 13-3**

5. In this dialog box, select the schemes to use for battery operation and AC operation.

6. To add or modify the schemes, select **Edit Schemes**.

A dialog box appears and displays an overview of the existing schemes, as shown in Figure 13-4.

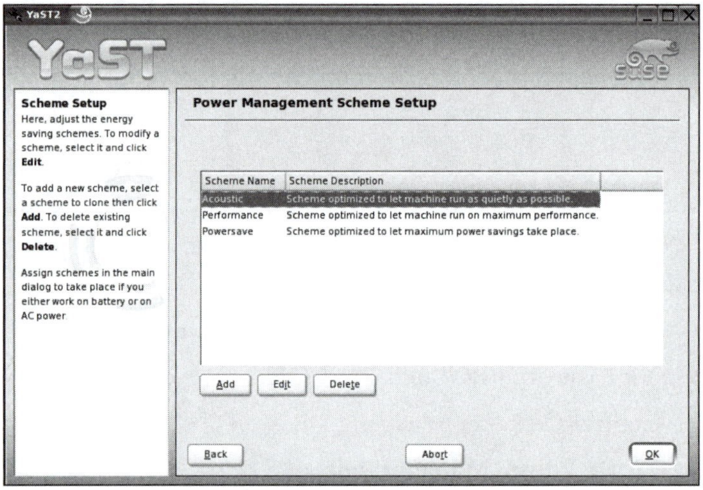

**Figure 13-4**

7. (Optional) To modify a scheme, select it; then select **Edit**.

   *or*

8. (Optional) To create a new scheme, select **Add**.

   In both cases, the dialog box that appears is the same, as shown in Figure 13-5.

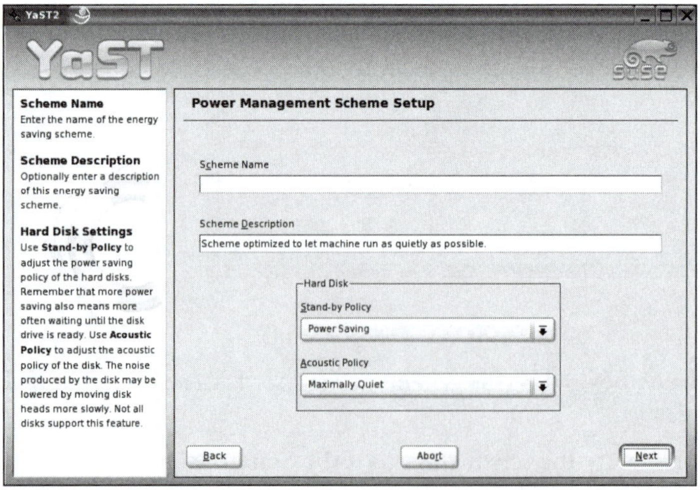

**Figure 13-5**

9. Enter a suitable name and description for the new or edited scheme.

10. For the hard disk, define a **Standby Policy** for maximum performance or for energy saving.

    The **Acoustic Policy** controls the noise level of the hard disk.

11. Select **Next**.

    The CPU and Cooling Policy dialog box appears.

12. CPU comprises the options **CPU Frequency Scaling** and **Throttling**.

    Use these options to define if and to what extent the CPU frequency may be throttled.

13. Cooling Policy determines the cooling method.

14. Complete all settings for the scheme; then select **OK**.

    You are returned to the start dialog box.

15. In the Start dialog box, assign the custom scheme to one of the two operating modes.

16. To activate your settings and exit this dialog box, select **OK**.

You can also set gobal power management settings from the intial dialog box by selecting **Battery Warnings** or **ACPI Settings**. Complete the following:

1. Select **Battery Warnings**.

   A dialog box for the battery charge level appears, as shown in Figure 13-6.

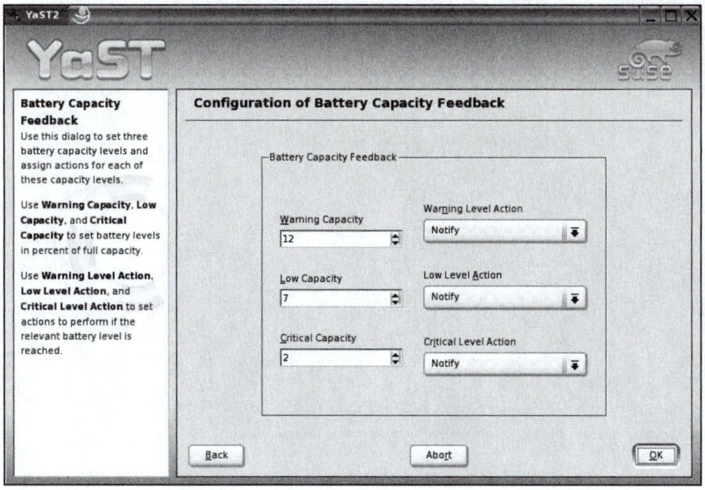

**Figure 13-6**

The BIOS of your system notifies the operating system whenever the charge level drops under certain configurable limits.

2. In this dialog box, define three limits:

- **Warning Capacity**

- **Low Capacity**

- **Critical Capacity**

Specific actions are triggered when the charge level drops under these limits.

Usually, the first two states merely trigger a notification to the user.

The third critical level triggers a suspend, as the remaining energy is not sufficient for continued system operation.

3. Select suitable charge levels and the respective actions.

4. Select **OK**.

You are returned to the Start dialog box.

5. To access the dialog box for configuring the ACPI buttons, select **ACPI Settings**.

The dialog box in Figure 13-7 appears.

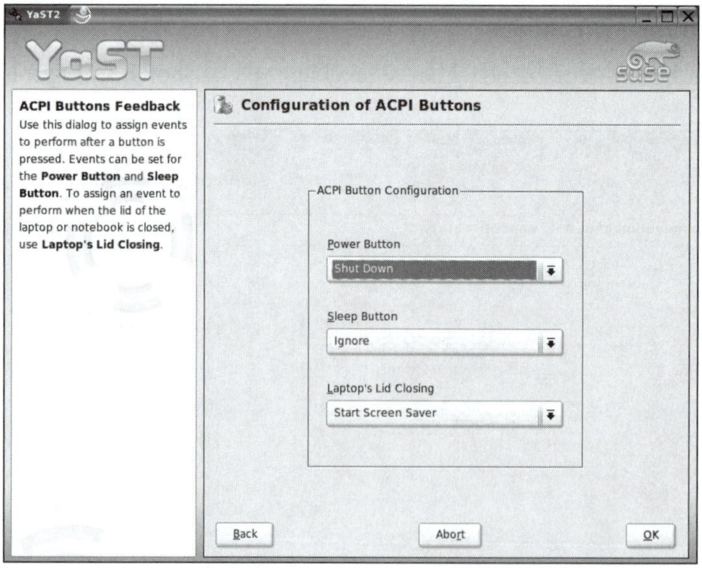

**Figure 13-7**

The settings for the ACPI buttons determine how the system should respond to the actuation of certain switches.

6. Configure the system response to pressing the power button, pressing the sleep button, and closing the laptop lid.

7. To complete the configuration, select **OK**.

   You are returned to the Start dialog box.

8. To exit the module and confirm your power management settings, select **OK**.

## OBJECTIVE 7    UNDERSTAND MASS STORAGE

While desktops are usually delivered with one IDE hard disk and a CD-ROM/DVD drive and/or CD/DVD burner, servers are often equipped with different mass storage devices that provide better fault tolerance.

In this section, you learn to

- Understand IDE and SCSI
- Understand RAID

## Understand IDE and SCSI

Common technologies to connect peripheral devices permanently to a computer are

- IDE
- SCSI

Connecting devices at runtime is possible using USB or FireWire. These technologies are covered in *Mobile Hardware*.

### IDE

The usual desktop computer comes with IDE (Integrated Device Electronics, more formally called Advanced Technology Attachment or ATA) hard disks.

ATAPI (ATA Packet Interface) devices like CD-ROM drives use the same interface on the motherboard as the IDE/ATA hard disks.

A maximum of four devices (such as hard disks, CD-ROM drives, and CD/DVD burners) can be connected to current motherboards.

Recent improvements include Serial ATA (SATA) hard disks that allow higher transfer rates to and from the disk.

### SCSI

SCSI is a technology that allows you to connect devices such as hard disks, tape drives, CD-ROM/DVD drives and burners, and scanners to computers.

13

Advantages of SCSI compared to IDE are a higher data transfer rate and a higher number of devices (7 or 15, depending on the SCSI standard, see Types of SCSI) that can be connected to the bus.

While in theory the handling of SCSI is not really complicated, in practice strange effects can occur, like that are devices connected to the bus but not visible to the operating system, or single devices turning up twice.

These phenomena are usually caused by one of the following:

- Improper electrical termination of the SCSI bus
- Incorrect cable lengths
- SCSI ID conflicts

Traditionally SCSI disks are more expensive than IDE hard disks of comparable capacity.

While IDE disks have caught up on performance over the years, SCSI disks are still considered more reliable.

Since SCSI disks are used mainly in servers, not desktops, they are usually designed for higher temperature tolerance, to run at higher speed (revolutions per minute) and tend to produce more noise.

## Understand RAID

If there is only one disk in a computer, data on it is lost if the disk fails.

If this happens, you have to replace the disk and restore the data from backup tapes. This usually means a downtime of at least several hours. To reduce this downtime or ideally eliminate it, use disk arrays.

RAID (Redundant Array of Independent Disks) combines several hard disk partitions to one virtual hard disk to increase performance or data security.

One way of implementing RAID is to use special hardware controllers to which the SCSI or IDE hard disks are connected.

The controller controls the hard disks and the organization of the data structures according to the set RAID level. To the operating system the hardware RAID appears as a hard disk like any other.

Another way to implement RAID is to use software RAID with the help of the drivers in the Linux kernel.

Of the six separate RAID levels originally defined, the Linux kernel supports the three most common levels (0, 1, and 5).

By means of this approach, individual hard disk partitions are combined to a multiple disk device (such as /dev/md0).

In practice, these partitions should be located on separate hard disks. However, for training purposes they may also be located on the same disk.

In this section, you learn about:

- RAID Levels
- Configuring RAID

## RAID Levels

There are various RAID levels. The more common ones are

- **RAID 0.** In contrast to what is implied by the name RAID, RAID 0 does not provide any redundancy.

  RAID 0 merely distributes the data across multiple partitions to achieve higher data throughput rates.

  The disadvantage: If one hard disk in this array fails, all data is lost.

  This kind of data management is also referred to as *striping*.

- **RAID 1.** RAID 1 increases the data security by maintaining an exact mirror of the data on one disk on the other disk.

  If one disk fails, all data continues to be fully available on the other disk.

  A further advantage is the increased read speed.

  The disadvantages are the increased costs (two hard disks with 50 GB each merely provide a total capacity of 50 GB) and the somewhat reduced write speed.

  This kind of data management is often referred to as *mirroring*.

- **RAID 5.** In terms of performance and redundancy, RAID 5 is an optimized compromise between the other two levels.

  The capacity corresponds to the sum of the capacities of the utilized disks minus the capacity of one disk (provided the disks are of the same size).

  Similar to RAID 0, the data are distributed across the hard disks.

  In RAID 5, the data security is implemented by parity blocks stored on one of the partitions.

  If one disk fails, its contents can be reconstructed from the data on the other disks.

  However, if two disks fail at the same time, all data are lost.

 RAID is in no way intended as a replacement for a backup strategy.

CAUTION

13

The purpose of RAID 1 or 5 is to reduce downtime and increase availability in the event of a hard disk failure.

A failed hard disk can be replaced (depending on the machine even while it is up and running) and the RAID is rebuilt with no data loss.

However, if two hard disks fail at the same time all data on a RAID 5 array are lost.

If a user deletes a file it is gone as well, RAID or no RAID.

Both scenarios require a functioning backup and restore mechanism.

## Configuring RAID

A hardware RAID is configured using the tools provided by the vendor of the controller.

With SLES, a Linux software RAID can be set up using YaST.

Later changes, like replacing a hard disk or adding a hot spare, are done using the command **mdadm.**

The following topics are described:

- Use YaST to Set up RAID
- Use mdadm to Administer RAID

**Use YaST to Set up RAID**    To set up RAID using YaST, do the following:

1. Select **YaST -> System -> Partitioner**.

2. Create three partitions with partition type Linux RAID (0xFD), as shown in Figure 13-8.

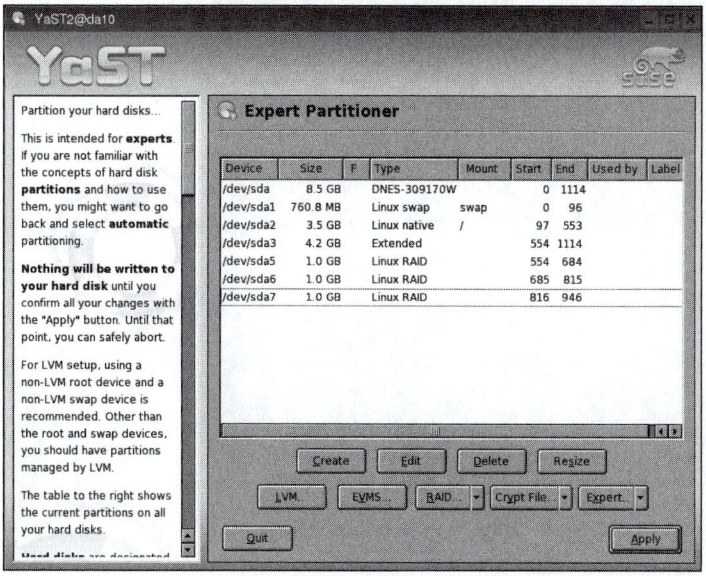

**Figure 13-8**

On a production system, these partitions should reside on separate hard disks.

3. Selecting **RAID** starts the RAID wizard that guides you through the steps to create a RAID.

4.  Select the type of RAID; then select **Next**, as shown in Figure 13-9.

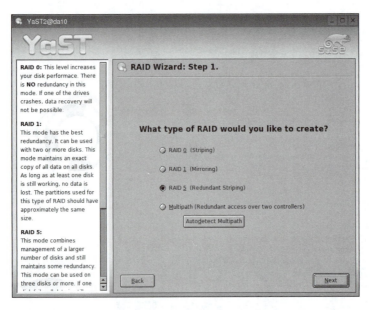

**Figure 13-9**

In the next dialog box, shown in Figure 13-10, the partitions that should be part of the RAID are selected. For RAID 5 a minimum of three partitions is required.

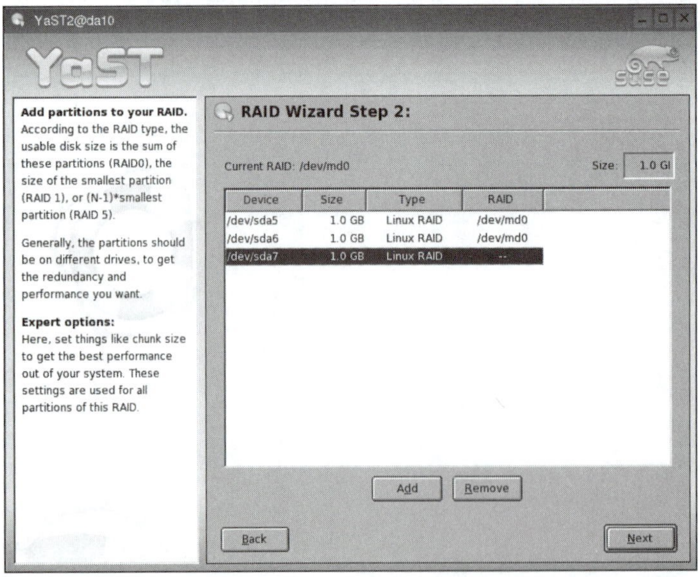

**Figure 13-10**

5. In the next dialog box, shown in Figure 13-11, set RAID parameters and then select **Next**.

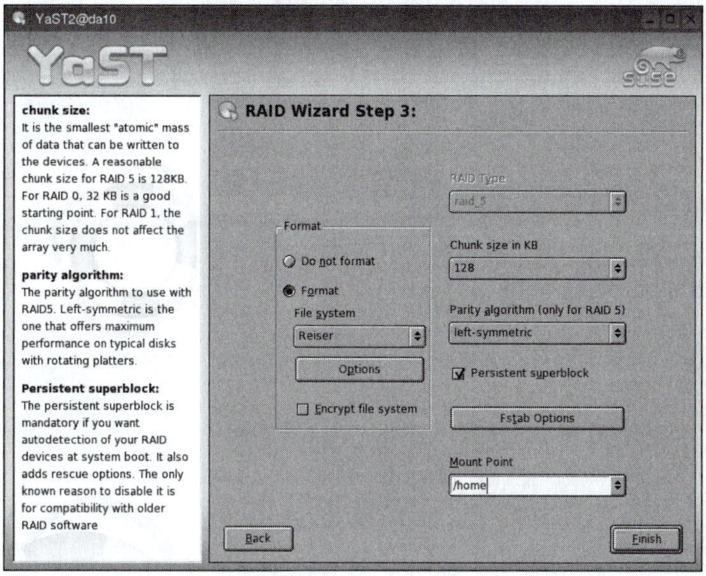

**Figure 13-11**

13

Usually the default values are adequate, only the mount point has to be modified according to your requirements.

6. Selecting **Finish** returns you to the YaST partitioner, which displays the new configuration, as shown in Figure 13-12.

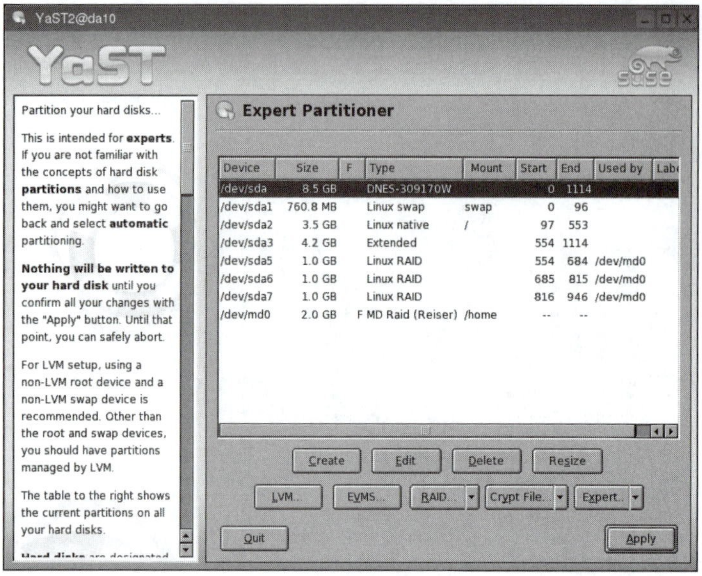

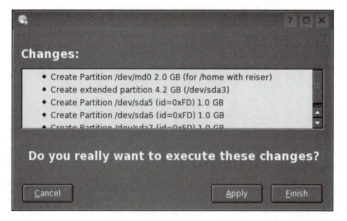

**Figure 13-12**

7. Selecting **Apply** brings up a final warning, shown in Figure 13-13.

**Figure 13-13**

8. Selecting **Apply** applies the changes and returns to the partitioner, while **Finish** applies them and leaves the partitioner, as shown in Figure 13-14.

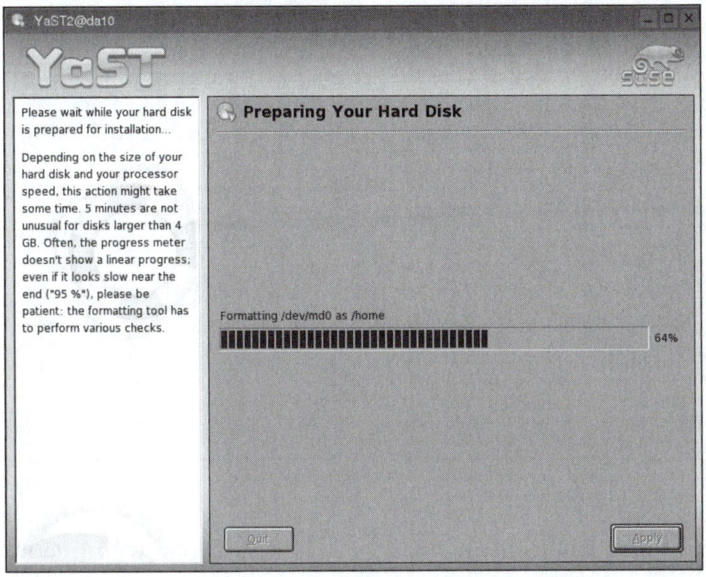

**Figure 13-14**

Now a file system is created on **/dev/md0** and an appropriate entry is made in **/etc/fstab**.

**Use mdadm to Administer RAID**    If a hard disk that is part of a RAID failed, it has to be replaced.

Let's assume the disk /dev/sda7 (in this example all partitions are on the same disk, but the procedure is the same for several disks; only the partitions have different labels) is faulty and you want to replace it by /dev/sda8. You will have to take the following steps to achieve this:

1. Mark the disk as faulty (**-f**) and remove it (**-r**) from the array:

```
da10:~ # mdadm /dev/md0 -f /dev/sda7
mdadm: set /dev/sda7 faulty in /dev/md0
da10:~ # mdadm /dev/md0 -r /dev/sda7
mdadm: hot removed /dev/sda7
```

2. Depending on your hardware you can replace the disk while the machine is running, or you have to shut down the system to replace the disk.

3. Next, add the new disk to (**-a**) the array.

Restoring parity information takes some time, but the RAID array can be used anyway:

```
da10:~ # mdadm /dev/md0 -a /dev/sda8
mdadm: hot added /dev/sda8
da10:~ # cat /proc/mdstat
Personalities : [raid5]
md0 : active raid5 sda8[3] sda6[1] sda5[0]
      2104320 blocks level 5, 128k chunk, algorithm 2 [3/
2] [UU_]
      [=>..................]  recovery =  6.4% (67872/
1052160) finish=5.3min speed=3085K/sec
```

**NOTE**

For more information, see the man page (**man mdadm**) and in the Software RAID howto in /usr/share/doc/packages/raidtools/software-RAID-HOWTO.html.

## CHAPTER SUMMARY

❑ CPUs process most instructions in a computer and work closely with data in RAM.

❑ All other hardware devices in a computer must have a unique IRQ channel and I/O address to communicate with the processor. They may optionally use DMA to bypass certain processor operations.

❑ Peripheral components typically interface with the computer mainboard using a data bus such as ISA or PCI. These peripheral components typically store their configuration using EPROM or EEPROM chips.

❑ Hardware information can be gathered from files in the /**proc** and /**sys** directories, YaST, and the /**var/log/boot.msg** file as well as the **lspci**, **hwinfo**, and **hdparm** commands.

❑ Devices that contain a device driver compiled in the Linux kernel typically have a device file in the /dev directory. The /**dev** directory contains entries made available by udev, which uses the **sysfs** filesystem and allows hotpluggable devices to be managed by entries in the /**sys** directory. Hotplug agent programs execute when these devices are plugged into or removed from the system. You can use the **hwup**, **hpdown**, and **hotplug** commands to manually execute hotplug agents.

❑ Devices that do not contain a device driver compiled into the Linux kernel typically have their device driver inserted into the Linux kernel as a module during system initialization using the **modprobe** command.

❑ Sound is typically provided by ALSA on Linux systems. You can modify the PCM digital output or balance for sound devices and play sound, video, and MIDI files using ALSA utilities.

❑ Most video media files require a codec for proper playback. DVDs require a CSS decoder for proper playback.

- You can manage PCMCIA cards using YaST, the scripts in the /etc/pcmcia and /etc/hotplug directories, or the **cardctl**, **pcic_probe**, and **lspci** commands.

- USB supports 127 devices at a speed of 12 Mbps (version 1.1) or 480 Mbps (version 2.0). The /proc/bus/usb directory lists USB device information.

- IEEE 1394(Firewire) is provided by the **ohci1394.ko** module and supports up to 64 devices at speeds of 400 Mbps (version 1) or 800 Mbps (version 2).

- CD images may be created using the **mkisofs** command and written to CDs using the **cdrecord** and **cdrdao** programs.

- Linux computers traditionally used the APM daemon to conserve energy and shut down hardware components for portable computers that supported APM in the BIOS.

- Today, ACPI modules and the ACPI daemon are used on most computers to perform the same functions as APM and also provide various power saving modes using the powersave daemon. ACPI is enabled by default in SLES.

- You can troubleshoot APM and ACPI using the parameters at the boot manager prompt. Specific power-saving functions may be configured using YaST and the /etc/sysconfig/powersave/common file.

- Most data is stored on IDE and SCSI devices. IDE devices use the ATAPI standard to transfer data. SCSI devices interface with a SCSI bus and controller (host adapter) that has its own BIOS. There are three categories of SCSI devices, which differ in bus size and speed.

- RAID may be used to combine IDE and SCSI hard disks to share volumes and make volumes fault tolerant. You can configure RAID during installation or after installation using YaST or the **mdadm** command.

**13**

## Key Terms

**/dev/modem** — A symbolic link that points to the device used for the modem on a Linux system.

**/etc/hotplug** — A directory that stores scripts for hotpluggable hardware.

**/etc/hotplug** — A file that lists hotplug agents.

**/etc/pcmcia** — A directory that stores PCMCIA configuration scripts.

**/etc/sysconfig/powersave/common** — A file used to define power saving options for ACPI.

**/proc** — A directory that contains most hardware device information on a Linux system.

**/sys** — A directory that contains hardware configuration information on a Linux system.

**/var/log/boot.msg** — A file that contains startup messages from the Linux kernel.

**acpid** — The ACPI daemon.

**Advanced Linux Sound Architecture (ALSA)** — A set of components and utilities that provides for sound playback in Linux.

**Advanced Technology Attachment Packet Interface (ATAPI)** — Allows devices to use an IDE bus.

**alsamixer command** — A text-based sound mixer program.

**alsamixergui command** — A graphical sound mixer program.

**aplay command** — Plays WAV files.

**APM (Advanced Power Management)** — A BIOS feature that shuts off power to peripheral devices which are not being used to save electricity; commonly used on laptop portable computers.

**apm command** — Displays information about APM, such as battery levels, and starts power saving modes.

**apmd** — The APM daemon.

**apmsleep command** — Configures suspend mode in APM.

**arecord command** — Records audio information in WAV files.

**Basic Input Output System (BIOS)** — The ROM chip on a mainboard used to initialize system hardware and search for operating system loaders.

**bus** — A term representing the pathway that information takes from one hardware device to another via a mainboard.

**Cardbus card** — A type of PCMCIA card that uses a 32-bit data bus.

**cardctl command** — Views and controls PCMCIA cards.

**cdrdao command** — Writes to recordable CD media in DAO mode.

**cdrecord command** — Writes to recordable CD media.

**Central Processing Unit (CPU)** — An integrated circuit board used to perform the majority of all calculations on a computer system; also known as a processor or microprocessor.

**Content Scrambling System (CSS)** — The encryption used for DVD media.

**devfs** — A special filesystem used for the /dev directory on UNIX and Linux systems.

**Direct Memory Access (DMA)** — Allows peripheral devices the ability to bypass the CPU and talk directly with other peripheral components to enhance performance.

**dmesg command** — Used to view the contents of /var/log/boot.msg.

**Electronically Erasable Programmable Read Only Memory (EEPROM)** — A type of ROM whose information store can not only be erased and rewritten as a whole, but can be modified singly, leaving other portions intact.

**Erasable Programmable Read Only Memory (EPROM)** — A type of ROM whose information store can be erased and rewritten, but only as a whole.

**flash drives** — A storage medium that uses EEPROM chips to store data.

**hdparm command** — Displays and sets hard disk parameters.

**host adapter** — A device that controls other devices on the system (e.g., SCSI host adapters control SCSI hard disks).

**hotplug** — Describes the ability to add or remove hardware to or from a computer while the computer and operating system are functional.

**hotplug agent** — A program that is executed when a hotplug event occurs.

**hotplug command** — Used to handle hotplug events.

**hwdown command** — Removes a kernel module based on a hotplug event.

**hwinfo command** — Displays a report of the hardware devices in your system.

**hwup command** — Loads a kernel module based on a hotplug event.

**I/O (Input/Output) address** — The small working area of RAM where the CPU can pass information to and receive information from a device.

**I/O (Input/Output) port** — See I/O address.

**IEEE1394 (Firewire)** — A mainboard connection technology, developed by Apple Computer Inc. in 1995, that supports data transfer speeds of up to 800MB per second.

**Industry Standard Architecture (ISA)** — An older motherboard connection slot designed to allow peripheral components an interconnect, and which transfers information at a speed of 8MHz.

**Integrated Drive Electronics (IDE)** — Also known as ATA (Advanced Technology Attachment), it consists of controllers that control the flow of information to and from up to four hard disks connected to the mainboard via a ribbon cable.

**Interrupt Request (IRQ)** — Specifies a unique channel from a device to the CPU.

**kbatmon command** — Displays information about APM, such as battery levels, and starts power-saving modes in a graphical desktop environment.

**lsmod command** — Displays kernel modules.

**lspci command** — Displays PCI devices on the system.

**mainboard** — A circuit board that connects all other hardware components together via slots or ports on the circuit board; also called a motherboard.

**mdadm command** — Used to manage RAID volumes.

**mirroring** — A RAID configuration that creates duplicates of information on two hard drives.

**mkisofs command** — Creates ISO filesystems and ISO filesystem images.

**modprobe command** — Inserts a module into the Linux kernel.

**PC Card** — A type of PCMCIA card that uses a 16-bit data bus.

**PCI (Peripheral Component Interconnect)** — The most common motherboard connection slot found in computers today, which can transfer information at a speed of 33MHz and use DMA (Direct Memory Access).

**pcic_probe command** — Views the type of removable card controller on the system.

**PCMCIA (Personal Computer Memory Card International Association)** — A mainboard connection technology that allows a small card to be inserted with the electronics necessary to provide a certain function.

**peripheral** — Components that attach to the mainboard of a computer and provide a specific function such as a video card, mouse, or keyboard.

**Pulse Code Modulation (PCM)** — A method for playing digital audio data.

**RAID 0** — See **striping**.

**RAID 1** — See **mirroing**.

**RAID 5** — A RAID configuration that spreads data across several hard disks and uses parity information to prevent data loss in the event of hard disk failure.

**Random Access Memory (RAM)** — A computer chip that stores information for use by the CPU when there is power to the system.

**13**

**Read-Only Memory (ROM)** — A computer chip able store information in a static permanent manner, even when there is no power to the system.

**Redundant Array of Inexpensive Disks (RAID)** — A configuration of hard disks used for faster access or redundancy.

**rmmod command** — Removes a module from the Linux kernel.

**Small Computer Systems Interface (SCSI)** — Consists of controllers that can connect several SCSI hard disk drives to the mainboard and control the flow of data to and from the SCSI hard disks.

**striping** — A RAID configuration that spreads data across several hard disks to speed up access time.

**sysfs** — A virtual file system created by the Linux kernel used to configure system devices.

**udev** — Used to manage the /dev directory and create device files for hotplug devices based on hotplug events.

**USB (Universal Serial Bus)** — A mainboard connection technology that allows data transfer speeds of up to 480MB per second and is used for many peripheral components today such as mice, printers, and scanners.

**xapm command** — Displays battery level for APM in a graphical desktop environment.

## REVIEW QUESTIONS

1. What IRQ is typically used by the first IDE controller on your system?

   _____

2. What file can you view to verify the IRQ in Question 1? _____

3. What command can you use to view detailed information about IDE devices on your computer? _____

4. Which of the following commands may be used to insert a module into the Linux kernel?

   a. lsmod module

   b. insertmod module

   c. modprobe module

   d. rmmod module

5. What software component must you have to play back a certain type of video media? _____

6. What command can you use to view the PCMCIA card in your portable computer?

   _____

7. What filesystem must be supported by a Linux kernel in order to use hotplug devices such as USB and IEE1394?

    a. devfs

    b. udf

    c. sysfs

    d. udev

8. Which of the following commands may be used to record to CD media in DAO mode? (Choose all that apply.)

    a. daocd

    b. cdrecord –dao

    c. cdrdao

    d. mkisofs

9. What file contains custom battery states for ACPI?_____

10. Which of the following RAID implementations provide disk redundancy? (Choose all that apply.)

    a. RAID 0

    b. RAID 1

    c. RAID 5

    d. RAID 9

13

## DISCOVERY EXERCISES

### Obtaining System Hardware Information

**DISCOVERY**

Log in to tty1 as the root user. Using the files and commands in this chapter, prepare a detailed log of the types of hardware devices in your computer and the resources that they use (IRQ, I/O Address, DMA). Next, insert any hotplug devices into your system and note their configuration. In your log, identify the source of the information for future reference. When finished, log out of tty1.

### Kernel Modules

**DISCOVERY**

Log in to tty1 as the root user. Use the **modprobe dummy** command to insert a sample module into the Linux kernel. Next, use the **lsmod** command to view the module. What other modules are listed and why? Use the **rmmod dummy** command to remove the module from the kernel and log out of tty1.

## APM and ACPI

Log in to tty1 as the root user. Using the files and commands in this chapter, determine whether your system uses APM or ACPI. Next, view the various files in the /etc/sysconfig/ powersave directory to view the current power-saving schemes. Then, use YaST to change the power-saving settings on your system and note any changes in the files within the /etc/sysconfig/powersave directory. When finished, log out of tty1.

## Recording to CD Media

Log in to tty1 as the root user. Provided you have a CD burner in your computer, use the **mkisofs** command to create an ISO image of the files in your home directory. Next, write this ISO image to a CD using the **cdrecord** utility. When finished, log out of tty1.

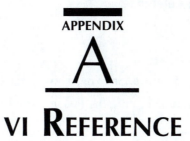
# VI REFERENCE

This appendix contains a short description of

- vi Modes

and commands for the following tasks:

- Save File, Quit
- Move Cursor
- Insert Text
- Delete Text
- Change Text
- Copy (Yank) and Paste
- Use Buffer
- Use Marker
- Search and Replace
- Use Regular Expressions
- Repeat
- Use Regions
- Work with Files
- Others

## vi Modes

- **Command mode.** Start mode of vi, for entering commands.
- **Insert mode.** For entering text; is started by a change or insert command and left again by pressing **Esc**.
- **Command line mode.** For entering commands in the command line; commands are run only by pressing **Return**.

## Save File, Quit

To save files and quit vi, use the commands shown in Table A-1.

**Table A-1**

| Command | Description |
|---|---|
| :x or :wq | Save and close |
| :q | Close if nothing was changed |
| :q! | Close, ignore changes |

## Move Cursor

To move the cursor, use the commands shown in Table A-2.

**Table A-2**

| Command | Description |
|---|---|
| :h, j, k, l | Left, down, up, right |
| w | Beginning of the next word |
| W | Beginning of the next word separated by space |
| b | Beginning of the previous word |
| B | Beginning of the previous word separated by a space |
| e | End of the next word |
| E | End of the next word separated by a space |
| 0, $ | Beginning, end of line |
| 1G, G | Beginning, end of file |
| $n$G | Go to line $n$ |
| f$c$, F$c$ | Forwards, back to the character $c$ |
| H, M, L | Go to top, middle, end of page |

A

# Insert Text

To insert text, use the commands shown in Table A-3.

**Table A-3**

| Command | Description |
|---------|-------------|
| i, I | Insert text before the cursor, at beginning of line |
| a, A | After cursor, at end of line |
| o, O | Insert new line below, above cursor |
| r, R | Replace one, many characters |

# Delete Text

All delete commands start with d, followed by a movement command, as described in Table A-4.

**Table A-4**

| Command | Description |
|---------|-------------|
| dw, db | Delete the word after, before the cursor |
| D | Delete to end of the line |
| dd or :d | Delete line |
| x, X | Delete current, previous character |

# Change Text

The change command starts with c, followed by a movement command, as described in Table A-5.

**Table A-5**

| Command | Description |
|---------|-------------|
| cw | Change a word |
| C | Change text to the end of the line |
| cc | Change entire line |

## Copy (Yank) and Paste

Most copying commands are performed by pressing y, followed by a movement command, as described in Table A-6.

**Table A-6**

| Command | Description |
|---|---|
| y$ | Copy (yank) text to end of line |
| yy or :y | Copy line |
| p | Insert text after the current cursor position or line |
| P | Insert text before current cursor position or line |

## Use Buffer

Buffer names can be used for each delete, modification, copy, or re-insert command.

The general form is "*c*, whereby *c* can be any small letter.

For example, "**adw** deletes a word and saves it to buffer a. It can then be restored with the re-insert command "**ap**.

## Use Marker

Markers can be set on all lines in a file.

Any small letter is a permitted marker name.

Markers can also be used in regions.

To use markers, the commands shown in Table A-7 are available.

**Table A-7**

| Command | Description |
|---|---|
| m*c* | Set marker |
| '*c* | Go to marker |

## Search and Replace

To search and replace, use the commands shown in Table A-8.

**Table A-8**

| Command | Description |
|---|---|
| /*string*, ?*string* | Search forward, backward |
| n, N | Repeat search in the same, opposite direction |
| r, s | Replace character with a different character, string |

**Table A-8**   (continued)

| Command | Description |
|---|---|
| cc, C | Replace line, rest of line |
| :s/old/new/options | Search for old and replace with new |
| g, c | Options: all occurrences in a line, confirm |
| & | Repeat the last ":s" command |

## Use Regular Expressions

The keystrokes shown in Table A-9 are available.

**Table A-9**

| Command | Description |
|---|---|
| . (dot) | Any character apart from "new line" |
| * | 0 or more occurrences |
| [...] | Any character from a group of characters |
| [^ ...] | Any character not from the group of characters |
| ^, $ | Beginning, end of a line |
| \<, \> | Beginning, end of a word |
| \(...\) | Group |
| \n | Contents of the nth group |

## Repeat

For almost every command a repeat factor can be given, specifying how often it should be performed.

For example, **5dw** deletes five words and **3fe** moves the cursor to the third occurrence of the character e.

Even inserts can be repeated in this way, for example, to insert the same line 50 times.

## Use Regions

You can use regions for most commands in the command line mode, which then limit the commands to the corresponding lines.

For example, **:3,7d** deletes lines 3–7.

Regions are often used with the replace command :s; for example, **:.,$s/old/new/g** performs replacements from the current line to the end.

The commands shown in Table A-10 are available.

**Table A-10**

| Command | Description |
|---|---|
| :*n,m* | Lines *n-m* |
| :. | Current lines |
| :$ | Last line |
| :'*c* | Marker *c* |
| :% | All lines |
| :g/*string*/ | All matching lines |

## Work with Files

To work with files, use the commands shown in Table A-11.

**Table A-11**

| Command | Description |
|---|---|
| :w *file* | Save *file* (current file if no name is given) |
| :r *file* | Insert *file* after the current line |
| :n, :N | Change to the next file, previous file |
| :e *file* | Edit *file* |
| :e! | Reload file (despite changes) |
| !!*program* | Replace line with *program* output |

## Others

Table A-12 shows further useful commands.

**Table A-12**

| Command | Description |
|---|---|
| ~ | Switch to upper case/lower case |
| J | Join lines together |
| . (dot) | Repeat last command |
| :u | Undo last change |
| u, U | Undo all changes in the current line |
| :! | Switch into a shell (shell escape) |

# Glossary

**&** — A special character used to start a program in the background.

**&&** — A special operator that executes the command on the right side if the command on the left side exited with a zero exit status.

**. (period)** — A special character used to indicate the user's current directory in the directory tree.

**. (root domain)** — The root domain of DNS.

**. command** — Used to execute a file in the current shell environment.

**.rhosts** — A file that lists user accounts on certain remote UNIX or Linux computers. These users can connect to your computer using the r-tools without specifying a username or password; instead, they will be automatically logged in as your user account.

**.xinitrc** — A file that contains information used to control the X Window System.

**.xsession** — A file that contains the default window manager or desktop environment to load when starting the X Window System.

**.. (double period)** — Special characters used to represent the user's parent directory in the directory tree.

**\** — A special character used to protect the following character from shell interpretation.

**/** — The single root directory in Linux.

**/bin directory** — Contains binary commands for use by all users.

**/boot directory** — Contains the Linux kernel and files used by the boot loader.

**/boot/grub/grub.conf** — The GRUB configuration file in most Linux distributions.

**/boot/grub/menu.lst** — The GRUB configuration file in SLES.

**/dev directory** — Contains device files.

**/dev/modem** — A file that is used to identify the port that a modem uses. It is typically a shortcut to /dev/ttyS0 or /dev/ttyS1.

**/dev/ttyS0** — A file that is used to identify the first serial port on a Linux computer. It is called COM1 in Windows.

**/dev/ttyS1** — A file that is used to identify the second serial port on a Linux computer. It is called COM2 in Windows.

**/etc directory** — Contains system-specific configuration files.

**/etc/aliases** — Contains mail aliases for user accounts.

**/etc/apache2/httpd.conf** — The main Apache configuration file.

**/etc/at.allow** — A file that lists users who can use the at command.

**/etc/at.deny** — A file that lists users who cannot use the at command.

**/etc/bash.bashrc** — A bash shell configuration file used to create aliases for all users on the system.

**/etc/cron.d** — A directory that contains additional system cron tables.

**/etc/crontab** — The system cron table.

**/etc/cups/cupsd.conf** — The main CUPS configuration file.

**/etc/cups/lpoptions** — The file that stores system-wide print options set by the root user.

**/etc/cups/ppd** — The directory that stores the active PPD files used for a particular printer.

**/etc/cups/printers.conf** — Contains CUPS printer definitions.

**/etc/default/passwd** — A file that contains default values used when changing passwords, such as encryption algorithm.

**/etc/default/useradd** — A file that contains default values used when creating user accounts.

**/etc/defaultdomain** — A file that stores the default NIS domain name.

**/etc/dhcpd.conf** — The DHCP daemon configuration file.

**/etc/exports** — The file that lists exported directories on an NFS server.

**/etc/fstab** — A file used to store information used to mount filesystems.

**/etc/group** — The file that stores the list of system groups, their GIDs, and members.

**/etc/grub.conf** — The file that contains information about GRUB components.

**/etc/gshadow** — A file that is typically used on older Linux computers. It can contain encrypted group passwords.

**/etc/HOSTNAME** — A file that contains the name of the host.

**/etc/hosts** — A local file that contains host names and their respective IP addresses.

**/etc/hosts.allow** — A text file used by tcpd listing hosts that are allowed to connect to network daemons.

**/etc/hosts.deny** — A text file used by tcpd listing hosts that are not allowed to connect to network daemons.

**/etc/hosts.equiv** — A file that contains a list of remote Linux or UNIX computers. Users on these computers can run the r-tools and specify your computer without providing a username or password; instead, they will be automatically logged in as the same user on your computer.

**/etc/hotplug** — A directory that stores scripts for hot-pluggable hardware.

**/etc/hotplug** — A file that lists hotplug agents.

**/etc/inetd.conf** — The main configuration file for inetd.

**/etc/init.d** — The directory that contains the scripts used to start most daemons.

**/etc/init.d/network** — The script that activates network interfaces at system initialization.

**/etc/init.d/skeleton** — A sample script that may be copied to create scripts used to start a daemon.

**/etc/inittab** — The configuration file for the init daemon.

**/etc/issue** — A text file containing banner text that is displayed before you log into a command-line virtual terminal.

**/etc/issue.net** — A text file containing banner text that is displayed before you log in to a command-line terminal from across the network.

**/etc/lilo.conf** — The LILO configuration file.

**/etc/login.defs** — A file that stores defaults for user logins and user account creation.

**/etc/logrotate.conf** — The configuration file for the logrotate command. Additional configuration files for logrotate may be in the /etc/logrotate.d directory.

**/etc/logrotate.d** — This directory contains additional configuration files for the logrotate command.

**/etc/motd** — A text file containing banner text that is displayed after you log in to a command-line terminal.

**/etc/mtab** — A file that contains a list of mounted filesystems.

**/etc/named.conf** — A file that lists the type of zones hosted on the DNS server and the location of the zone files.

**/etc/networks** — A file used for local network name resolution.

**/etc/nsswitch.conf** — A file that determines when NIS maps are used to configure system information.

**/etc/passwd** — A file that stores information about user accounts on the Linux system including the UID, primary GID, home directory, and login shell.

**/etc/pcmcia** — A directory that stores PCMCIA configuration scripts.

**/etc/permissions.easy** — A file that lists the least secure file permission restrictions for system files.

**/etc/permissions.local** — A file that lists user-defined file permission restrictions for system files.

**/etc/permissions.paranoid** — A file that lists the most secure file permission restrictions for system files.

**/etc/permissions.secure** — A file that lists secure file permission restrictions for system files.

**/etc/profile** — A bash shell configuration file that is read for all users on the system.

**/etc/rc.d/rc** — The script that executes files in the /etc/rc.d/rc.d directories.

**/etc/rc.d/rc.d** — The directories used by the init daemon to start and kill daemons in each runlevel.

**/etc/resolv.conf** — A file that lists up to three DNS servers and which may be contacted to resolve a remote host name to an IP address.

**/etc/samba/smb.conf** — The main Samba configuration file.

**/etc/security/limits.conf** — A file that lists user resource limits.

**/etc/sendmail.cf** — The main Sendmail configuration file.

**/etc/shadow** — The file that typically contains encrypted passwords and password expiry information for user accounts on the system.

**/etc/shells** — A file that lists valid system shells such as /bin/bash.

**/etc/skel** — A directory that contains files and directories that are copied to all new users' home directories when they are created.

**/etc/ssh/ssh_config** — The system-wide ssh client program configuration file.

**/etc/ssh/sshd_config** — The SSH daemon configuration file.

**/etc/sudoers** — A file that lists the users who are allowed to run certain commands as other users.

**/etc/sysconfig/network** — The directory that contains most network configuration information.

**/etc/sysconfig/network/config** — A file that stores information about how network interfaces are handled by the system.

**/etc/sysconfig/network/ifcfg-ppp0** — A file that stores the configuration of your modem for use when connecting to the Internet.

**/etc/sysconfig/network/ifcfg-template** — A template file that may be used to create the TCP/IP configuration for a network interface.

**/etc/sysconfig/network/ifroute-*interface*** — A file that stores static routes for a specific *interface*.

**/etc/sysconfig/network/providers/*providername*** — A file that stores the information used to connect to an Internet Service Provider including the username, password, and phone number.

**/etc/sysconfig/network/routes** — A file that stores static routes for use on the system.

**/etc/sysconfig/powersave/common** — A file used to define power saving options for ACPI.

**/etc/sysconfig/syslog** — A file that contains parameters for the syslogd daemon.

**/etc/sysconfig/ypserv** — Stores NIS server options.

**/etc/syslog.conf** — The main configuration file for the syslogd daemon.

**/etc/X11/XF86Config** — The configuration file used by the X server.

**/etc/X11R6/bin/xvidtune** — A utility that can be used to fine tune X server settings such as screen dimensions and screen refresh rates.

**/etc/xinetd.conf** — The main configuration file for xinetd. It loads configuration files from the /etc/xinetd.d directory.

**/etc/xinetd.d** — The directory that stores most xinetd configurations.

**/etc/yp.conf** — A file that stores the location of NIS servers.

**/etc/ypserv.conf** — The main NIS server configuration file.

**/home directory** — Default location for user home directories.

**/lib directory** — Contains shared program libraries (used by the commands in /bin and /sbin) as well as kernel modules.

**/media directory** — Used for accessing (mounting) disks such as floppy disks and CD-ROMs.

**/mnt directory** — Used for accessing (mounting) disks such as floppy disks and CD-ROMs.

**/opt directory** — Stores additional software programs.

**/proc** — A directory that contains most hardware device information on a Linux system.

**/proc directory** — Contains process and kernel information.

**/proc/sys/net/ipv4/ip_forward** — A file that is used to enable routing on a router.

**/root directory** — The root user's home directory.

**/sbin directory** — Contains system binary commands used for administration.

**/srv/www/htdocs** — The default location for Web site content in Apache.

**/sys** — A directory that contains hardware configuration information on a Linux system.

**/sys directory** — Contains current system information.

**/tmp directory** — Holds temporary files created by programs.

**/use/X11R6/bin/XFree86** — The X server program in SLES. The /usr/X11R6/bin/X and /var/X11R6/bin/X files are shortcuts to this file that are used for program compatibility.

**/usr directory** — Contains most system commands and utilities.

**/usr/share/cups/model** — The directory that stores sample PPD files used for a particular printer.

**/usr/share/doc** — A directory that stores most command, file, system, and program information on a Linux system.

**/usr/X11R6/bin/xf86config** — A text-based X server configuration utility that comes with XFree86 version 4.

**/var directory** — Contains log files and spools.

**/var/lib/dhcp/db/dhcpd.leases** — The file that contains current DHCP leases on a DHCP server.

**/var/lib/named** — The directory that stores zone files in SLES.

**/var/lib/nfs/etab** — A file that lists currently exported directories on an NFS server.

**/var/log/boot.msg** — A text file that lists system initialization messages.

**/var/log/cups/access_log** — A CUPS log file that stores information about network print requests.

**/var/log/cups/error_log** — A CUPS log file that stores information about the CUPS daemon.

**/var/log/faillog** — A data file that lists failed login attempts.

**/var/log/lastlog** — A data file that lists recent login attempts.

**/var/log/mail** — A text file that lists message from the mail system.

**/var/log/messages** — The default log file for the DNS daemon.

**/var/log/wtmp** — A data file that lists successful login attempts.

**/var/spool/cron/allow** — A file that lists users who can use the crontab command.

**/var/spool/cron/deny** — A file that lists users who cannot use the crontab command.

**/var/spool/cron/tabs** — The directory used to store user crontabs.

**/var/spool/cups** — The default print queue directory in SLES.

**/var/spool/mail** — The default location for local e-mails.

**/var/yp/Makefile** — A file whose settings are used to create NIS maps.

**/var/yp/nicknames** — A file that contains aliases for NIS maps.

**/var/yp/securenets** — A file on a NIS server that lists valid networks for NIS clients.

**/var/yp/ypservers** — A file on a NIS master server that lists NIS slave servers.

**;** — A special character that acts as a command terminator and can be used to chain commands together on the command line.

**|** — A special character used to send Standard Output from one command to the Standard Input of another command.

**| |** — A special operator that executes the command on the right side if the command on the left side exited with a nonzero exit status.

**~** — A special character that refers to the current user's home directory.

**~ (tilde)** — A character used to represent a user's home directory.

**~/.alias** — A bash shell configuration file that is used to store aliases.

**~/.bash_history** — A bash shell configuration file that is used to store previously executed commands.

**~/.bash_login** — A bash shell configuration file that is read if ~/.bash_profile does not exist.

**~/.bash_profile** — A bash shell configuration file that is read following /etc/profile.

**~/.bashrc** — A bash shell configuration file that is read at login and when nonlogin shells are started.

**~/.forward** — An MTA file used to configure e-mail handling options.

**~/.lpoptions** — The file that stores user-defined print options.

**~/.procmailrc** — A file that contains Procmail e-mail filtering criteria.

**~/.profile** — A bash shell configuration file that is read if ~/.bash_profile and ~/.bash_login do not exist.

**~/.ssh/config** — The ssh client program configuration file.

**'…' (single quotes)** — Used to protect all enclosed text from shell interpretation.

**"…" (double quotes)** — Used to protect all enclosed text except $, \, and ` characters from shell interpretation.

**<** — A special character used to redirect Standard Input from a file.

**>** — A special character used to redirect Standard Output and Standard Error to a file.

**absolute path** — The full name to a certain file or directory, starting from the root directory.

**accept command** — Allows print jobs to enter the print queue.

**acpid** — The ACPI daemon.

**Address record (A)** — A DNS record that identifies hosts within a domain.

**Advanced Intrusion Detection Environment (AIDE)** — A common Host Based IDS used to monitor key system files.

**Advanced Linux Sound Architecture (ALSA)** — A set of components and utilities that provides for sound playback in Linux.

**Advanced Technology Attachment Packet Interface (ATAPI)** — Allows devices to use an IDE bus.

**alias command** — Used to create special alias variables.

**aliases** — Special variables that may be used to execute commands in a shell.

**allocation groups** — Sections of a block within an XFS filesystem.

**alsamixer command** — A text-based sound mixer program.

**alsamixergui command** — A graphical sound mixer program.

**Apache** — The default Web server software in SLES.

**aplay command** — Plays WAV files.

**APM (Advanced Power Management)** — A BIOS feature that shuts off power to peripheral devices that are not being used to save electricity; commonly used on laptop portable computers.

**apm command** — Displays information about APM, such as battery levels, and starts power saving modes.

**apmd** — The APM daemon.

**apmsleep command** — Configures suspend mode in APM.

**apropos command** — Used to search the manual pages by keyword.

**aquota.group** — A file that stores group quota information for a filesystem.

**aquota.user** — A file that stores user quota information for a filesystem.

**arecord command** — Records audio information in WAV files.

**ark** — A graphical program that may be used to archive files and directories.

**ARPANET** — The network that led to the development of the Internet. It stands for Advanced Research Projects Agency Network.

**arpwatch** — A common Network Based IDS used to identify network attacks by monitoring the ARP cache.

**ASCII files** — Files that contain text that adheres to the American Standard Code for Information Interchange.

**at command** — Used to schedule commands to run at a certain time in the future.

**atq command** — Used to view scheduled at jobs.

**atrm command** — Used to remove a scheduled at job.

**Audit Record Generation and Utilization System (Argus)** — A common Network Based IDS used to identify network attacks by monitoring network transactions.

**authoritative answer** — A name resolution response from a DNS server where the DNS server contained the appropriate record in its zone database.

**awk command** — Used to search for and display text using a variety of different formatting options.

**B+ tree** — A structure used to organize files on a filesystem for fast access.

**background process** — A process that runs unnoticed in your terminal and does not interfere with your command-line interface.

**baseline performance** — The average performance of a computer under normal working conditions.

**Basic Input Output System (BIOS)** — The ROM chip on a mainboard used to initialize system hardware and search for operating system loaders.

**Berkeley Internet Name Domain (BIND)** — The reference implementation for DNS.

**bg command** — Used to start a process in the background.

**block** — The unit of data commonly used by a filesystem.

**block-oriented device file** — A device file that specifies that information be transferred to the device in a block-by-block manner to a formatted filesystem.

**Blowfish** — An encryption method used to encrypt Linux passwords.

**boot loader** — See **boot manager**.

**boot manager** — The program used to load and start the operating system kernel at system startup.

**broadcast** — A message destined for all computers on a TCP/IP network.

**bunzip2 command** — Used to decompress files that have been compressed with bzip2.

**bus** — A term representing the pathway that information takes from one hardware device to another via a mainboard.

**bzip2 command** — A common compression utility in Linux.

**cache** — An area of memory that stores information obtained from resolving DNS names. Entries are kept in the cache for the time period specified by the TTL.

**caching-only server** — A DNS server that is not authoritative for any zones. It only answers DNS queries where the answers come from other DNS servers.

**cancel command** — Used to remove a print job from the print queue.

**Canonical NAME (CNAME)** — An alias for an A record in DNS.

**Cardbus card** — A type of PCMCIA card that uses a 32-bit data bus.

**cardctl command** — Views and controls PCMCIA cards.

**cat command** — Used to display (or concatenate) the entire contents of a text file to the screen.

**cd command** — Used to change the current directory in the directory tree.

**cdrdao command** — Writes to recordable CD media in DAO mode.

**cdrecord command** — Writes to recordable CD media.

**Central Processing Unit (CPU)** — An integrated circuit board used to perform the majority of all calculations on a computer system; also known as a processor or microprocessor.

**chains** — Collections of firewall rules that may be used to match network traffic.

**character-oriented device file** — A device file that specifies that information be transferred to the device in a character-by-character manner.

**chgrp (change group) command** — Used to change the group owner of a file or directory.

**child process** — A program that is executed by another process, such as a shell.

**chkconfig** — Used to configure the daemons that start in a runlevel.

**chkconfig command** — Used to set the startup status of a service in Linux.

**chmod (change mode) command** — Used to change the mode (permissions) of a file or directory.

**chown (change owner) command** — Used to change the owner and group owner of a file or directory.

**cinternet command** — Typically used to dial your modem to establish an Internet connection. It can also be used to close an Internet connection.

**Class A address** — An IP address that uses the first byte to identify the TCP/IP network.

**Class B address** — An IP address that uses the first two bytes to identify the TCP/IP network.

**Class C address** — An IP address that uses the first three bytes to identify the TCP/IP network.

**Class D address** — An IP address that is used for communicating to several hosts simultaneously, using multicast packets.

**Class E address** — An IP address that cannot be used on a TCP/IP network and is intended for research purposes only.

**Classless Inter-Domain Routing (CIDR)** — A standard that allows the subdivision of traditional Class A, B, and C networks into subnets.

**client application** — The application program that receives keyboard and mouse input from the X server and sends screen output to the X server. It may run on the same or a different computer than the X sever. It is also called the X client.

**command mode** — A mode in the vi editor that allows you to perform any available text editing task that is not related to inserting text into the document.

**Common Internet File System (CIFS)** — A file- and printer-sharing protocol used by Windows systems.

**Common Unix Printing System (CUPS)** — The default printing system in SLES.

**container** — An LDAP object used to organize leaf objects.

**Content Scrambling System (CSS)** — The encryption used for DVD media.

**cp command** — Used to create copies of files and directories.

**cpio (copy in and out) command** — A command-line utility that may be used to archive files and directories.

**cron** — The system service that executes commands regularly in the future based on information in crontabs.

**crontab (cron table)** — A file specifying the commands to be run by the cron daemon and the schedule to run them.

**crontab command** — Used to view and edit user cron tables.

**CUPS Web Administration Tools** — A series of CUPS administration utilities that may be accessed using a Web browser on port 631.

**daemon process** — A system process that is not associated with a terminal.

**Data Encryption Standard (DES)** — The default encryption method used in SLES for passwords.

**dd command** — Used to copy files to an alternate location using a particular format or method.

**default gateway** — The router that connects a network to other networks. Packets whose destination networks are not included in the routing table are sent to the default gateway.

**default route** — See **default gateway**.

**Dennis Ritchie** — The creator of the C programming language that was adopted by the UNIX operating system.

**dependencies** — The prerequisite software required by a software package.

**desktop environment** — A set of software components that standardize the look and feel of the desktop. There are two standard GUI desktop environments available in most Linux distributions: KDE and GNOME.

**devfs** — A special filesystem used for the /dev directory on UNIX and Linux systems.

**device file** — A file used to identify hardware devices such as hard disks and serial ports.

**df command** — Displays disk usage by file system.

**dhcpd** — The DHCP server daemon.

**dig command** — Used to perform and test name resolution using a variety of options.

**Direct Memory Access (DMA)** — Allows peripheral devices the ability to bypass the CPU and talk directly with other peripheral components to enhance performance.

**directories** — Special files that are used to organize other files on the filesystem.

**Directory Information Tree (DIT)** — The hierarchical structure of an LDAP database.

**disable command** — Prevents print jobs in the print queue from being sent to the printer.

**DISPLAY** — A variable that stores the default display name for your system.

**display name** — A name used by the X Window System to determine the location of the X server to use.

**Distinguished Name (DN)** — A full pathname to an LDAP leaf object.

**dmesg command** — Used to view the contents of /var/log/boot.msg.

**DNS server** — A server that contains records for hosts on a network. It may be queried to resolve a host name to an IP address.

**dnsdomainname command** — Used to display the domain name of a host.

**domain** — The name in DNS that identifies the organization and which exists under the TLD.

**Domain Name System (DNS)** — The naming system used on the Internet. Each host is identified by a host name and domain name.

**du command** — Displays disk usage by directory.

**dumpe2fs command** — Used to obtain filesystem information from Ext2 and Ext3 filesystems.

**Dynamic Host Configuration Protocol (DHCP)** — A protocol that is used to assign TCP/IP configuration information to a host on the network.

**echo command** — Used to display or echo output to the terminal screen; it may be used to view the contents of variables.

**edquota command** — Used to specify quota limits for users and groups.

**effective group** — See **primary group**.

**egrep command** — A variant of the grep command used to search files for patterns using extended regular expressions.

**Electronically Erasable Programmable Read Only Memory (EEPROM)** — A type of ROM whose information store can not only be erased and rewritten as a whole, but can be modified singly, leaving other portions intact.

**enable command** — Allows print jobs in the print queue to be sent to the printer.

**env command** — Used to display a list of exported environment variables.

**environment variables** — Variables that are available to subshells and that store information commonly accessed by the system or programs executing on the system.

**Erasable Programmable Read Only Memory (EPROM)** — A type of ROM whose information store can be erased and rewritten, but only as a whole.

**Ethereal** — A graphical program used to capture and examine packets on the network.

**Ethernet** — The standard method used to access network media today. Most network adapters on networks use Ethernet.

**Evolution** — A common Linux MUA.

**Exim** — A common MTA on Linux systems.

**exit command** — Quits the current shell.

**exit status** — The hidden value that is returned by a program following execution. It is also called the return value.

**export command** — Used to create and view environment variables.

**exportfs command** — Used to temporarily export directories on an NFS server.

**Ext2** — The traditional filesystem used on older Linux systems.

**Ext3** — A journaling version of the Ext2 filesystem.

**faillog command** — Displays the contents of /var/log/faillog.

**fdisk command** — Used to create, delete, and modify hard disk partitions.

**fg command** — Used to force a background process to run in the foreground.

**FIFOs** — See named pipes.

**filesystem** — A structure used to organize blocks on a device such that they can be used by the operating system to store data.

**Filesystem Hierarchy Standard (FHS)** — A standard outlining the location of set files and directories on a Linux system.

**find command** — Used to find files on the filesystem using various criteria.

**finger command** — Displays information about local user accounts.

**firewall** — A software feature that allows a host to drop IP packets that meet a certain criteria.

**flash drives** — A storage medium that uses EEPROM chips to store data.

**foreground process** — A process that runs in your terminal and must finish execution before you receive your shell prompt.

**forking** — The process whereby a shell creates a subshell to execute a child process.

**forward resolution** — A name resolution request that desires the IP address for a particular FQDN.

**forwarding server** — A DNS server that forwards any DNS queries it cannot resolve to another DNS server on the network.

**free command** — A utility that can be run within a command-line Linux interface; it displays information about memory usage on your system.

**fsck command** — Used to check and repair filesystems.

**Fully Qualified Domain Name (FQDN)** — A complete name that identifies a host computer in DNS. It consists of a host name (or computer name) followed by subdomain/domain names and a TLD (e.g., www.west.africa.com).

**fuser command** — Used to identify users and processes using a particular file or directory.

**gdm** — A program that is used to display a GNOME-style graphical login screen.

**General Electric Comprehensive Operating System (GECOS)** — Represents a description of a user account stored in the comments field of /etc/passwd.

**getty** — A program used to display a login prompt on a character-based terminal.

**GNOME** — A common Linux desktop environment that uses the GNOME window manager. GNOME stands for GNU Object Model Environment.

**GNOME window manager** — The window manager used by the GNOME desktop.

**GNU Public License (GPL)** — A legal license under which the Linux kernel and most Linux software is published; it allows for open development and distribution of software.

**grace period** — The amount of time a user can exceed a quota limit.

**Grand Unified Boot Loader (GRUB)** — The default boot manager in SLES.

**graphical applications** — Programs that send their output to a graphical user interface.

**graphical user interface (GUI)** — An interface that allows users to manipulate icons to control the operating system and run application programs.

**grep (Global Regular Expression Print) command** — Searches files for patterns of characters using regular expression metacharacters.

**group** — When referring to a long file or directory listing, it represents the group ownership of a file or directory.

**Group ID (GID)** — A number that is used by the Linux operating system to uniquely identify a system group. The root group always has a GID of 0.

**groupadd command** — Used to add a group to the system.

**groupdel command** — Used to delete a group from the system.

**groupmod command** — Used to modify the name, membership, or GID of a group on the system.

**gunzip command** — Used to decompress files that have been compressed with gzip.

**gzip command** — A common compression utility in Linux.

**halt command** — Used to quickly bring a system to runlevel 0.

**hard limit** — A quota limit that cannot be exceeded.

**hard link** — A file that points to another file's inode.

**hdparm command** — Displays and sets hard disk parameters.

**head command** — Displays the first set of lines of a text file; by default, the head command displays the first 10 lines.

**hidden files** — Files that are not normally displayed to the user via common filesystem commands; hidden files have filenames that start with a period.

**history command** — Used to view and recall previously executed commands.

**home directory** — The directory on your hard disk that you have full permissions to and are placed in by default. It is typically /home/*username*.

**host** — A computer or device that can communicate on a network.

**host adapter** — A device that controls other devices on the system (e.g., SCSI host adapters control SCSI hard disks).

**Host Based IDS** — A software system that detects changes to key system files to identify a security breach.

**host command** — Used to perform and test name resolution.

**host ID** — The part of an IP address that uniquely identifies a host on a network.

**hostname command** — Used to display and set the host name of the computer.

**hotplug** — Describes the ability to add or remove hardware to or from a computer while the computer and operating system are functional.

**hotplug agent** — A program that is executed when a hotplug event occurs.

**hotplug command** — Used to handle hotplug events.

**howto files** — A document that contains the steps for common Linux procedures.

**hwdown command** — Removes a kernel module based on a hotplug event.

**hwinfo command** — Displays a report of the hardware devices in your system.

**hwup command** — Loads a kernel module based on a hotplug event.

**I/O (Input/Output) address** — The small working area of RAM where the CPU can pass information to and receive information from a device.

**I/O (Input/Output) port** — See **I/O address**.

**id command** — Displays the UID and GIDs for the current user account.

**IEEE1394 (Firewire)** — A mainboard connection technology, developed by Apple Computer Inc. in 1995, that supports data transfer speeds of up to 800MB per second.

**ifconfig command** — Used to view, configure, and manage IP addresses on a network interface.

**ifdown command** — Used to deactivate a network interface.

**ifstatus command** — Used to display the status of a network interface.

**ifup command** — Used to activate a network interface.

**Industry Standard Architecture (ISA)** — An older motherboard connection slot designed to allow peripheral components an interconnect, and which transfers information at a speed of 8MHz.

**inetd** — The Internet Super Daemon used to start other network daemons on Linux systems.

**info command** — Used to search the info pages.

**info pages** — A database that contains information about the syntax and usage of commands and files, organized in a document-like format with links to other information.

**init** — The first daemon started by the Linux kernel; it is responsible for starting and stopping other daemons.

**init command** — Used to change the system runlevel.

**inode** — The portion of a file that stores information on the file's attributes, access permissions, location, ownership, and file type.

**insert mode** — A mode in the vi editor that allows you to insert text into the document.

**insserv command** — Used to enable scripts that are used to start daemons.

**Integrated Drive Electronics (IDE)** — Also known as ATA (Advanced Technology Attachment), it consists of controllers that control the flow of information to and from up to four hard disks connected to the mainboard via a ribbon cable.

**Internet Control Message Protocol (ICMP)** — A part of the TCP/IP protocol suite that is used to relay information about network communications.

**Internet Message Access Protocol (IMAP)** — A protocol used to obtain e-mails from an e-mail server.

**Internet Printing Protocol (IPP)** — A printing protocol that allows print jobs to be sent across the Internet using a Web browser.

**Internet Protocol (IP) address** — A unique address used to identify a computer on a TCP/IP network.

**Internet Protocol (IP) packet** — A unit of information sent on a TCP/IP network.

**Interrupt Request (IRQ)** — Specifies a unique channel from a device to the CPU.

**Interval-controlled daemon** — A daemon that is started at a certain time on a regular basis.

**Intrusion Detection System (IDS)** — A software system designed to check for evidence of security threats and breaches.

**IP aliases** — Additional IP addresses that are assigned to a network interface.

**ip command** — Used to view, configure, and manage network interfaces and the routing table.

**ipchains command** — Used to configure firewall rules on network interfaces in older versions of Linux.

**iptables command** — Used to configure firewall rules on network interfaces in SLES.

**IPv4** — The current version of the TCP/IP protocol suite.

**IPv6** — A new version of the TCP/IP protocol suite that contains a larger address space and improvements to routing and security.

**JFS** — A journaling filesystem that supports large filesystem sizes.

**job** — See **background process**.

**job ID** — The ID given to a background process that may be used in commands that manipulate the process during execution.

**jobs command** — Used to view background processes in your terminal.

**journaling** — A filesystem feature that records all filesystem transactions in a small transaction log on the filesystem for tracking and troubleshooting purposes.

**kbatmon command** — Displays information about APM, such as battery levels, and starts power-saving modes in a graphical desktop environment.

**KDE** — A common Linux desktop environment that uses the KDE window manager. KDE stands for K Desktop Environment.

**KDE Control Panel** — The panel at the bottom of the KDE desktop that is used to start applications. It is also called the KDE Kicker.

**KDE Info Center** — A graphical utility that displays system information.

**KDE Kicker** — See **KDE Control Panel**.

**KDE menu** — The main menu used to start applications in the KDE desktop. It is invoked by pressing the leftmost button on the KDE Control Panel.

**KDE System Guard** — A graphical utility that may be used to view and control processes.

**KDE window manager (kwin)** — The window manager used by the KDE desktop.

**kdf command** — Starts the KDiskFree utility.

**KDiskFree** — A graphical utility that displays free space by filesystem.

**kdm** — A program that is used to display a KDE-style graphical login screen. It is the default login manager in SLES.

**Ken Thompson** — The original creator of the UNIX operating system.

**kernel** — The core component of the Linux operating system; SLES uses the 2.6.5 version of the Linux kernel.

**KFind** — A graphical utility that may be used to find files and directories on the filesystem.

**kill command** — Used to send a signal to a process by PID or job ID.

**killall command** — Used to send a signal to a process by name.

**kinfocenter command** — Starts the KDE Info Center utility.

**Kinternet** — A graphical utility that can be used to dial your modem to establish an Internet connection. It can also be used to close an Internet connection.

**KMail** — A common Linux MUA.

**Konqueror** — The default directory navigation utility and Web browser that is included with KDE.

**Konsole** — An application that emulates a command-line terminal within the KDE desktop.

**kprinter** — A graphical utility that is invoked when a graphical application creates a print job. It may also be used to change printing options, such as resolution.

**last command** — Displays the most recent users who have logged in to the system from entries in /var/log/wtmp.

**lastlog command** — Displays the most recent users who have logged in to the system from entries in /var/log/lastlog.

**leaf** — An LDAP object that represents a network resource.

**less command** — Used to display text files in a page-by-page fashion. It also is used to display the contents of manual pages.

**Lightweight Directory Access Protocol (LDAP)** — A protocol used to provide central authentication and distribute information to network computers.

**lilo command** — Used to reinstall the LILO boot manager after configuration changes.

**Line Printer Daemon (LPD)** — A common printing protocol used on older Linux and UNIX computers.

**links** — Files that point to other files on the filesystem.

**Linus Torvalds** — The creator of the Linux operating system kernel.

**Linux Loader (LILO)** — The traditional boot manager used on Linux systems. The 64-bit version of this boot loader is called ELILO.

**ll command** — An alias for the ls -l command; it gives a long file listing.

**ln (link) command** — Used to create hard and symbolic links.

**locate command** — Used to locate files from a file database.

**logcheck** — A utility that may be used to locate and extract anomalies in log files.

**login manager** — A program that provides a graphical login screen for users to log in. Following a successful log in, the login manager starts an X server, window manager, and desktop environment.

**login shell** — The program that provides a command prompt and executes user commands. The default shell in SLES is the Bourne Again Shell (/bin/bash).

**logrotate command** — Used to archive log files using entries in the /etc/logrotate.conf file and other configuration files that may exist in the /etc/logrotate.d directory.

**logsurfer** — A utility that may be used to check log files for certain patterns and trigger actions.

**lookup table** — A Postfix file used to process e-mails.

**loopback** — An IP address that is used to test the local host.

**lp command** — Used to create a print job.

**lpadmin command** — Used to create and manage CUPS printers.

**lpoptions command** — Used to create or change printing options, such as resolution.

**lppasswd** — Used to create CUPS passwords and access to the CUPS Web Administration Tools.

**lpq command** — Used to view print jobs in the print queue.

**lpr command** — Used to create a print job.

**lprm command** — Used to remove a print job from the print queue.

**lpstat command** — Used to view print jobs in the print queue.

**ls command** — Used to list the files in a given directory.

**lsmod command** — Displays kernel modules.

**lsof command** — Used to list processes and the files that they have opened on the filesystem.

**lspci command** — Displays PCI device attributes.

**mail command** — An MUA available on most Linux systems.

**Mail Delivery Agent (MDA)** — A program that stores e-mails for later access.

**Mail eXchanger (MX)** — A DNS record that identifies the e-mail servers for a domain.

**Mail Transfer Agent (MTA)** — A server program that relays e-mail on the Internet. It is commonly called a mail server.

**Mail User Agent (MUA)** — An e-mail reader program.

**mailq command** — Lists mail in the Postfix/Sendmail mail queue.

**mailstats command** — Displays e-mail statistics.

**mainboard** — A circuit board that connects all other hardware components together via slots or ports on the circuit board; also called a motherboard.

**major device number** — A number used in a device file that determines the location of the device driver in the Linux kernel for a particular device.

**make command** — Used to compile source code into programs according to a makefile.

**make install command** — Used to copy a compiled program to the correct location on the filesystem.

**makefile** — A file created by a configuration script that contains settings used when compiling source code.

**makemap command** — Generates lookup tables for Sendmail information.

**man command** — Used to search the manual pages.

**manual pages** — A database that contains information about the syntax and usage of commands and files.

**maps** — NIS database files containing information that is central to the network, such as user accounts and host names.

**master server** — A DNS server that contains a read-write copy of the zone database.

**master server** — A NIS server that contains the maps used to configure NIS clients.

**mdadm command** — Used to manage RAID volumes.

**Message Digest 5 (MD5)** — An encryption method used to encrypt Linux passwords.

**metacharacters** — Characters that have special meaning on your system when typed at a command prompt.

**metadata** — The section of a filesystem that is not used to store user data.

**minor device number** — A number used in a device file that determines the instance of the particular device.

**mirroring** — A RAID configuration that creates duplicates of information on two hard drives.

**mkdir command** — Used to create directories.

**mkfs command** — Used to create most filesystems in Linux.

**mkisofs command** — Creates ISO filesystems and ISO filesystem images.

**mkpasswd command** — Used to create an encrypted password string.

**mkreiserfs command** — Used to create ReiserFS filesystems.

**modprobe command** — Inserts a module into the Linux kernel.

**mount command** — Used to mount a device to a mount point directory.

**mount point** — A directory to which a device is mounted.

**mounting** — The process of associating a device (e.g., CD-ROM) to a directory (e.g., /media/cdrom). Once a device has been mounted, it may be accessed by navigating to the appropriate directory.

**mt (magnetic tape) command** — Used to manage tape devices.

**MULTICS** — An operating system that originated in 1965 and developed into the UNIX operating system.

**Multipurpose Internet Mail Extensions (MIME)** — A standard used for attaching files to e-mails.

**multiuser** — A feature of the Linux operating system that allows multiple users to interact with it simultaneously.

**Mutt** — A common Linux MUA.

**mv (move) command** — Used to move/rename files and directories.

**name resolution** — The process where an FQDN is associated with its IP address.

**name server** — See **DNS server**.

**Name Server (NS)** — A DNS record that identifies a DNS server that is authoritative for the zone.

**named** — The DNS/BIND daemon in Linux.

**named pipes** — Temporary connections that send information from one command or process in memory to another; they are also represented by files on the filesystem. Named pipes are also called FIFO (First In First Out) files.

**Nautilus** — The default directory navigation utility that is included with GNOME.

**ncurses** — A standard used by menu-based programs that are run within a command-line terminal.

**Nessus** — A program that may be used to monitor security settings on network computers.

**NetBIOS** — A Windows protocol that uses unique, 15-character computer names to identify network hosts.

**netcat command** — Used to test communication among hosts using TCP or UDP.

**netmask (network mask)** — See **subnet mask**.

**netstat command** — Displays network statistics and open ports.

**Network Based IDS** — A software system that detects patterns in network traffic and log files to identify a security breach or attack.

**Network File System (NFS)** — A file-sharing protocol used by UNIX and Linux systems.

**network ID** — The part of an IP address that identifies the network a host is on.

**Network Information Service (NIS)** — A service that allows the centralization of Linux and UNIX configuration.

**newaliases command** — It converts the plain text /etc/aliases file into the /etc/aliases.db database file for use by the system.

**newgrp command** — Used to change the current primary group for a user account.

**NFS client** — A computer that accesses exported files on an NFS server using the NFS protocol.

**NFS server** — A computer that hosts (exports) files using the NFS protocol.

**nice command** — Used to change the priority of a process as it is started.

**nice value** — Represents the priority of a process. A higher nice value reduces the priority of the process.

**NIS client** — A computer that authenticates or obtains its configuration information from a master or slave NIS server.

**nmblookup command** — Displays NetBIOS computer names for hosts.

**node** — See **host**.

**nohup command** — Used to prevent a process from stopping when the shell that started it has exited.

**nonauthoritative answer** — A name resolution response from a DNS server where the DNS server had to query other DNS servers in order to find the appropriate record.

**nonlogin shell** — A shell that is started by an existing shell.

**normal files** — Commonly used files such as text files, graphic files, data files, and executable programs.

**nslookup command** — Used to perform and test name resolution using a variety of options.

**object** — A component of an LDAP database. The two main object types are container objects and leaf objects.

**object class** — A type of object within an LDAP database.

**one-way hash algorithm** — An algorithm that encrypts data but cannot be used to decrypt it. It is also called a trapdoor algorithm.

**other** — When referring to a long file or directory listing, it represents all users on the Linux system that are not the owner or a member of the group on the file or directory.

**owner** — The user whose name appears in a long listing of a file or directory and who typically has the most permissions to that file or directory.

**package** — A group of software programs that provide a certain functionality on an SLES system.

**parent process** — A process that has started another process.

**Parent Process ID (PPID)** — The PID of the parent process.

**partition** — A physical division of a hard disk drive.

**passwd command** — Used to modify user passwords and expiry information as well as lock and unlock user accounts.

**PATH** — A variable that stores a list of directories that will be searched in order when commands are executed without an absolute or relative pathname.

**PC Card** — A type of PCMCIA card that uses a 16-bit data bus.

**PCI (Peripheral Component Interconnect)** — The most common motherboard connection slot found in computers today, which can transfer information at a speed of 33MHz and use DMA (Direct Memory Access).

**pcic_probe command** — Views the type of removable card controller on the system.

**PCMCIA (Personal Computer Memory Card International Association)** — A mainboard connection technology that allows a small card to be inserted with the electronics necessary to provide a certain function.

**peripheral** — Components that attach to the mainboard of a computer and provide a specific function such as a video card, mouse, or keyboard.

**Pine** — A common Linux MUA.

**ping command** — Used to test network connectivity using ICMP.

**pipe** — A string of commands connected by pipe (|) characters.

**platform** — A set of common hardware components on which an operating system can be run. The most common one today is the Intel i386 32-bit platform.

**Pluggable Authentication Modules (PAM)** — A set of components that allow programs to access user account information.

**PoinTeR (PTR)** — A DNS record that identifies the FQDN associated with an IP address for reverse resolution.

**policy** — The action that is applied for packets that do not match a chain rule.

**portmapper** — The service that provides for RPCs in Linux.

**PortSentry** — A common Network Based IDS used to identify network attacks by listening to multiple TCP/IP ports.

**POSIX** — An industry standard that defines operating system interface components. It stands for Portable Operating System Interface.

**Post Office Protocol (POP)** — A protocol used to obtain e-mails from an e-mail server. POP3 is the latest version of POP.

**postalias command** — A postfix program that performs the same function as the newaliases command.

**postcat command** — Displays contents of files in the Postfix mail queue.

**postconf command** — Displays and sets Postfix variables.

**postdrop command** — Creates files in the postdrop directory.

**Postfix** — A common MTA on Linux systems.

**postfix command** — Checks for Postfix configuration problems.

**postmap command** — Generates lookup tables for Postfix information.

**PostScript Printer Description (PPD)** — A printing format that is widely used by many printers and printing systems.

**postsuper command** — Cleans up unused files in the Postfix queue directories.

**poweroff command** — Used to quickly bring a system to runlevel 0 and power off the system.

**preemptive multitasking** — A feature of the Linux operating system that allows several processes to run simultaneously; the Linux kernel determines how much time each process has to execute.

**primary group** — The group specified for a user in the /etc/passwd file that becomes the group owner on newly created files and directories.

**private host key** — A string of characters that is used to decrypt information that is encrypted using a public host key.

**process** — A program currently loaded into memory and running on the CPU.

**Process ID (PID)** — A unique identifier assigned to every process.

**Procmail** — A common MDA on Linux systems.

**program** — A file that may be executed to create a process.

**ps command** — Used to list processes that are running on the system.

**pstree command** — Used to list processes that are running on the system as well as their parent and child relationships.

**public host key** — A string of characters that is used to encrypt information.

**Pulse Code Modulation (PCM)** — A method for playing digital audio data.

**pwck command** — Used to check the validity of the /etc/passwd and /etc/shadow files.

**pwconv command** — Used to enable the use of the /etc/shadow file.

**pwd (print working directory) command** — Used to display the current directory in the directory tree.

**pwunconv command** — Used to disable the use of the /etc/shadow file.

**Qmail** — A common MTA on Linux systems.

**Qt** — A standard toolkit used to create GUI programs within a desktop environment.

**queue** — A directory used to store print jobs before they are sent to the physical printer.

**quotacheck command** — Used to update the quota database files.

**quotaoff command** — Used to deactivate disk quotas.

**quotaon command** — Used to activate disk quotas.

**quotas** — Filesystem usage limits that may be imposed upon users and groups.

**RAID 0** — See **striping**.

**RAID 1** — See **mirroing**.

**RAID 5** — A RAID configuration that spreads data across several hard disks and uses parity information to prevent data loss in the event of hard disk failure.

**Random Access Memory (RAM)** — A computer chip that stores information for use by the CPU when there is power to the system.

**rcp** — Used to copy files to and from remote computers.

**rcp command** — Used to copy files from one remote Linux or UNIX computer to another across a network.

**Read-Only Memory (ROM)** — A computer chip able store information in a static permanent manner, even when there is no power to the system.

**reboot command** — Used to quickly bring a system to runlevel 6.

**Red Hat Package Manager (RPM)** — A format used to distribute software packages on most Linux systems.

**redirection** — The process of changing the default locations of Standard Input, Standard Output, and Standard Error to or from a file.

**Redundant Array of Inexpensive Disks (RAID)** — A configuration of hard disks used for faster access or redundancy.

**regular expressions** — Special metacharacters used to match patterns of text within text files; they are commonly used by many text tool commands such as grep.

**ReiserFS** — A journaling filesystem that uses B+ tree structures and has fast data access.

**reiserfsck command** — Used to check and repair ReiserFS filesystems.

**reject command** — Prevents print jobs from entering the print queue.

**Relative Distinguished Name (RDN)** — The simple name of an object in LDAP.

**relative path** — The name of a target directory relative to your current directory in the tree.

**Remote Procedure Call (RPC)** — A routine that is executed on a remote computer.

**renice command** — Used to change the priority of a running process.

**repquota command** — Used to produce a report on quotas for a particular filesystem.

**resolver** — A host that requests name resolution using DNS.

**return value** — See **exit status**.

**reverse resolution** — A name resolution request that desires the FQDN for a particular IP address.

**rlogin** — Used to obtain a shell on a remote computer.

**rlogin command** — Used to obtain a command-line interface from a remote Linux or UNIX computer on the network.

**rm command** — Used to remove files and directories.

**rmdir command** — Used to remove empty directories.

**rmmod command** — Removes a module from the Linux kernel.

**route command** — Used to view and modify the routing table.

**router** — A device that is used to relay packets from one network to another.

**routing** — The process of sending IP packets from one IP network to another.

**routing table** — A table that is stored on each host and which contains a list of local and remote networks and routers.

**rpcinfo command** — Displays RPC ports and their associated services.

**rpm command** — Used to install, remove, and find information on RPM software packages.

**rsh** — Used to obtain a shell or run a program on a remote computer.

**rsh command** — Used to run programs on remote Linux or UNIX computers.

**rsync command** — Used to copy files and directories to a different location on the local computer or to a remote computer across a network.

**r-tools** — A series of utilities that was commonly used to access, copy files to, and run programs on remote UNIX and Linux computers. The most common r-tools are rlogin, rsh, and rcp.

**runlevel** — A category that describes the number and type of daemons on a Linux system.

**runlevel 3** — A system state that allows you to log in to tty1 through tty6, but does not contain a graphical login screen on tty7.

**runlevel 5** — A system state that allows you to log in to tty1 through tty7. It is the default system state in SLES.

**runlevel command** — Used to display the current and most recent runlevel.

**Samba** — A set of services in Linux that provides the SMB and CIFS protocols for file- and printer-sharing with Windows computers.

**SaX2** — The main X server configuration utility in SLES.

**scanlogd** — A common Network Based IDS used to identify network attacks by listening to traffic sent on multiple ports.

**schema** — The list of object and object properties for an LDAP database.

**search patterns** — Special characters that may be used to match multiple filenames. Also known as wildcards.

**seccheck** — A package that contains a series of scripts that may be used to check for security vulnerabilities on your system.

**Secure SHell (SSH)** — A software service that provides an encrypted shell session to and from remote computers.

**sed command** — Used to search for and manipulate text.

**Sendmail** — A common MTA on Linux systems.

**Server Level Security** — A Samba share security level that requires a valid login to another server in order to access a shared directory.

**Server Message Block (SMB)** — A file- and printer-sharing protocol used by Windows systems.

**set command** — A command used to view all variables in the shell.

**Set Group ID (SGID)** — A special permission set on executable files and directories. When you run an executable program that has the SGID permission set, you become the group owner of the executable file for the duration of the program. On a directory, the SGID sets the group that gets attached to newly created files.

**Set User ID (SUID)** — A special permission set on executable files. When you run an executable program that has the SUID permission set, you become the owner of the executable file for the duration of the program.

**Share Level Security** — A Samba share security level that requires a password in order to access a shared directory.

**shared libraries** — Files that store common functions used by most programs on the system.

**shell** — The Linux command interpreter.

**shell variables** — Variables that are only available in the current shell and which store information commonly accessed by the system or your current shell.

**showmount command** — Displays exported directories on an NFS server.

**shutdown command** — Used to change to runlevel 0 at a certain time.

**signal** — A termination request that is sent to a process.

**Signal-controlled daemon** — A daemon that is started when an event occurs on the system.

**Simple Mail Transfer Protocol (SMTP)** — The protocol used to send e-mails to MTAs on the Internet.

**slave server** — A DNS server that contains a read-only copy of the zone database obtained from a master server via a zone transfer.

**slave server** — A NIS server that contains a copy of the maps from the master server and uses them to configure NIS clients.

**Small Computer Systems Interface (SCSI)** — Consists of controllers that can connect several SCSI hard disk drives to the mainboard and control the flow of data to and from the SCSI hard disks.

**smbclient command** — Used to view and access Windows file and printer shares.

**smbpasswd command** — Sets a Windows-formatted password for Linux user accounts.

**smbstatus command** — Displays current Samba server connections.

**Snort** — A common Network Based IDS used to identify network traffic attacks.

**socket** — An established network connection between two hosts. TCP uses STREAM sockets, whereas UDP uses DGRAM sockets.

**sockets** — Named pipes connecting processes on two different computers; they can also be represented by files on the filesystem.

**soft limit** — A quota limit that can be exceeded for a certain period of time.

**soft link** — See **symbolic link**.

**source command** — Used to execute a file in the current shell environment.

**SSH** — A utility that can be used to access a remote computer in a secure manner by encrypting any data it sends across the network. SSH stands for Secure Shell.

**ssh command** — Used to obtain a shell from a remote SSH server.

**Standard Error** — Represents any error messages generated by a command.

**Standard Input** — Represents information input to a command during execution.

**Standard Output** — Represents the desired output from a command.

**Start Of Authority (SOA)** — A DNS record that identifies zone-specific information and zone transfer settings.

**startx command** — Used to start the X server and default desktop environment from a command-line terminal.

**static route** — Identifies a remote network and the router that must be used to forward packets to it.

**stderr** — See **Standard Error**.

**stdin** — See **Standard Input**.

**stdout** — See **Standard Output**.

**Sticky bit** — A special permission that is set on directories that prevents users from removing files that they do not own.

**striping** — A RAID configuration that spreads data across several hard disks to speed up access time.

**su (switch user) command** — Used to open a new shell as a different user account.

**subdomain** — The name in DNS that identifies a division of an organization and which exists under the domain and TLD.

**subnet (sub-network)** — A division of a Class A, B, or C network.

**subnet mask** — A number used to determine which portions of an IP address are the network ID and host ID.

**subshell** — A shell started by the current shell.

**sudo command** — Used to run commands as another user via entries in /etc/sudoers.

**sulogin** — A program used to display a login prompt on a character-based terminal for the root user only in runlevel 1.

**superblock** — The section of a filesystem that stores the filesystem structure.

**SUSE HelpCenter** — A GUI help program that contains information about the SUSE Linux operating system.

**SUSEfirewall** — A graphical firewall utility in YaST.

**sux (switch user X) command** — Used to open a new shell that can execute graphical programs as a different user account.

**symbolic link** — A pointer to another file on the same or another filesystem; commonly referred to as a shortcut or soft link.

**sysfs** — A virtual file system created by the Linux kernel used to configure system devices.

**syslogd** — The daemon responsible for most logging on Linux systems. It stands for System Log Daemon.

**Tab Window Manager (twm)** — A small, stand-alone window manager that uses few system resources and which may be used instead of the KDE or GNOME desktop. When you invoke the Tab Window Manager, you are said to be in failsafe mode.

**tail command** — A Linux command used to display the last set number of lines of text in a file; by default, the tail command displays the last 10 lines of the file.

**tar (tape archiver) command** — A command-line utility that may be used to archive files and directories.

**TCP wrapper (tcpd)** — A small program that is used to start network daemons via inetd or xinetd. It provides additional security by using the /etc/hosts.allow and /etc/hosts.deny files to control access.

**TCP/IP** — The default network protocol used on Linux systems. It stands for Transmission Control Protocol / Internet Protocol.

**tcpdchk command** — Reports on the configuration of the tcpd program.

**tcpdmatch command** — Used to test the behavior of the tcpd program.

**tcpdump command** — Used to capture and examine IP packets on the network.

**tee command** — Used to copy data from Standard Input to both Standard Output and a specified file.

**testparm command** — Checks the syntax of /etc/samba/smb.conf.

**text-based applications** — Programs that send their output to a command-line user interface.

**Thunderbird** — A common Linux MUA.

**Time To Live (TTL)** — The amount of time a name resolution result is cached on the computer. The default TTL is set in the SOA in the zone file on the DNS server.

**top command** — A utility that can be run from a command-line Linux interface; it displays the processes that are currently using the most CPU time on your system.

**Top Level Domain (TLD)** — The first level of names underneath the root domain in DNS.

**touch command** — Used to create new files. It was originally used to update the timestamp on a file.

**traceroute command** — Used to identify the route an IP packet takes to a remote host.

**Transport Control Protocol (TCP)** — A part of the TCP/IP protocol suite that provides reliable communication between hosts on a network.

**Transport Control Protocol / Internet Protocol (TCP/IP)** — A suite of protocols that are used to communicate with other computers on a network.

**trapdoor algorithm** — See **one-way hash algorithm**.

**Tripwire** — A common Host Based IDS used to identify changes to key system files.

**type command** — Used to determine the type of program for a command. The type command can be used to identify aliases and their target commands.

**udev** — Used to manage the /dev directory and create device files for hotplug devices based on hotplug events.

**ulimit command** — Used to set resource limits for user accounts.

**umask** — A system variable that sets permissions for newly created files.

**umask command** — Used to view and change the system umask.

**umount command** — Used to unmount a device from a mount point directory.

**unalias command** — Used to destroy an alias in memory.

**UNIX** — The operating system developed in 1969 that provided the basis for modern operating systems such as Linux.

**unset command** — Used to destroy a variable in memory.

**updatedb** — Used to create and update the database used by the locate command.

**USB (Universal Serial Bus)** — A mainboard connection technology that allows data transfer speeds of up to 480MB per second and is used for many peripheral components today such as mice, printers, and scanners.

**user** — When referring to a long file or directory listing, it represents the owner of that file or directory.

**User Datagram Protocol (UDP)** — A part of the TCP/IP protocol suite that provides fast but unreliable communication between hosts on a network.

**User ID (UID)** — A number that is used by the Linux operating system to uniquely identify a user account. The root user always has a UID of 0.

**User Level Security** — A Samba share security level that requires a valid Linux login in order to access a shared directory.

**user process** — A process that is begun by a user and runs on a terminal.

**useradd command** — Used to add a user account to the system.

**userdel command** — Used to remove a user account from the system.

**usermod command** — Used to modify the properties of a user account on the system.

**users** — The default group that all new users are placed in on an SLES system.

**variable** — An area of memory used to store information; variables are created from entries in files when the shell is first created after login and are destroyed when the shell is exited upon logout.

**VFAT** — A Linux version of the Microsoft FAT filesystem.

**vi editor** — The most common text editor on Linux and UNIX systems.

**vim (vi improved) editor** — An enhanced version of the vi editor that is common on Linux systems today.

**virtual desktops** — Separate workspaces that you can use within a desktop environment such as KDE or GNOME.

**virtual terminals** — The system components that allow you to log in to and interact with a command-line user interface. You can use and switch between six virtual terminals by default on most Linux systems (tty1–tty6).

**vmstat command** — A utility that can be run from a command-line Linux interface; it displays process, memory, paging, and CPU activity statistics for your system.

**w command** — Displays the users currently logged in to the system and their processes.

**whatis command** — Used to display the basic usage of a command from the manual pages database.

**whereis command** — Displays the location, manual pages, and source code for a command.

**which command** — Used to locate files that exist within directories listed in the PATH variable.

**who command** — Displays the users currently logged in to the system. It can also be used to display the contents of the /var/log/wtmp file.

**whoami command** — Displays the name for the current user account.

**wildcards** — See **search patterns**.

**window manager** — The component of the X Window System that controls the look and feel of windows on the desktop.

**workgroup** — A name that identifies a group of computers in a Windows network that are not part of a domain.

**World Wide Web (WWW)** — A naming convention for Internet services that may be queried using a Web browser.

**X server** — The component of the X Window System that accepts information from client applications and draws graphical images to the screen.

**X Window System** — The set of software components that provides a graphical user interface in Linux.

**xapm command** — Displays battery level for APM in a graphical desktop environment.

**xdm** — A program that is used to display a graphical login screen.

**XF86Setup** — An X server configuration utility used in older versions of XFree86.

**XFree86** — A free version of the X Window System that is used by SLES.

**XFS** — A journaling filesystem that uses allocation groups to manage data.

**xinetd** — The Extended Internet Super Daemon used to start other network daemons on Linux systems. It is the default Internet Super Daemon used in SLES.

**YaST** — The main system configuration utility in SUSE Linux. It is also used to perform the SUSE Linux installation process. YaST stands for Yet another Setup Tool.

**YaST Runlevel Editor** — A graphical program that may be used to configure the daemons that start in each runlevel.

**ypbind** — The NIS client program. This program also runs on NIS servers.

**ypcat command** — Displays the contents of NIS maps.

**ypdomainname command** — Used to set the NIS domain name for a computer.

**ypinit command** — The NIS slave server program.

**ypmatch command** — Used to query NIS maps for specific information.

**yppasswd command** — Used to change a user password on a NIS server.

**yppoll command** — Displays NIS map ID numbers.

**yppush command** — Copies NIS maps from master servers to slave servers.

**ypserv** — The NIS server program.

**ypwhich command** — Displays the NIS server used by a host.

**zcat command** — Used to view the contents of text files that have been compressed with gzip.

**zone** — A specific domain in DNS that is represented by file on a DNS server that contains the records used for name resolution.

**zone transfer** — The process whereby a master DNS server sends zone information to a slave DNS server.

# Index

## SYMBOLS

' ' (single quotes), use in code, 250
" " (double quotes), use in code, 250
& (ampersand), start background program character, 385
&& operator, 249
.. (double period), use in directories, 201
. (period), use in directories, 201
/ (slashes) in file paths, 145
; (semicolons)
    command terminator, 249
    comments in BIND, 459
~ (tilde)
    home directory shortcut, 150
    use in directories, 159, 202
| (pipe) character, 250
| | (double pipe) operator, 250

## A

absolute paths, 145, 202
accept command, 540
access permissions, controls
    modifying, 279–283
    printer restrictions, 527–531
    configuring for TCP wrapper, 620
accessing
    info pages, 81
    manual pages, 76–79
    SUSE HelpCenter, 84
accounts, user. *See* user accounts
ACPI power management, 750–754, 20
acpid daemon, 753, 773

adding
    file permissions, 276–277
    programs using GNOME, 64
    programs with KDE Control Panel, 58
    users, user accounts, 102, 267–268
Address record (A), 540
addresses, hardware, 707, 711
administering
    groups with YaST, 104–106
    RAID, 771–772
Advanced Intrusion Detection Environment (AIDE), 693, 697
Advanced Linux Sound Architecture (ALSA), 720–722, 773
Advanced Power Management. *See* APM
Advanced Technology Attachment Packet Interface (ATAPI), 773
agents, mail, 586–587
AIDE (Advanced Intrusion Detection Environment), 693, 697
alias command, 227–229, 250
~/.alias configuration file, 250
~/.alias file, 228
aliases
    assigning computer, 464
    configuring IP, 447–448
    described, 250
    IP, 412–413
Allman, Eric, 593
allocation groups, 295, 328
ALSA (Advanced Linux Sound Architecture), 720–722, 725, 773
alsamixer, alsamixergui commands, 722, 723, 774

ampersand (&), start background program character, 385
Apaches
    adding Web Server, 639
    described, 634
    installing, starting, 630–632
aplay command, 726, 774
APM (Advanced Power Management), 747–754, 774
apm command, 774
apmd daemon, 749–750, 774
apmsleep command, 750, 774
applications
    client, 69
    creating icons on desktop for, 57
    graphical, described, 69
    sound, Linux, 720–725
    starting on X server, 123–124
    text-based, described, 70
apropos command, 79, 89
aquota.group. aquota.user files, 285, 328
archiving
    files, 186–193
    log files, 668–670
arecord command, 726, 774
Argus (Audit Record Generation and Utilization System), 695, 697
ark archiving program, using, 186–188, 202
ARPANET (Advanced Research Projects Agency Network), 450, 451, 540
arpwatch, 695, 697
ASCII files, 202
Asian character support, 18

**807**